S0-ACR-401

The Works of John Dryden

General Editor

H. T. SWEDENBERG, JR.

Associate General Editor

EARL MINER

Textual Editor

VINTON A. DEARING

VOLUME TEN

EDITOR

Maximillian E. Novak

TEXTUAL EDITOR

George Robert Guffey

CATHERINE OF BRAGANZA AS SAINT CATHERINE
MEZZOTINT BY RICHARD TOMPSON
AFTER THE PAINTING BY JACOB HUYSMANS
Courtesy of the Trustees of the British Museum

109622

v. 10

PR
3410
F5.6

VOLUME X

The Works
of John Dryden

Plays

THE TEMPEST
TYRANNICK LOVE
AN EVENING'S LOVE

University of California Press
Berkeley   Los Angeles   London
1970

GOSHEN COLLEGE LIBRARY
GOSHEN, INDIANA 46526

UNIVERSITY OF CALIFORNIA PRESS
Berkeley and Los Angeles, California

UNIVERSITY OF CALIFORNIA PRESS, LTD.
London, England

The copy texts of this edition have been drawn in the
main from the Dryden Collection of the
William Andrews Clark Memorial Library

Copyright © 1970 by The Regents of the University of California
Printed in the United States of America
ISBN: 0-520-01589-4
Library of Congress Catalog Card Number: 55-7149
Designed by Ward Ritchie

Acknowledgments

The staff members of the William Andrews Clark Memorial Library—William Conway, the librarian, Edna C. Davis, Elizabeth Angelico, Patrick McCloskey, Virginia Wong, and Neady Taylor—deserve our first acknowledgment of gratitude, since for the past five years we have depended upon their knowledge, called continually for their assistance, and, doubtless, at times exhausted their patience. When we kept hundreds of books out of circulation in our cubicles, the Clark staff never complained, and though their joy at the completion of our task must be nearly equal to our own, they have never shown us and our assistants anything but the warmest courtesy. They made the Clark Library into something closer to a second home than a second office, and thanks to the atmosphere they created, our coffee breaks and lunches became congenial moments for exchanging ideas, not only between ourselves and those assisting us on this volume, but with such distinguished visiting scholars as James Sutherland, Samuel Monk, Charles Ward, and Emmett Avery.

We also wish to thank the staffs of the University of California, Los Angeles, Library, the Henry E. Huntington Library, and the British Museum for their expert service; the Research Committee of the University of California, Los Angeles, and the John Simon Guggenheim Memorial Foundation for the generous grants and fellowships that enabled us to complete the necessary research; Professor John Crow of the University of London for obtaining some much needed materials for us; Professor John Loftis of Stanford University for his helpful advice on problems of staging.

We owe a special debt of gratitude to those of our students and staff at UCLA who have helped us with more general problems: to William Jacquith, David Latt, Stephen Noble, Michael Seidel, Nick Havranek, and Jeanette Wallin for research assistance; to Melanie Rangno for her conscientious work in typing the manuscript as well as for her general scholarly assistance; and to our editorial assistant, Mrs. Geneva Phillips, for her care in preparing the manuscript and for her unique

method of prodding us into getting things done without caus-
ing us to lose our collective sense of humor. Finally, we are
grateful to Mrs. Grace H. Stimson of the University of California
Press for the skill and attention she bestowed upon this volume
as it proceeded through the press.

M. E. N.
G. R. G.

Los Angeles
June 1969

Contents

Illustrations

THE TEMPEST

OR

THE ENCHANTED ISLAND

THE
TEMPEST,
OR THE
Enchanted Island.
A
COMEDY.

As it is now Acted at his Highnefs the Duke of *York's*
THEATRE.

LONDON,

Printed by *J. M.* for *Henry Herringman* at the *Blew
Anchor* in the *Lower-walk* of the *New-Exchange*.
MDCLXX.

TITLE PAGE OF THE FIRST EDITION (MACDONALD 73A)

PREFACE
TO THE
ENCHANTED ISLAND.

THE *writing of Prefaces to Plays was probably invented by some very ambitious Poet, who never thought he had done enough: Perhaps by some Ape of the* French *Eloquence, who uses to make a business of a Letter of gallantry, an examen of a Farce; and in short, a great pomp and ostentation of words on every trifle. This is certainly the talent of that Nation, and ought not to be invaded by any other. They do that out of gayety which would be an imposition upon us.*

We may satisfie our selves with surmounting them in the
10 *Scene, and safely leave them those trappings of writing, and flourishes of the Pen, with which they adorn the borders of their Plays, and which are indeed no more than good Landskips to a very indifferent Picture. I must proceed no farther in this argument, lest I run my self beyond my excuse for writing this. Give me leave therefore to tell you, Reader, that I do it not to set a value on any thing I have written in this Play, but out of gratitude to the memory of Sir* William D'avenant, *who did me the honour to joyn me with him in the alteration of it.*

It was originally Shakespear's: *a Poet for whom he had par-*
20 *ticularly a high veneration, and whom he first taught me to admire. The Play it self had formerly been acted with success in the* Black-Fryers: *and our excellent* Fletcher *had so great a value for it, that he thought fit to make use of the same Design, not much varied, a second time. Those who have seen his* Sea-Voyage, *may easily discern that it was a Copy of* Shakespear's Tempest: *the Storm, the desart Island, and the Woman who had never seen a Man, are all sufficient testimonies of it. But* Fletcher *was not the only Poet who made use of* Shakespear's *Plot: Sir* John Suckling, *a profess'd admirer of our Author, has follow'd*
30 *his footsteps in his* Goblins; *his* Regmella *being an open imita-*

---

3 French] *French* Q, F. [These and other sigla are identified in the Textual Notes.]   17 D'avenant] Davenant Q, F.

tion of Shakespear's Miranda; *and his Spirits, though counter-feit, yet are copied from* Ariel. *But Sir* William D'avenant, *as he was a man of quick and piercing imagination, soon found that somewhat might be added to the Design of* Shakespear, *of which neither* Fletcher *nor* Suckling *had ever thought: and therefore to put the last hand to it, he design'd the Counterpart to* Shake-spear's *Plot, namely that of a Man who had never seen a Woman; that by this means those two Characters of Innocence and Love might the more illustrate and commend each other. This ex-*
10 *cellent contrivance he was pleas'd to communicate to me, and to desire my assistance in it. I confess that from the very first moment it so pleas'd me, that I never writ any thing with more delight. I must likewise do him that justice to acknowledge, that my writing received daily his amendments, and that is the rea-son why it is not so faulty, as the rest which I have done without the help or correction of so judicious a friend. The Comical parts of the Saylors were also his invention, and for the most part his writing, as you will easily discover by the style. In the time I writ with him I had the opportunity to observe somewhat*
20 *more neerly of him than I had formerly done, when I had only a bare acquaintance with him: I found him then of so quick a fancy, that nothing was propos'd to him, on which he could not suddenly produce a thought extreamly pleasant and surprizing: and those first thoughts of his, contrary to the old* Latine *Prov-erb, were not alwaies the least happy. And as his fancy was quick, so likewise were the products of it remote and new. He borrowed not of any other; and his imaginations were such as could not easily enter into any other man. His corrections were sober and judicious: and he corrected his own writings much*
30 *more severely than those of another man, bestowing twice the time and labour in polishing which he us'd in invention. It had perhaps been easie enough for me to have arrogated more to my self than was my due in the writing of this Play, and to have pass'd by his name with silence in the publication of it, with the same ingratitude which others have us'd to him, whose Writings he hath not only corrected, as he has done this, but has had a*

---

greater inspection over them, and sometimes added whole Scenes together, which may as easily be distinguish'd from the rest, as true Gold from counterfeit by the weight. But besides the unworthiness of the action which deterred me from it (there being nothing so base as to rob the dead of his reputation) I am satisfi'd I could never have receiv'd so much honour in being thought the Author of any Poem how excellent soever, as I shall from the joining my imperfections with the merit and name of Shakespear *and Sir* William D'avenant.

10 Decemb. 1.
  1669.

JOHN DRYDEN.

Prologue to the *Tempest,* or the *Enchanted Island.*

As when a *Tree's cut down the secret root*
Lives under ground, and thence new Branches shoot;
So, from old Shakespear's *honour'd dust, this day*
Springs up and buds a new reviving Play:
Shakespear, *who (taught by none) did first impart*
To Fletcher *Wit, to labouring* Johnson *Art.*
He Monarch-like gave those his subjects law,
And is that Nature which they paint and draw.
Fletcher *reach'd that which on his heights did grow,*
10 *Whilst* Johnson *crept and gather'd all below.*
This did his Love, and this his Mirth digest:
One imitates him most, the other best.
If they have since out-writ all other men,
'Tis with the drops which fell from Shakespear's *Pen.*
The Storm which vanish'd on the Neighb'ring shore,
Was taught by Shakespear's *Tempest first to roar.*
That innocence and beauty which did smile
In Fletcher, *grew on this* Enchanted Isle.
But Shakespear's *Magick could not copy'd be,*
20 *Within that Circle none durst walk but he.*
I must confess 'twas bold, nor would you now,
That liberty to vulgar Wits allow,
Which works by Magick supernatural things:
But Shakespear's *pow'r is sacred as a King's.*
Those Legends from old Priest-hood were receiv'd,
And he then writ, as people then believ'd.
But, if for Shakespear *we your grace implore,*
We for our Theatre shall want it more:
Who by our dearth of Youths are forc'd t'employ
30 *One of our Women to present a Boy.*
And that's a transformation you will say

2 *shoot;*] F; ~ᴧ Q.   4 *Play:*] ~ . Q, F.

Exceeding all the Magick in the Play.
Let none expect in the last Act to find,
Her Sex transform'd from man to Woman-kind.
What e're she was before the Play began,
All you shall see of her is perfect man.
Or if your fancy will be farther led,
To find her Woman, it must be abed.

Dramatis Personæ.

Alonzo Duke of *Savoy,* and Usurper of the Dukedom
    of *Mantua.*
Ferdinand his Son.
Prospero right Duke of *Millain.*
Antonio his Brother, Usurper of the Dukedom.
Gonzalo a Nobleman of *Savoy.*
Hippolito, one that never saw Woman, right Heir of
    the Dukedom of *Mantua.*
Stephano Master of the Ship.
Mustacho his Mate.
Trincalo Boatswain.
Ventoso a Mariner.
Several Mariners.
A Cabbin-Boy.
Miranda and⎤ (Daughters to *Prospero*) that never
Dorinda   ⎦   saw man.
Ariel an aiery Spirit, attendant on *Prospero.*
Several Spirits, Guards to *Prospero.*
Caliban and   ⎤
Sycorax his Sister⎦ Two Monsters of the Isle.

Nobleman] F; Noble man Q.   Spirits,] ∼∧ Q, F.
Caliban and] F; *Caliban* Q.

FRONTISPIECE OF *The Tempest* IN
The Works of Mr. William Shakespeare
ED. NICHOLAS ROWE (1709)

THE

ENCHANTED ISLAND.

ACT I. SCENE I.

Enter Mustacho *and* Ventoso.

Vent. What, a Sea comes in?
Must. A hoaming Sea! we shall have foul weather.

Enter Trincalo.

Trinc. The Scud comes against the Wind, 'twill blow hard.

Enter Stephano.

Steph. Bosen!
Trinc. Here, Master what cheer?
Steph. Ill weather! let's off to Sea.
Must. Let's have Sea-room enough, and then let it blow the Devils head off.
Steph. Boy!

Enter Cabin-boy.

10   *Boy.* Yaw, yaw, here Master.
Steph. Give the Pilot a dram of the Bottle.
                                [Exeunt Stephano *and* Boy.

ACT I. SCENE I.] ACT I. Q, F.
1 What,] ∼ᴧ Q, F.
2–2+ *s.d.* weather. / *Enter*] F; ∼ . [∼ Q (*s.d. at right margin*).
9–9+ *s.d.* Boy! / *Enter*] F; ∼ ! [∼ Q (*s.d. at right margin*).

Enter Mariners and pass over the Stage.

Trinc. Heigh, my hearts, chearly, chearly, my hearts, yare, yare.

Enter Alonzo, Antonio, Gonzalo.

Alon. Good Bosen have a care; where's the Master?
Play the men.
Trinc. Pray keep below.
Anto. Where's the Master, Bosen?
Trinc. Do you not hear him? you mar our labour: keep your
Cabins, you help the storm.
20   *Gonz.* Nay, good friend be patient.
Trinc. I, when the Sea is: hence; what care these roarers for
the name of Duke? to Cabin; silence; trouble us not.
Gonz. Good friend, remember whom thou hast aboard.
Trinc. None that I love more than my self: you are a Coun-
sellour, if you can advise these Elements to silence: use your
wisdom: if you cannot, make your self ready in the Cabin for
the ill hour. Cheerly good hearts! out of our way, Sirs.
                    [*Exeunt* Trincalo *and Mariners.*
Gonz. I have great comfort from this Fellow; methinks his
complexion is perfect Gallows; stand fast, good fate, to his hang-
30 ing; make the Rope of his destiny our Cable, for our own does
little advantage us; if he be not born to be hang'd we shall be
drown'd.   [*Exeunt* Alonzo, Antonio, *and* Gonzalo.

Enter Trincalo *and* Stephano.

Trinc. Up aloft Lads. Come, reef both Top-sails.
Steph. Let's weigh, Let's weigh, and off to Sea.
                    [*Ex.* Stephano.

Enter two Mariners and pass over the Stage.

---

32 *s.d. Exeunt* Alonzo, Antonio, *and* Gonzalo] *Exit* Q, F.

Trinc. Hands down! man your main-Capstorm.
[*Exeunt two Mariners.*

Enter Mustacho *and* Ventoso *at the other door.*

Must. Up aloft! and man your jeere-Capstorm.
Vent. My Lads, my hearts of Gold, get in your Capstorm-Bar.
Hoa up, hoa up, *&c.*   [*Exeunt* Mustacho *and* Ventoso.

Enter Stephano.

Steph. Hold on well! hold on well! nip well there;
40 Quarter-Master, get's more Nippers.   [*Exit* Stephano.

Enter two Mariners and pass over again.

Trinc. Turn out, turn out all hands to Capstorm!
You dogs, is this a time to sleep?
Heave together Lads.   [Trincalo *whistles.*
[*Exeunt two Mariners.*
Must. within. Our Viall's broke.
Vent. within. 'Tis but our Vial-block has given way. Come
heave Lads! we are fix'd again. Heave together Bullyes.

Enter Stephano.

Steph. Cut off the Hamocks! cut off the Hamocks, come my
Lads: Come Bullys, chear up! heave lustily.
The Anchor's a peek.
50   *Trinc.* Is the Anchor a peek?
Steph. Is a weigh! Is a weigh!
Trinc. Up aloft my Lads upon the Fore-Castle!
Cat the Anchor, cat him.
All within. Haul Catt, Haul Catt, *&c.* Haul Catt, haul: haul,
Catt, haul. Below.

35+ *s.d.* [*Exeunt two Mariners.*] *omitted from* Q, F.
36 jeere-Capstorm] seere-Capstorm Q, F.   41 Capstorm!] ~ ? Q, F.
43+ *s.d. two Mariners*] Mustacho *and* Ventoso Q, F.
48 Bullys] F; *Bullys* Q.   53 Cat . . . cat] Cut . . . cut Q, F.

Steph. Aft, Aft! and loose the Misen!
Trinc. Get the Misen-tack aboard. Haul Aft Misen-sheat!

Enter Mustacho.

Must. Loose the main Top-sail!
Steph. Furle him again, there's too much Wind.
60   *Trinc.* Loose Fore-sail! Haul Aft both sheats! trim her right
afore the Wind. Aft! Aft! Lads, and hale up the Misen here.
Must. A Mackrel-Gale, Master.
Steph. Port hard, port! the Wind grows scant, bring the Tack
aboard Port is. Star-board, star-board, a little steady; now steady,
keep her thus, no neerer you cannot come.

Enter Ventoso.

Vent. Some hands down: the Guns are loose.   [*Ex.* Must.
Trinc. Try the Pump, try the Pump!   [*Exit* Ventoso.

Enter Mustacho *at the other door.*

Must. O Master! six foot Water in Hold.
Steph. Clap the Helm hard aboard! Flat, flat, flat in the Fore-
70 sheat there.   [*Exit* Mustacho.
Trinc. Over-haul your fore-boling.
Steph. Brace in the Lar-board.   [*Exit.*
Trinc. A curse upon this howling,   [*A great cry within.*
They are louder than the weather.

Enter Antonio *and* Gonzalo.

Yet again, what do you here! shall we give o're, and drown? ha'
you a mind to sink?
   Gonz. A Pox o' your throat, you bawling, blasphemous, uncharitable dog.
   Trinc. Work you then.

---

63 *Steph.*] *Steph. within.* Q, F.   70 there. [*Exit* Mustacho.] there. Q, F.
74–74+ *s.d.* weather. / *Enter*] ~ . [~ Q, F (*s.d. at right margin*).

80   *Anto.* Hang, Cur, hang, you whorson insolent noise-maker, we are less afraid to be drown'd than thou art.

  Trinc. Brace off the Fore-yard.   [*Exit.*

  Gonz. I'le warrant him for drowning, though the Ship were no stronger than a Nut-shell, and as leaky as an unstanch'd Wench.

Enter Alonzo *and* Ferdinand.

  Ferd. For my self I care not, but your loss brings a thousand Deaths to me.

  Alonzo. O name not me, I am grown old, my Son; I now am tedious to the world, and that, by use, is so to me: but, *Ferdi-*
90 *nand,* I grieve my subjects loss in thee: Alas! I suffer justly for my crimes, but why thou shouldest————O Heaven!

                               [*A cry within.*

Heark, farewel my Son! a long farewel!

  Ferd. Some lucky Plank, when we are lost by shipwrack, waft hither, and submit it self beneath you.

Your blessing, and I dye contented.   [*Embrace and Exeunt.*

Enter Trincalo, Mustacho, *and* Ventoso.

  Trinc. What, must our mouths be cold then?

  Vent. All's lost. To prayers, to prayers.

  Gonz. The Duke and Prince are gone within to prayers. Let's assist them.

100   *Must.* Nay, we may e'ne pray too; our case is now alike.

  Ant. We are meerly cheated of our lives by Drunkards. This wide-chopt Rascal: would thou might'st lye drowning The long washing of ten Tides.

           [*Exeunt* Trincalo, Mustacho, *and* Ventoso.

  Gonz. He'll be hang'd yet, though every drop of water swears against it; now would I give ten thousand Furlongs of Sea for one Acre of barren ground, Long-heath, Broom-furs, or any

---

95+ *s.d. and*] F; and Q.   96 What,] ∼ₐ Q, F.
102 wide-chopt] wide chopt Q, F.   104 be] F; he Q.

thing. The wills above be done, but I would fain dye a dry
death.   [*A confused noise within.*
    Ant. Mercy upon us! we split, we split.
110   *Gonz.* Let's all sink with the Duke, and the young Prince.
                                                    [*Exeunt.*

Enter Stephano, Trincalo.

    Trinc. The Ship is sinking.   [*A new cry within.*
    Steph. Run her ashore!
    Trinc. Luffe! luffe! or we are all lost! there's a Rock upon the
Star-board Bow.
    Steph. She strikes, she strikes! All shift for themselves.
                                                    [*Exeunt.*

SCENE II.

Enter Prospero *and* Miranda.

    Prosp. Miranda! where's your Sister?
    Miran. I left her looking from the pointed Rock, at the walks
end, on the huge beat of Waters.
    Prosp. It is a dreadful object.
    Mir. If by your Art, my dearest Father, you have put them in
this roar, allay 'em quickly.
Had I been any God of power, I would have sunk the Sea into
the Earth, before it should the Vessel so have swallowed.
    Prosp. Collect your self, and tell your piteous heart,
10 There's no harm done.
    Mir. O woe the day!
    Prosp. There is no harm:
I have done nothing but in care of thee,
My Daughter, and thy pretty Sister:
You both are ignorant of what you are,
Not knowing whence I am, nor that I'm more

SCENE II.] *omitted from* Q, F.

Than *Prospero,* Master of a narrow Cell,
And thy unhappy Father.
    Mir. I ne're indeavour'd to know more than you were pleas'd
20 to tell me.
    Prosp. I should inform thee farther: wipe thou thine Eyes,
have comfort; the direful spectacle of the wrack, which touch'd
the very virtue of compassion in thee, I have with such a pity
safely order'd, that not one creature in the Ship is lost.
    Mir. You often, Sir, began to tell me what I am,
But then you stopt.
    Prosp. The hour's now come;
Obey, and be attentive. Canst thou remember a time before we
came into this Cell? I do not think thou canst, for then thou
30 wert not full three years old.
    Mir. Certainly I can, Sir.
    Prosp. Tell me the image then of any thing which thou dost
keep in thy remembrance still.
    Mir. Sir, had I not four or five Women once that tended me?
    Prosp. Thou hadst, and more, *Miranda:* what see'st thou else
in the dark back-ward, and abyss of Time?
If thou remembrest ought e're thou cam'st here, then, how thou
cam'st thou may'st remember too.
    Mir. Sir, that I do not.
40   *Prosp.* Fifteen Years since, *Miranda,* thy Father was the Duke
of *Millain,* and a Prince of power.
    Mir. Sir, are not you my Father?
    Prosp. Thy Mother was all virtue, and she said, thou wast my
Daughter, and thy Sister too.
    Mir. O Heavens! what foul play had we, that we hither came,
or was't a blessing that we did?
    Prosp. Both, both, my Girl.
    Mir. How my heart bleeds to think what you have suffer'd.
But, Sir, I pray proceed.
50   *Prosp.* My Brother, and thy Uncle, call'd *Antonio,* to whom I
trusted then the manage of my State, while I was wrap'd with

---

28 attentive.] ~ , Q, F.   41 *Millain*] Millan Q, F.

secret Studies: That false Uncle————Do'st thou attend me
Child?

Mir. Sir, most heedfully.

Prosp. Having attain'd the craft of granting suits, and of denying them; whom to advance, or lop, for over-toping, soon was
grown the Ivy which did hide my Princely Trunck, and suckt
my verdure out: thou attend'st not.

Mir. O good Sir, I do.

60 *Prosp.* I thus neglecting worldly ends, and bent to closeness,
and the bettering of my mind, wak'd in my false Brother an evil
Nature:
He did believe
He was indeed the Duke, because he then did execute the out-
ward face of Soveraignty. Do'st thou still mark me?

Mir. Your story would cure deafness.

Prosp. To have no screen between the part he plaid, and
whom he plaid it for; he needs would be Absolute *Millain,* and
Confederates (so dry he was for Sway) with *Savoy's* Duke, to give
70 him Tribute, and to do him homage.

Mir. False man!

Prosp. This Duke of *Savoy* being an Enemy,
To me inveterate, strait grants my Brother's suit,
And on a night
Mated to his design, *Antonio* opened the Gates of *Millain,* and
i'th' dead of darkness, hurri'd me thence with thy young Sister,
and thy crying self.

Mir. But wherefore did they not that hour destroy us?

Prosp. They durst not, Girl, in *Millain,* for the love my peo-
80 ple bore me; in short, they hurri'd us away to *Savoy,* and thence
aboard a Bark at *Nissa's* Port: bore us some Leagues to Sea,
where they prepar'd a rotten Carkass of a Boat, not rigg'd, no
Tackle, Sail, nor Mast; the very Rats instinctively had quit it:
they hoisted us, to cry to Seas which roar'd to us; to sigh to

---

52–53 Uncle————Do'st . . . Child?] Uncle (do'st . . . Child?) Q, F.
68 *Millain*] *Millan* Q, F.   75 *Millain*] *Millan* Q, F.
79 *Millain*] *Millan* Q, F.   79 for] F; For Q.

Winds, whose pity sighing back again, did seem to do us loving
wrong.

Mir. Alack! what trouble was I then to you?

Prosp. Thou and thy Sister were two Cherubins, which did
preserve me: you both did smile, infus'd with fortitude from
90 Heaven.

Mir. How came we ashore?

Prosp. By Providence Divine,
Some food we had, and some fresh Water, which a Nobleman
of *Savoy,* called *Gonzalo,* appointed Master of that black design, gave us; with rich Garments, and all necessaries, which
since have steaded much: and of his gentleness (knowing I lov'd
my Books) he furnisht me from mine own Library, with Volumes which I prize above my Dukedom.

Mir. Would I might see that man.

100 *Prosp.* Here in this Island we arriv'd, and here have I your
Tutor been. But by my skill I find that my mid-Heaven doth
depend on a most happy Star, whose influence if I now court
not, but omit, my Fortunes will ever after droop: here cease
more question, thou art inclin'd to sleep: 'tis a good dulness,
and give it way; I know thou canst not chuse.   [*She falls asleep.*
Come away my Spirit: I am ready now, approach,
My *Ariel,* Come.

Enter Ariel.

Ariel. All hail, great Master, grave Sir, hail; I come to answer
thy best pleasure, be it to fly, to swim, to shoot into the fire, to
110 ride on the curl'd Clouds; to thy strong bidding, task *Ariel* and
all his qualities.

Prosp. Hast thou, Spirit, perform'd to point the Tempest that
I bad thee?

Ariel. To every Article.

93 Nobleman] F; Noble man Q.   106 approach,] $\sim_\wedge$ Q, F.
107–107+ *s.d.* Come. / Enter] F; $\sim$. [$\sim$ Q (*s.d. at right margin*).
108 hail, . . . hail;] $\sim_\wedge$ . . . $\sim$, Q, F.

I boarded the Duke's Ship, now on the Beak, now in the Waste,
the Deck, in every Cabin; I flam'd amazement, and sometimes
I seem'd to burn in many places on the Top-Mast, the Yards and
Bore-sprit; I did flame distinctly.

Prosp. My brave Spirit!

120 Who was so firm, so constant, that this coil did not infect his
Reason?

Ariel. Not a soul
But felt a Feaver of the mind, and play'd some tricks of despe-
ration; all, but Mariners, plung'd in the foaming brine, and
quit the Vessel: the Duke's Son, *Ferdinand,* with hair upstairing
(more like Reeds than Hair) was the first man that leap'd; cry'd,
Hell is empty, and all the Devils are here.

Prosp. Why that's my Spirit;
But was not this nigh Shore?

130 *Ariel.* Close by, my Master.

Prosp. But, *Ariel,* are they safe?

Ariel. Not a hair perisht.
In Troops I have dispers'd them round this Isle.
The Duke's Son I have landed by himself, whom I have left
warming the air with sighs, in an odde angle of the Isle, and
sitting, his arms he folded in this sad knot.

Prosp. Say how thou hast dispos'd the Mariners of the Duke's
Ship, and all the rest of the Fleet.

Ariel. Safely in Harbour

140 Is the Duke's Ship; in the deep Nook, where once thou call'dst
Me up at midnight to fetch Dew from the
Still vext *Bermoothes,* there she's hid;
The Mariners all under hatches stow'd;
Whom, with a charm, join'd to their suffer'd labour,
I have left asleep: and for the rest o'th' Fleet
(Which I disperst) they all have met again,
And are upon the *Mediterranean* Float,
Bound sadly home for *Italy;*

---

127 *in romans in Q, F.*   130 by,] F; ~∧ Q.
140–145 Ship; . . . hid; . . . stow'd; . . . asleep:]   ~ , . . . ~ , . . . ~ , . . .
~ , Q, F.

Supposing that they saw the Duke's Ship wrackt,
150 And his great person perish.
    Prosp. Ariel, thy charge
Exactly is perform'd, but there's more work:
What is the time o'th' day?
    Ariel. Past the mid-season.
    Prosp. At least two Glasses: the time 'tween six and now must
by us both be spent most preciously.
    Ariel. Is there more toyl? since thou dost give me pains, let
me remember thee what thou hast promis'd, which is not yet
perform'd me.
160   *Prosp.* How now, *Moodie?*
What is't thou canst demand?
    Ariel. My liberty.
    Prosp. Before the time be out? no more.
    Ariel. I prethee!
Remember I have done thee faithful service,
Told thee no lyes, made thee no mistakings,
Serv'd without or grudge, or grumblings:
Thou didst promise to bate me a full year.
    Prosp. Dost thou forget
170 From what a torment I did free thee?
    Ariel. No.
    Prosp. Thou dost, and think'st it much to tread the Ooze
Of the salt deep:
To run against the sharp wind of the North,
To do my business in the Veins of the Earth,
When it is bak'd with Frost.
    Ariel. I do not, Sir.
    Prosp. Thou ly'st, malignant thing! hast thou forgot the foul
Witch *Sycorax,* who with age and envy was grown into a Hoop?
180 hast thou forgot her?
    Ariel. No Sir!
    Prosp. Thou hast; where was she born? speak, tell me.
    Ariel. Sir, in *Argier.*
    Prosp. Oh, was she so! I must
Once every Month recount what thou hast been, which thou

forgettest. This damn'd Witch *Sycorax* for mischiefs manifold,
and sorceries too terrible to enter humane hearing, from *Argier*
thou knowst was banisht: but for one thing she did, they would
not take her life: is not this true?

190   *Ariel.* I, Sir.

       Prosp. This blew-ey'd Hag was hither brought with child,
And here was left by th' Saylors: thou, my slave,
As thou report'st thy self, wast then her servant;
And 'cause thou wast a spirit too delicate
To act her earthy and abhorr'd commands,
Refusing her grand Hests, she did confine thee,
By help of her more potent Ministers,
(In her unmitigable rage) into a cloven Pine;
Within whose rift imprison'd, thou didst painfully

200 Remain a dozen years; within which space she dy'd,
And left thee there; where thou didst vent thy
Groans, as fast as Mill-wheels strike.
Then was this Isle (save for two Brats, which she did
Litter here, the brutish *Caliban,* and his twin Sister,
Two freckel'd-hag-born Whelps) not honour'd with
A humane shape.

       Ariel. Yes! *Caliban* her Son, and *Sycorax* his Sister.

       Prosp. Dull thing, I say so; he, that *Caliban,* and she that
Sycorax, whom I now keep in service. Thou best knowst what

210 torment I did find thee in; thy groans did make Wolves howl,
and penetrate the breasts of ever angry Bears: it was a torment
to lay upon the damn'd, which *Sycorax* could ne're again undo:
It was my Art, when I arriv'd, and heard thee, that made the
Pine to gape and let thee out.

       Ariel. I thank thee, Master.

       Prosp. If thou more murmurest, I will rend an Oak,
And peg thee in his knotty Entrails, till thou
Hast howld away twelve Winters more.

---

190 I,] F; ~ₐ Q.
192–198 Saylors: . . . servant; . . . commands, . . . Pine;]   ~ , . . . ~ , . . .
~ ; . . . ~ , Q, F.
210–211 in; . . . Bears:] ~ , . . . ~ , Q, F.   217 thee] F; the Q.

Ariel. Pardon, Master,
230 I will be correspondent to command, and be
A gentle spirit.
　　Prosp. Do so, and after two days I'le discharge thee.
　　Ariel. That's my noble Master.
What shall I do? say? what? what shall I do?
　　Prosp. Be subject to no sight but mine; invisible to
Every eye-ball else: hence with diligence.
My daughter wakes. Anon thou shalt know more.　　[*Ex.* Ariel.
Thou hast slept well my child.
　　Mir. The sadness of your story put heaviness in me.
230　*Prosp.* Shake it off; come on, I'le now call *Caliban,* my slave,
Who never yields us a kind answer.
　　Mir. 'Tis a creature, Sir, I do not love to look on.
　　Prosp. But as 'tis, we cannot miss him; he does make our Fire,
fetch in our Wood, and serve in Offices that profit us. What hoa!
Slave! *Caliban!* thou Earth thou, speak.
　　Calib. within. There's Wood enough within.
　　Prosp. Come forth, I say, there's other business for thee.
Come thou Tortoise, when?

Enter Ariel.

Fine apparition, my quaint *Ariel,*
240 Hark in thy ear.
　　Ariel. My Lord it shall be done.　　　　　　　　　　　[*Exit.*
　　Prosp. Thou poisonous Slave, got by the Devil himself upon
thy wicked Dam, come forth.

Enter Caliban.

　　Calib. As wicked Dew, as e're my Mother brush'd with Ra-
ven's Feather from unwholsome Fens, drop on you both: A
South-west blow on you, and blister you all o're.

234　us. What] ∼ : what Q, F (What F).
238–238+　*s.d.* when? / *Enter*] ∼ ? [∼ Q, F (*s.d. at right margin*).
243–243+　*s.d.* forth. / *Enter*] ∼ . [∼ Q, F (*s.d. at right margin*).

Prosp. For this besure, to night thou shalt have Cramps, side-stitches, that shall pen thy breath up; Urchins shall prick thee till thou bleed'st: thou shalt be pinch'd as thick as Honey-
250 Combs, each pinch more stinging than the Bees which made 'em.

Calib. I must eat my dinner: this Island's mine by *Sycorax* my Mother, which thou took'st from me. When thou cam'st first, thou stroak'st me, and mad'st much of me, would'st give me Water with Berries in't, and teach me how to name the bigger Light, and how the less, that burn by day and night; and then I lov'd thee, and shew'd thee all the qualities of the Isle, the fresh-Springs, brine-Pits, barren places, and fertil. Curs'd be I, that I did so: All the Charms of *Sycorax,* Toads, Beetles, Batts, light
260 on thee, for I am all the Subjects that thou hast. I first was mine own Lord; and here thou stay'st me in this hard Rock, whiles thou dost keep from me the rest o'th' Island.

Prosp. Thou most lying Slave, whom stripes may move, not kindness: I have us'd thee (filth that thou art) with humane care, and lodg'd thee in mine own Cell, till thou didst seek to violate the honour of my Children.

Calib. Oh ho, Oh ho, would't had been done: thou did'st prevent me, I had peopl'd else this Isle with *Calibans.*

Prosp. Abhor'd Slave!
270 Who ne're would any print of goodness take, being capable of all ill: I pity'd thee, took pains to make thee speak, taught thee each hour one thing or other; when thou didst not (Savage) know thy own meaning, but would'st gabble, like a thing most brutish, I endow'd thy purposes with words which made them known: But thy wild race (though thou did'st learn) had that in't, which good Natures could not abide to be with: therefore wast thou deservedly pent up into this Rock.

Calib. You taught me language, and my profit by it is, that I know to curse: the red botch rid you for learning me your lan-
280 guage.

---

267 would't had] would t'had Q, F.

Prosp. Hag-seed hence!
Fetch us in fewel, and be quick
To answer other business: shrugst thou (malice)?
If thou neglectest or dost unwillingly what I command,
I'le wrack thee with old Cramps, fill all thy bones with
Aches, make thee roar, that Beasts shall tremble
At thy Din.
    Calib. No prethee!
[*Aside.*] I must obey. His Art is of such power,
290 It would controul my Dam's God, *Setebos,*
And make a Vassal of him.
    Prosp. So Slave, hence.
                [*Exeunt* Prospero *and* Caliban *severally.*

Enter Dorinda.

Dor. Oh Sister! what have I beheld?
Mir. What is it moves you so?
Dor. From yonder Rock,
As I my Eyes cast down upon the Seas,
The whistling winds blew rudely on my face,
And the waves roar'd; at first I thought the War
Had bin between themselves, but strait I spy'd
300 A huge great Creature.
    Mir. O you mean the Ship.
    Dor. Is't not a Creature then? it seem'd alive.
    Mir. But what of it?
    Dor. This floating Ram did bear his Horns above;
All ty'd with Ribbands, ruffling in the wind,
Sometimes he nodded down his head a while,
And then the Waves did heave him to the Moon;
He clamb'ring to the top of all the Billows,
And then again he curtsy'd down so low,
310 I could not see him: till, at last, all side-long

---

283 (malice)?] (∼)∧ Q, F.   289 [*Aside.*] I] I Q, F.
310 side-long] side long Q, F.

With a great crack his belly burst in pieces.

 Mir. There all had perisht
Had not my Father's magick Art reliev'd them.
But, Sister, I have stranger news to tell you;
In this great Creature there were other Creatures,
And shortly we may chance to see that thing,
Which you have heard my Father call, a Man.

 Dor. But what is that? for yet he never told me.

 Mir. I know no more than you: but I have heard
320 My Father say we Women were made for him.

 Dor. What, that he should eat us, Sister?

 Mir. No sure, you see my Father is a man, and yet
He does us good. I would he were not old.

 Dor. Methinks indeed it would be finer, if we two
Had two young Fathers.

 Mir. No Sister, no, if they were young, my Father
Said that we must call them Brothers.

 Dor. But pray how does it come that we two are not Brothers
then, and have not Beards like him?

330 *Mir.* Now I confess you pose me.

 Dor. How did he come to be our Father too?

 Mir. I think he found us when we both were little, and grew
within the ground.

 Dor. Why could he not find more of us? pray Sister, let you
and I look up and down one day, to find some little ones for us
to play with.

 Mir. Agreed; but now we must go in. This is the hour
Wherein my Father's Charm will work,
Which seizes all who are in open Air:
340 Th' effect of his great Art I long to see,
Which will perform as much as Magick can.

 Dor. And I, methinks, more long to see a Man.   [*Exeunt.*

---

321 us,] F; ~ₐ Q.   334 Sister,] sisterₐ Q, F (Sister F).
342 Man. [*Exeunt.*] F; Man. Q.

ACT II. SCENE I.

Enter Alonzo, Antonio, Gonzalo, *Attendants.*

Gonz. Beseech your Grace be merry; you have cause, so have
we all, of joy for our strange scape: then wisely, good Sir, weigh
our sorrow with our comfort.

Alonz. Prithee peace! you cram these words into my Ears
against my stomack. How can I rejoyce, when my dear Son, perhaps this very moment, is made a meal to some strange Fish?

Ant. Sir, he may live,
I saw him beat the billows under him, and ride upon their
backs; he trod the Water, whose enmity he flung aside, and
10 breasted the most swoln surge that met him; his bold head
'bove the contentious waves he kept, and oar'd himself with his
strong arms to shore: I do not doubt he came alive to land.

Alonz. No, no, he's gone, and you and I, *Antonio,* were those
who caus'd his death.

Ant. How could we help it?

Alonz. Then, then, we should have helpt it, when thou be-
trayedst thy Brother *Prospero,* and *Mantua's* Infant, Sovereign
to my power: And when I, too ambitious, took by force anothers
right; then lost we *Ferdinand,* then forfeited our Navy to this
20 Tempest.

Ant. Indeed we first broke truce with Heav'n;
You to the waves an Infant Prince expos'd,
And on the waves have lost an only Son;
I did usurp my Brother's fertile lands, and now
Am cast upon this desert Isle.

Gonz. These, Sir, 'tis true, were crimes of a black Dye,
But both of you have made amends to Heav'n,
By your late Voyage into *Portugal,*
Where, in defence of Christianity,

ACT II. SCENE I.] ACT II. Q, F.
5   stomack. How] ∼ , how Q, F.   10–12   him; . . . shore:] ∼ , . . . ∼ , Q, F.

30 Your valour has repuls'd the *Moors* of *Spain.*
        Alonz. O name it not, *Gonzalo.*
No act but penitence can expiate guilt.
Must we teach Heaven what price to set on Murthers?
What rate on lawless power, and wild ambition?
Or dare we traffick with the Powers above,
And sell by weight a good deed for a bad?   [*Musick within.*
        Gonz. Musick! and in the air! sure we are shipwrackt on the
Dominions of some merry Devil.
        Ant. This Isle's inchanted ground, for I have heard
40 Swift voices flying by my Ear, and groans
Of lamenting Ghosts.
        Alonz. I pull'd a Tree, and Blood pursu'd my hand. O Hea-
ven! deliver me from this dire place, and all the after actions of
my life shall mark my penitence and my bounty.
Heark!   [*A Dialogue within sung in parts.*
The sounds approach us.

        1. D. *Where does proud* Ambition *dwell?*
        2.   *In the lowest Rooms of Hell.*
        1.   *Of the damn'd who leads the Host?*
50   2.   *He who did oppress the most.*
        1.   *Who such Troops of damned brings?*
        2.   *Most are led by fighting Kings.*
                Kings who did Crowns unjustly get,
                Here on burning Thrones are set.
        Chor.   *Kings who did Crowns,* &c.

        Ant. Do you hear, Sir, how they lay our Crimes before us?
        Gonz. Do evil Spirits imitate the good,
In shewing men their sins?
        Alonz. But in a different way,
60 Those warn from doing, these upbraid 'em done.

---

32 guilt.] ~ , Q, F.   42 hand.] ~ ; Q, F.
47 1.] F; ~∧ Q.   47 D.] D. Q, F.
47 *Where does proud*] Where does proud Q, F.
47–55 *dwell? . . . Crowns,*] *words of song in romans in* Q, F.
55 Chor.] *Chor.* Q, F.   55 &c.] *&c.* Q, F.

1.   *Who are the Pillars of* Ambitions *Court?*
2.   Grim Deaths *and* Scarlet Murthers *it support.*
1.   *What lyes beneath her feet?*
2.   *Her footsteps tread,*
       On Orphans tender breasts, and Brothers dead.
1.   *Can Heaven permit such Crimes should be*
       Rewarded with felicity?
2.   *Oh no! uneasily their Crowns they wear,*
       And their own guilt amidst their Guards they fear.
       Cares when they wake their minds unquiet keep,
70   *And we in visions lord it o're their sleep.*
Cho. *Oh no! uneasily their Crowns,* &c.

Alonz. See where they come in horrid shapes!

Enter the two that sung, in the shape of Devils, placing
themselves at two corners of the Stage.

Ant. Sure Hell is open'd to devour us quick.
1. D. Say Brother, shall we bear these mortals hence?
2.   First let us shew the shapes of their offence.
1.   We'll muster then their crimes on either side.
Appear! appear! their first begotten, *Pride.*

Enter Pride.

Pride. Lo! I am here, who led their hearts astray,
And to *Ambition* did their minds betray.

Enter Fraud.

---

61   *Who are the Pillars of*] Who are the Pillars of Q, F.
61–62   *Court? . . . and . . . it support.*] *in romans in* Q, F.
63–71   *What . . . Crowns,*] *words of song in romans in* Q, F.
71   *Cho.*] Cho. Q, F.   71   &c.] *&c.* Q, F.
74–76   *1. . . . 2. . . . 1.*] 1. . . . 2. . . . 1. Q, F.   76   side.] ∼ : Q, F.
77–77+   *Pride. / Enter* Pride] Pride. [*Enter Pride* Q, F (*s.d. at right margin*).
79   *Ambition*] Ambition Q, F.
79–79+   *s.d.* betray. / *Enter* Fraud] ∼ . [*Enter Fraud* Q, F (*s.d. at right margin*).

80　　*Fraud.* And guileful *Fraud* does next appear,
　　Their wandring steps who led,
　　When they from virtue fled,
　　And in my crooked paths their course did steer.

Enter Rapine.

　　Rap. From *Fraud* to *Force* they soon arrive,
　　Where *Rapine* did their actions drive.

Enter Murther.

　　Murd. There long they cannot stay,
　　Down the deep precipice they run,
　　And to secure what they have done,
　　To murder bend their way.
　　　　　　After which they fall into a round encompassing the
　　　　　　　　Duke, &c. Singing.

90　　　　　　　　*Around, around, we pace*
　　　　　　　　About this cursed place,
　　　　　　　　Whilst thus we compass in
　　　　　　　　These mortals and their sin.　　　　*Dance.*
　　　　　　　　　　　　[*All the spirits vanish.*
　　Ant. Heav'n has heard me! they are vanish'd.
　　Alonz. But they have left me all unmann'd;
　　I feel my sinews slacken'd with the fright,
　　And a cold sweat trills down o're all my limbs,
　　As if I were dissolving into Water.
　　O *Prospero!* my crimes 'gainst thee sit heavy on my heart.
100　　*Ant.* And mine, 'gainst him and young *Hippolito.*

80　*Fraud* does] Fraud does Q, F.
83–83+　*s.d.* steer. / *Enter* Rapine] ∼ . [*Enter Rapine* Q, F (*s.d. at right mar-*
gin).
84　*Fraud*] Fraud Q, F.　　　　　　84　*Force*] Force Q, F.
85　*Rapine*] Rapine Q, F.
85–85+　*s.d.* drive. / *Enter* Murther] ∼ . [*Enter Murther* Q, F (*s.d. at right*
margin).
89+　*s.d.* &c.] F; *&c.* Q.　　　　　　95　unmann'd] unman'd Q, F.

   Gonz. Heav'n have mercy on the penitent!
   Alonz. Lead from this cursed ground;
The Seas, in all their rage, are not so dreadful.
This is the Region of despair and death.
   Gonz. Shall we not seek some food?
   Alonz. Beware all fruit but what the birds have peid,
The shadows of the Trees are poisonous too:
A secret venom slides from every branch.
My conscience doth distract me, O my Son!
110 Why do I speak of eating or repose,
Before I know thy fortune?   [*Exeunt.*

SCENE II.

Enter Ferdinand, *and* Ariel, *invisible, playing and singing.*

Ariel's *Song.*

     Come unto these yellow sands
        And then take hands.
     Curtsy'd when you have and kiss'd,
        The wild waves whist.
Foot it featly here and there, and sweet sprights bear
        the Burthen.   [Burthen dispersedly.
Hark! hark! Bow-waugh; *the watch-dogs bark,*
     Bow-waugh.
   Ariel. Hark! hark! I hear the strain of strutting Chanticleer
10   *Cry* Cock a doodle do.

   Ferd. Where should this Musick be? i'th' Air, or th' Earth?
It sounds no more, and sure it waits upon some God
O'th' Island, sitting on a bank weeping against the Duke

SCENE II.] *omitted from Q, F.*
7–8 Bow-waugh . . . Bow-waugh] *Bow-waugh . . . Bow-waugh* Q, F.
9 Chanticleer] *Chanticleer* Q, F.
10 Cock a doodle do] *Cock a doodle do* Q, F.

My Father's wrack. This musick hover'd o're me
On the waters, allaying both their fury and my passion
With charming Airs; thence I have follow'd it (or it
Hath drawn me rather) but 'tis gone;
No, it begins again.

Ariel. *Song.*

Full Fathoms five thy Father lyes,
20   *Of his bones is Coral made:*
Those are Pearls that were his eyes;
     Nothing of him that does fade,
But does suffer a Sea-change
Into something rich and strange:
Sea-Nymphs hourly ring his knell,
Heark now I hear 'em, Ding dong Bell.

                              [*Burthen, Ding dong.*
Ferd. The mournful Ditty mentions my drown'd Father,
This is no mortal business, nor a sound which the
Earth owns: I hear it now before me,
30 However I will on and follow it.   [*Ex.* Ferd. *and* Ariel.

SCENE III.

Enter Stephano, Mustacho, Ventoso.

Vent. The Runlet of Brandy was a loving Runlet, and floated
after us out of pure pity.
   Must. This kind Bottle, like an old acquaintance, swam after
it. And this Scollop-shell is all our Plate now.
   Vent. 'Tis well we have found something since we landed.
I prethee fill a soop, and let it go round.
Where hast thou laid the Runlet?

---

21 *eyes;*] ~ , Q, F.   25 *his knell*] *his* Q, F.
26 Ding dong Bell] *Ding dong Bell* Q, F.
SCENE III.] *omitted from Q, F.*

Must. I'th' hollow of an old Tree.

Vent. Fill apace,

10   We cannot live long in this barren Island, and we may
Take a soop before death, as well as others drink
At our Funerals.

Must. This is prize-Brandy, we steal Custom, and it costs nothing. Let's have two rounds more.

Vent. Master, what have you sav'd?

Steph. Just nothing but my self.

Vent. This works comfortably on a cold stomach.

Steph. Fill's another round.

Vent. Look! *Mustacho* weeps. Hang losses as long as we have
20   Brandy left. Prithee leave weeping.

Steph. He sheds his Brandy out of his eyes: he shall drink no
more.

Must. This will be a doleful day with old *Bess.* She gave me
a gilt Nutmeg at parting. That's lost too. But as you say, hang
losses. Prithee fill agen.

Vent. Beshrew thy heart for putting me in mind of thy Wife,
I had not thought of mine else, Nature will shew it self,
I must melt. I prithee fill agen, my Wife's a good old jade,
And has but one eye left: but she'll weep out that too,
30   When she hears that I am dead.

Steph. Would you were both hang'd for putting me in
thought of mine. But well, If I return not in seven years to my
own Country, she may marry agen: and 'tis from this Island
thither at least seven years swimming.

Must. O at least, having no help of Boat nor Bladders.

Steph. Whoe're she marries, poor soul, she'll weep a nights
when she thinks of *Stephano.*

Vent. But Master, sorrow is dry! there's for you agen.

Steph. A Mariner had e'en as good be a Fish as a Man, but for
40   the comfort we get ashore: O for any old dry Wench now I am
wet.

Must. Poor heart! that would soon make you dry agen: but

---

31   putting me] F; putting Q.

all is barren in this Isle: here we may lye at Hull till the Wind
blow Nore and by South, e're we can cry *a Sail, a Sail* at sight of
a white Apron. And therefore here's another soop to comfort us.

 Vent. This Isle's our own, that's our comfort, for the Duke,
the Prince, and all their train are perished.

 Must. Our Ship is sunk, and we can never get home agen: we
must e'en turn Salvages, and the next that catches his fellow
50 may eat him.

 Vent. No, no, let us have a Government; for if we live well
and orderly, Heav'n will drive the Shipwracks ashore to make
us all rich, therefore let us carry good Consciences, and not eat
one another.

 Steph. Whoever eats any of my subjects, I'le break out his
Teeth with my Scepter: for I was Master at Sea, and will be
Duke on Land: you *Mustacho* have been my Mate, and shall be
my Vice-Roy.

 Vent. When you are Duke you may chuse your Vice-Roy; but
60 I am a free Subject in a new Plantation, and will have no Duke
without my voice. And so fill me the other soop.

 Steph. whispering. Ventoso, dost thou hear? I will advance
thee, prithee give me thy voice.

 Vent. I'le have no whisperings to corrupt the Election; and
to show that I have no private ends, I declare aloud that I will
be Vice-Roy, or I'le keep my voice for my self.

 Must. Stephano, hear me, I will speak for the people, because
there are few, or rather none in the Isle to speak for themselves.
Know then, that to prevent the farther shedding of Christian
70 blood, we are all content *Ventoso* shall be Vice-Roy, upon condition I may be Vice-Roy over him. Speak good people, are you
well agreed? what, no man answer? well, you may take their
silence for consent.

 Vent. You speak for the people, *Mustacho?* I'le speak for 'em,
and declare generally with one voice, one word and all; that
there shall be no Vice-Roy but the Duke, unless I be he.

 Must. You declare for the people, who never saw your face!
Cold Iron shall decide it.   [*Both draw.*

---

44 *a Sail, a Sail*] a Sail, a Sail Q, F. 62 hear?] ∼ , Q, F.

Steph. Hold, loving Subjects: we will have no Civil war dur-
80 ing our Reign: I do hereby appoint you both to be my Vice-
Roys over the whole Island.

    Both. Agreed! agreed!

    Enter Trincalo *with a great bottle, half drunk.*

    Vent. How! *Trincalo* our brave Bosen!

    Must. He reels: can he be drunk with Sea-water?

    Trinc. sings. I shall no more to Sea, to Sea,
             Here I shall dye ashore.
This is a very scurvy tune to sing at a man's funeral,
But here's my comfort.   [*Drinks.*
    Sings. The Master, the Swabber, the Gunner, and I,
90   *The Surgeon, and his Mate,*
      Lov'd Mall, Meg, *and* Marrian, *and* Margery,
       But none of us car'd for Kate.
      For she had a tongue with a tang,
      Wou'd cry to a Saylor, go hang:
      She lov'd not the savour of Tar nor of Pitch,
      Yet a Taylor might scratch her where e're she did itch.
This is a scurvy Tune too, but here's my comfort agen. [*Drinks.*
    Steph. We have got another subject now; welcome,
Welcome into our Dominions!
100   *Trinc.* What Subject, or what Dominions? here's old Sack
Boys: the King of good fellows can be no subject.
I will be Old *Simon* the King.
    Must. Hah, old Boy! how didst thou scape?
    Trinc. Upon a Butt of Sack, Boys, which the Saylors
Threw overboard: but are you alive, hoa! for I will
Tipple with no Ghosts till I'm dead: thy hand *Mustacho,*
And thine *Ventoso;* the storm has done its worst:
Stephano alive too! give thy Bosen thy hand, Master.
    Vent. You must kiss it then, for, I must tell you, we have

---

85–86 *I* . . . [*italics*] . . . *ashore*] F; *in romans in* Q.
89–94 *The* . . . [*to*] . . . *Saylor,*] F; *romans and italics reversed in* Q.
95–96 *as in* F; *in romans in* Q.

110 chosen him Duke in a full Assembly.

Trinc. A Duke! where? what's he Duke of?

Must. Of this Island, man. Oh *Trincalo* we are all made, the Island's empty; all's our own, Boy; and we will speak to his Grace for thee, that thou may'st be as great as we are.

Trinc. You great? what the Devil are you?

Vent. We two are Vice-Roys over all the Island; and when we are weary of Governing thou shalt succeed us.

Trinc. Do you hear, *Ventoso,* I will succeed you in both your places before you enter into 'em.

120 *Steph. Trincalo,* sleep and be sober; and make no more up-roars in my Country.

Trinc. Why, what are you, Sir, what are you?

Steph. What I am, I am by free election, and you *Trincalo* are not your self; but we pardon your first fault,
Because it is the first day of our Reign.

Trinc. Umph, were matters carried so swimmingly against me, whilst I was swimming, and saving my self for the good of the people of this Island?

Must. Art thou mad *Trincalo,* wilt thou disturb a settled
130 Government?

Trinc. I say this Island shall be under *Trincalo,* or it shall be a Common-wealth; and so my Bottle is my Buckler, and so I draw my Sword. [*Draws.*

Vent. Ah *Trincalo,* I thought thou hadst had more grace,
Than to rebel against thy old Master,
And thy two lawful Vice-Roys.

Must. Wilt not thou take advice of two that stand
For old Counsellors here, where thou art a meer stranger
To the Laws of the Country.

140 *Trinc.* I'll have no Laws.

Vent. Then Civil-War begins. [Vent. Must. *draw.*

Steph. Hold, hold, I'le have no blood shed,
My Subjects are but few: let him make a rebellion
By himself; and a Rebel, I Duke *Stephano* declare him:

128 Island?] ∼ . Q, F.
141 s.d. Vent. Must. *draw*] Vent. Must. draw Q, F.

Vice-Roys, come away.

   Trinc. And Duke *Trincalo* declares, that he will make open war wherever he meets thee or thy Vice-Roys.

[Ex. Steph. Must. Vent.

Enter Caliban with wood upon his back.

   Trinc. Hah! who have we here?

   Calib. All the infections that the Sun sucks up from Fogs,
150 Fens, Flats, on *Prospero* fall; and make him by inch-meal a Disease: his spirits hear me, and yet I needs must curse; but they'l not pinch, fright me with Urchin shows, pitch me i'th' mire, nor lead me in the dark out of my way, unless he bid 'em: but for every trifle he sets them on me; sometimes like Baboons they mow and chatter at me, and often bite me; like Hedge-hogs then they mount their prickles at me, tumbling before me in my barefoot way. Sometimes I am all wound about with Adders, who with their cloven tongues hiss me to madness. Hah! yonder stands one of his spirits sent to torment me.

160   *Trinc.* What have we here, a man, or a fish?
This is some Monster of the Isle; were I in *England,*
As once I was, and had him painted,
Not a Holy-day fool there but would give me
Six-pence for the sight of him; well, if I could make
Him tame, he were a present for an Emperour.
Come hither pretty Monster, I'le do thee no harm.
Come hither!

   Calib. Torment me not;
I'le bring thee Wood home faster.

170   *Trinc.* He talks none of the wisest, but I'le give him
A dram o'th' Bottle, that will clear his understanding.
Come on your ways Master Monster, open your mouth.
How now, you perverse Moon-calf! what,
I think you cannot tell who is your friend!
Open your chops, I say.   [*Pours Wine down his throat.*

   Calib. This is a brave God, and bears cœlestial Liquor,

<hr>

151 curse;] ∼ , Q, F.   161–162 Isle; . . . painted,] ∼ , . . . ∼ ; Q, F.

I'le kneel to him.

 Trinc. He is a very hopeful Monster. Monster, what say'st thou, art thou content to turn civil and sober, as I am? for then
180 thou shalt be my subject.

 Calib. I'le swear upon that Bottle to be true; for the liquor is not Earthly: did'st thou not drop from Heaven?

 Trinc. Only out of the Moon, I was the man in her when time was.———[*Aside.*] By this light, a very shallow Monster.

 Calib. I'le shew thee every fertile inch i'th' Isle, and kiss thy foot: I prithee be my God, and let me drink.　　[*Drinks agen.*

 Trinc. Well drawn, Monster, in good faith.

 Calib. I'le shew thee the best Springs, I'le pluck thee Berries, I'le fish for thee, and get thee wood enough:
190 A curse upon the Tyrant whom I serve, I'le bear him
No more sticks, but follow thee.

 Trinc. The poor Monster is loving in his drink.　　[*Aside.*

 Calib. I prithee let me bring thee where Crabs grow,
And I with my long Nails, will dig thee Pig-nuts,
Shew thee a Jay's Nest, and instruct thee how to snare
The Marmazet; I'le bring thee to cluster'd Filberds;
Wilt thou go with me?

 Trinc. This Monster comes of a good natur'd race.　　[*Aside.*
Is there no more of thy kin in this Island?

200 *Calib.* Divine, here is but one besides my self;
My lovely Sister, beautiful and bright as the full Moon.

 Trinc. Where is she?

 Calib. I left her clambring up a hollow Oak,
And plucking thence the dropping Honey-Combs.
Say my King, shall I call her to thee?

 Trinc. She shall swear upon the Bottle too.
If she proves handsom she is mine: here Monster,
Drink agen for thy good news; thou shalt speak
A good word for me.　　[*Gives him the Bottle.*
210 *Calib.* Farewel, old Master, farewel, farewel.

Sings. No more Dams I'le make for Fish,
     Nor fetch in firing at requiring,
     Nor scrape Trencher, nor wash Dish;
     Ban, Ban, Cackaliban
     Has a new Master, get a new man.
Heigh-day, Freedom, freedom!
    Trinc. Here's two subjects got already, the Monster,
And his Sister: well, Duke *Stephano,* I say, and say agen,
Wars will ensue, and so I drink.   [*Drinks.*
220 From this worshipful Monster, and Mistress
Monster, his Sister,
I'le lay claim to this Island by Alliance.
Monster, I say thy Sister shall be my Spouse:
Come away Brother Monster, I'le lead thee to my Butt
And drink her health.   [*Exeunt.*

SCENE IV.

Enter Prospero *alone.*

    Prosp. 'Tis not yet fit to let my Daughters know I kept
The infant Duke of *Mantua* so near them in this Isle,
Whose Father dying bequeath'd him to my care,
Till my false Brother (when he design'd t'usurp
My Dukedom from me) expos'd him to that fate
He meant for me. By calculation of his birth
I saw death threat'ning him, if, till some time were
Past, he should behold the face of any Woman:
And now the danger's nigh.————*Hippolito!*

Enter Hippolito.

211–215   *No . . . [to] . . . man]* F; *italics and romans reversed in Q.*
213   *Dish;]* F; Dish, Q.   216   *indented as part of Caliban's song in Q, F.*
220–221   Mistress Monster,] ~ , ~∧ Q, F.   222   Alliance.] ~ : Q, F.
SCENE IV.] *omitted from Q, F.*   9   nigh.————] nigh: Q, F.
9–9+   s.d. *Hippolito! / Enter]* ~ ! [~ Q, F (*s.d. at right margin*).

10   *Hip.* Sir, I attend your pleasure.
        Prosp. How I have lov'd thee from thy infancy,
Heav'n knows, and thou thy self canst bear me witness,
Therefore accuse not me for thy restraint.
        Hip. Since I knew life, you've kept me in a Rock,
And you this day have hurry'd me from thence,
Only to change my Prison, not to free me.
I murmur not, but I may wonder at it.
        Prosp. O gentle Youth, Fate waits for thee abroad,
A black Star threatens thee, and death unseen
20 Stands ready to devour thee.
        Hip. You taught me not to fear him in any of his shapes:
Let me meet death rather than be a Prisoner.
        Prosp. 'Tis pity he should seize thy tender youth.
        Hip. Sir, I have often heard you say, no creature liv'd
Within this Isle, but those which Man was Lord of;
Why then should I fear?
        Prosp. But here are creatures which I nam'd not to thee,
Who share man's soveraignty by Nature's Laws,
And oft depose him from it.
30   *Hip.* What are those Creatures, Sir?
        Prosp. Those dangerous enemies of men call'd women.
        Hip. Women! I never heard of them before.
But have I Enemies within this Isle, and do you
Keep me from them? do you think that I want
Courage to encounter 'em?
        Prosp. No courage can resist 'em.
        Hip. How then have you, Sir,
Liv'd so long unharm'd among them?
        Prosp. O they despise old age, and spare it for that reason:
40 It is below their conquest, their fury falls
Alone upon the young.
        Hip. Why then the fury of the young should fall on them again.
Pray turn me loose upon 'em: but, good Sir,
What are women like?
        Prosp. Imagine something between young men and Angels:

25   of;] ~ , Q. F.

Fatally beauteous, and have killing Eyes;
Their voices charm beyond the Nightingales;
They are all enchantment; those who once behold 'em,
Are made their slaves for ever.
50   *Hip.* Then I will wink and fight with 'em.
     Prosp. 'Tis but in vain, for when your eyes are shut,
They through the lids will shine, and pierce your soul;
Absent, they will be present to you.
They'l haunt you in your very sleep.
     Hip. Then I'le revenge it on 'em when I wake.
     Prosp. You are without all possibility of revenge;
They are so beautiful that you can ne're attempt,
Nor wish to hurt them.
     Hip. Are they so beautiful?
60   *Prosp.* Calm sleep is not so soft, nor Winter Suns,
Nor Summer Shades so pleasant.
     Hip. Can they be fairer than the Plumes of Swans?
Or more delightful than the Peacocks Feathers?
Or than the gloss upon the necks of Doves?
Or have more various beauty than the Rain-bow?
These I have seen, and without danger wondred at.
     Prosp. All these are far below 'em: Nature made
Nothing but Woman dangerous and fair:
Therefore if you should chance to see 'em,
70 Avoid 'em streight, I charge you.
     Hip. Well, since you say they are so dangerous,
I'le so far shun 'em as I may with safety of the
Unblemish'd honour which you taught me.
But let 'em not provoke me, for I'm sure I shall
Not then forbear them.
     Prosp. Go in and read the Book I gave you last.
To morrow I may bring you better news.
     Hip. I shall obey you, Sir.   [*Exit* Hippolito.
     Prosp. So, so; I hope this lesson has secur'd him,
80 For I have been constrain'd to change his Lodging

46–47 Eyes; . . . Nightingales;] F; ~ , . . . ~ , Q.
48   enchantment;] F; ~ , Q.   56   revenge;] F; ~ , Q.

From yonder Rock where first I bred him up,
And here have brought him home to my own Cell,
Because the Shipwrack happen'd near his Mansion.
I hope he will not stir beyond his limits,
For hitherto he hath been all obedience:
The Planets seem to smile on my designs,
And yet there is one sullen cloud behind;
I would it were disperst.

Enter Miranda *and* Dorinda.

How, my daughters! I thought I had instructed
90 Them enough.————Children! retire;
Why do you walk this way?
    Mir. It is within our bounds, Sir.
    Prosp. But both take heed, that path is very dangerous.
Remember what I told you.
    Dor. Is the man that way, Sir?
    Prosp. All that you can imagine ill is there,
The curled Lyon, and the rugged Bear
Are not so dreadful as that man.
    Mir. Oh me, why stay we here then?
100   *Dor.* I'le keep far enough from his Den, I warrant him.
    Mir. But you have told me, Sir, you are a man;
And yet you are not dreadful.
    Prosp. I child! but I am a tame man; old men are tame
By Nature, but all the danger lies in a wild
Young man.
    Dor. Do they run wild about the Woods?
    Prosp. No, they are wild within Doors, in Chambers,
And in Closets.
    Dor. But Father, I would stroak 'em and make 'em gentle,
110 Then sure they would not hurt me.

---

87 behind;] ~ , Q, F.
88–88+ *s.d.* disperst. / *Enter*] ~ . [~ Q, F (*s.d. at right margin*).
90 enough.————] ~ :∧ Q, F.   96 ill is] F; is ill Q.

Prosp. You must not trust them, Child: no woman can come
Neer 'em but she feels a pain full nine Months:
Well I must in; for new affairs require my
Presence: be you, *Miranda,* your Sister's Guardian.

[*Exit* Prospero.

Dor. Come, Sister, shall we walk the other way?
The man will catch us else, we have but two legs,
And he perhaps has four.

Mir. Well, Sister, though he have; yet look about you
And we shall spy him e're he comes too near us.

120   *Dor.* Come back, that way is towards his Den.

Mir. Let me alone; I'le venture first, for sure he can
Devour but one of us at once.

Dor. How dare you venture?

Mir. We'll find him sitting like a Hare in's Form,
And he shall not see us.

Dor. I, but you know my Father charg'd us both.

Mir. But who shall tell him on't? we'll keep each
Others Counsel.

Dor. I dare not for the world.

130   *Mir.* But how shall we hereafter shun him, if we do not
Know him first?

Dor. Nay I confess I would fain see him too. I find it in my
Nature, because my Father has forbidden me.

Mir. I, there's it, Sister; if he had said nothing I had been
quiet. Go softly, and if you see him first, be quick and becken
me away.

Dor. Well, if he does catch me, I'le humble my self to him,
And ask him pardon, as I do my Father,
When I have done a fault.

140   *Mir.* And if I can but scape with life, I had rather be in pain
nine Months, as my Father threatn'd, than lose my longing.

[*Exeunt.*

115   way?] ∼ , Q, F.   134   Sister;] ∼ , Q, F.

SCENE V.

The Scene changes, and discovers Hippolito *in a Cave*
walking, his face from the Audience.

Hip. Prospero has often said that Nature makes
Nothing in vain: why then are women made?
Are they to suck the poyson of the Earth,
As gaudy colour'd Serpents are? I'le ask that
Question, when next I see him here.

Enter Miranda *and* Dorinda *peeping.*

Dor. O Sister, there it is, it walks about like one of us.
Mir. I, just so, and has legs as we have too.
Hip. It strangely puzzles me: yet 'tis most likely
Women are somewhat between men and spirits.
10   *Dor.* Heark! it talks, sure this is not it my Father meant,
For this is just like one of us: methinks I am not half
So much afraid on't as I was; see, now it turns this way.
Mir. Heaven! what a goodly thing it is!
Dor. I'le go nearer it.
Mir. O no, 'tis dangerous, Sister! I'le go to it.
I would not for the world that you should venture.
My Father charg'd me to secure you from it.
Dor. I warrant you this is a tame man, dear Sister,
He'll not hurt me, I see it by his looks.
20   *Mir.* Indeed he will! but go back, and he shall eat me first:
Fye, are you not asham'd to be so much inquisitive?
Dor. You chide me for't, and wou'd give your self.
Mir. Come back, or I will tell my Father.
Observe how he begins to stare already.
I'le meet the danger first, and then call you.
Dor. Nay, Sister, you shall never vanquish me in kindness.

SCENE V.] *omitted from* Q, F.   13 is!] ~ ? Q, F.

I'le venture you, no more than you will me.
> *Prosp. within. Miranda,* Child, where are you?
> *Mir.* Do you not hear my Father call? go in.
30   *Dor.* 'Twas you he nam'd, not me; I will but say my Prayers,
And follow you immediately.
> *Mir.* Well, Sister, you'l repent it.   [*Exit* Miranda.
> *Dor.* Though I dye for't, I must have th'other peep.
> *Hip. seeing her.* What thing is that? sure 'tis some Infant of
the Sun, dress'd in his Fathers gayest Beams, and comes to play
with Birds: my sight is dazl'd, and yet I find I'm loth to shut
my Eyes.
I must go nearer it————but stay a while;
May it not be that beauteous murderer, Woman,
40 Which I was charg'd to shun? Speak, what art thou?
Thou shining Vision!
> *Dor.* Alas I know not; but I'm told I am a Woman;
Do not hurt me, pray, fair thing.
> *Hip.* I'd sooner tear my eyes out, than consent to do you any
harm; though I was told a Woman was my Enemy.
> *Dor.* I never knew what 'twas to be an Enemy, nor can I
e're prove so to that which looks like you: for though I have
been charg'd by him (whom yet I never disobey'd) to shun your
presence, yet I'd rather dye than lose it; therefore I hope you
50 will not have the heart to hurt me: though I fear you are a man,
that dangerous thing of which I have been warn'd; pray tell
me what you are.
> *Hip.* I must confess, I was inform'd I am a man,
But if I fright you, I shall wish I were some other Creature.
I was bid to fear you too.
> *Dor.* Ay me! Heav'n grant we be not poyson to each other!
Alas, can we not meet but we must die?
> *Hip.* I hope not so! for when two poysonous Creatures,
Both of the same kind, meet, yet neither dies.
60 I've seen two Serpents harmless to each other,
Though they have twin'd into a mutual Knot:
If we have any venome in us, sure, we cannot be more

---

28   you?] F; ~ ! Q.   52   are.] ~ ? Q, F.

Poysonous, when we meet, than Serpents are.
You have a hand like mine, may I not gently touch it?

[*Takes her hand.*

Dor. I've touch'd my Father's and my Sister's hands
And felt no pain; but now, alas! there's something,
When I touch yours, which makes me sigh: just so
I've seen two Turtles mourning when they met;
Yet mine's a pleasing grief; and so methought was theirs;
70 For still they mourn'd, and still they seem'd to murmur too,
And yet they often met.

Hip. Oh Heavens! I have the same sense too: your hand
Methinks goes through me; I feel at my heart,
And find it pleases, though it pains me.

Prosp. within. Dorinda!

Dor. My Father calls agen, ah, I must leave you.

Hip. Alas, I'm subject to the same command.

Dor. This is my first offence against my Father,
Which he, by severing us, too cruelly does punish.

80 *Hip.* And this is my first trespass too: but he hath more
Offended truth than we have him:
He said our meeting would destructive be,
But I no death but in our parting see. [*Exeunt several ways.*

ACT III. SCENE I.

Enter Prospero *and* Miranda.

Prosp. Excuse it not, *Miranda,* for to you (the elder, and, I
thought the more discreet) I gave the conduct of your Sister's
actions.

Mir. Sir, when you call'd me thence, I did not fail to mind
her of her duty to depart.

Prosp. How can I think you did remember hers, when you
forgot your own? did you not see the man whom I commanded
you to shun?

ACT III. SCENE I.] ACT III. Q, F.

Mir. I must confess I saw him at a distance.

10 *Prosp.* Did not his Eyes infect and poyson you?
What alteration found you in your self?

Mir. I only wondred at a sight so new.

Prosp. But have you no desire once more to see him?
Come, tell me truly what you think of him.

Mir. As of the gayest thing I ever saw, so fine that it appear'd
more fit to be belov'd than fear'd, and seem'd so near my kind,
that I did think I might have call'd it Sister.

Prosp. You do not love it?

Mir. How is it likely that I should, except the thing had first
20 lov'd me?

Prosp. Cherish those thoughts: you have a gen'rous soul;
And since I see your mind not apt to take the light
Impressions of a sudden love, I will unfold
A secret to your knowledge.
That Creature which you saw, is of a kind which
Nature made a prop and guide to yours.

Mir. Why did you then propose him as an object of terrour
to my mind? you never us'd to teach me any thing but God-like
truths, and what you said I did believe as sacred.

30 *Prosp.* I fear'd the pleasing form of this young man
Might unawares possess your tender breast,
Which for a nobler Guest I had design'd;
For shortly, my *Miranda,* you shall see another of his kind,
The full blown-flower, of which this youth was but the
Op'ning-bud. Go in, and send your sister to me.

Mir. Heav'n still preserve you, Sir.   [*Ex.* Miranda.

Prosp. And make thee fortunate.
Dorinda now must be examin'd too concerning this
Late interview. I'm sure unartful truth lies open
40 In her mind, as Crystal streams their sandy bottom show.
I must take care her love grow not too fast,
For innocence is Love's most fertile soil,
Wherein he soon shoots up and widely spreads;

---

14 him.] ~ ? Q, F.
43 spreads;] ~ , Q, F.

GOSHEN COLLEGE LIBRARY
GOSHEN, INDIANA 46526

Nor is that danger which attends *Hippolito* yet overpast.

Enter Dorinda.

Prosp. O, come hither, you have seen a man to day,
Against my strict command.
  Dor. Who I? indeed I saw him but a little, Sir.
  Prosp. Come, come, be clear. Your Sister told me all.
  Dor. Did she? truly she would have seen him more than I,
50 But that I would not let her.
  Prosp. Why so?
  Dor. Because, methought, he would have hurt me less
Than he would her. But if I knew you'd not be angry
With him, I could tell you, Sir, that he was much to blame.
  Prosp. Hah! was he to blame?
Tell me, with that sincerity I taught you, how you became so
bold to see the man.
  Dor. I hope you will forgive me, Sir, because I did not see him
much till he saw me. Sir, he would needs come in my way, and
60 star'd, and star'd upon my face; and so I thought I would be re-
veng'd of him, and therefore I gaz'd on him as long; but if I
e're come neer a man again———
  Prosp. I told you he was dangerous; but you would not be
warn'd.
  Dor. Pray be not angry, Sir, if I tell you, you are mistaken in
him; for he did me no great hurt.
  Prosp. But he may do you more harm hereafter.
  Dor. No, Sir, I'm as well as e're I was in all my life,
But that I cannot eat nor drink for thought of him.
70 That dangerous man runs ever in my mind.
  Prosp. The way to cure you, is no more to see him.
  Dor. Nay, pray, Sir, say not so; I promis'd him
To see him once agen; and you know, Sir,
You charg'd me I should never break my promise.
  Prosp. Wou'd you see him who did you so much mischief?

44+ *s.d. Enter*] [~ Q, F (*s.d. at right margin*).   57 man.] ~ ? Q, F.
72 Nay, . . . so;] ~ᴧ . . . ~ , Q, F.

Dor. I warrant you I did him as much harm as he did me,
For when I left him, Sir, he sigh'd so as it griev'd
My heart to hear him.
    Prosp. Those sighs were poysonous, they infected you:
80 You say they griev'd you to the heart.
    Dor. 'Tis true; but yet his looks and words were gentle.
    Prosp. These are the Day-dreams of a maid in love,
But still I fear the worst.
    Dor. O fear not him, Sir,
I know he will not hurt you for my sake;
I'le undertake to tye him to a hair,
And lead him hither as my Pris'ner to you.
    Prosp. Take heed, *Dorinda,* you may be deceiv'd;
This Creature is of such a Salvage race,
90 That no mild usage can reclaim his wildness;
But, like a Lyon's whelp bred up by hand,
When least you look for't, Nature will present
The Image of his Fathers bloody Paws,
Wherewith he purvey'd for his couching Queen;
And he will leap into his native fury.
    Dor. He cannot change from what I left him, Sir.
    Prosp. You speak of him with too much passion; tell me
(And on your duty tell me true, *Dorinda*)
What past betwixt you and that horrid creature?
100   *Dor.* How, horrid, Sir? if any else but you should call it so,
indeed I should be angry.
    Prosp. Go to! you are a foolish Girl; but answer to what I ask,
what thought you when you saw it?
    Dor. At first it star'd upon me and seem'd wild,
And then I trembled; yet it look'd so lovely, that when
I would have fled away, my feet seem'd fasten'd to the ground;
Then it drew near, and with amazement askt
To touch my hand; which, as a ransom for my life,
I gave: but when he had it, with a furious gripe
110 He put it to his mouth so eagerly, I was afraid he

102   Go to] Go too Q, F.   105   trembled;] $\sim$, Q, F.
106   ground;] $\sim$, Q, F.

Would have swallow'd it.

    Prosp. Well, what was his behaviour afterwards?

    Dor. He on a sudden grew so tame and gentle,
That he became more kind to me than you are;
Then, Sir, I grew I know not how, and touching his hand
Agen, my heart did beat so strong as I lackt breath
To answer what he ask'd.

    Prosp. You have been too fond, and I should chide you for it.

    Dor. Then send me to that creature to be punisht.

120   *Prosp.* Poor Child! thy passion like a lazy Ague
Has seiz'd thy blood, instead of striving thou humour'st
And feed'st thy languishing disease: thou fight'st
The Battels of thy Enemy, and 'tis one part of what
I threatn'd thee, not to perceive thy danger.

    Dor. Danger, Sir?
If he would hurt me, yet he knows not how:
He hath no Claws, nor Teeth, nor Horns to hurt me,
But looks about him like a Callow-bird
Just straggl'd from the Nest: pray trust me, Sir,

130 To go to him agen.

    Prosp. Since you will venture,
I charge you bear your self reserv'dly to him,
Let him not dare to touch your naked hand,
But keep at distance from him.

    Dor. This is hard.

    Prosp. It is the way to make him love you more;
He will despise you if you grow too kind.

    Dor. I'le struggle with my heart to follow this,
But if I lose him by it, will you promise

140 To bring him back agen?

    Prosp. Fear not, *Dorinda;*
But use him ill and he'l be yours for ever.

    Dor. I hope you have not couzen'd me agen.   [*Exit* Dorinda.

    Prosp. Now my designs are gathering to a head.
My spirits are obedient to my charms.
What, *Ariel!* my servant *Ariel,* where art thou?

146+   *s.d. Enter*] F; [~ Q (*s.d. at right margin*).

Enter Ariel.

Ariel. What wou'd my potent Master? here I am.
Prosp. Thou and thy meaner fellows your last service
Did worthily perform, and I must use you in such another
150 Work: how goes the day?
  Ariel. On the fourth, my Lord, and on the sixth you said our
work should cease.
  Prosp. And so it shall;
And thou shalt have the open air at freedom.
  Ariel. Thanks my great Lord.
  Prosp. But tell me first, my spirit,
How fares the Duke, my Brother, and their followers?
  Ariel. Confin'd together, as you gave me order,
In the Lime-Grove which weather-fends your Cell;
160 Within that Circuit up and down they wander,
But cannot stir one step beyond their compass.
  Prosp. How do they bear their sorrows?
  Ariel. The two Dukes appear like men distracted, their
Attendants brim-full of sorrow mourning over 'em;
But chiefly, he you term'd *the good Gonzalo*:
His tears run down his Beard, like Winter-drops
From Eaves of Reeds; your Vision did so work 'em,
That if you now beheld 'em, your affections
Would become tender.
170   *Prosp.* Dost thou think so, Spirit?
  Ariel. Mine would, Sir, were I humane.
  Prosp. And mine shall:
Hast thou, who art but air, a touch, a feeling of their
Afflictions, and shall not I (a man like them, one
Who as sharply relish passions as they) be kindlier
Mov'd than thou art? though they have pierc'd
Me to the quick with injuries, yet with my nobler
Reason 'gainst my fury I will take part;
The rarer action is in virtue than in vengeance.

165 *the good*] the good Q, F.   167 Reeds;] $\sim$, Q, F.

180 Go, my *Ariel,* refresh with needful food their
Famish'd bodies. With shows and cheerful
Musick comfort 'em.
    Ariel. Presently, Master.
    Prosp. With a twinckle, *Ariel.*
    Ariel. Before you can say *come* and *go,*
And breath twice, and cry *so, so,*
Each spirit tripping on his toe,
Shall bring 'em meat with mop and moe;
Do you love me, Master, I, or no?
190   *Prosp.* Dearly, my dainty *Ariel,* but stay, spirit;
What is become of my Slave *Caliban,*
And *Sycorax* his Sister?
    Ariel. Potent Sir!
They have cast off your service, and revolted
To the wrack'd Mariners, who have already
Parcell'd your Island into Governments.
    Prosp. No matter, I have now no need of 'em;
But, spirit, now I stay thee on the Wing;
Haste to perform what I have given in charge:
200 But see they keep within the bounds I set 'em.
    Ariel. I'le keep 'em in with Walls of Adamant,
Invisible as air to mortal Eyes,
But yet unpassable.
    Prosp. Make hast then.   [*Exeunt severally.*

SCENE II.

Enter Alonzo, Antonio, Gonzalo.

    Gonz. I am weary, and can go no further, Sir;
My old Bones ake: here's a Maze trod indeed
Through forth-rights and Meanders: by your patience

---

185 *come . . . go*] come . . . go Q, F.   186 *so, so*] so; so Q, F.
188 moe;] ∼ , Q, F.
SCENE II.] *omitted from* Q, F.
1–3 Sir; . . . ake: . . . Meanders:] ∼, . . . ∼ , . . . ∼ , Q, F.

I needs must rest.
   Alonz. Old Lord, I cannot blame thee, who am my self seiz'd
With a weariness to the dulling of my Spirits:
Sit and rest.   [*They sit.*
Even here I will put off my hope, and keep it no longer
For my Flatterers: he is drown'd whom thus we
10 Stray to find, and the Sea mocks our frustrate
Search on Land: well! let him go.
   Ant. Do not for one repulse forego the purpose
Which you resolv'd t'effect.
   Alonz. I'm faint with hunger, and must despair
Of food, Heav'n hath incens'd the Seas and
Shores against us for our crimes.   [*Musick.*
What! Harmony agen, my good friends, heark!
   Anto. I fear some other horrid apparition.
Give us kind Keepers, Heaven I beseech thee!
20   *Gonz.* 'Tis chearful Musick, this, unlike the first;
And seems as 'twere meant t'unbend our cares,
And calm your troubled thoughts.

Ariel invisible Sings.

> *Dry those eyes which are o'reflowing,*
> *All your storms are over-blowing:*
> *While you in this Isle are bideing,*
> *You shall feast without providing:*
> *Every dainty you can think of,*
> *Ev'ry Wine which you would drink of,*
> *Shall be yours; all want shall shun you,*
> 30   *Ceres blessing so is on you.*

   Alonz. This voice speaks comfort to us.
   Ant. Wou'd 'twere come; there is no Musick in a Song
To me, my stomack being empty.
   Gonz. O for a heavenly Vision of Boyl'd,
Bak'd, and Roasted!

   Enter eight fat Spirits, with Cornu-Copia *in their hands.*

Alonz. Are these plump shapes sent to deride our hunger?

Gonz. No, no: it is a Masque of fatten'd Devils, the
Burgo-Masters of the lower Region.   [*Dance and vanish.*
O for a Collop of that large-haunch'd Devil
40 Who went out last!

Ant. going to the door. My Lord, the Duke, see yonder.
A Table, as I live, set out and furnisht
With all varieties of Meats and fruits.

Alonz. 'Tis so indeed, but who dares tast this feast,
Which Fiends provide, perhaps, to poyson us?

Gonz. Why that dare I; if the black Gentleman be so ill-
natur'd, he may do his pleasure.

Ant. 'Tis certain we must either eat or famish,
I will encounter it, and feed.
50 *Alonz.* If both resolve, I will adventure too.

Gonz. Then good my Lord, make haste,
And say no Grace before it, I beseech you,
Because the meat will vanish strait, if, as I fear,
An evil Spirit be our Cook.   [*Exeunt.*

SCENE III.

Enter Trincalo *and* Caliban.

Trinc. Brother Monster, welcome to my private Palace.
But where's thy Sister, is she so brave a Lass?

Calib. In all this Isle there are but two more, the Daughters
of the Tyrant *Prospero;* and she is bigger than 'em both. O here
she comes; now thou may'st judge thy self, my Lord.

Enter Sycorax.

Trinc. She's monstrous fair indeed. Is this to be my Spouse?
well, she's Heir of all this Isle (for I will geld Monster). The

Trincalos, like other wise men, have anciently us'd to marry for
Estate more than for beauty.   [*Aside.*
10   *Sycorax.* I prithee let me have the gay thing about thy neck,
and that which dangles at thy wrist.
          [Sycorax *points to his Bosens Whistle, and his Bottle.*
    Trinc. My dear Blobber-lips; this, observe my Chuck, is a
badge of my Sea-Office; my fair Fuss, thou dost not know it.
    Syc. No, my dread Lord.
    Trinc. It shall be a Whistle for our first Babe, and when the
next Shipwrack puts me again to swimming, I'le dive to get a
Coral to it.
    Syc. I'le be thy pretty child, and wear it first.
    Trinc. I prithee sweet Babby, do not play the wanton, and
20 cry for my goods e're I'm dead. When thou art my Widow, thou
shalt have the Devil and all.
    Syc. May I not have the other fine thing?
    Trinc. This is a sucking-Bottle for young *Trincalo.*
    Calib. This is a God-a-mighty liquor, I did but drink thrice
of it, and it hath made me glad e're since.
    Syc. He is the bravest God I ever saw.
    Calib. You must be kind to him, and he will love you.
I prithee speak to her, my Lord, and come neerer her.
    Trinc. By this light, I dare not till I have drank: I must
30 Fortifie my stomack first.
    Syc. I shall have all his fine things when I'm a Widow.
               [*Pointing to his Bottle, and Bosens Whistle.*
    Calib. I, but you must be kind and kiss him then.
    Trinc. My Brother Monster is a rare Pimp.   [*Aside.*
    Syc. I'le hug thee in my arms, my Brother's God.
    Trinc. Think o' thy soul *Trincalo,* thou art a dead man if
this kindness continue.
    Calib. And he shall get thee a young *Sycorax.* Wilt thou not,
my Lord?

---

9 beauty. [*Aside.*] beauty. Q, F.   19 Babby,] ~∧ Q, F.
24 God-a-mighty] F; God a mighty Q.   33 Pimp. [*Aside.*] Pimp. Q, F.
37 *Sycorax.* Wilt] ~ , wilt Q, F.

Trinc. Indeed I know not how, they do no such thing in my
40 Country.

Syc. I'le shew thee how: thou shalt get me twenty *Sycoraxes;*
and I'le get thee twenty *Calibans.*

Trinc. Nay, if they are got, she must do't all her self, that's
certain.

Syc. And we will tumble in cool Plashes, and the soft Fens,
Where we will make us Pillows of Flags and Bull-rushes.

Calib. My Lord, she would be loving to thee, and thou wilt
not let her.

Trinc. Ev'ry thing in its season, Brother Monster; but you
50 must counsel her; fair Maids must not be too forward.

Syc. My Brother's God, I love thee; prithee let me come to
thee.

Trinc. Subject Monster, I charge thee keep the Peace between us.

Calib. Shall she not taste of that immortal Liquor?

Trinc. Umph! that's another question: for if she be thus
flipant in her Water, what will she be in her Wine?

Enter Ariel *(invisible) and changes the Bottle which*
stands upon the ground.

Ariel. There's Water for your Wine.   [*Exit* Ariel.
Trinc. Well! since it must be so.   [*Gives her the Bottle.*
60 How do you like it now, my Queen that   [*She drinks.*
Must be?

Syc. Is this your heavenly liquor? I'le bring you to a River of
the same.

Trinc. Wilt thou so, Madam Monster? what a mighty Prince
shall I be then! I would not change my Dukedom to be great
Turk *Trincalo.*

Syc. This is the drink of Frogs.

Trinc. Nay, if the Frogs of this Island drink such, they are
the merryest Frogs in Christendom.

70   *Calib.* She does not know the virtue of this liquor:

57+   *s.d. Enter*] [~ Q, F (*s.d. at right margin*).   65   then!] ~ ? Q, F.

I prithee let me drink for her.

Trinc. Well said, Subject Monster.   [Caliban *drinks.*

Calib. My Lord, this is meer water.

Trinc. 'Tis thou hast chang'd the Wine then, and drunk it up,
Like a debauch'd Fish as thou art. Let me see't,
I'le taste it my self. Element! meer Element! as I live.
It was a cold gulp such as this which kill'd my famous
Predecessor, old *Simon* the King.

Calib. How does thy honour? prithee be not angry, and I will
80 lick thy shoe.

Trinc. I could find in my heart to turn thee out of my Dominions for a liquorish Monster.

Calib. O my Lord, I have found it out; this must be done by
one of *Prospero's* spirits.

Trinc. There's nothing but malice in these Devils, I never
lov'd 'em from my Childhood. The Devil take 'em, I would it
had bin holy-water for their sakes.

Syc. Will not thy mightiness revenge our wrongs, on this
great Sorcerer? I know thou wilt, for thou art valiant.

90   *Trinc.* In my Sack, Madam Monster, as any flesh alive.

Syc. Then I will cleave to thee.

Trinc. Lovingly said, in troth: now cannot I hold out against
her. This Wife-like virtue of hers, has overcome me.

Syc. Shall I have thee in my arms?

Trinc. Thou shalt have Duke *Trincalo* in thy arms:
But prithee be not too boistrous with me at first;
Do not discourage a young beginner.   [*They embrace.*
Stand to your Arms, my Spouse,
And subject Monster;

          Enter Stephano, Mustacho, *and* Ventoso.

100 The Enemy is come to surprise us in our Quarters.
You shall know, Rebels, that I'm marry'd to a Witch,

---

78   Predecessor,] ∼∧ Q, F.
99–99+   *s.d.* Monster; / *Enter* Stephano, Mustacho, *and* Ventoso.] ∼ ; [*Ent.*
Steph. Must. Vent. Q, F (*Enter* F; *s.d. at right margin*).
101   know, Rebels,] ∼∧ ∼∧ Q, F.

And we have a thousand Spirits of our party.

    Steph. Hold! I ask a Truce; I and my Vice-Roys
(Finding no food, and but a small remainder of Brandy)
Are come to treat a peace betwixt us,
Which may be for the good of both Armies,
Therefore *Trincalo* disband.

    Trinc. Plain *Trincalo*, methinks I might have been a Duke in
your mouth, I'le not accept of your Embassy without my title.

110   *Steph.* A title shall break no squares betwixt us.
Vice-Roys, give him his stile of Duke, and treat with him,
Whilst I walk by in state.

        [*Ventoso and* Mustacho *bow whilst* Trincalo *puts on his Cap.*

    Must. Our Lord and Master, Duke *Stephano,* has sent us
In the first place to demand of you, upon what
Ground you make war against him, having no right
To Govern here, as being elected only by
Your own voice.

    Trinc. To this I answer, that having in the face of the world
Espous'd the lawful Inheritrix of this Island,

120 Queen *Blouze* the first, and having homage done me,
By this hectoring Spark her Brother, from these two
I claim a lawful Title to this Island.

    Must. Who, that Monster? he a Hector?

    Calib. Lo! how he mocks me, wilt thou let him, my Lord?

    Vent. Lord! quoth he: the Monster's a very natural.

    Syc. Lo! lo! agen; bite him to death I prithee.

    Trinc. Vice-Roys! keep good tongues in your heads
I advise you, and proceed to your business, for I have
Other affairs to dispatch of more importance betwixt

130 Queen Slobber-Chops and my self.

    Must. First and foremost, as to your claim that you have
answer'd.

    Vent. But second and foremost, we demand of you,
That if we make a peace, the Butt also may be
Comprehended in the Treaty.

110   us.] ~ : Q, F.   125 *Lord*] Lord Q, F.

Must. Is the Butt safe, Duke *Trincalo?*

Trinc. The Butt is partly safe: but to comprehend it in the
Treaty, or indeed to make any Treaty, I cannot, with my honour, without your submission. These two, and the Spirits under
140   me, stand likewise upon their honours.

Calib. Keep the liquor for us, my Lord, and let them drink
Brine, for I will not show 'em the quick freshes of the Island.

Steph. I understand, being present, from my Embassadors
what your resolution is, and ask an hours time of deliberation,
and so I take our leave; but first I desire to be entertain'd at
your Butt, as becomes a Prince, and his Embassadors.

Trinc. That I refuse, till acts of Hostility be ceas'd.
These Rogues are rather Spies than Embassadors;
I must take heed of my Butt. They come to pry
150   Into the secrets of my Dukedom.

Vent. Trincalo you are a barbarous Prince, and so farewel.
                                        [*Exeunt* Steph. Must. Vent.

Trinc. Subject Monster! stand you Sentry before my Cellar;
my Queen and I will enter and feast our selves within.

Syc. May I not marry that other King and his two subjects,
to help you anights?

Trinc. What a careful Spouse have I! well! if she does
Cornute me, the care is taken.
When underneath my power my foes have truckl'd,
To be a Prince, who would not be a Cuckold?   [*Exeunt.*

SCENE IV.

Enter Ferdinand, *and* Ariel (*invisible.*)

Ferd. How far will this invisible Musician conduct
My steps? he hovers still about me, whether
For good or ill I cannot tell, nor care I much;
For I have been so long a slave to chance, that

---

138   cannot,] F; ∼∧ Q.   152   you] F; your Q.
156   I!] ∼? Q, F.   SCENE IV.] *omitted from Q, F.*

I'm as weary of her flatteries as her frowns:
But here I am——
  Ariel. Here I am.
  Ferd. Hah! art thou so? the Spirit's turn'd an Eccho:
This might seem pleasant, could the burthen of my
10 Griefs accord with any thing but sighs.
And my last words, like those of dying men,
Need no reply. Fain I would go to shades, where
Few would wish to follow me.
  Ariel. Follow me.
  Ferd. This evil Spirit grows importunate,
But I'le not take his counsel.
  Ariel. Take his counsel.
  Ferd. It may be the Devil's counsel. I'le never take it.
  Ariel. Take it.
20   *Ferd.* I will discourse no more with thee,
Nor follow one step further.
  Ariel. One step further.
  Ferd. This must have more importance than an Eccho.
Some Spirit tempts to a precipice.
I'le try if it will answer when I sing
My sorrows to the murmurs of this Brook.
    He Sings.
        Go thy way.
  Ariel.   *Go thy way.*
  Ferd.   *Why should'st thou stay?*
30   Ariel.   *Why should'st thou stay?*
  Ferd. *Where the Winds whistle, and where the streams creep,*
    Under yond Willow-tree, fain would I sleep.
      Then let me alone,
      For 'tis time to be gone.
  Ariel.   *For 'tis time to be gone.*
  Ferd. *What cares or pleasures can be in this Isle?*
    Within this desart place
    There lives no humane race;
  Fate cannot frown here, nor kind fortune smile.

---

5 frowns:] ~ , Q, F.   11 men,] ~ₐ Q, F.

40   Ariel. *Kind Fortune smiles, and she*
            Has yet in store for thee
            Some strange felicity.
            Follow me, follow me,
            And thou shalt see.
      Ferd. I'le take thy word for once;
      Lead on Musician.   *[Exeunt and return.*

SCENE V.

Scene changes, and discovers Prospero *and* Miranda.

Prosp. Advance the fringed Curtains of thine Eyes, and say
what thou seest yonder.
      Mir. Is it a Spirit?
Lord! how it looks about! Sir, I confess it carries a brave form.
But 'tis a Spirit.
      Prosp. No Girl, it eats and sleeps, and has such senses as we
have. This young Gallant, whom thou see'st, was in the wrack;
were he not somewhat stain'd with grief (beauty's worst Can-
cker) thou might'st call him a goodly person; he has lost his
10 company, and strays about to find 'em.
      Mir. I might call him a thing divine, for nothing natural I
ever saw so noble.
      Prosp. It goes on as my Soul prompts it.———*[Aside to*
Ariel.] Spirit, fine Spirit, I'le free thee within two days for this.
      Ferd. She's sure the Mistress, on whom these airs attend. Fair
Excellence, if, as your form declares, you are divine, be pleas'd
to instruct me how you will be worship'd; so bright a beauty
cannot sure belong to humane kind.
      Mir. I am, like you, a mortal, if such you are.
20   *Ferd.* My language too! O Heavens! I am the best of them
who speak this speech, when I'm in my own Country.
      Prosp. How, the best? what wert thou if the Duke of *Savoy*
heard thee?

SCENE V.] *omitted from Q, F.*
13-14 it.———*[Aside to* Ariel.] . . . fine Spirit,] it: . . . fine Spirit. Q, F.

Ferd. As I am now, who wonders to hear thee speak of *Savoy:*
he does hear me, and that he does I weep; my self am *Savoy,*
whose fatal Eyes (e're since at ebbe) beheld the Duke my Father
wrackt.

 Mir. Alack! for pity.

 Prosp. At the first sight they have chang'd Eyes, dear *Ariel,*
30 I'le set thee free for this. [*Aside.*]————Young Sir, a word.
With hazard of your self you do me wrong.

 Mir. Why speaks my Father so urgently?
This is the third man that e're I saw, the first whom
E're I sigh'd for; sweet Heaven move my Father
To be inclin'd my way.

 Ferd. O! if a Virgin! and your affection not gone forth,
I'le make you Mistress of *Savoy.*

 Prosp. Soft, Sir! one word more.
[*Aside.*] They are in each others powers, but this swift
40 Bus'ness I must uneasie make, lest too light
Winning make the prize light.————One word more.
Thou usurp'st the name not due to thee, and hast
Put thy self upon this Island as a spy to get the
Government from me, the Lord of it.

 Ferd. No, as I'm a man.

 Mir. There's nothing ill can dwell in such a Temple;
If th' Evil Spirit hath so fair a house,
Good things will strive to dwell with it.

 Prosp. No more. Speak not you for him, he's a Traytor.
50 Come! thou art my Pris'ner and shalt be in
Bonds. Sea-water shalt thou drink, thy food
Shall be the fresh-Brook-Muscles, wither'd Roots,
And Husks, wherein the Acorn cradl'd; follow.

 Ferd. No, I will resist such entertainment
Till my Enemy has more power.

     [*He draws, and is charm'd from moving.*

25 weep;] ∼ , Q, F.
30 this. [*Aside.*]————Young] this————young, Q, F (young∧ F).
34 for;] ∼ , Q, F.   39 [*Aside.*] They] They Q, F.
41 light.————One] ∼∧————one Q, F. 46 Temple;] ∼ , Q, F.
49 Traytor.] ∼ , Q, F.   53 cradl'd] crawl'd Q, F.

Mir. O dear Father! make not too rash a tryal
Of him, for he's gentle and not fearful.
    Prosp. My child my Tutor! put thy Sword up, Traytor,
Who mak'st a show, but dar'st not strike: thy
60 Conscience is possest with guilt. Come from
Thy Ward, for I can here disarm thee with
This Wand, and make thy Weapon drop.
    Mir. 'Beseech you, Father.
    Prosp. Hence: hang not on my Garment.
    Mir. Sir, have pity,
I'le be his Surety.
    Prosp. Silence! one word more shall make me chide thee,
If not hate thee: what, an advocate for an
Impostor? sure thou think'st there are no more
70 Such shapes as his?
To the most of men this is a *Caliban,*
And they to him are Angels.
    Mir. My affections are then most humble,
I have no ambition to see a goodlier man.
    Prosp. Come on, obey:
Thy Nerves are in their infancy agen, and have
No vigour in them.
    Ferd. So they are:
My Spirits, as in a Dream, are all bound up:
80 My Father's loss, the weakness which I feel,
The wrack of all my friends, and this man's threats,
To whom I am subdu'd, would seem light to me,
Might I but once a day through my Prison behold this maid:
All corners else o'th' Earth let liberty make use of:
I have space enough in such a Prison.
    Prosp. aside. It works.————[*To* Ferd.] Come on.
Thou hast done well, fine *Ariel.*————[*To* Ferd.] Follow me.
Heark what thou shalt more do for me.   [*Whispers* Ariel.

---

58 up,] ~∧ Q, F.   63 you,] ~∧ Q, F.
86 *Prosp. aside.* . . . works.————[*To* Ferd.] Come on.] *Prosp.* . . . works;
come on: Q, F.
87 *Ariel.*————[*To* Ferd.] Follow] *Ariel:* follow Q, F.

Mir. Be of comfort!
90 My Father's of a better nature, Sir,
Than he appears by speech: this is unwonted
Which now came from him.

 Prosp. Thou shalt be as free as Mountain Winds:
But then exactly do all points of my command.

 Ariel. To a Syllable.   *[Exit* Ariel.

 Prosp. to Mir. Go in that way, speak not a word for him:
I'le separate you.   *[Exit* Miranda.

 Ferd. As soon thou may'st divide the waters
When thou strik'st 'em, which pursue thy bootless blow,
100 And meet when 'tis past.

 Prosp. Go practise your Philosophy within,
And if you are the same you speak your self,
Bear your afflictions like a Prince.————That Door
Shews you your Lodging.

 Ferd. 'Tis in vain to strive, I must obey.   *[Exit* Ferd.

 Prosp. This goes as I would wish it.
Now for my second care, *Hippolito.*
I shall not need to chide him for his fault,
His passion is become his punishment.
110 Come forth, *Hippolito.*

Enter Hippolito.

Hip. entring. 'Tis *Prospero's* voice.

 Prosp. Hippolito! I know you now expect I should severely chide you: you have seen a woman in contempt of my commands.

 Hip. But, Sir, you see I am come off unharm'd;
I told you, that you need not doubt my courage.

 Prosp. You think you have receiv'd no hurt.

 Hip. No, none Sir.
Try me agen, when e're you please I'm ready:
120 I think I cannot fear an Army of 'em.

103 Prince.] ~∧ Q, F.   105 *s.d. Exit]* F; ~ . Q.
110–110+ *s.d. Hippolito. / Enter]* ~ . [~ Q, F *(s.d. at right margin).*

Prosp. How much in vain it is to bridle Nature!   [*Aside.*
Well! what was the success of your encounter?
   Hip. Sir, we had none, we yielded both at first,
For I took her to mercy, and she me.
   Prosp. But are you not much chang'd from what you were?
   Hip. Methinks I wish and wish! for what I know not,
But still I wish.————Yet if I had that woman,
She, I believe, could tell me what I wish for.
   Prosp. What wou'd you do to make that Woman yours?
130   *Hip.* I'd quit the rest o'th' world that I might live alone with
Her, she never should be from me.
We two would sit and look till our eyes ak'd.
   Prosp. You'd soon be weary of her.
   Hip. O, Sir, never.
   Prosp. But you'l grow old and wrinckl'd, as you see me now,
And then you will not care for her.
   Hip. You may do what you please, but, Sir, we two can never
possibly grow old.
   Prosp. You must, *Hippolito.*
140   *Hip.* Whether we will or no, Sir, who shall make us?
   Prosp. Nature, which made me so.
   Hip. But you have told me her works are various;
She made you old, but she has made us young.
   Prosp. Time will convince you,
Mean while be sure you tread in honours paths,
That you may merit her, and that you may not want
Fit occasions to employ your virtue: in this next
Cave there is a stranger lodg'd, one of your kind,
Young, of a noble presence, and as he says himself,
150 Of Princely birth; he is my Pris'ner and in deep
Affliction: visit, and comfort him; it will become you.
   Hip. It is my duty, Sir.   [*Exit* Hippolito.
   Prosp. True, he has seen a woman, yet he lives; perhaps I took
the moment of his birth amiss, perhaps my Art it self is false: on

---

127 wish.————Yet] ~ ∧————yet Q, F.   132 two] F; too Q.
147–151 virtue: . . . birth; . . . Affliction:] ~ , . . . ~ , . . . ~ , Q, F.
153 lives;] ~ , Q, F.

what strange grounds we build our hopes and fears; mans life is
all a mist, and in the dark, our fortunes meet us.
If Fate be not, then what can we foresee,
Or how can we avoid it, if it be?
If by free-will in our own paths we move,
160 How are we bounded by Decrees above?
Whether we drive, or whether we are driven,
If ill 'tis ours, if good the act of Heaven.   [*Exit* Prospero.

SCENE VI.

Scene, a Cave.

Enter Hippolito *and* Ferdinand.

Ferd. Your pity, noble youth, doth much oblige me,
Indeed 'twas sad to lose a Father so.
   Hip. I, and an only Father too, for sure you said
You had but one.
   Ferd. But one Father! he's wondrous simple!   [*Aside.*
   Hip. Are such misfortunes frequent in your world,
Where many men live?
   Ferd. Such we are born to.
But gentle youth, as you have question'd me,
10 So give me leave to ask you, what you are.
   Hip. Do not you know?
   Ferd. How should I?
   Hip. I well hop'd I was a man, but by your ignorance
Of what I am, I fear it is not so.
Well, *Prospero!* this is now the second time   [*Aside.*
You have deceiv'd me.
   Ferd. Sir, there is no doubt you are a man:

155 fears;] ∼ , Q, F.   SCENE VI.] *omitted from Q, F.*
s.d. Scene, a Cave. / Enter . . . Ferdinand.] F; *Enter . . .* Ferdinand. / *Scene,
a Cave.* Q.
10 are.] ∼ ? Q, F.   14 so.] ∼ : Q, F.
15 time [*Aside.*] time Q, F.

But I would know of whence?

Hip. Why, of this world; I never was in yours.

20   *Ferd.* Have you a Father?

Hip. I was told I had one, and that he was a man, yet I have bin so much deceived, I dare not tell't you for a truth; but I have still been kept a Prisoner for fear of women.

Ferd. They indeed are dangerous, for since I came I have beheld one here, whose beauty pierc'd my heart.

Hip. How did she pierce? you seem not hurt.

Ferd. Alas! the wound was made by her bright eyes,
And festers by her absence.
But to speak plainer to you, Sir, I love her.

30   *Hip.* Now I suspect that love's the very thing, that I feel too! pray tell me truly, Sir, are you not grown unquiet since you saw her?

Ferd. I take no rest.

Hip. Just, just my disease.
Do you not wish you do not know for what?

Ferd. O no! I know too well for what I wish.

Hip. There, I confess, I differ from you, Sir:
But you desire she may be always with you?

Ferd. I can have no felicity without her.

40   *Hip.* Just my condition! alas, gentle Sir,
I'le pity you, and you shall pity me.

Ferd. I love so much, that if I have her not,
I find I cannot live.

Hip. How! do you love her?
And would you have her too? that must not be:
For none but I must have her.

Ferd. But perhaps, we do not love the same:
All beauties are not pleasing alike to all.

Hip. Why, are there more fair Women, Sir,
50   Besides that one I love?

Ferd. That's a strange question. There are many more besides that beauty which you love.

19   world;] ~ , Q, F.   49   Why,] ~ ∧ Q, F.

Hip. I will have all of that kind, if there be a hundred of 'em.

Ferd. But noble youth, you know not what you say.

Hip. Sir, they are things I love, I cannot be without 'em:
O, how I rejoyce! more women!

Ferd. Sir, if you love you must be ty'd to one.

Hip. Ty'd! how ty'd to her?

Ferd. To love none but her.

60 *Hip.* But, Sir, I find it is against my Nature.
I must love where I like, and I believe I may like all,
All that are fair: come! bring me to this Woman,
For I must have her.

    Ferd. His simplicity
Is such that I can scarce be angry with him.   *[Aside.*
Perhaps, sweet youth, when you behold her,
You will find you do not love her.

Hip. I find already I love, because she is another Woman.

Ferd. You cannot love two women, both at once.

70 *Hip.* Sure 'tis my duty to love all who do resemble
Her whom I've already seen. I'le have as many as I can,
That are so good, and Angel-like, as she I love.
And will have yours.

    Ferd. Pretty youth, you cannot.

Hip. I can do any thing for that I love.

Ferd. I may, perhaps, by force restrain you from it.

Hip. Why, do so if you can. But either promise me
To love no Woman, or you must try your force.

Ferd. I cannot help it, I must love.

80 *Hip.* Well, you may love, for *Prospero* taught me friendship
too: you shall love me and other men if you can find 'em, but
all the Angel-women shall be mine.

    Ferd. I must break off this conference, or he will
Urge me else beyond what I can bear.
Sweet youth! some other time we will speak
Further concerning both our loves; at present
I am indispos'd with weariness and grief,
And would, if you are pleas'd, retire a while.

---

77 Why,] ~∧ Q, F.   80 Well,] ~∧ Q, F.

Hip. Some other time be it; but, Sir, remember
90 That I both seek and much intreat your friendship,
For next to Women, I find I can love you.
    Ferd. I thank you, Sir, I will consider of it.   [*Exit* Ferdinand.
    Hip. This Stranger does insult and comes into my
World to take those heavenly beauties from me,
Which I believe I am inspir'd to love,
And yet he said he did desire but one.
He would be poor in love, but I'le be rich:
I now perceive that *Prospero* was cunning;
For when he frighted me from woman-kind,
100 Those precious things he for himself design'd.   [*Exit.*

ACT IV.   SCENE I.

Enter Prospero, *and* Miranda.

Prosp. Your suit has pity in't, and has prevail'd.
Within this Cave he lies, and you may see him:
But yet take heed; let Prudence be your Guide;
You must not stay, your visit must be short.   [*She's going.*
One thing I had forgot; insinuate into his mind
A kindness to that youth, whom first you saw;
I would have friendship grow betwixt 'em.
    Mir. You shall be obey'd in all things.
    Prosp. Be earnest to unite their very souls.
10   *Mir.* I shall endeavour it.
    Prosp. This may secure *Hippolito* from that dark danger
which my art forebodes; for friendship does provide a double
strength t'oppose th' assaults of fortune.   [*Exit* Prospero.

Enter Ferdinand.

Ferd. To be a Pris'ner where I dearly love, is but a double
tye; a Link of fortune joyn'd to the chain of love; but not to see

ACT IV. SCENE I.] ACT IV. Q, F.

her, and yet to be so near her, there's the hardship; I feel my self as on a Rack, stretch'd out, and nigh the ground, on which I might have ease, yet cannot reach it.

    Mir. Sir! my Lord? where are you?

20   *Ferd.* Is it your voice, my Love? or do I dream?

    Mir. Speak softly, it is I.

    Ferd. O heavenly Creature! ten times more gentle, than your Father's cruel, how on a sudden all my griefs are vanish'd!

    Mir. I come to help you to support your griefs.

    Ferd. While I stand gazing thus, and thus have leave to touch your hand, I do not envy freedom.

    Mir. Heark! heark! is't not my Father's voice I hear? I fear he calls me back again too soon.

    Ferd. Leave fear to guilty minds: 'tis scarce a virtue when it is
30 paid to Heaven.

    Mir. But there 'tis mix'd with love, and so is mine; yet I may fear, for I am guilty when I disobey my Fathers will in loving you too much.

    Ferd. But you please Heav'n in disobeying him, Heav'n bids you succour Captives in distress.

    Mir. How do you bear your Prison?

    Ferd. 'Tis my Palace while you are here, and love and silence wait upon our wishes; do but think we chuse it, and 'tis what we would chuse.

40   *Mir.* I'm sure what I would.

But how can I be certain that you love me?

Look to't; for I will dye when you are false.

I've heard my Father tell of Maids, who dy'd,

And haunted their false Lovers with their Ghosts.

    Ferd. Your Ghost must take another form to fright me,

This shape will be too pleasing: do I love you?

O Heav'n! O Earth! bear witness to this sound,

If I prove false———

    Mir. Oh hold, you shall not swear;

50 For Heav'n will hate you if you prove forsworn.

    Ferd. Did I not love, I could no more endure this undeserved captivity, than I could wish to gain my freedom with the loss of you.

Mir. I am a fool to weep at what I'm glad of: but I have a suit to you, and that, Sir, shall be now the only tryal of your love.

Ferd. Y'ave said enough, never to be deny'd, were it my life; for you have far o'rebid the price of all that humane life is worth.

60   *Mir.* Sir, 'tis to love one for my sake, who for his own deserves all the respect which you can ever pay him.

Ferd. You mean your Father: do not think his usage can make me hate him; when he gave you being, he then did that which cancell'd all these wrongs.

Mir. I meant not him, for that was a request which if you love I should not need to urge.

Ferd. Is there another whom I ought to love?
And love him for your sake?

Mir. Yes, such a one, who for his sweetness and his goodly
70 shape, (if I, who am unskill'd in forms, may judge) I think can scarce be equall'd: 'Tis a youth, a Stranger too as you are.

Ferd. Of such a graceful feature, and must I for your sake love?

Mir. Yes, Sir, do you scruple to grant the first request I ever made? he's wholly unacquainted with the world, and wants your conversation. You should have compassion on so meer a stranger.

Ferd. Those need compassion whom you discommend, not whom you praise.

80   *Mir.* I only ask this easie tryal of you.

Ferd. Perhaps it might have easier bin
If you had never ask'd it.

Mir. I cannot understand you; and methinks am loth
To be more knowing.

Ferd. He has his freedom, and may get access, when my

---

52   than] F; then Q.   69   Yes,] ~∧ Q, F.

Confinement makes me want that blessing.
I his compassion need, and not he mine.
     Mir. If that be all you doubt, trust me for him.
He has a melting heart, and soft to all the Seals
90 Of kindness; I will undertake for his compassion.
     Ferd. O Heavens! would I were sure I did not need it.
     Mir. Come, you must love him for my sake: you shall.
     Ferd. Must I for yours, and cannot for my own?
Either you do not love, or think that I do not:
But when you bid me love him, I must hate him.
     Mir. Have I so far offended you already,
That he offends you only for my sake?
Yet sure you would not hate him, if you saw
Him as I have done, so full of youth and beauty.
100   *Ferd.* O poyson to my hopes!
When he did visit me, and I did mention this   [*Aside.*
Beauteous Creature to him, he did then tell me
He would have her.
     Mir. Alas, what mean you?
     Ferd. aside. It is too plain: like most of her frail Sex, she's false,
But has not learnt the art to hide it;
Nature has done her part, she loves variety:
Why did I think that any Woman could be innocent,
Because she's young? No, no, their Nurses teach them
110 Change, when with two Nipples they divide their
Liking.
     Mir. I fear I have offended you, and yet I meant no harm:
But if you please to hear me————   [*A noise within.*
Heark! Sir! now I am sure my Father comes, I know
His steps; dear Love retire a while, I fear
I've stay'd too long.
     Ferd. Too long indeed, and yet not long enough: oh jealousie!
Oh Love! how you distract me!   [*Exit* Ferdinand.
     Mir. He appears displeas'd with that young man, I know

100–101 hopes! / . . . this [*Aside.*] hopes! [*Aside.* / . . . this Q, F.
105   *Ferd. aside.*] *Ferd.* Q, F.   118 me!] ~? Q, F.
118   s.d. Ferdinand.] F; ~ₐ Q.

120 Not why: but, till I find from whence his hate proceeds,
I must conceal it from my Fathers knowledge,
For he will think that guiltless I have caus'd it;
And suffer me no more to see my Love.

Enter Prospero.

Prosp. Now I have been indulgent to your wish,
You have seen the Prisoner?
Mir. Yes.
Prosp. And he spake to you?
Mir. He spoke; but he receiv'd short answers from me.
Prosp. How like you his converse?
130   *Mir.* At second sight
A man does not appear so rare a Creature.
Prosp. aside. I find she loves him much because she hides it.
Love teaches cunning even to innocence,
And where he gets possession, his first work is to
Dig deep within a heart, and there lie hid,
And like a Miser in the dark to feast alone.
But tell me, dear *Miranda,* how does he suffer
His imprisonment?
Mir. I think he seems displeas'd.
140   *Prosp.* O then 'tis plain his temper is not noble,
For the brave with equal minds bear good
And evil fortune.
Mir. O, Sir, but he's pleas'd again so soon
That 'tis not worth your noting.
Prosp. To be soon displeas'd and pleas'd so suddenly again,
Does shew him of a various froward Nature.
Mir. The truth is, Sir, he was not vex'd at all, but only
Seem'd to be so.
Prosp. If he be not and yet seems angry, he is a dissembler,
150 Which shews the worst of Natures.
Mir. Truly, Sir, the man has faults enough; but in my con-
science that's none of 'em. He can be no dissembler.

123–123+   *s.d.* Love. / *Enter*] F; ∼ . [∼ Q (*s.d. at right margin*).

Prosp. aside. How she excuses him, and yet desires that I should judge her heart indifferent to him!———Well, since his faults are many, I am glad you love him not.

Mir. 'Tis like, Sir, they are many,
But I know none he has, yet let me often see him
And I shall find 'em all in time.

Prosp. I'le think on't.
160 Go in, this is your hour of Orizons.

Mir. aside. Forgive me, truth, for thus disguising thee; if I can make him think I do not love the stranger much, he'll let me see him oftner.   [*Exit* Miranda.

Prosp. Stay! stay———I had forgot to ask her what she has said
Of young *Hippolito:* Oh! here he comes! and with him
My *Dorinda.*

Enter Hippolito *and* Dorinda.

I'le not be seen, let
Their loves grow in secret.   [*Exit* Prospero.

Hip. But why are you so sad?

Dor. But why are you so joyful?

170 *Hip.* I have within me all, all the various Musick of
The Woods. Since last I saw you I have heard brave news!
I'le tell you, and make you joyful for me.

Dor. Sir, when I saw you first, I through my eyes drew
Something in, I know not what it is;
But still it entertains me with such thoughts
As makes me doubtful whether joy becomes me.

Hip. Pray believe me;
As I'm a man, I'le tell you blessed news.
I have heard there are more Women in the World,
180 As fair as you are too.

Dor. Is this your news? you see it moves not me.

Hip. And I'le have 'em all.

---

154 him!———Well] him? well Q, F (Well F).
166 *Dorinda.* / *Enter . . . Dorinda.* / I'le . . . let] *Dorinda.* I'le . . . let
[*Ent. . . .* Dorinda. Q, F (*Enter* F).

Dor. What will become of me then?

Hip. I'le have you too.

But are not you acquainted with these Women?

 Dor. I never saw but one.

 Hip. Is there but one here?

This is a base poor world, I'le go to th' other;

I've heard men have abundance of 'em there.

90 But pray where is that one Woman?

 Dor. Who, my Sister?

 Hip. Is she your Sister? I'm glad o' that: you shall help me to

her, and I'le love you for't.   [*Offers to take her hand.*

 Dor. Away! I will not have you touch my hand.

My Father's counsel which enjoyn'd reservedness, [*Aside.*

Was not in vain I see.

 Hip. What makes you shun me?

 Dor. You need not care, you'l have my Sisters hand.

 Hip. Why, must not he who touches hers touch yours?

200 *Dor.* You mean to love her too.

 Hip. Do not you love her?

Then why should not I do so?

 Dor. She is my Sister, and therefore I must love her:

But you cannot love both of us.

 Hip. I warrant you I can:

Oh that you had more Sisters!

 Dor. You may love her, but then I'le not love you.

 Hip. O but you must;

One is enough for you, but not for me.

210 *Dor.* My Sister told me she had seen another;

A man like you, and she lik'd only him;

Therefore if one must be enough for her,

He is that one, and then you cannot have her.

 Hip. If she like him, she may like both of us.

 Dor. But how if I should change and like that man?

Would you be willing to permit that change?

 Hip. No, for you lik'd me first.

 Dor. So you did me.

 Hip. But I would never have you see that man;

220 I cannot bear it.

    Dor. I'le see neither of you.

    Hip. Yes, me you may, for we are now acquainted;
But he's the man of whom your Father warn'd you:
O! he's a terrible, huge, monstrous creature,
I am but a Woman to him.

    Dor. I will see him,
Except you'l promise not to see my Sister.

    Hip. Yes, for your sake I needs must see your Sister.

    Dor. But she's a terrible, huge Creature too; if I were not
230 Her Sister she would eat me; therefore take heed.

    Hip. I heard that she was fair, and like you.

    Dor. No, indeed, she's like my Father, with a great Beard,
'Twould fright you to look on her,
Therefore that man and she may go together,
They are fit for no body but one another.

    Hip. looking in. Yonder he comes with glaring eyes, fly! fly!
Before he sees you.

    Dor. Must we part so soon?

    Hip. Y'are a lost Woman if you see him.

240   *Dor.* I would not willingly be lost, for fear you
Should not find me. I'le avoid him.   [*Exit* Dorinda.

    Hip. She fain would have deceived me, but I know her
Sister must be fair, for she's a Woman;
All of a Kind that I have seen are like to one
Another: all the Creatures of the Rivers and
The Woods are so.

Enter Ferdinand.

    Ferd. O! well encounter'd, you are the happy man!
Y'have got the hearts of both the beauteous Women.

    Hip. How! Sir? pray, are you sure on't?

250   *Ferd.* One of 'em charg'd me to love you for her sake.

    Hip. Then I must have her.

---

228 Yes,] ~ᴧ Q, F.   237 Before] F; before Q.
246–246+   *s.d. so. / Enter*] F; ~ . [~ Q (*s.d. at right margin*).

Ferd. No, not till I am dead.

Hip. How dead? what's that? but whatsoe're it be
I long to have her.

Ferd. Time and my grief may make me dye.

Hip. But for a friend you should make haste; I ne're ask'd
Any thing of you before.

Ferd. I see your ignorance;
And therefore will instruct you in my meaning.
260 The Woman, whom I love, saw you and lov'd you.
Now, Sir, if you love her you'l cause my death.

Hip. Besure I'le do't then.

Ferd. But I am your friend;
And I request you that you would not love her.

Hip. When friends request unreasonable things,
Sure th'are to be deny'd: you say she's fair,
And I must love all who are fair; for, to tell
You a secret, Sir, which I have lately found
Within my self, they all are made for me.

270 *Ferd.* That's but a fond conceit: you are made for one, and
one for you.

Hip. You cannot tell me, Sir.
I know I'm made for twenty hundred Women,
(I mean if there so many be i'th' World)
So that if once I see her I shall love her.

Ferd. Then do not see her.

Hip. Yes, Sir, I must see her.
For I wou'd fain have my heart beat again,
Just as it did when I first saw her Sister.

280 *Ferd.* I find I must not let you see her then.

Hip. How will you hinder me?

Ferd. By force of Arms.

Hip. By force of Arms?
My Arms perhaps may be as strong as yours.

Ferd. He's still so ignorant that I pity him, and fain
Would avoid force. [*Aside.*]————Pray, do not see her, she was

269   self,] ~ ; Q, F.   272   Sir.] F; ~ , Q.
273   Women,] ~ . Q, F.   286   force. [*Aside.*]————Pray] force: pray Q, F.

Mine first; you have no right to her.

Hip. I have not yet consider'd what is right, but, Sir,
I know my inclinations are to love all Women:
290 And I have been taught that to dissemble what I
Think is base. In honour then of truth, I must
Declare that I do love, and I will see your Woman.

Ferd. Wou'd you be willing I should see and love your
Woman, and endeavour to seduce her from that
Affection which she vow'd to you?

Hip. I wou'd not you should do it, but if she should
Love you best, I cannot hinder her.
But, Sir, for fear she shou'd, I will provide against
The worst, and try to get your Woman.

300 *Ferd.* But I pretend no claim at all to yours;
Besides you are more beautiful than I,
And fitter to allure unpractis'd hearts.
Therefore I once more beg you will not see her.

Hip. I'm glad you let me know I have such beauty.
If that will get me Women, they shall have it
As far as e're 'twill go: I'le never want 'em.

Ferd. Then since you have refused this act of friendship,
Provide your self a Sword; for we must fight.

Hip. A Sword, what's that?

310 *Ferd.* Why such a thing as this.

Hip. What should I do with it?

Ferd. You must stand thus, and push against me,
While I push at you, till one of us fall dead.

Hip. This is brave sport,
But we have no Swords growing in our World.

Ferd. What shall we do then to decide our quarrel?

Hip. We'll take the Sword by turns, and fight with it.

Ferd. Strange ignorance! you must defend your life,
And so must I: but since you have no Sword
320 Take this; [*Gives him his sword.*] for in a corner of my Cave
I found a rusty one, perhaps 'twas his who keeps

---

320 [*Gives . . . sword.*] for . . . Cave] for . . . Cave [*Gives . . . sword.* Q, F.

Me Pris'ner here: that I will fit:
When next we meet prepare your self to fight.
   Hip. Make haste then, this shall ne're be yours agen.
I mean to fight with all the men I meet, and
When they are dead, their Women shall be mine.
   Ferd. I see you are unskilful; I desire not to take
Your life, but if you please we'll fight on
These conditions; He who first draws bloud,
330 Or who can take the others Weapon from him,
Shall be acknowledg'd as the Conquerour,
And both the Women shall be his.
   Hip. Agreed,
And ev'ry day I'le fight for two more with you.
   Ferd. But win these first.
   Hip. I'le warrant you I'le push you.   [*Exeunt severally.*

SCENE II.

Enter Trincalo, Caliban, Sycorax.

   Calib. My Lord, I see 'em coming yonder.
   Trinc. Who?
   Calib. The starv'd Prince, and his two thirsty Subjects,
That would have our Liquor.
   Trinc. If thou wert a Monster of parts I would make thee
My Master of Ceremonies, to conduct 'em in.
The Devil take all Dunces, thou hast lost a brave
Employment by not being a Linguist, and for want
Of behaviour.
10   *Syc.* My Lord, shall I go meet 'em? I'le be kind to all of 'em,
Just as I am to thee.
   Trinc. No, that's against the fundamental Laws of my Duke-
dom: you are in a high place, Spouse, and must give good Ex-

SCENE II.] *omitted from Q, F.*

ample. Here they come, we'll put on the gravity of Statesmen, and be very dull, that we may be held wise.

Enter Stephano, Ventoso, Mustacho.

Vent. Duke *Trincalo,* we have consider'd.

Trinc. Peace, or War?

Must. Peace, and the Butt.

Steph. I come now as a private person, and promise to live
20 peaceably under your Government.

Trinc. You shall enjoy the benefits of Peace; and the first Fruits of it, amongst all civil Nations, is to be drunk for joy. *Caliban* skink about.

Steph. I long to have a Rowse to her Graces health, and to the *Haunse in Kelder,* or rather Haddock in *Kelder,* for I guess it will be half Fish.   [*Aside.*

Trinc. Subject *Stephano* here's to thee; and let old quarrels be drown'd in this draught.   [*Drinks.*

Steph. Great Magistrate, here's thy Sisters health to thee.
[*Drinks to* Caliban.
30 *Syc.* He shall not drink of that immortal liquor,
My Lord, let him drink water.

Trinc. O sweet heart, you must not shame your self to day.
Gentlemen Subjects, pray bear with her good Huswifry:
She wants a little breeding, but she's hearty.

Must. Ventoso here's to thee. Is it not better to pierce the Butt, than to quarrel and pierce one anothers bellies?

Vent. Let it come Boy.

Trinc. Now wou'd I lay greatness aside, and shake my heels, if I had but Musick.

40 *Calib.* O my Lord! my Mother left us in her Will a hundred Spirits to attend us, Devils of all sorts, some great roaring Devils, and some little singing Sprights.

Syc. Shall we call? and thou shalt hear them in the Air.

Trinc. I accept the motion: let us have our Mother-in-Law's Legacy immediately.

---

22   joy.] ~ : Q, F.

Calib. sings. We want Musick, we want Mirth,
　　　Up, Dam, and cleave the Earth,
　　　We have now no Lords that wrong us,
　　　Send thy merry Sprights among us.
　　　　　　　　　　　　　　　[*Musick heard.*
50　*Trinc.* What a merry Tyrant am I, to have my
Musick and pay nothing for't! come, hands, hands,
Let's lose no time while the Devil's in the
Humour.   [*A Dance.*
　Trinc. Enough, enough: now to our Sack agen.
　Vent. The Bottle's drunk.
　Must. Then the Bottle's a weak shallow fellow if it be drunk
first.
　Trinc. Caliban, give Bottle the belly full agen. [*Exit* Caliban.
　Steph. May I ask your Grace a question? pray is that hectoring
60　Spark, as you call'd him, flesh or fish?
　Trinc. Subject, I know not, but he drinks like a fish.

　　　　　　　　　Enter Caliban.

　Steph. O here's the Bottle agen; he has made a good voyage,
Come, who begins a Brindis to the Duke?
　Trinc. I'le begin it my self: give me the Bottle; 'tis my
Prerogative to drink first; *Stephano,* give me thy hand,
Thou hast been a Rebel, but here's to thee.   [*Drinks.*
Prithee why should we quarrel? shall I swear
Two Oaths? by Bottle, and by Butt I love thee:
In witness whereof I drink soundly.
70　*Steph.* Your Grace shall find there's no love lost,
For I will pledge you soundly.
　Trinc. Thou hast been a false Rebel, but that's all one;
Pledge my Grace faithfully.
　Steph. I will pledge your Grace *Up se Dutch.*

46–49　*We . . .* [*italics*] *. . . us*] F; *in romans in* Q.
47　*Up, Dam,*] Up Dam Q; *Up Dam* F.　　　　51　for't!] ∼? Q, F.
51　come,] F; ∼∧ Q.　　　　58　agen. [*Exit* Caliban.] agen. Q, F.
61　Subject,] ∼∧ Q, F.　　　　61+　*s.d. Enter*] [∼ Q, F (*s.d. at right margin*).
66　thee.] ∼ , Q, F.　　　　74　*Up se Dutch*] Up se Dutch Q, F.

Trinc. But thou shalt not pledge me before I have drunk
agen; would'st thou take the Liquor of Life out of my hands?
I see thou art a piece of a Rebel still, but here's to thee.
[*Drinks.*]———Now thou shalt have it.   [Stephano *drinks.*
      Vent. We loyal Subjects may be choak'd for any drink we can
80 get.
      Trinc. Have patience good people, you are unreasonable,
you'd be drunk as soon as I. *Ventoso* you shall have your time,
but you must give place to *Stephano.*
      Must. Brother *Ventoso,* I am afraid we shall lose our places.
The Duke grows fond of *Stephano,* and will declare him
Vice-Roy.
      Steph. I ha' done my worst at your Graces Bottle.
      Trinc. Then the Folks may have it. *Caliban*
Go to the Butt, and tell me how it sounds.   [*Exit* Caliban.
90 Peer *Stephano,* dost thou love me?
      Steph. I love your Grace and all your Princely Family.
      Trinc. 'Tis no matter, if thou lov'st me; hang my Family:
Thou art my Friend, prithee tell me what
Thou think'st of my Princess.
      Steph. I look on her as on a very noble Princess.
      Trinc. Noble? indeed she had a Witch to her Mother, and the
Witches are of great Families in *Lapland,* but the Devil was her
Father, and I have heard of the Mounsor *De-Viles* in *France;*
but look on her beauty, is she a fit Wife for Duke *Trincalo?*
100 mark her behaviour too, she's tippling yonder with the serving-
men.
      Steph. An please your Grace she's somewhat homely, but
that's no blemish in a Princess. She is virtuous.
      Trinc. Umph! virtuous! I am loth to disparage her;
But thou art my Friend, canst thou be close?
      Steph. As a stopt Bottle, an't please your Grace.

              Enter Caliban *agen with a Bottle.*

76 agen;] ∼ , Q, F.   76 hands?] ∼ ; Q, F.
77–78 thee. [*Drinks.*]———Now] thee, now Q, F.
89 sounds. [*Exit* Caliban.] sounds: Q, F.   92 matter,] ∼∧ Q, F.
94 Princess.] F; ∼ ? Q.   106+ s.d. Enter] [∼ Q, F (*s.d. at right margin*).

Trinc. Why then I'le tell thee, I found her an hour ago under
an Elder-tree, upon a sweet Bed of Nettles, singing Tory, Rory,
and Ranthum, Scantum, with her own natural Brother.

10 *Steph.* O Jew! make love in her own Tribe?

Trinc. But 'tis no matter, to tell thee true, I marry'd her to be
a great man and so forth: but make no words on't, for I care not
who knows it, and so here's to thee agen. Give me the Bottle,
Caliban! did you knock the Butt? how does it sound?

Calib. It sounds as though it had a noise within.

Trinc. I fear the Butt begins to rattle in the throat and is de-
parting: give me the Bottle.   [*Drinks.*

Must. A short life and a merry I say. [Steph. *whispers* Sycorax.

Syc. But did he tell you so?

20 *Steph.* He said you were as ugly as your Mother, and that he
Marry'd you only to get possession of the Island.

Syc. My Mothers Devils fetch him for't.

Steph. And your Fathers too, hem!————[*To* Calib.] Skink
about his Graces health agen.————O if you would but cast an
eye of pity upon me————

Syc. I will cast two eyes of pity on thee, I love thee more than
Haws, or Black-berries; I have a hoard of Wildings in the Moss,
my Brother knows not of 'em; But I'le bring thee where they
are.

30 *Steph. Trincalo* was but my man when time was.

Syc. Wert thou his God, and didst thou give him Liquor?

Steph. I gave him Brandy and drunk Sack my self; wilt thou
leave him, and thou shalt be my Princess?

Syc. If thou canst make me glad with this Liquor.

Steph. I warrant thee we'll ride into the Country where it
grows.

Syc. How wilt thou carry me thither?

Steph. Upon a Hackney-Devil of thy Mothers.

Trinc. What's that you will do? hah! I hope you have not
40 betray'd me? How does my Pigs-nye?   [*To* Sycorax.

---

113   agen. Give] agen, give Q, F.
123–124   hem!————[*To* Calib.] Skink . . . agen.————] hem! skink . . . agen.
Q, F (Skink F).
127   Black-berries;] F; ∼ , Q.

Syc. Be gone! thou shalt not be my Lord, thou say'st
I'm ugly.

Trinc. Did you tell her so?————Hah! he's a Rogue, do not
believe him chuck.

Steph. The foul words were yours: I will not eat 'em for you.

Trinc. I see if once a Rebel, then ever a Rebel. Did I receive
thee into grace for this? I will correct thee with my Royal Hand.

[*Strikes* Stephano.

Syc. Dost thou hurt my love?   [*Flies at* Trincalo.

Trinc. Where are our Guards? Treason, Treason!

[Vent. Must. Calib. *run betwixt.*

150   *Vent.* Who took up Arms first, the Prince or the People?

Trinc. This false Traytor has corrupted the Wife of my Bosom.————[*Whispers* Mustacho *hastily.*] Mustacho, strike on
my side, and thou shalt be my Vice-Roy.

Must. I'm against Rebels! *Ventoso,* obey your Vice-Roy.

Vent. You a Vice-Roy?   [*They two fight off from the rest.*

Steph. Hah! Hector Monster! do you stand neuter?

Calib. Thou would'st drink my Liquor, I will not help thee.

Syc. 'Twas his doing that I had such a Husband, but I'le claw
him.   [Syc. *and* Calib. *fight,* Syc. *beating him off the Stage.*

160   *Trinc.* The whole Nation is up in Arms, and shall I stand
idle?   [Trincalo *beats off* Stephano *to the door. Exit* Stephano.
I'le not pursue too far,
For fear the Enemy should rally agen and surprise my Butt in
the Cittadel; well, I must be rid of my Lady *Trincalo,* she will
be in the fashion else; first Cuckold her Husband, and then sue
for a separation, to get Alimony.   [*Exit.*

---

143 so?————Hah] ~_∧_————hah Q, F (Hah F).
151–152 Bosom.————[*Whispers . . . hastily.*] *Mustacho,*] Bosom. / [*Whispers
. . . hastily. / Mustacho*_∧_ Q, F.
154 *Ventoso,*] F; ~_∧_ Q.

SCENE III.

Enter Ferdinand, Hippolito, (*with their swords drawn.*)

Ferd. Come, Sir, our Cave affords no choice of place,
But the ground's firm and even: are you ready?
Hip. As ready as your self, Sir.
Ferd. You remember on what conditions we must fight?
Who first receives a Wound is to submit.
Hip. Come, come, this loses time, now for the
Women, Sir.　　　　　　[*They fight a little,* Ferdinand *hurts him.*
Ferd. Sir, you are wounded.
Hip. No.
10　*Ferd.* Believe your blood.
Hip. I feel no hurt, no matter for my blood.
Ferd. Remember our Conditions.
Hip. I'le not leave, till my Sword hits you too.
　　　　　　　　[Hip. *presses on,* Ferd. *retires and wards.*
Ferd. I'm loth to kill you, you are unskilful, Sir.
Hip. You beat aside my Sword, but let it come as near
As yours, and you shall see my skill.
Ferd. You faint for loss of blood, I see you stagger,
Pray, Sir, retire.
Hip. No! I will ne're go back————
20 Methinks the Cave turns round, I cannot find————
Ferd. Your eyes begin to dazle.
Hip. Why do you swim so, and dance about me?
Stand but still till I have made one thrust.
　　　　　　　　　　　[Hippolito *thrusts and falls.*
Ferd. O help, help, help!
Unhappy man! what have I done?
Hip. I'm going to a cold sleep, but when I wake
I'le fight agen. Pray stay for me.　　　　　　[*Swounds.*

SCENE III.] *omitted from* Q, F.

Ferd. He's gone! he's gone! O stay sweet lovely Youth!
Help, help!

Enter Prospero.

30   *Prosp.* What dismal noise is that ?
   Ferd. O see, Sir, see!
What mischief my unhappy hand has wrought.
   Prosp. Alas! how much in vain doth feeble Art endeavour
To resist the will of Heaven!   [*Rubs* Hippolito.
He's gone for ever; O thou cruel Son of an
Inhumane Father! all my designs are ruin'd
And unravell'd by this blow.
No pleasure now is left me but Revenge.
   Ferd. Sir, if you knew my innocence————
40   *Prosp.* Peace, peace,
Can thy excuses give me back his life?
What *Ariel!* sluggish spirit, where art thou?

Enter Ariel.

   Ariel. Here, at thy beck, my Lord.
   Prosp. I, now thou com'st, when Fate is past and not to be
Recall'd. Look there, and glut the malice of
Thy Nature, for as thou art thy self, thou
Canst not be but glad to see young Virtue
Nipt i'th' Blossom.
   Ariel. My Lord, the Being high above can witness
50 I am not glad; we Airy Spirits are not of temper
So malicious as the Earthy,
But of a Nature more approaching good:
For which we meet in swarms, and often combat
Betwixt the Confines of the Air and Earth.
   Prosp. Why did'st thou not prevent, at least foretell,

29–29+ *s.d.* help! / *Enter*] F; ～ ! [～ Q (*s.d. at right margin*).
34 Heaven!] ～ ? Q, F.
42–42+ *s.d.* thou? / *Enter*] F; ～ ? [～ Q (*s.d. at right margin*).
50–52 glad; . . . good:] ～ , . . . ～ . Q, F.

This fatal action then?
   Ariel. Pardon, great Sir,
I meant to do it, but I was forbidden
By the ill Genius of *Hippolito,*
60 Who came and threatn'd me if I disclos'd it,
To bind me in the bottom of the Sea,
Far from the lightsome Regions of the Air,
(My native fields) above a hundred years.
   Prosp. I'le chain thee in the North for thy neglect,
Within the burning Bowels of Mount *Hecla;*
I'le sindge thy airy wings with sulph'rous flames,
And choak thy tender nostrils with blew smoak;
At ev'ry Hick-up of the belching Mountain
Thou shalt be lifted up to taste fresh Air,
70 And then fall down agen.
   Ariel. Pardon, dread Lord.
   Prosp. No more of pardon than just Heav'n intends thee
Shalt thou e're find from me: hence! flye with speed,
Unbind the Charms which hold this Murtherer's
Father, and bring him with my Brother streight
Before me.
   Ariel. Mercy, my potent Lord, and I'le outfly thy thought.
                              [*Exit* Ariel.
   Ferd. O Heavens! what words are those I heard?
Yet cannot see who spoke 'em: sure the Woman
80 Whom I lov'd was like this, some aiery Vision.
   Prosp. No, Murd'rer, she's, like thee, of mortal mould,
But much too pure to mix with thy black Crimes;
Yet she had faults and must be punish'd for 'em.
Miranda and *Dorinda!* where are ye?
The will of Heaven's accomplish'd: I have
Now no more to fear, and nothing left to hope;
Now you may enter.

           Enter Miranda *and* Dorinda.

65–67 *Hecla; . . . smoak;*] *Heila, . . .* ~ , Q, F.   86 hope;] ~ , Q, F.
87–87+ *s.d.* enter. / *Enter*] F; ~ . [~ Q (*s.d. at right margin*).

Mir. My Love! is it permitted me to see you once again?

Prosp. You come to look your last; I will

90 For ever take him from your Eyes.
But, on my blessing, speak not, nor approach him.

Dor. Pray, Father, is not this my Sisters man?
He has a noble form; but yet he's not so excellent
As my *Hippolito.*

Prosp. Alas poor Girl, thou hast no man: look yonder;
There's all of him that's left.

Dor. Why, was there ever any more of him?
He lies asleep, Sir, shall I waken him?

　　　　　　　[*She kneels by* Hippolito, *and jogs him.*

Ferd. Alas! he's never to be wak'd agen.

100 *Dor.* My Love, my Love! will you not speak to me?
I fear you have disples'd him, Sir, and now
He will not answer me; he's dumb and cold too,
But I'le run streight, and make a fire to warm him.

　　　　　　　[*Exit* Dorinda *running.*

Enter Alonzo, Gonzalo, Antonio, *and* Ariel (*invisible.*)

Alonz. Never were Beasts so hunted into toyls,
As we have been pursu'd by dreadful shapes.
But is not that my Son? O *Ferdinand!*
If thou art not a Ghost, let me embrace thee.

Ferd. My Father! O sinister happiness! Is it
Decreed I should recover you alive, just in that

110 Fatal hour when this brave Youth is lost in Death,
And by my hand?

Ant. Heaven! what new wonder's this?

Gonz. This Isle is full of nothing else.

Alonz. I thought to dye, and in the walks above,
Wand'ring by Star-light, to have sought thee out;
But now I should have gone to Heaven in vain,
Whilst thou art here behind.

97　Why,] ~ʌ Q. F.　　　　　　102　me;] ~ , Q. F.
103+　*s.d.* Antonio, *and*] Antonio. Q. F.

Ferd. You must indeed in vain have gone thither
To look for me. Those who are stain'd with such black
120 Crimes as mine, come seldom there.
    Prosp. And those who are, like him, all foul with guilt,
More seldom upward go. You stare upon me as
You ne're had seen me; have fifteen years
So lost me to your knowledge, that you retain
No memory of *Prospero?*
    Gonz. The good old Duke of *Millain!*
    Prosp. I wonder less, that thou *Antonio* know'st me not,
Because thou did'st long since forget I was thy Brother,
Else I never had bin here.
130   *Ant.* Shame choaks my words.
    Alonz. And wonder mine.
    Prosp. For you, usurping Prince,   [*To* Alonzo.
Know, by my Art, you shipwrackt on this Isle,
Where, after I a while had punish'd you, my vengeance
Wou'd have ended; I design'd to match that Son
Of yours with this my Daughter.
    Alonz. Pursue it still, I am most willing to't.
    Prosp. So am not I. No marriages can prosper
Which are with Murd'rers made; look on that Corps;
140 This, whilst he liv'd, was young *Hippolito,* that
Infant Duke of *Mantua,* Sir, whom you expos'd
With me; and here I bred him up till that blood-thirsty
Man, that *Ferdinand*——
But why do I exclaim on him, when Justice calls
To unsheath her Sword against his guilt?
    Alonz. What do you mean?
    Prosp. To execute Heav'ns Laws.
Here I am plac'd by Heav'n, here I am Prince,
Though you have dispossess'd me of my *Millain.*
150 Blood calls for blood; your *Ferdinand* shall dye,
And I in bitterness have sent for you
To have the sudden joy of seeing him alive,

123 ne're] F; n'ere Q.   135 ended;] ∼ , Q, F.
139 Corps;] ∼ , Q, F.

And then the greater grief to see him dye.

Alonz. And think'st thou I or these will tamely stand
To view the execution?   [*Lays hand upon his Sword.*

Ferd. Hold, dear Father! I cannot suffer you
T'attempt against his life who gave her being
Whom I love.

Prosp. Nay then, appear my Guards!———[*Aside.*] I thought
no more to

160 Use their aids; (I'm curs'd because I us'd it)
                              [*He stamps, and many Spirits appear.*
But they are now the Ministers of Heaven,
Whilst I revenge this murder.

Alonz. Have I for this found thee my Son, so soon agen
To lose thee? *Antonio, Gonzalo,* speak for pity:
He may hear you.

Ant. I dare not draw that blood upon my self, by
Interceding for him.

Gonz. You drew this judgment down when you usurp'd
That Dukedom which was this dead Prince's right.

170 *Alonz.* Is this a time t'upbraid me with my sins, when
Grief lies heavy on me? y'are no more my friends,
But crueller than he, whose sentence has
Doom'd my Son to death.

Ant. You did unworthily t'upbraid him.

Gonz. And you do worse t'endure his crimes.

Ant. Gonzalo we'll meet no more as friends.

Gonz. Agreed *Antonio:* and we agree in discord.

Ferd. to Mir. Adieu my fairest Mistress.

Mir. Now I can hold no longer; I must speak.

180 Though I am loth to disobey you, Sir,
Be not so cruel to the man I love,
Or be so kind to let me suffer with him.

Ferd. Recall that Pray'r, or I shall wish to live,
Though death be all the mends that I can make.

Prosp. This night I will allow you, *Ferdinand,* to fit
You for your Death, that Cave's your Prison.

_____
159 then, . . . Guards!———[*Aside.*] I] then∧ . . . Guards∧———I Q, F.

Alonz. Ah, *Prospero!* hear me speak. You are a Father,
Look on my age, and look upon his youth.
  Prosp. No more! all you can say is urg'd in vain,
190 I have no room for pity left within me.
Do you refuse! help, *Ariel,* with your fellows
To drive 'em in; *Alonzo* and his Son bestow in
Yonder Cave, and here *Gonzalo* shall with
Antonio lodge.   [*Spirits drive 'em in, as they are appointed.*

Enter Dorinda.

  Dor. Sir, I have made a fire, shall he be warm'd?
  Prosp. He's dead, and vital warmth will ne're return.
  Dor. Dead, Sir, what's that?
  Prosp. His soul has left his body.
  Dor. When will it come agen?
200   *Prosp.* O never, never!
He must be laid in Earth, and there consume.
  Dor. He shall not lye in earth, you do not know
How well he loves me: indeed he'l come agen;
He told me he would go a little while,
But promis'd me he would not tarry long.
  Prosp. He's murder'd by the man who lov'd your Sister.
Now both of you may see what 'tis to break
A Father's precept; you would needs see men, and by
That sight are made for ever wretched.
210 *Hippolito* is dead, and *Ferdinand* must dye
For murdering him.
  Mir. Have you no pity?
  Prosp. Your disobedience has so much incens'd me, that
I this night can leave no blessing with you.
Help to convey the body to my Couch,
Then leave me to mourn over it alone.
                    [*They bear off the body of* Hippolito.

Enter Miranda, *and* Dorinda *again,* Ariel *behind 'em.*

191   help, *Ariel,*] ∼ₐ ∼ₐ Q, F.   216+   *s.d. again,*] ∼ . Q, F.

Ariel. I've bin so chid for my neglect by *Prospero,*
That I must now watch all and be unseen.
　　Mir. Sister, I say agen, 'twas long of you
220 That all this mischief happen'd.
　　Dor. Blame not me for your own fault, your
Curiosity brought me to see the man.
　　Mir. You safely might have seen him and retir'd, but
You wou'd needs go near him and converse, you may
Remember my Father call'd me thence, and I call'd you.
　　Dor. That was your envy, Sister, not your love;
You call'd me thence, because you could not be
Alone with him your self; but I am sure my
Man had never gone to Heaven so soon, but
230 That yours made him go.   [*Crying.*
　　Mir. Sister, I could not wish that either of 'em shou'd
Go to Heaven without us, but it was his fortune,
And you must be satisfi'd.
　　Dor. I'le not be satisfi'd: My Father says he'l make
Your man as cold as mine is now, and when he
Is made cold, my Father will not let you strive
To make him warm agen.
　　Mir. In spight of you mine never shall be cold.
　　Dor. I'm sure 'twas he that made me miserable,
240 And I will be reveng'd. Perhaps you think 'tis
Nothing to lose a man.
　　Mir. Yes, but there is some difference betwixt
My *Ferdinand,* and your *Hippolito.*
　　Dor. I, there's your judgment. Your's is the oldest
Man I ever saw except it were my Father.
　　Mir. Sister, no more. It is not comely in a Daughter,
When she says her Father's old.
　　Dor. But why do I stay here, whilst my cold Love
Perhaps may want me?
250 I'le pray my Father to make yours cold too.
　　Mir. Sister, I'le never sleep with you agen.

231　Sister,] ~∧ Q, F.　　　　　　　233　satisfi'd.] ~ ? Q, F.
251　I'le] F; I'e Q.

Dor. I'le never more meet in a Bed with you,
But lodge on the bare ground and watch my Love.
  Mir. And at the entrance of that Cave I'le lye,
And eccho to each blast of wind a sigh.
        [*Exeunt severally, looking discontentedly on one another*
  Ariel. Harsh discord reigns throughout this fatal Isle,
At which good Angels mourn, ill Spirits smile;
Old *Prospero,* by his Daughters rob'd of rest,
Has in displeasure left 'em both unblest.
260 Unkindly they abjure each others bed,
To save the living, and revenge the dead.
Alonzo and his Son are Pris'ners made,
And good *Gonzalo* does their crimes upbraid.
Antonio and *Gonzalo* disagree,
And wou'd, though in one Cave, at distance be.
The Seamen all that cursed Wine have spent,
Which still renew'd their thirst of Government;
And, wanting subjects for the food of Pow'r,
Each wou'd to rule alone the rest devour.
270 The Monsters *Sycorax* and *Caliban*
More monstrous grow by passions learn'd from man.
Even I not fram'd of warring Elements,
Partake and suffer in these discontents.
Why shou'd a mortal by Enchantments hold
In chains a spirit of ætherial mould?
Accursed Magick we our selves have taught,
And our own pow'r has our subjection wrought!   [*Exit.*

ACT V. SCENE I.

Enter Prospero *and* Miranda.

  Prosp. You beg in vain; I cannot pardon him,
He has offended Heaven.
  Mir. Then let Heaven punish him.

———
ACT V. SCENE I.] ACT V. Q, F.

Prosp. It will by me.

Mir. Grant him at least some respite for my sake.

Prosp. I by deferring Justice should incense the Deity
Against my self and you.

    Mir. Yet I have heard you say, The Powers above are slow
In punishing; and shou'd not you resemble them?

10   *Prosp.* The Powers above may pardon or reprieve,
As Sovereign Princes may dispense with Laws,
Which we, as Officers, must execute. Our Acts of grace
To Criminals are Treason to Heavens prerogative.

    Mir. Do you condemn him for shedding blood?

    Prosp. Why do you ask that question? you know I do.

    Mir. Then you must be condemn'd for shedding his,
And he who condemns you, must dye for shedding
Yours, and that's the way at last to leave none living.

    Prosp. The Argument is weak, but I want time
20 To let you see your errours; retire, and, if you love him,
Pray for him.   [*He's going.*

    Mir. O stay, Sir, I have yet more Arguments.

    Prosp. But none of any weight.

    Mir. Have you not said you are his Judge?

    Prosp. 'Tis true, I am; what then?

    Mir. And can you be his Executioner?
If that be so, then all men may declare their
Enemies in fault; and Pow'r without the Sword
Of Justice, will presume to punish what e're
30 It calls a crime.

    Prosp. I cannot force *Gonzalo* or my Brother, much
Less the Father, to destroy the Son; it must
Be then the Monster *Caliban,* and he's not here;
But *Ariel* strait shall fetch him.

Enter Ariel.

---

9 punishing;] ~ , Q, F.
32–33 Father, . . . Son; . . . here;] ~∧ . . . ~ , . . . ~ , Q, F.
34–34+ s.d. him. / *Enter*] F; ~ . [~ Q (*s.d. at right margin*).

Ariel. My potent Lord, before thou call'st, I come,
To serve thy will.
    Prosp. Then Spirit fetch me here my salvage Slave.
    Ariel. My Lord, it does not need.
    Prosp. Art thou then prone to mischief, wilt thou be thy self
40 the Executioner?
    Ariel. Think better of thy aiery Minister, who
For thy sake, unbid, this night has flown
O're almost all the habitable World.
    Prosp. But to what purpose was all thy diligence?
    Ariel. When I was chidden by my mighty Lord for my
Neglect of young *Hippolito,* I went to view
His body, and soon found his soul was but retir'd,
Not sally'd out, and frighted lay at skulk in
Th' inmost corner of his scarce-beating heart.
50   *Prosp.* Is he not dead?
    Ariel. Hear me my Lord! I prun'd my wings, and, fitted for
a journey, from the next Isles of our *Hesperides,* I gather'd Moly
first, thence shot my self to *Palestine,* and watch'd the trickling
Balm, which caught, I glided to the *British* Isles, and there the
purple Panacea found.
    Prosp. All this to night?
    Ariel. All this, my Lord, I did,
Nor was *Hippolito's* good Angel wanting, who
Climbing up the circle of the Moon,
60 While I below got Simples for the Cure, went to
Each Planet which o're-rul'd those Herbs,
And drew it's virtue to increase their pow'r:
Long e're this hour had I been back again,
But that a Storm took me returning back
And flag'd my tender Wings.
    Prosp. Thou shalt have rest my spirit,
But hast thou search'd the wound?
    Ariel. My Lord I have, and 'twas in time I did it; for
The soul stood almost at life's door, all bare

---

54 *British*] F; British Q.

70 And naked, shivering like Boys upon a Rivers
Bank, and loth to tempt the cold air; but I took
Her and stop'd her in; and pour'd into his mouth
The healing juice of vulnerary Herbs.

Prosp. Thou art my faithful servant.

Ariel. His only danger was his loss of blood, but now
He's wak'd, my Lord, and just this hour
He must be dress'd again, as I have done it.
Anoint the Sword which pierc'd him with this
Weapon-Salve, and wrap it close from air till
80 I have time to visit him again.

Prosp. It shall be done. Be it your task, *Miranda,* because your
Sister is not present here, while I go visit your
Dear *Ferdinand,* from whom I will a while conceal
This news, that it may be more welcome.

Mir. I obey you, and with a double duty, Sir: for now
You twice have given me life.

Prosp. My *Ariel,* follow me.   [*Exeunt severally.*

SCENE II.

Hippolito *discovered on a Couch,* Dorinda *by him.*

Dor. How do you find your self?

Hip. I'm somewhat cold, can you not draw me nearer
To the Sun? I am too weak to walk.

Dor. My Love, I'le try.

                    [*She draws the chair nearer the Audience.*
I thought you never would have walk'd agen,
They told me you were gone away to Heaven;
Have you bin there?

Hip. I know not where I was.

Dor. I will not leave you till you promise me you

---

71 air;] ~ , Q, F.   81 done. Be] done, be Q, F.
SCENE II.] *omitted from* Q, F.
s.d. Hippolito] F (*s.d. at right margin*); [~ Q (*s.d. at right margin*).
3 Sun? . . . walk.] ~ , . . . ~ ? Q, F.

10 Will not dye agen.

    Hip. Indeed I will not.

    Dor. You must not go to Heav'n unless we go together,
For I've heard my Father say that we must strive
To be each others Guide, the way to it will else
Be difficult, especially to those who are so young.
But I much wonder what it is to dye.

    Hip. Sure 'tis to dream, a kind of breathless sleep
When once the Soul's gone out.

    Dor. What is the Soul?

20   *Hip.* A small blew thing that runs about within us.

    Dor. Then I have seen it in a frosty morning run
Smoaking from my mouth.

    Hip. But if my soul had gone, it should have walk'd upon
A Cloud just over you, and peep'd, and thence I would have
Call'd you.

    Dor. But I should not have heard you, 'tis so far.

    Hip. Why then I would have rain'd and snow'd upon you,
And thrown down Hail-stones gently till I hit you,
And made you look at least. But dear *Dorinda*

30 What is become of him who fought with me?

    Dor. O, I can tell you joyful news of him,
My Father means to make him dye to day,
For what he did to you.

    Hip. That must not be, my dear *Dorinda;* go and beg your
Father he may not dye, it was my fault he hurt me,
I urg'd him to it first.

    Dor. But if he live, he'll never leave killing you.

    Hip. O no! I just remember when I fell asleep I heard
Him calling me a great way off, and crying over me as

40 You wou'd do; besides we have no cause of quarrel now.

    Dor. Pray how began your difference first?

    Hip. I fought with him for all the Women in the World.

    Dor. That hurt you had was justly sent from Heaven,
For wishing to have any more but me.

35   Father] F; ~ , Q.   39   off,] F; ~ ; Q.
40   do;] ~ , Q, F.

Hip. Indeed I think it was, but I repent it: the fault
Was only in my blood; for now 'tis gone, I find
I do not love so many.

Dor. In confidence of this, I'le beg my Father, that he
May live; I'm glad the naughty blood, that made
50 You love so many, is gone out.

Hip. My Dear, go quickly, lest you come too late.

[*Exit* Dor.

Enter Miranda *at the other door, with* Hippolito's
Sword wrapt up.

Hip. Who's this who looks so fair and beautiful, as
Nothing but *Dorinda* can surpass her? O!
I believe it is that Angel, Woman,
Whom she calls Sister.

Mir. Sir, I am sent hither to dress your wound,
How do you find your strength?

Hip. Fair Creature, I am faint with loss of blood.

Mir. I'm sorry for't.

60 *Hip.* Indeed and so am I, for if I had that blood, I then
Should find a great delight in loving you.

Mir. But, Sir, I am anothers, and your love is given
Already to my Sister.

Hip. Yet I find that if you please I can love still a little.

Mir. I cannot be unconstant, nor shou'd you.

Hip. O my wound pains me.

Mir. I am come to ease you.   [*She unwraps the Sword.*

Hip. Alas! I feel the cold air come to me,
My wound shoots worse than ever.

                    [*She wipes and anoints the Sword.*

70 *Mir.* Does it still grieve you?

Hip. Now methinks there's something laid just upon it.

Mir. Do you find no ease?

Hip. Yes, yes, upon the sudden all the pain
Is leaving me, sweet Heaven how I am eas'd!

45-46 it: . . . blood;] ~ , . . . ~ , Q, F.   49 live;] ~ , Q, F.

Enter Ferdinand *and* Dorinda *to them.*

Ferd. to Dor. Madam, I must confess my life is yours,
I owe it to your generosity.
    Dor. I am o'rejoy'd my Father lets you live, and proud
Of my good fortune, that he gave your life to me.
    Mir. How? gave his life to her?
80   *Hip.* Alas! I think she said so, and he said he ow'd it
To her generosity.
    Ferd. But is not that your Sister with *Hippolito?*
    Dor. So kind already?
    Ferd. I came to welcome life, and I have met the
Cruellest of deaths.
    Hip. My dear *Dorinda* with another man?
    Dor. Sister, what bus'ness have you here?
    Mir. You see I dress *Hippolito.*
    Dor. Y'are very charitable to a Stranger.
90   *Mir.* You are not much behind in charity, to beg a pardon
For a man, whom you scarce ever saw before.
    Dor. Henceforward let your Surgery alone, for I had
Rather he should dye, than you should cure his wound.
    Mir. And I wish *Ferdinand* had dy'd before
He ow'd his life to your entreaty.
    Ferd. to Hip. Sir, I'm glad you are so well recover'd, you
Keep your humour still to have all Women.
    Hip. Not all, Sir; you except one of the number,
Your new Love there, *Dorinda.*
100   *Mir.* Ah *Ferdinand!* can you become inconstant?
If I must lose you, I had rather death should take
You from me than you take your self.
    Ferd. And if I might have chose, I would have wish'd
That death from *Prospero,* and not this from you.
    Dor. I, now I find why I was sent away,
That you might have my Sisters company.
    Hip. Dorinda, kill me not with your unkindness,
This is too much, first to be false your self,

79 her?] ~ ! Q, F.   98 Sir;] ~ , Q, F.

And then accuse me too.

110   *Ferd.* We all accuse each other, and each one denys their guilt,
I should be glad it were a mutual errour.
And therefore first to clear my self from fault,
Madam, I beg your pardon, while I say I only love
Your Sister.   [*To* Dorinda.
       Mir. O blest word!
I'm sure I love no man but *Ferdinand.*
       Dor. Nor I, Heav'n knows, but my *Hippolito.*
       Hip. I never knew I lov'd so much, before I fear'd
Dorinda's constancy; but now I am convinc'd that

120   I lov'd none but her, because none else can
Recompence her loss.
       Ferd. 'Twas happy then you had this little tryal.
But how we all so much mistook, I know not.
       Mir. I have only this to say in my defence: my Father sent
Me hither, to attend the wounded Stranger.
       Dor. And *Hippolito* sent me to beg the life of *Ferdinand.*
       Ferd. From such small errours, left at first unheeded,
Have often sprung sad accidents in love:
But see, our Fathers and our friends are come

130   To mix their joys with ours.

Enter Prospero, Alonzo, Antonio, Gonzalo.

Alon. to Prosp. Let it no more be thought of, your purpose
Though it was severe was just. In losing *Ferdinand*
I should have mourn'd, but could not have complain'd.
       Prosp. Sir, I am glad kind Heaven decreed it otherwise.
       Dor. O wonder!
How many goodly Creatures are there here!
How beauteous mankind is!
       Hip. O brave new World that has such people in't!
       Alon. to Ferd. Now all the blessings of a glad Father

140   Compass thee about,
And make thee happy in thy beauteous choice.
       Gonz. I've inward wept, or should have spoke e're this.

Look down sweet Heav'n, and on this Couple drop
A blessed Crown, for it is you chalk'd out the
Way which brought us hither.
 Ant. Though penitence forc'd by necessity can scarce
Seem real, yet dearest Brother I have hope
My blood may plead for pardon with you, I resign
Dominion, which 'tis true I could not keep,
150 But Heaven knows too I would not.
 Prosp. All past crimes I bury in the joy of this
Blessed day.
 Alonz. And that I may not be behind in justice, to this
Young Prince I render back his Dukedom,
And as the Duke of *Mantua* thus salute him.
 Hip. What is it that you render back? methinks
You give me nothing.
 Prosp. You are to be Lord of a great People,
And o're Towns and Cities.
160 *Hip.* And shall these people be all Men and Women?
 Gonz. Yes, and shall call you Lord.
 Hip. Why then I'le live no longer in a Prison, but
Have a whole Cave to my self hereafter.
 Prosp. And that your happiness may be compleat,
I give you my *Dorinda* for your Wife, she shall
Be yours for ever, when the Priest has made you one.
 Hip. How can he make us one, shall I grow to her?
 Prosp. By saying holy words you shall be joyn'd in marriage
To each other.
170 *Dor.* I warrant you those holy words are charms.
My Father means to conjure us together.
 Prosp. to his daughter. My *Ariel* told me, when last night you
   quarrel'd,
You said you would for ever part your beds,
But what you threaten'd in your anger, Heaven
Has turn'd to Prophecy;
For you, *Miranda,* must with *Ferdinand,*
And you, *Dorinda,* with *Hippolito* lye in

One Bed hereafter.

Alonz. And Heaven make those Beds still fruitful in
180 Producing Children to bless their Parents
Youth, and Grandsires age.

Mir. to Dor. If Children come by lying in a Bed, I wonder you
And I had none between us.

Dor. Sister it was our fault, we meant like fools
To look 'em in the fields, and they it seems
Are only found in Beds.

Hip. I am o'rejoy'd that I shall have *Dorinda* in a Bed,
We'll lye all night and day together there,
And never rise again.

190 *Ferd. aside to him. Hippolito!* you yet are ignorant of your
great
Happiness, but there is somewhat which for
Your own and fair *Dorinda's* sake I must instruct
You in.

Hip. Pray teach me quickly how Men and Women in your
World make love, I shall soon learn
I warrant you.

Enter Ariel *driving in* Steph. Trinc. Must. Vent. Calib. Syc.

Prosp. Why that's my dainty *Ariel,* I shall miss thee,
But yet thou shalt have freedom.

Gonz. O look, Sir, look, the Master and the Saylors——
200 The Bosen too——my Prophecy is out, that if
A Gallows were on land, that man could ne're
Be drown'd.

Alonz. to Trinc. Now Blasphemy, what not one Oath ashore?
Hast thou no mouth by land? why star'st thou so?

Trinc. What, more Dukes yet, I must resign my Dukedom,
But 'tis no matter, I was almost starv'd in't.

Must. Here's nothing but wild Sallads without Oyl or Vinegar.

Steph. The Duke and Prince alive! would I had now our

196+ *s.d. Enter*] F; [~ Q (*s.d. at right margin*).   199 look, the] ~∧ ~ Q, F.
201 ne're] F; n'ere Q.   205 What,] ~∧ Q, F.

gallant Ship agen, and were her Master, I'd willingly give all
210 my Island for her.
    Vent. And I my Vice-Roy-ship.
    Trinc. I shall need no hangman, for I shall e'en hang
My self, now my friend Butt has shed his
Last drop of life. Poor Butt is quite departed.
    Ant. They talk like mad men.
    Prosp. No matter, time will bring 'em to themselves, and
Now their Wine is gone they will not quarrel.
Your Ship is safe and tight, and bravely rigg'd,
As when you first set Sail.
220   *Alonz.* This news is wonderful.
    Ariel. Was it well done, my Lord?
    Prosp. Rarely, my diligence.
    Gonz. But pray, Sir, what are those mishapen Creatures?
    Prosp. Their Mother was a Witch, and one so strong
She would controul the Moon, make Flows
And Ebbs, and deal in her command without
Her power.
    Syc. O *Setebos!* these be brave Sprights indeed.
    Prosp. to Calib. Go Sirrah to my Cell, and as you hope for
230 Pardon, trim it up.
    Calib. Most carefully. I will be wise hereafter.
What a dull fool was I to take those Drunkards
For Gods, when such as these were in the world!
    Prosp. Sir, I invite your Highness and your Train
To my poor Cave this night; a part of which
I will imploy in telling you my story.
    Alonz. No doubt it must be strangely taking, Sir.
    Prosp. When the morn draws I'le bring you to your Ship,
And promise you calm Seas and happy Gales.
240 My *Ariel,* that's thy charge: then to the Elements
Be free, and fare thee well.
    Ariel. I'le do it Master.
    Sings.   *Where the Bee sucks there suck I,*
            In a Cowslips Bell, I lye,

---

233   world!] ∼ ? Q, F.

There I couch when Owls do cry,
On the Swallows wing I flye
After Summer merrily.
Merrily, merrily shall I live now
Under the Blossom that hangs on the Bough.

250   *Syc.* I'le to Sea with thee, and keep thee warm in thy Cabin.

Trinc. No my dainty Dy-dapper, you have a tender constitu-
tion, and will be sick a Ship-board. You are partly Fish and may
swim after me. I wish you a good Voyage.

Prosp. Now to this Royal Company, my servant, be visible,
And entertain them with a Dance before they part.

Ariel. I have a gentle Spirit for my Love,
Who twice seven years hath waited for my Freedom,
It shall appear and foot it featly with me.
Milcha, my Love, thy *Ariel* calls thee.

Enter Milcha.

260   Milcha. Here!   [*They dance a Saraband.*
Prosp. Henceforth this Isle to the afflicted be
A place of Refuge as it was to me;
The Promises of blooming Spring live here,
And all the Blessings of the rip'ning year;
On my retreat let Heaven and Nature smile,
And ever flourish the *Enchanted Isle.*   [*Exeunt.*

259–259+   s.d. thee. / *Enter*] F; ∼ . [∼ Q (*s.d. at right margin*).

Epilogue.

GALLANTS, *by all good signs it does appear,*
That Sixty Seven's a very damning year,
For Knaves abroad, and for ill Poets here.

Among the Muses there's a gen'ral rot,
The Rhyming Mounsieur *and the* Spanish *Plot:*
Defie or Court, all's one, they go to Pot.

The Ghosts of Poets walk within this place,
And haunt us Actors wheresoe're we pass,
In Visions bloodier than King Richard's *was.*

For this poor wretch he has not much to say,
But quietly brings in his part o'th' Play,
And begs the favour to be damn'd to day.

He sends me only like a Sh'riffs man here
To let you know the Malefactor's neer;
And that he means to dye, en Cavalier.

For if you shou'd be gracious to his Pen,
Th' Example will prove ill to other men,
And you'll be troubled with 'em all agen.

FINIS.

10

5   Mounsieur] *Mounsieur* Q, F.   5   Spanish] *Spanish* Q, F.

TYRANNICK LOVE

OR

THE ROYAL MARTYR

Tyrannick Love,

OR THE

Royal Martyr.

A

TRAGEDY.

As it is Acted by his Majesties Servants, at the
THEATRE ROYAL.

BY

JOHN DRYDEN, Servant to his
MAJESTY.

Non jam prima peto———*neq; vincere certo;*
Extremum rediiffe pudet.———*Virg.*

LONDON,

Printed for H. *Herringman*, at the Sign of the *Blew Anchor* in the
Lower Walk of the *New Exchange.* 1670.

TITLE PAGE OF THE FIRST EDITION (MACDONALD 74A)

To the most Illustrious Prince, James, *Duke of* Monmouth
and Bucclugh, *one of His Majesties most Honourable
Privy-Council, and Knight of the most Noble
Order of the Garter,* &c.

SIR,

THE favourable Reception which your Excellent Lady af-
forded to one of my former Plays, has encourag'd me to
double my presumption, in addressing this to your
Graces Patronage. So dangerous a thing it is to admit a Poet into
your Family, that you can never afterwards be free from the
chiming of ill Verses, perpetually sounding in your ears, and
more troublesom than the neighbourhood of Steeples. I have
been favourable to my self in this expression; a zealous Fanatick
10 would have gone farther; and have called me the Serpent, who
first presented the fruit of my Poetry to the Wife, and so gain'd
the opportunity to seduce the Husband. Yet I am ready to avow
a Crime so advantagious to me; but the World, which will condemn my boldness, I am sure will justifie and applaude my
choice. All men will joyn with me in the adoration which I pay
you, they would wish only I had brought you a more noble
Sacrifice. Instead of an Heroick Play, you might justly expect
an Heroick Poem, filled with the past Glories of your Ancestors,
& the future certainties of your own. Heaven has already taken
20 care to form you for an Heroe. You have all the advantages of
Mind and Body, and an Illustrious Birth, conspiring to render
you an extraordinary Person. The *Achilles* and the *Rinaldo* are
present in you, even above their Originals; you only want a
Homer or a *Tasso* to make you equal to them. Youth, Beauty,
and Courage (all which you possess in the height of their perfection) are the most desirable gifts of Heaven: and Heaven is
never prodigal of such Treasures, but to some uncommon pur-

Caption: Illustrious] Q2–5, F, D; *Illustrious and High-born* Q1.
James,] Q3–5, F; ~∧ Q1–2, D.

pose. So goodly a Fabrick was never framed by an Almighty Architect for a vulgar Guest. He shewed the value which he set upon your Mind, when he took care to have it so nobly and so beautifully lodg'd. To a graceful fashion and deportment of Body, you have joyned a winning Conversation, and an easie Greatness, derived to you from the best, and best-belov'd of Princes. And with a great power of obliging, the world has observed in you, a desire to oblige, even beyond your power. This and all that I can say on so excellent and large a Subject, is
10 only History, in which Fiction has no part; I can employ nothing of Poetry in it, any more than I do in that humble protestation which I make, to continue ever

Your Graces most obedient

and most devoted Servant,

John Dryden.

6 best-belov'd] D; best belov'd Q1-5, F.

PREFACE.

I was mov'd to write this Play by many reasons: amongst others, the Commands of some Persons of Honour, for whom I have a most particular respect, were daily sounding in my ears, that it would be of good Example to undertake a Poem of this Nature. Neither were my own inclinations wanting to second their desires. I considered that pleasure was not the only end of Poesie; and that even the instructions of Morality were not so wholly the business of a Poet, as that the Precepts and Examples of Piety were to be omitted. For to leave that employment altogether to the Clergie, were to forget that Religion was first taught in Verse (which the laziness or dulness of succeeding Priesthood, turned afterwards into Prose.) And it were also to grant, which I never shall, that representations of this kind may not as well be conducing to Holiness, as to good Manners. Yet far be it from me, to compare the use of Dramatique Poesie with that of Divinity: I only maintain, against the Enemies of the Stage, that patterns of piety, decently represented, and equally removed from the extremes of Superstition and Prophaneness, may be of excellent use to second the Precepts of our Religion. By the Harmony of words we elevate the mind to a sense of Devotion, as our solemn Musick, which is inarticulate Poesie, does in Churches; and by the lively images of piety, adorned by action, through the senses allure the Soul: which while it is charmed in a silent joy of what it sees and hears, is struck at the same time with a secret veneration of things Celestial, and is wound up insensibly into the practice of that which it admires. Now, if, instead of this, we sometimes see on our Theaters, the Examples of Vice rewarded, or at least unpunished; yet it ought not to be an Argument against the Art, any more than the Extravagances and Impieties of the Pulpit in

---

5 *were . . . inclinations*] Q2–5, F, D; *was . . . inclination* Q1.
12 *Prose.) And*] Q2–5, F, D; ~ :) *and* Q1.
16 *maintain,*] Q2–5, F, D; ~ₐ Q1.   26 *wound*] Q2–5, F, D; *woond* Q1.

*the late times of Rebellion, can be against the Office and Dignity
of the Clergie.*

*But many times it happens, that Poets are wrongfully accused;
as it is my own Case in this very Play; where I am charged by
some ignorant or malicious persons, with no less Crimes than
Prophaneness and Irreligion.*

The part of Maximin, *against which these holy Cricks so
much declaim, was designed by me to set off the Character of S.*
Catharine. *And those who have read the* Roman *History, may*
10 *easily remember, that* Maximin *was not only a bloody Tyrant,
vastus corpore, animo ferus, as* Herodian *describes him; but also
a Persecutor of the Church, against which he raised the sixth
Persecution. So that whatsoever he speaks or acts in this Tragedy, is no more than a Record of his life and manners; a picture
as near as I could take it, from the Original. If with much pains
and some success I have drawn a deformed piece, there is as
much of Art, and as near an imitation of Nature, in a* Lazare *as
in a* Venus. Maximin *was an Heathen, and what he speaks
against Religion, is in contempt of that which he professed. He*
20 *defies the Gods of* Rome, *which is no more than S.* Catharine
*might with decency have done. If it be urged, that a person of
such principles who scoffes at any Religion, ought not to be
presented on the Stage; why then are the lives and sayings of so
many wicked and prophane persons recorded in the Holy Scrip-
tures? I know it will be answered, That a due use may be made
of them; that they are remembred with a Brand of Infamy fixt
upon them; and set as Sea-marks for those who behold them to
avoid. And what other use have I made of* Maximin? *have I
proposed him as a pattern to be imitated, whom even for his im-*
30 *piety to his false Gods I have so severely punished? Nay, as if I
had foreseen this Objection I purposely removed the Scene of
the Play, which ought to have been at* Alexandria *in* Egypt,
(where S. Catharine *suffered) and laid it under the Walls of*
Aquileia *in* Italy, *where* Maximin *was slain; that the punishment of his Crime might immediately succeed its execution.*

This, Reader, is what I owed to my just defence, and the due

9   Roman] Q3-5, F, D; *Roman* Q1-2.   24   *persons*] Q5, F; ~ , Q1-4, D.
32   *Play,*] Q4-5, F; ~ꞈ Q1-3, D.   34   *slain;*] F; ~ , Q1; ~ : Q2-5, D.

reverence of that Religion which I profess, to which all men,
who desire to be esteemed good or honest, are obliged: I have
neither leisure nor occasion to write more largely on this sub-
ject, because I am already justified by the sentence of the best
and most discerning Prince in the World, by the suffrage of all
unbiass'd Judges; and above all, by the witness of my own Con-
science, which abhors the thought of such a Crime; to which I
ask leave to add my outward Conversation, which shall never
be justly taxed with the Note of Atheism or Prophaneness.
10 *In what else concerns the Play, I shall be brief: for the faults*
of the writing and contrivance, I leave them to the mercy of the
Reader. For I am as little apt to defend my own Errours, as to
find those of other Poets. Only I observe, that the great Censors
of Wit and Poetry, either produce nothing of their own, or
what is more ridiculous than any thing they reprehend. Much of
ill Nature, and a very little Judgment, go far in finding the
mistakes of Writers.
I pretend not that any thing of mine can be Correct: This
Poem, especially, which was contrived and written in seven
20 *weeks, though afterwards hindred by many accidents from a*
speedy representation, which would have been its best excuse.
Yet the Scenes are every where unbroken, and the unities of
place and time more exactly kept, than perhaps is requisite in a
Tragedy; or at least then I have since preserv'd them in the
Conquest of Granada.
I have not every where observed the equality of numbers, in
my Verse; partly by reason of my haste; but more especially be-
cause I would not have my sense a slave to Syllables.
'Tis easie to discover, that I have been very bold in my altera-
30 *tion of the Story, which of it self was too barren for a Play: and,*
that I have taken from the Church two Martyrs, in the persons
of Porphyrius *and the Empress, who suffered for the Christian*
Faith, under the Tyranny of Maximin.
I have seen a French *Play, called the* Martyrdom of S. Cath-

2   honest,] Q5, D; ~_∧ Q1–4, F.   16   in] Q2–5, F, D; in the Q1.
25   Conquest of] F; *Conquest of* Q1–5, D.
34   French] Q3–4, D; *French* Q1–2, Q5, F.
34   Martyrdom of S.] *Martyrdom of S.* Q1–5, F, D.

arine; *but those who have read it, will soon clear me from stealing out of so dull an Author.* I *have only borrowed a mistake
from him, of one* Maximin *for another: for finding him in the*
French *Poet, called the Son of a* Thracian *Herds-man, and an*
Alane *Woman, I too easily believed him to have been the same*
Maximin *mentioned in* Herodian. *Till afterwards consulting*
Eusebius *and* Metaphrastes, *I found the* French-man *had betrayed me into an Errour (when it was too late to alter it) by
mistaking that first* Maximin *for a second, the Contemporary of*
10 Constantine the Great, *and one of the Usurpers of the Eastern
Empire.*

*But neither was the other name of my Play more fortunate:
for as some who had heard of a Tragedy of* S. Catharine, *imagined I had taken my plot from thence; so others, who had heard
of another Play called* L'Amour Tyrannique, *with the same
ignorance, accused me to have borrow'd my design from it, because I have accidentally given my Play the same Title, not
having to this day seen it: and knowing only by report, that such
a Comedy is extant in* French, *under the name of Monsieur*
20 Scudery.

*As for what I have said of Astral or Aerial Spirits it is no in-
vention of mine, but taken from those who have written on that
Subject. Whether there are such Beings or not, it concerns not
me; 'tis sufficient for my purpose, that many have believed the
affirmative: and that these Heroick Representations, which are
of the same Nature with the Epick, are not limited, but with
the extremest bounds of what is credible.*

*For the little Critiques who pleas'd themselves with thinking
they have found a flaw in that line of the Prologue,* (And he who
30 servilely creeps after sence, is safe, *&c.*) *as if I patroniz'd my own
nonsence, I may reasonably suppose they have never read*
Horace. Serpit humi tutus, *&c. are his words: He who creeps*

---

4   French] Q3–5, F, D; *French* Q1–2.
4   Thracian] Q3–5, F, D; *Thracian* Q1–2.
7   French-man] Q3–5, F, D; *French-man* Q1–2.
10 the Great] Q3–5, F; *the Great* Q1–2, D.
19 French] Q3–5, F, D; *French* Q1–2.   28–32 *omitted from* Q*1*.
30 safe, *&c.*] Q3–5, F, D; ~∧ &c. Q2.   32 tutus,] Q3–5, F, D; ~∧ Q2.

after plaine, dull, common sence, is safe from committing ab-
surdities; but, can never reach any heighth, or excellence of wit:
and sure I could not meane that any excellence were to be
found in nonsence. With the same ignorance or malice, they
would accuse me for useing empty armes, when I writ of a Ghost
or shadow: which has onely the appearance of a body or limbs;
and is empty or voyd of flesh and blood; and vacuis amplectitur
ulnis was an expression of Ovids on the same subject. Some foole
before them had charg'd me in the Indian Emperour with non-
10 sence in these words, And follow fate which does too fast pursue;
which was borrow'd from Virgil in the XIth of his Æneids,
Eludit gyro interior, sequiturque sequentem. I quote not these
to prove that I never writ Nonsence, but onely to show that
they are so unfortunate as not to have found it.

Vale.

1–15 *omitted from Q1*.   5 *useing*] Q5, F; ~ , Q2–4, D.
8 ulnis] ~ , Q2–5, F, D.
10–11 pursue; *which*] Q4–5, F; ~ . *Which* Q2, D; ~ : *which* Q3.
11 *XIth*] *xith* Q2; *11th* Q3–5, F; *sixth* D.
11 Æneids] D; *Æneids* Q2–5, F.   13 *writ*] Q3–5, F; *write* Q2, D.

Prologue.

SELF-LOVE (*which never rightly understood*)
 Makes Poets still conclude their Plays are good:
 And malice in all Criticks raigns so high,
That for small Errors, they whole Plays decry;
So that to see this fondness, and that spite,
You'd think that none but Mad-men judge or write.
Therefore our Poet, as he thinks not fit
T' impose upon you what he writes for Wit,
So hopes that leaving you your censures free, ⎫
You equal Judges of the whole will be: ⎬
They judge but half who only faults will see. ⎭
Poets, like Lovers, should be bold and dare,
They spoil their business with an over-care.
And he who servilely creeps after sence,
Is safe, but ne're will reach an Excellence.
Hence 'tis, our Poet in his conjuring,
Allow'd his Fancy the full scope and swing.
But when a Tyrant for his Theme he had,
He loos'd the Reins, and bid his Muse run mad:
And though he stumbles in a full career;
Yet rashness is a better fault than fear.
He saw his way; but in so swift a pace,
To chuse the ground, might be to lose the race.
They then who of each trip th' advantage take,
Find but those Faults which they want Wit to make.

10

20

8 *you*] Q3–5, F; ∼ , Q1–2, D.
12 *Poets, . . . Lovers,*] Q3–5, F, D (*Poets*∧ D); ∼∧ . . . ∼∧ Q1–2.
16 *'tis,*] Q4–5, F; ∼∧ Q1–3, D.

Persons Represented.

Maximin, *Tyrant of* Rome.	**By** Major *Mohun.*
Porphyrius, *Captain of the Prætorian Bands.*	Mr. *Hart.*
Charinus, *the Emperour's Son.*	Mr. *Harris.*
Placidius, *a great Officer.*	Mr. *Kynaston.*
Valerius, ⎫ *Tribunes of the Army.* ⎫	Mr. *Lydall.*
Albinus, ⎭	Mr. *Littlewood.*
Nigrinus, *a Tribune and Conjurer.*	Mr. *Beeston.*
Amariel, *Guardian-Angel to S.* Catharine.	Mr. *Bell.*
Apollonius, *a Heathen Philosopher.*	Mr. *Cartwright.*
Berenice, *Wife to* Maximin.	**By** Mrs. *Marshall.*
Valeria, *Daughter to* Maximin.	Mrs. *Ellen Guyn.*
S. Catharine, *Princess of* Alexandria.	Mrs. *Hughes.*
Felicia, *her Mother.*	Mrs. *Knepp.*
Erotion, ⎫ *Attendants.* ⎫	Mrs. *Uphill.*
Cydnon, ⎭	Mrs. *Eastland.*

SCENE, *The Camp of* Maximin, *under the Walls of* Aquileia.

Apollonius, *a Heathen Philosopher.*] Q2–5, F, D; *omitted from Q1.*
Mr. *Cartwright.*] Q2–5, F, D; *omitted from Q1.*
SCENE,] Q3–5, F; ~∧ Q1–2, D.
Maximin] Q4–5, F; *Maximin* Q1–3, D.
under the Walls of Aquileia] F; under the Walls of *Aquileia* Q1–5, D.

TYRANNICK LOVE;

OR, THE

ROYAL MARTYR.

ACT I. SCENE I.

A Camp or Pavilion Royal.

Enter Maximin, Charinus, Placidius, Albinus,
Valerius, Apollonius, *Guards.*

Max. Thus far my Arms have with success been crown'd;
And found no stop, or vanquish'd what they found.
The *German* Lakes my Legions have o're-past,
With all the bars which Art or Nature cast:
My Foes, in watry Fastnesses inclos'd,
I sought, alone, to their whole War expos'd,
Did first the depth of trembling Marshes sound,
And fix'd my Eagles in unfaithful ground:
By force submitted to the *Roman* sway
10 Fierce Nations, and unknowing to obey:
And now, for my reward, ungrateful *Rome*
For which I fought abroad, rebels at home.
  Alb. Yet 'tis their fear which does this War maintain:
They cannot brook a Martial Monarchs Raign:
Your Valour would too much their sloth accuse;
And therefore, like themselves, they Princes chuse.

---

s.d. *Enter*] D; *omitted from Q1–5, F.*   3 *German*] F, D; German Q1–5.
6 expos'd,] F; ~ . Q1–4, D; ~∧ Q5.   9 *Roman*] F, D; Roman Q1–5.
15 would too much their sloth] Q3–5, F; would their sloth too much Q1–2, D.

Placid. Two, tame, gown'd Princes, who at ease, debate
In lazy Chairs, the business of the State:
Who reign but while the people they can please,
20 And only know the little Arts of Peace.
     Char. In fields they dare not fight where Honour calls;
But breathe a faint defiance from their Walls.
The very noise of War their Souls does wound;
They quake, but hearing their own Trumpets sound.
     Val. An easie Summons but for form they wait,
And to your Fame will open wide the gate.
     Placid. I wish our Fame that swift success may find;
But Conquests, Sir, are easily design'd:
However soft within themselves they are,
30 To you they will be valiant by despair:
For having once been guilty, well they know
To a revengeful Prince they still are so.
     Alb. 'Tis true, that, since the Senates succours came,
They grow more bold.
     *Max.*_____ That Senate's but a name:
Or they are Pageant Princes which they make:
That pow'r they give away, they would partake.
Two equal pow'rs, two different ways will draw,
While each may check, and give the other Law.
True, they secure propriety and peace;
40 But are not fit an Empire to increase.
When they should aid their Prince, the Slaves dispute;
And fear success should make him absolute.
They let Foes conquer, to secure the State,
And lend a Sword, whose edge themselves rebate.
     Char. When to increase the Gods you late are gone,
I'le swiftly chuse to dye, or reign alone:
But these half-Kings our courage cannot fright;
The thrifty State will bargain e're they fight:
Give just so much for every Victory;
50 And rather lose a fight, than over-buy.
     Max. Since all delays are dangerous in War,
Your men, *Albinus,* for assault prepare:

Crispinus and *Menephilus,* I hear
Two Consulars, these *Aquileians* chear;
By whom they may, if we protract the time,
Be taught the courage to defend their crime.
    Placid. Put off th' assault but only for this day;
No loss can come by such a small delay.
    Char. We are not sure to morrow will be ours:
60 Wars have, like Love, their favourable hours:
Let us use all; for if we lose one day,
That white one, in the crowd, may slip away.
    Max. Fates dark recesses we can never find;
But Fortune at some hours to all is kind;
The lucky have whole days, which still they choose;
Th' unlucky have but hours, and those they lose.
    Placid. I have consulted one, who reads Heav'ns doom,
And sees, as present, things which are to come.
'Tis that *Nigrinus,* made by your command
70 A Tribune in the new *Panonian* Band.
Him have I seen, (on *Isters* Banks he stood,
Where last we winter'd) bind the head-long flood
In sudden ice; and where most swift it flows,
In chrystal nets, the wond'ring fishes close.
Then, with a moments thaw, the streams inlarge,
And from the Mesh the twinkling Guests discharge.
In a deep vale, or near some ruin'd wall
He would the Ghosts of slaughter'd Souldiers call;
Who, slow, to wounded bodies did repair,
80 And loth to enter, shiver'd in the air;
These his dread Wand did to short life compel,
And forc'd the Fates of Battels to foretel.
    Max. 'Tis wond'rous strange! But, good *Placidius,* say,
What prophesies *Nigrinus* of this day?
    Placid. In a lone Tent, all hung with black, I saw
Where in a Square he did a Circle draw:
Four Angles, made by that circumference,

---

61 day,] Q4–5, F; ~ ; Q1–3, D.   70 *Panonian*] F, D; Panonian Q1–5.

Bore holy words inscrib'd, of mystick sence.
When first a hollow wind began to blow,
90 The Sky grew black, and belli'd down more low;
Around the fields did nimble Lightning play,
Which offer'd us by fits, and snatch'd the day.
'Midst this, was heard the shrill and tender cry
Of well-pleas'd Ghosts, which in the storm did fly;
Danc'd to and fro, and skim'd along the ground,
Till to the Magick Circle they were bound.
They coursing it, while we were fenc'd within,
We saw this dreadful Scene of Fate begin.
       Char. Speak without fear; what did the Vision shew?
100   *Placid.* A Curtain drawn presented to our view
A Town besieg'd; and on the neighb'ring Plain
Lay heaps of visionary Souldiers slain.
A rising mist obscur'd the gloomy head
Of one, who in Imperial Robes lay dead.
Near this, in Fetters stood a Virgin, crown'd;
Whom many *Cupids* strove in vain to wound:
A voice *to morrow,* still *to morrow* rung:
Another *Iö; Iö, Pæan* sung.
       Char. Visions and Oracles still doubtful are,
110 And ne're expounded till th' event of War.
The Gods fore-knowledge on our Swords will wait:
If we fight well, they must fore-show good Fate.

                   To them a Centurion.

       Cent. A rising dust which troubles all the air,
And this way travels, shows some Army near.
       Char. I hear the sound of Trumpets from afar. [*Exit* Albinus.
       Max. It seems the voice of Triumph, not of War.

                   To them Albinus *again.*

_____

90 low;] F; ∼ , Q1–5, D.   100 view] F; ∼ , Q1–5, D.
107 *to morrow . . . to morrow*] F; to morrow . . . to morrow Q1–5, D.

Alb. Health and success our Emperour attends:
The Forces marching on the Plain, are friends.
Porphyrius, whom you *Ægypts* Prætor made,
120 Is come from *Alexandria* to your aid.
  Max. It well becomes the conduct and the care
Of one so fam'd and fortunate in War.
You must resign, *Placidius,* your Command;
To him I promis'd the Prætorian Band.
Your duty in your swift compliance show,
I will provide some other charge for you.
  Placid. May *Cæsar's* pleasure ever be obey'd
With that submission, which by me is paid.
Now all the Curses envy ever knew,
130 Or could invent, *Porphyrius* pursue.   *Aside.*
  Alb. Placidius does too tamely bear his loss;   [*To* Charinus.
This new pretender will all pow'r ingross:
All things must now by his direction move;
And you, Sir, must resign your Father's love.
  Char. Yes; every name to his repute must bow;
There grow no Bayes for any other brow.
He blasts my early Honour in the bud,
Like some tall Tree the Monster of the Wood.
O're-shading all which under him would grow,
140 He sheds his venim on the Plants below.
  Alb. You must some noble action undertake;
Equal with his your own renown to make.
  Char. I am not for a slothful envy born,
I'll do't this day, in the dire Visions scorn.
He comes: We two, like the twin Stars appear;
Never to shine together in one Sphere.   *Exit cum* Alb.

Enter Porphyrius *attended.*

Max. Porphyrius, welcome, welcome as the light
To cheerful Birds; or as to Lovers, night.

---

123 Command;] F; ∼ , Q1–5; ∼∧ D.
138 Wood.] Q3–5; ∼ , Q1–2, D; ∼ : F.   148 Lovers,] Q2–5, F, D; ∼∧ Q1.

Welcome as what thou bring'st me, Victory.

50   *Por.* That waits, Sir, on your Arms, and not on me.
You left a Conquest more than half atchiev'd;
And for whose easiness I almost griev'd.
Yours only the *Ægyptian* Laurels are;
I bring you but the reliques of your War.
The Christian Princess to receive your doom,
Is from her Conquer'd *Alexandria* come.
Her Mother in another Vessel sent,
A Storm surpriz'd; nor know I the event:
Both from your bounty must receive their state;

60 Or must on your triumphant Chariot wait.

    Max. From me they can expect no grace, whose minds
An execrable superstition blinds.

    Apoll. The Gods who rais'd you to the Worlds Command,
Require these Victims from your grateful hand.

    Por. To minds resolv'd, the threats of Death are vain;
They run to fires, and there enjoy their pain:
Not *Mucius* made more hast his hand t'expose
To greedy flames, than their whole bodies those.

    Max. How, to their own destruction, they are blind!

70 Zeal is the pious madness of the mind.

    Por. They all our fam'd Philosophers defy;
And would our Faith by force of reason try.

    Apoll. I beg it, Sir, by all the pow'rs Divine,
That in their right, this Combat may be mine.

    Max. It shall; and fifty Doctors of our Laws
Be added to you, to maintain the cause.

Enter Berenice *the Empress,* Valeria *Daughter to the*
Emperour, Erotion.

    Placid. The Empress and your Daughter, Sir, are here.
    Por. What dangers in those charming Eyes appear!
                              Aside, looking on the Empress.

_____

175 Laws] F; ~ , Q1-5, D.   177 here.] Q3-5, F, D; ~ , Q1-2.
178+ *s.d. Aside, looking*] *Looking* Q1-5, F, D.

How my old wounds are open'd at this view!
180 And in my murd'rers presence bleed anew!
　　Max. I did expect your coming to partake　　*To the Ladies.*
The general gladness which my Triumphs make.
You did *Porphyrius* as a Courtier know,
But as a Conquerour behold him now.
　　Ber. You know (I read it in your blushing face)　　*To* Por.
To merit, better than receive a grace:
And I know better silently to own,
Than with vain words to pay your service done.
　　Por. Princes, like Gods, reward e're we deserve;
　　　　　　　　　　　　Kneeling to kiss her hand.
190 And pay us in permitting us to serve.
Oh might I still grow here, and never move!　　　　(*Lower.*)
　　Ber. How dangerous are these extasies of Love!
He shows his passion to a thousand Eyes!
He cannot stir, nor can I bid him rise!
That word my heart refuses to my tongue!　　　　*Aside.*
　　Max. Madam, you let the General kneel too long.
　　Por. Too long, as if Eternity were so!　　　　*Aside.*
　　Ber. Rise, good *Porphyrius,* (since it must be so.)　　*Aside.*
　　Por. Like Hermits from a Vision I retire;　　*Rising.*
200 With Eyes too weak to see what I admire.　　*Aside.*
　　Vale. The Empress knows your worth; but, Sir, there be
　　　　　　　　　To Porphyrius, *who kisses her hand.*
Those who can value it as high as she.
And 'tis but just, (since in my Fathers cause
You fought) your Valour should have my applause.
　　Placid. O Jealousie, how art thou Eagle-ey'd!
She loves; and would her Love in praises hide:
How am I bound this Rival to pursue,
Who ravishes my Love and Fortune too!　　　　*Aside.*
　　　　　　　A Dead March within, and Trumpets.
　　Max. Somewhat of mournful, sure, my Ears does wound;

191　*s.d. Lower]* F, D; *lower* Q1–5.　　199　*s.d. Rising]* Q3–5, F, D; *rising* Q1–2.
201　*Vale.] Val.* Q1–5, F, D.　　　　201　be] Q3–5, F, D; ∼ , Q1–2.
203　cause] F, D; ∼ , Q1–5.

10 Like the hoarse murmurs of a Trumpets sound,
And Drums unbrac'd, with Souldiers broken cryes.

Enter Albinus.

Albinus, Whence proceeds this dismal noise?
    Alb. Too soon you'l know what I want words to tell.
    Max. How fares my Son? Is my *Charinus* well?
Not answer me! Oh my prophetique fear!
    Alb. How can I speak; or how, Sir, can you hear?
Imagine that which you would most deplore,
And that which I would speak is it, or more.
    Max. Thy mournful message in thy looks I read:
20 Is he (oh that I live to ask it) dead?
    Alb. Sir————
    Max. Stay; if thou speak'st that word, thou speak'st thy last:
Some God now, if he dares, relate what's past:
Say but he's dead, that God shall mortal be.
    Alb. Then, what I dare not speak, look back and see.

Charinus *born in dead by Souldiers.*

    Max. See nothing, Eyes, henceforth, but Death and wo;
You've done me the worst office you can do.
You've shown me Destinies prepost'rous crime;
An unripe fate; disclos'd e're Nature's time.
30   *Placid.* Asswage, great Prince, your passion, lest you show
There's somewhat in your Soul which Fate can bow.
    Por. Fortune should by your greatness be controul'd:
Arm your great mind, and let her take no hold.
    Max. To tame Philosophers teach constancy;
There is no farther use of it in me.
Gods (but why name I you!
All that was worth a pray'r to you, is gone:)
I ask not back my Vertue, but my Son.

---

226 wo;] F; ~ , Q1–5, D.   228 You've] Q3–5, F, D; Youv'e Q1–2.
237 you,] Q3–5, F; ~∧ Q1–2, D.

Alb. His too great thirst of fame his ruine brought,
240 Though, Sir, beyond all humane force he fought.
     Placid. This was my Vision of this fatal day!
     Alb. With a fierce hast he led our Troops the way:
While fiery showrs of Sulphur on him rain'd;
Nor left he till the Battlements he gain'd:
There with a Forest of their Darts he strove,
And stood like *Capaneus* defying *Jove;*
With his broad Sword the boldest beating down,
While Fate grew pale lest he should win the Town,
And turn'd the Iron leafs of its dark Book,
250 To make new dooms; or mend what it mistook;
Till, sought by many Deaths, he sunk though late,
And by his fall asserted doubtful Fate.
     Vale. Oh my Dear Brother! whom Heav'n let us see,
And would not longer suffer him to be!
     Max. And didst not thou a Death with Honour chuse,

                                        To Alb.

But impudently liv'st to bring this news?
After his loss how did'st thou dare to breath?
———But thy base Ghost shall follow him in death.
A decimation I will strictly make
260 Of all who my *Charinus* did forsake.
And of each Legion each Centurion
Shall dye.———*Placidius,* see my pleasure done.
     Por. Sir, you will lose by this severity
Your Souldiers hearts.
     Max. —————— Why, they take Pay to dye.
     Por. Then spare *Albinus* only.
     Max. ————————— I consent
To leave his life to be his punishment.
Discharg'd from trust, branded with infamy,

---

239 brought,] Q4–5, F; ~ . Q1–3, D.
240 all humane force] Q2–5, F, D; humanity Q1.
245–246 strove, . . . *Jove;*] ~ ; . . . ~ . Q1–5, F, D.
248 Town,] Q4–5, F; ~ . Q1–3, D.   250 mistook;] ~ . Q1–5, F, D.
251 Till,] F; ~ʌ Q1–5, D.   262 dye.] F; ~ : Q1–5, D.
267 trust,] F; ~ ; Q1–5, D.   267 infamy,] Q3, F; ~ʌ Q1–2, D; ~ . Q4–5.

Let him live on, till he ask leave to dye.
   Ber. Let me petition for him.
   Max. —————————————— I have said:
70 And will not be intreated, but obey'd.
But, Empress, whence does your compassion grow?
   Ber. You need not ask it, since my birth you know.
The Race of *Antonin's* was nam'd the Good:
I draw my pity from my Royal Blood.
   Max. Still must I be upbraided with your Line?
I know you speak it in contempt of mine.
But your late Brother did not prize me less,
Because I could not boast of Images.
And the Gods own'd me more, when they decreed
80 A *Thracian* Shepherd should your Line succeed.
   Ber. The Gods! O do not name the pow'rs divine,
They never mingled their Decrees with thine.
My Brother gave me to thee for a Wife,
And for my Dowry thou didst take his life.
   Max. The Gods by many Victories have shown,
That they my merits and his death did own.
   Ber. Yes; they have own'd it; witness this just day,
When they begin thy mischiefs to repay.
See the reward of all thy wicked care,
290 Before thee thy succession ended there.
Yet but in part my Brothers Ghost is pleas'd:
Restless till all the groaning world be eas'd.
For me, no other happiness I owne
Than to have born no Issue to thy Throne.
   Max. Provoke my rage no farther, lest I be
Reveng'd at once upon the Gods and thee.
   Por. aside. What horrid tortures seize my lab'ring mind!
O, only excellent of all thy kind!
To hear thee threatned while I idle stand:

---

279 more,] Q3-5, F, D; ~∧ Q1-2.   280 *Thracian*] D; Thracian Q1-5, F.
287 day,] F, D; ~ ; Q1-5.   293 me,] F; ~ ; Q1-5, D.
297 *Por. aside.* . . . mind!] *Por. aside.*] . . . mind! Q1-5, F; *Por.* . . . Mind!
[*Aside.* D.

300 Heav'n! was I born to fear a Tyrants hand?
    Max. to Ber. Hence from my sight,———thy blood, if thou
          dost stay,———
    Ber. Tyrant! too well to that thou know'st the way. (*Going.*)
    Por. Let baser Souls from falling Fortunes flye:
  I'le pay my duty to her, though I dye.   *Exit leading her.*
    Max. What made *Porphyrius* so officious be?
  The action look'd as done in scorn of me.
    Vale. It did, indeed, some little freedom show;
  But somewhat to his Services you owe.
    Max. Yet, if I thought it his presumption were———
310 *Placid.* Perhaps he did not your displeasure hear.
    Max. My anger was too loud, not to be heard.
    Placid. I'm loth to think he did it not regard.
    Max. How, not regard!
    Vale. —————————— *Placidius,* you foment
  On too light grounds my Father's discontent.
  But when an action does two faces wear,
  'Tis Justice to believe what is most fair.
  I think, that knowing what respect there rests
  For her late Brother in the Souldiers breasts,
  He went to serve the Emp'rour: and design'd
320 Only to calm the tempest in her mind,
  Lest some Sedition in the Camp should rise.
    Max. I ever thought him loyal as he's wise.
  Since therefore, all the Gods their spight have shown
  To rob my Age of a successive Throne;
  And you, who now remain
  The only Issue of my former bed,
  In Empire cannot by your Sex succeed:
  To bind *Porphyrius* firmly to the State,
  I will this day my *Cæsar* him create:
330 And, Daughter, I will give him you for Wife.

---

302   *s.d. Going*] Q3–5, F, D; *going* Q1–2.   307   *Vale.*] *Val.* Q1–5, F, D.
313   *Vale.*] *Val.* Q1–5, F, D.
313   [*rule*] *Placidius*] [*rule omitted*] ∼ Q1–5, F, D.
325   you,] F; ∼∧ Q1–5, D.   326   bed,] Q3–5, F, D; ∼∧ Q1–2.

Vale. O day, the best and happiest of my life!
Placid. O day, the most accurst I ever knew!   *Aside.*
Max. See to my Son perform'd each Funeral due:
Then to the toyls of War we will return;
And make our Enemies our losses mourn.   *Exeunt.*

ACT II. SCENE I.

The Royal Camp.

Enter Berenice, Porphyrius.

Ber. *Porphyrius,* you too far did tempt your Fate,
In owning her the Emperour does hate.
'Tis true, your duty to me it became;
But, praising that, I must your conduct blame.
     Por. Not to have own'd my zeal at such a time,
Were to sin higher than your Tyrants crime.
     Ber. 'Twas too much my disgrace t'accompany;
A silent wish had been enough for me.
     Por. Wishes are aids, faint Servants may supply,
10 Who ask Heav'n for you what themselves deny.
Could I do less than my respect to pay,
Where I before had giv'n my heart away?
     Ber. You fail in that respect you seem to bear,
When you speak words unfit for me to hear.
     Por. Yet you did once accept those vows I paid.
     Ber. Those vows were then to *Berenice* made;
But cannot now be heard without a sin,
When offer'd to the Wife of *Maximin.*
     Por. Has, then, the change of Fortune chang'd your will?
20 Ah! why are you not *Berenice* still?
To *Maximin* you once declar'd your hate;
Your Marriage was a Sacrifice to th' State:

---

331   *Vale.*] *Val.* Q1–5, F, D.   *s.d. Enter*] D; *omitted from Q1–5, F.*
s.d. Berenice, Porphyrius] Q4–5, D; *Berenice, Porphyrius* Q1–3, F.

Your Brother made it to secure his Throne,
Which this man made a step to mount it on.
  Ber. Whatever *Maximin* has been, or is,
I am to bear, since Heav'n has made me his.
For wives, who must themselves of pow'r devest,
When they love blindly, for their peace love best.
  Por. If mutual love be vow'd when faith you plight,
30 Then he, who forfeits first, has lost his right.
  Ber. Husbands a forfeiture of love may make;
But what avails the forfeit none can take?
As in a general wreck
The Pirate sinks with his ill-gotten gains,
And nothing to anothers use remains:
So, by his loss, no gain to you can fall;
The Sea, and vast destruction swallows all.
  Por. Yet he, who from the shore, the wreck descrys,
May lawfully inrich him with the prize.
40   *Ber.* Who sees the wreck can yet no title plead,
Till he be sure the Owner first is dead.
  Por. If that be all the claim I want to love,
This Pirate of your heart I'le soon remove;
And, at one stroke, the world and you set free.
  Ber. Leave to the care of Heav'n that world and me.
  Por. Heav'n, as its instrument, my courage sends.
  Ber. Heav'n ne'r sent those who fight for private ends.
We both are bound by trust, and must be true;
I to his Bed, and to his Empire you.
50 For he who to the bad betrays his trust,
Though he does good, becomes himself unjust.
  Por. When *Brutus* did from *Cæsar Rome* redeem,
The Act was good.
  Ber. ———— But was not good in him.
You see the Gods adjudg'd it Parricide,
By dooming the event on *Cæsar's* side.
'Tis vertue not to be oblig'd at all;
Or not conspire our Benefactors fall.

---

36 fall;] Q3–5, F; ∼ : Q1–2, D.   46 instrument,] Q4–5, F; ∼∧ Q1–3, D.

Por. You doom me then to suffer all this ill,
And yet I doom my self to love you still.
60   *Ber.* Dare not *Porphyrius* suffer then with me,
Since what for him I for my self decree?
     Por. How can I bear those griefs you disapprove?
     Ber. To ease 'em, I'le permit you still to love.
     Por. That will but haste my death, if you think fit
Not to reward, but barely to permit.
Love without hope does like a torture wound,
Which makes me reach in pain, to touch the ground.
     Ber. If hope, then, to your life so needful be,
Hope still.
     Por. ___ Blest News!
     Ber. _____ But hope, in Heav'n, not me.
70   *Por.* Love is too noble such deceits to use.
Referring me to Heav'n, your gift I lose.
So Princes cheaply may our wants supply,
When they give that their Treasurers deny.
     Ber. Love blinds my Vertue: if I longer stay,
It will grow dark, and I shall lose my way.
     Por. One kiss from this fair hand can be no sin;
I ask not that you gave to *Maximin.*
In full reward of all the pains I've past,
Give me but one.
     Ber. _____ Then let it be your last.
80   *Por.* 'Tis gone!
Like Souldiers prodigal of their Arrears,
One minute spends the Pay of many years.
———Let but one more be added to the sum,
And pay at once for all my pains to come.
     Ber. Unthrifts will starve if we before-hand give:
                        [*Pulling back her hand.*
I'le see you shall have just enough to live.

                 Enter Erotion.

85+   *s.d. hand.*] Q3–5, F, D; ~ .] Q1–2.

Ero. Madam, the Emperour is drawing near;
And comes, they say, to seek *Porphyrius* here.
    Ber. Alas!
    Por.————I will not ask what he intends;
90 My life, or death, alone on you depends.
    Ber. I must withdraw; but must not let him know   *Aside.*
How hard the precepts of my Vertue grow!
But what e're Fortune is for me design'd,
Sweet Heav'n, be still to brave *Porphyrius* kind!
                                              Exit cum Erotio.
    Por. She's gone unkindly, and refus'd to cast
One glance to feed me for so long a fast.

           Enter Maximin, Placidius, *Guards.*

    Max. Porphyrius, since the Gods have ravish'd one,
I come in you to seek another Son.
Succeed him then in my Imperial state;
100 Succeed in all, but his untimely fate.
If I adopt you with no better grace,
Pardon a fathers tears, upon my face,
And give 'em to *Charinus* memory:
May they not prove as ominous to thee.
    Por. With what misfortunes Heav'n torments me still!
Why must I be oblig'd to one so ill?   *[Aside.*
    Max. Those offers which I made you, Sir, were such,
No private man should need to ballance much.
    Por. Who durst his thoughts to such ambition lift? *[Kneeling.*
110 The greatness of it made me doubt the gift.
The distance was so vast, that to my view
It made the object seem at first untrue;
And now 'tis near, the sudden excellence
Strikes through, and flashes on my tender sence.
    Max. Yet Heav'n and Earth, which so remote appear,
                                              [Raising him.

---

90 alone] F; ~ , Q1–5, D.   94+   *s.d.* Erotio] Q3–5, F; *Erotio* Q1–2; *Erotion* D.
115+   *s.d. Raising]* F, D; *raising* Q1–5.
115+   *s.d. him.]* Q3–5, F, D; ~ .] Q1–2.

Are by the Air, which flows betwixt 'em, near.
And 'twixt us two my Daughter be the chain,
One end with me, and one with you remain.
   Por. You press me down with such a glorious Fate,

                                        [*Kneeling again.*
120 I cannot rise against the mighty weight.
Permit I may retire some little space,
And gather strength to bear so great a grace.   [*Exit bowing.*
   Placid. How Love and Fortune lavishly contend,
Which should *Porphyrius* wishes most befriend!
The mid-stream's his; I, creeping by the side,
Am shoulder'd off by his impetuous Tide.   [*Aside.*

        Enter Valerius *hastily.*

   Val. I hope my business may my haste excuse;
For, Sir, I bring you most surprizing news.
The Christian Princess in her Tent confers
130 With fifty of your learn'd Philosophers;
Whom with such Eloquence she does perswade,
That they are Captives to her reasons made.
I left 'em yielding up their vanquish'd cause,
And all the Souldiers shouting her applause;
Ev'n *Apollonius* does but faintly speak,
Whose voice the murmurs of th' assistants break.
   Max. Conduct this Captive Christian to my Tent;
She shall be brought to speedy punishment.   [*Exit* Valerius.
I must in time some remedy provide,
140 Lest this contagious Errour spread too wide.
   Placid. T' infected zeal you must no mercy show:
For, from Religion, all Rebellions grow.
   Max. The silly crowd, by factious Teachers brought
To think that Faith untrue their youth was taught,
Run on in new Opinions blindly bold;

119+ *s.d. again.*] Q3–5, F, D; ∼ .] Q1–2.
138–139 punishment. [*Exit* Valerius. / . . . provide,] F; punishment. / . . .
provide, [*Exit* Valerius. Q1–5, D.
143 Teachers] D; ∼ , Q1–5, F.

Neglect, contemn, and then assault the old.
Th' infectious madness seizes every part,
And from the head distils upon the heart.
And first they think their Princes faith not true,
150 And then proceed to offer him a new;
Which if refus'd, all duty from 'em cast,
To their new Faith they make new Kings at last.
    Placid. Those ills by Male-contents are often wrought,
That by their Prince their duty may be bought.
They head those holy Factions which they hate,
To sell their duty at a dearer rate.
But, Sir, the Tribune is already here
With your fair Captive.
    Max. ——————— Bid 'em both appear.

        Enter S. Catharine, Valerius, Apollonius, *Guards.*

See where she comes with that high Air and meen,
160 Which marks, in bonds, the greatness of a Queen.
What pity 'tis!————but I no charms must see
In her who to our Gods is enemy.————
Fair foe of Heav'n, whence comes this haughty pride,   [*To her.*
Or is it Frenzy does your mind misguide
To scorn our Worship, and new Gods to find?
    S. Cath. Nor pride nor frenzy, but a setled mind,
Enlightned from above, my way does mark.
    Max. Though Heav'n be clear, the way to it is dark.
    S. Cath. But where our Reason with our Faith does go,
170 We're both above enlightned, and below.
But Reason with your fond Religion fights,
For many Gods are many Infinites:
This to the first Philosophers was known,
Who, under various names, ador'd but one;
Though your vain Poets after did mistake,
Who ev'ry Attribute a God did make.
And so obscene their Ceremonies be,

───────────

166 mind,] F, D; ~ ; Q1-5.   174 one;] ~ . Q1-5, F, D.

As good men loath, and *Cato* blush'd to see.
   Max. War is my Province; Priest, why stand you mute?
180 You gain by Heav'n, and therefore should dispute.
   Apol. In all Religions, as in ours, there are
Some solid truths, and some things popular.
The popular in pleasing Fables lye,
The truths, in precepts of Morality.
And these to humane life are of that use,
That no Religion can such Rules produce.
   S. Cath. Then let the whole Dispute concluded be
Betwixt these Rules and Christianity.
   Apol. And what more noble can your Doctrine preach,
190 Than Vertues which Philosophy does teach?
To keep the passions in severest awe,
To live to Reason, (Nature's greatest Law)
To follow Vertue, as its own reward;
And good and ill, as things without, regard.
   S. Cath. Yet few could follow those strict Rules they gave;
For humane life will humane frailties have;
And love of Vertue is but barren praise,
Airy as Fame: nor strong enough to raise
The actions of the Soul above the sence.
200 Vertue grows cold without a recompence.
We vertuous acts as duty do regard;
Yet are permitted to expect reward.
   Apol. By how much more your Faith reward assures,
So much more frank our Virtue is than yours.
   S. Cath. Blind men! you seek ev'n those rewards you blame:
But ours are solid; yours an empty name.
Either to open praise your Acts you guide,
Or else reward your selves with secret pride.
   Apol. Yet still our Moral virtues you obey;
210 Ours are the Precepts though apply'd your way.
   S. Cath. 'Tis true, your virtues are the same we teach;
But in our practice they much higher reach.

---

205 *S.*] Q3–5, F, D; S. Q1–2.   206 yours] Q3–5, F, D; your's Q1–2.
211 *S.*] Q3–5, F, D; S. Q1–2.

You but forbid to take anothers due;
But we forbid ev'n to desire it too.
Revenge of injuries you Virtue call;
But we forgiveness of our wrongs extoll:
Immodest deeds you hinder to be wrought,
But we proscribe the least immodest thought.
So much your Virtues are in ours refin'd,
220 That yours but reach the actions, ours the mind.
      Max. Answer in short to what you heard her speak. [*To* Apol.
      Apol. Where Truth prevails, all arguments are weak.
To that convincing power I must give place:
And with that Truth, that Faith I will embrace.
      Max. O Traytor to our Gods; but more to me;
Dar'st thou of any Faith but of thy Princes be?
But sure thou rav'st; thy foolish Errour find:
Cast up the poyson that infects thy mind;
And shun the Torments thou art sure to feel.
230   *Apol.* Nor fire, nor torture, nor revenging Steel
Can on my Soul the least impression make:
How gladly, Truth, I suffer for thy sake!
Once I was ignorant of what was so;
But never can abandon Truth I know:
My Martyrdom I to thy Crown prefer;
Truth is a Cause for a Philosopher.
      S. Cath. Lose not that Courage which Heav'n does inspire;
                                        [*To* Apollonius.
But fearless go to be baptiz'd in fire.
Think 'tis a Triumph, not a danger near:
240 Give him your blood; but give him not a tear.
Go, and prepare my Seat: and hovering be
Near that bright space which is reserv'd for me.
      Max. Hence with the Traytor; bear him to his Fate.
      Apol. Tyrant, I fear thy pity, not thy hate:
A Life Eternal I by Death obtain.
      Max. Go, carry him, where he that Life may gain.
                          Ex. Apollonius, Valerius, *and Guards.*

---

214 ev'n] Q2, D; e'vn Q1; even Q3–5, F.
224 Truth,] Q3–5, F; ~∧ Q1–2, D.   237 S.] Q3–5, F, D; S. Q1–2.

Placid. From this Enchantress all these ills are come:
You are not safe till you pronounce her doom.
Each hour she lives a Legion sweeps away;
250 She'll make your Army Martyrs in a day.
    Max. 'Tis just: this Christian Sorceress shall dy:
(Would I had never prov'd her Sorcery:)
Not that her charming Tongue this change has bred;
I fear 'tis something that her Eyes have sed.
I love: and am asham'd it should be seen.   [*Aside.*
    Placid. Sir, shall she dy?
    Max. ———————————— Consider she's a Queen.
    Placid. Those claims in *Cleopatra* ended were.
    Max. How many *Cleopatra's* live in her!   [*Aside.*
    Placid. When you condemn'd her, Sir, she was a Queen.
260   *Max.* No, Slave; she only was a Captive then.
    S. Cath. My joyful Sentence you defer too long.
    Max. I never knew that Life was such a wrong.
But if you needs will dy:————it shall be so.
————Yet think it does from your perversness flow.
Men say, indeed, that I in Blood delight;
But you shall find————. Haste, take her from my sight.
————For *Maximin* I have too much confest: [*Aside.*
And for a Lover not enough exprest.
Absent, I may her Martyrdom decree;
270 But one look more will make that Martyr me.
                         [*Exit S.* Catharine *guarded.*
    Placid. What is it, Sir, that shakes your mighty mind?
    Max. Somewhat I am asham'd that thou shouldst find.
    Placid. If it be Love which does your Soul possess————
    Max. Are you my Rival that so soon you guess?
    Placid. Far, mighty Prince, be such a crime from me;
                                        [*Kneeling.*
Which, with the pride, includes impiety.

---

261   too] Q2–5, F, D; to Q1.   266   find————.] ~————‸ Q1–5, F, D.
267   confest: [*Aside.*] confest: Q1–5, F, D.
270+   s.d. *guarded.*] Q3–5, F, D; *Guarded.*] Q1–2.
275   me;] D; ~ . Q1–2; ~ , Q3–5, F.
275+   s.d. *Kneeling.*] Q3–5, F, D; ~ .] Q1–2.

Could you forgive it, yet the Gods above
Would never pardon me a Christian Love.
   Max. Thou ly'st:————there's not a God inhabits there,
280 But for this Christian would all Heav'n forswear.
Ev'n *Jove* would try more shapes her Love to win: ⎤
And in new birds, and unknown beasts would sin; ⎬
At least, if *Jove* could love like *Maximin.* ⎦
   Placid. A Captive, Sir, who would a Martyr dye?
   Max. She courts not death, but shuns Captivity.
Great gifts, and greater promises I'le make;
And what Religion is't, but they can shake?
She shall live high:————Devotion in distress
Is born, but vanishes in happiness.   *Exit* Maximin.
290   *Placid. solus.* His Son forgot, his Empress unappeas'd;
How soon the Tyrant with new Love is seiz'd!
Love various minds does variously inspire:
He stirs in gentle Natures, gentle fire;
Like that of Incense on the Altars laid:
But raging flames tempestuous Souls invade.
A fire which every windy passion blows;
With pride it mounts, and with revenge it glows.
But I accurs'd, who servilely must move;
And sooth his passion, for his Daughters Love!
300 Small hope, 'tis true, attends my mighty care;
But of all passions Love does last despair.   *Exit.*

ACT III.   SCENE I.

The Royal Pavilion.

Enter Maximin, Placidius, *Guards and Attendants.*

   Max. This Love that never could my youth engage,
Peeps out his coward head to dare my age.

---

293   Natures,] Q3–5; Natures∧ Q1–2, F; Nature's∧ D.
299   passion,] F; ∼∧ Q1–5, D.   300   care;] D; ∼ . Q1–5; ∼ , F.
s.d. Enter] omitted from Q1–5, F, D.

Where hast thou been thus long, thou sleeping form,
That wak'st like drowsie Sea-men in a storm?
A sullen hour thou chusest for thy birth:
My Love shoots up in tempests, as the Earth
Is stirr'd and loosen'd in a blust'ring wind,
Whose blasts to waiting flowers her womb unbind.
     Placid. Forgive me, if I say your passions are
10   So rough, as if in Love you would make War.
But Love is soft——
And with soft beauty tenderly complies;
In lips it laughs, and languishes in eyes.
     Max. There let it laugh; or, like an Infant, weep:
I cannot such a supple passion keep.
Mine, stiff with age, and stubborn as my arms,
Walks upright; stoops not to, but meets her charms.
     Placid. Yet fierceness suits not with her gentle kind;
They brave assaults, but may be undermin'd.
20   *Max.* Till I in those mean Arts am better read,
Court thou, and fawn, and flatter in my stead.

Enter S. Catharine.

She comes; and now, methinks, I could obey:
Her form glides through me, and my heart gives way:
This Iron heart, which no impression took
From Wars, melts down, and runs, if she but look.
                             Exit Maximin.
     Placid. Madam, I from the Emperour am come
T'applaude your Vertue, and reverse your doom.
He thinks, whatever your Religion be,
This Palm is owing to your constancy.
30   *S. Cath.* My constancy from him seeks no renown;
Heav'n, that propos'd the course, will give the Crown.
     Placid. But Monarchs are the Gods Vicegerents here;
Heav'n gives rewards; but what it gives they bear:

---

19   assaults,] F; ～ ; Q1–4, D; ～∧ Q5.
24   Iron heart] Q2–5, F, D; Ironheart Q1.

From Heav'n to you th' *Ægyptian* Crown is sent,
Yet 'tis a Prince who does the gift present.
   S. Cath. The Deity I serve, had he thought fit,
Could have preserv'd my Crown unconquer'd yet:
But when his secret Providence design'd
To level that, he levell'd too my mind;
40 Which, by contracting its desires, is taught
The humble quiet of possessing nought.
   Placid. To Stoicks leave a happiness so mean:
Your Vertue does deserve a nobler Scene.
You are not for obscurity design'd:
But, like the Sun, must cheer all humane kind.
   S. Cath. No happiness can be where is no rest:
Th' unknown, untalk'd of man is only blest.
He, as in some safe Cliff, his Cell does keep,
From thence he views the labours of the Deep:
50 The Gold-fraught Vessel which mad tempests beat,
He sees now vainly make to his retreat:
And, when from far, the tenth wave does appear,
Shrinks up in silent joy, that he's not there.
   Placid. You have a Pilot who your Ship secures;
The Monarch both of Earth and Seas is yours,
He who so freely gives a Crown away,
Yet asks no tribute but what you may pay.
One smile on him a greater wealth bestows,
Than *Ægypt* yields, when *Nilus* overflows.
60   *S. Cath.* I cannot wholly innocent appear,
Since I have liv'd such words as these to hear.
O Heav'n, which dost of chastity take care!———
   Placid. Why do you lose an unregarded pray'r?
If happiness, as you believe, be rest,
That quiet sure is by the Gods possest:———
'Tis greatness to neglect, or not to know
The little business of the world below.
   S. Cath. This doctrine well befitted him who thought
A casual world was from wild Atoms wrought:
70 But such an order in each chance we see,

---

34 *Ægyptian*] D; Ægyptian Q1–5, F.   55 yours,] ~. Q1–5, F, D.

(Chain'd to its cause, as that to its decree,)
That none can think a workmanship so rare,
Was built or kept without a Workman's care.

> *To them* Maximin, *Attendants, and Guards.*

  Max. Madam, you from *Placidius* may have heard
Some news, which will your happiness regard.
For what a greater happiness can be
Than to be courted, and be lov'd by me?
Th' *Ægyptian* Crown I to your hands remit;
And, with it, take his heart who offers it. *She turns aside.*
80 Do you my person and my gift contemn?
  S. Cath. My hopes pursue a brighter Diadem.
  Max. Can any brighter than the *Roman* be?
I find my proffer'd Love has cheapned me:
Since you neglect to answer my desires,
Know, Princess, you shall burn in other fires.
————Why should you urge me to so black a deed?
Think all my anger did from Love proceed.
  S. Cath. Nor threats nor promises my mind can move:
Your furious anger, nor your impious Love.
90 *Max.* The Love of you can never impious be;
You are so pure————
That in the Act 'twould change th' impiety.
Heav'n would unmake it sin.————
  S. Cath. I take my self from thy detested sight:
To my respect thou hast no longer right:
Such pow'r in bonds true piety can have,
That I command, and thou art but a Slave. *Exit S.* Cath.
  Max. To what a height of arrogance she swells!
Pride or ill nature still with Vertue dwells;
100 Her death shall set me free this very hour;
————But is her death within a Lovers pow'r?
Wild with my rage, more wild with my desire,

76–77 *omitted from Q1.*   78 *Ægyptian*] F, D; Ægyptian Q1–5.
82 *Roman*] Q3–4, F, D; Roman Q1–2, Q5.   93 sin.]~ʌ Q1–5, F, D.
97 *s.d. Exit*] Q5; ~ . Q1–4, F; *Ex.* D.

Like meeting tides————but mine are tides of fire.
What petty promise was't that caus'd this frown?
　　Placid. You heard: no less than the *Ægyptian* Crown.
　　Max. Throw *Ægypt*'s by, and offer in the stead;
Offer————the Crown on *Berenice*'s head.
I am resolv'd to double till I win;
About it straight, and send *Porphyrius* in.　　　*Exit* Placid.
110　We look like Eagles tow'ring in the Sky;
While her high flight still raises mine more high.

　　　　　　　To him Porphyrius.

　　Por. I come, Sir, to expect your great commands.
　　Max. My happiness lyes only in thy hands.
And, since I have adopted thee my Son,
I'le keep no secret from thy breast unknown:
Led by the int'rest of my rising Fate,
I did espouse this Empress whom I hate:
And therefore with less shame I may declare,
That I the Fetters of thy Captive wear.
120　　*Por.* Sir, you amaze me with so strange a Love.
　　Max. Pity, my Son, those flames you disapprove.
The cause of Love can never be assign'd;
'Tis in no face, but in the Lover's mind.
　　Por. Yet there are Beauties which attract all hearts;
And all mankind lyes open to their darts:
Whose Soveraignty, without dispute, we grant;
Such Graces, sure, your Empress does not want.
　　Max. Beauty has bounds,————
And can no more to every heart be so,
130　Than any Coin through every Land can go.
Some secret Grace, which is but so to me,
Though not so great, may yet more pow'rful be:
All guard themselves when stronger Foes invade;⎤
Yet, by the weak, surprizes may be made:　　　⎬
But you, my Son, are not to judge, but aid.　　⎦

105　*Ægyptian*] F, D; Ægyptian Q1-5.

Por. What is it, Sir, you can require of me?

Max. I would from *Berenice*'s bonds be free:
This yoke of Marriage from us both remove,
Where two are bound to draw, though neither love.

40 *Por.* Neither the Gods nor man will give consent
To put in practice your unjust intent.

Max. Both must consent to that which I decree.

Por. The Souldiers love her Brother's memory;
And for her sake some Mutiny will stir.

Max. Our parting therefore————shall be sought by her.
Go, bid her sue for a Divorce, or dye;
I'le cut the knot, if she will not untye:
Haste to prepare her, and thy self return;
Thy *Hymen*'s Torch this day with mine shall burn.   *Exit.*

50 *Por.* Rather my Funeral-torch;————for though I know
Valeria's fair, and that she loves me too,
'Gainst her my Soul is arm'd on every part:
Yet there are secret Rivets to my heart;
Where *Berenice*'s Charms have found the way;
Subtile as Lightnings, but more fierce than they.
How shall I this avoid, or gain that Love!
So near the Rock, I to the Port must move.

To him Valeria *attended.*

Vale. Porphyrius, now my joy I may express,
Nor longer hide the Love I must possess.

160 Should I have stay'd till Marriage made us one,
You might have thought it was by duty done;
But of my heart I now a present make;
And give it you e're it be yours to take.
Accept it as when early fruit we send:
And let the rareness the small gift commend.

Por. Great Monarchs, like your Father, often give

What is above a Subject to receive:
But faithful Officers should countermand,
And stop the gift that passes through their hand:
170 And to their Prince, that mass of wealth restore,
Which lavish'd thus, would make whole Nations poor.
    Vale. But to this gift a double right you have:
My Father gives but what before I gave.
    Por. In vain you such unequal presents make,
Which I still want capacity to take.
Such fatal bounty once the *Gaules* did show;
They threw their Rings, but threw their Targets too.
Bounty so plac'd, does more like ruine look;
You pour the Ocean on a narrow Brook.
180   *Vale.* Yet, if your Love before prepares a Boat,
The stream so pour'd, drowns not, but makes it float.
    Por. But when the Vessel is on Quick-sands cast,
The flowing tide does more the sinking hast.
    Vale. And on what Quick-sands can your heart be thrown?
Can you a Love besides *Valeria's* own?
    Por. If he who at your feet his heart would lay,
Be met with first, and robb'd upon the way,
You may indeed the Robbers strength accuse,
But pardon him who did the Present lose.
190   *Vale.* Who is this Thief that does my right possess?
Name her, and then we of her strength may guess.————
From whence does your unwonted silence come?
    Por. She bound and gagg'd me, and has left me dumb.
    Vale. But of my wrongs I will aloud complain:
False man, thou would'st excuse thy self in vain:
For thee I did a Maidens blush forsake;
And own'd a Love thou hast refus'd to take.
    Por. Refus'd it!————like a Miser midst his store,
Who grasps and grasps, till he can hold no more,
200 And when his strength is wanting to his mind,

172 *Vale.*] *Val.* Q1–5, F, D.   180 *Vale.*] *Val.* Q1–5, F, D.
184 *Vale.*] *Val.* Q1–5, F, D.   190 *Vale.*] *Val.* Q1–5, F, D.
193 gagg'd] Q3–5, F, D; gag'd Q1–2.   194 *Vale.*] *Val.* Q1–5, F, D.

Looks back, and sighs on what he left behind.

Vale. No, I resume that heart thou didst possess;
My Father shall my injuries redress:
With me thou losest his Imperial Crown,
And speedy death attends upon his frown.

Por. You may revenge your wrongs a nobler way;
Command my death, and I will soon obey.

Vale. No, live; for on thy life my cure depends:
In Debters deaths all obligation ends:
210 'Twill be some ease Ungrateful thee to call;
And, Bankrupt-like, say, trusting him lost all.

Por. Upbraided thus, what gen'rous man would live!
But Fortune will revenge what you forgive.
When I refuse, (as in few hours I must)
This offer'd grace, your Father will be just.

Vale. Be just! say rather he will cruel prove,
To kill that only person I can love.
Yet so it is!————
Your int'rest in the Army is so high,
220 That he must make you his, or you must dye!
It is resolv'd! who e're my Rival be,   *Aside after a pause.*
I'le show that I deserve him more than she.
And if at last he does ingrateful prove,
My constancy it self rewards my Love.   *Exit.*

Por. She's gone, and gazing round about, I see
Nothing but death, or glorious misery;
Here Empire stands, if I could Love displace;
There, hopeless Love, with more Imperial Grace:
Thus, as a sinking Hero compass'd round,
230 Beckens his bravest Foe for his last wound,
And him into his part of Fame does call,
I'le turn my face to Love, and there I'le fall.

To him Berenice, Erotion.

202   *Vale.*] *Val.* Q1–5, F, D.   208   *Vale.*] *Val.* Q1–5, F, D.
216   *Vale.*] *Val.* Q1–5, F, D.

Ber. I come, *Porphyrius,* to congratulate
This happy change of your exalted Fate:
You to the Empire are, I hear, design'd;
And fair *Valeria* must th' Alliance bind.

    Por. Would Heav'n had my succession so decreed,
That I in all might *Maximin* succeed!
He offers me th' Imperial Crown, 'tis true:
240 I would succeed him, but it is in you.

    Ber. In me! I never did accept your Love;
But you, I see, would handsomly remove:
And I can give you leave without a frown:
I always thought you merited a Crown.

    Por. I never sought that Crown but on your brow;
But you with such indiff'rence would allow
My change, that you have kill'd me with that breath:
I feel your scorn cold as the hand of death.

    Ber. You'l come to life in your *Valeria's* arms:
250 'Tis true, I cannot boast of equal Charms;
Or if I could, I never did admit
Your Love to me, but only suffer'd it.
I am a Wife, and can make no return;
And 'twere but vain, in hopeless fires to burn.

    Por. Unkind! can you whom only I adore,
Set open to your Slave the Prison-door?
You use my heart just as you would afford
A fatal freedom to some harmless bird,
Whom, breeding, you ne're taught to seek its food;
260 And now let flye to perish in the Wood.

    Ber. Then, if you will love on, and disobey,
And lose an Empire for my sake, you may.
Will a kind look from me pay all this score?
For you well know you must expect no more.

    Por. All I deserve it will, not all I wish:
But I will brave the Tyrants rage, for this.
If I refuse, my death must needs ensue;

---

246   indiff'rence] Q2–5, F, D; indifference Q1.
263–264   score ? . . . more.] F; $\sim$, . . . $\sim$? Q1–5, D.

But you shall see that I dare dye for you.
 Ber. Would you for me,
70 A Beauty, and an Empire too deny?
I love you now so well————that you shall dye.
Dye mine; 'tis all I can with honour give:
Nor should you dye, if after, I would live.
But when your Marriage and your Death I view,
That makes you false, but this will keep you true.
 Por. Unbind thy brows, and look abroad to see,
O mighty Love, thy mightiest Victory!
 Ber. And yet————is there no other way to try?
'Tis hard to say I love, and let you dye.
80 *Por.* Yes, there remains some help which you might give,
If you, as I would dye for Love, would live.
 Ber. If death for Love be sweet, sure life is more:
Teach me the means your safety to restore.
 Por. Your Tyrant the *Ægyptian* Princess loves;
And to that height his swelling passion moves,
That, fearing in your death the Souldiers force,
He from your bed does study a Divorce.
 Ber. Th' *Ægyptian* Princess I disputing heard,
And as a Miracle her mind regard.
90 But yet I wish that this Divorce be true.   *Gives her hand.*
 Por. 'Tis, Madam, but it must be sought by you.
By this he will all Mutinies prevent;
And this, as well, secures your own content.
 Ber. I hate this Tyrant, and his bed I loath;
But, once submitting, I am ty'd to both:
Ty'd to that Honour, which all Women owe,
Though not their Husbands person, yet their vow.
Something so sacred in that bond there is,
That none should think there could be ought amiss:
100 And if there be, we should in silence hide
Those faults, which blame our choice when they are spy'd.
 Por. But, since to all the world his crimes are known,

<hr>

284 *Ægyptian*] F, D; Ægyptian Q1–5.   288 *Ægyptian*] F, D; Ægyptian Q1–5.
288 heard] Q3–5, F, D; hard Q1–2.

And, by himself the Civil War's begun,
Would you th' advantage of the fight delay,
If, striking first, you were to win the day?
    Ber. I would, like *Jews* upon their Sabbath, fall:
And rather than strike first, not strike at all.
    Por. Against your self you sadly prophesie:
You either this Divorce must seek, or dye.
310   *Ber.* Then death from all my griefs shall set me free.
    Por. And would you rather chuse your death, than me?
    Ber. My earthy part————
Which is my Tyrants right, death will remove,
I'le come all Soul and Spirit to your Love.
With silent steps I'le follow you all day;
Or else before you, in the Sun-beams, play.
I'le lead you thence to melancholy Groves,
And there repeat the Scenes of our past Loves.
At night, I will within your Curtains peep;
320 With empty arms embrace you while you sleep.
In gentle dreams I often will be by;
And sweep along, before your closing eye.
All dangers from your bed I will remove;
But guard it most from any future Love.
And when at last, in pity, you will dye,
I'le watch your Birth of Immortality:
Then, Turtle-like, I'le to my Mate repair;
And teach you your first flight in open Air.
                    Exit Berenice *cum* Erotio.
    Por. She has but done what Honour did require:
330 Nor can I blame that Love, which I admire.
But then her death!
I'le stand betwixt, it first shall pierce my heart:
We will be stuck together on his dart.
But yet the danger not so high does grow:
I'le charge death first, perhaps repulse him too.
But, if o'repow'r'd, I must be overcome;
Forc'd back, I'le fight each inch into my Tomb.   *Exit.*

---

306 *Jews*] F, D; Jews Q1–5.   306 Sabbath,] Q3–4; ~∧ Q1–2, Q5, F, D.
337 Forc'd back] Q2–5, F, D; Forc'dback Q1.

ACT IV.   SCENE I.

Indian *Cave.*

Enter Placidius, Nigrinus. Nigrinus *with two drawn Swords,
held upward in his hands.*

Placid. All other means have fail'd to move her heart;
Our last recourse is, therefore, to your Art.
    Nig. Of Wars, and Bloodshed, and of dire Events,
Of Fates, and fighting Kings, their Instruments,
I could with greater certainty foretell;
Love only does in doubts and darkness dwell.
For, like a wind, it in no quarter stays;
But points and veers each hour a thousand ways.
On Women Love depends, and they on Will;
10 Chance turns their Orb while Destiny sits still.
    Placid. Leave nothing unattempted in your pow'r:
Remember you oblige an Emperour.
    Nig. An earthy Fiend by compact me obeys;
But him to light intents I must not raise.
Some Astral forms I must invoke by pray'r,
Fram'd all of purest Atoms of the Air;
Not in their Natures simply good or ill;
But most subservient to bad Spirits will.
Nakar of these does lead the mighty Band,
20 For eighty Legions move at his Command:
Gentle to all, but, far above the rest,
Mild *Nakar* loves his soft *Damilcar* best.
In Aery Chariots they together ride;
And sip the dew as through the Clouds they glide:
These are the Spirits which in Love have pow'r.
    Placid. Haste, and invoke 'em in a happy hour.
    Nig. And so it proves: for, counting sev'n from Noon,

s.d. Indian] D; *Indian* Q1–5, F.   *s.d.* Enter] D; *omitted from Q1–5, F.*
15   pray'r] Q2–5, F, D; prayer Q1.

'Tis *Venus* hour, and in the wexing Moon.
With Chalk I first describe a Circle here,
30 Where these Ætherial Spirits must appear.
Come in, come in; for here they will be strait:
Around, around, the place I fumigate:
My fumigation is to *Venus,* just:
The Souls of Roses, and red Corals dust:
A lump of *Sperma Ceti;* and to these
The stalks and chips of *Lignum Alöes.*
And, last, to make my fumigation good,
'Tis mixt with Sparrows brains, and Pigeons blood.
                                   Nigrinus *takes up the Swords.*
They come, they come, they come! I hear 'em now.
40   *Placid.* A death-like damp sits cold upon my brow:
And misty vapours swim before my sight.
     Nig. They come not in a shape to cause your fright.

          Nakar *and* Damilcar *descend in Clouds, and sing.*

     Nakar. *Hark, my* Damilcar, *we are call'd below!*
     Dam. *Let us go, let us go!*
Go to relieve the care
Of longing Lovers in despair!
     Nakar. *Merry, merry, merry, we sail from the East*
Half tippled at a Rain-bow Feast.
     Dam. *In the bright Moon-shine while winds whistle loud,*
50 *Tivy, tivy, tivy, we mount and we fly,*
All racking along in a downy white Cloud:
And lest our leap from the Skie should prove too far,
We slide on the back of a new-falling Star.
     Nakar. *And drop from above,*
In a Gelly of Love!
     Dam. *But now the Sun's down, and the Element's red,*
The Spirits of Fire against us make head!
     Nakar. *They muster, they muster, like Gnats in the Air:*
Alas! I must leave thee, my Fair;
60 *And to my light Horse-men repair.*

    Dam. *O stay, for you need not to fear 'em to night;*
The wind is for us, and blows full in their sight:
And o're the wide Ocean we fight!
Like leaves in the Autumn our Foes will fall down;
And hiss in the Water————
    Both. *And hiss in the Water and drown!*
    Nakar. *But their men lye securely intrench'd in a Cloud:*
And a Trumpeter-Hornet to battel sounds loud.
    Dam. *Now Mortals that spie*
70 *How we tilt in the Skie*
With wonder will gaze;
And fear such events as will ne're come to pass!
    Nakar. *Stay you to perform what the man will have done.*
    Dam. *Then call me again when the Battel is won.*
    Both. *So ready and quick is a Spirit of Air*
To pity the Lover, and succour the fair,
That, silent and swift, the little soft God
Is here with a wish, and is gone with a nod.

           The Clouds part, Nakar *flies up, and* Damilcar *down.*

    Nig. I charge thee, Spirit, stay; and by the pow'r
                                   [*To* Damilcar.
80 Of *Nakar's* Love, and of this holy Wand,
On the North quarter of my Circle stand:
(Sev'n foot around for my defence I take!)
To all my questions faithful answers make,
So may'st thou live thy thousand years in peace;
And see thy Aery progeny increase:
So may'st thou still continue young and fair,
Fed by the blast of pure Ætherial Air.
And, thy full term expir'd, without all pain
Dissolve into thy Astral source again.
90   *Dam.* Name not my hated Rival *Gemory,*
And I'le speak true whate're thy questions be.

79+ *s.d.* Damilcar.] Q3–5, F, D; ∼ .] Q1–2.
80   Wand,] Q3, Q5, F; ∼ᴧ Q1–2, D; ∼ . Q4.

Nig. Thy Rivals hated name I will refrain:
Speak, shall the Emperour his love obtain?
   Dam. Few hours shall pass before your Emperour shall be
Possess'd of that he loves, or from that love be free.
   Placid. Shall I enjoy that Beauty I adore?
   Dam. She, Suppliant-like, e're long, thy succour shall implore:
And thou with her thou lov'st in happiness may'st live:
If she not dies before, who all thy joys can give.
100   *Nig.* Say, what does the *Ægyptian* Princess now?
   Dam. A gentle slumber sits upon her brow.
   Nig. Go, stand before her in a golden dream:
Set all the pleasures of the world to show,
And in vain joys let her loose spirit flow.
   Dam. Twice fifty Tents remove her from your sight,
But I'll cut through 'em all with rays of light:
And covering other objects to your eyes,
Show where intranc'd in silent sleep she lies.

   Damilcar *stamps, and the Bed arises with S.* Catharine *in it.*

Dam. singing. *You pleasing dreams of Love and sweet delight,*
110   *Appear before this slumbring Virgins sight:*
                 Soft visions set her free
                 From mournful piety.
                 Let her sad thoughts from Heav'n retire;
                 And let the Melancholy Love
                 Of those remoter joys above
                 Give place to your more sprightly fire.
                 Let purling streams be in her fancy seen;
                 And flowry Meads, and Vales of chearful green:
                 And in the midst of deathless Groves
120   *Soft sighing wishes ly,*
                 And smiling hopes fast by,
                 And just beyond 'em ever-laughing Loves.

                 A Scene of a Paradise is discovered.

---

97   She,] F; ~ᴧ Q1–5, D.   100   *Ægyptian*] D; Ægyptian Q1–5, F.
106   'em] Q4, D; e'm Q1–3; them Q5, F.   122   'em] Q3–5, F, D; e'm Q1–2.
122   *ever-laughing*] Q4–5, F, D; *ever laughing* Q1–3.

Placid. Some pleasing objects do her mind employ;
For on her face I read a wandring Joy.

SONG.

Dam.   *Ah how sweet it is to love,*
       Ah how gay is young desire!
       And what pleasing pains we prove
       When we first approach Loves fire!
         Pains of Love be sweeter far
130   *Than all other pleasures are.*

       Sighs which are from Lovers blown,
       Do but gently heave the Heart:
       Ev'n the tears they shed alone
       Cure, like trickling Balm, their smart.
         Lovers when they lose their breath,
         Bleed away in easie death.

       Love and Time with reverence use,
       Treat 'em like a parting friend:
       Nor the golden gifts refuse
140   *Which in youth sincere they send:*
         For each year their price is more,
         And they less simple than before.

       Love, like Spring-tides full and high,
       Swells in every youthful vein:
       But each Tide does less supply,
       Till they quite shrink in again:
         If a flow in Age appear,
         'Tis but rain, and runs not clear.

   At the end of the Song a Dance of Spirits. After which Amariel,
     the Guardian-Angel of S. Catharine, *descends to soft Musick,*
     with a flaming Sword. The Spirits crawl off the Stage amaz-
     edly, and Damilcar *runs to a corner of it.*

---

134   *Balm,*] F, D, d, M3; ~∧ Q1–5, f1, b1–3, M4–5.

Amar. From the bright Empire of Eternal day,
150 Where waiting minds for Heav'ns Commission stay,
Amariel flies.———[*To S.* Cath.] A darted Mandate came
From that great will which moves this mighty Frame,
Bid me to thee, my Royal charge, repair,
To guard thee from the Dæmons of the Air;
My flaming Sword above 'em to display,
(All keen and ground upon the edge of day;)
The flat to sweep the Visions from thy mind,
The edge to cut 'em through that stay behind.
———Vain Spirits, you that shunning Heav'ns high noon,
160 Swarm here beneath the concave of the Moon,
What folly, or what rage your duty blinds,
To violate the sleep of holy minds?
Hence, to the task assign'd you here below:
Upon the Ocean make loud Tempests blow:
Into the wombs of hollow Clouds repair,
And crush out Thunder from the bladder'd Air.
From pointed Sun-beams take the Mists they drew,
And scatter 'em again in pearly dew:
And of the bigger drops they drain below,
170 Some mould in Hail, and others stamp in Snow.
Dam. Mercy, bright Spirit, I already feel
The piercing edge of thy immortal steel:
Thou, Prince of day, from Elements Art free;
And I all body when compar'd to thee.
Thou tread'st th' Abyss of light!
And where it streams with open eyes canst go:
We wander in the Fields of Air below:
Changlings and Fooles of Heav'n: and thence shut out,
Wildly we roam in discontent about:
180 Gross-heavy-fed, next man in ignorance and sin,
And spotted all without; and dusky all within.
Without thy Sword I perish by thy sight,
I reel, and stagger, and am drunk with light.

---

151 flies.———[*To S.* Cath.] A] flies: (a Q1–5, F, D (A D).
158–159 behind. / ———Vain] behind.) / Vain Q1–5, F, D.

Ama. If e're again thou on this place art found,
Full fifty years I'le chain thee under ground;
The damps of Earth shall be thy daily food;
All swoln and bloated like a dungeon toad:
And when thou shalt be freed, yet thou shalt ly ⎫
Gasping upon the ground, too faint to fly;   ⎬
190 And lag below thy fellows in the sky.   ⎭
Dam. O pardon, pardon this accursed deed,
And I no more on Magick fumes will feed;
Which drew me hither by their pow'rful steams.
Ama. Go expiate thy guilt in holy dreams.   [*Ex.* Dam.
But thou, sweet Saint, henceforth disturb'd no more [*To S.* Cath.
With dreams not thine, thy thoughts to Heav'n restore.
                    The Angel ascends, and the Scene shuts.
Nig. Some holy Being does invade this place,
And from their duty does my Spirits chase.
I dare no longer near it make abode:
200 No Charms prevail against the Christians God.   *Exit.*
Placid. How doubtfully these Specters Fate foretell!
In double sense, and twi-light truth they dwell:
Like fawning Courtiers for success they wait,
And then come smiling and declare for Fate.

        Enter Maximin *and* Porphyrius, *attended by* Valerius
                    and Guards.

But see, the Tyrant and my Rival come:
I, like the Fiends, will flatter in his doom:
None but a Fool distastful truth will tell,
So it be new and please, 'tis full as well.
            Placid. *whispers with the Emperour who seems pleas'd.*
Max. You charm me with your news, which I'le reward:
210 By hopes we are for coming joys prepar'd:
Possess her Love, or from that Love be free————

194–195 Go . . . / But . . . more [*To S.* Cath.] D; *to S. Cath.* Go . . . / But
. . . more Q1–5; Go . . . / *To S.* Cath.] But . . . more F.
211 *in romans in Q1–5, F, D.*

Heav'n speaks me fair: if she as kind can prove,
I shall possess, but never quit my Love.
Go, tell me when she wakes.——— *Exit* Placidius.
        Porphyrius *seems to beg something of him.*
————————————*Porphyrius,* no;
She has refus'd, and I will keep my vow.
   Por. For your own sake your cruel vow defer;
The time's unsafe, your Enemies are near.
And to displease your men when they should fight———
   Max. My looks alone my Enemies will fright;
220 And o're my men I'le set my careful Spies,
To watch Rebellion in their very eyes.
No more, I cannot bear the least reply.
   Por. Yet, Tyrant, thou shalt perish e're she dye.   *Aside.*

Enter Valeria.

Valeria here! how Fortune treats me still
With various harms, magnificently ill!
   Max. Valeria, I was sending to your Tent,   *To* Valeria.
But my Commands your presence does prevent.
This is the hour, wherein the Priest shall joyn
Your holy Loves, and make *Porphyrius* mine.
230 *Vale. aside.* Now hold, my Heart, and *Venus* I implore,
Be Judge if she he loves deserves him more.
   Por. aside. Past hope! and all in vain I would preserve
My life, not for my self, but her I serve.
   Vale. I come, great Sir, your justice to demand. *To the Emp.*
   Max. You cannot doubt it from a Fathers hand.
   Por. Sir, I confess before her Suit be known;
And, by my self condemn'd, my crime I own.
I have refus'd———
   Vale. ————————Peace, peace, while I confess
I have refus'd thee for unworthiness.
240 *Por.* I am amaz'd.

214 wakes.] ∼∧ Q1–5, F, D.   226 *s.d.* Valeria] Q3–5, F, D; *Valeria* Q1–2.
230 *Vale.*] *Val.* Q1–5, F, D.   234 *Vale.*] *Val.* Q1–5, F, D.
238 *Vale.*] *Val.* Q1–5, F, D.

Max. _____What Riddles do you use?
Dare either of you my Commands refuse?
   Vale. Yes, I dare owne how e're 'twas wisely done
T'adopt so mean a person for your Son:
So low you should not for your Daughter chuse:
And therefore, Sir, this Marriage I refuse.
   Max. You lik'd the choice when first I thought it fit.
   Vale. I had not then enough consider'd it.
   Max. And you have now consider'd it too much:
Secrets of Empire are not safe to touch.
250   *Por.* Let not your mighty anger rise too high;
'Tis not *Valeria* merits it, but I.
My own unworthiness so well I knew,
That from her Love I consciously withdrew.
   Vale. Thus rather than endure the little shame
To be refus'd, you blast a Virgins name.
You to refuse, and I to be deny'd!
Learn more discretion, or be taught less pride.
   Por. O Heav'n, in what a Lab'rinth am I led!
I could get out, but she detains the thred!
260 Now I must wander on till I can see,
Whether her pity or revenge it be!   *Aside.*
   Max. With what childs anger do you think you play?
I'le punish both, if either disobey.
   Vale. Since all the fault was mine, I am content
Porphyrius should not share the punishment.
   Por. Blind that I was till now, that could not see,
'Twas all th' effect of generosity.
She loves me, ev'n to suffer for my sake;
And on her self would my refusal take.   *Aside.*
270   *Max.* Children to serve their Parents int'rest, live.   *To* Val.
Take heed what doom against your self you give.
   Por. Since she must suffer, if I do not speak,
'Tis time the Laws of Decency to break.

---

242 *Vale.*] *Val.* Q1–5, F, D.   247 *Vale.*] *Val.* Q1–5, F, D.
254 *Vale.*] *Val.* Q1–5, F, D.   258 Lab'rinth] Q2–5, F, D; Labyrinth Q1.
264 *Vale.*] *Val.* Q1–5, F, D.

She told me, Sir, that she your choice approv'd:
And (though I blush to owne it) said she lov'd,
Lov'd me desertless, who, with shame, confest
Another flame had seiz'd upon my brest.
Which when, too late, the generous Princess knew,
And fear'd your justice would my crime pursue,
280 Upon her self she makes the Tempest fall,
And my refusal her contempt would call.
  Vale. He raves, Sir, and to cover my disdain,
Unhandsomly would his denial feign.
And all means failing him, at last would try
T'usurp the credit of a scorn, and dye.
But————let him live:————his punishment shall be
The grief his pride will bring for losing me.
  Max. You both obnoxious to my justice are;
And, Daughter, you have not deserv'd my care.
290 'Tis my Command you strictly guarded be,
Till your fantastick quarrel you agree.
  Por. Sir————
  Max. ————I'le not hear you speak, her crime is plain,
She owns her pride which you perhaps may feign.
She shall be Pris'ner till she bend her mind
To that which is for both of you design'd.
  Vale. You'l find it hard my free-born will to bound.
  Max. I'le find that pow'r o're wills which Heav'n ne're found.
Free will's a cheat in any one but me:
In all but Kings 'tis willing slavery,
300 An unseen Fate which forces the desire,
The will of Puppets danc'd upon a wyre.
A Monarch is
The Spirit of the World in every mind;
He may match Wolves to Lambs, and make it kind.
Mine is the business of your little Fates:

---

275 lov'd,] Q4-5, F; ~ . Q1-3, D.   282 *Vale.*] *Val.* Q1-5, F, D.
292 [*rule*] I'le] [*rule omitted*] ~ Q1-5, F, D.
294 Pris'ner] F; Prisoner Q1-5, D.
296 *Vale.*] *Val.* Q1-5, F, D.   299 slavery,] ~ . Q1-5, F, D.
300 desire,] Q4-5, F; ~ : Q1-3, D.

And though you war, like petty wrangling States,
You're in my hand; and when I bid you cease,
You shall be crush'd together into peace.
    Vale. aside. Thus by the world my courage will be priz'd;
310 Seeming to scorn, who am, alas, despis'd:
Dying for Love's, fulfilling Honour's Laws;
A secret Martyr while I owne no cause.   *Exit* Valeria.
    Max. Porphyrius, stay; there's something I would hear:
You said you lov'd, and you must tell me where.
    Por. All Heav'n is to my sole destruction bent.   *Aside.*
    Max. You would, it seems, have leisure to invent.
    Por. Her name in pity, Sir, I must forbear,
Lest my offences you revenge on her.
    Max. My promise for her life I do engage.
320   *Por.* Will that, Sir, be remember'd in your rage?
    Max. Speak, or your silence more my rage will move;
'Twill argue that you rival me in Love.
    Por. Can you believe that my ambitious flame
Should mount so high as *Berenice*'s name?
    Max. Your guilt dares not approach what it would hide;
But draws me off, and (Lapwing-like) flies wide.
'Tis not my Wife, but Mistress you adore:
Though that affronts, yet this offends me more.
Who courts my Wife———
330 Does to my Honour more injurious prove;
But he who courts my Mistress, wrongs my Love.
    Por. Th' *Ægyptian* Princess ne're could move my heart.
    Max. You could not perish by a nobler Dart.
    Por. Sir, I presume not beauties to compare;
But in my eye, my Princess is as fair.
    Max. Your Princess! then it seems, though you deny
Her name you love, you owne her quality.
    Por. Though not by Birth or Title so; yet she
Who rules my heart, a Princess is to me.
340   *Max.* No, no———

---

309 *Vale.*] *Val.* Q1–5, F, D.
332 *Ægyptian*] F, D; Egyptian Q1 (*cancel*), Q2–5.

'Tis plain that word you unawares did use,
And told a truth which now you would excuse.
Besides my Wife and Mistress, here are none
Who can the Title of a Princess owne.
    Por. There is one more———
Your Daughter, Sir: let that your doubt remove.
    Max. But she is not that Princess whom you love.
    Por. I nam'd not Love, though it might doubtful seem;
She's fair; and is that Princess I esteem.
350   *Max.* Go, and to passion your esteem improve,
While I command her to receive your Love.   *Exit* Por.

Enter S. Catharine.

    S. Cath. I come not now, as Captive to your pow'r,
To beg; but as high Heav'ns Embassadour,
The Laws of my Religion to fulfill:
Heav'n sends me to return you good for ill.
Your Empress to your Love I would restore;
And to your mind the peace it had before.
    Max. While in anothers name you Peace declare,
Princess, you in your own proclaim a War.
360 Your too great pow'r does your design oppose;
You make those breaches which you strive to close.
    S. Cath. That little beauty which too much you prize
Seeks not to move your heart, or draw your eyes:
Your Love to *Berenice* is due alone:
Love, like that pow'r which I adore, is one.
When fixt to one, it safe at Anchor rides,
And dares the fury of the winds and tides:
But losing once that hold, to the wide Ocean born,
It drives away at will, to every wave a scorn.
370   *Max.* If to new persons I my Love apply,
The Stars and Nature are in fault, not I:
My Loves are like my old Prætorian Bands,

354   fulfill] Q1 (*cancelandum*), Q3–4; fulfil Q1 (*cancel*), Q2, Q5, F, D.

Whose Arbitrary pow'r their Prince commands:
I can no more make passion come or go,
Than you can bid your *Nilus* ebb or flow.
'Tis lawless, and will love, and where it list:
And that's no sin which no man can resist:
Those who impute it to me as a crime,
Would make a God of me before my time.
380   *S. Cath.* A God, indeed, after the *Roman* style,
An Eagle mounting from a kindled Pile:
But you may make your self a God below:
For Kings who rule their own desires are so.
You roam about, and never are at rest,
By new desires, that is, new torments, still possest;
Qualmish and loathing all you had before,
Yet with a sickly appetite to more.
As in a fev'rish dream you still drink on;
And wonder why your thirst is never gone.
390 Love, like a ghostly Vision haunts your mind;
'Tis still before you what you left behind.
       Max. How can I help those faults which Nature made?
My appetite is sickly and decay'd,
And you forbid me change, the sick mans ease;
Who cannot cure, must humour his disease.
       S. Cath. Your mind should first the remedy begin;
You seek without, the Cure that is within.
The vain experiments you make each day,
To find content, still finding it decay,
400 Without attempting more, should let you see
That you have sought it where it ne're could be.
But when you place your joys on things above,
You fix the wand'ring Planet of your Love:
Thence you may see
Poor humane kind all daz'd in open day,

---

380 *Roman*] Q3–4, F, D; Roman Q1–2, Q5.
384–386 rest, . . . possest; . . . before,] ∼ ; . . . ∼ . . . . ∼ : Q1–5, F, D.
394 change, the . . . ease;] ∼ (∼ . . . ∼) Q1–5, F, D.

Erre after bliss, and blindly miss their way:
The greatest happiness a Prince can know,
Is to love Heav'n above, do good below.

To them Berenice *and Attendants.*

Ber. That happiness may *Berenice* find,
410 Leaving these empty joys of Earth behind:
And this frail Being, where so short a while
Th' unfortunate lament, and prosp'rous smile.
Yet a few days, and those which now appear
In youth and beauty like the blooming year,
In life's swift Scene shall change; and cares shall come,
And heavy age, and death's relentless doom.
    S. Cath. Yet man, by pleasures seeks that Fate which he would
        shun;
And, suck'd in by the stream, does to the Whirl-pool run.
    Max. How, Madam, are you to new ways inclin'd?   *To* Ber.
420 I fear the Christian Sect perverts your mind.
    Ber. Yes, Tyrant, know that I their Faith embrace,
And owne it in the midst of my disgrace.
That Faith, which abject as it seems to thee,
Is nobler than thy Purple Pageantry:
A Faith, which still with Nature is at strife,
And looks beyond it to a future life;
A Faith which vitious Souls abhor and fear,
Because it shows Eternity too near.
And therefore every one——
430 With seeming scorn of it the rest deceives:
All joyning not to owne what each believes.
    S. Cath. O happy Queen! whom pow'r leads not astray,
Nor youth's more pow'rful blandishments betray.
    Ber. Your Arguments my reason first inclin'd,
And then your bright example fix'd my mind.
    Max. With what a holy Empress am I blest,

425–426 strife, . . . life;] ~ ; . . . ~ . Q1–5, F, D.
428 too] Q2–5, F, D; to Q1.

What scorn of Earth dwells in her heav'nly brest!
My Crown's too mean; but he whom you adore,
Has one more bright of Martyrdom in store.
440 She dyes, and I am from the envy freed: *Aside.*
She has, I thank her, her own death decreed.
No Souldier now will in her rescue stir;
Her death is but in complaisance to her.
I'le haste to gratifie her holy will;
Heav'n grant her zeal may but continue still.
Tribune, a Guard to seize the Empress strait,   *To* Val.
Secure her Person Pris'ner to the State.   *Exit* Maximin.
       Val. going to her. Madam, believe 'tis with regret I come
To execute my angry Prince's doom.

                      Enter Porphyrius.

450   *Por.* What is it I behold! Tribune, from whence
Proceeds this more than barbarous insolence?
       Val. Sir, I perform the Emperour's Commands.
       Por. Villain, hold off thy sacrilegious hands,
Or by the Gods———retire without reply:
And, if he asks who bid thee, say 'twas I.
                      Valerius *retires to a distance.*
       Ber. Too generously your safety you expose
To save one moment her whom you must lose.
       Por. 'Twixt you and death ten thousand lives there stand;
Have courage, Madam, the Prætorian Band
460 Will all oppose your Tyrants cruelty.
       S. Cath. And I have Heav'n implor'd she may not dye.
As some to witness truth Heav'ns call obey;
So some on Earth must, to confirm it, stay.
       Por. What Faith, what Witness is it that you name?
       Ber. Knowing what she believes, my Faith's the same.
       Por. How am I cross'd what way so e're I go!
To the unlucky every thing is so.

---

446 Tribune . . . strait, *To* Val.] D; *To Val.* Tribune . . . strait, Q1–5, F
(*line indented*).

Now, Fortune, thou hast shown thy utmost spight:
The Souldiers will not for a Christian fight.
470 And, Madam, all that I can promise now,
Is but to dye before death reaches you.

    Ber. Now death draws near, a strange perplexity
Creeps coldly on me, like a fear to dye:
Courage, uncertain dangers may abate;
But who can bear th' approach of certain Fate?

    S. Cath. The wisest and the best some fear may show;
And wish to stay, though they resolve to go.

    Ber. As some faint Pilgrim standing on the shore,
First views the Torrent he would venture o're;
480 And then his Inn upon the farther ground,
Loth to wade through, and lother to go round:
Then dipping in his staff do's tryal make,
How deep it is; and, sighing, pulls it back:
Sometimes resolv'd to fetch his leap; and then
Runs to the Bank, but there stops short agen;
So I at once——
Both heav'nly Faith, and humane fear obey;
And feel before me in an unknown way.
For this blest Voyage I with joy prepare;
490 Yet am asham'd to be a stranger there.

    S. Cath. You are not yet enough prepar'd to dye:
Earth hangs too heavy for your Soul to flye.

    Por. One way (and Heav'n I hope inspires my mind)
I for your safety in this straight can find:
But this fair Queen must farther my intent.

    S. Cath. Name any way your reason can invent.

    Por. to Ber. Though your Religion (which I cannot blame,
Because my secret Soul avows the same)
Has made your life a forfeit to the Laws,
500 The Tyrants new-born passion is the cause.
Were this bright Princess once remov'd away,
Wanting the food, the flame would soon decay.
And I'le prepare a faithful Guard this night
T'attend her person, and secure her flight.

Ber. to S. Cath. By this way I shall both from death be freed,
And you unforc'd to any wicked deed.
 S. Cath. Madam, my thoughts are with themselves at strife;
And Heav'n can witness how I prize your life:
But 'tis a doubtful conflict I must try
510 Betwixt my pity and my piety.
Staying, your precious life I must expose:
Going, my Crown of Martyrdom I lose.
 Por. Your equal choice when Heav'n does thus divide,
You should, like Heav'n, still lean on mercy's side.
 S. Cath. The will of Heav'n, judg'd by a private brest,
Is often what's our private interest.
And therefore those, who would that will obey,
Without their int'rest must their duty weigh.
As for my self, I do not life despise;
520 But as the greatest gift of Nature prize.
My Sex is weak, my fears of death are strong;
And whate're is, its Being would prolong.
Were there no sting in death, for me to dye,
Would not be conquest, but stupidity.
But if vain Honour can confirm the Soul,
And sense of shame the fear of death controul,
How much more then should Faith uphold the mind,
Which, showing death, shows future life behind?
 Ber. Of death's contempt Heroick proofs you give;
530 But, Madam, let my weaker Vertue live.
Your Faith may bid you your own life resign;
But not when yours must be involv'd with mine.
Since, then, you do not think me fit to dye,
Ah, how can you that life I beg, deny!
 S. Cath. Heav'n does in this my greatest tryal make,
When I for it, the care of you forsake.
But I am plac'd, as on a Theater, ⎫
Where all my Acts to all Mankind appear, ⎬
To imitate my constancy or fear. ⎭
540 Then, Madam, judge what course I should pursue,

---

522 its] Q3–5, F, D; it's Q1–2. 531 you] Q3–5, F; ∼ , Q1–2, D.

When I must either Heav'n forsake, or you.
   Por. Were saving *Berenice's* life a sin,
Heav'n had shut up your flight from *Maximin.*
   S. Cath. Thus, with short Plummets Heav'ns deep will we
      sound,
That vast Abyss where humane Wit is drown'd!
In our small Skiff we must not launce too far;
We here but Coasters, not Discov'rers are.
Faith's necessary Rules are plain and few;
We, many, and those needless Rules pursue:
550 Faith from our hearts into our heads we drive;
And make Religion all Contemplative.
You, on Heav'ns will may witty glosses feign;
But that which I must practise here, is plain:
If the All-great decree her life to spare,
He will the means, without my crime, prepare.   *Exit S.* Cath.
   Por. Yet there is one way left! it is decreed,
To save your life, that *Maximin* shall bleed.
'Midst all his Guards I will his death pursue,
Or fall a Sacrifice to Love and you.
560   *Ber.* So great a fear of death I have not shown,
That I would shed his blood to save my own.
My fear is but from humane frailty brought;
And never mingled with a wicked thought.
   Por. 'Tis not a Crime, since one of you must dye;
Or is excus'd by the necessity.
   Ber. I cannot to a Husband's death consent;
But, by revealing, will your crime prevent:
The horrour of this deed——
Against the fear of death has arm'd my mind;
570 And now less guilt in him than you I find:
If I a Tyrant did detest before,
I hate a Rebel and a Traitor more:
Ungrateful man——
Remember whose Successor thou art made,

---

555   will . . . crime,] F, D; ~ , . . . ~∧ Q1–5.
556   decreed,] F; ~∧ Q1–5, D.   557   life,] Q4–5, F; ~∧ Q1–3, D.

And then thy Benefactors life invade.
Guards, to your charge I give your Pris'ner back:
And will from none but Heav'n my safety take.
                 Exit with Valerius *and Guards.*
    Por. solus. 'Tis true, what she has often urg'd before;
He's both my Father and my Emperour!

580 O Honour, how can'st thou invent a way
To save my Queen, and not my trust betray!
Unhappy I that e're he trusted me!
As well his Guardian-Angel may his Murd'rer be.
And yet————let Honour, Faith, and Vertue flye,
But let not Love in *Berenice* dye.
She lives!————
That's put beyond dispute, as firm as Fate:
Honour and Faith let Argument debate.

      Enter Maximin *and* Valerius *talking, and Guards.*

    Max. 'Tis said; but I am loth to think it true,   *To* Porphy.

590 That my late Orders were contemn'd by you:
That *Berenice* from her Guards you freed.
    Por. I did it, and I glory in the deed.
    Max. How, glory my Commands to disobey!
    Por. When those Commands would your Renown betray.
    Max. Who should be Judge of that Renown you name
But I?
    Por.————Yes, I, and all who love your fame.
    Max. Porphyrius, your replies are insolent.
    Por. Sir, they are just, and for your service meant.
If, for Religion you our lives will take;

600 You do not the offenders find, but make.
All Faiths are to their own believers just;
For none believe, because they will, but must.
Faith is a force from which there's no defence;
Because the Reason it does first convince.

---

576   Guards,] ~ᴧ Q1–5, F, D.   589   *Max.*] Q2–5, F, D; ~ᴧ Q1.
596   Yes,] D; ~ᴧ Q1–5, F.

And Reason Conscience into fetters brings;
And Conscience is without the pow'r of Kings.
　Max. Then Conscience is a greater Prince than I:
At whose each erring call a King may dye.
Who Conscience leaves to its own free command,
610 Puts the worst Weapon in a Rebels hand.
　Por. Its Empire, therefore, Sir, should bounded be;
And but in acts of its Religion, free:
Those who ask Civil pow'r and Conscience too,
Their Monarch to his own destruction woo.
With needful Arms let him secure his peace;
Then, that wild beast he safely may release.
　Max. I can forgive these liberties you take,
While but my Counsellor your self you make:
But you first act your sense, and then advise:
620 That is, at my expence you will be wise.
My Wife, I for Religion do not kill;
But she shall dye———because it is my will.
　Por. Sir, I acknowledge I too much have done;
And therefore merit not to be your Son:
I render back the Honours which you gave;
My liberty's the only gift I crave.
　Max. You take too much:———but, e're you lay it down,
Consider what you part with in a Crown:
Monarchs of cares in Policy complain,
630 Because they would be pity'd while they raign;
For still the greater troubles they confess,
They know their pleasures will be envy'd less.
　Por. Those joys I neither envy nor admire;
But beg I from the troubles may retire.
　Max. What Soul is this which Empire cannot stir!
Supine and tame as a Philosopher!
Know then, thou wert adopted to a Throne,
Not for thy sake so much as for my own.
My thoughts were once about thy death at strife;

611　Its] Q3–5, F, D; It's Q1–2.　　　　611　therefore,] Q4–5, F, D; ～ₐ Q1–3.
612　its] Q3–5, F, D; it's Q1–2.

40 And thy succession's thy reprieve for life.
    Por. My life and death are still within your pow'r:
But your succession I renounce this hour.
Upon a bloody Throne I will not sit;
Nor share the guilt of Crimes which you commit.
    Max. If you are not my *Cæsar,* you must dye.
    Por. I take it as the nobler Destiny.
    Max. I pity thee, and would thy faults forgive:
But thus presuming on, thou canst not live.
    Por. Sir, with your Throne your pity I restore;
50 I am your Foe; nor will I use it more.
Now all my debts of gratitude are paid,
I cannot trusted be, nor you betray'd.   *Is going.*
    Max. Stay, stay! in threat'ning me to be my Foe,
You give me warning to conclude you so.
Thou to succeed a Monarch in his Seat!

Enter Placidius.

No, Fool, thou art too honest to be great!
Placidius, on your life this Pris'ner keep:
Our enmity shall end before I sleep.
    Placid. I still am ready, Sir, when e're you please,
                                   To Porphy.
60 To do you such small services as these.
    Max. The sight with which my eyes shall first be fed,
Must be my Empress and this Traitors head.
    Por. Where e're thou standst I'le level at that place
My gushing blood, and spout it at thy face.
Thus, not by Marriage, we our blood will joyn:
Nay, more, my arms shall throw my head at thine.
                           Exit guarded.
    Max. There, go adoption:———I have now decreed
That *Maximin* shall *Maximin* succeed:
Old as I am, in pleasures I will try
670 To waste an Empire yet before I dye:

666   Nay,] Q5, F; ~∧ Q1–4, D.

Since life is fugitive, and will not stay,
I'le make it flye more pleasantly away.   *Exit.*

ACT V.   SCENE I.

Enter Valeria, Placidius.

Vale. If, as you say, you silently have been
So long my Lover, let my pow'r be seen:
One hours discourse before *Porphyrius* dye,
Is all I ask, and you too may be by.
    Placid. I must not break
The order, which the Emperour did sign.
    Vale. Has then his hand more pow'r with you than mine?
    Placid. This hand if given, would far more pow'rful be
Than all the Monarchs of the World to me:
10 But 'tis a bait which would my heart betray;
And, when I'm fast, will soon be snatcht away.
    Vale. O say not so; for I shall ever be
Oblig'd to him who once obliges me.
    Placid. Madam, I'le wink, and favour your deceit:
But know, fair Coz'ner, that I know the cheat:
Though to these eyes I nothing can refuse,
I'le not the merit of my ruine lose:
It is enough I see the hook, and bite:
But first I'le pay my death with my delight.
                          [*Kisses her hand, and Exit.*
20   *Vale.* What can I hope from this sad interview!
And yet my brave design I will pursue.
By many signs I have my Rival found:
But Fortune him, as deep as me does wound.

---

s.d. Enter] D; *omitted from* Q1–5, F.
s.d. Valeria, Placidius] Q4–5, D; *Valeria, Placidius* Q1–3, F.
1   *Vale.*] *Val.* Q1–5, F, D.   7   *Vale.*] *Val.* Q1–5, F, D.
12 *Vale.*] *Val.* Q1–5, F, D.   19+   s.d. *Exit.*] Q3–5, F, D; ∼ .] Q1–2.
20 *Vale.*] *Val.* Q1–5, F, D.

For, if he loves the Empress, his sad Fate
More moves my pity, than his scorn my hate.

To her Placidius *with* Porphyrius.

Placid. I am, perhaps, the first
Who forc'd by Fate, and in his own despight,
Brought a lov'd Rival to his Mistress sight.
    Vale. But, in revenge, let this your comfort be,
30 That you have brought a man who loves not me.
However, lay your causeless envy by;
He is a Rival who must quickly dye.
    Por. And yet I could with less concernment bear
That death of which you speak, than see you here.
So much of guilt in my refusal lyes,
That Debtor-like, I dare not meet your eyes.
    Vale. I do not blame you, if you love elsewhere:
And, would to Heav'n, I could your suff'rings bear;
Or once again could some new way invent
40 To take upon my self your punishment:
I sent for you, to let you know that still
(Though now I want the pow'r) I have the will.
    Placid. Can all this Ocean of your kindness be
Pour'd upon him, and not one drop on me?
    Vale. 'Tis pour'd; but falls from this ungrateful man,
Like drops of water from a rising Swan.
Upon his breast no sign of wet remains;
He bears his Love more proudly than his Chains.
    Por. This thankless man his death will soon remove,
50 And quickly end so undeserv'd a Love.
    Vale. Unthankful as you are, I know not why,
But still I love too well to see you dye.
Placidius, can you love, and see my grief,
And for my sake not offer some relief?
    Placid. Not all the Gods his ruine shall prevent;

Your kindness does but urge his punishment.
Besides, what can I for his safety do?
He has declar'd himself your Father's Foe.
    Vale. Give out he is escap'd, and set him free:
60 And, if you please, lay all the fault on me.
    Por. O do not on those terms my freedom name:
Freed by your danger I should dye with shame.
    Placid. I must not farther by your pray'rs be won.   *To her.*
All I could do I have already done.
    Vale. To bring *Porphyrius* only to my sight,
Was not to show your pity, but your spight:
Would you but half oblige her you adore?
You should not have done this, or should do more.
    Placid. Alas, what hope can there be left for me,
70 When I must sink into the Mine I see?
My heart will fall before you, if I stay;
Each word you speak saps part of it away.
———Yet all my Fortune on his death is set: *Aside.*
And he may love her, though he loves not yet.
He must———and yet she says he must not dye:
O, if I could but wink, I could deny.

                To them Albinus.

    Alb. The Emperour expects your Pris'ner strait:
And, with impatience, for his death does wait.
    Placid. Nay, then it is too late my Love to weigh.   *Exit* Alb.
80 Your pardon, Madam, if I must obey.
    Por. I am prepar'd, he shall not long attend.
    Vale. Then here my pray'rs, and my submissions end.
Placidius, know, that hour in which he dyes,
My death (so well I love) shall wait on his.

57 Besides, what can I] Q2–5, F, D (Besides∧ Q2; What F); Besides——— /
What is it I can Q1.   59 *Vale.*] *Val.* Q1–5, F, D.
63 pray'rs] F; prayers Q1–5, D.   65 *Vale.*] *Val.* Q1–5, F, D.
72 away.] ∼ .——— Q1–2, D; ∼∧——— Q3–5, F.
73 set: *Aside.*] set: Q1–5, F, D.   82 *Vale.*] *Val.* Q1–5, F, D.
82 here] Q2–5, F; hear Q1, D.   83 *Placidius,*] F; ∼∧ Q1–5, D.

Placid. O, Madam, do not fright me with your death!

Vale. My life depends alone upon his breath.

But, if I live in him, you do not know

How far my gratitude to you may go.

I do not promise———but it so may prove,

90 That gratitude, in time, may turn to Love.

Try me———

  Placid. ——— Now I consider it, I will: *Musing a little.*

'Tis in your pow'r to save him or to kill.

I'le run the hazard to preserve his life,

If, after that, you vow to be my Wife.

  Vale. Nay, good *Placidius*, now you are too hard:

Would you do nothing but for meer reward?

Like Usurers to men in want you prove,

When you would take Extortion for my Love.

  Placid. You have concluded then that he must dye.

              [*Going with* Porphy.

00 *Vale.* O stay, if no price else his life can buy,

My Love a ransom for his life I give:

     [*Holding her Handkerchief before her face.*

Let my *Porphyrius* for another live.

  Por. You too much value the small merchandise:

My life's o're-rated, when your Love's the price.

Enter Albinus.

  Alb. I long have list'ned to your generous strife,

As much concern'd for brave *Porphyrius* life:

For mine I to his favour ow'd this day;

Which with my future Service I will pay.

  Placid. Lest any your intended flight prevent,

110 I'le lead you first the back-way to my Tent:

Thence, in disguise, you may the City gain,

While some excuse for your escape I feign.

---

86 *Vale.*] *Val.* Q1–5, F, D.   95 *Vale.*] *Val.* Q1–5, F, D.
99+ s.d. Porphy.] Q3–5, F, D; ~ .] Q1–2. 100 *Vale.*] *Val.* Q1–5, F, D.
101+ s.d. face.] Q3–5, F, D; ~ .] Q1–2.

Vale. Farewel, I must not see you when you part:

[*Turning her face away.*

For that last look would break my tender heart.

Yet————let it break————I must have one look more:

[*Looking on him.*

Nay, now I'm less contented than before.

For that last look draws on another too;

Which sure I need not to remember you.

For ever————yet I must one glance repeat:

120 But quick and short as starving people eat.

So much humanity dwells in your brest,

Sometimes to think on her who loves you best.

Por. My wandring steps where ever Fortune bear,

Your memory I in my breast will wear:

Which, as a precious Amulet, I still

Will carry, my defence and guard from ill.

Though to my former vows I must be true,

I'le ever keep one Love entire for you;

That Love which Brothers with chaste Sisters make:

130 And by this Holy kiss, which now I take

From your fair hand————

[*Going, he takes her hand and kisses it.*

This common Sun which absent both shall see,

Shall ne're behold a breach of Faith in me.

Vale. Go, go, my death will your short vows restore:

You've said enough, and I can hear no more.

Exit Valeria *one way, and* Porphy. *and* Alb. *another.*

Placid. Love and good Nature, how do you betray!

Misleading those who see and know their way!

I, whom deep Arts of State could ne're beguile,

Have sold my self to ruine for a smile.

---

113   *Vale.*] *Val.* Q1–5, F, D.   113+   *s.d. away.*] Q3–5, F, D; ~ .] Q1–2.
115+   *s.d. him.*] Q3–5, F, D; ~ .] Q1–2.   124   wear:] F; ~ . Q1–5, D.
128   you;] ~ . Q1–5, F, D.
131+   *s.d.* [*Going . . . it.*] Q4–5, F, D (*s.d. at line 122*); [*Going . . . it*∧] Q1–2
(*s.d. at line 122*); [*Going . . . it.*] Q3 (*s.d. at line 122*).
134   *Vale.*] *Val.* Q1–5, F, D.

140 Nay, I am driv'n so low, that I must take
That smile, as Alms, giv'n for my Rivals sake.

Enter Maximin *talking with* Valerius, *and* Guards.

Max. And why was I not told of this before?
Val. Sir, she this evening landed on the shore.
For with her Daughter being Pris'ner made,
She in another Vessel was convey'd.
Max. Bring hither the *Ægyptian* Princess strait.   *To* Placid.
And you, *Valerius,* on her Mother wait.   *Exit* Valerius.
Placid. The Mother of th' *Ægyptian* Princess here!
Max. Porphyrius death I will a while defer;
150 And this new opportunity improve
To make my last effort upon her Love.———   *Exit* Placidius.
Those who have youth may long endure to court;
But he must swiftly catch whose Race is short.
I in my Autumn do my Siege begin;
And must make haste e're Winter comes, to win.
This hour———no longer shall my pains endure:
Her Love shall ease me, or her death shall cure.

Enter at one door Felicia *and* Valerius, *at the other*
S. Catharine *and* Placidius.

S. Cath. O, my dear Mother!
Fel. ————————— With what joy I see
My dearest Daughter from the Tempest free.
160   *S. Cath.* Dearer than all the joys vain Empire yields,
Or then to youthful Monarchs conquer'd fields.
Before you came———my Soul

---

141   sake.] Q2–5, F, D; sake. / He, like a secret Worm, has eat his way; / And,
lodg'd within, does on the kernel prey: / I creep without; and hopeless to
remove / Him thence, wait only for the husk of Love. Q1.
141+   s.d. Valerius, *and* Guards.] Valerius. Q1–5, F, D.
146   *Ægyptian*] F, D; Ægyptian Q1–5.
148   *Ægyptian*] F, D; Ægyptian Q1–5.   149   defer;] Q3–5, F; ∼ . Q1–2, D.

All fill'd with Heav'n did earthly joys disdain,
But you pull back some part of me again.
Placid. You see, Sir, she can owne a joy below.
Max. It much imports me that this truth I know.
Fel. How dreadful death does on the waves appear!
Where Seas we only see, and Tempests hear.
Such frightful Images did then pursue
170 My trembling Soul, that scarce I thought of you.
    Placid. All Circumstances to your wish combine: *To* Max.
Her fear of death advances your design.
    Fel. But to that only pow'r we serve I pray'd,
Till he, who bid it rise, the Tempest laid.
    Max. You are a Christian then!   *To* Felicia.
For death this very hour you must prepare:
I have decreed no Christians life to spare.
    Fel. For death! I hope you but my courage try:
Whatever I believe, I dare not dye.
180 Heav'n does not, sure, that Seal of Faith require;
Or, if it did, would firmer thoughts inspire.
A Womans witness can no credit give
To Truths Divine, and therefore I would live.
    Max. I cannot give the life which you demand:
But that and mine are in your Daughter's hand:
Ask her, if she will yet her Love deny;
And bid a Monarch, and her Mother dye.
    Fel. Now, mighty Prince, you cancel all my fear:
My life is safe, when it depends on her.
190 How can you let me languish thus in pain!   *To* S. Cath.
Make haste to cure those doubts which yet remain.
Speak quickly, speak and ease me of my fear.
    S. Cath. Alas, I doubt it is not you I hear.
Some wicked Fiend assumes your voice and face,
To make frail Nature triumph over Grace.

---

163   disdain,] Q4–5, F; ~ . Q1–3; ~ : D.
168   Tempests] Q3–5, F, D; Tempest Q1–2.
171   combine: *To* Max.] combine: Q1–5, F, D.
190   s.d. Cath.] Q2–5, F, D; *Cath.* Q1.

It cannot be————
That she who taught my Childhood Piety,
Should bid my riper age my Faith deny:
That she who bid my hopes this Crown pursue,
Should snatch it from me when 'tis just in view.

    Fel. Peace, peace, too much my age's shame you show:
How easie 'tis to teach! how hard to do!
My lab'ring thoughts are with themselves at strife:
I dare not dye, nor bid you save my life.

    Max. You must do one, and that without delay;
Too long already for your death I stay:
I cannot with your small concerns dispence;
For deaths of more importance call me hence.
Prepare to execute your office strait.   *To his Guards.*

    Fel. O stay, and let 'em but one minute wait.
Such quick Commands for death you would not give,
If you but knew how sweet it were to live.

    Max. Then bid her love.

    Fel. ————————— Is duty grown so weak,
                             To S. Cath.
That Love's a harder word than Death to speak?

    S. Cath. Oh!————

    Fel. Mistake me not, I never can approve
                       [*Privately to S.* Cath.
A thing so wicked as the Tyrants Love.
I ask you would but some false promise give,
Only to gain me so much time to live.

    S. Cath. That promise is a step to greater sin:
The hold once lost, we seldom take agen.
Each bound to Heav'n we fainter Essays make:
Still losing somewhat till we quite go back.

    Max. Away, I grant no longer a reprieve.

    Fel. O do but beg my life, and I may live.   *To S.* Cath.
Have you not so much pity in your brest?

---

212   If you but] Q2–5, F, D; (Ah) if you Q1.
216+   s.d. Privately] Q3–5, F, D; *privately* Q1–2.
216+   s.d. Cath.] Q3–5, F, D; ~ .] Q1–2.

He stays to have you make it your request.

    S. Cath. To beg your life———

Is not to ask a grace of *Maximin:*

230 It is a silent bargain for a sin.

Could we live always, life were worth our cost;

But now we keep with care what must be lost.

Here we stand shiv'ring on the Bank, and cry,

When we should plunge into Eternity.

One moment ends our pain;

And yet the shock of death we dare not stand,

By thought scarce measur'd, and too swift for sand:

'Tis but because the Living death ne're knew,

They fear to prove it as a thing that's new.

240 Let me th' Experiment before you try,

I'le show you first how easie 'tis to dye.

    Max. Draw then that Curtain, and let death appear,

And let both see how easie 'twill be there.

              The Scene opens, and shews the Wheel.

    Fel. Alas, what torments I already feel!

    Max. Go, bind her hand and foot beneath that Wheel:

Four of you turn the dreadful Engine round;

Four others hold her fast'ned to the ground:

That by degrees her tender breasts may feel,

First the rough razings of the pointed steel:

250 Her Paps then let the bearded Tenters stake,

And on each hook a gory Gobbet take;

Till th' upper flesh by piece-meal torn away,

Her beating heart shall to the Sun display.

    Fel. My dearest Daughter, at your feet I fall;   *Kneeling.*

Hear, Oh yet hear your wretched Mothers call.

Think, at your Birth, ah think what pains I bore,

And can your eyes behold me suffer more?

You were the Child which from your infancy

I still lov'd best, and then you best lov'd me.

260 About my neck your little arms you spred.

---

251 take;] ～ . Q1–5, F, D.   254 Daughter,] D; ～∧ Q1–5, F.

Nor could you sleep without me in the bed;
But sought my bosom when you went to rest,
And all night long would lye across my brest.
Nor without cause did you that fondness show:
You may remember when our *Nile* did flow;
While on the Bank you innocently stood,
And with a Wand made Circles in the flood,
That rose, and just was hurrying you to death,
When I, from far, all pale and out of breath,
270 Ran and rusht in————
And from the waves my floating pledge did bear,
So much my Love was stronger than my fear.
But you————
    Max. Woman, for these long tales your life's too short.
Go, bind her quickly, and begin the sport.   *To his Guards.*
    Fel. No, in her arms my Sanctuary's plac'd:
                       [Running to her Daughter.
Thus I will cling for ever to her waste.
    Max. What, must my will by women be controll'd?
Haste, draw your Weapons, and cut off her hold.
280   *S. Cath.* Thus my last duty to you let me pay.
                         [Kissing her Mother.
Yet, Tyrant, I to thee will never pray.
Though hers to save I my own life would give,
Yet by my sin, my Mother shall not live.
To thy foul lust I never can consent;
Why dost thou then defer my punishment?
I scorn those Gods thou vainly dost adore:
Contemn thy Empire, but thy Bed abhor.
If thou would'st yet a bloodier Tyrant be,
I will instruct thy rage, begin with me.
90   *Max.* I thank thee that thou dost my anger move:
It is a Tempest that will wreck my Love.

261   bed;] Q4–5, F, D; ∼ . Q1–2; ∼ , Q3.   269   breath,] Q3–5, F; ∼ᴧ Q1–2, D.
274   short.] ∼ ; Q1–5, F, D.   275   sport. *To his Guards.*] sport. Q1–5, F, D.
276+   *s.d. Daughter.*] Q3–5, F, D; ∼ .] Q1–2.
278   What,] Q3–5, F, D; ∼ᴧ Q1–2.   280   pay.] ∼ : Q1–5, F, D.
280+   *s.d. Mother.*] Q3–5, F, D; ∼ .] Q1–2.

I'le pull thee hence, close hidden as thou art,
                    [*Claps his hand to his breast.*
And stand with my drawn Sword before my heart.
Yes, you shall be obey'd, though I am loth.
Go, and while I can bid you, bind 'em both.   *To his Guards.*
Go, bind 'em e're my fit of Love return:
Fire shall quench fire, and anger Love shall burn.
Thus I prevent those follies I should do;
And 'tis the nobler Fever of the two.

300   *Fel.* Torn piece by piece, alas what horrid pains!
       S. Cath. Heav'n is all mercy, who that death ordains.
And that which Heav'n thinks best is surely so:
But bare and naked, shame to undergo,
'Tis somewhat more than death!
Expos'd to lawless eyes I dare not be,
My modesty is sacred, Heav'n, to thee.
Let not my body be the Tyrant's spoil;
Nor hands nor eyes thy purity defile.

Amariel *descends swiftly with a flaming Sword, and strikes at*
the Wheel, which breaks in pieces; then he ascends again.

       Max. Is this th' effect of all your boasted skill?   *To* Valerius.
310 These brittle toys to execute my will?
A Puppet-show of death I only find,
Where I a strong and sinewy pain design'd.
By what weak infant was this Engine wrought?
       Val. From *Bilbilis* the temper'd steel was brought:
Metall more tough the Anvil ne're did beat,
Nor, from the Forge, did hissing waters heat.
       Placid. I saw a Youth descend all Heav'nly fair, ⎤
Who in his hand a flaming Sword did bear,   ⎬
And, Whirlwind-like, around him drove the Air.   ⎦

292+   s.d. breast.] Q3-5, F, D; ~ .] Q1-2.   294   loth.] ~ , Q1-5; ~ ; F, D.
295   both. To his Guards.] both. Q1-5, F, D.
306   Heav'n,] Q4-5, F, D; ~ʌ Q1-3.
308+   s.d. pieces;] Q3-5, F; ~ , Q1-2, D.
309   skill? To Valerius.] skill? Q1-5, F, D.

320 At his rais'd arm the rigid Iron shook;
    And, bending backwards, fled before the stroke.
       Max. What! Miracles, the tricks of Heav'n to me?
    I'le try if she be wholly Iron-free.
    If not by Sword, then she shall dye by fire;
    And one by one her Miracles I'le tire.
    If proof against all kind of death she be,
    My Love's immortal, and she's fit for me.
       S. Cath. No, Heav'n has shown its pow'r, and now thinks fit
    Thee to thy former fury to remit.
330 Had Providence my longer life decreed,
    Thou from thy passion hadst not yet been freed.
    But Heav'n, which suffer'd that, my Faith to prove,
    Now to its self does vindicate my Love.
    A pow'r controls thee which thou dost not see;
    And that's a Miracle it works in thee.
       Max. The truth of this new Miracle we'll try;
    To prove it, you must take the pains to dye.
    Bring me their heads——
       Fel. That mercy, Tyrant, thou deny'st to me,
340 At thy last breath may Heav'n refuse to thee.
    My fears are going, and I death can view:
    I see, I see him there thy steps pursue,
    And with a lifted arm and silent pace,
    Stalk after thee, just aiming in his chace.
       S. Cath. No more, dear Mother; ill in death it shows
    Your peace of mind by rage to discompose:
    No streak of blood (the reliques of the Earth)
    Shall stain my Soul in her immortal birth;
    But she shall mount all pure, a white, and Virgin mind;
350 And full of all that peace, which there she goes to find.
                Exeunt S. Catharine *and* Felicia, *with* Valerius
                and Guards. The Scene shuts.
    Max. She's gone, and pull'd my heart-strings as she went.
                              Aside.

---

323 Iron-free] Q3–5, F; Iron free Q1–2, D.   342 pursue,] F, D; ∼. Q1–5.
345 Mother;] D; ∼, Q1–5, F.   351–351+ went. / *Aside.*] went. Q1–5, F, D.

Were penitence no shame, I could repent.
Yet 'tis of bad example she should live;
For I might get th' ill habit to forgive.
Thou soft Seducer of my heart, away———
Who ling'ring would'st about its confines stay
To watch when some Rebellion would begin;
And ready at each sigh to enter in.
In vain; for thou
360 Dost on the outside of the body play,
And when drawn nearest, shalt be whirl'd away.
What ails me, that I cannot lose thy thought!
Command the Empress hither to be brought;   *To* Placid.
I in her death shall some diversion find,
And rid my thoughts at once of woman-kind.
    Placid. 'Tis well he thinks not of *Porphyrius* yet.   *Aside. Exit.*
    Max. How hard it is this Beauty to forget!
My stormy rage has only shook my will:
She crept down lower, but she sticks there still.
370 Fool that I am to struggle thus with Love!
Why should I that which pleases me remove?
True, she should dye were she concern'd alone;
But I love, not for her sake, but my own.
Our Gods are Gods 'cause they have pow'r and will;
Who can do all things, can do nothing ill.
Ill is Rebellion 'gainst some higher pow'r:
The World may sin, but not its Emperour.
My Empress then shall dye, my Princess live;
If this be sin, I do my self forgive.

             To him Valerius.

380   *Val.* Your will's obey'd; for, mighty Emperour,
The Princess and her Mother are no more.
    Max. She is not dead!
    Val. ——————— Great Sir, your will was so.
    Max. That was my will of half an hour ago.

---

379 sin] Q2–5, F, D; ill Q1.   380 for,] Q3–5, F; ~∧ Q1–2, D.

But now 'tis alter'd; I have chang'd her Fate,
She shall not dye.
    Val. —————— Your pity comes too late.
Betwixt her Guards she seem'd by Bride-men led, ⎤
Her cheeks with cheerful blushes were o'respred, ⎬
When, smiling, to the Ax she bow'd her head. ⎦
Just at the stroke———
390 Ætherial musick did her death prepare;
Like joyful sounds of Spousals in the Air.
A radiant light did her crown'd Temples guild,
And all the place with fragrant scents was fill'd.
The Balmy mist came thick'ning to the ground,
And sacred silence cover'd all around.
But when (its work perform'd) the Cloud withdrew,
And day restor'd us to each others view,
I sought her head to bring it on my Spear;
In vain I sought it, for it was not there.
400 No part remain'd; but from afar our sight
Discover'd in the Air long tracks of light;
Of charming Notes we heard the last rebounds,
And Musick dying in remoter sounds.
    Max. And dost thou think
This lame account fit for a Love-sick King?
Go———from the other World a better bring.
            [*Kills him, then sets his foot on him, and speaks on.*
When in my breast two mighty passions strove,
Thou had'st err'd better in obeying Love.
'Tis true, that way thy death had follow'd too,
410 But I had then been less displeas'd than now.
Now I must live unquiet for thy sake;
And this poor recompence is all I take.   *Spurns the body.*

Here the Scene opens and discovers Berenice *on a Scaffold, the
    Guards by her, and amongst them* Porphyrius *and* Albinus,
    like* Moors, *as all the Guards are.* Placidius *enters, and
    whispers the Emperour whilst* Porphyrius *speaks.*

406+ *s.d. speaks on.*] Q3–4, D; *speaks on.*] Q1–2; *speaks.* Q5, F (*speaks*ᴧ Q5).
409 too,] Q5, F; ~ . Q1–4, D.   412+ *s.d.* Moors] *Moors* Q1–5, F, D.

Por. From *Berenice* I cannot go away;
But, like a Ghost, must near my Treasure stay.
    Alb. Night and this shape secure us from their eyes.
    Por. Have courage then for our bold enterprise.
Duty and Faith no tye on me can have,
Since I renounc'd those Honours which he gave.
    Max. The time is come we did so long attend,   *To* Berenice.
420 Which must these discords of our Marriage end.
Yet, *Berenice,* remember you have been
An Empress, and the Wife of *Maximin.*
    Ber. I will remember I have been your Wife;
And therefore, dying, beg from Heav'n your life:
Be all the discords of our Bed forgot,
Which, Vertue witness, I did never spot.
What errors I have made, though while I live
You cannot pardon, to the dead forgive.
    Max. How much she is to piety inclin'd!
430 Behead her while she's in so good a mind.   *To his Guards.*
    Por. Stand firm, *Albinus,* now the time is come
To free the Empress.
    Alb. ———— And deliver *Rome.*
    Por. Within I feel my hot blood swell my heart,
And generous tremblings in each outward part.
'Tis done.———Tyrant, this is thy latest hour.

                 Porphyrius *and* Albinus *draw, and are*
                       making at the Emperour.

    Ber. Look to your self, my Lord the Emperour:
Treason, help, help, my Lord!

             Maximin *turns and defends himself, the Guards*
                 set on Porphyrius *and* Albinus.

    Max. Disarm 'em, but their lives I charge you spare.
                    After they are disarm'd.
Unmask 'em, and discover who they are.
440 Good Gods! is it *Porphyrius* whom I see?

---

421   Yet, *Berenice,*] Q3–5, F, D (Yet$_\wedge$ D); $\sim_\wedge \sim_\wedge$ Q1–2.
427   live] Q3–5, F; $\sim$, Q1–2, D.
430   mind. *To his Guards.*] mind. Q1–5, F, D.   435   done.] $\sim_\wedge$ Q1–5, F, D.
440   Gods! . . . see?] Q4–5, F; $\sim$, . . . $\sim$! Q1–3, D.

Placid. I wonder how he gain'd his liberty.

Max. Traytor!

Por. ———— Know, Tyrant, I can hear that name
Rather than Son, and bear it with less shame.
Traytor's a name which, were my arm yet free,
The *Roman* Senate would bestow on thee.
Ah, Madam, you have ruin'd my design,   *To* Ber.
And lost your life; for I regard not mine.
Too ill a Mistress, and too good a Wife.

Ber. It was my duty to preserve his life.

50 *Max.* Now I perceive   *To* Porphyrius.
In what close walks your mind so long did move:
You scorn'd my Throne, aspiring to her Love.

Ber. In death I'le owne a Love to him so pure;
As will the test of Heav'n it self endure:
A Love so chast, as Conscience could not chide;
But cherisht it, and kept it by its side:
A Love which never knew a hot desire,
But flam'd as harmless as a lambent fire:
A Love which pure from Soul to Soul might pass,
60 As light transmitted through a Crystal glass:
Which gave *Porphyrius* all without a sin;
Yet kept entire the Right of *Maximin.*

Max. The best return that I to both can make,
Shall be to suffer for each others sake.

Por. Barbarian, do not dare her blood to shed,
Who from my vengeance sav'd thy cursed head:
A flight no Honour ever reach'd before;
And which succeeding Ages will adore.

Ber. Porphyrius, I must dye!
470 That common debt to Nature paid must be;

---

444 which,] Q3–5, F, D; ∼∧ Q1–2.   445 *Roman*] F, D; Roman Q1–5.
446 Ah . . . design, *To* Ber.] D; *To Ber.* Ah . . . design, Q1–5, F (*line in-*
dented).
450 *s.d.* Porphyrius.] Q3–5, F; Porphyriu∧ Q1; ∼∧ Q2; Por. D.
454–460 endure: . . . side: . . . fire: . . . glass:] ∼ . . . . ∼ . . . . ∼ . . . . ∼ .
Q1–5, F, D.
459 which] Q3–5, F; ∼ , Q1–2, D.   465 *Barbarian*] D; Barbarian Q1–5, F.
466 head:] ∼ . Q1–5, F, D.   469 *Porphyrius,*] Q3–5, F, D; ∼∧ Q1–2.

But I have left a debt unpaid to thee.
To *Maximin*————
I have perform'd the duty of a Wife;
But, saving his, I cast away thy life.
Ah, what ill Stars upon our Loves did shine,
That I am more thy Murd'rer than he mine.
   Max. Make haste.
   Por. So hasty none in execution are,
But they allow the dying time for pray'r.
480 Farewel, sweet Saint, my pray'r shall be to you:
My Love has been unhappy, but 'twas true.
Remember me! Alas what have I sed?
You must dye too!
But yet remember me when you are dead.
   Ber. If I dye first, I will————
Stop short of Heav'n, and wait you in a Cloud;
For fear we lose each other in the crowd.
   Por. Love is the only Coyn in Heav'n will go:
Then take all with you, and leave none below.
490   *Ber.* 'Tis want of knowledge, not of Love, I fear,
Lest we mistake when bodies are not there;
O as a mark that I could wear a Scroul,
With this Inscription, *Berenice's Soul.*
   Por. That needs not, sure, for none will be so bright,
So pure, or with so small allays of light.
   Max. From my full eyes fond tears begin to start;
Dispatch, they practise treason on my heart.
   Por. Adieu: this farewel sigh I as my last bequeath,
Catch it, 'tis Love expiring in a breath.
500   *Ber.* This sigh of mine shall meet it half the way,
As pledges giv'n that each for other stay.

                Enter Valeria *and* Cydon.

---

485   first,] Q3–5, F, D; ~∧ Q1–2.   490   fear,] Q4–5, F; ~ . Q1–3, D.
491   there;] ~ , Q1–5, F, D.   493   *Soul*] Soul Q1–5, F, D.
497   heart.] Q2–5, F, D; heart. / *Porphyrius kisses his hand, and blows it to*
Berenice saying, Q1.
499   breath.] Q2–5, F, D; breath. / *Berenice kissing hers in the same manner.*
Q1.   501+   *s.d.* Cydon] Q2–5, F, D; Cydon *her Woman* Q1.

Vale. What dismal Scene of Death is here prepar'd!

Max. Now strike.

Vale. ————— They shall not strike till I am heard.

Max. From whence does this new impudence proceed,
That you dare alter that which I decreed?

Vale. Ah, Sir, to what strange courses do you fly,
To make your self abhorr'd for cruelty!
The Empire groans under your bloody Reign,
And its vast body bleeds in ev'ry vein.

10 Gasping and pale, and fearing more, it lyes;
And now you stab it in the very eyes:
Your *Cæsar* and the Partner of your Bed;
Ah who can wish to live when they are dead?
If ever gentle pity touch'd your brest————
I cannot speak,————my tears shall speak the rest.

                     Weeping and sobbing.

Por. She adds new grief to what I felt before,
And Fate has now no room to put in more.

Max. Away, thou shame and slander of my blood.   *To* Vale.
Who taught thee to be pitiful or good?

520   *Vale.* What hope have I
The name of Vertue should prevail with him,
Who thinks ev'n it, for which I plead, a crime?
Yet Nature, sure, some Argument may be;
If them you cannot pity, pity me.

Max. I will, and all the World shall judge it so:
I will th' excess of pity to you show.
You ask to save
A dangerous Rebel, and disloyal Wife,
And I in mercy————will not take your life.

530   *Vale.* You more than kill me by this cruelty,
And in their persons bid your Daughter dye.

---

502   *Vale.*] *Val.* Q1–5, F, D.   503   *Vale.* [*rule*]] *Val.* [*rule omitted*] Q1–5, F, D.
506   *Vale.*] *Val.* Q1–5, F, D.
515   I] D; ————I Q1–5, F.   509   ev'ry] D; every Q1–5, F.
518   *s.d.* Vale.] Val. Q1–5, F; Valeria. D.   518   *Max.*] Q2–5, F, D; ~∧ Q1.
530   *Vale.*] *Val.* Q1–5, F, D.   520   *Vale.*] *Val.* Q1–5, F, D.

I honour *Berenice*'s Vertue much;
But for *Porphyrius* my Love is such,
I cannot, will not live when he is gone.
　　Max. I'le do that Cure for you which on my self is done.
You must, like me, your Lovers life remove;
Cut off your hope, and you destroy your Love.
If it were hard I would not bid you try
The Med'cine: but 'tis but to let him dye.
540 Yet since you are so soft, (which you call good)
And are not yet confirm'd enough in blood
To see his death;
Your frailty shall be favour'd with this grace,
That they shall suffer in another place.
If after they are dead, their memory
By any chance into your mind be brought,
Laugh, and divert it with some other thought.
Away with 'em.

　　　　　　　　　Exeunt Berenice, Porphyrius, Albinus
　　　　　　　　　　carried off by Guards.
　　Vale. Since pray'rs nor tears can bend his cruel mind,
　　　　　　　　　　　　　[Looking after Porphy.
550 Farewel, the best and bravest of Mankind;
How I have lov'd Heav'n knows; but there's a Fate,
Which hinders me from being fortunate.
My Father's Crimes hang heavy on my head,
And like a gloomy Cloud about me spread;
I would in vain be pious, that's a grace
Which Heav'n permits not to a Tyrant's race.
　　Max. Hence to her Tent the foolish Girl convey.
　　Vale. Let me be just before I go away.
Placidius, I have vow'd to be your Wife;
560 Take then my hand, 'tis yours while I have life.
One moment here, I must anothers be:
But this, *Porphyrius*, gives me back to thee.

              Stabs her self twice, and then Placidius
                  wrests the Dagger from her.

Placid. Help, help the Princess, help!
Max. What rage has urg'd this act which thou hast done?
Vale. Thou, Tyrant, and thy Crimes have pull'd it on.
Thou who canst death with such a pleasure see,
Now take thy fill, and glut thy sight in me.
But————I'le th' occasion of my death forget;
Save him I love, and be my Father yet.
570 I can no more————*Porphyrius,* my dear————
     Cyd. Alas, she raves, and thinks *Porphyrius* here.
     Vale. Have I not yet deserv'd thee now I dye?
Is *Berenice* still more fair than I?
Porphyrius, do not swim before my sight;
Stand still, and let me, let me aim aright.
Stand still but while thy poor *Valeria* dyes,
And sighs her Soul into her Lovers eyes.   *Dyes.*
     Placid. She's gone from Earth, and with her went away
All of the Tyrant that deserv'd to stay:
580 I've lost in her all joys that life can give;
And only to revenge her death would live.————   *Aside.*
     Cyd. The Gods have claim'd her, and we must resign.
     Max. What had the Gods to do with me or mine?
Did I molest your Heav'n?————
Why should you then make *Maximin* your Foe,
Who paid you Tribute, which he need not do?
Your Altars I with smoke of Gums did crown:
For which you lean'd your hungry nostrils down,
All daily gaping for my Incense there,
590 More than your Sun could draw you in a year.
And you for this these Plagues on me have sent;
But by the Gods, (by *Maximin,* I meant)
Henceforth I and my World
Hostility with you and yours declare:

565 *Vale.*] *Val.* Q1–5, F, D.   569 yet.] ~ : Q1–5, F, D.
572 *Vale.*] *Val.* Q1–5, F, D.   581 live.] ~∧ Q1–5, F, D.
588 down,] D; ~ . Q1–2; ~ : Q3–5, F.   592 *Maximin,*] D; ~∧ Q1–5, F.
594 declare:] Q3–5, F; ~ , Q1–2, D.

Look to it, Gods; for you th' Aggressors are.
Keep you your Rain and Sun-shine in your Skies,
And I'le keep back my flame and Sacrifice.
Your Trade of Heav'n shall soon be at a stand,
And all your Goods lie dead upon your hand.

600   *Placid.* Thus, Tyrant, since the Gods th' Aggressors are,
                                        [*Stabbing him.*
Thus by this stroke they have begun the War.
                              Maximin *struggles with him, and gets*
                                 the Dagger from him.
     Max. Thus I return the strokes which they have giv'n;
                                        [*Stabbing* Placid.
Thus, Traytor, thus; and thus I would to Heav'n.
                           Placidius *falls, and the Emperour staggers after him,*
                              and sits down upon him; the Guards come to help
                              the Emperour.
     Max. Stand off, and let me, e're my strength be gone,
Take my last pleasure of revenge alone.

                         Enter a Centurion.

     Cen. Arm, arm, the Camp is in a mutiny:
For *Rome* and Liberty the Souldiers cry.
Porphyrius mov'd their pity as he went,
To rescue *Berenice* from punishment,
610 And now he heads their new-attempted crime.
     Max. Now I am down, the Gods have watch'd their time.
You think————
To save your credit, feeble Deities;
But I will give my self the strength to rise.
                         He strives to get up, and being up, staggers.
It wonnot be.————

600+ s.d. him.] Q4–5, F, D; ~ .] Q1–3.
602+ s.d. Placid.] Q4–5, F, D; ~ .] Q1–3.   603 thus;] Q3–5, F; ~ , Q1–2, D.
603+ s.d. Placidius] Q2–5, F, D; *Stabbing upward with his Dagger.* Placidius
Q1.
603+ s.d. him;] Q3–5, F; ~ , Q1–2, D.
603+ s.d. come] Q2–5, F, D; *come in* Q1.   615 be.] ~ ∧ Q1–5, F, D.

My body has not pow'r my mind to bear.
I must return again————and conquer here.
Sits down upon the Body.

My coward Body does my will controul;
Farewel thou base Deserter of my Soul.
620 I'le shake this Carcass off, and be obey'd;
Reign an Imperial Ghost without its aid.
Go, Souldiers, take my Ensigns with you, fight,
And vanquish Rebels in your Soveraign's right:
Before I die————
Bring me *Porphyrius* and my Empress dead,
I would brave Heav'n, in my each hand a head.
    Placid. Do not regard a dying Tyrants breath.
[*To the Souldiers.*

He can but look revenge on you in death.
    Max. Vanquish'd, and dar'st thou yet a Rebel be?
630 Thus————I can more than look revenge on thee.
[*Stabs him again.*

    Placid. Oh, I am gone!   *Dyes.*
    Max. ————————— And after thee I go,
Revenging still, and following ev'n to th' other world my blow.
Stabs him again.

And shoving back this Earth on which I sit,
I'le mount————and scatter all the Gods I hit.   *Dyes.*

Enter Porphyrius, Berenice, Albinus, *Souldiers. Entring,*
    Porphyrius *looks on the Bodies and speaks.*

    Por. 'Tis done before, (this mighty work of Fate!)
And I am glad our Swords are come too late.
He was my Prince, and though a bloody one,
I should have conquer'd and have mercy shown.
Sheath all your Swords, and cease your enmity;
640 They are not Foes, but *Romans* whom you see.

616   pow'r] Q2–5, F, D; strength Q1.
627+   *s.d. Souldiers.*] Q3–5, F, D; ~ .] Q1–2.
634+   *s.d. Entring,* Porphyrius . . . *Bodies*] Porphyrius . . . *Bodies entring,*
Q1–5, F, D.

Ber. He was my Tyrant, but my Husband too;
And therefore duty will some tears allow.
   Por. Placidius here!
And fair *Valeria* new depriv'd of breath?
Who can unriddle this dumb-show of death?
   Cyd. When, Sir, her Father did your life deny,
She kill'd her self, that she with you might dye.
Placidius made the Emp'rours death his crime;
Who, dying, did revenge his death on him.

Porphyrius kneels and takes Valeria's hand.

650   *Por.* For thy dear sake, I vow each week I live,
One day to fasting and just grief I'le give:
And what hard Fate did to thy life deny,
My gratitude shall pay thy memory.
   Cen. Mean time to you belongs th' Imperial pow'r:
We with one voice salute you Emperour.
   Souldiers. Long live *Porphyrius* Emperour of the *Romans.*
   Por. Too much, my Country-men, your Love you show,
That you have thought me worthy to be so.
But, to requite that Love, I must take care
660 Not to ingage you in a Civil War.
Two Emperours at *Rome* the Senate chose,
And whom they chuse no *Roman* should oppose.
In Peace or War, let Monarchs hope or fear;
All my ambition shall be bounded here.

Kissing Berenice's hand.

   Ber. I have too lately been a Prince's Wife,
And fear th' unlucky Omen of the life.
Like a rich Vessel beat by storms to shore,
'Twere madness should I venture out once more.
Of glorious troubles I will take no part,
670 And in no Empire reign, but of your heart.
   Por. Let to the winds your golden Eagles flye,

[To the Souldiers.

---

650 sake, . . . live,] Q4–5, F, D; ~ₐ . . . ~ₐ Q1–3.
664+ *s.d. hand.*] Q1 *(some copies)*, Q2–5, F, D; ~ₐ Q1 *(period did not print in copy text).*
671+ *s.d. Souldiers.*] Q3–5, F, D; ~ .] Q1–2.

Your Trumpets sound a bloodless Victory:
Our Arms no more let *Aquileia* fear,
But to her Gates our peaceful Ensigns bear.
While I mix Cypress with my Myrtle Wreath:
Joy for your life, and mourn *Valeria's* Death.

Exeunt omnes.

------

674   Gates our peaceful Ensigns bear.] Q2-5, F, D; Gates———— / Our peaceful
Ensigns crown'd with Olives bear: Q1.

Epilogue.

Spoken by Mrs. *Ellen*, when she was to be
carried off dead by the Bearers.

To the Bearer. *Hold, are you mad? you damn'd confounded Dog,*
    I am to rise, and speak the Epilogue.
To the Audience. *I come, kind Gentlemen, strange news to*
    tell ye,
I am the Ghost of poor departed Nelly.
Sweet Ladies, be not frighted, I'le be civil,
I'm what I was, a little harmless Devil.
For after death, we Sprights have just such Natures
We had, for all the World, when humane Creatures;
And therefore I that was an Actress here,
10 *Play all my Tricks in Hell, a Goblin there.*
Gallants, look to't, you say there are no Sprights;
But I'le come dance about your Beds at nights.
And faith you'l be in a sweet kind of taking,
When I surprise you between sleep and waking.
To tell you true, I walk because I dye
Out of my Calling in a Tragedy.
O Poet, damn'd dull Poet, who could prove
So sensless! to make Nelly *dye for Love;*
Nay, what's yet worse, to kill me in the prime
20 *Of* Easter-*Term, in Tart and Cheese-cake time!*
I'le fit the Fopp; for I'le not one word say
T' excuse his godly out-of-fashion Play:
A Play which if you dare but twice sit out,
You'l all be slander'd, and be thought devout.

Epilogue.] Q5, F, D; ~∧ Q1–4.   7 *Sprights*] Q4–5, F, D; ~ , Q1–3.
7 *Natures*] Q2, D; ~ , Q1, Q3–5, F.   8 *had,*] Q4–5; ~∧ Q1–3, F, D.
18 *Love;*] Q2–4, D; ~ , Q1; ~ : Q5, F.
22 *out-of-fashion*] D; out of fashion Q1–5, F.   22 *Play:*] ~ . Q1–5, F, D.

NELL GWYN RISING FROM THE DEAD TO SPEAK
THE EPILOGUE TO *Tyrannick Love*
FROM *The Key to the Rehearsal* (1714) IN
GEORGE VILLIERS, DUKE OF BUCKINGHAM, *Works*, VOLUME II

But farewel, Gentlemen, make haste to me,
I'm sure e're long to have your company.
As for my Epitaph when I am gone,
I'le trust no Poet, but will write my own.

Here *Nelly* lies, who, though she liv'd a Slater'n,
30 Yet dy'd a Princess, acting in S. *Cathar'n.*

FINIS.

---

25 *But farewel,*] Q3–5, F; ~ , ~∧ Q1–2, D.

AN EVENING'S LOVE

OR

THE MOCK-ASTROLOGER

A N
Evening's Love,
OR THE
Mock-Aſtrologer.

Acted at the **THEATER ROYAL,**

BY HIS

MAJESTIES SERVANTS.

WRITTEN BY
JOHN DRYDEN,

Servant to His Majeſty.

Mallem Convivis quàm placuiſſe Cocis. Mart.

In the *SAVOY*,

Printed by *T. N.* for *Henry Herringman,* and are to be
ſold at the Anchor in the lower Walk of
the *New Exchange*, 1671.

TITLE PAGE OF THE FIRST EDITION (MACDONALD 75A)

TO HIS GRACE, *WILLIAM,* DUKE of *NEWCASTLE,*
One of his Majestie's most Honourable Privy Council;
and of the most noble Order of the Garter, *&c.*

May it please your Grace,

AMONGST *those few persons of Wit and Honour, whose fa-vourable opinion I have desir'd, your own vertue and my great obligations to your Grace, have justly given you the precedence. For what could be more glorious to me, than to have acquir'd some part of your esteem, who are admir'd and honour'd by all good men; who have been, for so many years together, the Pattern and Standard of Honor to the Nation: and whose whole life has been so great an example of Heroick ver-*
10 *tue, that we might wonder how it happen'd into an Age so cor-rupt as ours, if it had not likewise been a part of the former? as you came into the world with all the advantages of a noble Birth and Education, so you have rendred both yet more conspicuous by your vertue. Fortune, indeed, has perpetually crown'd your undertakings with success, but she has only waited on your valour, not conducted it. She has ministred to your glory like a slave, and has been led in triumph by it; or at most, while Hon-our led you by the hand to greatness, fortune only follow'd to keep you from sliding back in the ascent. That which* Plutarch
20 *accounted her favour to* Cymon *and* Lucullus, *was but her jus-tice to your Grace: and, never to have been overcome where you led in person, as it was more than* Hannibal *could boast, so it was all that providence could do for that party which it had resolv'd to ruine. Thus, my Lord, the last smiles of victory were on your armes: and, every where else, declaring for the Rebels, she seem'd to suspend her self, and to doubt, before she took her flight, whether she were able wholly to abandon that cause for which you fought.*

Caption: *WILLIAM*] D; WILLIAM Q1–3, F.
1 May it please your Grace,] F, D; *omitted from* Q*1–3*.
13 *both*] D; ∼ , Q1–3, F.
17 *it;*] Q3; ∼ . Q1; ∼ , Q2, F, D.
17 *most,*] Q2–3, F, D; ∼∧ Q1.
22 *boast,*] Q2–3, F, D; ∼ ; Q1.
27 *flight*] Q2–3, F, D; *fiight* Q1.

*But the greatest tryals of your Courage and Constancy were
yet to come: many had ventur'd their fortunes, and expos'd their
lives to the utmost dangers for their King and Country, who
ended their loyalty with the War: and submitting to the iniq-
uity of the times, chose rather to redeem their former plenty by
acknowledging an Usurper, than to suffer with an unprofitable
fidelity (as those meaner spirits call'd it) for their lawful Soveraign. But, as I dare not accuse so many of our Nobility, who
were content to accept their Patrimonies from the Clemency*
10 *of the* Conquerour, *and to retain only a secret veneration for
their Prince, amidst the open worship which they were forc'd
to pay to the Usurper, who had dethron'd him; so, I hope, I may
have leave to extoll that vertue which acted more generously;
and which was not satisfi'd with an inward devotion to Monarchy, but produc'd it self to view, and asserted the cause by
open Martyrdome. Of these rare patterns of loyalty your Grace
was chief: those examples you cou'd not find, you made. Some
few* Cato's *there were with you, whose invincible resolution
could not be conquer'd by* that usurping Cæsar: *your vertue*
20 *oppos'd it self to his fortune, and overcame it by not submitting
to it. The last and most difficult Enterprize he had to effect,
when he had conquer'd three Nations, was to subdue your
spirits: and he dy'd weary of that War, and unable to finish it.*

*In the mean time you liv'd more happily in your exile then
the other on his Throne: your loyalty made you friends and
servants amongst Forreigners: and you liv'd plentifully without
a fortune; for you liv'd on your own desert and reputation. The
glorious Name of the valiant and faithful* Newcastle *was a Patri-
mony which cou'd never be exhausted.*

30 *Thus, my Lord, the morning of your life was clear, and calm;
and, though it was afterwards overcast; yet, in that general
storm, you were never without a shelter. And now you are
happily arriv'd to the evening of a day as serene, as the dawn
of it was glorious: but such an evening as, I hope, and almost
prophesie, is far from night: 'Tis the Evening of a Summer's*

---

6   *than*] Q2–3, F, D; *then* Q1.   18   *you*,] Q2–3, F, D; ~∧ Q1.

Sun, which keeps the day-light long within the skies. The health of your body is maintain'd by the vigour of your mind: neither does the one shrink from the fatigue of exercise, nor the other bend under the pains of study. Methinks I behold in you an-other Caius Marius, *who in the extremity of his age, exercis'd himself almost every morning in the* Campus Martius, *amongst the youthful Nobility of* Rome. *And afterwards, in your retire-ments, when you do honour to Poetrie, by employing part of your leisure in it, I regard you as another* Silius Italicus, *who* having pass'd over his Consulship with applause, dismiss'd himself from business and from the Gown, and employ'd his age, amongst the shades, in the reading and imitation of* Virgil.

In which, lest any thing should be wanting to your happiness, you have, by a rare effect of Fortune, found, in the person of your excellent Lady, not only a Lover, *but a Partner of your studies: a Lady whom our Age may justly equal with the* Sappho *of the* Greeks, *or the* Sulpitia *of the* Romans: *who, by being taken into your bosome, seems to be inspir'd with your Genius; and by writing the History of your life in so masculine a style,* has already plac'd you in the Number of the Heroes. She has anticipated that great portion of Fame which envy often hinders a living vertue from possessing: which wou'd, indeed, have been given to your ashes, but with a latter payment: and, of which you could have no present use, except it were by a secret presage of that which was to come, when you were no longer in a possi-bility of knowing it. So that if that were a praise or satisfaction to the greatest of* Emperors, *which the most judicious of* Poets *gives him,*

Præsenti tibi maturos largimur honores, *&c.*

That the adoration which was not allowed to Hercules *and* Romulus *till after death, was given to* Augustus *living; then cer-tainly it cannot be deny'd but that your Grace has receiv'd a double satisfaction: the one, to see your self consecrated to im-mortality while you are yet alive: the other, to have your praises*

---

16 *studies: a*] ∼ . *A* Q1–3, F, D.   17 Romans: *who*] ∼ . *Who* Q1–3, F, D.
18–19 *Genius; and*] ∼ : *And* Q1–3, F, D.   29 *&c.*] Q3, F, D; &c. Q1–2.

celebrated by so dear, so just, and so pious an Historian.

'Tis the consideration of this that stops my pen: though I am loath to leave so fair a subject, which gives me as much field as Poetry cou'd wish; and yet no more than truth can justifie. But to attempt any thing of a Panegyrick were to enterprize on your Lady's right; and to seem to affect those praises, which none but the Dutchess of Newcastle *can deserve, when she writes the actions of her Lord. I shall therefore leave that wider space, and contract my self to those narrow bounds which best become my*
10 Fortune and Employment.

I am oblig'd, my Lord, to return you not only my own acknowledgements; but to thank you in the name of former Poets. The manes *of* Johnson *and* D'avenant *seem to require it from me, that those favours which you plac'd on them, and which they wanted opportunity to own in publick, yet might not be lost to the knowledge of Posterity, with a forgetfulness unbecoming of the Muses, who are the Daughters of Memory. And give me leave, my Lord, to avow so much of vanity, as to say, I am proud to be their Remembrancer: for, by relating how gracious*
20 *you have been to them, and are to me, I in some measure joyn my name with theirs: and the continu'd descent of your favours to me is the best title which I can plead for my succession. I only wish, that I had as great reason to be satisfi'd with my self, in the return of our common acknowledgements, as your Grace may justly take in the conferring them: for I cannot but be very sensible that the present of an ill Comedy, which I here make you, is a very unsuitable way of giving thanks for them, who themselves have written so many better. This pretends to nothing more than to be a foyl to those Scenes, which are compos'd*
30 *by the most noble Poet of our Age, and Nation: and to be set as a water-mark of the lowest ebb, to which the wit of my Predecessors has sunk and run down in me: but, though all of 'em have surpass'd me in the Scene; there is one part of glory in which I will not yield to any of them. I mean, my Lord, that honour and veneration which they had for you in their lives; and which I preserve after them, more holily than the Vestal fires were maintain'd from Age to Age; but with a greater degree of heat*

and of devotion than theirs, as being with more respect and
passion then they ever were,

Your GRACES most obliged, most

humble, and most obedient Servant,

JOHN DRYDEN.

---

2 *were,*] Q3, F, D; ~∧ Q1–2.   4 Servant,] Q3, F, D; ~∧ Q1–2.

PREFACE.

I had thought, Reader, in this Preface to have written somewhat concerning the difference betwixt the Playes of our
Age, and those of our Predecessors on the English Stage: to
have shewn in what parts of Dramatick Poesie we were excell'd
by Ben. Johnson, I mean, humour, and contrivance of Comedy;
and in what we may justly claim precedence of Shakespear and
Fletcher, namely in Heroick Playes: but this design I have
wav'd on second considerations; at least deferr'd it till I publish
the Conquest of Granada, where the discourse will be more
10 proper. I had also prepar'd to treat of the improvement of our
Language since Fletcher's and Johnson's dayes, and consequently
of our refining the Courtship, Raillery, and Conversation of
Playes: but as I am willing to decline that envy which I shou'd
draw on my self from some old Opiniatre judges of the Stage;
so likewise I am prest in time so much that I have not leisure, at
present, to go thorough with it. Neither, indeed, do I value a
reputation gain'd from Comedy, so far as to concern my self
about it any more than I needs must in my own defence: for I
think it, in it's own nature, inferiour to all sorts of Dramatick
20 writing. Low Comedy especially requires, on the Writers part,
much of conversation with the vulgar: and much of ill nature
in the observation of their follies. But let all men please themselves according to their several tastes: that which is not pleasant
to me may be to others who judge better: and, to prevent an accusation from my enemies, I am sometimes ready to imagine
that my disgust of low Comedy proceeds not so much from my
judgement as from my temper; which is the reason why I so
seldom write it; and that when I succeed in it, (I mean so far as
to please the Audience) yet I am nothing satisfi'd with what I
30 have done; but am often vex'd to hear the people laugh, and
clap, as they perpetually do, where I intended 'em no jest; while

9 Conquest of] *Conquest of* Q1–3, **F, D.**
10 *improvement*] Q2–3, F, D; *improvemeni* Q1.

they let pass the better things without taking notice of them. Yet even this confirms me in my opinion of slighting popular applause, and of contemning that approbation which those very people give, equally with me, to the Zany of a Mountebank; or to the appearance of an Antick on the Theatre, without wit on the Poets part, or any occasion of laughter from the Actor, besides the ridiculousness of his habit and his Grimaces.

But I have descended before I was aware, from Comedy to Farce; which consists principally of Grimaces. That I admire not any *Comedy equally with Tragedy, is, perhaps, from the sullenness of my humor; but that I detest those Farces, which are now the most frequent entertainments of the Stage, I am sure I have reason on my side. Comedy consists, though of low persons, yet of natural actions, and characters; I mean such humours, adventures, and designes, as are to be found and met with in the world. Farce, on the other side, consists of forc'd humours, and unnatural events. Comedy presents us with the imperfections of humane nature: Farce entertains us with what is monstruous and chimerical. The one causes laughter in those who can judge of men and manners, by the lively representation of their folly or corruption; the other produces the same effect in those who can judge of neither, and that only by its extravagances. The first works on the judgment and fancy; the latter on the fancy only: There is more of satisfaction in the former kind of laughter, and in the latter more of scorn. But, how it happens that an impossible adventure should cause our mirth, I cannot so easily imagine. Something there may be in the oddness of it, because on the Stage it is the common effect of things unexpected to surprize us into a delight: and that is to be ascrib'd to the strange appetite, as I may call it, of the fancy; which, like that of a longing Woman, often runs out into the most extravagant desires; and is better satisfi'd sometimes with Loam, or with the Rinds of Trees, than with the wholsome nourishments of life. In short, there is the same difference betwixt Farce and Comedy,*

---

11 *Farces*] Q2–3, F, D; *Farees* Q1.   17 *events.*] D; ~ : Q1–3, F.
18 *nature:*] D; ~ . Q1–3, F.   19 *chimerical. The*] D; ~ : *the* Q1–3, F.
20 *manners,*] D; ~ ; Q1–3, F.

as betwixt an *Empirique* and a true *Physitian:* both of them
may attain their ends; but what the one performs by hazard, the
other does by skill. And as the Artist is often unsuccessful, while
the Mountebank succeeds; so Farces more commonly take the
people than Comedies. For to write unnatural things, is the
most probable way of pleasing them, who understand not Nature. And a true Poet often misses of applause, because he
cannot debase himself to write so ill as to please his Audience.

    After all, it is to be acknowledg'd, that most of those Come-
10 dies, which have been lately written, have been ally'd too much
to Farce: and this must of necessity fall out till we forbear the
translation of French Plays: for their Poets wanting judgement
to make, or to maintain true characters, strive to cover their
defects with ridiculous Figures and Grimaces. While I say this
I accuse my self as well as others: and this very play would rise
up in judgment against me, if I would defend all things I have
written to be natural: but I confess I have given too much to the
people in it, and am asham'd for them as well as for my self,
that I have pleas'd them at so cheap a rate: not that there is any
20 thing here which I would not defend to an ill-natur'd judge:
(for I despise their censures, who I am sure wou'd write worse
on the same subject:) but because I love to deal clearly and
plainly, and to speak of my own faults with more criticism, than
I would of another Poets. Yet I think it no vanity to say that this
Comedy has as much of entertainment in it as many other which
have bin lately written: and, if I find my own errors in it, I am
able at the same time to arraign all my Contemporaries for
greater. As I pretend not that I can write humour, so none of
them can reasonably pretend to have written it as they ought.
30 Johnson was the only man of all Ages and Nations who has perform'd it well; and that but in three or four of his Comedies:
the rest are but a Crambe bis cocta; the same humours a little
vary'd and written worse: neither was it more allowable in him,
than it is in our present Poets, to represent the follies of particular persons; of which many have accus'd him. Parcere personis

---

16　*defend*] Q2–3, F, D; *de fend* Q1.   23　*than*] Q2–3, F, D; *then* Q1.
25　*it as*] Q2–3, F, D; *as it* Q1.   30　*who*] Q2–3, F, D; *wo* Q1.

dicere de vitiis *is the rule of Plays. And* Horace *tells you that the old Comedy amongst the* Grecians *was silenc'd for the too great liberties of the Poets.*

> ————In vitium libertas excidit & vim
> Dignam lege regi: lex est accepta chorusque
> Turpiter obticuit, sublato jure nocendi.

Of which he gives you the reason in another place: where having given the precept,

> Neve immunda crepent, ignominiosáque dicta:

10 *He immediately subjoyns,*

> Offenduntur enim, quibus est equus, & pater, & res.

But Ben. Johnson *is to be admir'd for many excellencies; and can be tax'd with fewer failings than any* English *Poet. I know I have been accus'd as an enemy of his writings; but without any other reason than that I do not admire him blindly, and without looking into his imperfections. For why should he only be exempted from those frailties, from which* Homer *and* Virgil *are not free? Or why should there be any* ipse dixit *in our Poetry, any more than there is in our Philosophy? I admire and applaud*

20 *him where I ought: those who do more do but value themselves in their admiration of him: and, by telling you they extoll* Ben. Johnson's *way, would insinuate to you that they can practice it. For my part I declare that I want judgement to imitate him: and shou'd think it a great impudence in my self to attempt it. To make men appear pleasantly ridiculous on the Stage was, as I have said, his talent: and in this he needed not the acumen of wit, but that of judgement. For the characters and representations of folly are only the effects of observation; and observation is an effect of judgment. Some ingenious men, for whom I have*

30 *a particular esteem, have thought I have much injur'd* Ben. Johnson *when I have not allow'd his wit to be extraordinary: but they confound the notion of what is witty with what is pleasant. That* Ben. Johnson's *Playes were pleasant he must want reason who denyes: But that pleasantness was not properly wit, or the sharpness of conceit; but the natural imitation of folly: which I confess to be excellent in it's kind, but not to be of that*

---

8   *precept,*] D; ∼ . Q1–3, F.

kind which they pretend. Yet if we will believe Quintilian *in his Chapter* de Movendo risu, *he gives his opinion of both in these following words.* Stulta reprehendere facillimum est; nam per se sunt ridicula: & a derisu non procul abest risus: sed rem urbanam facit aliqua ex nobis adjectio.

And some perhaps wou'd be apt to say of Johnson *as it was said of* Demosthenes; Non displicuisse illi jocos, sed non contigisse. *I will not deny but that I approve most the mixt way of Comedy; that which is neither all wit, nor all humour, but the*
10 *result of both: neither so little of humour as* Fletcher *shews, nor so little of love and wit, as* Johnson: *neither all cheat, with which the best Playes of the one are fill'd, nor all adventure, which is the common practice of the other. I would have the characters well chosen, and kept distant from interfaring with each other; which is more than* Fletcher *or* Shakespear *did: but I would have more of the* Urbana, venusta, salsa, faceta *and the rest which* Quintilian *reckons up as the ornaments of wit; and these are extremely wanting in* Ben. Johnson. *As for repartie in particular; as it is the very soul of conversation, so it is the*
20 *greatest grace of Comedy, where it is proper to the Characters: there may be much of acuteness in a thing well said; but there is more in a quick reply:* sunt, enim, longè venustiora omnia in respondendo quàm in provocando. *Of one thing I am sure, that no man ever will decry wit, but he who despairs of it himself; and who has no other quarrel to it but that which the* Fox *had to the* Grapes. *Yet, as Mr.* Cowley, *(who had a greater portion of it than any man I know) tells us in his Character of Wit, rather than all wit let there be none; I think there's no folly so great in any Poet of our Age as the superfluity and wast of wit*
30 *was in some of our predecessors: particularly we may say of* Fletcher *and of* Shakespear, *what was said of* Ovid, In omni ejus ingenio, facilius quod rejici, quàm quod adjici potest, invenies. *The contrary of which was true in* Virgil *and our incomparable* Johnson.

7–8 contigisse.] D; ∼, Q1–3, F.
10–11 *both: neither* . . . Johnson: *neither*] both. Neither . . . Johnson. Nei-ther Q1–3, F, D.

Some enemies of Repartie have observ'd to us, that there is a great latitude in their Characters, which are made to speak it: And that it is easier to write wit than humour; because in the characters of humour, the Poet is confin'd to make the person speak what is only proper to it: whereas all kind of wit is proper in the Character of a witty person. But, by their favour, there are as different characters in wit as in folly. Neither is all kind of wit proper in the mouth of every ingenious person. A witty Coward and a witty Brave must speak differently. Falstaffe and
10 the Lyar speak not like Don John in the Chances, and Valentine in Wit without Money. And Johnson's Truwit in the Silent Woman, is a Character different from all of them. Yet it appears that this one Character of Wit was more difficult to the Author, than all his images of humour in the Play: For those he could describe and manage from his observation of men; this he has taken, at least a part of it, from books: witness the Speeches in the first Act, translated verbatim out of Ovid de Arte Amandi; to omit what afterwards he borrowed from the sixth Satyre of Juvenal against Women.
20 However, if I should grant, that there were a greater latitude in Characters of Wit, than in those of Humour; yet that latitude would be of small advantage to such Poets who have too narrow an imagination to write it. And to entertain an Audience perpetually with Humour, is to carry them from the conversation of Gentlemen, and treat them with the follies and extravagances of Bedlam.
I find I have launch'd out farther than I intended in the beginning of this Preface, and that in the heat of writing, I have touch'd at something, which I thought to have avoided. 'Tis
30 time now to draw homeward: and to think rather of defending my self, than assaulting others. I have already acknowledg'd that this Play is far from perfect: but I do not think my self oblig'd to discover the imperfections of it to my Adversaries, any more than a guilty person is bound to accuse himself before his

5   *it: whereas*] D (*Whereas*); ~ . *Whereas* Q1–3, F.
9   *witty*] Q2–3, F, D; *wity* Q1.   10   Lyar] ~ , Q1–3, F, D.
17–18   *Amandi; to*] ~ . *To* Q1–3, F, D.
28   *Preface, and*] ~ . *And* Q1–3, F, D.

*Judges. 'Tis charg'd upon me that I make debauch'd persons
(such as they say my* Astrologer *and* Gamester *are) my Protagonists, or the chief persons of the* Drama; *and that I make them
happy in the conclusion of my Play; against the Law of Comedy,
which is to reward virtue and punish vice. I answer first, that I
know no such law to have been constantly observ'd in Comedy,
either by the Ancient or Modern Poets.* Chærea *is made happy
in the* Eunuch, *after having deflour'd a Virgin: and* Terence
generally does the same through all his Plays, where you per-*
10 *petually see, not only debauch'd young men enjoy their Mistresses, but even the Courtezans themselves rewarded and honour'd in the Catastrophe. The same may be observ'd in* Plautus
almost every where. Ben. Johnson *himself, after whom I may be
proud to erre, has given me more than once the example of it.
That in the* Alchemist *is notorious, where* Face, *after having
contriv'd and carried on the great cozenage of the Play, and continued in it without repentance to the last, is not only forgiven
by his Master, but inrich'd by his consent, with the spoiles of
those whom he had cheated. And, which is more, his Master*
20 *himself, a grave man, and a Widower, is introduc'd taking his
Man's counsel, debauching the Widow first, in hope to marry
her afterward. In the* Silent Woman, Dauphine, *(who with the
other two Gentlemen, is of the same Character with my* Celadon
in the Maiden Queen, *and with* Wildblood *in this) professes
himself in love with all the Collegiate Ladies: and they likewise
are all of the same Character with each other, excepting only
Madam* Otter, *who has something singular: yet this naughty*
Dauphine *is crown'd in the end with the possession of his Uncles
Estate, and with the hopes of enjoying all his Mistresses. And*
30 *his friend Mr.* Truwit *(the best Character of a Gentleman which*
Ben. Johnson *ever made) is not asham'd to pimp for him. As for*
Beaumont *and* Fletcher, *I need not alledge examples out of
them; for that were to quote almost all their Comedies. But now
it will be objected that I patronize vice by the authority of
former Poets, and extenuate my own faults by recrimination. I*

---

2 Astrologer] *Astrologer* Q1–3, F, D.   7 Chærea] F, D; Chœrea Q1–3.
8 Eunuch] D; *Eunuch* Q1–3, F.   27 *singular:*] D; ~ :) Q1–3, F.

answer that as I defend my self by their example; so that ex-
ample I defend by reason, and by the end of all Dramatique
Poesie. In the first place therefore give me leave to shew you
their mistake who have accus'd me. They have not distinguish'd,
as they ought, betwixt the rules of Tragedy and Comedy. In
Tragedy, where the Actions and Persons are great, and the
crimes horrid, the laws of justice are more strictly to be ob-
serv'd: and examples of punishment to be made to deterre man-
kind from the pursuit of vice. Faults of this kind have been rare
10 *amongst the Ancient Poets: for they have punish'd in* Oedipus,
and in his posterity, the sinne which he knew not he had com-
mitted. Medea *is the only example I remember at present, who*
escapes from punishment after murder. Thus Tragedie fulfils
one great part of its institution; which is by example to instruct.
But in Comedy it is not so; for the chief end of it is divertise-
ment and delight: and that so much, that it is disputed, I think,
by Heinsius, *before* Horace *his art of Poetry, whether instruc-*
tion be any part of its employment. At least I am sure it can be
but its secondary end: for the business of the Poet is to make you
20 *laugh: when he writes humour he makes folly ridiculous; when*
wit, he moves you, if not alwayes to laughter, yet to a pleasure
that is more noble. And if he works a cure on folly, and the
small imperfections in mankind, by exposing them to publick
view, that cure is not perform'd by an immediate operation. For
it works first on the ill nature of the Audience; they are mov'd
to laugh by the representation of deformity; and the shame of
that laughter, teaches us to amend what is ridiculous in our
manners. This being, then, establish'd, that the first end of
Comedie is delight, and instruction only the second; it may rea-
30 *sonably be inferr'd that Comedy is not so much oblig'd to the*
punishment of the faults which it represents, as Tragedy. For
the persons in Comedy are of a lower quality, the action is little,
and the faults and vices are but the sallies of youth, and the
frailties of humane nature, and not premeditated crimes: such
to which all men are obnoxious; not such as are attempted only
by few, and those abandonn'd to all sense of vertue: such as

---

35 *obnoxious;*] D; ∼ , Q1–3, F.　　　35 *such*] Q2–3, F, D; ∼ , Q1.

move pity and commiseration; not detestation and horror: such in short as may be forgiven, not such as must of necessity be punish'd. But, lest any man should think that I write this to make libertinism amiable; or that I car'd not to debase the end and institution of Comedy, so I might thereby maintain my own errors, and those of better Poets; I must farther declare, both for them and for my self, that we make not vicious persons happy, but only as heaven makes sinners so: that is by reclaiming them first from vice. For so 'tis to be suppos'd they are, when they re-
10 *solve to marry; for then enjoying what they desire in one, they cease to pursue the love of many. So* Chærea *is made happy by* Terence, *in marrying her whom he had deflour'd: And so are* Wildblood *and the* Astrologer *in this Play.*

There is another crime with which I am charg'd, at which I am yet much less concern'd, because it does not relate to my manners, as the former did, but only to my reputation as a Poet: A name of which I assure the Reader I am nothing proud; and therefore cannot be very solicitous to defend it. I am tax'd with stealing all my Playes, and that by some who should be the last
20 *men from whom I would steal any part of 'em. There is one answer which I will not make; but it has been made for me by him to whose Grace and Patronage I owe all things,*

   Et spes & ratio studiorum, in *Cæsare* tantum,

and without whose command they shou'd no longer be troubl'd with any thing of mine; that he only desir'd that they who accus'd me of theft would alwayes steal him Playes like mine. But though I have reason to be proud of this defence, yet I should wave it, because I have a worse opinion of my own Comedies than any of my Enemies can have. 'Tis true, that where ever I
30 *have lik'd any story in a Romance, Novel, or forreign Play, I have made no difficulty, nor ever shall, to take the foundation of it, to build it up, and to make it proper for the* English Stage. *And I will be so vain to say it has lost nothing in my hands: But it alwayes cost me so much trouble to heighten it for our*

1   *horror:*] ~ ; Q1–3, F, D.   22 *things,*] Q2–3, F, D; ~ . Q1.
23 tantum,] ~ . Q1–3, F, D.   24 *and*] D; *And* Q1–3, F.
25 *mine;*] Q2–3, F; ~ , Q1, D.   34 *it for*] D; ~ , ~ Q1–3; ~ ; ~ F.

Theatre (which is incomparably more curious in all the orna-
ments of Dramatick Poesie, than the French *or* Spanish) *that*
when I had finish'd my Play, it was like the Hulk of Sir Francis
Drake, *so strangely alter'd, that there scarce remain'd any Plank*
of the Timber which first built it. To witness this I need go no
farther than this Play: It was first Spanish, *and call'd* El Astrologo fingido; *then made* French *by the younger* Corneille: *and*
is now translated into English, *and in print, under the name of*
the Feign'd Astrologer. *What I have perform'd in this will best*
10 *appear by comparing it with those: you will see that I have re-*
jected some adventures which I judg'd were not divertising: that
I have heightned those which I have chosen, and that I have
added others which were neither in the French *nor* Spanish.
And besides you will easily discover that the Walk of the
Astrologer *is the least considerable in my Play: for the design of*
it turns more on the parts of Wildblood *and* Jacinta, *who are*
the chief persons in it. I have farther to add, that I seldome use
the wit and language of any Romance or Play which I undertake
to alter: because my own invention (as bad as it is) can furnish
20 *me with nothing so dull as what is there. Those who have call'd*
Virgil, Terence, *and* Tasso *Plagiaries (though they much injur'd*
them,) had yet a better colour for their accusation: For Virgil
has evidently translated Theocritus, Hesiod, *and* Homer, *in*
many places; besides what he has taken from Ennius *in his own*
language. Terence *was not only known to translate* Menander,
(which he avows also in his Prologues) but was said also to be
help't in those Translations by Scipio *the* African, *and* Lælius.
And Tasso, *the most excellent of modern Poets, and whom I*
reverence next to Virgil, *has taken both from* Homer *many*
30 *admirable things which were left untouch'd by* Virgil, *and from*
Virgil *himself where* Homer *cou'd not furnish him. Yet the*
bodies of Virgil's *and* Tasso's *Poems were their own: and so are*
all the Ornaments of language and elocution in them. The same
(if there were any thing commendable in this Play) I could say
for it. But I will come nearer to our own Countrymen. Most of
Shakespear's *Playes, I mean the Stories of them, are to be found*

18 *Romance*] Q3; ∼ , Q1–2, F, D.   27 *help't*] Q2–3, F, D; *help'* Q1.

in the Hecatommithi, *or hundred Novels of* Cinthio. *I have, my self, read in his* Italian, *that of* Romeo and Juliet, *the* Moor of Venice, *and many others of them.* Beaumont *and* Fletcher *had most of theirs from* Spanish Novels: *witness the* Chances, *the* Spanish Curate, Rule a Wife and have a Wife, *the* Little French Lawyer, *and so many others of them as compose the greatest part of their Volume in folio.* Ben. Johnson, *indeed, has design'd his Plots himself; but no man has borrow'd so much from the* Ancients *as he has done: And he did well in it, for he has there-*
10 *by beautifi'd our language.*

But these little Criticks *do not well consider what is the work of a Poet, and what the* Graces *of a Poem: The* Story *is the least part of either: I mean the foundation of it, before it is modell'd by the art of him who writes it; who formes it with more care, by exposing only the beautiful parts of it to view, than a skilful* Lapidary *sets a* Jewel. *On this foundation of the* Story *the Characters are rais'd: and, since no* Story *can afford Characters enough for the variety of the* English Stage, *it follows that it is to be alter'd, and inlarg'd, with new persons, accidents, and*
20 *designes, which wil almost make it new. When this is done, the forming it into* Acts, *and* Scenes, *disposing of actions and passions into their proper places, and beautifying both with descriptions, similitudes, and propriety of language, is the principal employment of the Poet; as being the largest field of fancy, which is the principall quality requir'd in him: For so much the word* ποιητὴς *imployes. Judgement, indeed, is necessary in him; but 'tis fancy that gives the life touches, and the secret graces to it; especially in serious Plays, which depend not much on observation. For to write humour in Comedy (which is the theft of*
30 *Poets from mankind) little of fancy is requir'd; the Poet observes only what is ridiculous, and pleasant folly, and by judging exactly what is so, he pleases in the representation of it.*

But in general, the employment of a Poet, is like that of a curious Gunsmith, or Watchmaker: the Iron or Silver is not his own; but they are the least part of that which gives the value: The price lyes wholly in the workmanship. And he who works

---

1 Hecatommithi] Hecatommuthi Q1-3, F, D.

dully on a Story, without moving laughter in a Comedy, or raising concernments in a serious Play, is no more to be accounted a
good Poet, than a Gunsmith of the Minories is to be compar'd
with the best workman of the Town.

But I have said more of this than I intended; and more, perhaps, than I needed to have done: I shall but laugh at them
hereafter, who accuse me with so little reason; and withall contemn their dulness, who, if they could ruine that little reputation I have got, and which I value not, yet would want both wit
and learning to establish their own; or to be rememberd in
after ages for any thing, but only that which makes them ridiculous in this.

Prologue.

W HEN *first our Poet set himself to write,*
     Like a young Bridegroom on his Wedding-night
     He layd about him, and did so bestir him,
His Muse could never lye in quiet for him:
But now his Honey-moon is gone and past,
Yet the ungrateful drudgery must last:
And he is bound, as civil Husbands do,
To strain himself, in complaisance to you:
To write in pain, and counterfeit a bliss,
Like the faint smackings of an after-kiss.
But you, like Wives ill pleas'd, supply his want;
Each writing Monsieur *is a fresh Gallant:*
And though, perhaps, 'twas done as well before,
Yet still there's something in a new amour.
Your several Poets work with several tools,
One gets you wits, another gets you fools:
This pleases you with some by-stroke of wit,
This finds some cranny, that was never hit.
But should these janty Lovers daily come
To do your work, like your good man at home,
Their fine small-timber'd wits would soon decay;
These are Gallants but for a Holiday.
Others you had who oftner have appear'd,
Whom, for meer impotence you have cashier'd:
Such as at first came on with pomp and glory,
But, overstraining, soon fell flat before yee.
Their useless weight with patience long was born,
But at the last you threw 'em off with scorn.

10   *after-kiss*] Q2–3, F, D; *after kiss* Q1, M1.
12   Monsieur] Q2–3, F, D; *Monsieur* Q1, M1.
18   *cranny,*] Q1 *(some copies),* Q2–3, F, D; ~∧ Q1 *(comma did not print in copy text),* M1.
19   *janty*] Q1 *(some copies),* Q2–3, F, D, M1; *jant* Q1 *("y" did not print in copy text).*

As for the Poet of this present night,
Though now he claims in you an Husbands right,
He will not hinder you of fresh delight.
He, like a Seaman, seldom will appear;
And means to trouble home but thrice a year:
That only time from your Gallants he'll borrow;
Be kind to day, and Cuckold him to morrow.

Persons Represented.

MEN.

By

Wildblood, ⎱ Two young *English* ⎱	Mr. *Hart.*
Bellamy, ⎰ Gentlemen. ⎰	Mr. *Mohun.*
Maskall, Their Servant.	Mr. *Shatterell.*
Don Alonzo de Ribera, an old *Spanish* Gentleman.	Mr. *Wintershall.*
Don Lopez de Gamboa, a young Noble *Spaniard.*	Mr. *Burt.*
Don Melchor de Guzman, A Gentleman of a great Family; but of a decay'd fortune.	Mr. *Lydall.*

WOMEN.

By

Donna Theodosia, ⎱ Daughters to ⎱	Mrs. *Bowtell.*
Donna Jacinta, ⎰ *Don Alonzo.* ⎰	Mrs. *Ellen Guynn.*
Donna Aurelia, Their Cousin.	Mrs. *Marshall;* and formerly by M^rs. *Quin.*
Beatrix, Woman and Confident to the two Sisters.	Mrs. *Knepp.*
Camilla, Woman to *Aurelia.*	Mrs. *Betty Slate.*

Servants to *Don Lopez,* and *Don Alonzo.*

The Scene *Madrid,* in the Year 1665.
The Time, the last Evening of the Carnival.

English] D; English Q1–3, F.   *Spanish*] Q2–3, F, D; Spanish Q1.
Spaniard] Q2–3, F, D; Spaniard Q1.   *Jacinta*] Jacintha Q1–3, F, D.
Cousin.] Q2–3, F, D; ∼∧ Q1.   Sisters.] Q2–3, F, D; ∼∧ Q1.
Time,] Q2–3, F, D; ∼∧ Q1.

AN
EVENING'S LOVE,

OR THE

MOCK-ASTROLOGER.

ACT I. SCENE I.

Don Lopez, and a Servant, walking over the Stage.
Enter another Servant, and follows him.

Ser. Don *Lopez?*
Lop. Any new business?
Ser. My Master had forgot this Letter;
Which he conjures you, as you are his friend,
To give *Aurelia* from him.
    Lop. Tell *Don Melchor* 'tis a hard task which he enjoyns me:
He knows I love her, and much more than he;
For I love her alone, but he divides
His passion betwixt two: Did he consider
10 How great a pain 'tis to dissemble love,
He would never practise it.
    Ser. He knows his fault; but cannot mend it.
    Lop. To make the poor *Aurelia* believe
He's gone for *Flanders,* whiles he lies conceal'd,
And every night makes visits to her Cousin;
When will he leave this strange extravagance?
    Ser. When he can love one more, or t'other less.

ACT] Q2–3, F, D; ~. Q1.   *s.d.* Don] *Don* Q1–3, F, D.
2 business?] Q1 *(corrected state)*, Q2–3, F, D; ~. Q1 *(uncorrected state)*.
3 Letter;] ~. Q1–3, F, D.   15 Cousin;] ~. Q1–3, F, D.

Lop. Before I lov'd my self, I promis'd him
To serve him in his love; and I'll perform it,
20 How e're repugnant to my own concernments.
    Serv. You are a noble Cavalier.   *Exit Servant.*

Enter Bellamy, Wildblood, Maskall.

2ᵈ· *Ser.* Sir, your Guests of the *English* Embassador's Retinue.
Lop. Cavaliers, will you please to command my Coach to take
the air this Evening?
Bell. We have not yet resolv'd how to dispose of our selves;
but however, we are highly acknowledging to you for your
civility.
Lop. You cannot more oblige me then by laying your commands on me.
30 *Wild.* We kiss your hands.   *Exit* Lopez *cum Servo.*
Bell. Give the *Don* his due, he entertain'd us nobly this Carnival.
Wild. Give the Devil the *Don* for any thing I lik'd in his
Entertainment.
Bell. I hope we had variety enough.
Wild. I, it look'd like variety, till we came to taste it; there
were twenty several dishes to the eye, but in the pallat nothing
but Spices. I had a mind to eat of a Pheasant, and as soon as I
got it into my mouth, I found I was chawing a limb of Cina-
40 mon; then I went to cut a piece of Kid, and no sooner it had
touch'd my lips, but it turn'd to red Pepper: at last I began to
think my self another kind of *Midas,* that every thing I touch'd
should be turn'd to Spice.
Bell. And for my part, I imagin'd his Catholick Majesty had
invited us to eat his *Indies.* But prethee let's leave the discourse
of it, and contrive together how we may spend the Evening;
for in this hot Country, 'tis as in the Creation, the Evening and
the Morning make the Day.

Wild. I have a little serious business.

50   *Bell.* Put it off till a fitter season: for the truth is, business is then only tollerable, when the world and the flesh have no baits to set before us for the day.

Wild. But mine perhaps is publick business.

Bell. Why, is any business more publick than drinking and wenching? Look on those grave plodding fellows, that pass by us as though they were meditating the reconquest of *Flanders:* fly 'em to a Mark, and I'll undertake three parts of four are going to their Courtezans. I tell thee, *Jack,* the whisking of a Silk-Gown, and the rash of a Tabby-Pettycoat, are as comfortable 60 sounds to one of these rich Citizens, as the chink of their Pieces of Eight.

Wild. This being granted to be the common design of humane kind, 'tis more than probable 'tis yours; therefore I'll leave you to the prosecution of it.

Bell. Nay, good *Jack,* mine is but a Mistress in Embrio; the possession of her is at least some ten dayes off, and till that time, thy company will be pleasant, and may be profitable to carry on the work. I would use thee like an under kind of Chymist, to blow the coals; 'twill be time enough for me to be alone when I 70 come to projection.

Wild. You must excuse me, *Frank;* I have made an appointment at the Gameing-house.

Bell. What to do there I prethee? to mis-spend that money which kind fortune intended for a Mistress? or to learn new Oaths and Curses to carry into *England?* that is not it.——— I heard you were to marry when you left home: perhaps that may be still running in your head, and keep you vertuous.

Wild. Marriage quoth a! what, dost thou think I have been bred in the Desarts of *Africk,* or among the Savages of *America?* 80 nay, if I had, I must needs have known better things than so; the light of Nature would not have let me gone so far astray.

Bell. Well! what think you of the *Prado* this Evening?

---

71   *Frank*] Q2–3, F, D; *Franck* Q1.   75   it.] ~∧ Q1–3, F, D.
78   what,] D; ~∧ Q1–3, F.

Wild. Pox upon't, 'tis worse than our contemplative *Hide-Park.*

Bell. O! but we must submit to the Custom of the Country for courtship: what ever the means are, we are sure the end is still the same in all places. But who are these?

Enter Don Alonzo de Ribera, *with his two Daughters* Theodosia *and* Jacinta, *and* Beatrix *their Woman, passing by.*

Theo. Do you see those strangers, Sister, that eye us so earnestly?

90 *Jac.* Yes, and I guess 'em to be feathers of the *English* Embassador's Train; for I think I saw 'em at the grand Audience ———And have the strangest temptation in the world to talk to 'em: A mischief on this modesty.

Beat. A mischief of this Father of yours that haunts you so.

Jac. 'Tis very true *Beatrix;* for though I am the younger Sister, I should have the grace to lay modesty first aside. However, Sister, let us pull up our Vails and give 'em an Essay of our faces. *They pull up their Vails, and pull 'em down agen.*

Wild. Ah *Bellamy!* undone, undone! dost thou see those 100 Beauties?

Bell. Prethee *Wildblood* hold thy tongue, and do not spoil my contemplation; I am undoing my self as fast as e're I can too.

Wild. I must go to 'em.

Bell. Hold Madman; dost thou not see their father? hast thou a mind to have our throats cut?

Wild. By a Hector of fourscore? Hang our throats; what, a Lover and cautious? *Is going towards them.*

Alon. Come away Daughters, we shall be late else.

110 *Bell.* Look you, they are on the wing already.

Wild. Prethee, dear *Frank,* let's follow 'em: I long to know who they are.

Mask. Let me alone, I'll dog 'em for you.

---

90 *English*] Q2–3, F, D; English Q1.
96–97 aside. However] ~ : however Q1–3, F, D (However D).
107 throats; what,] D; ~ , ~ʌ Q1–3, F (Throats; Q3).

Bell. I am glad on't, for my shooes so pinch me, I can scarce go a step farther.

Wild. Cross the way there lives a Shoomaker: away quickly, that we may not spoil our man's design.   *Ex.* Bell. Wild.

Alon. offers to go off. Now friend! what's your business to follow us?

20 *Mask.* Noble *Don;* 'tis only to recommend my service to you: A certain violent passion I have had for your worship since the first moment that I saw you.

Alon. I never saw thee before, to my remembrance.

Mask. No matter Sir; true love never stands upon ceremony.

Alon. Prethee begone my sawcie companion, or I'll clap an Alguazile upon thy heels; I tell thee I have no need of thy service.

Mask. Having no servant of your own, I cannot in good manners leave you destitute.

30 *Alon.* I'll beat thee if thou follow'st me.

Mask. I am your Spaniel Sir, the more you beat me, the better I'll wait on you.

Alon. Let me intreat thee to be gone; the boyes will hoot at me to see me follow'd thus against my will.

Mask. Shall you and I concern our selves for what the Boyes do, Sir? Pray do you hear the news at Court?

Alon. Prethee what's the news to thee or me?

Mask. Will you be at the next *Juego de cannas?*

Alon. If I think good.

40 *Mask.* Pray go on Sir, we can discourse as we walk together: And whither were you now a going, Sir?

Alon. To the Devil I think.

Mask. O! not this year or two, Sir, by your age.

Jac. My Father was never so match'd for talking in all his life before; he who loves to hear nothing but himself. Prethee, *Beatrix,* stay behind, and see what this impudent *Englishman* would have.

---

118 *Alon. . . . off.*] D; Alon. . . . *off.*———— Q1-2; Alon. . . . *off.* Q3; Alon. . . . *off*——— F.
123 before,] D; ∼ₐ Q1-3, F.   145 himself.] Q3; ∼ : Q1-2, F, D.
146 *Englishman*] Q2-3, F, D; Englishman Q1.

Beat. Sir! if you'll let my Master go, I'll be his pawn.

Mask. Well, Sir, I kiss your hand, in hope to wait on you

150 another time.

Alon. Let us mend our pace to get clear of him.

Theo. If you do not, he'll be with you agen, like *Atalanta* in
the fable, and make you drop another of your golden Apples.

Ex. Alon. Theod. Jacinta.

Maskall *whispers* Beatrix *the while.*

Beat. How much good language is here thrown away to make
me betray my Ladies?

Mask. If you will discover nothing of 'em, let me discourse
with you a little.

Beat. As little as you please.

Mask. They are rich I suppose.

160   *Beat.* Now you are talking of them agen: but they are as rich,
as they are fair.

Mask. Then they have the *Indies:* well, but their Names, my
sweet Mistress.

Beat. Sweet Servant, their Names are———

Mask. Their Names are———out with it boldly———

Beat. A secret not to be disclos'd.

Mask. A secret say you? Nay, then I conjure you, as you are a
Woman, tell it me.

Beat. Not a syllable.

170   *Mask.* Why then, as you are a Waiting-woman: as you are the
Sieve of all your Ladies Secrets, tell it me.

Beat. You lose your labour: nothing will strain through me.

Mask. Are you so well stop'd i'th' bottom?

Beat. It was enjoyn'd me strictly as a Secret.

Mask. Was it enjoyn'd thee strictly, and can'st thou hold it?
Nay then thou art invincible: but, by that face, that more than
ugly face, which I suspect to be under thy Vaile, disclose it to
me.

153+   *s.d.* Maskall] D; Maskal Q1-3, F.   162   Names,] Q3, D; ~∧ Q1-2, F.
164   Servant,] Q2-3, F, D; ~∧ Q1.   167   you,] Q3; ~∧ Q1-2, F, D.
168   Woman,] Q2-3, F; ~∧ Q1, D.   170   then,] Q2-3, F, D; ~∧ Q1.
171   Secrets,] Q2-3, F, D; ~∧ Q1.

Beat. By that Face of thine, which is a Natural Visor: I will
180 not tell thee.

Mask. By thy————

Beat. No more Swearing I beseech you.

Mask. That Woman's worth little that is not worth an Oath:
well, get thee gone, now I think on't thou shalt not tell me.

Beat. Shall I not? Who shall hinder me? They are *Don Alonzo
de Ribera's* Daughters.

Mask. Out, out: I'le stop my Eares.

Beat.————They live hard by, in the *Calle major.*

Mask. O infernal Tongue————

190 *Beat.* And are going to the next Chappel with their Father.

Mask. Wilt thou never have done tormenting me? in my
Conscience anon thou wilt blab out their Names too.

Beat. Their Names are *Theodosia* and *Jacinta.*

Mask. And where's your great Secret now?

Beat. Now I think I am reveng'd on you for running down
my poor old Master.

Mask. Thou art not fully reveng'd till thou hast told me thy
own Name too.

Beat. 'Tis *Beatrix,* at your service, Sir; pray remember I wait
200 on 'em.

Mask. Now I have enough, I must be going.

Beat. I perceive you are just like other Men; when you have
got your ends you care not how soon you are going.————Farewell,————you'l be constant to me————

Mask. If thy face, when I see it, do not give me occasion to be
otherwise.

Beat. You shall take a Sample that you may praise it when
you see it next.   (*She pulls up her Vail.*)

Enter Wildblood *and* Bellamy.

Wild. Look, there's your Dog with a Duck in's mouth.————
210 Oh she's got loose and div'd again.————   [*Exit* Beatrix.

---

188   *major*] Q3; *maior* Q1-2, F, D.   199   Sir;] Q3; ~ , Q1-2, F, D.
209   mouth.] ~ₐ Q1-3, F, D.

Bell. Well *Maskall,* What newes of the Ladies of the Lake?

Mask. I have learn'd enough to embarque you in an Adventure; they are Daughters to one *Don Alonzo de Ribera* in the *Calle major,* their Names *Theodosia* and *Jacinta,* and they are going to their Devotions in the next Chappel.

Wild. Away then, let us lose no time, I thank Heaven I never found my self better enclin'd to Godliness than at this present.———   *Exeunt.*

SCENE II.

A Chappel.

Enter Alonzo, Theodosia, Jacinta, Beatrix, *other Ladies and Cavaliers as at their Devotion.*

Alon. By that time you have told your Beads I'll be agen with you.   *Exit.*

Jac. Do you think the *English* Men will come after us?

Beat. Do you think they can stay from you?

Jac. For my part I feel a certain qualm upon my heart, which makes me believe I am breeding Love to one of 'em.

Theo. How, Love, *Jacinta,* in so short a time? *Cupids* Arrow was well feather'd to reach you so suddenly.

Jac. Faith, as good at first as at last Sister, 'tis a thing that must 10 be done, and therefore 'tis best dispatching it out o'th' way.

Theo. But you do not mean to tell him so whom you love?

Jac. Why should I keep my self and Servant in pain for that which may be cur'd at a dayes warning?

Beat. My Lady tells you true, Madam; long tedious Courtship may be proper for cold Countries, where their Frosts are long a thawing; but Heaven be prais'd we live in a warm Climate.

Theo. The truth is, in other Countries they have opportu-

SCENE II. / *A*] SCENE II. *A* Q1–3, F, D (SCENE Q3, F, D).
s.d. Ladies . . . *Cavaliers*] Q3, D; Ladies . . . Cavaliers Q1–2, F.
9 Faith,] Q3, D; ~∧ Q1–2, F.   14 Madam;] Q3; ~ , Q1–2, F, D.

nities for Courtship, which we have not; they are not mew'd
20 up with double Locks and Grated Windows, but may receive
Addresses at their leisure.

Jac. But our Love here is like our Grass; if it be not mow'd
quickly 'tis burnt up.

> *Enter* Bellamy, Wildblood, Maskall: *they look*
> *about 'em.*

Theo. Yonder are your Gallants, send you comfort of 'em:
I am for my Devotions.

Jac. Now for my heart can I think of no other Prayer, but
only that they may not mistake us.————Why Sister, Sister,
————will you Pray? What injury have I ever done you, that
you should Pray in my company? If your servant *Don Melchor*
30 were here, we should have you mind Heaven as little as the best
on's.

Beat. They are at a loss, Madam; shall I put up my Vail that
they may take aime?

Jac. No, let 'em take their Fortune in the dark: we shall see
what Archers these *English* are.

Bell. Which are they think'st thou?

Wild. There's no knowing them, they are all Children of
darkness.

Bell. I'll besworn they have one sign of Godliness among 'em,
40 there's no distinction of persons here.

Wild. Pox o' this blind-mans-buffe; they may be asham'd to
provoke a man thus by their keeping themselves so close.

Bell. You are for the youngest you say; 'tis the eldest has
smitten me. And here I fix; if I am right————happy man be
his dole.————   *By* Theodosia.

Wild. I'll take my fortune here.————   *By* Jacinta.
Madam, I hope a stranger may take the libertie without offence
to offer his devotions by you.

---

19 not;] Q3; ~ , Q1–2, F, D.   20 Windows,] ~ ; Q1–3, F, D.
27 us.] ~ʌ Q1–3, F, D.   32 Madam;] Q3; ~ , Q1–2, F, D.
44 fix;] ~ , Q1–3, F, D.

Jac. That, Sir, would interrupt mine, without being any
50 advantage to your own.

Wild. My advantage, Madam, is very evident; for the kind
Saint to whom you pray, may by the neighbourhood mistake my
devotions for yours.

Jac. O Sir! our Saints can better distinguish between the
prayers of a Catholick and a Lutheran.

Wild. I beseech you, Madam, trouble not your self for my
Religion; for though I am a Heretick to the men of your Country, to your Ladies I am a very zealous Catholick: and for forni-
cation and adulterie, I assure you I hold with both Churches.

60 *Theo. to Bell.* Sir, if you will not be more devout, be at least
more civil; you see you are observ'd.

Bell. And pray, Madam, what do you think the lookers on
imagine I am imploy'd about?

Theo. I will not trouble my self to guess.

Bell. Why, by all circumstances, they must conclude that I am
making love to you: and methinks it were scarce civil to give
the opinion of so much good company the lye.

Theo. If this were true, you would have little reason to thank
'em for their Divination.

70 *Bell.* Meaning I should not be lov'd again.

Theo. You have interpreted my riddle, and may take it for
your pains.

Enter Alonzo, *(and goes apart to his devotion.)*

Beat. Madam, your Father is return'd.

Bell. She has nettled me, would I could be reveng'd on her.

Wild. Do you see their Father? let us make as though we
talk'd to one another, that we may not be suspected.

Beat. You have lost your *Englishmen.*

Jac. No, no, 'tis but design I warrant you: you shall see these
Island Cocks wheel about immediately.

---

60 *to*] D; to Q1-3, F. 61 civil;] Q3; ~ , Q1-2, F, D.
72+ *s.d.* Alonzo] Q2-3, F, D; Alonso Q1.
72+ *s.d.* devotion.] Q3, D; ~ₐ Q1-2, F.
77 *Englishmen*] Q2-3, F, D; Englishmen Q1.

80   *Beat.* Perhaps they thought they were observ'd.

               The English *gather up close to them.*

Wild. to Bell. Talk not of our Countrie Ladies: I declare my self for the *Spanish* Beauties.

Bell. Prethee tell me what thou canst find to doat on in these *Castilians.*

Wild. Their wit and beauty.

Theo. Now for our Champion *St. Jago* for *Spain* there.

Bell. Faith, I can speak no such miracles of either; for their beautie 'tis much as the *Moores* left it; not altogether so deep a black as the true *Æthiopian:* A kind of beautie that is too 90 civil to the lookers on to do them any mischief.

Jac. This was your frowardness that provok'd him, Sister.

Theo. But they shall not carry it off so.

Bell. As for their wit, you may judge it by their breeding, which is commonly in a Nunnerie; where the want of mankind while they are there, makes them value the blessing ever after.

Theo. Prethee dear *Jacinta* tell me, what kind of creatures were those we saw yesterday at the Audience? Those I mean that look'd so like *Frenchmen* in their habits, but only became their Apishness so much worse.

100   *Jac. Englishmen* I think they call'd 'em.

Theo. Crie you mercy; they were of your wild *English* indeed, that is a kind of Northern Beast, that is taught its feats of activity in *Monsieurland,* and for doing 'em too lubberly, is laugh'd at all the world over.

Bell. Wildblood, I perceive the women understand little of discourse; their Gallants do not use 'em to't: they get upon their Gennits, and prance before their Ladies windows; there the Palfray curvets and bounds, and in short entertains 'em for his Master.

110   *Wild.* And this horse-play they call making love.

Beat. Your Father, Madam.———

Alon. Daughters! what Cavaliers are those which were talking by you?

———

80+   *s.d.* English] Q3, D; *English* Q1–2, F.   81   *to*] D; to Q1–3, F.

82   *Spanish*] Q2–3, F, D; Spanish Q1.   86   *St.*] Q2–3; St. Q1, F, D.

87   Faith,] Q2–3, F; ~∧ Q1, D.   111   Father,] Q3, D; ~∧ Q1–2, F.

Jac. *Englishmen,* I believe Sir, at their devotions.————
Cavalier, would you would try to pray a little better then you
have railly'd. *Aside to* Wildblood.

Wild. Hang me if I put all my devotions out of order for you:
I remember I pray'd but on *Tuesday* last, and my time comes
not till *Tuesday* next.

120 *Mask.* You had as good pray, Sir; she will not stir till you
have: Say any thing.

Wild. Fair Lady, though I am not worthy of the least of your
favours, yet give me the happiness this Evening to see you at
your fathers door, that I may acquaint you with part of my
sufferings. *Aside to* Jacinta.

Alon. Come Daughters, have you done?

Jac. Immediately Sir.————Cavalier, I will not fail to be
there at the time appointed, if it be but to teach you more wit,
henceforward, than to engage your heart so lightly.
Aside to Wildblood.

130 *Wild.* I have engag'd my heart with so much zeal and true
devotion to your divine beauty, that————

Alon. What means this Cavalier?

Jac. Some zealous ejaculation.

Alon. May the Saint hear him.

Jac. I'll answer for her.———— *Ex. Father and Daughters.*

Wild. Now *Bellamy,* what success?

Bell. I pray'd to a more Marble Saint than that was in the
Shrine; but you, it seems, have been successful.

Wild. And so shalt thou; let me alone for both.

140 *Bell.* If you'll undertake it, I will make bold to indulge my
love; and within this two hours be a desperate Inamorado. I
feel I am coming apace to it.

Wild. Faith, I can love at any time with a wish at my rate:
I give my heart according to the old law of pawns, to be return'd
me before sun-set.

---

114 devotions.————] ~ :∧ Q1–2, F, D; ~ ·∧ Q3.
116 s.d. *Aside*] Q2–3, D; *aside* Q1, F.
118–119 *Tuesday* . . . *Tuesday*] Q3, D; *Tuesday* . . . *Tuesday* Q1–2, F.
125 s.d. *Aside*] Q2–3, F, D; *aside* Q1.   129 than] Q3, F, D; then Q1–2.
129+ s.d. *Aside*] Q2–3, F, D; *aside* Q1.   143 Faith,] Q3; ~∧ Q1–2, F, D.

Bell. I love only that I may keep my heart warm; for a man's a pool if love stir him not; and to bring it to that pass, I first resolve whom to love, and presently after imagine I am in love; for a strong imagination is requir'd in a Lover as much as in a
150 Witch.

Wild. And is this all your Receipt?

Bell. These are my principal ingredients; as for Piques, Jealousies, Duels, Daggers, and Halters, I let 'em alone to the vulgar.

Wild. Prethee let's round the street a little; till *Maskall* watches for their Woman.

Bell. That's well thought on: he shall about it immediately.
> We will attempt the Mistress by the Maid:
> Women by women still are best betray'd.   *Exeunt.*

ACT II. SCENE I.

Enter Wildblood, Bellamy, Maskall.

Wild. Did you speak with her Woman?

Mask. Yes, but she was in hast, and bid me wait her hereabouts when she return'd.

Bell. Then you have discover'd nothing more?

Mask. Only, in general, that *Donna Theodosia* is engag'd elsewhere; so that all your Courtship will be to no purpose.————
[*To* Wild.] But for your Mistress, Sir, she is waded out of her depth in love to you already.

Wild. That's very hard, when I am scarce knee-deep with her:
10 'tis true, I have given her hold of my heart, but if she take not heed it will slip through her fingers.

Bell. You are Prince of the Soil, Sir, and may take your plea-

---

158–159   *as in Q3, F; not indented in Q1–2, D.*
ACT II. SCENE I.] D; ACT. II. Q1–2; ACT II. Q3, F.
s.d. Enter] Q3, D; *omitted from Q1–2, F.*
s.d. Wildblood, Bellamy, Maskall] Q3, F, D; *Wildblood, Bellamy, Maskall* Q1–2.
6   purpose.————] D; ~ ·∧ Q1–3, F.

sure when you please; but I am the Eve to your Holy-day, and must fast for being joyn'd to you.

Wild. Were I as thou art, I would content my self with having had one fair flight at her, without wearying my self on the wing for a retrieve; for when all's done the Quarry is but woman.

Bell. Thank you, Sir, you would fly 'em both your self, and while I turn tail, we should have you come gingling with your
20 bells in the neck of my Patridge; do you remember who incourag'd me to love, and promis'd me his assistance?

Wild. I, while there was hope *Frank,* while there was hope; but there's no contending with one's destiny.

Bell. Nay, it may be I care as little for her as another man; but while she flyes before me I must follow: I can leave a woman first with ease, but if she begins to fly before me, I grow opiniatre as the Devil.

Wild. What a secret have you found out! why, 'tis the nature of all mankind: we love to get our Mistresses, and purr over
30 'em, as Cats do over Mice, and then let 'em go a little way; and all the pleasure is, to pat 'em back again: But yours, I take it, *Frank,* is gone too far; prethee how long dost thou intend to love at this rate?

Bell. Till the evil constellation be past over me: yet I believe it would hasten my recovery if I knew whom she lov'd.

Mask. You shall not be long without that satisfaction.

Wild. 'St, the door opens; and two women are coming out.

Bell. By their stature they should be thy gracious Mistress and *Beatrix.*
40 *Wild.* Methinks you should know your Q. then and withdraw.

Bell. Well, I'll leave you to your fortune; but if you come to close fighting, I shall make bold to run in and part you.

Bellamy *and* Maskall *withdraw.*

Wild. Yonder she comes with full sails, i'faith; I'll hail her amain for *England.*

Enter Jacinta *and* Beatrix *at the other end of the Stage.*

---

28 out!] ∼? Q1-3, F, D.   28 why,] Q3; ∼∧ Q1-2, F, D.
43 sails,] Q3; ∼∧ Q1-2, F, D.

Beat. You do love him then?

Jac. Yes, most vehemently.

Beat. But set some bounds to your affection.

Jac. None but fools confine their pleasure: what Usurer ever thought his Coffers held too much? No, I'll give my self the
50 swinge, and love without reserve. If I'll keep a passion, I'll never starve it in my service.

Beat. But are you sure he will deserve this kindness?

Jac. I never trouble my self so long beforehand: Jealousies and disquiets are the dregs of an amour; but I'll leave mine before I have drawn it off so low: when it once grows troubled I'll give vent to a fresh draught.

Beat. Yet it is but prudence to try him first; no Pilot ventures on an unknown Coast without sounding.

Jac. Well, to satisfie thee I am content; partly too because I
60 find a kind of pleasure in laying baits for him.

Beat. The two great vertues of a Lover are constancy and liberality; if he profess those two, you may be happy in him.

Jac. Nay, if he be not Lord and Master of both those qualities I disown him.————But who goes there?

Beat. He, I warrant you, Madam; for his Servant told me he was waiting hereabout.

Jac. Watch the door, give me notice if any come.

Beat. I'll secure you, Madam.————   *Exit* Beatrix.

Jac. to Wild. What, have you laid an ambush for me?

70 *Wild.* Only to make a Reprisal of my heart.

Jac. 'Tis so wild, that the Lady who has it in her keeping, would be glad she were well rid on't: it does so flutter about the Cage. 'Tis a meer *Bajazet;* and if it be not let out the sooner, will beat out the brains against the Grates.

Wild. I am afraid the Lady has not fed it, and 'tis wild for hunger.

Jac. Or perhaps it wants company; shall she put another to it?

Wild. I; but then 'twere best to trust 'em out of the Cage together; let 'em hop about at libertie.

---

64   him.] ~∧ Q1–3, F, D.   69   *to*] D; to Q1–3, F.
69   What,] D; ~∧ Q1–3, F.

80 *Jac.* But if they should lose one another in the wide world!

Wild. They'll meet at night I warrant 'em.

Jac. But is not your heart of the nature of those Birds that breed in one Countrie, and goe to winter in another?

Wild. Suppose it does so; yet I take my Mate along with me. And now to leave our parables, and speak in the language of the vulgar, what think you of a voyage to merry *England?*

Jac. Just as *Æsop's* Frog did, of leaping into a deep Well in a drought: if he ventur'd the leap, there might be water; but if there were no water, how should he get out again?

90 *Wild.* Faith, we live in a good honest Country, where we are content with our old vices, partly because we want wit to invent more new. A Colonie of *Spaniards,* or spiritual *Italians* planted among us would make us much more racy. 'Tis true, our variety is not much; but to speak nobly of our way of living, 'tis like that of the Sun, which rises, and looks upon the same things he saw yesterday, and goes to bed again.

Jac. But I hear your women live most blessedly; there's no such thing as jealousie among the Husbands; if any man has horns, he bears 'em as loftily as a Stag, and as inoffensively.

100 *Wild.* All this I hope gives you no ill Character of the Country.

Jac. But what need we go into another Climate? as our love was born here, so let it live and die here, and be honestly buried in its native Country.

Wild. Faith, agreed with all my heart. For I am none of those unreasonable lovers, that propose to themselves the loving to eternity; the truth is, a month is commonly my stint; but in that month I love so dreadfully, that it is after a twelvemonths rate of common love.

110 *Jac.* Or would not a fortnight serve our turn? for in troth a month looks somewhat dismally; 'tis a whole *Ægyptian* year. If a Moon changes in my love I shall think my *Cupid* grown dull, or fallen into an Apoplexie.

Wild. Well, I pray heaven we both get off as clear as we imag-

90   Faith,] ~∧ Q1–3, F, D.   103   born here,] Q2–3, F, D; ~~ ; Q1.
105   Faith,] Q3, D; ~∧ Q1–2, F.   111   year. If] D; ~ , if Q1–2, F; ~ : If Q3.

ine; for my part I like your humour so damnably well, that I
fear I am in for a week longer than I propos'd; I am half afraid
your *Spanish* Planet, and my *English* one have been acquainted,
and have found out some by-room or other in the 12 houses: I
wish they have been honorable.

120   *Jac.* The best way for both were to take up in time; yet I am
afraid our forces are engag'd so far, that we must make a battel
on't. What think you of disobliging one another from this day
forward; and shewing all our ill humours at the first; which
Lovers use to keep as a reserve till they are married?

Wild. Or let us encourage one another to a breach by the
dangers of possession: I have a Song to that purpose.

Jac. Pray let me hear it: I hope it will go to the tune of one of
our *Passa-calles.*

SONG.

> *You charm'd me not with that fair face*
130   *Though it was all divine:*
> *To be anothers is the Grace,*
>   *That makes me wish you mine.*
> *The Gods and Fortune take their part*
>   *Who like young Monarchs fight;*
> *And boldly dare invade that heart*
>   *Which is anothers right.*
> *First mad with hope we undertake*
>   *To pull up every barr;*
> *But once possess'd, we faintly make*
140   *A dull defensive warr.*
> *Now every friend is turn'd a foe*
>   *In hope to get our store:*
> *And passion makes us Cowards grow,*
>   *Which made us brave before.*

Jac. Believe it, Cavalier, you are a dangerous person: do you
hold forth your gifts in hopes to make me love you less?

Wild. They would signifie little, if we were once married:

those gayeties are all nipt, and frost-bitten in the Marriage-bed,
i'faith.

150   *Jac.* I am sorry to hear 'tis so cold a place: but 'tis all one to us
who do not mean to trouble it: the truth is, your humor pleases
me exceedingly; how long it will do so, I know not; but so long
as it does, I am resolv'd to give my self the content of seeing you.
For if I should once constrain my self, I might fall in love in
good earnest: but I have stay'd too long with you, and would
be loth to surfeit you at first.

Wild. Surfet me, Madam? why, you have but Tantaliz'd me
all this while.

Jac. What would you have?

160   *Wild.* A hand, or lip, or any thing that you can spare; when
you have Conjur'd up a Spirit he must have some employment,
or he'll tear you a pieces.

Jac. Well, Here's my Picture; to help your contemplation in
my absence.

Wild. You have already the Original of mine: but some
revenge you must allow me: a Locket of Diamonds, or some
such trifle, the next time I kiss your hand.

Jac. Fie, fie; you do not think me mercinary! yet now I think
on't, I'll put you into our *Spanish* Mode of Love: our Ladies

170   here use to be the Banquiers of their Servants, and to have their
Gold in keeping.

Wild. This is the least trial you could have made of me: I
have some 300 Pistols by me; those I'll send you by my servant.

Jac. Confess freely; you mistrust me: but if you find the least
qualme about your Gold, pray keep it for a Cordial.

Wild. The Cordial must be apply'd to the heart, and mine's
with you Madam: Well; I say no more; but these are dangerous
beginings for holding on: I find my moneth will have more then
one and thirty dayes in't.

Enter Beatrix *running.*

---

157   Madam? why,] D; ∼ , ∼∧ Q1-2, F; ∼ ! ∼∧ Q3.
176   mine's] Q2-3, F, D; mines Q1.

180 *Beat.* Madam, your Father calls in hast for you; and is looking
you about the house.

Jac. Adieu Servant, be a good manager of your stock of Love,
that it may hold out your Moneth; I am afraid you'll wast so
much of it before to morrow night, that you'll shine but with a
quarter Moon upon me.

Wild. It shall be a Crescent.   *Exit* Wild., Jacinta *severally.*

      Beatrix *is going, and* Maskall *runs and stops her.*

Mask. Pay your ransome; you are my Prisoner.

Beat. What, do you fight after the *French* Fashion; take
Towns before you declare a Warr?

190 *Mask.* I should be glad to imitate them so far, to be in the
middle of the Country before you could resist me.

Beat. Well, what composition Monsieur?

Mask. Deliver up your Lady's secret; what makes her so cruel
to my Master?

Beat. Which of my Ladies, and which of your Masters? For
I suppose we are Factors for both of them.

Mask. Your eldest Lady, *Theodosia.*

Beat. How dare you press your Mistress to an inconvenience?

Mask. My Mistress? I understand not that language; the for-
200 tune of the Valet ever follows that of the Master; and his is
desperate; if his fate were alter'd for the better, I should not care
if I ventur'd upon you for the worse.

Beat. I have told you already *Donna Theodosia* loves another.

Mask. Has he no name?

Beat. Let it suffice he is born noble, though without a fortune.
His povertie makes him conceal his love from her Father; but
she sees him every night in private: and to blind the world,
about a fortnight agoe he took a solemn leave of her, as if he
were going into *Flanders:* in the mean time he lodges at the
210 house of *Don Lopez de Gamboa;* and is himself call'd *Don
Melchor de Guzman.*

186   *s.d.* Wild., . . . *severally.*] Q2–3, F, D; ~‸, . . . ~ , Q1.
186+   *s.d.* Maskall] D; Maskal Q1–3, F.   188   What,] Q3, D; ~‸ Q1–2, F.
207–208   world, . . . agoe] D; ~‸ . . . ~, Q1–3, F.

Mask. Don Melchor de Guzman! O heavens!

Beat. What amazes you!

Theo. within. Why, *Beatrix,* where are you?

Beat. You hear I am call'd; Adieu; and be sure you keep my Counsel.

Mask. Come, Sir, you see the Coast is clear.   *Ex.* Beatrix.

Enter Bellamy.

Bell. Clear, dost thou say? no 'tis full of Rocks and Quick-sands: yet nothing vexes me so much as that she is in love with
220 such a poor Rogue.

Mask. But that he should lodge privately in the same house with us! 'twas odly contriv'd of fortune.

Bell. Hang him Rogue, methinks I see him perching like an Owle by day, and not daring to flutter out till Moon-light. The Rascal invents love, and brews his complements all day, and broaches 'em at night; just as some of our dry wits do their stories before they come into company: well, if I could be re-veng'd on either of 'em.

Mask. Here she comes again with *Beatrix;* but good Sir mod-
230 erate your passion.

Enter Theodosia *and* Beatrix.

Bell. Nay, Madam, you are known; and must not pass till I have spoke with you.   Bellamy *lifts up* Theodosia's *Vail.*

Theo. This rudeness to a person of my quality may cost you dear. Pray when did I give you encouragement for so much familiarity?

Bell. When you scorn'd me in the Chappel.

Theo. The truth is, I deny'd you as heartily as I could; that I might not be twice troubled with you.

Bell. Yet you have not this aversion for all the world: how-
240 ever, I was in hope though the day frown'd, the night might prove as propitious to me as it is to others.

———

239–240 however,] D; ∼∧ Q1–3, F.

Theo. I have now a quarrell both to the Sun and Moon, because I have seen you by both their lights.

Bell. Spare the Moon I beseech you, Madam; she is a very trusty Planet to you.

Beat. O *Maskall* you have ruin'd me.

Mask. Dear Sir, hold yet. ·

Bell. Away.

Theo. Pray, Sir, expound your meaning; for I confess I am in
250 the dark.

Bell. Methinks you should discover it by Moon-light. Or if you would have me speak clearer to you, give me leave to wait on you at a midnight assignation; and that it may not be discover'd, I'll feign a voyage beyond sea, as if I were gone a Captaining to *Flanders.*

Mask. A pox on's memory, he has not forgot one syllable.

Theo. Ah *Beatrix,* you have betray'd and sold me.

Beat. You have betray'd and sold your self, Madam, by your own rashness to confess it; Heaven knows I have serv'd you but
260 too faithfully.

Theo. Peace, impudence; and see my face no more.

Mask. Do you know what work you have made, Sir?

Bell. Let her see what she has got by slighting me.

Mask. You had best let *Beatrix* be turn'd away for me to keep: if you do, I know whose purse shall pay for't.

Bell. That's a curse I never thought on: cast about quickly and save all yet. Range, quest, and spring a lie immediately.

Theo. to Beat. Never importune me farther; you shall go; there's no removing me.

270 *Beat.* Well; this is ever the reward of innocence————

(*Going.*)

Mask. Stay, guiltless Virgin, stay; thou shalt not go.

Theo. Why, who should hinder it?

Mask. That will I in the name of truth.————[*Aside.*] If this hard-bound lie would but come from me.————Madam, I must

---

244 Madam;] Q3; ∼ , Q1–2, F, D.   246 *Maskall*] D; *Maskal* Q1–3, F.
259 knows] Q2–3, F, D; know's Q1.   268 *Theo.*] Q2–3, F, D; ∼ ∧ Q1.
268 *to*] D; to Q1–3, F.   270+ *s.d. Going.*] Q3, D; *going*∧ Q1–2, F.
273–274 ————[*Aside.*] If . . . me.————] (If . . . me:) Q1–3, F, D.

tell you it lies in my power to appease this tempest with one word.

Beat. Would it were come once.

Mask. Nay, Sir, 'tis all one to me, if you turn me away uppon't; I can hold no longer.

280 *Theo.* What does the fellow mean?

Mask. For all your noddings, and your Mathematical grimaces. [*To* Bellamy.]————In short, Madam, my Master has been conversing with the Planets; and from them has had the knowledge of your affairs.

Bell. This Rogue amazes me.

Mask. I care not, Sir, I am for truth; that will shame you and all your Devils. In short, Madam, this Master of mine that stands before you, without a word to say for himself, so like an Oph, as I may say with reverence to him————

290 *Bell.* The Raskal makes me mad.

Mask. Is the greatest *Astrologer* in *Christendome.*

Theo. Your Master an *Astrologer?*

Mask. A most profound one.

Bell. Why you dog, do you consider what an improbable lie this is; which you know I can never make good: disgorge it you Cormorant, or I'll pinch your throat out.————

Takes him by the throat.

Mask. 'Tis all in vain, Sir, you are and shall be an *Astrologer* what e're I suffer: you know all things, see into all things, foretell all things; and if you pinch more truth out of me, I will

300 confess you are a Conjurer.

Bell. How, sirrah, a Conjurer?

Mask. I mean, Sir, the Devil is in your fingers: own it you had best, Sir, and do not provoke me farther; what, did not I see you an hour ago, turning over a great Folio with strange figures in it, and then muttering to your self like any Poet, and then naming *Theodosia*, and then staring up in the skie,

---

281–282 grimaces. [*To* Bellamy.]————In] grimaces, in Q1–3, F, D (Grimaces: Q3).
287 Devils. In] ∼ : in Q1–3, F, D (In D).
291 *Christendome*] Q3; Christendome Q1–2, F, D.
303 what,] D; ∼∧ Q1–3, F.

and then poring upon the ground? So that betwixt God and the Devil, Madam, he came to know your love.

While he is speaking, Bellamy *stops his mouth by fits.*

Bell. Madam, if ever I knew the least term in *Astrologie,* I am the arrantest Son of a whore breathing.

Beat. O, Sir, for that matter you shall excuse my Lady: Nay hide your tallents if you can, Sir.

Theo. The more you pretend ignorance, the more we are resolv'd to believe you skilfull.

Bell. You'll hold your tongue yet.

Mask. You shall never make me hold my tongue, except you conjure me to silence: what, did you not call me to look into a Chrystal, and there shew'd me a fair Garden, and a *Spaniard* stalking in his narrow breeches, and walking underneath a window? I should know him agen amongst a thousand.

Beat. Don Melchor, in my conscience, Madam.

Bell. This Rogue will invent more stories of me, than e're were father'd upon *Lilly.*

Mask. Will you confess then; do you think I'll stain my honor to swallow a lie for you?

Bell. Well, a pox on you, I am an *Astrologer.*

Beat. O, are you so, Sir?

Theo. I hope then, learned Sir, as you have been curious in enquiring into my secrets, you will be so much a Cavalier as to conceal 'em.

Bell. You need not doubt me, Madam; I am more in your power than you can be in mine: besides, if I were once known in Town, the next thing, for ought I know, would be to bring me before the fathers of the Inquisition.

Beat. Well, Madam, what do you think of me now; I have betray'd you, I have sold you; how can you ever make me amends for this imputation? I did not think you could have us'd me so.——   (*Cries and claps her hands at her.*)

307   ground? So] ∼ ; so Q1–3, F, D.
309   *Astrologie*] Q2–3, F; Astrologie Q1, D.   317   what,] Q3, D; ∼∧ Q1–2, F.
319–320 window?] Q2–3, F, D; ∼ ; Q1.
326   *Astrologer*] Q2–3, F; Astrologer Q1, D.   331   You] Q2–3, F, D; you Q1.

Theo. Nay, prethee *Beatrix* do not crie; I'll leave of my new
340 Gown to morrow, and thou shalt have it.

Beat. No, I'll crie eternally; you have taken away my good
name from me; and you can never make me recompence———
except you give me your new Gorget too.

Theo. No more words; thou shalt have it Girle.

Beat. O, Madam, your Father has surpriz'd us!

Enter Don Alonzo, *and frowns.*

Bell. Then I'll begone to avoid suspicion.

Theo. By your favour, Sir, you shall stay a little; the happiness of so rare an acquaintance, ought to be cherish'd on my
side by a longer conversation.

350 *Alon. Theodosia,* what business have you with this Cavalier?

Theo. That, Sir, which will make you as ambitious of being
known to him as I have been: under the habit of a Gallant he
conceals the greatest *Astrologer* this day living.

Alon. You amaze me Daughter.

Theo. For my own part I have been consulting with him
about some particulars of my fortunes past and future; both
which he has resolv'd me with that admirable knowledge———

Bell. Yes, faith, Sir, I was foretelling her of a disaster that
severely threatn'd her: and———[*Aside.*] One thing I foresee
360 already by my starrs, that I must bear up boldly, or I am lost.

Mask. to Bellamy. Never fear him, Sir; he's an ignorant fellow, and credulous I warrant him.

Alon. Daughter be not too confident in your belief; there's
nothing more uncertain than the cold Prophecies of these *Nostradamusses;* but of what nature was the question which you
ask'd him?

Theo. What should be my fortune in marriage.

Alon. And, pray, what did you answer, Sir?

Bell. I answer'd her the truth, that she is in danger of marry-
370 ing a Gentleman without a fortune.

357 knowledge———] Q3; ~ .——— Q1-2, F, D.
359-360 ———[*Aside.*] One . . . lost.] (one . . . lost.) Q1-3, F, D.
361 *to*] F, D; to Q1-3.

Theo. And this, Sir, has put me into such a fright————

Alon. Never trouble your self about it, Daughter; follow my advice and I warrant you a rich Husband.

Bell. But the starrs say she shall not follow your advice: if it happens otherwise I'll burn my folio Volumes, and my Manuscripts too, I assure you that, Sir.

Alon. Be not too confident, young man; I know somewhat in *Astrologie* my self; for in my younger years I study'd it; and though I say it, made some small proficience in it.

ᵎ⁰ *Bell.* Marry Heaven forbid.————   (*Aside.*)

Alon. And I could only find it was no way demonstrative, but altogether fallacious.

Mask. On what a Rock have we split our selves!

Bell. Now my ignorance will certainly come out!

Beat. Sir, remember you are old and crazie, Sir; and if the Evening Air should take you————beseech you Sir retire.

Alon. Knowledge is to be prefer'd before health; I must needs discusse a point with this learned Cavalier, concerning a difficult question in that Art, which almost gravels me.

ᵎ⁰ *Mask.* How I sweat for him, *Beatrix,* and my self too, who have brought him into this *Præmunire!*

Beat. You must be impudent; for our old man will stick like a burre to you, now he's in a dispute.

Alon. What Judgment may a man reasonably form from the trine Aspect of the two Infortunes in Angular houses?

Bell. That's a matter of nothing, Sir; I'll turn my man loose to you for such a question.————   (*Puts* Maskall *forward.*)

Alon. Come on, Sir, I am the quærent.

Mask. Meaning me, Sir! I vow to God, and your Worship

ᵎ⁰ knows it, I never made that Science my study in the least, Sir.

Bell. The gleanings of mine are enough for that: why, you impudent rogue you, hold forth your gifts, or I'll————What a devil, must I be pester'd with every trivial question, when there's not a Master in Town of any Science, but has his Usher for these mean offices?

Theo. Trie him in some deeper question, Sir; you see he will not put himself forth for this.

Alon. Then I'll be more abstruse with him. What think you, Sir, of the taking *Hyleg?* or of the best way of rectification for a
410 Nativity? have you been conversant in the *Centiloquium* of *Trismegistus?* what think you of *Mars* in the tenth when 'tis his own House, or of *Jupiter* configurated with malevolent Planets?

Bell. I thought what your skill was! to answer your question in two words, *Mars* rules over the Martial, and *Jupiter* over the Jovial; and so of the rest, Sir.

Alon. This every School-boy could have told me.

Bell. Why then you must not ask such School-boyes questions. ————But your Carkase, Sirrah, shall pay for this.

Aside to Maskall.

420 *Alon.* You seem not to understand the Terms, Sir.

Bell. By your favour, Sir, I know there are five of 'em; do not I know your *Michaelmas,* your *Hillary,* your *Easter,* your *Trinity,* and your *Long Vacation* term, Sir?

Alon. I do not understand a word of this *Jargon.*

Bell. It may be not, Sir; I believe the terms are not the same in *Spain* they are in *England.*

Mask. Did one ever hear so impudent an ignorance?

Alon. The terms of Art are the same every where.

Bell. Tell me that! you are an old man, and they are alter'd
430 since you studied them.

Alon. That may be I must confess; however if you please to discourse something of the Art to me, you shall find me an apt Scholar.

Enter a Servant to Alonzo.

---

408 him. What] ∼ : what Q1–3, F, D (What Q3, D).
411 *Trismegistus?*] Q3; ∼ : Q1–2, F, D.
419 ————But . . . this.] (But . . . this.)———— Q1–3, F, D (this.)∧ Q2–3, F).
419+ *s.d.* Maskall] D; Maskal Q1–3, F.
422–423 *Michaelmas . . . Hillary . . . Easter . . . Trinity . . . Long Vacation*] Q2–3, F, D; Michaelmas . . . Hillary . . . Easter . . . Trinity . . . Long Vacation Q1.
433+ *s.d. Servant*] F, D; Servant Q1–3.

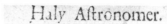

ILLUSTRATIONS FROM *The Book of Fortune* (1698)
See An Evening's Love, *II, i, 447–449*

GULIELMUS LILLIUS Astrologus *Natus Comitat: Leicest:*
1°.May 1602.

WILLIAM LILLY
FRONTISPIECE IN LILLY's *Christian Astrology* (1659)
See An Evening's Love, *II, i, 323, 475*

Ser. Sir,——— (*Whispers.*)

Alon. Sir, I am sorry a business of importance calls me hence; but I'll wait on you some other time, to discourse more at large of *Astrologie.*

Bell. Is your business very pressing?

Alon. It is, I assure you, Sir.

40 *Bell.* I am very sorry, for I should have instructed you in such rare secrets; I have no fault, but that I am too communicative.

Alon. I'll dispatch my business, and return immediately. Come away Daughter.

　　　　　Exeunt Alonzo, Theodosia, Beatrix, *Servus.*

Bell. A Devil on's learning; he had brought me to my last legs; I was fighting as low as ever was Squire *Widdrington.*

Mask. Who would have suspected it from that wicked Elder?

Bell. Suspected it? why 'twas palpable from his very Physnomy; he looks like *Haly,* and the spirit *Fircu* in the Fortunebook.

Enter Wildblood.

50 *Wild.* How now *Bellamy,* in wrath? prethee, what's the matter?

Bell. The story is too long to tell you; but this Rogue here has made me pass for an errant Fortune-teller.

Mask. If I had not, I am sure he must have past for an errant Mad-man; he had discover'd, in a rage, all that *Beatrix* had confess'd to me concerning her Mistresse's love; and I had no other way to bring him off, but to say he knew it by the Planets.

Wild. And art thou such an Oph to be vext at this? as the adventure may be manag'd it may make the most pleasant one
60 in all the Carnival.

Bell. Death! I shall have all *Madrid* about me within these two dayes.

434　s.d. *Whispers*] Q2–3, F, D; *whispers* Q1.
442–443　immediately. Come] ∼ ; come Q1–3, F, D.
443+　s.d. Alonzo, Theodosia, Beatrix] Q2–3, F, D; *Alonzo, Theodosia, Beatrix* Q1.
450　*Wild.*] Q2–3, F, D; *Widl.* Q1.　　　450　wrath?] Q2–3, F, D; ∼ , Q1.

Wild. Nay, all *Spain,* i'faith, as fast as I can divulge thee: not a Ship shall pass out from any Port, but shall ask thee for a wind; thou shalt have all the trade of *Lapland* within a Month.

Bell. And do you think it reasonable for me to stand defendant to all the impertinent questions that the Town can ask me?

Wild. Thou shalt do't boy: pox on thee, thou dost not know thine own happiness; thou wilt have the Ladies come to thee; 470 and if thou dost not fit them with fortunes, thou art bewitch'd.

Mask. Sir, 'tis the easiest thing in Nature; you need but speak doubtfully, or keep your self in general terms, and for the most part tell good rather than bad fortune.

Wild. And if at any time thou ventur'st at particulars, have an evasion ready like *Lilly;* as thus, it will infallibly happen if our sins hinder not. I would undertake with one of his Almanacks to give very good content to all *Christendom,* and what good luck fell not out in one Kingdom, should in another.

Mask. The pleasure on't will be to see how all his Customers 480 will contribute to their own deceiving; and verily believe he told them that, which they told him.

Bell. Umh! now I begin to taste it; I am like the drunken Tinker in the Play, a great Prince, and never knew it.

Wild. A great Prince, a great Turk; we shall have thee within these two dayes, do grace to the Ladies by throwing out a handkerchief; 'lif, I could feast upon thy fragments.

Bell. If the women come you shall be sure to help me to undergo the burden; for though you make me an *Astronomer* I am no *Atlas,* to bear all upon my back. But who are these?

Enter Musicians with disguises; and some in their hands.

490 *Wild.* You know the men if their Masquing habits were off; they are the Musick of our Embassadors Retinue: my project is to give our Mistresses a Serenade; this being the last Evening of the Carnival; and to prevent discovery, here are disguises for us too.————

Bell. 'Tis very well; come *Maskall* help on with 'em, while they tune their Instruments.

Wild. Strike up Gentlemen; we'll entertain 'em with a song *al' Angloise,* pray be ready with your *Chorus.*

SONG.

After the pangs of a desperate Lover,
When day and night I have sigh'd all in vain,
Ah what a pleasure it is to discover
In her eyes pity, who causes my pain!

2.

When with unkindness our love at a stand is,
And both have punish'd our selves with the pain,
Ah what a pleasure the touch of her hand is,
Ah what a pleasure to press it again!

3.

When the denyal comes fainter and fainter,
And her eyes give what her tongue does deny,
Ah what a trembling I feel when I venture,
Ah what a trembling does usher my joy!

4.

When, with a Sigh, she accords me the blessing,
And her eyes twinkle 'twixt pleasure and pain;
Ah what a joy 'tis beyond all expressing,
Ah what a joy to hear, Shall we again?

Enter Theodosia *and* Jacinta *above.*

Jacinta *throws down her handkerchief*
with a Favour ty'd to it.

---

507   *fainter,*] Q2–3, F, D, o1, d1–2, d5, f1–3; ~ ,, Q1; ~∧ M2–3.
514   Shall we again?] *shall we again!* Q1–3, F, D, f1–3, M2 (*Shall* f2–3; *again?* f1–3; *a gaine* M2); *it again!* o1, d1–2, d5, M3 (*again.* M3).
514+   s.d. *Enter*] omitted from *Q1–3, F, D.*
514+   s.d. Theodosia . . . Jacinta] Q2–3, F, D; *Theodosia . . . Jacinta* Q1.

Jac. Ill Musicians must be rewarded: there, Cavalier, 'tis to buy your silence.——— *Exeunt women from above.*

Wild. By this light, which at present is scarce an oath, an handkerchief and a favour.

Musick and Guittars tuning on the other side of the Stage.

Bell. Hark, *Wildblood,* do you hear; there's more melody; 520 on my life some *Spaniards* have taken up this Post for the same design.

Wild. I'll be with their Cats-guts immediately.

Bell. Prethee be patient; we shall lose the sport else.

Enter Don Lopez *and* Don Melchor *disguis'd, with Servants, and Musicians on the other side.*

Wild. 'Tis some Rival of yours or mine, *Bellamy:* for he addresses to this window.

Bell. Damn him, let's fall on then.

The two Spaniards *and the* English *fight: the* Spaniards *are beaten off the Stage; the Musicians on both sides and Servants fall confusedly one over the other. They all get off, only* Maskall *remains upon the ground.*

Mask. rising. So, all's past, and I am safe: a pox on these fighting Masters of mine, to bring me into this danger with their valours and magnanimities. When I go a Serenading again with 530 'em, I'll give 'em leave to make Fiddle-strings of my small-guts.

To him Don Lopez.

Lop. Who goes there?

Mask. 'Tis *Don Lopez* by his voice.

Lop. The same; and by yours you should belong to my two *English* Ghests. Did you hear no tumult hereabouts?

Mask. I heard a clashing of swords, and men a fighting.

523+ *s.d. Enter* Don] Don Q1–3, F, D.
526+ *s.d.* Maskall] D; Maskal Q1–3, F.
534 *English*] Q2–3, F, D; English Q1.

Lop. I had my share in't; but how came you here?

Mask. I came hither by my Masters order to see if you were in any danger.

Lop. But how could he imagine I was in any?

540   *Mask.* 'Tis all one for that, Sir, he knew it, by—Heaven, what was I agoing to say, I had like to have discover'd all!

Lop. I find there is some secret in't; and you dare not trust me.

Mask. If you will swear on your honor to be very secret, I will tell you.

Lop. As I am a Cavalier, and by my Beard, I will.

Mask. Then, in few words, he knew it by *Astrologie,* or Magick.

Lop. You amaze me! Is he conversant in the occult Sciences?

550   *Mask.* Most profoundly.

Lop. I alwayes thought him an extraordinary person; but I could never imagine his head lay that way.

Mask. He shew'd me yesterday in a glass a Ladies Maid at *London,* whom I well knew; and with whom I us'd to converse on a Pallet in a drawing-room, while he was paying his devotions to her Lady in the Bed-chamber.

Lop. Lord, what a treasure for a State were here! and how much might we save by this man, in Forreign Intelligence!

Mask. And just now he shew'd me how you were assaulted in 560 the dark by Foreigners.

Lop. Could you guess what Countrymen?

Mask. I imagin'd them to be *Italians.*

Lop. Not unlikely; for they play'd most furiously at our backsides.

Mask. I will return to my Master with the good news of your safety; but once again be secret; or disclose it to none but friends.————[*Aside.*] So, there's one Woodcock more in the Springe.————   *Exit.*

Lop. Yes, I will be very secret; for I will tell it only to one 570 person; but she is a woman. I will to *Aurelia,* and acquaint her

---

536   here?] Q2–3, F, D; ~ : Q1.   541   discover'd] Q2–3, F, D; disover'd Q1.
567   ————[*Aside.*] So] ————So Q1–3, F, D.

with the skill of this rare Artist: she is curious as all women
are; and, 'tis probable, will desire to look into the Glass to
see *Don Melchor,* whom she believes absent. So that by this
means, without breaking my oath to him, he will be discover'd
to be in Town. Then his intrigue with *Theodosia* will come to
light too, for which *Aurelia* will, I hope, discard him, and receive me. I will about it instantly:

> Success, in love, on diligence depends;
> No lazie Lover e're attain'd his ends.   *Exit.*

ACT III.   SCENE I.

Enter Bellamy, Maskall.

Bell. Then, they were certainly *Don Lopez* and *Don Melchor*
with whom we fought!

Mask. Yes, Sir.

Bell. And when you met *Lopez* he swallow'd all you told him?

Mask. As greedily, as if it had been a new Saints miracle.

Bell. I see 'twill spread.

Mask. And the fame of it will be of use to you in your next
amour: for the women, you know, run mad after Fortune-
tellers and Preachers.

10   *Bell.* But for all my bragging this amour is not yet worn off.
I find constancy, and once a night come naturally upon a man
towards thirty: only we set a face on't; and call our selves unconstant for our reputation.

Mask. But, What say the Starrs, Sir?

Bell. They move faster than you imagine; for I have got me
an *Argol,* and an *English-Almanack;* by help of which in one
half-hour I have learnt to Cant with an indifferent good grace:
Conjunction, Opposition, Trine, Square and *Sextile,* are now no
longer Bug-bears to me, I thank my Starrs for't.

Enter Wildblood.

ACT III. SCENE I.]   D; ACT. III. Q1; ACT III. Q2-3, F.
s.d. Bellamy, Maskall] Q2-3, F, D; *Bellamy, Maskall* Q1.
8   women, . . . know,] Q3; ~∧ . . . ~∧ Q1-2, F, D.

————Monsieur *Wildblood,* in good time! What, you have been taking pains too, to divulge my Tallent?

Wild. So successfully, that shortly there will be no talk in Town but of you onely: another Miracle or two, and a sharp Sword, and you stand fair for a New Prophet.

Bell. But where did you begin to blow the Trumpet?

Wild. In the Gaming-house: where I found most of the Town-wits; the Prose-wits playing, and the Verse-wits rooking.

Bell. All sorts of Gamesters are so Superstitious, that I need not doubt of my reception there.

Wild. From thence I went to the latter end of a Comedy, and there whisper'd it to the next Man I knew who had a Woman by him.

Mask. Nay, then it went like a Train of Powder, if once they had it by the end.

Wild. Like a Squib upon a Line, i'faith, it ran through one row, and came back upon me in the next: at my going out I met a knot of *Spaniards,* who were formally listening to one who was relating it: but he told the Story so ridiculously, with his Marginal Notes upon it, that I was forc'd to contradict him.

Bell. 'Twas discreetly done.

Wild. I, for you, but not for me. *What,* sayes he, *must such Boracho's as you, take upon you to villifie a Man of Science? I tell you, he's of my intimate Acquaintance, and I have known him long, for a prodigious person!*————When I saw my *Don* so fierce, I thought it not wisdom to quarrel for so slight a matter as your Reputation, and so withdrew.

Bell. A pox of your success! now shall I have my Chamber besieg'd to morrow morning: there will be no stiring out for me; but I must be fain to take up their Questions in a cleft-Cane, or a Begging-box, as they do Charity in Prisons.

Wild. Faith, I cannot help what your Learning has brought you to: Go in and study; I foresee you will have but few Holy-dayes: in the mean time I'll not fail to give the World an account of your indowments. Fare-well: I'll to the Gaming house.   *Exit* Wildblood.

25 Trumpet?] Q2–3, F, D; ∼ . Q1.   41 me. *What*] ∼ : What Q1–3, F, D.
41–44 *must* . . . [*italics*] . . . *person!*] must . . . [*romans*] . . . person∧ Q1–3, F, D.

Mask. O, Sir, here is the rarest adventure, and which is more, come home to you.

Bell. What is it?

Mask. A fair Lady and her Woman, wait in the outer Room
60 to speak with you.

Bell. But how know you she is fair?

Mask. Her Woman pluck'd up her Vaile when she spake to me; so that having seen her this evening, I know her Mistress to be *Donna Aurelia,* Cousin to your Mistress *Theodosia,* and who lodges in the same House with her: she wants a Starr or two I warrant you.

Bell. My whole Constellation is at her service: but what is she for a Woman?

Mask. Fair enough, as *Beatrix* has told me; but sufficiently
70 impertinent. She is one of those Ladies who make ten Visits in an afternoon; and entertain her they see, with speaking ill of the last from whom they parted: in few words, she is one of the greatest Coquette's in *Madrid:* and to show she is one, she cannot speak ten words without some affected phrase that is in fashion.

Bell. For my part I can suffer any impertinence from a woman, provided she be handsome: my business is with her Beauty, not with her Morals: let her Confessor look to them.

Mask. I wonder what she has to say to you!
80 *Bell.* I know not; but I sweat for fear I should be gravell'd.

Mask. Venture out of your depth, and plunge boldly Sir; I warrant you will swimm.

Bell. Do not leave me I charge you; but when I look mournfully upon you help me out.

Enter Aurelia *and* Camilla.

Mask. Here they are already.   [Aurelia *plucks up her vail.*

Aur. How am I drest to night, *Camilla?* is nothing disorder'd in my head?

Cam. Not the least hair, Madam.

---

79 you!] Q3; ~? Q1–2, F, D.

Aur. No? let me see: give me the Counsellor of the Graces.

90   *Cam.* The Counsellor of the Graces, Madam?

Aur. My Glass I mean: what, will you never be so spiritual as to understand refin'd language?

Cam. Madam!

Aur. Madam me no *Madam,* but learn to retrench your words; and say *Mam;* as *yes Mam,* and *no Mam,* as other Ladies Women do. *Madam!* 'tis a year in pronouncing.

Cam. Pardon me Madam.

Aur. Yet again ignorance: *par-don Madam,* fie fie, what a superfluity is there, and how much sweeter the Cadence is,

100 *parn me Mam!* and for *your Ladyship, your Laship.*———— Out upon't, what a furious indigence of Ribands is here upon my head! This dress is a Libel to my beauty; a meer Lampoon. Would any one that had the least revenue of common sense have done this?

Cam. Mam, the Cavalier approaches your Laship.

Bell. to Mask. Maskall, pump the woman; and see if you can discover any thing to save my credit.

Aur. Out upon it; now I should speak, I want assurance.

Bell. Madam, I was told you meant to honor me with your

110 Commands.

Aur. I believe, Sir, you wonder at my confidence in this visit: but I may be excus'd for waving a little modesty to know the only person of the Age.

Bell. I wish my skill were more to serve you, Madam.

Aur. Sir, you are an unfit judge of your own merits: for my own part I confess I have a furious inclination for the occult Sciences; but at present 'tis my misfortune———   [*Sighs.*

---

91   what,] D; ∼∧ Q1–3, F.
94–96   *Madam . . . Mam . . . yes Mam . . . no Mam . . . Madam*] Madam . . . Mam . . . yes Mam . . . no Mam . . . Madam Q1–3, F, D.
98   *par-don Madam*] par-don Madam Q1–3, F, D.
100   *parn me Mam . . . your Ladyship, your*] parn me Mam . . . your Ladyship, your Q1–3, F, D.
100   *Laship.*] Laship∧ Q1–3, F, D (∼ . F).   105   Mam,] Q2–3, F; ∼∧ Q1, D.
106   *to*] D; to Q1–3, F.   108   speak,] D; ∼∧ Q1–3, F.
117   *s.d. Sighs*] Q2–3, F, D; *sighs* Q1.

Bell. But why that sigh, Madam?

Aur. You might spare me the shame of telling you; since I
120 am sure you can divine my thoughts: I will therefore tell you
nothing.

Bell. What the Devil will become of me now!————[*Aside.*

Aur. You may give me an Essay of your Science, by declaring to me the secret of my thoughts.

Bell. If I know your thoughts, Madam, 'tis in vain for you
to disguise them to me: therefore as you tender your own satisfaction lay them open without bashfulness.

Aur. I beseech you let us pass over that chapter; for I am
shamefac'd to the last point: Since therefore I cannot put off
130 my modesty, succour it, and tell me what I think.

Bell. Madam, Madam, that bashfulness must be laid aside:
not but that I know your business perfectly; and will if you
please unfold it to you all, immediately.

Aur. Favour me so far, I beseech you, Sir; for I furiously
desire it.

Bell. But then I must call up before you a most dreadful
Spirit, with head upon head, and horns upon horns: therefore
consider how you can endure it.

Aur. This is furiously furious; but rather than fail of my
140 expectances, I'll try my assurance.

Bell. Well, then, I find you will force me to this unlawful,
and abominable act of Conjuration: remember the sin is yours
too.

Aur. I espouse the crime also.

Bell. I see when a woman has a mind to't, she'll never boggle
at a sin. Pox on her, what shall I do? [*Aside.*]————Well, I'll tell
you your thoughts, Madam; but after that expect no farther
service from me; for 'tis your confidence must make my Art succesful:————Well, you are obstinate, then; I must tell you
150 your thoughts?

Aur. Hold, hold, Sir, I am content to pass over that chapter
rather than be depriv'd of your assistance.

---

119 since] Q2–3, F, D; sioce Q1.   146 do? [*Aside.*]] do? Q1–3, F, D.

Bell. 'Tis very well; what need these circumstances between us two? Confess freely, is not love your business?

Aur. You have touch'd me to the quick, Sir.

Bell. La you there; you see I knew it; nay, I'll tell you more, 'tis a man you love.

Au. O prodigious Science! I confess I love a man most furiously, to the last point, Sir.

160 *Bell.* Now proceed Lady, your way is open; I am resolv'd I'll not tell you a word farther.

Aur. Well, then, since I must acquaint you with what you know much better than my self; I will tell you I lov'd a Cavalier, who was noble, young, and handsome; this Gentleman is since gone for *Flanders;* now whether he has preserv'd his passion inviolate or not, is that which causes my inquietude.

Bell. Trouble not your self, Madam; he's as constant as a Romance Hero.

Aur. Sir, your good news has ravish'd me most furiously; 170 but that I may have a confirmation of it, I beg only, that you would lay your commands upon his *Genius,* or *Idea,* to appear to me this night, that I may have my sentence from his mouth. This, Sir, I know is a slight effect of your Science, and yet will infinitely oblige me.

Bell. What the Devil does she call a slight effect! [*Aside.*]
————Why Lady, do you consider what you say? you desire me to shew you a man whom your self confess to be in *Flanders.*

Aur. To view him in a glass is nothing, I would speak with him in person, I mean his *Idea,* Sir.

180 *Bell.* I, but Madam, there is a vast sea betwixt us and *Flanders;* and water is an enemy to Conjuration: A witches horse you know, when he enters into water, returns into a bottle of hay again.

Aur. But, Sir, I am not so ill a *Geographer,* or to speak more

---

168 Hero] F, D; Heros Q1-3.   169 me most] S-S; most Q1-3, F, D.
175-176 [*Aside.*]————] [*aside*] Q1; [*Aside.*] Q2, D; [*Aside.* Q3 (*at right margin*);
(*aside.*) F.
180 I,] D; ∼∧ Q1-3, F.

properly, a *Chorographer,* as not to know there is a passage by
land from hence to *Flanders.*

Bell. That's true, Madam, but Magick works in a direct line.
Why should you think the Devil such an Ass to goe about?
'gad he'll not stir a step out of his road for you or any man.

190 *Aur.* Yes, for a Lady, Sir; I hope he's a person that wants not
that civility for a Lady: especially a spirit that has the honor
to belong to you, Sir.

Bell. For that matter he's your Servant, Madam; but his education has been in the fire, and he's naturally an enemy to water I assure you.

Aur. I beg his pardon for forgetting his Antipathy; but it
imports not much, Sir; for I have lately receiv'd a letter from
my Servant, that he is yet in *Spain;* and stays for a wind in
St. Sebastians.

200 *Bell.* Now I am lost past all redemption.———*Maskall*———
must you be smickering after Wenches while I am in calamity?

[*Aside.*

Mask. It must be he, I'll venture on't. [*Aside.*]———Alas Sir,
I was complaining to my self of the condition of poor *Don Melchor,* who you know is windbound at *St. Sebastians.*

Bell. Why you impudent Villain, must you offer to name
him publickly, when I have taken so much care to conceal him
all this while?

Aur. Mitigate your displeasure I beseech you; and without
making farther testimony of it, gratifie my expectances.

210 *Bell.* Well, Madam, since the Sea hinders not, you shall have
your desire. Look upon me with a fix'd eye———so———or
a little more amorously if you please.———Good. Now favour
me with your hand.

Aur. Is it absolutely necessary you should press my hand thus?

Bell. Furiously necessary, I assure you, Madam; for now I
take possession of it in the name of the *Idea* of *Don Melchor.*
Now, Madam, I am farther to desire of you, to write a Note to

---

201+ *s.d.* [*Aside.*] Q2-3, F, D; [*aside.*] Q1.
202 [*Aside.*]———] [*aside*] Q1; [*aside.*] Q2; [*Aside.* Q3 (*at right margin*);
(*Aside.*) F; [*Aside.*] D.

his Genius, wherein you desire him to appear, and this, we Men of Art, call a Compact with the *Idea's*.

220   *Aur.* I tremble furiously.

Bell. Give me your hand, I'll guide it.   [*They write.*

Mask. to Cam. Now, Lady mine, what think you of my Master?

Cam. I think I would not serve him for the world: nay, if he can know our thoughts by looking on us, we women are hypocrites to little purpose.

Mask. He can do that and more; for by casting his eyes but once upon them, he knows whether they are Maids, better than a whole Jury of Midwives.

230   *Cam.* Now Heaven defend me from him.

Mask. He has a certain small Familiar which he carries still about him, that never fails to make discovery.

Cam. See, they have done writing; not a word more, for fear he knows my voice.

Bell. One thing I had forgot, Madam; you must subscribe your name to't.

Aur. There 'tis; farewell Cavalier, keep your promise, for I expect it furiously.

Cam. If he sees me I am undone.   [*Hiding her face.*

240   *Bell. Camilla!*

Cam. starts and schreeks. Ah he has found me; I am ruin'd!

Bell. You hide your face in vain; for I see into your heart.

Cam. Then, sweet Sir, have pity on my frailty; for if my Lady has the least inkling of what we did last night, the poor Coachman will be turn'd away.   *Exit after her Lady.*

Mask. Well, Sir, how like you your New Profession?

Bell. Would I were well quit on't; I sweat all over.

Mask. But what faint-hearted Devils yours are that will not go by water! Are they all *Lancashire* Devils, of the brood of

250 *Tybert* and *Grimalkin*, that they dare not wet their feet?

Bell. Mine are honest land Devils, good plain foot Posts,

---

222   *to*] D; to Q1–3, F.   235   Madam;] ∼ , Q1–3, F, D.
249   water!] ∼ ? Q1–3, F, D.

that beat upon the hoof for me: but to save their labour, here take this, and in some disguise deliver it to *Don Melchor*.

Mask. I'll serve it upon him within this hour, when he sallyes out to his assignation with *Theodosia:* 'tis but counterfeiting my voice a little; for he cannot know me in the dark. But let me see, what are the words?   *Reads.*

Don Melchor, *if the Magique of love have any power upon your spirit, I conjure you to appear this night before me: you* 260 *may guess the greatness of my passion, since it has forc'd me to have recourse to Art: but no shape which resembles you can fright*

Aurelia.

Bell. Well, I am glad there's one point gain'd; for by this means he will be hindred to night from entertaining *Theodosia*. ———Pox on him, is he here again?

Enter Don Alonzo.

Alon. Cavalier *Ingles* I have been seeking you: I have a Present in my Pocket for you; read it by your Art and take it.

Bell. That I could do easily;———but to shew you I am gen- 270 erous, I'll none of your Present; do you think I am mercenary?

Alon. I know you will say now 'tis some Astrological question, and so 'tis perhaps.

Bell. I, 'tis the Devil of a question without dispute.

Alon. No 'tis within dispute: 'tis a certain difficulty in the Art; a Problem which you and I will discuss, with the arguments on both sides.

Bell. At this time I am not problematically given; I have a humour of complaisance upon me, and will contradict no man.

Alon. We'll but discuss a little.

280 *Bell.* By your favour I'll not discusse; for I see by the Stars that if I Dispute to day, I am infallibly threatned to be thought ignorant all my life after.

_____

276 sides.] Q2–3, F, D; ∼ , Q1.

Alon. Well, then, we'll but cast an eye together, upon my eldest Daughters Nativity.

Bell. Nativity!————

Alon. I know what you would say now, that there wants the Table of Direction for the five Hylegiacalls; the Ascendant, *Medium Cœli,* Sun, Moon, and *Sors:* but we'll take it as it is.

Bell. Never tell me that, Sir————

290 *Alon.* I know what you would say again, Sir————

Bell. 'Tis well you do, for I'll besworn I do not.————[*Aside.*

Alon. You would say, Sir————

Bell. I say, Sir, there is no doing without the Sun and Moon, and all that, Sir. And so you may make use of your Paper for your occasions. Come to a man of Art without [*Tears it.*] the Sun and Moon, and all that, Sir.————

Alon. 'Tis no matter; this shall break no squares betwixt us.

[*Gathers up the Torne Papers.*

I know what you would say now, that Men of parts are alwayes cholerick; I know it by my self, Sir.

[*He goes to match the Papers.*

Enter Don Lopez.

300 *Lop.* Don *Alonzo* in my house! this is a most happy opportunity to put my other design in execution; for if I can perswade him to bestow his Daughter on *Don Melchor,* I shall serve my Friend, though against his will: and, when *Aurelia* sees she cannot be his, perhaps she will accept my Love.   [*Aside.*

Alon. I warrant you, Sir, 'tis all piec'd right, both top, sides and bottom; for, look you, Sir, here was *Aldeboran,* and there *Cor Scorpii*————

Lop. Don *Alonzo,* I am happy to see you under my Roof: and shall take it————

288   *Sors*] F; Sors Q1–3; Stars D.   291   not.] ∼∧ Q1–3, F, D.
295–296   occasions. . . . without [*Tears it.*] . . . Sir.————] ∼ . . . . . ∼ [*tears it.*∧ . . . ∼∧———— Q1–2 (*Tears* Q2); ∼ . [*Tears it.*] . . . ∼ . . . ∼∧———— Q3; ∼ . . . . . ∼ [*tears it*∧] . . . ∼∧———— F; ∼ . . . . . ∼ . . . ∼∧————[*Tears it.*∧ D.
297   us.] Q2–3, F; ∼ : Q1, D.   299+   *s.d. Papers.*] Q2–3, F, D; ∼ , Q1.
299+   *s.d.* Don] Q2, F; *Don* Q1, Q3, D.   304   Love. [*Aside.*] Love. Q1–3, F, D.

310   *Alon.* I know what you would say, Sir, that though I am
your neighbour, this is the first time I have been here.————
[*To* Bellamy.] But, come, Sir, by *Don Lopez* his permission
let us return to our Nativity.

 Bell. Would thou wert there, in thy Mother's Belly again.
                   [*Aside.*

 Lop. But *Sennor*————   [*To* Alonzo.

 Alon. It needs not *Sennor;* I'll suppose your Compliment;
you would say that your house and all things in it are at my
service. But let us proceed without his interruption.

 Bell. By no means, Sir; this Cavalier is come on purpose to
320 perform the civilities of his house to you.

 Alon. But, good Sir————

 Bell. I know what you would say, Sir.

            Exeunt Bellamy *and* Maskall.

 Lop. No matter, let him go, Sir; I have long desir'd this
opportunity to move a Sute to you in the behalf of a Friend of
mine: if you please to allow me the hearing of it.

 Alon. With all my heart, Sir.

 Lop. He is a person of worth and vertue, and is infinitely
ambitious of the honour————

 Alon. Of being known to me; I understand you, Sir.

330 *Lop.* If you will please to favour me with your patience,
which I beg of you a second time.

 Alon. I am dumb, Sir.

 Lop. This Cavalier of whom I was speaking, is in Love————

 Alon. Satisfie your self, Sir, I'll not interrupt you.

 Lop. Sir, I am satisfied of your promise.

 Alon. If I speak one Syllable more, the Devil take me: speak
when you please.

311–312 ————[*To* Bellamy.] But, . . . Sir,] D; [*to Bellamy*————But, . . .
Sir, Q1–2 (*To* Bellamy. Q2); ————But$_\wedge$ . . . Sir, [*To* Bellamy.] Q3; [*to* bellamy.]
————But, . . . Sir, F.
314+ *s.d.* [*Aside.*] Q3, F, D; ————*Aside.* Q1–2.
315 *s.d.* [*To* Alonzo.] Q3, D; *to Alonzo.* Q1–2 (*in middle of line as dialogue*);
(*to Alonzo.*) F (*in middle of line*).
318 service. But] ~ : but Q1–3, F (service; F); Service: But D.
322+ *s.d.* Maskall] D; Maskal Q1–2, F; Mask. Q3.
336 more,] Q2–3, F, D; ~$_\wedge$ Q1.

Lop. I am going, Sir———

Alon. You need not speak twice to me to be silent: though I
340 take it somewhat ill of you to be tutor'd———

Lop. This eternal old Man will make me mad.   [*Aside.*

Alon. Why, when do you begin, Sir? How long must a man
wait for you? pray make an end of what you have to say
quickly, that I may speak in my turn too.

Lop. This Cavalier is in Love———

Alon. You told me that before, Sir; Do you speak Oracles
that you require this strict attention? either let me share the
talk with you or I am gone.

Lop. Why, Sir, I am almost mad to tell you, and you will
350 not suffer me.

Alon. Will you never have done, Sir? I must tell you, Sir,
you have tatled long enough; and 'tis now good Manners to
hear me speak. Here's a Torrent of words indeed; a very *im-*
petus dicendi; Will you never have done?

Lop. I will be heard in spight of you.

> *This next Speech of* Lopez, *and the next of* Alonzo's, *with*
> *both their Replies, are to be spoken at one time; both*
> *raising their voices by little and little, till they baul, and*
> *come up close to shoulder one another.*

Lop. There's one *Don Melchor de Guzman,* a Friend and Acquaintance of mine, that is desperately in Love with your eldest
Daughter *Donna Theodosia.*

Alon. at the same time. 'Tis the sentence of a Philosopher,
360 *Loquere ut te videam;* Speak that I may know thee; now if you
take away the power of speaking from me———

> *Both pause a little; then speak together again.*

Lop. I'll try the Language of the Law; sure the Devil cannot
out-talke that Gibberish.———For this *Don Melchor* of *Madrid*
aforesaid, as premised, I request, move, and supplicate, that you

---

338   Sir———] ~ ; Q1–2; ~ . Q3, F, D.   342   Why,] Q3; ~∧ Q1–2, F, D.
351   Sir?] Q3; ~ ; Q1–2, D; ~ : F.   354   *dicendi;*] Q3, D; ~ , Q1–2, F.
363   Gibberish.] ~∧ Q1–3, F, D.

would give, bestow, Marry, and give in Mariage, this your Daughter aforesaid, to the Cavalier aforesaid.————Not yet; thou Devil of a Man thou shalt be silent.————

[*Exit* Lopez *running.*

Alon. at the same time with Lopez *his last speech, and after* Lopez *is run out.* Oh, how I hate, abominate, detest and abhor,
370 these perpetual Talkers, Disputants, Controverters, and Duellers of the Tongue! But, on the other side, if it be not permitted to prudent men to speak their minds, appositely, and to the purpose and in few words————If, I say, the prudent must be Tongue-ty'd; then let Great Nature be destroy'd; let the order of all things be turn'd topsy-turvy; let the Goose devour the Fox; let the Infants preach to their Great-Grandsires; let the tender Lamb pursue the Woolfe, and the Sick prescribe to the Physician. Let Fishes live upon dry-land, and the Beasts of the Earth inhabit in the Water.————Let the fearful Hare————

Enter Lopez *with a Bell, and rings it in his ears.*

380 *Alon.* Help, help, murder, murder, murder!

Exit Alonzo *running.*
Lop. There was no way but this to be rid of him.

Enter a Servant.

Serv. Sir, there are some Women without in Masquerade; and, I believe, persons of Quality, who are come to Play here.
Lop. Bring 'em in with all respect.   [*Exit Servant.*

Enter again the Servant, after him Jacinta, Beatrix,
and other Ladies and Gentlemen; all Masqued.

---

366   aforesaid.————Not] ~_Λ————not Q1–3, F, D (Not Q3).
366   yet;] Q3; ~ , Q1–2, F, D.   367   silent.] Q3; ~_Λ Q1–2, F, D.
368   at] F; *At* Q1–3, D.
368–369   *Lopez . . . Lopez*] Lopez . . . Lopez Q1–3, F, D.
369   *out.*] Q2–3, F, D; ~_Λ Q1.   380   murder!] Q3, D; ~ . Q1–2, F.
384   s.d. [*Exit Servant.*] Q3; omitted from *Q1–2, F, D.*

Lop. Cavaliers, and Ladies, you are welcome: I wish I had more company to entertain you:———Oh, here comes one sooner then I expected.

Enter Wildblood *and* Maskall.

Wild. I have swept your Gaming-house, i'faith; *Ecce signum.*
[*Shows Gold.*

Lop. Well, here's more to be had of these Ladies, if it be
390 your fortune.

Wild. The first Stakes I would play for, should be their Vailes, and Visor Masques.

Jac. to Beat. Do you think he will not know us?

Beat. If you keep your Design of passing for an *African.*

Jac. Well, now I shall make an absolute trial of him; for, being thus incognita, I shall discover if he make Love to any of you. As for the Gallantry of his Serenade, we will not be indebted to him, for we will make him another with our Guittars.

400 *Beat.* I'll whisper your intention to the Servant, who shall deliver it to *Don Lopez.*   [Beatrix *whispers to the Servant.*

Serv. to Lopez. Sir, the Ladies have commanded me to tell you, that they are willing, before they Play, to present you with a Dance; and to give you an Essay of their Guittars.

Lop. They much honor me.

A DANCE.

After the Dance the Cavaliers take the Ladies and Court them.
Wildblood *takes* Jacinta.

Wild. While you have been Singing, Lady, I have been Praying: I mean, that your Face and Wit may not prove equal

---

387+   *s.d.* Maskall] D; Maskal Q1–3, F.   388   i'faith;] ～ , Q1–3, F, D.
401   *s.d. Servant*] Q3, F, D; Servant Q1–2.   402   *to*] Q3, D; to Q1–2, F.
405+   *s.d. Cavaliers . . . Ladies*] D; Cavaliers . . . Ladies Q1–3, F.
405+   *s.d.* Jacinta.] Q3, F, D; ～ ; Q1–2.

to your Dancing; for, if they be, there's a heart gone astray to my knowledge.

410   *Jac.* If you pray against me before you have seen me, you'll curse me when you have look'd on me.

Wild. I believe I shall have cause to do so, if your Beauty be as killing as I imagine it.

Jac. 'Tis true, I have been flatter'd in my own Country, with an opinion of a little handsomness; but, how it will pass in *Spain* is a question.

Wild. Why Madam, Are you not of *Spain?*

Jac. No, Sir, of *Marocco:* I onely came hither to see some of my Relations who are setled here, and turn'd *Christians,*
420   since the expulsion of my Countrymen the *Moors.*

Wild. Are you then a *Mahometan?*

Jac. A *Musullman* at your service.

Wild. A *Musullwoman* say you? I protest by your voice I should have taken you for a *Christian* Lady of my acquaintance.

Jac. It seems you are in love then: if so, I have done with you. I dare not invade the Dominions of another Lady; especially in a Country where my Ancestors have been so unfortunate.

Wild. Some little liking I might have, but that was onely a
430   morning-dew, 'tis drawn up by the Sun-shine of your Beauty: I find your *African-Cupid* is a much surer Archer then ours of *Europe.* Yet would I could see you; one look would secure your victory.

Jac. I'll reserve my Face to gratifie your imagination with it; make what head you please, and set it on my Shoulders.

Wild. Well, Madam, an eye, a nose, or a lip shall break no squares: the Face is but a spans breadth of beauty; and where there is so much besides, I'll never stand with you for that.

Jac. But, in earnest, Do you love me?

440   *Wild.* I, by *Alha* do I, most extreamly: you have Wit in abundance, you Dance to a Miracle, you Sing like an Angel, and I believe you look like a Cherubim.

Jac. And can you be constant to me?

---

434   it;] D; ∼ , Q1-3, F.

Wild. By *Mahomet,* can I.

Jac. You Swear like a *Turk,* Sir; but, take heed: for our Prophet is a severe punisher of Promise-breakers.

Wild. Your Prophet's a Cavalier; I honour your Prophet and his Law, for providing so well for us Lovers in the other World, Black Eyes, and Fresh-Maidenheads every day; go thy way little *Mahomet,* i'faith thou shalt have my good word. But, by his favour Lady, give me leave to tell you, that we of the Uncircumcised, in a civil way, as Lovers, have somewhat the advantage of your *Musullman.*

Jac. The Company are rejoyn'd, and set to play; we must go to 'em: Adieu, and when you have a thought to throw away, bestow it on your Servant *Fatyma.*   [*She goes to the Company.*

Wild. This Lady *Fatyma* pleases me most infinitely: now am I got among the *Hamets,* the *Zegrys,* and the *Bencerrages.* Hey, What work will the *Wildbloods* make among the *Cids* and the *Bens* of the *Arabians!*

Beat. to Jac. False, or true, Madam?

Jac. False as Hell; but by Heaven I'll fit him for't: Have you the high-running Dice about you?

Beat. I got them on purpose, Madam.

Jac. You shall see me win all their Mony; and when I have done, I'll return in my own person, and ask him for the money which he promis'd me.

Beat. 'Twill put him upon a streight to be so surpriz'd: but, let us to the Table; the Company stayes for us.

                                   [*The Company sit.*

Wild. What is the Ladies Game, Sir?

Lop. Most commonly they use Raffle. That is, to throw with three Dice, till Duplets and a chance be thrown; and the highest Duplets wins except you throw *In and In,* which is call'd Raffle; and that wins all.

Wild. I understand it. Come, Lady, 'tis no matter what I lose; the greatest stake, my heart, is gone already.   [*To* Jacinta.
                    They play: and the rest by couples.

---

461   true,] F, D; ~∧ Q1–3.   473   *and*] Q2–3, F; and Q1, D.
475   it.] ~ : Q1–3, F, D.   476   *s.d.* Jacinta] Q2–3, F, D; *Jacinta* Q1.

Wild. So, I have a good chance, two quaters and a sice.

Jac. Two sixes and a trey wins it.——— *Sweeps the money.*

Wild. No matter; I'll try my fortune once again: what have
480 I here, two sixes and a quater?———an hundred Pistols on
that throw.

Jac. I take you, Sir.———[*Aside.*] *Beatrix* the high running
Dice.———

Beat. Here Madam.———

Jac. Three fives: I have won you Sir.

Wild. I, the pox take me for't, you have won me: it would
never have vex'd me to have lost my money to a *Christian;*
but to a Pagan, an Infidel———

Mask. Pray, Sir, leave off while you have some money.

490 *Wild.* Pox of this Lady *Fatyma!* Raffle thrice together, I am
out of patience.

Mask. to him. Sir, I beseech you if you will lose, to lose *en
Cavalier.*

Wild. Tol de ra, tol de ra—pox and curse—tol de ra, *&c.*
What the Devil did I mean to play with this Brunet of *Afrique?*
The Ladies rise.

Wild. Will you be gone already Ladies?

Lop. You have won our money; but however, we are acknowledging to you for the honor of your company.

Jacinta *makes a sign of farewel to* Wildblood.

Wild. Farewell Lady *Fatyma. Exeunt all but* Wild. *and* Mask.

500 *Mask.* All the company took notice of your concernment.

Wild. 'Tis no matter; I do not love to fret inwardly, as
your silent losers do, and in the mean time be ready to choak
for want of vent.

Mask. Pray consider your condition a little; a younger
Brother in a foreign Country, living at a high rate, your money
lost, and without hope of a supply. Now curse if you think
good.

---

478 s.d. *Sweeps*] Q2–3, F, D; *sweeps* Q1.   480 here,] Q3, D; ~∧ Q1–2; ~ ? F.

482 [*Aside.*] *Beatrix*] *Beatrix* Q1–3, F, D.

487 *Christian*] Q2–3, F; Christian Q1, D.   488 Infidel] D; ~ . Q1–3, F.

492 *Mask.*] Q2–3, F, D; Mask. Q1.   497 however,] ~∧ Q1–3, F, D.

Wild. No, now I will laugh at my self most unmercifully:
for my condition is so ridiculous that 'tis past cursing. The
10 pleasantest part of the adventure is, that I have promis'd 300
pistols to *Jacinta:* but there is no remedy, they are now fair
Fatyma's.

Mask. Fatyma!

Wild. I, I, a certain *African* Lady of my acquaintance whom
you know not.

Mask. But who is here, Sir!

Enter Jacinta *and* Beatrix *in their own shapes.*

Wild. Madam, what happy star has conducted you hither to
night!————A thousand Devils of this fortune!   [*Aside.*
Jac. I was told you had Ladies here and fiddles; so I came
520 partly for the divertisement, and partly out of jealousie.

Wild. Jealousie! why sure you do not think me a Pagan, an
Infidel? But the company's broke up you see. Am I to wait upon
you home, or will you be so kind to take a hard lodging with me
to night?

Jac. You shall have the honor to lead me to my Father's.

Wild. No more words then, let's away to prevent discovery.

Beat. For my part I think he has a mind to be rid of you.

Wild. No: but if your Lady should want sleep, 'twould spoil
the lustre of her eyes to morrow. There were a Conquest lost.

530 *Jac.* I am a peaceable Princess, and content with my own; I
mean your heart, and purse; for the truth is, I have lost my
money to night in *Masquerade,* and am come to claim your
promise of supplying me.

Wild. You make me happy by commanding me: to morrow
morning my servant shall wait upon you with 300 pistols.

Jac. But I left my company with promise to return to play.

Wild. Play on tick, and lose the *Indies,* I'll discharge it all to
morrow.

Jac. To night, if you'll oblige me.

540 *Wild. Maskall,* go and bring me 300 pistols immediately.

518   ————A] D; ∧~ Q1-3, F.   518 *s.d. Aside*] Q2-3, F, D; *aside* Q1.

Mask. Are you mad Sir?

Wild. Do you expostulate you rascall! how he stares; I'll be hang'd if he have not lost my gold at play: if you have, confess you had best, and perhaps I'll pardon you; but if you do not confess I'll have no mercy: did you lose it?

Mask. Sir, 'tis not for me to dispute with you.

Wild. Why then let me tell you, you did lose it.

Jac. I, as sure as e're he had it, I dare swear for him: but commend to you for a kind Master, that can let your Servant play
550 off 300 pistols, without the least sign of anger to him.

Beat. 'Tis a sign he has a greater banck in store to comfort him.

Wild. Well, Madam, I must confess I have more then I will speak of at this time; but till you have given me satisfaction——

Jac. Satisfaction; why, are you offended, Sir?

Wild. Heaven! that you should not perceive it in me: I tell you I am mortally offended with you.

Jac. Sure 'tis impossible.

560 *Wild.* You have done nothing, I warrant, to make a man jealous: going out a gaming in *Masquerade,* at unseasonable hours, and losing your money, at play; that loss above all provokes me.

Beat. I believe you; because she comes to you for more.
                                                          [*Aside.*

Jac. Is this the quarrel? I'll clear it immediately.

Wild. 'Tis impossible you should clear it; I'll stop my ears if you but offer it. There's no satisfaction in the point.

Jac. You'll hear me?——

Wild. To do this in the beginning of an amour, and to a jealous servant as I am; had I all the wealth of *Peru,* I would not let
570 go one Maravedis to you.

Jac. To this I answer——

Wild. Answer nothing, for it will but inflame the quarrel

---

556 why,] D; ~∧ Q1–3, F.
559 *Jac.*] Q1 (*some copies*), Q2–3, F, D; *Jac*∧ Q1 (*period did not print in copy text*).
560 nothing, . . . warrant,] D; ~∧ . . . ~∧ Q1; ~∧ . . . ~ , Q2–3, F.
563+ *s.d. Aside.*] Q2–3, F, D; *Aside.*] Q1.

betwixt us: I must come to my self by little and little; and
when I am ready for satisfaction I will take it: but at present
it is not for my honor to be friends.

Beat. Pray let us neighbour Princes interpose a little.

Wild. When I have conquer'd, you may interpose; but at
present the mediation of all *Christendome* would be fruitless.

Jac. Though *Christendome* can do nothing with you, yet I
hope an *African* may prevail. Let me beg you for the sake of
the Lady *Fatyma.*

Wild. I begin to suspect that Lady *Fatyma* is no better than
she should be. If she be turn'd *Christian* again I am undone.

Jac. By *Alha* I am afraid on't too: By *Mahomet* I am.

Wild. Well, well, Madam, any man may be overtaken with
an oath; but I never meant to perform it with her: you know
no oathes are to be kept with Infidels. But———

Jac. No, the love you made was certainly a design of charitie
you had to reconcile the two Religions. There's scarce such another man in *Europe* to be sent Apostle to convert the *Moor*
Ladies.

Wild. Faith I would rather widen their breaches then make
'em up.

Jac. I see there's no hope of a reconcilement with you; and
therefore I give it o're as desperate.

Wild. You have gain'd your point, you have my money; and
I was only angry because I did not know 'twas you who had it.

Jac. This will not serve your turn, Sir; what I have got I have
conquer'd from you.

Wild. Indeed you use me like one that's conquer'd; for you
have plunder'd me of all I had.

Jac. I only disarm'd you for fear you should rebell again;
for if you had the sinews of warr I am sure you would be flying
out.

Wild. Dare but to stay without a new Servant till I am flush
again, and I will love you, and treat you, and present you at that

578 *Christendome*] Q2–3, F; Christendome Q1, D.
579 *Christendome*] Q2–3, F; Christendome Q1, D.
583 *Christian*] Christian Q1–3, F, D.

unreasonable rate; that I will make you an example to all un-believing Mistresses.

Jac. Well, I will trie you once more; but you must make haste
610 then, that we may be within our time; methinks our love is drawn out so subtle already, that 'tis near breaking.

Wild. I will have more care of it on my part, than the kindred of an old Pope have to preserve him.

Jac. Adieu; for this time I wipe off your score,
Till you're caught tripping in some new amour. [*Ex. Women.*

Mask. You have us'd me very kindly, Sir, I thank you.

Wild. You deserv'd it for not having a lye ready for my occa-sions. A good Servant should be no more without it, than a Souldier without his armes. But prethee advise me what's to be
620 done to get *Jacinta.*

Mask. You have lost her, or will lose her by your submitting: if we men could but learn to value our selves, we should soon take down our Mistresses from all their Altitudes, and make 'em dance after our Pipes, longer perhaps than we had a mind to't.————But I must make haste, or I shall lose *Don Mel-chor.*————

Wild. Call *Bellamy,* we'll both be present at thy enterprise: then I'll once more to the Gaming-house with my small stock, for my last refuge: if I win, I have wherewithall to mollifie
630 *Jacinta.*

　　　　　　If I throw out I'll bear it off with huffing;
　　　　　　And snatch the money like a Bulli-Ruffin.　　*Exeunt.*

ACT IV.　SCENE I.

Enter Bellamy, Wildblood: Maskall *in a visor.*

Bell. Here comes one, and in all probability it must be *Don Melchor* going to *Theodosia.*

614　score,] F, D; ~. Q1–3.
ACT IV. SCENE I.] D; ACT. IV. Q1; ACT IV. Q2–3, F.
s.d. Enter] D; *omitted from Q1–3, F.*
s.d. Bellamy, Wildblood: Maskall] Q3, F, D; *Bellamy, Wildblood: Maskall* Q1–2.

Mask. Stand close, and you shall see me serve the Writ upon him.

Enter Don Melchor.

Wild. Now, *Maskall.*

Mask. I stay'd here, Sir, by express order from the Lady *Aurelia,* to deliver you this Note; and to desire you from her to meet her immediately in the Garden.

Mel. Do you hear friend!

10   *Mask.* Not a syllable more, Sir, I have perform'd my orders.

Maskall *retires to his Masters.*

Mel. He's gone; and 'tis in vain for me to look after him. What envious Devil has discover'd to *Aurelia* that I am in Town? it must be *Don Lopez,* who to advance his own pretensions to her, has endeavour'd to ruine mine.

Wild. It works rarely.

Mel. But I am resolv'd to see *Aurelia;* if it be but to defeat him.   *Exit* Melchor.

Wild. Let's make haste after him; I long to see the end of this adventure.

20   *Mask.* Sir, I think I see some women coming yonder.

Bell. Well; I'll leave you to your adventures; while I prosecute my own.

Wild. I warrant you have made an assignation to instruct some Lady in the Mathematicks.

Bell. I'll not tell you my design; because if it does not succeed you shall not laugh at me.   *Exit* Bellamy.

Enter Beatrix; *and* Jacinta *in the habit of a* Mulatta.

Wild. Let us withdraw a little, and see if they will come this way.

4+   *s.d.* Don Melchor] Q3, F; *Don Melchor* Q1; Don *Melchor* Q2; *Don* Melchor D.

10+   *s.d.* Maskall] Maskal Q1–3, F; Mask. D.

13–14 pretensions] Q2–3, F, D; pretentensions Q1.

26+   *s.d.* Mulatta] D; *Mulatta* Q1–3, F.

Beat. We are right, Madam, 'tis certainly your *Englishman,*
30 and his Servant with him. But why this second triall, when you
engag'd to break with him, if he fail'd in the first?

Jac. 'Tis true, he has been a little inconstant; cholerick, or so.

Beat. And it seems you are not contented with those vices;
but are searching him for more. This is the folly of a bleeding
Gamester, who will obstinately pursue a losing hand.

Jac. On t'other side you would have me throw up my Cards
before the game be lost: let me make this one more triall, when
he has money whether he will give it me, and then if he
fails————

40 *Beat.* You'l forgive him agen.

Jac. He's already in Purgatory; but the next offence shall put
him in the pit past all redemption; prethee sing to draw him
nearer: Sure he cannot know me in this disguise.

Beat. Make haste then; for I have more Irons in the fire:
when I have done with you I have another assignation of my
Lady *Theodosia's* to *Don Melchor.*

SONG.

Calm was the Even, and cleer was the Skie,
  And the new budding flowers did spring,
When all alone went Amyntas *and I*
50   *To hear the sweet Nightingale sing;*
I sate, and he laid him down by me,
  But scarcely his breath he could draw;
For when with a fear he began to draw near,
  He was dash'd with A ha ha ha ha!

2.

He blush'd to himself, and lay still for a while,
  And his modesty curb'd his desire;
But streight I convinc'd all his fear with a smile,
  Which added new flames to his fire.

---

51 *me,*] o1a, o1b, d1–7, f1–3; ∼ ; Q1–3, F, D; ∼ᴧ M4–5; ∼ . M6.
54 A ha ha ha ha] *A ha ha ha ha* Q1–3, F, D, o1a, o1b, d1, d3–5, d7, f1–3,
M4–6; *a* ha ha ha ha d2, d6.

O Sylvia, *said he,* you are cruel,
60   To keep your poor Lover in awe;
Then once more he prest with his hand to my brest,
But was dash'd with A ha ha ha ha!

3.
I knew 'twas his passion that caus'd all his fear;
And therefore I pity'd his case:
I whisper'd him softly there's no body near,
And layd my cheek close to his face:
But as he grew bolder and bolder,
A Shepherd came by us and saw;
And just as our bliss we began with a kiss,
70   *He laugh'd out with* A ha ha ha ha!

Wild. If you dare be the *Sylvia,* Lady, I have brought you a
more confident *Amyntas,* than that bashful Gentleman in your
Song.———   *Goes to lay hold of her.*

Jac. Hold, hold; Sir, I am only an Ambassadress sent you from
a Lady, I hope you will not violate the Laws of Nations.

Wild. I was only searching for your Letters of Credence: but
methinks with that beauty you look more like a Herauld that
comes to denounce war to all mankind.———

Jac. One of the Ladies in the Masque to night has taken a
80 liking to you; and sent you by me this purse of gold, in recompence of that she saw you lose.

Wild. And she expects in return of it, that I should wait on
her; I'll do't. Where lives she? I am desperately in love with her.

Jac. Why, Can you love her unknown?

Wild. I have a Banque of Love, to supply every ones occa-

59   O] *O* Q1–3, F, D, o1a, o1b, d1–7, f1–3, M4–6.
59–60   you . . . [*to*] . . . awe] *in italics in Q1–3, F, D, o1a, o1b, d1–7, f1–3, M4–6.*
62   A ha ha ha ha!] *A ha ha ha ha.* Q1–3, F, D, o1a, o1b, d1, d3–5, d7, f1–3,
M4–6 (*ha!* F; *ha*ᴧ M6); *a ha ha ha ha.* d2, d6.
70   laugh'd] Q2–3, F, D; *laughd* Q1, M6; *burst* o1a, d1–6; *laughs* o1b, M4;
laught d7, f1–3, M5.
70   A ha ha ha ha!] *A ha ha ha ha.* Q1–3, F, D, o1a, o1b, d1, d3–5, d7, f1–3,
M4–6 (*ha!* F; *ha,* d3; *ha*ᴧ M6); *a ha ha ha ha.* d2, d6.
73   Song.] ∼ᴧ Q1–3, F, D.   83   do't.] Q3; ∼ , Q1–2, F, D.

sions; some for her, some for another, and some for you; charge what you will upon me, I pay all at sight, and without questioning who brought the Bill.

Jac. Heyday, You dispatch your Mistresses as fast, as if you
90 meant to o're-run all Woman-kind: sure you aime at the Universal-Monarchy.

Wild. Now I think on't, I have a foolish fancy to send thy Lady a taste of my love by thee.

Jac. 'Tis impossible your love should be so humble, to descend to a *Mulatta*.

Wild. One would think so, but I cannot help it. Gad, I think the reason is because there's something more of sin in thy colour then in ours. I know not what's the matter, but a *Turky-Cock* is not more provok'd at red, than I bristle at the sight of black.
100 Come, be kinder to me. Young, and slip an opportunity? 'Tis an Evening lost out of your life.

Jac. These fine things you have said over a thousand times; your cold Compliment's the cold Pye of love which you serve up to every new guest whom you invite.

Wild. Come; because thou art very moving, here's part of the Gold, which thou brought'st to corrupt me for thy Lady: truth is, I had promis'd a summ to a *Spanish* Lady————but thy eyes have allur'd it from me.

Jac. You'll repent to morrow.
110 *Wild.* Let to morrow starve: or provide for himself, as to night has done: to morrow is a cheat in love, and I will not trust it.

Jac. I, but Heaven that sees all things————

Wild. Heaven that sees all things will say nothing: that is, all eyes and no tongue; *Et la lune & les estoiles,*————you know the Song.

Jac. A poor slave as I am————

Wild. It has been always my humour to love downward. I love to stoop to my prey, and to have it in my power to Sowse
120 at when I please. When a man comes to a great Lady, he is

---

99 than] Q3, D; then Q1-2, F.

fain to approach her with fear and reverence; methinks there's something of Godliness in't.

Jac. Yet I cannot believe, but the meanness of my habit must needs scandalize you.

Wild. I'll tell thee my friend and so forth, that I exceedingly honour course Linnen; 'tis as proper sometimes in an under Garment, as a course Towel is to rub and scrub me.

Jac. Now I am altogether of the other side, I can love no where but above me: methinks the ratling of a Coach and six,
130 sounds more eloquently, than the best Harrangue a Wit could make me.

Wild. Do you make no more esteem of a Wit then?

Jac. His commendations serve onely to make others have a mind to me; He does but say Grace to me like a *Chaplain;* and like him is the last that shall fall on. He ought to get no more by it, than a poor Silk-weaver does by the Ribband which he workes, to make a Gallant fine.

Wild. Then what is a Gentleman to hope from you?

Jac. To be admitted to pass my time with, while a better
140 comes: to be the lowest step in my Stair-case, for a Knight to mount upon him, and a Lord upon him, and a Marquess upon him, and a Duke upon him, till I get as high as I can climb.

Wild. For ought I see, the Great Ladies have the Appetites which you Slaves should have; and you Slaves the Pride which ought to be in Ladies. For, I observe, that all women of your condition are like the women of the Play-house, still Piquing at each other, who shall go the best Drest, and in the Richest Habits: till you work up one another by your high flying, as the *Heron* and *Jerfalcon* do. If you cannot outshine your fellow
150 with one Lover, you fetch her up with another: and in short, all you get by it is onely to put Finery out of countenance; and to make the Ladies of Quality go plain, because they will avoid the Scandal of your bravery.

Beat. running in. Madam, come away; I hear company in the Garden.

---

130   than] Q3, F, D; then Q1–2.   136   than] Q3, F, D; then Q1–2.

Wild. You are not going?

Jac. Yes, to cry out a Rape if you follow me.

Wild. However, I am glad you have left your treasure behind you: farewel Fairie.

160   *Jac.* Farewel Changeling.————[*Aside.*] Come *Beatrix.*

[*Exeunt Women.*

Mask. Do you know how you came by this money, Sir? you think, I warrant, that it came by fortune.

Wild. No, Sirrah, I know it came by my own industry. Did not I come out diligently to meet this gold, in the very way it was to come? what could Fate do less for me? they are such thoughtless, and undesigning rogues as you, that make a drudge of poor providence, and set it a shifting for you. Give me a brave fellow like my self; that if you throw him down into the world, lights every where upon his legs, and helps himself without

170 being beholding to Fate, that is the Hospital of fools.

Mask. But after all your jollitie, what think you if it was *Jacinta* that gave it you in this disguise? I am sure I heard her call *Beatrix* as she went away.

Wild. Umh! thou awaken'st a most villainous apprehension in me! methought indeed I knew the voice; but the face was such an evidence against it! if it were so she is lost for ever.

Mask. And so is *Beatrix!*

Wild. Now could I cut my throat for madness.

Mask. Now could I break my neck for despair; if I could find

180 a precipice absolutely to my liking.

Wild. 'Tis in vain to consider on't. There's but one way; go you *Maskall,* and find her out, and invent some excuse for me, and be sure to beg leave I may come and wait upon her with the gold before she sleeps.

Mask. In the mean time you'l be thinking at your lodging.

Wild. But make haste then to relieve me; for I think over all my thoughts in half an hour.

Exit Maskall.

---

160 Changeling.————[*Aside.*]] ~ʌ———— Q1–3, F, D.
182 *Maskall*] D; *Maskal* Q1–3, F.   185 *Mask.*] Q2–3, F, D; *Mak.* Q1.
187+ *s.d.* Maskall] Q2–3, F, D; *Maskall* Q1.

Wild. solus. Hang't, now I think on't, I shall be but melan-
cholique at my Lodging, I'll go pass my hour at the Gaming-
house, and make use of this money while I have tools, to win
more to it. Stay, let me see, I have the box and throw. My *Don*
he sets me ten pistols; I nick him: ten more, I sweep them too.
Now in all reason he is nettled, and sets me twenty: I win them
too. Now he kindles, and butters me with forty. They are all my
own: in fine, he is vehement, and bleeds on to fourscore or an
hundred; and I not willing to tempt fortune, come away a
moderate winner of 200 pistols.

> *The Scene opens and discovers* Aurelia *and* Camilla: *be-
> hind them a Table and lights set on it. The Scene is a
> Garden with an Arbour in it.*

The Garden dore opens! How now, *Aurelia* and *Camilla* in expectation of *Don Melchor* at the Garden door; I'll away lest I
prevent the designe, and within this half hour come sailing
back with full pockets, as wantonly as a laden Galleon from
the *Indies*.   *Exit.*

Aur. But dost thou think the *Englishman* can keep his promise? for I confess I furiously desire to see the *Idea* of *Don
Melchor.*

Cam. But, Madam, if you should see him, it will not be he,
but the Devil in his likeness; and then why should you desire it?

Aur. In effect 'tis a very dark *Enigma;* and one must be very
spiritual to understand it. But be what it will, bodie or fantome,
I am resolv'd to meet it.

Cam. Can you do it without fear?

Aur. No; I must avow it, I am furiously fearful; but yet I am
resolv'd to sacrifice all things to my love. Therefore let us pass
over that chapter.   Don Melchor *without.*

Cam. Do you hear, Madam, there's one treading already;
how if it be he?

Aur. If it be he; that is to say his Specter, that is to say his
Fantome, that is to say his *Idea,* that is to say, He and not he.

---

188   *Wild.*] Q2–3, F, D; ∼∧ Q1.
214   *s.d.* Don Melchor] Q2–3, F, D (*Don*); *Don Melchor* Q1.
218   *Idea*] Idea Q1–3, F, D.

Cam. crying out. Ah, Madam, 'tis he himself; but he's as big
220 again as he us'd to be, with eyes like sawcers.————I'll save my
self.   *Runs under the table.*

Enter Don Melchor: *they both shreek.*

Aur. Oh heaven! humanitie is not able to support it.
                                                          [*Running.*
Mel. Dear *Aurelia,* what mean you?
Aur. The Tempter has imitated his voice too. Avoid, avoid,
Specter!
Cam. If he should find me under the table now!
Mel. Is it thus my Dear that you treat your Servant?
Aur. I am not thy Dear; I renounce thee, spirit of darkness.
Mel. This Spirit of darkness is come to see an Angel of light
230 by her command; and to assure her of his constancy, that he will
be hers eternally.
Aur. Away Infernal, 'tis not thee, 'tis the true *Don Melchor*
that I would see.
Mel. Hell and Furies.
Aur. Heaven and Angels! Ah————   [*Runs out shreeking.*
Mel. This is a riddle past my finding out, to send for me, and
then to shun me; but here's one shall resolve it for me. *Camilla,*
what dost thou there?
Cam. Help, help, I shall be carried away, bodily.
     She rises up, overthrows the Table and lights, and runs out.
     The Scene Shuts.
240 *Mel. alone.* Why *Aurelia, Camilla!* they are both run out of
hearing! This amazes me; what can the meaning of it be? Sure
she has heard of my unfaithfulness, and was resolv'd to punish
me by this contrivance! to put an affront upon me by this
abrupt departure, as I did on her by my seeming absence.

219   himself] Q2–3, F, D; nimself Q1.   221   self.] Q3, F, D; ~∧ Q1–2.
221   *s.d. Runs*] Q2–3, F, D; *runs* Q1.
222+   *s.d. Running*] Q2–3, F, D; *running* Q1.
224–225   too. Avoid, avoid, Specter!] too; avoid, avoid∧ Specter. Q1–3, F, D.
235   *s.d.* [*Runs*] Q2–3, F, D; *runs* Q1.   237   me.] ~ : Q1–3, F, D.
242   unfaithfulness] Q1 (*corrected state*), Q2–3, F, D; unfathfulness Q1 (*uncorrected state*).

Enter Theodosia *and* Beatrix.

Theo. Don *Melchor!* is it you my Love that have frighted *Aurelia* so terribly?

Mel. Alas, Madam, I know not; but coming hither by your appointment, and thinking my self secure in the night without disguise, perhaps it might work upon her fancie, because she 250 thought me absent.

Theo. Since 'tis so unluckily fallen out that she knows you are at *Madrid,* it can no longer be kept a secret; therefore you must now pretend openly to me, and run the risque of a denial from my Father.

Mel. O, Madam, there's no question but he'll refuse me: for alas, what is it he can see in me worthy of that honor? or if he should be so partial to me, as some in the world are, to think me valiant, learned, and not altogether a fool, yet my want of fortune would weigh down all.

260 *Theo.* When he has refus'd you his consent, I may with Justice dispose of my self; and that, while you are constant, shall never be to any but your self: in witness of which, accept this Diamond as a Pledge of my hearts firmness to you.

Beat. Madam, Your Father is coming this way.

Theo. 'Tis no matter; do not stir; since he must know you are return'd, let him now see you.

Enter Don Alonzo.

Alon. Daughter, What make you here at this unseasonable hour?

Theo. Sir,———

70 *Alon.* I know what you would say, That you heard a noise, and ran hither to see what it might be———Bless us! Who is this with you?

Mel. 'Tis your servant Don *Melchor;* just return'd from *St. Sebastians.*

266+   *s.d.* Don] *Don* Q1–3, F, D.   273   *Don*] Don Q1–3, F, D.
273   *St.*] Q2, F; St. Q1, Q3, D.

Alon. But, Sir, I thought you had been upon the Sea for *Flanders.*

Mel. I had so design'd it.

Alon. But, Why came you back from *St. Sebastians?*

Mel. As for that, Sir, 'tis not material———

280 *Theo.* An unexpected Law Sute has call'd him back from *St. Sebastians.*

Alon. And, How fares my Son-in-Law that lives there?

Melch. In Catholique health, Sir.

Alon. Have you brought no Letters from him?

Mel. I had, Sir, but I was set on by the way, by Pickerons: and, in spight of my resistance, rob'd, and my Portmantue taken from me.

Theo. And this was that which he was now desiring me to excuse to you.

290 *Alon.* If my Credit, Friends, or Counsel can do you any service in your Sute, I hope you will command them freely.

Mel. When I have dispatch'd some private business I shall not fail to trouble you; till then, humbly kisses your hands, the most oblig'd of your servants.——— *Exit* Melchor.

Alon. Daughter, now this Cavalier is gone, What occasion brought you out so late? I know what you would say, That it is Melancholy; a Tincture of the Hypocondriaque you mean: but, What cause have you for this Melancholy? give me your hand, and answer me without Ambages or Ambiguities.

300 *Theo.* He will find out I have given away my Ring.———I must prevent him. [*Aside.*]———Sir, I am asham'd to confess it to you; but, in hope of your indulgence, I have lost the Table Diamond you gave me.

Alon. You would say, The fear of my displeasure has caus'd this perturbation in you; well, do not disquiet your self too much, you say 'tis gone; I say so too. 'Tis stollen; and that by some Thief I take it: but, I will go and consult the *Astrologer* immediately. [*He is going.*

---

278 *St.*] Q2, F; St. Q1, Q3, D.
294 servants.] D; ~∧ Q1–3, F.
301 him. [*Aside.*]] him Q1–3, F, D.

280 *St.*] Q2, F; St. Q1, Q3, D.
300 Ring.] ~∧ Q1–3, F, D.

Theo. What have I done? to avoid one inconvenience, I have run into another: this Devil of an *Astrologer* will discover that *Don Melchor* has it.   [*Aside.*

Alon. When did you lose this Diamond? the minute and second I should know; but the hour will serve for the Degree ascending.

Theo. Sir, the precise time I know not; but, it was betwixt six and seven this evening, as near as I can guess.

Alon. 'Tis enough; by all the Stars I'll have it for you: Therefore go in, and suppose it on your finger.

Beat. I'll watch you at a distance, Sir, that my *Englishman* may have wherewithall to answer you.———   [*Aside.*

Exit Theo. Beat.

Alon. This melancholy wherewith my Daughter laboureth, is———a———I know what I would say, is a certain species of the Hysterical Diseases; or a certain motion, caused by a certain appetite, which at a certain time heaveth in her, like a certain motion of an Earthquake.———

Enter Bellamy.

Bell. This is the place, and very near the time that *Theodosia* appoints her meeting with *Don Melchor*. He is this night otherwise dispos'd of with *Aurelia*: 'Tis but trying my fortune to tell her of his Infidelity, and my love. If she yields she makes me happy; if not, I shall be sure *Don Melchor* has not planted the Armes of *Spain* in the Fort before me. However, I'll push my Fortune as sure as I am an *Englishman*.

Alon. Sennor *Ingles,* I know your voice, though I cannot perfectly discern you.

Bell. How the Devil come he to cross me?   [*Aside.*

Alon. I was just coming to have ask'd another Favour of you.

Bell. Without Ceremony command me, Sir.

Alon. My Daughter *Theodosia* has lost a fair Diamond from

320 you.] D; ~ᴧ Q1–3, F.   320 s.d. *Aside.*] Q2–3, D; ~ .] Q1; ~ᴧ) F.
325 Earthquake.] ~ᴧ Q1–3, F, D.   327 *Don*] Don Q1–3, F, D.
330 *Don*] Don Q1–3, F, D.   335 me? [*Aside.*] me? Q1–3, F, D.

her finger, the time betwixt six and seven this evening; now I
340 desire you, Sir, to erect a Scheme for it, and if it be lost, or
stollen, to restore it to me.————This is all, Sir.

Bell. There is no end of this old Fellow; thus will he baite
me from day to day, till my ignorance be found out.————
[*Aside.*

Alon. Now is he casting a Figure by the Art of Memory, and
making a Judgment of it to himself. This *Astrology* is a very
mysterious speculation.———— [*Aside.*

Bell. 'Tis a madness for me to hope I can deceive him longer.
Since then he must know I am no *Astrologer,* I'll discover it my
self to him, and blush once for all.———— [*Aside.*
350 *Alon.* Well, Sir, and what do the Stars hold forth? What sayes
nimble Master *Mercury* to the matter?

Bell. Sir, not to keep you longer in ignorance, I must inge-
niously declare to you that I am not the man for whom you take
me. Some smattering in *Astrology* I have; which my Friends, by
their indiscretion, have blown abroad, beyond my intentions.
But, you are not a person to be impos'd on like the vulgar:
therefore, to satisfie you in one word, my skill goes not farr
enough to give you knowledge of what you desire from me.

Alon. You have said enough, Sir, to perswade me of your
360 Science; if Fame had not publish'd it, yet this very humility of
yours were enough to confirm me in the beliefe of it.

Bell. Death, you make me mad, Sir: Will you have me Swear?
As I am a Gentleman, a man of the Town, one who wears good
Cloathes, Eates, Drinks, and Wenches abundantly; I am a
damn'd ignorant, and senceless Fellow.

Enter Beatrix.

Alon. How now Gentlewoman.————What, Are you going to
reliefe by Moonshine?

---

341 me.] ∼ᴧ Q1–3, F, D. 346 speculation.] D; ∼ᴧ Q1–3, F.
348 *Astrologer*] Q2–3, F; Astrologer Q1, D. 349 all.] D; ∼ᴧ Q1–3, F.
349 *s.d. Aside*] Q2–3, F, D; *aside* Q1. 360 Science;] Q3, D; ∼ , Q1–2, F.
366 Gentlewoman.] ∼ᴧ Q1–3, F, D.

Beat. I was going on a very charitable Office, to help a Friend that was gravell'd in a very doubtful business.

370 *Bell.* Some good newes, Fortune, I beseech thee.

Beat. But now I have found this learned Gentleman, I shall make bold to propound a Question to him from a Lady.

Alon. I will have my own Question first resolv'd.

Bell. O, Sir, 'tis from a Lady———

Beat. If you please, Sir, I'll tell it in your eare.———My Lady has given *Don Melchor* the Ring; in whose company her Father found her but just now at the Garden door.   [*In whisper.*

Bell. aloud. Come to me to morrow, and you shall receive an answer.———

380 *Beat.* Your Servant, Sir.———   [*Exit* Beatrix.

Alon. Sir, I shall take it very unkindly if you satisfie any other, and leave me in this perplexity.

Bell. Sir, if my knowledge were according———

Alon. No more of that, Sir, I beseech you.

Bell. Perhaps I may know something by my Art concerning it; but, for your quiet, I wish you would not press me.

Alon. Do you think I am not Master of my Passions?

Bell. Since you will needs know what I would willingly have conceal'd, the person who has your Diamond, is he whom you

390 saw last in your Daughters company.

Alon. You would say 'tis *Don Melchor de Guzman.* Who the Devil would have suspected him of such an action? But he is of a decay'd Family, and poverty it seems has inforc'd him to it: now I think on't better, he has e'en stoln it for a fee to bribe his Lawyer; to requite a lye with a theft: I'll seek him out, and tell him part of my mind before I sleep.   [*Exit* Alon.

Bell. So, once more I am at liberty: but this *Astrologie* is so troublesome a Science———would I were well rid on't.

Enter Don Lopez *and a Servant.*

375 eare.] ~ᴧ Q1–3, F, D.   376 *Don*] Don Q1–3, F, D.
379 answer.] D; ~ᴧ Q1–3, F.   380 Sir.] D; ~ , Q1–3, F.
391 Who] Q3, D; ~ , Q1–2, F.   394 better,] Q2–3, F, D; ~ᴧ Q1.
395 theft:] ~ ; Q1–3, F, D.   398+ *s.d. Servant*] Q2–3, F, D; Servant Q1.

Lop. *Astrologie* does he say? O Cavalier is it you? not finding
400 you at home I came on purpose to seek you out: I have a small
request to the Stars by your mediation.

Bell. Sir, for pity let 'em shine in quiet a little; for what for
Ladies and their Servants, and younger Brothers, they scarce
get a Holy-day in a twelvemoneth.

Lop. Pray pardon me, if I am a little curious of my destiny,
since all my happiness depends on your answer.

Bell. Well, Sir, what is it you expect?

Lop. To know whether my love to a Lady will be succesful.

Bell. 'Tis *Aurelia* he means. [*Aside.*]————Sir, in one word I
410 answer you, that your Mistress loves another: one who is your
friend: but comfort your self; the Dragons tail is between him
and home, he never shall enjoy her.

Lop. But what hope for me?

Bell. The Stars have partly assur'd me you shall be happy, if
you acquaint her with your passion, and with the double dealing of your friend, who is false to her.

Lop. You speak like an Oracle. But I have engag'd my promise to that friend to serve him in his passion to my Mistress.

Bell. We *English* seldom make such scruples; Women are not
420 compris'd in our Laws of friendship: they are *feræ naturæ;* our
common game, like Hare and Patridge: every man has equal
right to them, as he has to the Sun and Elements.

Lop. Must I then betray my friend?

Bell. In that case my friend is a *Turk* to me, if he will be so
barbarous as to retain two women to his private use; I will be
factious for all distressed Damsels; who would much rather have
their cause try'd by a full Jury, than a single Judge.

Lop. Well, Sir, I will take your counsel; and if I erre, the
fault be on love and you.———   *Exit* Lopez.

430 *Bell.* Were it not for love I would run out of the Town,
that's the short on't; for I have engag'd my self in so many promises for the Sun and Moon, and those little minc'd-meats of 'em,

399 you?] D; ~ ; Q1–3, F.   407 *Bell.*] Q2–3, F, D; ~ , Q1.
409 means. [*Aside.*]————] D; ~∧————(*aside*∧) Q1, F (*Aside* F); ~∧————
[*Aside.*] Q2; ~∧————[*Aside.*∧ Q3 (*at right margin*).
424 *Turk*] Q2–3, F, D; Turk Q1.   427 than] Q2–3, F; then Q1, D.

that I must hide before my day of payment comes. In the mean
time I forget *Theodosia;* but now I defie the Devil to hinder
me.

> *As he is going out he meets* Aurelia, *and almost*
> *justles her down. With her* Camilla *enters.*

Aur. What rudeness is this?

Bell. Madam *Aurelia,* is it you?

Aur. Monsieur *Bellamy!*

Bell. The same, Madam.

Aur. My Unkle told me he left you here: and indeed I came
hither to complain of you: for you have treated me so inhu-
manely that I have some reason to resent it.

Bell. What occasion can I have given you for a complaint?

Aur. Don Melchor, as I am inform'd by my Uncle, is effec-
tively at *Madrid:* so that it was not his *Idea,* but himself in person whom I saw: and since you knew this, why did you conceal
it from me?

Bell. When I spoke with you I knew it not: but I discover'd
it in the erecting of my figure. Yet if instead of his *Idea* I constrain'd himself to come, in spight of his resolution to remain
conceal'd, I think I have shown a greater effect of my art then
what I promis'd.

Aur. I render my self to so convincing an argument: but by
over-hearing a discourse just now betwixt my Cousin *Theodosia*
and her Maid, I find that he has conceal'd himself upon her
account, which has given me jealousie to the last point; for to
avow an incontestable truth, my Cousin is furiously handsome.

Bell. Madam, Madam, trust not your ears too far; she talk'd
on purpose that you might hear her: but I assure you the true
cause of *Don Melchor's* concealment, was not love of her, but
jealousie of you: he staid in private to observe your actions:
build upon't Madam, he is inviolably yours.

Aur. Then will he sacrifice my Cousin to me?

Bell. 'Tis furiously true Madam.

Aur. O most agreeable assurance!

Cam. Albricias, Madam, for my good news; *Don Melchor* is coming this way; I know him by his voice; but he is in company with another person.

Aur. It will not be convenient to give him any umbrage by
470 seeing me with another person; therefore I will go before; do you stay here and conduct him to my Appartment. Good-night Sir.   *Exit.*

Bell. I have promis'd *Don Lopez* he shall possess her; and I have promis'd her she shall possess *Don Melchor:* 'tis a little difficult I confess, as to the Matrimonial part of it: but if *Don Melchor* will be civil to her, and she be civil to *Don Lopez,* my credit is safe without the benefit of my Clergie. But all this is nothing to *Theodosia.*   *Exit* Bellamy.

Enter Don Alonzo *and* Don Melchor.

Cam. Don Melchor, a word in private.
480   *Mel.* Your pleasure, Lady. Sir, I will wait on you immediately.

Cam. I am sent to you from a fair Lady, who bears you no ill will. You may guess whom I mean.

Mel. Not by my own merits, but by knowing whom you serve: but I confess I wonder at her late strange usage when she fled from me.

Cam. That was only a mistake; but I have now, by her command, been in a thousand places in quest of you.

Mel. You overjoy me.

Cam. And where amongst the rest do you think I have been
490 looking you?

Mel. Pray refresh my memory.

Cam. In that same street, by that same shop; you know where, by a good token.

Mel. By what token?

Cam. Just by that shop where, out of your nobleness, you promis'd me a new Silk Gown.

466 *Albricias,*] Q3, F, D; ~∧ Q1–2.   477 this is] Q2–3, F, D; this Q1.
480 Lady.] Q3; ~ ; Q1–2, F, D.   492 where,] Q2–3, F; ~∧ Q1, D.

Mel. O, now I understand you.

Cam. Not that I press you to a performance———

Mel. Take this, and please your self in the choice of it.———

[*Gives her money.*

500 *Cam.* Nay, dear Sir, now you make me blush; in faith I———
am asham'd———I swear 'tis only because I would keep something for your sake.———But my Lady expects you immediately in her Appartment.

Mel. I'll wait on her if I can possibly.——— *Exit* Camilla.
But if I can prevail with *Don Alonzo* for his Daughter, then will
I again consider, which of the Ladies best deserves me. [*Aside.*]
———Sir, I beg your pardon for this rudeness in leaving you.

[*To* Alonzo.

Alon. I cannot possibly resolve with my self to tell him
openly he is a thief; but I'll guild the pill for him to swallow.

[*Aside.*

510 *Mel.* I believe he has discover'd our amour: how he surveys
me for a Son in law! [*Aside.*

Alon. Sir, I am sorry for your sake, that true nobility is not
alwayes accompanied with riches to support it in it's lustre.

Mel. You have a just exception against the Caprichiousness
of destiny; yet if I were owner of any noble qualities, (which
I am not) I should not much esteem the goods of fortune.

Alon. But pray conceive me, Sir, your father did not leave
you flourishing in wealth.

Mel. Only a very fair Seat in *Andalusia*, with all the pleasures
520 imaginable about it: that alone, were my poor deserts according,
which I confess they are not, were enough to make a woman
happy in it.

Alon. But give me leave to come to the point, I beseech you,

---

499 it.] Q3; ~ʌ Q1-2, F, D.
499+ *s.d.* [*Gives . . . money.*] Q2-3, F, D; ʌ~ . . . ~.] Q1 (*at left margin*).
502-503 immediately] Q2-3, F, D; immedeiately Q1.
504 possibly.] ~ʌ Q1-3, F, D.
506-507+ me. [*Aside.*]———Sir, . . . you. / [*To* Alonzo.] D; me.——— /
[*Aside.*] / *To* Alonzo. Sir, . . . you. Q1; me.——— / [*Aside.* / *To* Alonzo.
Sir, . . . you. Q2, F; meʌ———[*Aside.* / [*To* Alonzo.] Sir, . . . you. Q3.
509+ *s.d. Aside*] Q2-3, F, D; *aside* Q1.
511 law! [*Aside.*] Q3, D; law! Q1-2, F.   523 point,] Q2-3, F, D; ~ʌ Q1.

Sir. I have lost a Jewel which I value infinitely, and I hear it is in your possession: but I accuse your wants, not you, for it.

Mel. Your Daughter is indeed a Jewel, but she were not lost, were she in possession of a man of parts.

Alon. A pretious Diamond Sir.————

Mel. But a man of honor, Sir————

530   *Alon.* I know what you would say, Sir, that a man of honor is not capable of an unworthy action; but therefore I do not accuse you of the theft, I suppose the Jewel was only put into your hands.

Mel. By honorable wayes I assure you Sir.

Alon. Sir, Sir, will you restore my Jewel?

Mel. Will you please, Sir, to give me leave to be the unworthy possessor of her? I know how to use her with that respect————

Alon. I know what you would say, Sir, but if it belongs to our Family; otherwise I assure you it were at your service.

540   *Mel.* As it belongs to your Family I covet it; not that I plead my own deserts, Sir.

Alon. Sir, I know your deserts; but, I protest I cannot part with it: for, I must tell you, this Diamond Ring was originally my Great Grandfathers.

Mel. A Diamond Ring, Sir, do you mean?————

Alon. By your patience, Sir, when I have done you may speak your pleasure. I onely lent it to my Daughter; but, how she lost it, and how it came upon your Finger, I am yet *in tenebris.*

Mel. Sir————

550   *Alon.* I know it, Sir; but spare your self the trouble, I'll speak for you; you would say you had it from some other hand; I believe it, Sir.

Mel. But, Sir————

Alon. I warrant you, Sir, Ile bring you off without your speaking; from another hand you had it; and now Sir, as you say, Sir, and as I am saying for you, Sir, you are loath to part with it.

Mel. Good Sir,————let me————

Alon. I understand you already, Sir, that you have taken a

529   Sir————] Q3, D; ∼ . ∧ Q1–2, F.
537   respect————] Q3, F, D; ∼ .———— Q1–2.
548   *in tenebris*] Q2–3, F, D (in Q2, F); in tenebris Q1.

fancy to it, and would buy it; but, to that I answer as I did
560 before, that it is a Relique of my family: now, Sir, if you can
urge ought farther, you have liberty to speak without interruption.

Mel. This Diamond you speak on I confess————

Alon. But, What need you confess, Sir, before you are accus'd?

Mel. You promis'd you would hear me in my turn, Sir,
but————

Alon. But, as you were saying, it is needless, because I have
already spoken for you.

Mel. The truth is, Sir, I was too presumptuous to take this
570 Pledge from *Theodosia* without your knowledge; but, you will
pardon the invincible necessity, when I tell you————

Alon. You need not tell me, I know your necessity was the
reason of it, and that place and opportunity have caus'd your
error.

Mel. This is the goodest old man I ever knew; he prevents me
in my motion for his Daughter. [*Aside.*]————Since, Sir, you
know the cause of my errors, and are pleas'd to lay part of the
blame upon Youth and Opportunity; I beseech you favour me
so far, to accept me as fair *Theodosia* already has————

580 *Alon.* I conceive you, Sir, that I would accept of your excuse:
why, restore the Diamond and 'tis done.

Mel. More joyfully then I receiv'd it: and with it I beg the
honour to be receiv'd by you as your Son in Law.

Alon. My Son in Law! this is the most pleasant Proposition I
ever heard.

Mel. I am proud you think it so; but, I protest I think not I
deserve this honor.

Alon. Nor I, I assure you, Sir; marry my daughter————ha,
ha, ha.

590 *Mel.* But, Sir————

Alon. I know what you would say, Sir, that there is too much
hazard in the Profession of a Thief, and therefore you would
Marry my Daughter to become rich, without venturing your
Neck for't. I beseech you, Sir, steal on, be apprehended, and if

576 Daughter. [*Aside.*]————] Daughter. Q1–3, F; Daughter.———— D.
581 why,] Q3, D; ~ˌ Q1–2, F.

you please, be hang'd, it shall make no breach betwixt us. For
my part, I'll keep your Counsel, and so good night, Sir.
                                                          [*Exit* Alonzo.

Mel. Is the Devil in this old man, first to give me occasion
to confess my Love, and, when he knew it, to promise he would
keep my Counsel? But, Who are these? I'll not be seen; but to
600 my old appointment with *Theodosia,* and desire her to unriddle it.———   [*Exit* Melchor.

                Enter Maskall, Jacinta, Beatrix.

Mask. But, Madam, Do you take me for a man of Honour?
Jac. No.
Mask. Why there's it; if you had, I would have sworn that my
Master has neither done nor intended you any injury; I suppose
you'll grant he knew you in your disguise?
Beat. Nay, to know her, and use her so, is an aggravation of
his Crime.
Mask. Unconscionable *Beatrix!* Would you two have all the
610 Carnival to your selves? He knew you, Madam, and was resolv'd
to countermine you in all your Plots. But, when he saw you so
much piqued, he was too good natur'd to let you sleep in wrath,
and sent me to you to disabuse you: for, if the business had gone
on till to morrow, when *Lent* begins, you would have grown so
peevish (as all good Catholicks are with fasting) that the quarrel
would never have been ended.
Jac. Well; this mollifies a little: I am content he shall see me.
Mask. But, that you may be sure he knew you, he will bring
the Certificate of the Purse along with him.
620 *Jac.* I shall be glad to find him innocent.

            Enter Wildblood *at the other end of the Stage.*

Wild. No mortal man ever threw out so often. It could not
be me, it must be the Devil that did it: he took all the Chances,

---

601 it.] ∼∧ Q1–3, F, D.
601+ *s.d.* Maskall, Jacinta, Beatrix] Q2–3, F, D (Maskal Q2–3, F); *Maskal,
Jacinta, Beatrix* Q1.

and chang'd 'em after I had thrown 'em: but, I'le be even with him; for, I'll never throw one of his Dice more.

Mask. Madam, 'tis certainly my Master; and he is so zealous to make his peace, that he could not stay till I call'd him to you.————Sir————

Wild. Sirrah, I'll teach you more manners then to leave me another time: you Rogue, you have lost me two hundred Pistolls, you and the Devil your accomplice; you, by leaving me to my self, and he by tempting me to Play it off.

Mask. Is the wind in that door? here's like to be fine doings.

Wild. Oh mischiefe! am I fallen into her ambush? I must face it out with another quarrel.———— [*Aside.*

Jac. Your man has been treating your Accommodation; 'tis half made already.

Wild. I, On your part it may be.

Jac. He sayes you knew me.

Wild. Yes; I do know you so well, that my poor heart akes for't: I was going to bed without telling you my mind; but, upon consideration I am come————

Jac. To bring the Money with you.

Wild. To declare my grievances, which are great, and many.

Mask. Well, for impudence, let thee alone.

Wild. As in the first place————

Jac. I'll hear no Grievances; Where's the Money?

Beat. I; keep to that, Madam.

Wild. Do you think me a person to be so us'd?

Jac. We will not quarrel; Where's the Money?

Wild. By your favour we will quarrel.

Beat. Money, Money————

Wild. I am angry, and can hear nothing.

Beat. Money, Money, Money, Money.

Wild. Do you think it a reasonable thing to put on two disguises in a Night, to tempt a man?————[*Aside.*] Help me, *Maskall,* for I want Arguments abominably.————I thank

Heaven I was never so barbarously us'd in all my life.

Jac. He begins to anger me in good earnest.

Mask. A thing so much against the Rules of Modesty: so
660 undecent a thing.

Wild. I, so undecent a thing: nay, now I do not wonder at
my self for being angry. And then to wonder I should love her
in those disguises? to quarrel at the natural desires of humane
kind, assaulted by powerful temptations; I am inrag'd at
that———

Jac. Heyday! you had best quarrel too for my bringing you
the Money!

Wild. I have a grudging to you for't.———*Maskall,* the
Money, *Maskall;* now help or we are gone.   [*Aside.*
670 *Mask.* Would she offer to bring Money to you? first to affront
your poverty———

Wild. I; to affront my poverty. But, that's no great matter;
and then———

Mask. And then, to bring you Money———I stick fast, Sir.
                                                        [*Aside.*

Wild to Mask. Forward, you Dog, and invent, or I'll cut your
throat.———And then as I was saying, to bring me Money———

Mask. Which is the greatest and most sweet of all temptations;
and to think you could resist it: being also aggravated by her
680 handsomeness who brought it?

Wild. Resist it? no; I would she would understand it, I know
better what belongs to flesh and blood then so.

Beat. to Jac. This is plain confederacie; I smoak it; he came
on purpose to quarrel with you; break first with him and prevent it.

Jac. to Beat. If it be come to that once, the Devill take the

668–669 for't.———*Maskall, . . .* gone. [*Aside.*] for't: (*Maskall, . . .* gone.)
Q1–3, F, D.
674–674+ Money———I . . . Sir. / [*Aside.*] Money (I . . . Sir.) Q1–3, F, D.
675–676 *to Mask.* Forward, . . . throat.———And] (Forward, . . . throat;) and
Q1–3, F, D.
680 it?] Q2–3, F; ~ . Q1, D.   683 *to*] D; to Q1–3, F.
686 *to Beat.*] *omitted from* Q1–3, F, D.

hindmost; I'll not be last in love; for that will be a dishonour to my Sex.

Wild. And then————

690 *Jac.* Hold Sir; there needs no more: you shall fall out; and I'll gratifie you with a new occasion: I only try'd you in hope you would be false; and rather than fail of my design, brought gold to bribe you to't.

Beat. As people when they have an ill bargain, are content to lose by't, that they may get it off their hands.

Mask. Beatrix, while our principals are engag'd, I hold it not for our honor to stand idle.

Beat. With all my heart: please you let us draw off to some other ground.

700 *Mask.* I dare meet you on any Spot, but one.

Wild. I think we shall do well to put it to an issue; this is the last time you shall ever be troubled with my addresses.

Jac. The favour had been greater to have spar'd this too.

Mask. Beatrix, let us dispatch; or they'll break off before us.

Beat. Break as fast as thou wilt, I am as brittle as thou art for thy heart.

Wild. Because I will absolutely break off with you, I will keep nothing that belongs to you: therefore take back your Picture, and your Handkerchief.

710 *Jac.* I have nothing of yours to keep; therefore take back your liberal promises. Take 'em in imagination.

Wild. Not to be behind hand with you in your frumps, I give you back your Purse of Gold: take you that————in imagination.

Jac. To conclude with you, take back your oathes and protestations; they are never the worse for the wearing, I assure you: therefore take 'em, spick and span new, for the use of your next Mistress.

Mask. Beatrix, follow your leader; here's the sixpenny whittle 720 you gave me, with the Mutton haft: I can spare it, for knives are of little use in *Spain.*

Beat. There's your Cizars with the stinking brass chain to

716 wearing,] Q2–3, F, D; ~∧ Q1.

'em: 'tis well there was no love betwixt us; for they had been too dull to cut it.

Mask. There's the dandriffe Comb you lent me.

Beat. There's your ferret Ribbaning for garters.

Mask. I would never have come so near as to have taken 'em from you.

Beat. For your Letter, I have it not about me; but upon repu-
730 tation I'll burn it.

Mask. And for yours, I have already put it to a fitting imploy-
ment.———Courage, Sir; how goes the battel on your wing?

Wild. Just drawing off on both sides. Adieu *Spain.*

Jac. Farewel old *England.*

Beat. Come away in Triumph; the day's your own Madam.

Mask. I'll bear you off upon my shoulders, Sir; we have broke their hearts.

Wild. Let her go first then; I'll stay, and keep the honor of the Field.

740 *Jac.* I'll not retreat, if you stay till midnight.

Wild. Are you sure then we have done loving?

Jac. Yes, very sure; I think so.

Wild. 'Tis well you are so; for otherwise I feel my stomack a little maukish. I should have doubted another fit of love were coming up.

Jac. No, no; your inconstancy secures you enough for that.

Wild. That's it which makes me fear my own returning: nothing vexes me, but that you should part with me so slightly, as though I were not worth your keeping; well, 'tis a sign you
750 never lov'd me.

Jac. 'Tis the least of your care whether I did or did not: it may be it had been more for the quiet of my self, if I———but 'tis no matter, I'll not give you that satisfaction.

Wild. But what's the reason you will not give it me?

Jac. For the reason that we are quite broke off.

Wild. Why, are we quite broke off?

Jac. Why, are we not?

Wild. Well, since 'tis past, 'tis past; but a pox of all foolish quarrelling, for my part.

760　*Jac.* And a mischief of all foolish disguisements, for my part.

Wild. But if it were to do again with another Mistress, I would e'en plainly confess I had lost my money.

Jac. And if I had to deal with another Servant, I would learn more wit then to tempt him in disguises: for that's to throw a *Venice*-glass to the ground, to try if it would not break.

Wild. If it were not to please you, I see no necessity of our parting.

Jac. I protest I do it only out of complaisance to you.

Wild. But if I should play the fool and ask you pardon, you 770　would refuse it.

Jac. No, never submit, for I should spoil you again with pardoning you.

Mask. Do you hear this, *Beatrix?* they are just upon the point of accommodation; we must make haste or they'll make a peace by themselves; and exclude us from the Treaty.

Beat. Declare your self the Aggressor then; and I'll take you into mercy.

Wild. The worst that you can say of me is that I have lov'd you thrice over.

780　*Jac.* The prime Articles between *Spain* and *England* are seal'd; for the rest concerning a more strict alliance, if you please we'll dispute them in the Garden.

Wild. But in the first place let us agree on the Article of Navigation, I beseech you.

Beat. These Leagues offensive and defensive will be too strict for us, *Maskall:* a Treaty of commerce will serve our turn.

Mask. With all my heart; and when our loves are veering,
　　　We'll make no words, but fall to privateering.
　　　　　　　　　　　　Exeunt, the men leading the women.

759　quarrelling,] Q2-3, F; ~∧ Q1, D.
760　disguisements,] Q2-3, F; ~∧ Q1, D.
765　*Venice*-glass] Q2-3, F, D; Venice-glass Q1.
781　alliance,] D; ~ ; Q1-3, F.　　　　　784　Navigation,] Q2-3, F, D; ~∧ Q1.
788　*as in Q3; not indented in Q1-2, F, D.*
788+　*s.d. Exeunt*] Q2-3, F, D; Exeunt Q1.

ACT V. SCENE I.

Enter Lopez, Aurelia, *and* Camilla.

Lop. Tis true, if he had continu'd constant to you, I should have thought my self oblig'd in honor to be his friend; but I could no longer suffer him to abuse a person of your worth and beauty with a feign'd affection.

Aur. But is it possible *Don Melchor* should be false to love? I'll be sworn I did not imagine such a treacherie could have been in nature; especially to a Lady who had so oblig'd him.

Lop. 'Twas this, Madam, which gave me the confidence to wait upon you at an hour which would be otherwise unseason-
10 able.

Aur. You are the most obliging person in the world.

Lop. But to clear it to you that he is false; he is at this very minute at an assignation with your Cousin in the Garden; I am sure he was endeavouring it not an hour ago.

Aur. I swear this Evenings Air begins to incommode me extremely with a cold; but yet in hope of detecting this perjur'd man I am content to stay abroad.

Lop. But withall, you must permit me to tell you, Madam, that it is but just I should have some share in a heart which I
20 endeavour to redeem: in the Law of Arms you know that they who pay the ransome have right to dispose of the prisoner.

Aur. The prize is so very inconsiderable that 'tis not worth the claiming.

Lop. If I thought the boon were small, I would not importune my Princess with the asking it: but since my life depends upon the grant———

Cam. Mam, I must needs tell your Laship that *Don Lopez* has

ACT V. SCENE I.] D; ACT. V. Q1; ACT V. Q2–3, F.
s.d. *Enter*] D; *omitted from Q1–3, F.*
s.d. Lopez, Aurelia, . . . Camilla] Q3, F, D; *Lopez, Aurelia, . . . Camilla*
Q1–2.
9   upon you] Q2–3, F, D; upon Q1.   18   withall,] Q3; ~∧ Q1–2, F, D.
18   me to] Q2–3, F, D; me Q1.

deserv'd you: for he has acted all along like a Cavalier; and
more for your interest than his own; besides Mam, *Don Melchor*
30 is as poor as he is false: for my part I shall ne're endure to call
him Master.

Aur. *Don Lopez* go along with me, I can promise nothing,
but I swear I will do my best to disingage my heart from this
furious tender which I have for him.

Cam. If I had been a man I could never have forsaken you:
Ah those languishing casts, Mam; and that pouting lip of your
Laship, like a Cherry-bough weigh'd down with the weight of
fruit.

Aur. And that sigh too I think is not altogether disagreeable:
40 but something *charmante* and *mignonne.*

Cam. Well, *Don Lopez,* you'l be but too happy.

Lop. If I were once possessor————

Enter Bellamy *and* Theodosia.

Theo. O we are surpriz'd.

Bell. Fear nothing, Madam, I think I know 'em. *Don Lopez?*

Lop. Our famous *Astrologer,* how come you here!

Bell. I am infinitely happy to have met you with *Donna Aurelia,* that you may do me the favour to satisfie this Lady of
a truth which I can scarce perswade her to believe.

Lop. I am glad our concernments are so equal: for I have the
50 like favour to ask from *Donna Theodosia.*

Theo. *Don Lopez* is too noble to be refus'd any thing within
my power; and I am ready to do him any service after I have
ask'd my Cousin if ever *Don Melchor* pretended to her.

Aur. 'Tis the very question which I was furiously resolv'd
to have ask'd of you.

Theo. I must confess he has made some professions to me:
and withall, I will acknowledge my own weakness so far as to
tell you I have given way he should often visit me when the
world believ'd him absent.

60   *Aur.* O Cavalier *Astrologer;* how have you betrayd me! did you not assure me that *Don Melchor*'s tender and inclination was for me only?

   Bell. I had it from his Star, Madam, I do assure you, and if that twinkled false, I cannot help it: The truth is, there's no trusting the Planet of an inconstant man: his was moving to you when I look'd on't, and if since it has chang'd the course, I am not to be blam'd for't.

   Lop. Now, Madam, the truth is evident. And for this Cavalier he might easily be deceiv'd in *Melchor,* for I dare affirm it to 70 you both, he never knew to which of you he was most inclin'd: for he visited one, and writ letters to the other.

   Bell. to Theo. Then Madam I must claim your promise, (since I have discover'd to you that *Don Melchor* is unworthy of your favours) that you would make me happy, who amongst my many imperfections can never be guilty of such a falsehood.

   Theo. If I have been deceiv'd in *Melchor* whom I have known so long, you cannot reasonably expect I should trust you at a dayes acquaintance.

   Bell. For that, Madam, you may know as much of me in a 80 day as you can in all your life: all my humours circulate like my blood, at farthest within 24 hours. I am plain and true like all my Countrymen; you see to the bottom of me as easily as you do to the gravel of a clear stream in Autumn.

   Lop. You plead so well, Sir, that I desire you would speak for me too: my cause is the same with yours, only it has not so good an Advocate.

   Aur. Since I cannot make my self happy, I will have the glory to felicitate another: and therefore I declare I will reward the fidelity of *Don Lopez.*

90   *Theo.* All that I can say at present is, that I will never be *Don Melchors:* the rest, time and your service must make out.

   Bell. I have all I can expect, to be admitted as eldest Servant; as preferment falls I hope you will remember my seniority.

   Cam. Mam, *Don Melchor.*

---

64 is,] Q2–3, F, D; ∼ₐ Q1.   72 *to*] D; to Q1–3, F.
72 promise,] F, D; ∼ : Q1–3.   91 rest,] Q2–3, F; ∼ₐ Q1, D.

An Evening's Love

Aur. Cavaliers, retire a little; we shall see to which of us he will make his Court. *The men withdraw.*

Enter Don Melchor.

Don Melchor, I thought you had been a-bed before this time.

Mel. Fair *Aurelia,* this is a blessing beyond expectation to see you agen so soon.

00 *Aur.* What important business brought you hither?

Mel. Onely to make my peace with you before I slept. You know you are the Saint to whom I pay my devotions.

Aur. And yet it was beyond your expectances to meet me? This is furiously incongruous.

Theo. advancing. Don Melchor, whither were you bound so late?

Mel. What shall I say? I am so confounded that I know not to which of them I should excuse my self. *Aside.*

10 *Theo.* Pray answer me truly to one question: did you never make any addresses to my Cousin?

Mel. Fie, fie, Madam, there's a question indeed.

Aur. How, Monster of ingratitude, can you deny the Declaration of your passion to me?

Mel. I say nothing Madam.

Theo. Which of us is it for whom you are concern'd?

Mel. For that, Madam, you must excuse me; I have more discretion then to boast a Ladies favour.

Aur. Did you counterfeit an address to me?

Mel. Still I say nothing, Madam; but I will satisfie either of 20 you in private; for these matters are too tender for publick discourse.

Enter Lopez *and* Bellamy *hastily with their swords drawn.*

Bellamy and *Lopez!* This is strange!

---
95   Cavaliers,] Q3, D; ~∧ Q1–2, F.
96+   *s.d.* Don Melchor] *Don Melchor* Q1; *Don* Melchor Q2–3, F, D.
97   *Melchor,*] Q2–3, F, D; ~∧ Q1.   97   a-bed] Q3, F, D; a bed Q1–2.
110   Cousin?] Q2–3, F, D; ~ . Q1.   112   How,] Q3, D; ~∧ Q1–2; ~ ! F.
116   that,] Q3, F, D; ~∧ Q1–2.   122   *as in Q3, F, D; indented in Q1–2.*

Lop. Ladies, we would not have disturb'd you, but as we were walking to the Garden door, it open'd suddenly against us, and we confusedly saw by Moon-light, some persons entring, but who they were we know not.

Bell. You had best retire into the Garden-house, and leave us to take our fortunes, without prejudice to your reputations.

Enter Wildblood, Maskall, Jacinta, Beatrix.

Wild. to Jacinta entring. Do not fear, Madam, I think I heard
130 my friends voice.

Bell. Marry hang you, is it you that have given us this hot alarme?

Wild. There's more in't than you imagine, the whole house is up: for seeing you two, and not knowing you after I had entred the Garden-door, I made too much haste to get out again, and have left the key broken in it. With the noise one of the Servants came running in, whom I forc'd back; and doubtless he is gone for company, for you may see lights running through every Chamber.

140 *Theo. Jaci.* What will become of us?

Bell. We must have recourse to our former resolution. Let the Ladies retire into the Garden-house. And now I think on't you Gentlemen shall go in with 'em, and leave me and *Maskall* to bear the brunt on't.

Mask. Me, Sir? I beseech you let me go in with the Ladies too. Dear *Beatrix* speak a good word for me, I protest 'tis more out of love to thy company than for any fear I have.

Bell. You Dog, I have need of your wit and counsel. We have no time to deliberate. Will you stay, Sir?   [*To* Maskall.
150 *Mask.* No Sir, 'tis not for my safety.

Bell. Will you in Sir?   [*To* Melchor.

128+ *s.d.* Wildblood, Maskall, Jacinta, Beatrix] Q2–3, F, D; *Wildblood, Maskall, Jacinta, Beatrix* Q1.
129 *to*] Q2, F, D; to Q1, Q3.   132 alarme?] Q2–3, F, D; ~ . Q1.
137 running] Q2–3, F, D; runing Q1.   146 too. Dear] Q3; ~ ; dear Q1–2, F, D.
148 Dog,] Q3, D; ~∧ Q1–2, F.
149 *s.d. To* Maskall] Q2–3, F, D; *to Maskall* Q1.
151 *s.d. To* Melchor] Q2–3, F, D; *to Melchor* Q1.

Mel. No Sir, 'tis not for my honor, to be assisting to you:
I'll to *Don Alonzo,* and help to revenge the injury you are doing him.

Bell. Then we are lost, I can do nothing.

Wild. Nay, and you talk of honor, by your leave Sir.

                    [Falls upon him & throws him down.

I hate your *Spanish* honor ever since it spoyl'd our *English*
Playes, with faces about and t'other side.

Mel. What do you mean, you will not murder me?
160 Must valour be oppress'd by multitudes?

Wild. Come yarely my mates, every man to his share of the
burthen. Come yarly hay.

        The four men take him each by a limb, and carry
               him out, he crying murder.

Theo. If this *Englishman* save us now I shall admire his wit.

Beat. Good wits never think themselves admir'd till they are
well rewarded: you must pay him in *specie,* Madam; give him
love for his wit.

               Enter the Men again.

Bell. Ladies fear nothing, but enter into the Garden-house
with these Cavaliers.————

Mask. Oh that I were a Cavalier too!   *Is going with them.*
170   *Bell.* Come you back Sirrah.   *Stops him.*
Think your selves as safe as in a Sanctuary, only keep quiet
what ever happens.

Jac. Come away then, they are upon us.

               Exeunt all but Bell. *and* Mask.

Mask. Hark, I hear the foe coming: methinks they threaten
too, Sir; pray let me go in for a Guard to the Ladies and poor
Beatrix. I can fight much better when there is a wall betwixt
me and danger.

Bell. Peace, I have occasion for your wit to help me lie.

Mask. Sir, upon the faith of a sinner you have had my last

---

160 Must] Q1 *(corrected state),* Q2–3, F, D; *Mel.* Must Q1 *(uncorrected state).*
165 Madam;] ∼ , Q1–3, F, D.   168 Cavaliers.] ∼∧ Q1–3, F, D.

180 lye already; I have not one more to do me credit, as I hope to
be sav'd, Sir.

    Bell. Victore, victore; knock under you rogue, and confess
me Conquerour, and you shall see I'll bring all off.

Enter Don Alonzo *and six Servants; with lights
and swords drawn.*

    Alon. Search about there.

    Bell. Fear nothing, do but vouch what I shall say.

    Mask. For a passive lye I can yet do something.

    Alon. Stand: who goes there?

    Bell. Friends.

    Alon. Friends? who are you?

190   *Bell.* Noble *Don Alonzo,* such as are watching for your good.

    Alon. Is it you, Sennor *Ingles?* why all this noise and tu-
mult? where are my Daughters and my Neece? But in the
first place, though last nam'd, how came you hither, Sir?

    Bell. I came hither———by *Astrologie,* Sir.

    Mask. My Master's in, heavens send him good shipping with
his lye, and all kind Devils stand his friends.

    Alon. How, by *Astrologie,* Sir? meaning you came hither
by Art Magick.

    Bell. I say by pure *Astrologie* Sir, I foresaw by my Art a
200 little after I had left you that your Neece and Daughters would
this night run a risque of being carried away from this very
Garden.

    Alon. O the wonders of this speculation!

    Bell. Thereupon I call'd immediately for my sword and
came in all haste to advertise you; but I see there's no resist-
ing Destiny, for just as I was entring the Garden door I met
the Women with their Gallants all under sail and outward
bound.

    Mask. Thereupon what does me, he but draws by my ad-
210 vice———

---

180 credit,] Q2–3, F, D; ∼∧ Q1.   193 Sir?] F, D; ∼ . Q1–3.
194–199 *Astrologie . . . Astrologie . . . Astrologie*] Astrologie . . . Astrologie
. . . Astrologie Q1–3, F, D.
209 me,] F; ∼∧ Q1–3, D.

Bell. How now Mr. Raskall? are you itching to be in? [*Aside.*

Mask. Pray, Sir, let me go snip with you in this lye, and be not too covetous of honor? you know I never stood with you; now my courage is come to me I cannot resist the temptation.
[*Aside.*

Bell. Content; tell on.

Mask. So in short Sir, we drew, first I, and then my Master; but, being overpower'd, they have escap'd us, so that I think you may go to bed and trouble your self no further, for gone they are.

220   *Bell. You* tell a lye! you have curtail'd my invention: you are not fit to invent a lye for a Bawd when she would whedle a young Squire.   [*To* Maskall *aside.*

Alon. Call up the Officers of Justice, I'll have the Town search'd immediately.

Bell. 'Tis in vain, Sir; I know by my Art you'll never recover 'em: besides, 'tis an affront to my friends the Stars, who have otherwise dispos'd of 'em.

Enter a Servant.

Ser. Sir, the key is broken in the Garden-door, and the door lock'd, so that of necessitie they must be in the Garden yet.

230   *Alon.* Disperse your selves, some into the Wilderness, some into the Allyes, and some into the Parterre. You *Diego,* go trie to get out the key, and run to the Corigidore for his assistance: in the mean time I'll search the Garden-house my self.

Exeunt all the Servants but one.

Mask. I'll be unbetted again if you please Sir, and leave you all the honor of it.   [*To* Bellamy *aside.*

Alon. Come Cavalier, let us in together.

Bell. holding him. Hold Sir, for the love of heaven, you are not mad!

Alon. We must leave no place unsearch'd. A light there.

---

211 in? [*Aside.*] in? Q1–3, F, D.   214+ *s.d. omitted from Q1–3, F, D.*
216 Sir,] Q2–3, F, D; ∼∧ Q1.   220 *You*] You Q1–3, F, D.
222 Squire. [*To* Maskall *aside.*] Squire. Q1–3, F, D.
231 Parterre. You] ∼ : you Q1–3, F, D (You F, D).
237 Sir,] Q3, F, D; ∼∧ Q1–2.   238 mad!] F; ∼ . Q1–3, D.

240   *Bell.* Hold I say, do you know what you are undertaking?
and have you arm'd your self with resolution for such an adventure?

Alon. What adventure?

Bell. A word in private.———The place you would go into
is full of enchantments; there are at this time, for ought I
know, a Legion of spirits in it.

Alon. You confound me with wonder, Sir!

Bell. I have been making there my Magical operations, to
know the event of your Daughters flight: and, to perform it
250 rightly, have been forc'd to call up Spirits of several Orders:
and there they are humming like a swarm of Bees, some stalking
about upon the ground, some flying, and some sticking upon
the walls like Rear-mice.

Mask. The Devil's in him, he's got off again.   [*Aside.*

Alon. Now Sir I shall trie the truth of your friendship to me.
To confess the secret of my soul to you, I have all my life
been curious to see a Devil: And to that purpose have con'd
Agrippa through and through, and made experiment of all his
rules, *Pari die & incremento Lunæ,* and yet could never com-
260 pass the sight of one of these *Dæmoniums:* if you will ever
oblige me let it be on this occasion.

Mask. There's another storm arising.   [*Aside.*

Bell. You shall pardon me, Sir, I'll not expose you to that
peril for the world without due preparations of ceremony.

Alon. For that, Sir, I alwayes carry a Talisman about me;
that will secure me: and therefore I will venture in, a Gods
name, and defie 'em all at once.   [*Going in.*

Mask. How the pox will he get off from this?   [*Aside.*

Bell. Well, Sir, since you are so resolv'd, send off your Ser-
270 vant that there may be no noise made on't, and we'll take our
venture.

Alon. Pedro, leave your light, and help the fellows search
the Garden.   *Exit Servant.*

---

244 private.] ~‸ Q1–3, F, D.   254 again. [*Aside.*] again. Q1–3, F, D.
262 arising. [*Aside.*] arising. Q1–3, F, D. 266 in,] F, D; ~‸ Q1–3.
268 this? [*Aside.*] this? Q1–3, F, D.

Mask. What does my incomprehensible Master mean? [*Aside.*

Bell. Now I must tell you Sir, you will see that which will very much astonish you if my Art fail me not. [*Goes to the door.*] You Spirits and Intelligences that are within there, stand close, and silent, at your perril, and fear nothing, but appear in your own shapes, boldly.————*Maskall open the door.*

Maskall *goes to one side of the Scene, which draws, and discovers* Theo. Jac. Aur. Beat. Cam. Lop. Wild. *standing all without motion in a rank.*

280 Now Sir what think you?

Alon. They are here, they are here: we need search no farther. Ah you ungratious baggages!   [*Going toward them.*

Bell. Stay, or you'll be torn in pieces: these are the very shapes I Conjur'd up, and truly represent to you in what company your Niece and Daughters are, this very moment.

Alon. Why, are they not they? I durst have sworn that some of 'em had been my own flesh and blood.————Look; one of them is just like that rogue your Camrade.

Wildblood shakes his head and frowns at him.

Bell. Do you see how you have provok'd that *English* Devil:
290 take heed of him; if he gets you once into his clutches:————
Wildblood embracing Jacinta.

Alon. He seems to have got possession of the Spirit of my *Jacinta* by his hugging her.

Bell. Nay, I imagin'd as much: do but look upon his physiognomy, you have read *Baptista Porta:* has he not the leer of a very lewd debauch'd Spirit?

Alon. He has indeed: Then there's my Neece *Aurelia,* with the Spirit of *Don Lopez;* but that's well enough; and my Daughter *Theodosia* all alone: pray how comes that about?

Bell. She's provided for with a Familiar too: one that is in
300 this very room with you, and by your Elbow; but I'll shew you him some other time.

---

274 mean? [*Aside.*] mean? Q1–3, F, D.
276 s.d. [*Goes . . . door.*]] Q2–3, F, D; ∧~ . . . ~·∧ Q1.
279 *Maskall open the door*] Q3, D (*Maskal* Q3); Maskal *open the door* Q1–2,
F (*printed as s.d.*).
286 Why,] Q3, D; ~∧ Q1–2, F.   287 blood.] ~∧ Q1–3, F, D.

Alon. And that Baggage *Beatrix,* how I would swinge her if I had her here; I lay my life she was in the Plot for the flight of her Mistresses. [*Bea. claps her hands at him.*

Bell. Sir you do ill to provoke her: for being the Spirit of a Woman, she is naturally mischievous: you see she can scarce hold her hands from you already.

Mask. Let me alone to revenge your quarrel upon *Beatrix:* if e're she come to light I'll take a course with her, I warrant 310 you Sir.

Bell. Now come away Sir, you have seen enough: the Spirits are in pain whilst we are here: we keep 'em too long condens'd in bodies: if we were gone they would rarifie into air immediately. *Maskall* shut the door.

Maskall *goes to the Scene and it closes.*
Alon. Monstrum hominis! O prodigie of Science!

Enter two Servants with Don Melchor.

Bell. Now help me with a lye *Maskall,* or we are lost. [*Aside.*
Mask. Sir, I could never lie with man or woman in a fright.
Ser. Sir, we found this Gentleman bound and gagg'd, and he desir'd us to bring him to you with all haste imaginable.
320 *Mel.* O Sir, Sir, your two Daughters and your Niece————
Bell. They are gone, he knows it. But are you mad Sir to set this pernicious wretch at libertie?
Mel. I endeavour'd all that I was able————
Mask. Now Sir I have it for you. [*Aside to his Master.*]————
He was endeavouring indeed to have got away with 'em: for your Daughter *Theodosia* was his prize: but we prevented him, and left him in the condition in which you see him.
Alon. I thought somewhat was the matter that *Theodosia* had not a Spirit by her, as her Sister had.
330 *Bell.* This was he I meant to shew you.

---

304   s.d. *claps*] Q2–3, F, D; *Claps* Q1.   309   her,] D; ~∧ Q1–3, F.
316   lost. [*Aside.*] lost. Q1–3, F, D.   321   gone,] Q3, D; ~∧ Q1–2, F.
321   it. But] ~ : but Q1–3, F, D (But F, D).
324   you. [*Aside . . . Master.*]————] you∧————*Aside . . . Master.* Q1–2; you∧
————[*Aside . . . Master.* Q3; you∧————[*Aside . . . Master.*] F, D.

Mel. Do you believe him Sir?

Bell. No, no, believe *him,* Sir: you know his truth ever since he stole your Daughters Diamond.

Mel. I swear to you by my honor.

Alon. Nay, a thief I knew him, and yet after that, he had the impudence to ask me for my Daughter.

Bell. Was he so impudent? The case is plain Sir, put him quickly into custody.

Mel. Hear me but one word Sir, and I'll discover all to you.

340   *Bell.* Hear him not Sir: for my Art assures me if he speaks one syllable more, he will cause great mischief.

Alon. Will he so? I'll stop my ears, away with him.

Mel. Your Daughters are yet in the Garden, hidden by this fellow and his accomplices.

Alon. at the same time drowning him. I'll stop my ears, I'll stop my ears.

Bell. Mask. at the same time also. A thief, a thief, away with him.   *Servants carry* Melchor *off struggling.*

Alon. He thought to have born us down with his confi-
350 dence.

Enter another Servant.

Ser. Sir, with much ado we have got out the key and open'd the door.

Alon. Then, as I told you, run quickly to the Corigidor, and desire him to come hither in person to examine a malefactor.

Wildblood *sneezes within.*

Alon. Hark, what noise is that within? I think one sneezes.

Bell. One of the Devils I warrant you has got a cold with being so long out of the fire.

Alon. Bless his Devilship, as I may say.

Wildblood *sneezes again.*

Ser. to Don Alonzo. This is a mans voice, do not suffer your
360 self to be deceiv'd so grosly, Sir.

332 *him,*] Q2–3, F, D; ~∧ Q1.   345 *Alon.*] F, D; Alon. Q1–3.
347 *Bell. Mask.*] F, D; Bell. Mask. Q1–3.   358 Devilship,] Q2–3, F, D; ~∧ Q1.
359 *to*] D; to Q1–3, F.

Mask. A mans voice, that's a good one indeed! that you should live to these years and yet be so silly as not to know a man from a Devil.

Alon. There's more in't than I imagin'd: hold up your Torch and go in first, *Pedro,* and I'll follow you.

Mask. No, let me have the honor to be your Usher.

           Takes the Torch and goes in.

Mask. within. Help, help, help!

Alon. What's the matter?

Bell. Stir not upon your life Sir.

    Enter Maskall *again without the Torch.*

370 *Mask.* I was no sooner entred, but a huge Giant seiz'd my Torch, and fell'd me along, with the very whiffe of his breath as he past by me.

Alon. Bless us!

Bell. at the door to them within. Pass out now while you have time in the dark: the Officers of Justice will be here immediately, the Garden-door is open for you.

Alon. What are you muttering there Sir?

Bell. Only dismissing these Spirits of darkness, that they may trouble you no further. Go out I say.

    They all come out upon the Stage, groaping their way.
    Wildblood *falls into* Alonzo's *hands.*

380 *Alon.* I have caught some body; are these your Spirits? Another light quickly, *Pedro.*

Mask. slipping between Alonzo and Wildblood. 'Tis *Maskall* you have caught, Sir; do you mean to strangle me that you press me so hard between your Arms?

Alon. letting Wildblood go. Is it thee *Maskall?* I durst have sworn it had been another.

---

366 No,] Q2–3, F, D; ~ᴧ Q1.   367 help!] D; ~ . Q1–3, F.
374 *Bell.*] F, D; Bellᴧ Q1; Bell. Q2–3.
379 further. Go] ~ : go Q1–3, D (Go D); ~ ; go F.
382 *Mask. . . . Alonzo . . . Wildblood*] D; Mask. . . . Alonzo . . . Wildblood Q1–3, F (*Mask.* Q2, F).
385 *Alon. . . . Wildblood*] F, D (Wildblood F); Alon. . . . Wildblood Q1–3.

Bell. Make haste now before the Candle comes.

                          Aurelia *falls into* Alonzo's *armes.*

Alon. Now I have another.

Aur. 'Tis *Maskall* you have caught Sir.

390   *Alon.* No I thank you Niece, this artifice is too gross! I know your voice a little better. What ho, bring lights there.

Bell. Her impertinence has ruin'd all.

Enter Servants with lights and swords drawn.

Ser. Sir, the Corigidor is coming according to your desire: in the mean time we have secur'd the Garden doors.

Alon. I am glad on't: I'll make some of 'em severe examples.

Wild. Nay then as we have liv'd merrily, so let us die together: but we'll shew the *Don* some sport first.

Theo. What will become of us!

Jac. We'll die for company: nothing vexes me but that I
400 am not a man to have one thrust at that malicious old father of mine before I go.

Lop. Let us break our way through the Corigidor's band.

Jac. A match, i'faith: we'll venture our bodies with you: you shall put the baggage in the middle.

Wild. He that pierces thee, I say no more, but I shall be somewhat angry with him.————[*To* Alonzo.] In the mean time I arrest you Sir, in the behalf of this good company. As the Corigidor uses us, so we'll use you.

Alon. You do not mean to murder me!

410   *Bell.* You murder your self if you force us to it.

Wild. Give me a Razor there, that I may scrape his weeson, that the bristles may not hinder me when I come to cut it.

Bell. What need you bring matters to that extremity? you have your ransome in your hand: here are three men, and there are three women; you understand me.

Jac. If not, here's a sword and there's a throat: you understand me.

---

391 ho,] Q3, F, D; ~ᴀ Q1-2.   403 match,] ~ᴀ Q1-3, F, D.
406 him.————[*To* Alonzo.] In] D (him:); him: [*to Alonzo*] in Q1; him: [*To* Alonzo.] in Q2-3 (Alonzoᴀ] Q3); him: (*To* Alonzo) In F.

Alon. This is very hard!

Theo. The propositions are good, and marriage is as hon-
420 orable as it us'd to be.

Beat. You had best let your Daughters live branded with the
name of Strumpets: for what ever befalls the men, that will
be sure to be their share.

Alon. I can put them into a Nunnery.

All the Women. A Nunnery!

Jac. I would have thee to know, thou graceless old man,
that I defie a Nunnery: name a Nunnery once more, and I disown thee for my Father.

Lop. You know the Custome of the Country, in this case
430 Sir: 'tis either death or marriage: the business will certainly be
publick; and if they die they have sworn you shall bear 'em
company.

Alon. Since it must be so, run *Pedro* and stop the Corigidor:
tell him it was only a Carnival merriment, which I mistook for a
Rape and Robbery.

Jac. Why now you are a dutiful Father again, and I receive
you into grace.

Bell. Among the rest of your mistakes, Sir, I must desire you
to let my *Astrologie* pass for one: my Mathematicks, and Art
440 Magick were only a Carnival device; and now that's end-
ing, I have more mind to deal with the flesh than with the
devil.

Alon. No *Astrologer!* 'tis impossible!

Mask. I have known him, Sir, this seven years, and dare
take my oath he has been alwayes an utter stranger to the Stars:
and indeed to any thing that belongs to heaven.

Lop. Then I have been cozen'd among the rest.

Theo. And I; but I forgive him.

Beat. I hope you will forgive me, Madam; who have been
450 the cause on't; but what he wants in *Astrologie* he shall make
up to you some other way, I'll pass my word for him.

Alon. I hope you are both Gentlemen?

---

443 *Astrologer*] Q2–3, F; Astrologer Q1, D.
450 *Astrologie*] Q2–3, F; Astrologie Q1, D.   451 way,] Q2–3, F, D; ∼∧ Q1.

Bell. As good as the *Cid* himself, Sir.

Alon. And for your Religion, right *Romanes*———

Wild. As ever was *Marc Anthony.*

Alon. For your fortunes and courages———

Mask. They are both desperate, Sir; especially their fortunes.

Theo. to Bell. You should not have had my consent so soon,
460 but only to revenge my self upon the falseness of *Don Melchor.*

Aur. I must avow that gratitude for *Don Lopez* is as prevalent
with me as revenge against *Don Melchor.*

Alon. Lent you know begins to morrow; when that's over
marriage will be proper.

Jac. If I stay till after *Lent,* I shall be to marry when I have
no love left: I'll not bate you an Ace of to night, Father:
I mean to bury this man e're *Lent* be done, and get me another
before *Easter.*

Alon. Well, make a night on't then.   [*Giving his Daughters.*
470 *Wild. Jacinta Wildblood,* welcome to me: since our Starres
have doom'd it so, we cannot help it: but 'twas a meer trick of
Fate to catch us thus at unawares; to draw us in with a *what
do you lack* as we pass'd by: had we once separated to night,
we should have had more wit than ever to have met again to
morrow.

Jac. 'Tis true we shot each other flying: we were both upon
wing I find; and had we pass'd this Critical minute, I should
have gone for the *Indies,* and you for *Greenland* e're we had met
in a bed upon consideration.

80 *Mask.* You have quarrell'd twice to night without bloodshed,
'ware the third time.

Jac. A propos! I have been retrieving an old Song of a Lover
that was ever quarrelling with his Mistress: I think it will fit
our amour so well, that if you please I'll give it you for an

453   *Cid*] Cid Q1–3, F, D.   454   *Romanes*] Q2–3, F, D; Romanes Q1.
459   *to*] Q2, D; to Q1, Q3, F.   461   gratitude] F, D; ~ , Q1–3.
463–467   *Lent . . . Lent . . . Lent*] Q2–3, F; Lent . . . Lent . . . Lent Q1, D.
468   *Easter*] Q2–3, F, D; Easter Q1.   471   so,] Q2–3, F, D; ~∧ Q1.
472   unawares;] F; ~ : Q1–3, D.
472–473   *what do you lack*] what do you lack Q1–3, F, D.

Epithalamium: and you shall sing it. *Gives him a Paper.*

Wild. I never sung in all my life; nor ever durst trie when I was alone, for fear of braying.

Jac. Just me, up and down; but for a frolick let's sing together: for I am sure if we cannot sing now, we shall never have 490 cause when we are married.

Wild. Begin then; give me my Key, and I'll set my voice to't.

Jac. Fa la, fa la, fa la.

Wild. Fala, fala, fala. Is this your best, upon the faith of a Virgin?

Jac. I, by the Muses, I am at my pitch.

Wild. Then do your worst: and let the company be judge who sings worst.

Jac. Upon condition the best singer shall wear the breeches: 500 prepare to strip Sir; I shall put you into your drawers presently.

Wild. I shall be reveng'd with putting you into your smock anon; *St. George* for me.

Jac. St. James for me: come start Sir.

SONG.

Damon. *Celimena, of my heart,*
None shall e're bereave you:
If, with your good leave, I may
Quarrel with you once a day,
I will never leave you.

2.

Celimena. *Passion's but an empty name*
510 *Where respect is wanting:*
Damon you mistake your ayme;
Hang your heart, and burn your flame,
If you must be ranting.

---

494 best,] Q2–3, F, D; ∼∧ Q1.   496 I,] D; ∼∧ Q1–3, F.
502–503 *St. . . . St.*] Q2; St. . . . St. Q1, Q3, F, D.

3.

Damon. *Love as dull and muddy is,*
          As decaying liquor:
          Anger sets it on the lees,
          And refines it by degrees,
          Till it workes it quicker.

4.

Celimena. *Love by quarrels to beget*
          Wisely you endeavour;
          With a grave Physician's wit,
          Who to cure an Ague fit
          Put me in a Feavor.

5.

Damon. *Anger rouzes love to fight,*
          And his only bayt is,
          'Tis the spurre to dull delight,
          And is but an eager bite,
          When desire at height is.

6.

Celimena. *If such drops of heat can fall*
          In our wooing weather;
          If such drops of heat can fall,
          We shall have the Devil and all
          When we come together.

Wild. Your judgement Gentlemen: a Man or a Maid?

Bell. And you make no better harmony after you are married then you have before, you are the miserablest couple in *Christendome.*

Wild. 'Tis no great matter; if I had had a good voice she would have spoil'd it before to morrow.

---

521   *wit,*] Q3, F, D, o2–6, d1–2, d5; ~∧ Q1, M7; ~ . Q2.
537   *Christendome*] Christendome Q1–3, F, D.

540   *Bell.* When *Maskall* has married *Beatrix,* you may learn of her.

   Mask. You shall put her life into a Lease then.

   Wild. Upon condition that when I drop into your house from hunting, I may set my slippers at your door, as a *Turk* does at a *Jews,* that you may not enter.

   Beat. And while you refresh your self within, he shall wind the horn without.

   Mask. I'll throw up my Lease first.

   Bell. Why, thou would'st not be so impudent, to marry *Bea-*
550 *trix* for thy self only?

   Beat. For all his ranting and tearing now, I'll pass my word he shall degenerate into as tame and peaceable a Husband as a civil Woman would wish to have.

Enter Don Melchor *with a Servant.*

   Mel. Sir——

   Alon. I know what you would say, but your discoverie comes too late now.

   Mel. Why, the Ladies are found.

   Aur. But their inclinations are lost I can assure you.

   Jac. Look you Sir, there goes the game: your Plate-fleet
560 is divided; half for *Spain,* and half for *England.*

   Theo. You are justly punish'd for loving two.

   Mel. Yet I have the comfort of a cast Lover: I will think well of my self; and despise my Mistresses.   *Exit.*

DANCE.

   Bell. Enough, enough; let's end the Carnival abed.

   Wild. And for these Gentlemen, when e're they try,
      May they all speed as soon, and well as I.

                        Exeunt Omnes.

---

549 Why,] F, D; ~∧ Q1-3.   549–550 *Beatrix*] Q2-3, F, D; ~ : Q1.
557 Why,] F, D; ~∧ Q1-3.

Epilogue.

M Y *part being small, I have had time to day,*
To mark your various censures of our Play:
First, looking for a Judgement or a Wit,
Like Jews *I saw 'em scatter'd through the Pit:*
And where a knot of Smilers lent an eare
To one that talk'd, I knew the foe was there.
The Club of jests went round; he who had none
Borrow'd o'th' next, and told it for his own:
Among the rest they kept a fearfull stir,
In whisp'ring that he stole th' Astrologer;
And said, betwixt a French *and* English *Plot*
He eas'd his half-tir'd Muse, on pace and trot.
Up starts a Monsieur *new come o're; and warm*
In the French *stoop; and the pull-back o'th' arm;*
Morbleu dit il, *and cocks,* I am a rogue
But he has quite spoil'd the *feint Astrologue.*
Pox, *sayes another;* here's so great a stir
With a son of a whore Farce that's regular,
A rule where nothing must decorum shock!
Dam' me 'ts as dull as dining by the clock.
An Evening! why the devil should we be vext
Whither he gets the Wench this night or next?
When I heard this, I to the Poet went,
Told him the house was full of discontent,
And ask'd him what excuse he could invent.
He neither swore nor storm'd as Poets do,
But, most unlike an Author, vow'd 'twas true.
Yet said, he us'd the French *like Enemies,*

8 *o'th'*] Q2–3, F, D; *oth'* Q1.   10 Astrologer] Q2–3, F, D; *Astrologer* Q1.
13 Monsieur] Q2–3, F, D; *Monsieur* Q1.   14 *o'th'*] Q2–3, F, D; *oth'* Q1.
15 *Morbleu*] Morbleu Q1–3, F, D.
15–16 I . . . [*to*] . . . the] *in italics in Q1–3, F, D.*   17 Pox] *Pox* Q1–3, F, D.
17–22 here's . . . [*to*] . . . next?] *in italics in Q1–3, F, D.*

And did not steal their Plots, but made 'em prize.
But should he all the pains and charges count
Of taking 'em, the bill so high wou'd mount,
That, like Prize goods, which through the Office come,
He could have had 'em much more cheap at home.
He still must write; and Banquier-like, each day
Accept new Bills, and he must break, or pay.
When through his hands such sums must yearly run,
You cannot think the Stock is all his own.
His haste his other errors might excuse;
But there's no mercy for a guilty Muse:
For like a Mistress, she must stand or fall,
And please you to a height, or not at all.

FINIS.

COMMENTARY

List of Abbreviated References

Agrippa: Cornelius Agrippa, *Three Books of Occult Philosophy,* trans. J. F., 1651

Allen: Ned Bliss Allen, *The Sources of John Dryden's Comedies,* Ann Arbor, 1935

"Anti-Scot": "A Discourse concerning the Nature and Substance of Devils and Spirits," appended to Scot (*q.v.*)

Brunel: Antoine de Brunel, *A Journey into Spain,* 1670

Case: Arthur E. Case, *A Bibliography of English Poetical Miscellanies, 1521–1750,* Oxford, 1935

Cox: Nicholas Cox, *The Gentleman's Recreation,* 1677

D&M: C. L. Day and E. B. Murrie, *English Song-Books, 1651–1702: A Bibliography,* Oxford, 1940

Downes: John Downes, *Roscius Anglicanus,* 1708

ELH: A Journal of English Literary History

ELN: English Language Notes

Evelyn, *Diary: The Diary of John Evelyn,* ed. E. S. de Beer, Oxford, 1955

Furness: William Shakespeare, *The Tempest,* ed. Horace Howard Furness, Variorum ed., 1892

Gabalis: N. de Montfaçon de Villars, *Comte de Gabalis,* trans. "The Brothers," 1913

Gentleman's Dictionary: Georges Guillet de Saint-Georges, *Gentleman's Dictionary,* 1705

Herodian: Herodian, *History of the Roman Empire,* trans. Edward C. Echols, Berkeley and Los Angeles, 1961

HLQ: Huntington Library Quarterly

Hobbes, *English Works:* Thomas Hobbes, *The English Works,* ed. William Molesworth, 1839–1845

JEGP: Journal of English and Germanic Philology

Jonson, *Works: Ben Jonson,* ed. C. H. Herford and Percy Simpson, Oxford, 1925–1952

Kermode: William Shakespeare, *The Tempest,* ed. Frank Kermode, Arden ed., 5th ed., rev., Cambridge, Mass., 1954

Kinsley: *The Poems of John Dryden,* ed. James Kinsley, Oxford, 1958

Lancaster: Henry C. Lancaster, *A History of French Dramatic Literature in the Seventeenth Century,* Baltimore, 1929–1942

Macdonald: Hugh Macdonald, *John Dryden: A Bibliography of Early Editions and of Drydeniana,* Oxford, 1939

MLN: Modern Language Notes

MLR: Modern Language Review

MP: Modern Philology

N&Q: Notes and Queries

Noyes: *Poetical Works of Dryden,* ed. George R. Noyes, rev. ed., Cambridge, Mass., 1950

OED: Oxford English Dictionary
Ogg: David Ogg, *England in the Reign of Charles II*, 2d ed., Oxford, 1955
Paracelsus: Theophrastus von Hohenheim, *A Book on Nymphs, Sylphs, Pygmies and Salamanders, and on the other Spirits*, trans. Henry Sigerest, in *Four Treatises*, ed. Henry Sigerest, Baltimore, 1941
Partridge: John Partridge, *An Astrological Vade Mecum*, 1679
PMLA: Publications of the Modern Language Association of America
PQ: Philological Quarterly
RES: Review of English Studies
SB: Studies in Bibliography
Scot: Reginald Scot, *The Discovery of Witchcraft*, 1665
Shadwell, *Works:* Thomas Shadwell, *The Complete Works*, ed. Montague Summers, 1927
SP: Studies in Philology
Spingarn: *Critical Essays of the Seventeenth Century*, ed. J. E. Spingarn, reissue, Bloomington, Ind., 1957
S-S: *The Works of John Dryden*, ed. Sir Walter Scott and George Saintsbury, 1882–1893
Stanley: Thomas Stanley, *The History of Philosophy*, 1655–1660
Summers: Dryden's *Dramatic Works*, ed. Montague Summers, 1931
Term Catalogues: The Term Catalogues, ed. Edward Arber, 1903–1906
Tilley: M. P. Tilley, *A Dictionary of the Proverbs in England in the Sixteenth and Seventeenth Centuries*, Ann Arbor, 1950
Van Lennep: *The London Stage, 1660–1800*, Part 1: 1660–1700, ed. William Van Lennep, with Critical Introduction by Emmett L. Avery and Arthur H. Scouten, Carbondale, Ill., 1965
W&M: Gertrude L. Woodward and James G. McManaway, *A Check List of English Plays, 1641–1700*, Chicago, 1945
Ward, *Letters: The Letters of John Dryden*, ed. Charles E. Ward, Durham, N.C., 1942
Ward, *Life:* Charles E. Ward, *The Life of John Dryden*, Chapel Hill, 1961
Watson: *John Dryden: Of Dramatic Poesy and Other Critical Essays*, ed. George Watson, 1962
Wilson: John Harold Wilson, *All the King's Ladies*, Chicago, 1958
Works: Dryden's works in the present edition

The Tempest

On 7 November 1667, at a time when the great Lord Chancellor Clarendon was about to be removed from office, Samuel Pepys and the court
took time out to attend the first performance of John Dryden and Sir
William Davenant's alteration of Shakespeare's *The Tempest* by the
Duke's Company in Lincoln's Inn Fields. Pepys's enthusiastic response
was unquestionably representative of the feelings of the audience:

> . . . at noon resolved with Sir W. Pen to go see "The
> Tempest," an old play of Shakespeare's, acted, I hear,
> the first day; and so my wife, and girl, and W. Hewer by
> themselves, and Sir W. Pen and I afterwards by our-
> selves; and forced to sit in the side balcone over against
> the musique-room at the Duke's house, close by my Lady
> Dorset and a great many great ones. The house mighty
> full; the King and Court there: and the most innocent
> play that ever I saw; and a curious piece of musique in
> an echo of half sentences, the echo repeating the former
> half, while the man goes on to the latter; which is mighty
> pretty. The play [has] no great wit, but yet good, above
> ordinary plays. Thence home with [Sir] W. Pen, and
> there all mightily pleased with the play; and so to supper
> and to bed, after having done at the office.

Pepys was to record seeing *The Tempest* seven more times,[1] objecting
once to the tediousness of the "seaman's part" and another time to the
dancing of Mrs. Gosnell, but always delighting in the songs. He decided
that no matter how often he saw the play, he would continue to enjoy it.
When he went to see the production by the rival King's Company of a
somewhat similar play, John Fletcher and Philip Massinger's *The Sea
Voyage*, he complained that it was "but a mean play compared with 'The
Tempest,' at the Duke of York's house." [2]

Pepys's admiration for the Dryden-Davenant alteration should be
considered carefully. He did not admire the play because Shakespeare
wrote it; rather he approached it with suspicion because it had "no great
wit," such as might have been expected from a Restoration comedy. And
far from finding the play "defiled" and "degraded," in the manner of
some modern critics, he thought it "the most innocent play" he had ever
seen. We should be careful to avoid making Pepys's standards our own,
but in this instance his reaction to the play has the advantage of anteced-

---

[1] On 13 November, 12 December 1667; 6 January, 3 February, 30 April, 11
May 1668; 21 January 1669. Pepys praised the play twice for its unique
"variety."

[2] 25 March 1668.

ing the era of Shakespeare idolatry and of coming from an age whose sexual morality was not very different from our own.

The Dryden-Davenant version of *The Tempest* was entered in the *Stationers' Register* by Henry Herringman on 8 January 1670 as a "Trage-Comedy" and announced in the *Term Catalogues* (I, 26) on 17 February. It was published at about the same time with a preface by Dryden dated 1 December 1669 and without a cast. Some of the main roles, however, can be assigned. Henry Harris played Ferdinand,[3] Edward Angel played Stephano,[4] Cave Underhill was Trincalo,[5] Mary Davis appeared as Ariel, and Jane Long probably played Hippolito.[6] These players became so closely identified with their roles that Underhill was nicknamed Prince Trincalo, Pepys was upset when Mrs. Gosnell appeared instead of Mary Davis, and the writer of an elegy on Angel asked,

Who shall play Stephano now? your Tempest's gone
To raise new Storms i' th' hearts of every one.[7]

When Pepys remarked in his *Diary* on 25 March 1668 that *The Sea Voyage,* or *The Storm* (as it was renamed), was inferior to the Dryden-Davenant *Tempest,* he was drawing a comparison that was obvious enough to contemporaries. Dryden argued in his preface that Fletcher's play *"was a Copy of* Shakespear's Tempest" and referred to it in his prologue as *"The Storm which vanish'd on the Neighb'ring shore,"* implying that the production of the King's Company had little success because Fletcher was incapable of capturing Shakespeare's poetic genius.[8] The King's Company put on a production of *The Sea Voyage* as *The Storm* on 25 September 1667, just five weeks before the first performance of the Dryden-Davenant revised *Tempest;* it had a run of only three days.[9] Two other performances recorded by Van Lennep were in even

---

[3] Pepys asked Harris for the words of the "Echo Song" which Ferdinand sings as a duet with Ariel; the music was written by John Banister and Pelham Humphrey (see Pepys, *Diary,* 11 May 1668; W. J. Lawrence, "Purcell's Music for *The Tempest,*" *N&Q,* 10th ser., II [1904], 164–165).

[4] See C. B., "An Elegy upon That Incomparable Comedian, Mr. Edward Angell," in *A Little Ark,* ed. G. Thorn-Drury (1921), pp. 38–39.

[5] Van Lennep, p. 123.

[6] Pepys supplies the evidence for Mrs. Davis' appearance in *The Tempest.* On 21 January 1669 he lamented her disappearance and severely criticized her replacement, Mrs. Gosnell. Pepys does not mention what part the two ladies played, but it was probably that of Ariel, since both actresses were known for their singing and dancing. The assumption that Mrs. Long played Hippolito is based entirely on John Downes's remark concerning her success in breeches parts. See Wilson, pp. 140, 146, 166; Downes, p. 27.

[7] *A Little Ark,* p. 38.

[8] *The Sea Voyage* was printed in the folio collections of the plays of Beaumont and Fletcher published in 1647 and 1679. In his dedicatory poem, "On the Dramatick Poems of Mr John Fletcher" (Francis Beaumont and John Fletcher, *Comedies and Tragedies* [1647], sig. C2), Robert Gardiner suggests that the play was written by Fletcher. The attribution of some parts to Massinger was made after Dryden's lifetime.

[9] Van Lennep, p. 118.

closer proximity to performances of *The Tempest*.[10] It is possible that the two companies were deliberately sustaining a rivalry from the very beginning. That Thomas Killigrew should have learned about the coming production of *The Tempest* and put on a similar play seems somewhat more likely than that Dryden and Davenant should have bothered with extensive revisions of Shakespeare's play on such short notice. Even allowing that the Dryden-Davenant *Tempest* was not extraordinarily elaborate, especially in comparison with the "operatic" version of 1674, it still required some new music and some stage effects.

Dryden's collaboration with Davenant probably began at the end of the summer or in the early autumn of 1667. Dryden had worked on the Duke of Newcastle's *Sir Martin Mar-all* for Davenant and the Duke's Company during the early part of the summer, and this contact with the older poet presumably resulted in their joint effort on *The Tempest*.[11] It is likely, as Dryden stated, that Davenant's role was limited to suggestions for a character like Hippolito, to the writing of some sections concerned with the sailors, and to a general supervision.[12] If so, Dryden is overly generous in his homage to Davenant in the preface, which was written toward the end of 1669 after Davenant's death and after the dead laureate had been satirized by Richard Flecknoe in *Sir William D'avenant's Voyage to the Other World* (1668). Flecknoe follows the tradition of Lucian and his seventeenth-century imitators, Quevedo and Boccalini, in showing Davenant's reception by the poets of Elysium. They laugh at him for his pretensions to genius and express their anger at his attacks upon them. "Nay even Shakespear," wrote Flecknoe, "whom he thought to have found his greatest Friend, was as much offended with him as any of the rest, for so spoiling and mangling of his Plays." [13] Flecknoe's postscript, addressed to the actors of the Duke's Company, explains that he published his lampoon to show them it was not so vicious as had been rumored and ends with a threat to attack them if they do not stop murmuring against him: "If you like it not, take heed hereafter how you disoblige Him, who can not onely write for you, but against you too." [14]

Dryden's preface was written in this vituperative atmosphere. Flecknoe had not only attacked Davenant, the manager of the Duke's Company, but the preceding year he had viciously ridiculed Thomas Killigrew, the manager of the rival company. Thus Dryden's attack on a certain *"Ape*

---

[10] *Ibid.*, pp. 131, 136.

[11] Ward (*Life*, pp. 48–53) suggests that the collaboration may have begun in the latter part of spring, 1667.

[12] See Hazleton Spencer, *Shakespeare Improved* (1927), pp. 193–204. For an example of the opposing view that Dryden's share in the revision was very small, see *Shakespeare Adaptations*, ed. Montague Summers (1922), p. xli.

[13] Richard Flecknoe, *Sir William D'avenant's Voyage to the Other World* (1668), pp. 8–9.

[14] *Ibid.*, p. 15. For a general discussion of Flecknoe's pamphlet, see A. K. Croston's introduction to the reprint in *Theatre Miscellany*, Luttrell Reprints no. 14 (1953), pp. 51–58.

of the French *Eloquence"* is almost certainly directed against Flecknoe.[15]
And his defense of Davenant's fancy and imagination must be viewed
more as a gesture of kindness toward the Duke's Company and their
former manager than as a straightforward evaluation of Davenant's role
in the revision of *The Tempest* or of his excellence as a poet. Under the
circumstances it seems likely that Dryden would have overstated rather
than minimized Davenant's share in altering Shakespeare's play. Moreover, Dryden's resentment toward Flecknoe for the vision of Shakespeare's
anger at the spoiling of his plays should not be underestimated. In the
preface, therefore, Dryden extols the imaginative qualities of Davenant
which made him capable of adding to Shakespeare's *"Design,"* and argues
for a continuity from Shakespeare to his putative son Davenant, the dead
laureate, and to Dryden, the new laureate. That *The Tempest* was always
printed in lists of Dryden's plays while being excluded from the folio
collection of Davenant's writings published in 1673 may be an indication
that Dryden regarded his own contribution as the major part in the
revision.[16]

The new *Tempest* was a popular play. Its initial run of at least seven
consecutive acting days was followed by nine recorded performances before the end of April 1674, when new alterations, mostly cuts in the
text and additional music, transformed a play with a great deal of music
and dancing into a colossally successful, spectacular dramatic opera.[17]
Pepys reported the "house very full" when he attended a performance of
the play on 12 December 1667, and it was acted before royalty four
times.[18] The "operatic *Tempest"* included many of the Dryden-Davenant
additions, particularly the large part devoted to the lovers, Hippolito and
Dorinda, and these characters remained on the stage until 1838.[19]
Although many nineteenth- and twentieth-century critics would have
agreed with the argument that the changes made by Dryden and Davenant
represented "a typhoid of the entire system," there is evidence to show
the existence of considerable audience resistance to restoring the original.[20] Francis Gentleman, editor of the Bell edition of Shakespeare

---

[15] See Maximillian E. Novak, "Dryden's 'Ape of the French Eloquence' and
Richard Flecknoe," *Bulletin of the New York Public Library*, LXXII (1968),
499–506.

[16] See, for example, Herringman's list in the 1686 edition of *Tyrannick Love*,
sig. I4. Admittedly the 1673 folio of Davenant's writings was incomplete, but
Dryden did, in effect, claim the revised *Tempest*. Gerard Langbaine classified
it with Dryden's revision of *Troilus and Cressida* and accused Dryden of becoming wealthy by stealing from Shakespeare. Langbaine's classification, which
appears in his first volume on the stage, was retained by Gildon. See Langbaine's *Momus Triumphans* (1688), p. 7; *An Account of the English Dramatick
Poets* (Oxford, 1691), p. 141; and *The Lives and Characters of the English
Dramatick Poets*, rev. Charles Gildon (1699), p. 47.

[17] Van Lennep, pp. 123–126, 128, 131, 133–136, 154, 156, 176.

[18] *Ibid.*, pp. 123, 124, 131.

[19] See G. C. D. Odell, *Shakespeare from Betterton to Irving* (1920), II, 200–201.

[20] *Ibid.*, I, 233. For Garrick's effort to eliminate the Dryden-Davenant version,

(1774), suggested that far from destroying Shakespeare's play, Dryden and Davenant had produced "a better acting play," and further noted: "Of Shakespeare's original we may say, it is more nervous and chaste, but not so well supplied with humour or business as Dryden's."[21] Gentleman thought the handling of the sailors in the Dryden-Davenant version more probable than in Shakespeare's play and advised a judicious combination of the original with Dryden and Davenant's changes. Such a version was produced successfully in 1789 by John Philip Kemble.[22] In spite of adverse criticism, Hippolito and Dorinda remained on the stage, a tribute to Dryden and Davenant's understanding of popular taste in comedy, until William Macready's enormously successful production of Shakespeare's original on 13 October 1838.[23]

Most of the performances of *The Tempest* during the Restoration and the eighteenth century were probably based on the operatic *Tempest,* first produced in April 1674 and described by John Downes:

> The Tempest, or the Inchanted Island, made into an Opera by Mr. Shadwell, having all New in it; as Scenes, Machines; particularly, one Scene Painted with Myriads of Ariel Spirits; and another flying away, with a Table Furnisht out with Fruits, Sweetmeats and all sorts of Viands; just when Duke Trinculo and his Companions, were going to Dinner; all things perform'd in it so Admirably well, that not any succeeding Opera got more Money.[24]

see George Winchester Stone, "Shakespeare's *Tempest* at Drury Lane during Garrick's Management," *Shakespeare Quarterly,* VII (1956), 1–7. See also Charles Hogan, *Shakespeare in the Theatre, 1701–1800* (1952), I, 422–425.

[21] William Shakespeare, *Plays* (1774), III, 6 (sig. X2). On the witty dialogue of Antonio, Sebastian, and Gonzalo at the beginning of the second act, which had been cut by Dryden and Davenant, Gentleman commented (p. 24): "There are near three pages of the scene succeeding this speech, in the original, very properly left out, as they are strangely trifling, and therefore not worthy of either utterance or perusal."

[22] In the Kemble version advertised on the title page as "written by Shakespeare; with additions from Dryden as compiled by J. P. Kemble," Mustacho and Ventoso were eliminated along with Shakespeare's Sebastian, while Neptune and Amphitrite from Shadwell's masque of 1674 were retained. For a full discussion of the revisions of *The Tempest* between 1667 and 1789, see George Guffey's introduction to a reprint collection of various versions of the play (*After The Tempest,* Augustan Reprint Society, Special Publication, 1969).

[23] Alfred Bunn, Macready's rival, claimed that his own production of *The Tempest* on 5 October 1833, which included Hippolito and Dorinda, was superior to Macready's, which "owed all the attraction it possessed to the novelty of Miss P. Horton 'My gentle Ariel,' singing while suspended in the air" (*The Stage: Both Before and Behind the Curtain* [1840], I, 134; III, 98, 252). But reviewers criticized Bunn for using some of Dryden and Davenant's "inconsistent and unnatural additions" (see, e.g., *Literary Gazette,* 12 October 1833, p. 652).

[24] Downes, pp. 34–35.

Downes's information is at least partly correct, but many of the details of the new production remain in doubt. First, it is unlikely that Dryden had anything to do with it, since he had signed a contract with the King's Company in May 1668 to provide three plays a year.[25] Also his reaction to the operatic version was hostile, as is clearly shown by his remarks in "A Prologue spoken at the Opening of the New House, Mar. 26. 1674":

> . . . *French* Machines have ne'r done *England* good:
> I wou'd not prophesie our Houses Fate:
> But while vain Shows and Scenes you over-rate,
> 'Tis to be fear'd——
> That as a Fire the former House o'rethrew,
> Machines and Tempests will destroy the new.[26]

Many years later he could speak of *The Tempest* in detached and general terms as a kind of opera, but even though many of his textual revisions and his characters were retained, Dryden's tone of distant praise suggests that he did not regard the spectacle put together in 1674 as his own work.[27]

The authorship debate has raged ever since the operatic *Tempest* was claimed for Shadwell in 1904 with the assertion that scholars had previously failed to distinguish between a comedy and an opera.[28] Next came a denial that Shadwell's claim had been established, along with a countersuggestion that the Dryden-Davenant version itself may have been an opera of a sort.[29] It has also been suggested that Thomas

---

[25] James M. Osborn, *John Dryden: Some Biographical Facts and Problems* (1965), pp. 202–207; Ward, *Life*, p. 57.

[26] *Works*, I, 150. For variant readings and a discussion of Dryden's sneer at the Duke's Company, see Helene Maxwell Hooker, "Dryden's and Shadwell's *Tempest*," *HLQ*, VI (1943), 224–228.

[27] See the preface to *Albion and Albanius* (1685, sig. b2; Watson, II, 41–42).

[28] The debate was embittered from the start by W. J. Lawrence's attack on William Cummings and his insistence that Sir Ernest Clarke had plagiarized from Lawrence's writings on the subject. See W. J. Lawrence, "Did Thomas Shadwell Write an Opera on 'The Tempest'?" *Anglia*, XXVII (1904), 205–217; Lawrence, "Purcell's Music for *The Tempest*," pp. 164–165; William Cummings, "Purcell's Music for *The Tempest*," *N&Q*, 10th ser., II (1904), 270–271; Lawrence, "Purcell's Music for *The Tempest*," *N&Q*, 10th ser., II (1904), 329–330; William Barclay Squire, "Purcell's Dramatic Music," *Sammelbände der Internationalen Musik Gesellschaft*, V (1904–05), 552–555; Squire, "The Music of Shadwell's *Tempest*" (with musical notations), *Musical Quarterly*, VII (1921), 565–578; Ernest Clarke, "The 'Tempest' as an 'Opera,'" *Athenaeum* (1906), pp. 222–223; Lawrence, "Shadwell's Opera of 'The Tempest,'" *Anglia*, XXIX (1906), 539; Lawrence, in *The Elizabethan Playhouse and Other Studies*, 1st ser. (1912), pp. 191–206. For a list of writings on the music for *The Tempest*, see James McManaway, "Songs and Masques in *The Tempest*," *Theatre Miscellany*, Luttrel Reprints no. 14 (1953), p. 78.

[29] G. Thorn-Drury, "Shadwell and the Operatic *Tempest*," *RES*, III (1927), 204. Thorn-Drury argued for the operatic quality of the Dryden-Davenant version after his doubts on Shadwell's part in the operatic *Tempest* had been

Betterton may have done most of the work,[30] and again, that the operatic version was a group effort.[31] The latter seems extremely likely in spite of Downes's sweeping attribution of the changes to Shadwell.[32]

If Dryden and Davenant turned Shakespeare's play somewhat more in the direction of traditional comedy, they nevertheless retained many operatic elements. When, in the preface to *Albion and Albanius* (1685), Dryden used *The Tempest* as an example of "a Tragedy mix'd with *Opera;* or a *Drama* Written in blank Verse, adorn'd with Scenes, Machines, Songs, and Dances," he was probably referring to the operatic *Tempest*, but his remarks are pertinent to his own version. He distinguishes between the operatic form and a play on the grounds that the former "is suppos'd to be conducted sometimes by supernatural means, or Magick." [33] If we can rely on this definition, Dryden must have regarded his and Davenant's revision of *The Tempest* as partly operatic in nature. Although Dryden gave no indication that he was connected with the operatic version, his choice of it as an example suggests that even after the demands of spectacle and music had caused severe cutting and some inartistic juggling of scenes, he experienced pleasure in seeing his Dorinda and Hippolito as popular stage characters.[34] He probably would

attacked by D. M. Walmsley. See Thorn-Drury, "Some Notes on Dryden," *RES*, I (1925), 187, 324–330; Walmsley, "Shadwell and the Operatic *Tempest*," *RES*, II (1926), 463–466; Walmsley, "Shadwell and the Operatic *Tempest*," *RES*, III (1927), 451–453.

[30] Charles E. Ward, "*The Tempest: A Restoration Opera Problem,*" *ELH*, XIII (1946), 119–130.

[31] William Milton warns against "attempting to decide who 'wrote' such a hodgepodge as the Tempest of 1674" ("Tempest in a Teapot," *ELH*, XIV [1947], 218), and McManaway, remarking on the way new music and lyrics were added, compares the operatic version with "a modern musical show" ("Songs and Masques," *Theatre Miscellany*, pp. 79–80).

[32] Through the identification of the contemporary musician, Pietro Reggio, Shadwell's part in writing the song, "Arise Ye Subterranean Winds," has long been known. But new evidence supporting the theory that the operatic *Tempest* was a group effort has been drawn from Elkanah Settle's comments in his *Notes and Observations on the Empress of Morocco Revised* (1674) (see Maximillian E. Novak, "Elkanah Settle's Attacks on Thomas Shadwell and the Authorship of the 'Operatic *Tempest*,'" *N&Q*, CCXIII [1968], 263–265). There is something to be said, moreover, for the argument that the Dryden-Davenant version was itself close to being an opera. *The Tempest* was Shakespeare's most spectacular and most musical play, and we must remember that Pepys was delighted by the dancing, music, and "variety" of the Dryden-Davenant version. The collaborators dropped a few of Shakespeare's songs, the elaborate masque of Iris, Juno, and Ceres, and such effects as the "quaint device" (III, iii) by which the banquet vanished. But they adapted one part of the masque for the lovely lyric beginning *"Dry those eyes which are o'reflowing"* (III, ii) and added an antimasque as well as various songs and dances. Pepys admired the "echo" song and the dance of the sailors, while the dance of *"eight fat Spirits, with Cornu-Copia in their hands"* did not escape the satire of the authors of *The Rehearsal.*

[33] *Albion and Albanius* (1685), sig. b2; Watson, II, 41.

[34] Thomas Davies suggested that Dryden's quarrel with Shadwell had its

have liked some of the new music added by Henry Purcell around 1695, but what he would have made of the "Dialogue between Cupid and Bacchus," which was announced with the play in 1707, or of the "Grand Devils Dance" of 1727 is hard to say.[35] Dryden and Davenant were the last writers to contribute significant artistic changes to *The Tempest.* From a purely literary standpoint, the operatic *Tempest,* by Shadwell or anyone else, is a myth.

Dryden's collaboration with Davenant on *The Tempest* was the first of his adaptations of Shakespeare. A decade later he was to state his indebtedness to Shakespeare's genius in the preface to *All for Love* (1678), and in the spring of 1679 his adaptation of Shakespeare's *Troilus and Cressida* was first performed. Dryden had probably concluded that Shakespeare was the great master of the English stage considerably before he began working with Davenant in 1667, and he did much toward making his contemporaries agree with him. What seems obvious enough to us was not at all clear at a time when Fletcher was more popular than Shakespeare on the stage and Jonson received greater acclaim from the learned critics. If Dryden was telling the truth about being converted into an admirer of Shakespeare's by Davenant, the conversion must have taken place long before their collaboration on *The Tempest.* In his dedication of *The Rival Ladies* (1664), Dryden had stated that in spite of "some Errors not to be avoided in that Age" Shakespeare "had undoubtedly a larger Soul of Pœsie than ever any of our Nation," [36] and he may have written the encomium on Shakespeare in *Of Dramatick Poesie* at least a year before working with Davenant.[37]

But Davenant was both the foremost repository of information about Shakespeare and his most ardent advocate, and it is not improbable that at some point the older poet should have convinced Dryden of Shakespeare's greatness. Davenant had already adapted Shakespeare's *Measure for Measure* and *Much Ado About Nothing* into a single comedy, *The Law against Lovers,* probably first performed in February 1662; and sometime shortly before November 1664 he staged an adaptation of *Macbeth.*[38] Dryden's brief connection with the Duke's Company began with what must have been the uncongenial task of revising the Duke of Newcastle's *Sir Martin Mar-all,* which was just the kind of play he had always attacked—a French farce; but there is no reason to doubt Dryden's

origins in his envy of the success of Shadwell's "operatic *Tempest,*" but whatever pique Dryden may have felt because of a successful production by the rival company while he was a shareholder in the King's Company had long passed by 1685 (see John Downes, *Roscius Anglicanus,* ed. Davies [1789], p. 44).

[35] See Van Lennep, p. 441. See also *The London Stage, 1660–1800,* Pt. II: 1700–1729, ed. Emmett L. Avery (1960), Vol. I, p. 136; Vol. II, p. 927.

[36] *Works,* VIII, 99.

[37] Charles Ward (*Life,* pp. 46, 58) sets the date of composition in late summer or early autumn of 1665. The essay was published in May or June 1668.

[38] Van Lennep, pp. 36, 47, 85.

statement in the preface to *The Tempest* that he undertook the writing of the parts of Hippolito and Dorinda with great *"delight"* or that he enjoyed working with Davenant.

Some of the reasons behind Dryden's extraordinary encomium on Davenant in the prefatory note have already been examined, but it would be a mistake to be too skeptical of every part of the preface. That Davenant suggested the *"excellent contrivance"* of having a character like Hippolito—a man who had never seen a woman—to balance his female counterpart, Miranda, seems very likely, since Davenant preferred to balance his plots with parallel characters. It is also believable that the *"Comical parts of the Saylors"* were his invention, but how much of the writing Davenant actually did is difficult to say. Dryden's casual remark that Davenant's hand is easily detectable is highly questionable. In fact, the extremely racy and sexually suggestive scenes with Sycorax are very unlike Davenant and very much like Dryden.[39] And if Dryden was perfectly honest about his *"gratitude to the memory of Sir* William D'avenant*"* and his high opinion of Davenant's poetic talents in 1669, he was certainly to change his mind in the future. There can be little doubt that Dryden either wrote or polished the lines in Sir William Soame's translation of Boileau's *Art of Poetry* which are critical of Davenant's poetry:

> Then D'Avenant came; who, with a new found Art,
> Chang'd all, spoil'd all, and had his way apart:
> His haughty Muse all others did despise,
> And thought in Triumph to bear off the Prize,
> Till the Sharp-sighted Critics of the Times
> In their Mock-*Gondibert* expos'd his Rhimes;
> The Lawrels he pretended did refuse,
> And dash'd the hopes of his aspiring Muse.
> This head-strong Writer, falling from on high,
> Made following Authors take less Liberty.[40]

It may be possible to see a suggestion of this criticism in Dryden's compliment: *"He borrowed not of any other; and his imaginations were such as could not easily enter into any other man."* If this hypothesis seems too much the product of hindsight, we can at least be certain that Dryden's sly parody of Davenant's *Gondibert* in *Mac Flecknoe* (1. 82) several years

---

[39] Hazleton Spencer has argued cogently that "D'Avenant was almost a prude where verbal grossness was to be dealt with. Dryden, on the other hand, is one of the loosest of the English dramatists." But while Spencer uses these facts as evidence for Dryden's major part in the undertaking, he accepts Dryden's word on the composition of the sections concerning the sailors, though these scenes are surely marked by the most obvious "verbal grossness." The Duke of Buckingham and his friends undoubtedly had Dryden in mind when they had Bayes boast: "I make 'em all talk bawdy—ha, ha, ha!—beastly, downright bawdy upon the stage, 'y gad—ha, ha, ha!—but with an infinite deal of wit, that I must say." See Spencer, *Shakespeare Improved*, p. 202; *The Rehearsal*, III, v, 145.

[40] *Art of Poetry* (1683), p. 8; Kinsley, I, 335.

later was no accident. Whatever his opinion of Davenant may have been in 1669, Dryden was careful to separate himself from those who, like Flecknoe, were *"so base as to rob the dead of his reputation"* and to identify himself as heir to the laureateship.

From the comments of numerous critics on the Dryden-Davenant *Tempest,* one might think that the collaborators had set out deliberately to destroy the play and to ruin Shakespeare's reputation.[41] Yet Dryden's magnificent prologue, which boasts proudly of Shakespeare's superiority to Fletcher and Jonson, should remove any lingering suspicion of Dryden and Davenant's intentions. Dryden presents Shakespeare as the archetypal natural artist, rooted in nature like a tree and possessing the magical force of nature. Jonson and Fletcher could capture only part of Shakespeare's brilliance:

> But Shakespear's *Magick could not copy'd be,*
> *Within that Circle none durst walk but he.*

The collaborators had no intention of destroying the *"innocence and beauty"* of Shakespeare's play, but they did realize that their contemporaries would have regarded it as old-fashioned. They apologize for Shakespeare's use of magic by giving the historical explanation that Shakespeare wrote for a naïve age. And the belief in Shakespeare as the very *"Nature"* that the playwrights strove to imitate opened the possibility of improving Shakespeare by the polish of art. Dryden and Davenant wrote a *"new reviving Play,"* a remaking of Shakespeare's *Tempest* in a manner they thought would amuse the audience sitting in Lincoln's Inn Fields on the seventh day of November 1667, and also in a manner they did not hesitate to set next to Shakespeare's. If they seem insensitive to the organic unity, to the balance of beauty in Shakespeare's art, it was because both Dryden and Davenant lived under a new artistic dispensation now called neoclassicism.

In his *Defence of the Epilogue* (1672), Dryden remarked that one of Shakespeare's faults was that plays like *The Winter's Tale, Love's Labour's Lost,* and *Measure for Measure* "were either grounded on impossibilities, or at least, so meanly written, that the Comedy neither caus'd your mirth, nor the serious part your concernment." [42] The major departures from Shakespeare's *Tempest* are directed toward resolving these problems. Whereas Shakespeare had merged the separate elements of his play in such a way that ultimate problems of sin and redemption, freedom and slavery, love and hatred, music and discord, storm and calm, illusion and reality are resolved by the magic powers of Prospero,[43] Dryden and Davenant tried to separate the disparate

---

[41] See, e.g., Furness, p. viii; Frederick Kilbourne, *Alterations and Adaptations of Shakespeare* (1906), pp. 27, 32; Spencer, *Shakespeare Improved,* pp. 86–87, 203.

[42] *Conquest of Granada* (1672), p. 163; Watson, I, 172.

[43] This way of resolving problems has led critics to search for mystical or allegorical interpretations of *The Tempest* (see, e.g., A. D. Nuttall, *Two Concepts of Allegory* [1967]).

elements and to simplify what had been ambiguous before. The relationships in Shakespeare's play are connected by a series of correspondences. The revolt of Caliban, Trinculo, and Stephano against authority is paralleled by that of Antonio and Sebastian and (in the past) Antonio and Alonzo. Dryden and Davenant drop Sebastian and make Antonio and Alonzo penitent from their first arrival on the island. They are sympathetic figures, and we are concerned with Prospero's acceptance of their penitence rather than with the change in Alonzo during the play. We are even more concerned with what seems to be the death of one of the lovers. And we are amused by the complete buffoonery of the sailors. Dryden and Davenant attempt to bring clarity to Shakespeare's play by dividing the characters and their actions along lines of class and decorum inherent in the concept of literary genre. They might knowingly violate French neoclassical ideals, however, by joining tragic and comic themes in the same play; and they deliberately avoid the kind of organic unity to be found in Shakespeare. Comic and tragic themes are tied together not by metaphoric relationships but by the turns of plot.

Viewed in this way, the structural changes of the Dryden-Davenant version followed the logic of comedy and tragicomedy during the Restoration. Almost every play had at least three couples whose love might be measured on a descending scale, from platonic down to the purely sensual. *The Tempest* is set on an enchanted island, but as Thomas Duffet's *The Mock Tempest,* a parody of the operatic *Tempest* produced in 1674, revealed, a bawdy London setting could easily transform the *"innocence and beauty"* of which Dryden boasted into complete obscenity. Duffet's farce is instructive also in showing how much Dryden and Davenant, and for that matter even Shakespeare, depended on the magical qualities of Prospero's island to achieve their effects.[44] Dryden and Davenant structured their play in terms of contemporary tragicomedy, but their concept of the island and its relationship to the theme of innocence and experience was the main factor in determining how their characters would act and think. Shakespeare saw certain comic, sexual implications in the encounter between Ferdinand and Miranda, but he stressed the purity of their love. Davenant and Dryden retained much of Shakespeare's approach; Miranda and Ferdinand "have chang'd Eyes" in the revised *Tempest* as in Shakespeare's. But Dryden and Davenant were too much the product of their times not to see the sexual drives behind the most innocent love, and like their contemporaries they regarded this very human attribute as potentially very comic.[45]

---

[44] Duffet's settings are a bordello and a house of correction for prostitutes, Bridewell. In Duffet's parody the tone of *The Tempest* is lowered in a variety of ways, from having Prospero enter at one point eating bread and butter to having several of the prostitutes debate the physiological effects of venereal disease.

[45] Anne Ferry puts this idea neatly, if somewhat unsympathetically, when she writes that "Dryden transposes the ideal of pastoral innocence into an image of prurient ignorance" (*Milton and the Miltonic Dryden* [1968], p. 91).

Sir Walter Scott complained that "Miranda's simplicity is converted into indelicacy, and Dorinda talks the language of prostitution before she has ever seen a man." [46] That is to say, Dryden and Davenant reveal the sexual longings of the characters through their language before they themselves are aware of the precise meaning of their words and desires. The Dryden-Davenant heroines feel a natural drive toward physical contact with men, though they are entirely ignorant of the implications of their feelings. Admittedly they are sexually innocent only in a technical sense, but such a concept is surely as understandable to our age as it was to the Restoration.[47] In regarding the "peculiar colouring" thrown over Miranda and Dorinda as suggestive of prostitution, Scott merely revealed the perverse repressions of his period and the absurd burden of sexual purity it imposed upon women.[48] Both Miranda and Dorinda fall in love immediately, and if their love is partly sexual, they nevertheless reveal both their fidelity to the men they love and the depth of their feelings. Their conduct, Dryden and Davenant are saying, with perhaps a hint of irony, reveals true innocence.

Hippolito, the *"Man who had never seen a Woman,"* is also connected with the theme of innocence, ignorance, and experience, but Dryden and Davenant seem to have put more thought into his creation, for he was a typical, indeed a symbolic, figure in the seventeenth century. Although Prospero jests with Dorinda about the "wild Young man" who is not wild in the woods but "within Doors, in Chambers, And in Closets," Dryden and Davenant are serious enough concerning their variation on the theme of the wild man—the natural man raised in isolation and outside the laws of civilization.[49] Pedro Calderón's magnificent *La Vida Es Sueño* (1635) also brings such an innocent suddenly into society, and Baltasar Gracián's *El Criticón* (1651–1657) develops an entire allegory out of Andrenio's discovery of the world after leaving the cave on the island where he has grown up in complete isolation.[50] The wild man, or the

[46] S-S, I, 91.

[47] James Sutherland maintains that "Dryden pays lip service to 'pretty innocence' while revelling in innuendo," but Dryden and Davenant make no effort to conceal the awakening sexuality of the two ingenues, who are just about as innocent as the sophisticated Restoration drama allowed anyone to be (see *English Literature in the Late Seventeenth Century* [1969], p. 99).

[48] S-S, I, 91.

[49] For a discussion of this mythic figure, see Richard Bernheimer, *Wild Men in the Middle Ages* (1952).

[50] Calderón's *En Esta Vida Todo Es Verdad y Todo Mentira*, written in 1659 and printed in 1664, has four characters who could qualify as wild men, including the tyrant, Focas, who claims that he was raised by wolves near Etna:

> Leche de lobas, infante
> me alimentó allí en mi tierna
> edad, y en mi vida adulta
> en veneno de sus yerbas;
> en cuya bruta crïanza
> dudó la naturaleza
> si era fiera o si era hombre,
> y resolvió, al ver que era

natural man, continued a popular figure, whether in plays like *Muce-dorus* or in chapbook versions of *Valentine and Orson*.[51]
Dryden's own fascination with the myth of natural man is beyond question. His Montezuma in *The Indian Queen* was raised by Garrucca and taught to live the life of nature, and his later character, Almanzor, could make the famous boast:

I am as free as Nature first made man,
'Ere the base Laws of Servitude began
When wild in woods the noble Savage ran.[52]

In many ways the Adam of Dryden's *The State of Innocence* seems

---

hombre y fiera, que creciese
para rey de hombres y fieras.

Herman Grimm argued that Dryden and Davenant had taken the Dorinda-Hippolito plot and several other hints from the Calderón play, and his opinion was adopted unquestionably by Furness in his edition of Shakespeare's *Tempest*. But Montague Summers dismissed these charges (Summers, II, 147), arguing that "given the situation, the coincidence in thought is almost inevitable." Summers was unquestionably right, though he did not elaborate on what might be a fascinating exercise in archetypal criticism or the study of the influence of the seventeenth-century *Weltanschauung* on writers in England and Spain. Very much like Dryden and Davenant is the way Calderón's Astolfo warns his two wild foster sons, Heraclio and Leonido, of the dangers of women and their dual nature. In spite of Astolfo's advice, Heraclio finds that his body trembles at the very mention of the word *mujer*, and his first encounter with a woman, Cintia, leaves him astonished by her beauty. When she asks him questions, he shows his ignorance, but defends himself by a Socratic excuse worthy of Dryden's Adam in *The State of Innocence:*

Cin. ¿Nada sabes?
Her.   No, indignada,
culpa tus iras me den;
que no sabe poco quien
sabe que no sabe nada.

When Leonido sees the magician's daughter, Libia, there is the same combination of naïve wonder at her beauty and fear of her power. This play has all of Calderón's preoccupation with illusion and reality, which finds its best English equivalent in Shakespeare's *The Tempest*, and contains a magician to raise a storm, a prince returned to his throne after being brought up as a wild man, and even a duel between Heraclio and Leonido to parallel that between Hippolito and Ferdinand. Calderón's play suggests that the changes made by Dryden and Davenant in *The Tempest* were not so much associated with the license of the Restoration stage as with the pre-occupation with certain themes common to all western European literature at the time. See Grimm, "Shakespeare's Sturm in der Bearbeitung von Dryden und Davenant," in *Fünfzehn Essays* (Berlin, 1875), pp. 183–224; Furness, pp. ix, 346–347; Pedro Calderón de la Barca, *Obras Completas*, ed. Angel Valbuena Briones, I (5th ed.; 1966), 1110, 1115–1119 (Jornada I).
[51] These works, with their traditional wild men, were extremely popular throughout the seventeenth century. During the following century the myth dissipated in the direction of philosophical tales in the manner of John Kirby's *Automathes*, island adventures like *Robinson Crusoe*, and works dramatizing the life of the noble savage.
[52] *Conquest of Granada* (1672), p. 7; S-S, IV, 43.

closer to the traditional natural man of the period than to Milton's progenitor of the human race. But whatever license Dryden permitted himself, any Adam must inevitably be tested by the biblical account; on the other hand, a natural man like Montezuma or Hippolito could be used to illustrate those general maxims about the human race of which the period was so fond. Thus the natural man became a subject of interest for writers on politics and society from Hobbes to Rousseau, and there is no reason to doubt that Dryden enjoyed the task assigned him by Davenant. *"I confess that from the very first moment it so pleas'd me,"* wrote Dryden in the preface to *The Tempest,* *"that I never writ any thing with more delight."* What is surprising is that Dryden's rendering of Hippolito is so limited in scope. Although Hippolito may be seen as contributing another dimension to Shakespeare's concept of freedom, since like Ariel and Caliban he is seeking to expand his experience of his world, the particular nature of his experience within the play is limited to an awareness of the existence of women and a desire to test his courage against another man—in short, limited to love and honor. The natural man, as evolved by Dryden, seems to be a simple compound of concupiscible and irascible passions. Lacking a full understanding of sex and love, Hippolito nevertheless desires to possess every woman and to remove every obstacle that hinders realization of his goal. Although his quarrel and fight with Ferdinand may be viewed as the product of Hippolito's naïveté or innocence, both men—the natural man and the civilized man—are motivated by the same sexual drive for possession and conquest. With the shedding of his blood Hippolito loses something of the force of his sex drive along with his physical strength. His wound has much the same effect upon him as the laws of society would have: they weaken his powers and force him to content himself with one woman. Polygamy is good enough for the natural man (the wild man, an animalistic version of natural man, was famous for his sexual powers) or for the patriarchs, but it cannot be carried over to Western civilization. The taming of Hippolito is roughly equivalent to the change in Almanzor in *The Conquest of Granada*—the shift from a hero of will, asserting his superiority over both society and his environment, to a man capable of living in civilization.[53]

Like Dorinda and Miranda, Hippolito is provided with language full of sexual puns (e.g., "turn me loose upon 'em"), but today there would be less objection than Sir Walter Scott displayed to such unconscious wit proceeding from the libido.[54] Dryden sometimes moves from this kind of wit to a poetic rendering of innocence in his best manner:

[53] John H. Winterbottom, "The Development of the Hero in Dryden's Tragedies," *JEGP,* LII (1953), 161–173. Fujimura's arguments concerning the naturalistic basis of passion in Dryden's heroic plays have, in some ways, better application to Hippolito and the revised *Tempest* than to Dryden's "serious" plays (Thomas H. Fujimura, "The Appeal of Dryden's Heroic Plays," *PMLA,* LXXV [1960], 37–45).

[54] For the classic discussion of the underlying sexual motive for such wit, see Sigmund Freud, *Wit and Its Relation to the Unconscious,* in *The Basic Writings of Sigmund Freud,* trans. A. A. Brill (1938), pp. 692–697.

> *Hip.* Are they so beautiful?
> *Prosp.* Calm sleep is not so soft, nor Winter Suns,
> Nor Summer Shades so pleasant.
> *Hip.* Can they be fairer than the Plumes of Swans?
> Or more delightful than the Peacocks Feathers?
> Or than the gloss upon the necks of Doves?
> Or have more various beauty than the Rain-bow?
> These I have seen, and without danger wondred at.

At their worst Dryden and Davenant's double entendres are no more shocking than those found in modern comedies or in typical nightclub entertainment. To Scott, sexual puns must have seemed more offensive coming from the women than from Hippolito, but they are seldom more obscene than Dorinda's response to Prospero's warnings concerning wild men:

> *Dor.* But Father, I would stroak 'em, and make 'em gentle,
> Then sure they would not hurt me.
> *Prosp.* You must not trust them, Child: no woman can come
> Neer 'em but she feels a pain full nine Months.

Such warnings do not prevent Dorinda and Miranda from fighting over the opportunity to see that "goodly thing," a man. Admittedly Dryden and Davenant bring Shakespeare's romantic picture of ideal love down to earth, but Shakespeare himself occasionally introduced reality into his Arcadias; and there is no reason to suspect Pepys's sense of the "innocence" of the Dryden-Davenant version. It is not so innocent as Shakespeare's play, but it is certainly innocent enough for a modern audience.

Just as Dryden and Davenant attempted to heighten comic effects throughout the romantic parts of *The Tempest,* so they also revised the roles of Stephano, Trincalo, and Caliban in the direction of comedy. In doing so they cut out the sections containing Gonzalo's speech on utopia, the witty attacks on Gonzalo by Sebastian and Antonio, and the attempted assassination of Alonzo. The deletions revealed good dramatic sense on the part of the collaborators, for enjoyable as these parts are to read, they are difficult to sustain on the stage. Sebastian is dropped entirely, but the utopian theme undergoes a comic metamorphosis. Trincalo and Stephano are changed from jester and butler to sailors, given two companions, Mustacho and Ventoso, and made the center of political interest. The revolt of this symbolic rabble is enlarged and provided with the comic force that Dryden liked to expend upon his scenes of mob rule and insurrection. Trincalo, like Sancho Panza almost starved in his kingdom, and Stephano, struggling over the favors of the monstrous Sycorax, strike one as wittier and more amusing than Shakespeare's drunken would-be rulers.[55] And to a certain extent they are true to

---

[55] John Genest observed, with some justice, that Dryden and Davenant had made Trincalo and Stephano less individualized than Shakespeare's characters and had "transferred a great part of Stephano's character to Trincalo" (*Some Account of the English Stage from the Restoration in 1660 to 1830* [Bath, 1832], IV, 236).

Shakespeare's rendering of the insurrections among Sir George Somers'
crew on the island of Bermuda. Although it is very likely that Shakespeare
had read about the wreck of the *Sea Adventure* on the coast of the
Bermudas in 1609, he took from the story only some hints for his play.
The tale of Carter, Waters, and Chard in Bermuda—the vivid account of
three men alone on an island fighting for a kingdom (an episode that
occurred after Shakespeare's death)—was available to Dryden and Davenant in a number of voyage narratives. In short, Dryden and Davenant's
expansion of the roles of the sailors is ascribable partly to their effort to
make *The Tempest* more comic and partly to the increased interest in,
and knowledge about, Shakespeare's archetypal island of rebellion.[56]

Francis Gentleman thought Dryden's sailors more "characteristic" than
Shakespeare's usurpers,[57] and certainly Dryden's version of Shakespeare's
bawdy sea ballad, "The Master, the Swabber, the Gunner, and I," seems
more appropriate to the boatswain, Trincalo, than to the jester, Trinculo.
The addition of Mustacho and Ventoso provides comic heightening, not
so much in the dialogue as in the stage action. It is likely that their roles
lay mainly in farcical grimaces and the kind of stage action associated
with *commedia dell'arte*. Shakespeare's indebtedness to the scenari of the
Italian comedians has been disputed, but there can be no question that
Dryden and Davenant saw them as characters out of Italian or French
farce. Although the names, Mustacho and Ventoso, are not to be found
among the traditional characters of the *commedia dell'arte*, their ante-
cedents are unmistakable. Davenant had already experimented with
French farce, and it is hard to resist the temptation to believe that
James Nokes, who had been so successful as Sir Martin Mar-all a few
months before, joined Angel and Underhill in contributing something to
the farcical nature of the subplot.[58] Stripped of much of Shakespeare's
poetic powers, the revolt of the drunken, hungry sailors and the monstrous
Caliban and Sycorax seems very close indeed to scenari like *The Great
Magician* and *Arcadia Enchanted*.[59]

Much that is added by way of comedy may be discovered in the char-

---

[56] See Samuel Purchas, *Purchas his Pilgrimes* (Glasgow ed., 1905–1907), XIX,
13–38.

[57] Shakespeare, *Plays* (1774), III, sig. X2.

[58] In a series of prologues attacking farce, Edward Howard brought all three
together on the stage to have them frightened by the ghost of Ben Jonson, the
defender of true comedy (*The Womens Conquest* [1671], sigs. c2v–c4).

[59] K. M. Lea, *Italian Popular Comedy* (1934), II, 434, 444–453, 649–657, 670–
674. Kermode is skeptical of the arguments put forward by Lea and others,
and while he does not resolve the problem, he concludes that it is "safe only
to say that no matter what is proved in the end, it is very unlikely that the
interpretation of *The Tempest* will be seriously affected." Although the origins
of Shakespeare's drunken jester and butler are obscure, there can be no
question that Dryden and Davenant would have known something about
commedia dell'arte, if only through the familiar sight of a mountebank's zanni.
Dryden was always contemptuous of the grimaces that still make up much
farce, but Davenant and his company experimented with French farce soon
after a French troop visited England in 1661. With Nokes, Angel, and Under-

acter of Sycorax and in the rivalry between Trincalo and Stephano for her hand and, with it, political control of the island. Monstrous as she is, Sycorax is made to embody all the sensuality that Western man has always imagined to be characteristic of women of dark-skinned races. By 1668 polygamous, polyandrous, and even incestuous societies had been discovered by voyagers, and Sycorax is a typically libertine object lesson in the conventional and regional nature of monogamy. Sycorax is interested solely in sex, whether with Trincalo, his subjects, or her own brother. Some critics have found Sycorax unpleasant, but the kind of remarks made at her expense in the play are undeniably amusing and are traditionally the basis of low comedy and music-hall humor.[60] Unmoved by epithets like "Queen *Blouze*" or "Queen Slobber-Chops," she keeps her eyes on the men. Her next to final line, Dryden and Davenant's comic version of "O brave new world," has distinct sexual overtones. "O *Setebos!*" she says, "these be brave Sprights indeed." Her true opposite is neither Miranda nor Dorinda, but rather Milcha, the faithful, ethereal companion of Ariel who has waited fourteen years for Ariel's freedom. In the Dryden-Davenant version Milcha utters only the word "Here" and closes the play with a dance. She was an ideal female spirit for an opera, and her role increased with each revision of the operatic *Tempest.*

These major changes in the conceptual nature and structure of Shakespeare's play were accompanied by appropriate changes in the dialogue, but some of the revisions were fairly typical of the kind thought necessary in adapting an old play to the Restoration stage. It has been argued that the categories that worked well enough for most adaptations of Shakespeare during this period did not seem applicable to *The Tempest* and that "such portions of Shakespeare's text as were retained suffered little alteration." [61] A comparison of the Dryden-Davenant version with the Arden edition of *The Tempest*, however, reveals that the changes were more apparent than this comment suggests. The most significant may be classified as follows:

1. Modernization

    a. Shakespeare, I, ii, 41:
        Out three years old
    Dryden-Davenant, I, ii, 30:
        full three years old

    b. Shakespeare, I, ii, 56:
        Thy mother was a piece of virtue
    Dryden-Davenant, I, ii, 43:
        Thy Mother was all virtue

2. Metrical changes

    a. Shakespeare, I, ii, 25–33:
        Lie there, my Art. Wipe thou thine eyes; have comfort.

---

hill, the Duke's Company could easily outshine its rival in low comedy. See Kermode, pp. lxvi–lxix; Leo Hughes, *A Century of English Farce* (1956), pp. 47–49, 72–74.
  [60] See, e.g., Hazleton Spencer, *Shakespeare Improved*, p. 193.   [61] *Ibid.,* p. 202.

The direful spectacle of the wrack, which touch'd
The very virtue of compassion in thee,
I have with such provision in mine Art
So safely ordered, that there is no soul—
No, not so much perdition as an hair
Betid to any creature in the vessel
Which thou heard'st cry, which thou saw'st sink. Sit down;
For thou must now know farther.

Dryden-Davenant, I, ii, 21–24:

I should inform thee farther; wipe thou thine Eyes,
have comfort; the direful spectacle of the wrack,
which touch'd the very virtue of compassion in
thee, I have with such a pity safely order'd, that
not one creature in the Ship is lost.

   b. Shakespeare, I, ii, 274–284:

she did confine thee,
By help of her more potent ministers,
And in her most unmitigable rage,
Into a cloven pine; within which rift
Imprison'd thou didst painfully remain
A dozen years; within which space she died,
And left thee there; where thou didst vent thy groans
As fast as mill-wheels strike. Then was this island—
Save for the son that she did litter here,
A freckled whelp hag-born—not honour'd with
A human shape.

Dryden-Davenant, I, ii, 196–206:

she did confine thee,
By help of her more potent Ministers,
(In her unmitigable rage) into a cloven Pine;
Within whose rift imprison'd, thou didst painfully
Remain a dozen years; within which space she dy'd,
And left thee there; where thou didst vent thy
Groans, as fast as Mill-wheels strike.
Then was this Isle (save for two Brats, which she did
Litter here, the brutish *Caliban,* and his twin Sister,
Two freckel'd-hag-born Whelps) not honour'd with
A humane shape.

3. Grammatical corrections

   a. Shakespeare, I, ii, 492–494:

To whom I am subdued, are but light to me,
Might I but through my prison once a day
Behold this maid.

Dryden-Davenant, III, v, 82–83:

To whom I am subdu'd, would seem light to me,
Might I but once a day through my Prison behold this maid.

   b. Shakespeare, I, ii, 149:

To cry to th' sea that roar'd to us

Dryden-Davenant, I, ii, 84:
    to cry to Seas which roar'd to us
4. Efforts to achieve clarity
    a. Shakespeare, I, ii, 21–22:
                More to know
        Did never meddle with my thoughts.
    Dryden-Davenant, I, ii, 19–20:
        I ne're indeavour'd to know more than you were
        pleas'd to tell me.
    b. Shakespeare, I, i, 15:
        Nay, good, be patient.
    Dryden-Davenant, I, i, 20:
        Nay, good friend be patient.
5. Decorum and attempts at greater elegance
    a. Shakespeare, I, ii, 472:
        My foot my tutor?
    Dryden-Davenant, III, v, 58:
        My child my Tutor!
    b. Shakespeare, I, ii, 424–430:
                Most sure the goddess
        On whom these airs attend! Vouchsafe my prayer
        May know if you remain upon this island;
        And that you will some good instruction give
        How I may bear me here: my prime request,
        Which I do last pronounce, is, O you wonder!
        If you be maid or no?
    Dryden-Davenant, III, v, 15–18:
        She's sure the Mistress, on whom these airs attend.
        Fair Excellence, if, as your form declares, you
        are divine, be pleas'd to instruct me how you will be
        worship'd; so bright a beauty cannot sure belong to
        humane kind.
6. General toning down and concision
    a. Shakespeare, V, i, 1–3:
        Now does my project gather to a head:
        My charms crack not; my spirits obey; and time
        Goes upright with his carriage. How's the day?
    Dryden-Davenant, III, i, 144–146:
        Now my designs are gathering to a head.
        My spirits are obedient to my charms.
        What, *Ariel!* my servant *Ariel,* where art thou?
    b. Shakespeare, I, ii, 79–87:
        Being once perfected how to grant suits,
        How to deny them, who t' advance, and who
        To trash for over-topping, new created
        The creatures that were mine, I say, or chang'd 'em,
        Or else new form'd 'em; having both the key
        Of officer and office, set all hearts i' th' state

To what tune pleas'd his ear; that now he was
The ivy which had hid my princely trunk,
And suck'd my verdure out on 't. Thou attend'st not?
Dryden-Davenant, I, ii, 55–58:
Having attain'd the craft of granting suits, and
of denying them; whom to advance, or lop, for
over-toping, soon was grown the Ivy which did hide
my Princely Trunck, and suckt my verdure out: thou
attend'st not.

7. Attempts to correct errors and improve technical knowledge
   a. *Shakespeare,* I, i, 6:
      Take in the topsail.
      Dryden-Davenant, I, i, 33:
      . . . reef both Top-sails.
   b. *Shakespeare,* I, ii, 181:
      I find my zenith doth depend
      Dryden-Davenant, I, ii, 101–102:
      I find that my mid-Heaven doth depend

8. Excision of offenses against piety or audience sensibilities
   a. *Shakespeare,* I, ii, 116:
      O the heavens!
      Dryden-Davenant, I, ii, 71:
      False man!
   b. *Shakespeare,* I, ii, 366–367:
      The red plague rid you
      For learning me your language!
      Dryden-Davenant, I, ii, 279–280:
      . . . the red botch rid you for learning me your
      language.

The most important alteration is in the versification. Dryden and Davenant attempted to smooth out Shakespeare's line, but they frequently achieved the desired effect by changing Shakespeare's blank verse to a rhythmic prose. The rendering in prose may have been the fault of the printer, but the extent to which such passages resist reconstruction into blank verse suggests that it was the preference of the collaborators. The passage cited at *2b* above, where the demands of clarity and the addition of a sister for Caliban forced certain revisions, was printed as verse, though there is no consistent effort to retain blank verse throughout the play, either in passages revised from Shakespeare or in sections added by Dryden and Davenant.[62]

---

[62] In a note on the lines at the beginning of the fifth act of the Dryden-Davenant *Tempest,* George Saintsbury remarked in exasperation: "It is, however, still incredible, that at the very height of Dryden's power in versifying, he would have permitted himself this shambling doggrel, which may be versified in several ways, but all bad" (S-S, III, 207). Attempts to reline both the revised passages of Shakespeare and the contributions of Dryden and Davenant to make them into blank verse lead to the inevitable conclusion that

The most distinctive grammatical alterations were merely correcting tenses and substituting "which" for "that," but the changes designed to enhance elegance and decorum often required more complicated solutions. Ferdinand's speech to Miranda (5*b*) has been revised to be more suitable for a young prince, but the impetus behind the change may be a need to eliminate Shakespeare's pun on Miranda's name.[63] Although some changes defy classification, few appear to be capricious. Theobald thought that a speech transferred from Miranda to Prospero on grounds of decorum probably revealed Shakespeare's true intention, and who is to say whether Ferdinand would be more likely to be "warming" or "cooling" the air of the enchanted island with his sighs?[64]

What is the result of these changes? Unquestionably, Dryden and Davenant succeeded in making *The Tempest* into a viable play for Restoration audiences at a time when the original would have been regarded as old-fashioned and unentertaining. They shaped a play that is more amusing than Shakespeare's, but only at the cost of reducing the

---

neither Davenant nor the young Dryden was so poor a poet as to intend these passages to be read as anything but prose. Most of such efforts have been expended (frequently through editorial error) on the edition of 1674 and are, therefore, less useful for our purposes than they might be. For a recent example, see Christopher Spencer, *Five Restoration Adaptations of Shakespeare* (1965), p. 437. For discussions of the versification of the 1674 edition and a useful list of parallel passages, see Max Rosbund, *Dryden als Shakespeare-Bearbeiter* (Halle, 1882), pp. 47–69; Otto Witt, *The Tempest, or The Enchanted Island. A Comedy by John Dryden, 1670. The Sea-Voyage. A Comedy by Beaumont and Fletcher, 1647. The Goblins' Tragi-Comedy by Sir John Suckling, 1646. in ihren Verhältnis zu Shakspere's "Tempest" und den übrigen Quellen* (Rostock, 1899), pp. 69–86.

[63] Dryden had argued just the year before in his preface to *Annus Mirabilis*, dated 10 November 1666 (*Works*, I, 53), that "the gingle of a . . . poor *Paranomasia*" should not be confused with true wit, and he had not changed his mind in 1693, when he compared puns with "Garbidge" in his *Discourse of Satire* (1693, p. xliii; Watson, II, 139). See also George C. Branam, *Eighteenth-Century Adaptations of Shakespearean Tragedy*, University of California Publications, English Studies no. 14 (1956), pp. 85–94.

[64] Lewis Theobald, ed., *The Works of Shakespeare* (1733), I, 18. Cf. Dryden-Davenant, I, ii, 269, with Arden ed., I, ii, 353; and Dryden-Davenant, I, ii, 135, with Arden ed., I, ii, 222. In Prospero's command to Miranda, "Advance the fringed Curtains of thine Eyes, and say what thou seest yonder" (III, v, 1–2), Dryden and Davenant preserved with little variation the only passage from Shakespeare to appear in Pope's *Peri Bathous*. Pope used Shakespeare's lines as emended by Dryden and Davenant, literalizing them under the heading, "See who is there?" He obviously thought the lines elegant to the point of absurdity, classifying them under that mixture of the "CUMBROUS" and "BUSKIN" styles which, when working together, produce "Bathos in perfection." If Dryden and Davenant saw little wrong with Shakespeare's image except the syntax, Thomas Duffet did. He parodied its précieuse quality aptly as "Advance the frizled frouzes of thine Eyes, and glout on yon fair thing." See Alexander Pope, *Works*, ed. W. Elwin and W. Courthope (1886), X, 393; Duffet, *The Mock Tempest* (1675), p. 44 (V, ii).

spiritual dimension of Shakespeare's drama. Prospero's internal conflict, and his external conflict with his enemies, are diminished to an element of the plot; in his magical power over the spiritual forces of the island, there is little indication of control over himself. That this demythifying of Prospero was entirely deliberate there can be no doubt. The near death of Hippolito dramatizes Prospero's inability to control his environment and reduces him to a very human and a very severe judge; the Shakespearean themes of forgiveness, grace, and redemption are replaced by the hocus-pocus of weapon salves and the off-color buffoonery of the sailors. The sense of expansive symbolic meanings in Shakespeare's play could not have escaped Dryden and Davenant, but it was not an effect that their age appreciated. Nor can it be said that either Dryden or Davenant appreciated Shakespeare's symbolism. The magical effects within the play are not reduced, but the magic of the play has disappeared. The power of Shakespeare's play is epitomized in speeches like Gonzalo's summary of the plot action (V, i, 205–213):

> Was Milan thrust from Milan, that his issue
> Should become Kings of Naples? O, rejoice
> Beyond a common joy! and set it down
> With gold on lasting pillars: in one voyage
> Did Claribel her husband find at Tunis,
> And Ferdinand, her brother, found a wife
> Where he himself was lost, Prospero his dukedom
> In a poor isle, and all of us ourselves
> When no man was his own.

Dryden and Davenant delete this speech to make room for the sexual clowning that precedes the coming marriages of the couples.

Both Dryden and Davenant felt a sincere admiration for Shakespeare, and the prologue as well as the preface expresses ideas that Dryden was to repeat in his later criticism. Shakespeare was the great, natural magician of poetry,

> *He Monarch-like gave those his subjects law,*
> *And is that Nature which they paint and draw,*

but a writer from another age—a less refined age. The drama of the Restoration was to be concerned with the passions and the will operating within the world. A Prospero entirely at peace with himself, the world, and Heaven would lack the necessary emotion for the contemporary stage. Dryden and Davenant show him in a variety of postures: calm, angry, vengeful. He tries to dominate his small world by his power, but he has little control over the passions of Miranda, Dorinda, and Hippolito. In the comic routines he is often reduced to being a straight man, a role that not only diminishes his stature but alters his relation to the destructive forces on the island. Whereas Shakespeare never allows the threats to the happy and comic solution of his play to go beyond "comic apprehension," [65] the collaborators remove from Prospero his power over the

---

[65] R. S. Crane, "The Concept of Plot and the Plot of *Tom Jones*," in *Critics and Criticism*, ed. R. S. Crane (1952), p. 641.

happy resolution of the play and thereby direct the entire rhythm of *The Tempest* away from cosmic comedy and toward traditional tragicomedy. There is little doubt that it is Dryden rather than Davenant who has Prospero engage in an argument with Miranda on capital punishment, pardons, and the separation of the offices of judge and executioner at the very moment of greatest excitement, when Ferdinand is about to be executed for the murder of Hippolito.[66] Prospero does not drown his book, abjure his art, and vow that every third thought shall be of the grave; instead he returns to political power having arranged a clever method of uniting several kingdoms. In short, he is changed from a symbolic magician-king-artist to a magician-politician.

Whether or not Shakespeare thought of Prospero as a magus, he is certainly given power that Dryden and Davenant would never have allowed an earthly monarch.[67] Indeed, he seems capable of an almost godlike power. In contrast with Shakespeare's Prospero, the Prospero of Dryden and Davenant is puzzled by the operation of fate. Pondering the fact that the stars have decreed the danger that will confront Hippolito if he beholds the face of a woman, he says:

> If by free-will in our own paths we move,
> How are we bounded by Decrees above?
> Whether we drive, or whether we are driven,
> If ill 'tis ours, if good the act of Heaven.

The wonder of Shakespeare's Prospero is his complete control over the operations of fate.[68] The Prospero of Dryden and Davenant has about as much control over the lives and loves of his daughters and his ward as have most of the exasperated fathers of Restoration comedy.

Also changed is Prospero's relationship with Ariel. As in Shakespeare's play, Ariel has been rescued from the enchantments of Sycorax by Prospero's magic, but whereas Shakespeare's Ariel acts entirely as Prospero's agent, the Ariel of Dryden and Davenant is more strictly an independent agent. At the end of the fourth act, Ariel is allowed to summarize the action from his perspective and comment on the cosmic significance of the discord on the island, on the sorrowing of the "good Angels" and the rejoicing of the forces of evil. He questions the reason for his loss of freedom, a loss he has suffered, ironically enough, because of the knowledge the spirits have imparted to mankind. Not only is Ariel a more substantial character than in Shakespeare's *Tempest*, but he raises a point that has larger implications within the play. For it is Ariel and the elemental spirits who work the magic, not their master. Hippolito's

---

[66] As Dr. Johnson remarked, "The favourite exercise of his mind was ratiocination; and, that argument might not be too soon at an end, he delighted to talk of liberty and necessity, destiny and contingence" (*Lives of the Poets*, ed. George B. Hill [1905], I, 459).

[67] Frances Yates, *Giordano Bruno and the Hermetic Tradition* (1964), p. 357.

[68] The confession of Prospero, in the Dryden-Davenant version, that he is "curs'd" because he commands spirits seems completely alien to Shakespeare's play.

life is saved by Ariel acting in conjunction with the angelic forces and "unbid" by Prospero. Whereas it is Prospero to whom Shakespeare gives a magnificent speech abjuring his "rough magic," Dryden and Davenant allow the weight of the most effective poetry to fall upon Ariel, as he describes his flight through the world to find the drugs with which to cure Hippolito, the flight of Hippolito's guardian angel to the planets that rule over Hippolito's fate, and finally, his own arrival just in time to save Hippolito's life, as

> The soul stood almost at life's door, all bare
> And naked, shivering like Boys upon a Rivers
> Bank, and loth to tempt the cold air . . .[69]

What should be apparent is that the revised *Tempest* is not merely a botched version of Shakespeare's play, but a *Tempest* reshaped to suit a view of man's relation to the universe compatible with the age, with its theater, and with the views of Dryden and Davenant. Although Alonzo and Antonio have sinned and Prospero forgives them, the mysterious and suggestive religious implications of Shakespeare's play are reduced to the comic dimensions of human existence. Caliban does not say that he will "seek for grace," and there is no sinister and unrepentant figure like Shakespeare's Antonio. Even an elemental spirit like Ariel must be aided by the heavenly powers. And Prospero's ability to command a spirit falls far short of a power to control human destiny. In his soliloquy near the end of the third act, Prospero maintains that "mans life is all a mist, and in the dark, our fortunes meet us." All we really know, he concludes, is that whatever happiness man meets in life proceeds from Heaven.

In attacking the Dryden-Davenant version, the editor of the Variorum edition of Shakespeare's *Tempest* quotes Gotthold Lessing's warning: "Upon the most insignificant of his beauties there is an impress stamped which to all the world proclaims: 'I am SHAKESPEARE's!' Woe to the alien beauty who presumes to place herself beside it." [70] Lessing was cautioning writers not to plagiarize from Shakespeare, and his position is not significantly different from Dryden's acknowledgment in the prologue that Shakespeare's *"Magick"* could not be imitated.[71] Yet it was precisely the magic that Dryden and Davenant dropped. In the prologue Dryden also praises Jonson for borrowing from Shakespeare his concept of comedy and art, and Fletcher for taking his wit and scenes of love. The Dryden-Davenant *Tempest* moves in the direction of heightening these very elements. There is more wit, more love, more mirth, and,

---

[69] In *Tyrannick Love* (V, i, 231–234), Dryden put a similar description into the mouth of Saint Catherine:

> Could we live always, life were worth our cost;
> But now we keep with care what must be lost.
> Here we stand shiv'ring on the Bank, and cry,
> When we should plunge into Eternity.

[70] Furness, p. ix.

[71] See *Hamburg Dramaturgy*, trans. Helen Zimmern (1962), pp. 173–175.

in the sense of mechanical plotting, more art. Shakespeare's "insubstantial pageant" reminding us that "We are such stuff / As dreams are made on" is gone. But once we accept the idea that Dryden and Davenant have created a tragicomedy in the Restoration mode, we can appreciate just how good some of their verse is. And we can see that Caliban is still Shakespeare's Caliban,[72] that Ariel, though changed substantially, is perhaps as interesting as Shakespeare's Ariel, and that the play itself is both moving and comic.

PREFACE

The title of the play as given in the preface may be a conscious attempt to echo the title of a magnificent spectacle performed at Versailles on 8 May 1664 and published that year as *Les Plaisirs de l'Ile enchantée* (see Molière, *Œuvres*, ed. Eugène Despois and Paul Mesnard, IV [1912], 91–268; see also Ronald McKerrow, *An Introduction to Bibliography* [1928], p. 91).

P. 3: ll. 3–4 *Ape of the French Eloquence*. Dryden may be referring specifically to Richard Flecknoe, whose *Miscellania, or, Poems of All Sorts, with Divers Other Pieces*, printed in 1653, commences with a dedication in French and contains in the "Address to the Reader" a good deal of self-praise: "I have been Accurate enough to expose nothing to the publique, but what I could venture on my credite having suppresst many pieces, which others have thought worthy of the light, as being a severer censurer of mine owne Worke, then thou canst possibly be. . . ." The Flecknoe volume includes a letter of gallantry, poems, translations, essays, and characters. In the preface to *The Damoiselles à la Mode*, the piece that Dryden may be attacking in his mention of *"an examen of a Farce,"* Flecknoe praises himself for his skillful translation of Molière's parody of précieuse diction in spite of difficulties that had hitherto proved insurmountable. "I have not only made the Language of the Author, English, but even the spirit, life, and quickness of it too," wrote Flecknoe without a shred of modesty. If Dryden was indeed referring to Flecknoe, he may have had two reasons for his attack. He may have assumed that the "R. F." who criticized him in *A Letter from a Gentleman to the Honourable Ed. Howard Esq* (1668) was really Richard

---

[72] Dryden expressed his genuine admiration for Shakespeare's imaginative genius in creating Caliban "with a Language, and a character, which will suit him, both by Fathers and Mothers side: he has all the discontents, and malice of a Witch, and of a Devil; besides a convenient proportion of the deadly sins; Gluttony, Sloth, and Lust, are manifest; the dejectedness of a slave is likewise given him, and the ignorance of one bred up in a Desart Island" (see *The Grounds of Criticism in Tragedy*, prefixed to *Troilus and Cressida* [1679, sig. b1; Watson, I, 253]). In this passage Dryden shows himself at his best as a critic, and there is nothing in his delineation of Caliban which is not perfectly in keeping with Shakespeare's creation. Caliban, as unquestionably a figure more comprehensible to the Restoration than Shakespeare's Prospero, needed less revision.

Flecknoe, and he may have resented Flecknoe's satire on his friend and collaborator in *Sir William D'avenant's Voyage to the Other World* (1668). Significantly enough, Flecknoe made two attacks on Dryden's critical positions in the new edition of his poems, *Epigrams of All Sorts* (1671), pp. 51, 52.

3:9–10 *surmounting them in the Scene.* This confident assertion of the superiority of the English theater to the French is best seen in connection with the debate between Samuel Sorbière and Thomas Sprat over the respective merits of the two nations. Sprat, in replying to Sorbière's remarks on the failure of English dramatists to follow the unities and to observe decorum, defended the English stage as superior entertainment and superior imitation of reality (*Observations on Mons. de Sorbier's Voyage into England* [1665], pp. 246–256). Like Dryden, Sprat attacked the "swelling Metaphors, wherewith some of our Neighbors, who most admire themselves do still adorn their Books" (*ibid.,* p. 265). See also George Williamson, "The Occasion of *An Essay of Dramatic Poesy*," *MP,* XLIV (1946), 1–9.

3:11–12 *borders of their Plays.* Compared with the unadorned printed English plays, the French volumes were extremely elaborate, often containing a frontispiece and illustrations before each act in addition to the customary devices separating scenes and acts from one another.

3:12 *good Landskips.* Dryden takes the customary position of the time that landscapes should merely provide the background for more important subjects, and he probably shared with many of his contemporaries the contempt for what Kenneth Clark calls the "landscape of fact." Speaking of the background landscapes of Italian artists, Clark remarks that "none of these painters considered that the recording of a true visual impression of nature was a sufficient end in itself. . . . All theories of Art—and theories abounded—insisted that the value of a painting depended on the moral or historical importance of its subject." Although Clark is correct in stressing this disapproval among the art critics, Dutch landscape had a considerable vogue in England in Dryden's day. See Clark, *Landscape into Art* (1963), pp. 25–26; Henry and Margaret Ogden, *English Taste in Landscape in the Seventeenth Century* (1955).

3:20 *high veneration.* Davenant's reverence for Shakespeare appears not only in his poem, "In Remembrance of Master William Shakespeare," which depicts the Avon mourning the poet's death, and in his revisions of *Macbeth* and *The Tempest,* but also in his willingness to be thought Shakespeare's illegitimate son. Whether or not Aubrey's account of Davenant's tolerance of this story or the story itself contained any truth, it is nevertheless a fact, as Arthur Nethercot points out, that "in his own day Will Davenant was regarded as the repository of a greater and more authentic mass of Shakespeareana than any other living man" (see John Aubrey, *Brief Lives,* ed. Andrew Clark [1898], I, 204; Nethercot, *Sir William D'Avenant* [1938], p. 5).

3:21–22 *acted . . . in the Black-Fryers.* Kermode (pp. 150–153) considers Dryden's suggestion very likely and argues that although *The Tempest* may have been performed in three theaters between 1611 and

1613 "the Blackfriars was the natural home of the play." Gerald Bentley (*The Jacobean and Caroline Stage* [1941]) does not include *The Tempest* among those plays of Shakespeare for which there is evidence of performance. The omission does not mean that the play was never performed during the time that Davenant would have been frequenting Blackfriars Theatre, but it may suggest that *The Tempest* was not one of Shakespeare's more popular plays.

3:24–25 *Sea-Voyage*. This play by John Fletcher, licensed on 2 June 1622, was probably produced shortly thereafter. Most critics have agreed that either Fletcher collaborated with Philip Massinger or that Massinger revised Fletcher's play later. *The Sea Voyage,* first printed in the folio of Beaumont and Fletcher in 1647, was revived by the King's Company on 25 September 1667, less than two weeks before the first performance of the Dryden-Davenant *Tempest,* and it continued running as a rival attraction. Perhaps knowing that their rivals were intending to stage an elaborate production of *The Tempest,* the King's Company had decided to gain the initiative. But Pepys's reaction to the two plays was probably fairly common. ". . . with my wife to the King's playhouse to see 'The Storme,' which we did, but without much pleasure," wrote Pepys on 25 March 1668, "it being but a mean play compared with 'The Tempest,' at the Duke of York's house, though Knepp did act her part of grief very well." Dryden's contention that Fletcher's play was a *"Copy of* Shakespear's*"* is an exaggeration. Fletcher unquestionably drew his inspiration from Shakespeare, but many similarities between the two plays were common properties of the seventeenth-century imagination. See Otto Witt, *The Tempest, or The Enchanted Island. A Comedy by John Dryden, 1670. The Sea-Voyage. . . . The Goblins' Tragi-Comedy . . . in ihren Verhältnis zu Shakspere's "Tempest"* . . . (Rostock, 1899), pp. 87–113.

3:30 *Goblins*. Suckling's *The Goblins* may have been performed as early as 1637, but it first appears in a list of plays that were the property of the King's Men. The first printed edition was published in 1646. After the Restoration the play was revived by the King's Company and performed on 24 January, 22 May, and 21 November 1667. Pepys remarked that the performance in May attracted a full house. Although Dryden was probably correct about the influence of *The Tempest* on Suckling's play, Ruth Wallerstein ("Suckling's Imitation of Shakespeare," *RES,* XIX [1943], 290–295) finds that "the fundamental design and substance of the play are difficult to compare with those of *The Tempest* because of the intellectual and dramatic triviality of *The Goblins.*" See Van Lennep, pp. 101, 109, 124; and Witt, *Shakspere's "Tempest,"* pp. 114–138.

3:30 *Regmella*. Actually Reginella.

4:7 *Man who had never seen a Woman*. Nethercot (*D'Avenant,* pp. 399–400) traces this idea back to Davenant's *The Platonick Lovers* (1636), in which a soldier named Gridonel has been raised in complete innocence of women and sex.

4:21–22 *so quick a fancy*. Compliments to Davenant's gift of imagination were frequent in the period. Cowley wrote:

Thy Fancy, like a Flame, her way does make:
And leaves bright tracks for following Pens to take.

Endymion Porter mentions his "lofty fancy" and William Habington his "bright fancie." See William Davenant, *Works* (1673), [Pt. I], pp. 30, 202–203.

4:24–25 *Latine Proverb.* Cicero, *Philippics,* XII, ii, 5: Posteriores enim cogitationes, ut aiunt, sapientiores solent esse (Loeb trans.: "For the later thoughts, as the saying is, are usually the wiser").

4:29 *corrected his own writings.* Evidence for this statement may be found in Davenant's revisions of *Gondibert* (see D. H. Woodward, "The Manuscript Corrections and Printed Variants in the Quarto Edition of *Gondibert," The Library,* 5th ser., XX [1965], 298–309).

PROLOGUE

5 *Shakespear, who (taught by none).* The concept of Shakespeare as a natural poet in contrast with the learned playwrights, Jonson and Beaumont and Fletcher, probably received its strongest impetus from the remarks of Jonson in his poem prefaced to the first folio. Milton was to speak of Shakespeare's "native Wood-notes wilde," and Leonard Digges, in a dedicatory poem prefixed to the 1640 edition of Shakespeare's *Poems,* argued that

Poets are borne not made, when I would prove
This truth, the glad remembrance I must love
Of never dying Shakespeare, who alone,
Is argument enough to make that one.

Although Jonson also stressed Shakespeare's craft, Dryden, in the preface to *All for Love* (1678, sig. b4v; Watson, I, 231), refers specifically to Jonson as the source for the concept of Shakespeare's want of learning. Dryden praises Shakespeare for his artistry, but the kind of art meant has little to do with the neoclassical rules. For Dryden, Shakespeare's true genius lay in his natural ability to create character and to move the passions. See *The Grounds of Criticism in Tragedy* prefixed to *Troilus and Cressida* (1679, sig. b1v; Watson, I, 254–255). For a general discussion of this point, see Edward Niles Hooker, ed., *The Critical Works of John Dennis* (1939), II, 429.

6 *To Fletcher Wit, to labouring Johnson Art.* Cf. John Denham, "On Mr. John Fletcher's Workes," in Francis Beaumont and John Fletcher, *Comedies and Tragedies* (1647), sig. b1v:

Then was wits Empire at the fatall height,
When labouring and sinking with its weight,
From thence a thousand lesser Poets sprong
Like petty Princes from the fall of Rome.
When JOHNSON, SHAKESPEARE, and thy self did sit,
And sway'd in the Triumvirate of wit—
Yet what from JOHNSONS oyle and sweat did flow,
Or what more easie nature did bestow
On SHAKESPEARES gentler Muse, in thee full growne

Their Graces both appeare, not so, that none
Can say here Nature ends, and Art begins
But mixt like th'Elements, and borne like Twins,
So interweav'd, so like, so much the same,
None this meere Nature, that meere Art can name.

See also Richard Flecknoe, *A Short Discourse of the English Stage* (1664), in Spingarn, II, 93–94: "To compare our English Dramatick Poets together, without taxing them, Shakespeare excelled in a natural Vein, Fletcher in Wit, and Johnson in Gravity and ponderousness of Style, whose onely fault was he was too elaborate, and had he mixt less erudition with his Playes, they had been more pleasant and delightful then they are. Comparing him with Shakespear, you shall see the difference betwixt Nature and Art and with Fletcher the difference betwixt Wit and Judgement: Wit being an exuberant thing, like Nilus, never more commendable then when it overflowes; but Judgement, a stayed and reposed thing, always containing it self within its bounds and limits."

The idea of a "Triumvirate of wit" was common enough before Dryden's grouping in this prologue and his amplification in *Of Dramatick Poesie,* but there was little agreement on the details. Milton leaves out Beaumont and Fletcher, and in the Beaumont and Fletcher folio, James Howell and George Buck include Chapman in their grouping. Joseph Howe compares Fletcher only with Jonson. Nor was the praise always in favor of Shakespeare. Plays of Beaumont and Fletcher, as Dryden pointed out (*Of Dramatick Poesie* [1668, p. 49; Watson, I, 69]), were performed twice as often as those of Shakespeare. William Cartwright (*Plays and Poems,* ed. G. Blakemore Evans [1951], pp. 520–521) argued that, compared with Fletcher's, Jonson's love scenes were "cold and frosty" and Shakespeare's wit was "Old fashion'd." And Jonson had an ardent champion in Thomas Shadwell.

7 *gave those his subjects law.* Cf. *Of Dramatick Poesie* (1668, p. 50; Watson, I, 68–70), where Dryden argues that Shakespeare was "the Homer or Father of our Dramatick poets" because later playwrights learned so much from him.

8 *And is that Nature.* See *Of Dramatick Poesie* (1668, p. 47; Watson, I, 67): "All the Images of Nature were still present to him, and he drew them not laboriously, but luckily; when he describes any thing, you more than see it, you feel it too. Those who accuse him to have wanted learning, give him the greater commendation: he was naturally learn'd; he needed not the spectacles of Books to read Nature; he look'd inwards, and found her there." In the prologue to *Julius Caesar,* which Dryden wrote either wholly or in part, the unconscious aspect of Shakespeare's art is emphasized:

Such Artless beauty lies in Shakespeare's wit,
'Twas well in spight of him whate're he writ.
His Excellencies came and were not sought,
His words like casual Atoms made a thought:
Drew up themselves in Rank and File, and writ,
He wond'ring how the Devil it were such wit.

Thus like the drunken Tinker in his Play
He grew a Prince and never knew which way.
But the prologue to *The Tempest* allows Shakespeare the natural wisdom
of the artist, and Dryden expresses much the same view in his *Discourse
of Satire* (1693, p. ii; Watson, II, 74).

Dryden's attitude to Shakespeare may be reflecting a number of sources.
In suggesting that a poet might become great by copying nature directly,
without imitating any literary models, Dryden may have been influenced
by the "moderns" among the Italian critics. His attitude may also be
based upon Shakespeare's popularity and universal acceptance in England
—the same position from which Dryden criticized Scaliger's attack on
Homer and three thousand years of critical opinion (see the dedication
of *Examen Poeticum* [1693, sig. A5; Watson, II, 158]). Certainly there is
a resemblance between Dryden's defense of Shakespeare and the arguments used to defend Homer. Finally, Dryden may be relying upon or
reflecting Longinus' concept of the superiority of the great writer with
flaws over the dull but correct writer. For a good discussion of nature
as an attribute of the artist, see Arthur Lovejoy, "Nature as Aesthetic
Norm," in *Essays in the History of Ideas* (1960), pp. 72–73; Bernard
Weinberg, *A History of Literary Criticism in the Italian Renaissance*
(1961), II, 988–989.

11 *This did his Love.* A common praise lavished on Fletcher; Robert
Herrick closed his poem, "Upon Master Fletchers Incomparable Playes"
(*Poetical Works,* ed. F. W. Moorman [1915], p. 415), with the line, "None
writes lov's passion in the world, like Thee." Dryden stressed this aspect
of Fletcher also in *The Grounds of Criticism in Tragedy* (1679, sig. b5;
Watson, I, 260): ". . . the excellency of that poet [Shakespeare] was, as I
have said, in the more manly passions; Fletcher's in the softer: Shakespeare writ better betwixt man and man; Fletcher betwixt man and
woman: consequently the one described friendship better; the other love:
yet Shakespeare . . . had an universal mind, which comprehended all
characters and passions; Fletcher a more confined and limited: for though
he treated love in perfection, yet honour, ambition, revenge, and generally
all the stronger passions, he either touched not, or not masterly."

12 *One imitates him most.* In *The Grounds of Criticism in Tragedy*
(1679, sig. b1; Watson, I, 253) Dryden argued that Fletcher borrowed his
characterization entirely from Shakespeare, that the imitation was inferior to the original, and that to "imitate Fletcher is but to copy after
him who was a copier."

15–16 *The Storm . . . Tempest.* A punning reference to Fletcher's
The Sea Voyage acted by the King's Company on 25 September 1667 at
the Theatre Royal (*the Neighb'ring shore*). Like Shakespeare's *Tempest,*
Fletcher's play begins with a violent storm.

17 *That innocence and beauty.* Clarinda in *The Sea Voyage,* like
Miranda in *The Tempest,* has, at the beginning of the play, never seen
a man.

20 *Within that Circle.* Dryden may be referring to the stage direction
following V, i, 57 in Shakespeare's *Tempest,* in which Ariel drives Alonso
and his followers into a magic circle where they stand charmed and in-

sensible to Prospero's musings. But it is more likely that Dryden is referring to the circle in which the magician stands when calling down spirits. The entire metaphor compares the power of the imaginative poet with that of a magician or a priest. See "Anti-Scot," pp. 43, 72; Scot, p. 222.

30 *Women to present a Boy.* "The role was that of Hippolito, which was probably taken in 1667 by Moll Davis" (Summers, II, 486).

DRAMATIS PERSONÆ

Changes in the characters include making Alonzo the duke of Savoy instead of the king of Naples. Savoy, when it controlled Piedmont, bordered on Milan. Shakespeare's Trinculo is changed to Trincalo, the name of the countryman in Thomas Tomkis' *Albumazar* (1615), an adaptation of Giambattista della Porta's *Lo Astrologo* (1606). There are three possible reasons for the name change: the collaborators may have considered the name Trincalo closer to the buffoonery of Italian comedy; they may have felt that it sounded more suggestive of the quantity of liquor imbibed by the sailors; or they may have thought in terms of a nautical pun on "trink," a fisherman's net, or on *trinca*, a nautical term in Italian and Spanish for a rope or cable. Tomkis' play was probably in their minds, since Dryden wrote a prologue for the Duke's Company's revival of *Albumazar* on 22 February 1668, a little more than two months after the first performance of *The Tempest.* For some speculation about Tomkis' use of the name Trincalo see Hugh G. Dick, ed., *Albumazar: A Comedy (1615) by Thomas Tomkis,* University of California Publications in English no. 13 (1944), p. 162. For the names of Shakespeare's Trinculo and Stephano, see Kermode, p. lxviii.

Ventoso and Mustacho, the names of the new companions of Stephano and Trincalo, are obviously intended to echo names from *commedia dell'arte,* though they are not to be found among the many standard characters of Italian comedy. Ventoso's name suggests both wind and flatulence. Mustacho's role was probably played by an actor wearing an excessively large moustache. Caliban's sister, Sycorax, is named after her mother, the witch of Shakespeare's play. The names of the new lovers are probably generic. Hippolito's is suggestive enough of a young man who is ignorant of society and is threatened with death if he ever beholds a woman; presumably the collaborators thought it sufficiently close to the Hippolytus of Greek myth and Euripides for that purpose. (Fletcher and Massinger make a somewhat wry use of the name Hippolita, the classical queen of the Amazons, for a man-hungry woman in *The Sea Voyage.*) Dorinda's name has less specific associations, but Dryden and Davenant may have been trying to underline her simplicity with a hint of the word "Doric."

I, i

2 *hoaming.* Tempestuous. In his edition of Dryden, Scott changed this word to "foaming," but the *OED* merely decided that the meaning was doubtful because no evidence of previous usage could be found and only

one instance after Dryden was discovered. Summers (II, 487), however, found a second example in Milburn's translation of *The First Book of Virgil's Aeneid* (1688).

3 *The Scud comes against the Wind.* Light clouds being driven rapidly before the wind. A contemporary manual for seamen notes: "Sometimes when there is but little winde, there will come a contrary Sea, and presently the winde after it, whereby we may judge that from whence it came was much winde, for commonly before any great storm the Sea will come that way." Dryden and Davenant, trying to picture the moment at which the wind and the sea change direction with an approaching storm, were probably more accurate than the notes of F. M. Green suggest (see Furness, pp. viii–ix, 392). See also John Smith, *The Sea-Mans Grammar* (1653), p. 41; Henry Mainwaring, *The Seaman's Dictionary*, in *The Life and Works of Sir Henry Mainwaring*, ed. G. E. Manwaring and W. G. Perrin (1922), II, 162.

4–5 *Bosen . . . Master.* The duties of the boatswain and the master are clear enough from the beginning of the play. The boatswain was to supervise the work of the "several gangs and companies" of the crew. The master, Stephano, operated as the captain of the ship; Nathaniel Butler complained that masters often assumed the title of captain. Apparently the master was personally in charge of the stern of the ship, and the boatswain of the area before the mainmast. See Butler, *Boteler's Dialogues*, ed. W. G. Perrin (1929), pp. 16, 31. See also "The Master's Whistle," *Mariner's Mirror*, IV (1914), 201; William Monson, *Naval Tracts*, ed. M. Oppenheim (1913), IV, 32.

6 *let's off to Sea.* The ship is at anchor. Much of the action on the ship at the beginning centers on Stephano's attempt to get the anchor up and the ship out to sea in order to provide what Mustacho calls "Searoom," distance enough from land to avoid being driven ashore.

10–13 *Yaw, yaw, . . . yare, yare.* "Yaw" is probably a corruption of "yare," which means ready, alert, active.

11+ *s.d. pass over the Stage.* This direction does not necessarily mean that the mariners have actually left the stage. Here they are merely ordered to be alert and to remain on what is supposed to be the middle of the ship until further orders direct them offstage toward what serves as the bow or the stern. For a similar kind of stage directions, see John Suckling, *The Goblins*, in *Works*, ed. W. C. Hazlitt (1892), II, 24–25. For a discussion of entrances and exits through the four doors of the Theatre Royal, see Montague Summers, *The Restoration Theatre* (1934), pp. 126–149.

15 *Play the men.* "Upton remarked (*Critical Observations on Shakespeare*, 1746, p. 241), 'It should be *ply* the men: keep them to their business.' . . . Upton may be right; *O.E.D.* (*s.v. ply*) *does* support this usage. In Elizabethan pronunciation, *ply* and *play* differed less than they do now" (Kermode, p. 4). The order to the boatswain, who was charged with keeping the men at work and "in peace," suggests that Alonzo was nervous at seeing the men standing around. Although it may indicate merely Alonzo's concern about the storm, it is also the first hint of the

theme of rebellion which pervades the play. See *Boteler's Dialogues,* p. 16.

21 *roarers.* Noisy and unruly waves.

29 *complexion.* "Meant external appearance, much as it does still, though it retained something of a technical meaning, so that here one might gloss it 'physical appearance as an index of temperament'" (Kermode, p. 5).

29–30 *hanging.* Cf. the proverb, "He that is born to be hanged shall never be drowned" (Tilley, B139).

32 *s.d. Exeunt Alonzo, Antonio, and Gonzalo.* It is clear that all the noblemen leave the stage at this time.

33 *reef both Top-sails.* Changed from Shakespeare's "Take in the topsail." Since Davenant had had experience as a sailor, and Dryden had studied the technicalities of sailing when writing *Annus Mirabilis (Works,* I, 52), the description of the ship in storm is likely to show technical improvements over Shakespeare's original. John Smith (*Sea-Mans Grammar,* p. 38) tells how to handle a ship in a storm: "It over casts, we shall have winde, fowl weather, settle your top sailes, take in the spret-saile, in with your top-sailes, . . . lash sure the ordnance, strike your top-masts to the cap, make it sure with your sheeps feet. A storme, let us lie at Trie with our main course, that is, to hale the tacke aboord, the sheat close aft the boling set up, and the helme tied cloase aboord. When that will not serve then try the mizen, if that split, or the storm grow so great she cannot bear it; then hull, which is to bear no sail, but to strike a hull is when they would lie obscurely in the Sea, or stay for some consort, lash sure the helme a lee, and so a good ship will lie at ease under the Sea as we terme it." To reef was to gather up the top part of the square sail with the reef points—small ropes set in the sail for this purpose—and tie it to the yard. The ship must be under sail before the anchor is weighed in order to prevent it from drifting, but the sails are not set full. The ship in the play has three masts, fore, main, and mizzen. The topsails being reefed are those on the foremast and the mainmast and are the only sails set at this point. See *Gentleman's Dictionary,* sigs. Ggg5*v*–Ggg6.

35 *Hands down! man your main-Capstorm.* Part of the crew has been ordered aloft; others are being sent below to the deck parallel with the hawseholes through which the anchor passes. The main capstan, located behind the mainmast, was used to aid the crew in heaving up the anchor. According to Mainwaring (*Seaman's Dictionary,* II, 116) the main capstan was used "chiefly to weigh . . . anchors and generally to hoist or strike-down topmasts, or to heave in any thing of weight . . . or indeed to strain any rope that requires great force."

36 *jeere-Capstorm.* The "seere" of the first edition (and hence of the folio) was almost certainly a compositor's error for "jeere" or a misreading of the manuscript *j* for an *s;* Summers' suggestion (II, 487) that it was caused "by a j being printed upside down as a long s" is less likely. Mainwaring (*Seaman's Dictionary,* II, 169) writes that the jeer capstan "hath its name from the jeer [a three-strand rope] which is ever brought to this capstan to be heaved-at by. It stands in the waist in the hatchway, and serves for many other uses; as to heave upon the viol, or

hold off the cable from the main capstan." It seems likely that the jeer capstan is here being used to help weigh the anchor rather than to raise the foremast with the jeer rope. See *Boteler's Dialogues*, p. 83.

37 *Capstorm-Bar.* "Capstan-Bars, are the Bars or Pieces of Wood, that are put into the Capstan-holes, to heave up any thing of weight into the Ship, by the help of as many Men, as can well stand at them" (*Gentleman's Dictionary*, sig. Aaa7).

39–40 *nip . . . Nippers.* To nip is to tie, compress, or catch between two surfaces or points. "Nippers," writes Mainwaring (*Seaman's Dictionary*, II, 191), "are small ropes (about a fathom and a half or two fathom long) with a little truck at one end (or some have only a wale knot, the use whereof is to hold off the cable from the main capstan, or the jeer-capstan, when the cable is either so slippy or so great that they cannot strain it, to hold it off, with their hands only." R. Morton Nance suggests ("The Voyol," *Mariner's Mirror*, XXXII [1946], 59–60) some of the difficulties encountered in attaching the anchor cable to the voyol (or viol): "Each man busied in putting them on had a boy to help him by walking aft with the loose ends of his nipper as the cable came in, and casting it off as it drew near the fore hatch, to carry it right forward where it was put round the cable and the voyol again."

44 *Our Viall's broke.* See Mainwaring, *Seaman's Dictionary*, II, 191: "A Violl. When the anchor is in such stiff ground that we cannot weigh it, or else that the sea goes so high that the main capstan cannot purchase in the cable, then, for more help, we take a hawser and open one strand, and so put it into nippers (some seven or eight, a fathom distant from each other) and with these nippers we bind fast the hawser to the cable; and so bring this hawser to the jeer capstan and heave upon it, and this will purchase more than the main capstan can. The Violl is fastened together at both ends with an eye and a wale knot, or else two eyes seized together." The voyol block was a single-sheaved pulley through which the voyol passed. For excellent diagrams of the way the voyol was attached to the anchor cable, see R. Morton Nance, "The Development of the Capital Ship-Mangers," *Mariner's Mirror*, VI (1916), 122–123; Nance, "The Voyol," p. 61.

46 *fix'd.* Secured.

47 *Cut off the Hamocks.* T. D. Manning, editor of the *Mariner's Mirror*, has tentatively suggested, in a reply to our query, that "the hammocks were stowed in 'nettings' on the upper deck, and in an emergency they might well be cut adrift."

49 *The Anchor's a peek.* That is, "when a Ship, being about to weigh, come so over her anchor, that the Cable is Perpendicular between the Hawse and the Anchor" (*Gentleman's Dictionary*, sig. Fff3v).

53 *Cat the Anchor.* Bring the anchor up to the forecastle. "Cut the Anchor," which appeared in the first edition, is an obvious error. See F. M. Green's note in Furness, p. 394.

56 *loose the Misen.* Stephano begins by preparing the ship for an ordinary wind in loosing both the mizzen and the main topsail, but he

quickly discovers his error (see *Gentleman's Dictionary*, sigs. Ggg5*v*–Ggg6*v*).

57 *Get the Misen-tack aboard.* Secure the rope attached to the lower forward edge of the mizzen sail (see Mainwaring, *Seaman's Dictionary*, II, 240–241).

57 *Haul Aft Misen-sheat.* Pull the ropes attached to the lower after edge of the mizzen sail to set the sail (see Mainwaring, *Seaman's Dictionary*, II, 223–224).

60–61 *trim her right afore the Wind.* Arrange the sails so as to set them perpendicular to the wind's direction (R. H. Dana, *The Seaman's Manual* [1844], p. 120).

61 *hale up the Misen.* The mizzen might be the sail of last resort to use in a storm before deciding to "hull" or ride out the storm with only the foresail. According to *Boteler's Dialogues* (p. 162), however, the mizzen ought to be hauled down during a tempest. If the foresail was blown away, the ship usually abandoned everything but a small sail or "fore-bonnet" (see Smith, *Sea-Mans Grammar*, p. 40; *Gentleman's Dictionary*, sig. Ggg6*v*).

62 *Mackrel-Gale.* A "strong breeze such as mackerel are best caught in" (*OED*). Mustacho is being either ironic or simply imperturbable.

63 The stage direction *within* (following the name tag) has been deleted here because Stephano, the master, has just been addressed by Mustacho and is clearly on deck. Perhaps he calls offstage through one of the proscenium doors or perhaps he steps through one of them for a moment. Either explanation is possible, as Stephano is shouting orders to the helmsman who theoretically is offstage.

63 *Port hard, port.* Stephano is conning the ship (giving directions to the helmsman) in the prescribed manner for a ship going before the wind. The order is to turn the helm to the left to make the ship move to starboard, or right. See *Boteler's Dialogues*, p. 78; William Mountaine, *The Seaman's Vade-mecum* (1744), p. 3.

64 *Port is.* Saintsbury emended to "Port it is," but there is an obvious analogy with *Is a weigh* in l. 51. Mainwaring (*Seaman's Dictionary*, p. 131) is vague about the words used to keep a ship on course; he suggests "steady," "as you go, and such like."

65 *no neerer you cannot come.* See *Gentleman's Dictionary*, sig. Eee8: "Near! no Near! a Word of Command from him that Con's [guides] the ship, to the Man at Helm, requiring him to let her fall to the Leeward." At this point the ship is "spooming" or riding before the wind with only the foresail.

69–70 *flat in the Fore-sheat.* See *Gentleman's Dictionary*, sig. Ccc4*v*: "that is, hale in the Fore-Sail by the Sheat, as near the Ship's Side as possible: This is done when a Ship will not fall off from the Wind."

71 *Over-haul your fore-boling.* "The fore-bowline is a rope connecting the luff of the fore-sail (or forward edge) to the cathead, or part of the bow, forward of the sail, so that that part of the sail shall be kept well forward as a ship is staying. Thus when the wind is ahead in this

manoeuvre, the fore-sail is kept aback (with the wind on its fore side) which drives the head of the ship round on the other tack" (Summers, II, 488).

72 *Brace in the Lar-board.* "Brace in (or up) to larboard, to haul the yards sharp up on the port tack so that the ship may sail closer to the wind" (Summers, II, 488).

77–78 *blasphemous, uncharitable dog.* This line is retained from Shakespeare's play, though there is no evidence of blasphemy. Summers (II, 488) maintains that Gonzalo is referring to Trincalo's slighting remarks on the importance of a king in a storm at sea, but Kermode (p. 6) suggests that in the original certain oaths may have been deleted in accordance with the act of 1606 prohibiting their use onstage. Dryden and Davenant may have thought that Gonzalo was referring to Trincalo's remarks on Alonzo, since the prologue states that "Shakespear's *pow'r is sacred as a King's,*" but they changed Shakespeare's "A plague . . ." to "A curse upon this howling" (l. 73), perhaps to clarify the line.

82 *Brace off the Fore-yard.* "Means ease off the lee braces and take in the slack on the weather braces, so that the yard is not pointing so sharp fore and aft; in consequence of the ship being kept a little more off the wind" (Summers, II, 489).

84–85 *unstanch'd Wench.* A rather complex pun on menstruation retained from Shakespeare.

96 *must our mouths be cold.* Dryden and Davenant probably understood this expression to mean "must we die" rather than thinking that Shakespeare was referring either to drinking or to prayers. Their interpretation is suggested by their reversing the position of the line (l. 97) referring to prayer and by their showing the crew as already having had their "dram." For a discussion of this problem in Shakespeare's play, see Furness, p. 19; Kermode, p. 7.

101 *meerly.* Utterly.

102 *wide-chopt Rascal.* "He that hath a great and broad mouth is shameless, a great babler and lyar, a carrier of false tales, very foolish, impudent, couragious, but perfidious withal" (Richard Saunders, *Saunders' Physiognomie, and Chiromancie, Metoposcopie* [1671], p. 196). See also Bartholomeus Cocles, *A Brief and Most Pleasant Epitomye of the Whole Art of Phisiognomie,* trans. Thomas Hyll (1656), sig. B8.

103 *long washing of ten Tides.* Under a sentence passed by the English court of admiralty, pirates were to be hanged on the shore at low-water mark and remain there until three tides had "overwashed them." The addition of the word "long" in the Dryden-Davenant version indicates their awareness of Shakespeare's exaggeration (see Furness, p. 19).

110 *Let's all sink with the Duke.* Shakespeare gave this speech to Anthony, but Dryden and Davenant may have felt that such an expression of loyalty was more suitable for Gonzalo.

113 *Luffe.* Bring the head of the ship nearer to the wind in order to stop its progress.

I, ii

17 *narrow*. Small, with the implication of poverty.

19 *I ne're indeavour'd*. Dryden and Davenant reduce much of the blank verse of this section to prose and cut the highly poetic removal of Prospero's magic garment. They may have objected to Shakespeare's verbiage in Miranda's

More to know
Did never meddle with my thoughts.

57–58 *Ivy which . . . suckt my verdure out*. See John Parkinson, *Theatrum Botanicum: The Theater of Plants* (1640), p. 678: "The climing Ivie groweth up with a thicke wooddy trunke or body, sometimes as bigge as ones arme, shooting forth on all sides many wooddy branches, and groweth sometimes alone by it selfe . . . but usually climeth up by trees, and as the branches rise sendeth forth divers small rootes into the body, or branches of the tree whereby it climeth up, or into the chinkes or joynts of stone walls, whereon it runneth so strongly, fastning them therein, that it draweth the nourishment out of the tree and thereby killeth it by consuming the life and moisture thereof. . . ." Dryden and Davenant shape this passage into a single metaphor taken from gardening; Shakespeare's original passage included imagery from hunting and music as well. Cf. Furness, pp. 33–35.

69 *dry*. Eager.

81 *Nissa's Port*. Nice. Dryden and Davenant attempt to correct Shakespeare's vagueness about geography by changing the enemy from Naples to Savoy. Nice (sometimes called Nizza or Nizze) was under the control of Savoy in Dryden's time.

96 *steaded*. Stood in good stead.

101 *mid-Heaven*. Shakespeare has "zenith," but Dryden and Davenant supply the more technical astronomical term. For an example of propitious judgments, according to midheaven, see Partridge, pp. 183–188.

109 *be it to fly*. As Kermode notes (p. 22), Ariel is given the ability to move in all the four elements, being also capable of doing "business in the Veins of the Earth." To both Shakespeare and his revisers Ariel would represent one of the elemental beings or middle spirits. For a description of such spirits see Paracelsus, *Three Books of Philosophy* (1657), pp. 11–20.

111 *qualities*. Dryden and Davenant changed Shakespeare's "quality" presumably because they misread his meaning and assumed that he was ungrammatically using the word to denote mental or moral attributes. In Shakespeare's play, Ariel is referring to his train of lesser spirits.

112 *perform'd to point*. Executed exactly.

115 *Beak*. "Beak, or Beak-Head of a Ship, is that Part without the Ship, before the Fore-Castle, which is fasten'd to the Stem, supported by the Main-Knee: 'Tis commonly Carv'd and Painted, and is a great Ornament to the Ship, besides other necessary Uses" (*Gentleman's Dictionary*, sig. Aaa2v).

116 *I flam'd amazement*. A reference to St. Elmo's fire.

118 *Bore-sprit.* "Bow-Sprit, or Bolt-Sprit, is a kind of Mast resting slop-wise on the head of the Main-Stem, and having its lower end fasten'd to the Partners of the Fore-mast, and farther supported by the Fore-stay: It carries the Sprit-sail, Sprit-top-sail, and Jack-staff: And its Length is usually the same with the Fore-Mast" (*Gentleman's Dictionary*, sig. Aaa5).

120 *coil.* Confusion.

125 *upstairing.* Standing on end.

132 *Not a hair perisht.* One of a magician's powers was his ability to prevent men from sinking into water (see Laurent Bordelon, *A History of the Ridiculous Extravagancies of Monsieur Oufle* [1711], pp. 272–273).

136 *in this sad knot.* Ariel probably accompanied this statement with an appropriate gesture.

142 *Still vext Bermoothes.* This mention of Bermuda is the only one in the play, and its retention from Shakespeare shows that Dryden and Davenant could still expect their audience to recall the legends of magic and enchantment which once surrounded that island. Kermode (pp. xxvi–xxx, 24) argues that William Strachey's *True Reportory of the Wracke,* the most vivid account of the wreck of George Somers and his crew on the island, may well have been read in manuscript by Shakespeare; the Restoration audience, of course, would have had direct access to it through Samuel Purchas, *Hakluytus Posthumus, or Purchas his Pilgrimes* (1625). Strachey says that "such tempests, thunders, and other fearfull objects are seene and heard about them, that they be called commonly The Devils Ilands, and are feared and avoyded of all sea travellers alive, above any other place in the world," but denies that they are "given over to Devils and wicked Spirits" and argues that they are perfect for human habitation. The political development of Bermuda was turbulent from the very start, and Strachey reports sentiments among the sailors anticipatory of the Levellers. Such accounts probably influenced Fletcher's *The Sea Voyage,* which in turn influenced the Dryden-Davenant revisions of *The Tempest.* See Samuel Purchas, *Purchas his Pilgrimes* (Glasgow ed., 1905–1907), XIX, 13–38; John Smith, *The General Historie of the Bermudas,* in *Works,* ed. Edward Arber (Birmingham, 1884), pp. 625–688.

147 *Float.* Flood, sea.

155 *two Glasses.* Two o'clock.

160 *Moodie.* Scot (pp. 222, 226–228) says that the spirit, Balkin, becomes "wearied if the action wherein he is employed continue longer than an hour," but many commentators have confused the control of elemental spirits with the binding of infernal spirits. In Davenant's *The Temple of Love* (1634) the elemental spirits enter in an antimasque and are kept distinct from the devils. "Anti-Scot" (p. 50) states that "considered in themselves, their Nature is wholly harmless, as to ought that may be called innate Evill, having nothing in them that is eternal as the Soul of Man: and consequently nothing in them that is able to make them capable of enjoying Heaven, or induring the torments of Hell." He also tends to regard the impatient Balkin as an elemental spirit of earth

rather than a devil. Prospero actually seems to preserve Ariel as his servant by appealing to his sense of gratitude as it might operate in a free moral agent rather than by treating him as a slave in bondage. The use of italics here, not present in Shakespeare folios, may indicate that the collaborators thought that Moodie was a nickname for Ariel. See Davenant, *Dramatic Works,* ed. James Maidment and W. H. Logan (Edinburgh, 1872–1874), I, 295–296; Furness, p. 57.

175–176 *Veins . . . bak'd with Frost.* Kermode (p. 26) suggests that this description is "Not metaphorical, but in accordance with contemporary cosmology."

179 *Sycorax.* Dryden and Davenant probably accepted Shakespeare's creation as a quintessential witch, but for discussions of the origin of the name see Furness, pp. 58–59; Kermode, p. 26.

183 *Argier.* Algiers. Shakespeare's spelling would have been contemporary for Dryden and Davenant (see *The Adventures of (Mr. T. S.) an English Merchant . . . with a Description of the Kingdom of Argiers* [1670]).

184 *Oh, was she so.* Shakespeare's use of a question mark here instead of the exclamation point leads Kermode (p. 27) to speculate on whether Prospero is being sarcastic or is preparing to contradict Ariel. Dryden and Davenant assume that he is being sarcastic.

191 *blew-ey'd Hag.* Two major theories have been offered for this description of Sycorax, which has been retained by Dryden and Davenant: (1) it alludes to the eyelid and is an indication of Sycorax' pregnancy; (2) it has some association with "blear-eyed," a common characteristic of witches. The first theory may explain why Sycorax was not executed for her crimes in Algiers, but the second gives a good indication of her powers. Agrippa (p. 101) wrote:

> Now the instrument of Fascination is the spirit, *viz.* a certain pure, lucid subtile vapour, generated of the purer blood, by the heat of the heart. This doth alwaies send forth through the eyes, rayes like to it self; Those rayes being sent forth, do carry with them a spirituall vapour, and that vapour a blood, as it appears in bleer, and red eyes, whose raies being sent forth to the eyes of him that is opposite, and looks upon them, carries the vapour of the corrupt blood, together with it self, by the contagion of which it doth infect the eyes of the beholder with the like disease. So the eye being opened, and intent upon any one with a strong imagination, doth dart its beams, which are the Vehiculum of the spirit into the eyes of him that is opposite to him, which . . . possesseth the breast of him that is stricken, wounds the heart and infects his spirit.

It seems likely that Shakespeare's description is directly related to Sycorax' pregnancy, but any statement about a witch's eyes would remind the audience of one of her main powers. For other theories, see Kermode, p. 167.

196 *Hests.* Commands, behests.

197 *more potent Ministers.* The forces of hell commanded by Sycorax in order to bind Ariel, an astral spirit. Paracelsus, though describing the elemental spirits as independent of the infernal spirits, notes that they may be intimidated by the latter and that the gnomes, who dwell in the earth, being closest in location to the infernal forces, are frequently subject to their powers. Prospero suggests a distinction between Sycorax, who practices goety, or black magic, and himself, a practitioner of theurgy, or divine magic. Scot (p. 280) dismisses the claims of the theurgists: "There is yet another Art professed by these cosening Conjurors, which some fond Divines affirm to be more honest and lawful than Necromancy, which is called Theurgie; wherein they work by good Angels. Howbeit their Ceremonies are altogether Papistical and Superstitious, consisting in cleanliness partly of the mind, partly of the body, and partly of things about and belonging to the body. . . ." Scot was certainly correct in suspecting someone like Cornelius Agrippa, who dabbled in black magic despite all his claims to the contrary. But magic found defenders among the Hermetists and the Rosicrucians. In 1651 Hardick Warren defended true magic as a way of reaching religious truth (*Magick and Astrology Vindicated* [1651], p. 2): "And it is too true as one saith that many men abhor the name and word (Magos) because of Simon Magus, who being not indeed Magus, but Goes (that is) familiar with evil spirits, usurped that Title. For Magick, Conjuring, and Witchery, are far differing Arts, which Pliny being ignorant of, scoffed thereat: But Magus is a Persian word, whereby is expresst such a one as is altogether conversant in divine things; And (as Plato affirmeth) that the Art of Magick is an Art of worshipping of God. And sometimes the word Magus is a Name of him that is a God by Nature, and sometimes of him that is conversant in the service and worship of God." Seemingly the problem of magic, infernal and divine, was as current intellectually for the Restoration audience as for Shakespeare's. See Paracelsus, pp. 229–231, 240; Paracelsus, *Three Books of Philosophy,* p. 39; Agrippa, pp. 1–2. For relevant discussions of magic, see Frances Yates, *Giordano Bruno and the Hermetic Tradition* (1964); D. P. Walker, *Spiritual and Demonic Magic* (1958).

202 *strike.* Strike the water.

207 *Yes! Caliban.* Dryden and Davenant add an exclamation point to suggest Ariel's excitement. Some critics have taken Ariel's repetition in Shakespeare's original as an indication of his inattention (see Furness, p. 63).

212 *could ne're again undo.* Kermode (p. 27) suggests an affinity between the metamorphosis of Fradubio into a tree and Sycorax' charm, but Ariel is not transformed; he is entrapped in the same way that a spirit may be entrapped in a crystal. Since this operation is the work of a conjuror or a theurgist rather than of a witch, it is impossible for Sycorax to release the spirit (see Scot, p. 250).

220 *correspondent.* Obedient.

238 *when.* An expression of extreme impatience.

242 *got by the Devil.* Part of the ceremony of witchcraft was actual copulation with Satan; Merlin was reputed to be the offspring of such a union (for a full discussion, see Scot, pp. 39, 41–48).

243 *wicked.* Baneful.

245–246 *A South-west.* Shakespeare means a pestilence-bearing wind. See also Agrippa (p. 17): "Notus is the Southern Wind, cloudy, moist, warm, and sickly."

248 *Urchins.* Goblins in the shape of hedgehogs. Speaking of the way men are terrified by the tales they hear in childhood, Scot (p. 85) complains: "They have so frayed us with Bul-beggers, Spirits, Witches, Urchens, Elves, Hags, Fairies, Satyrs . . . that we are afraid of our own shadows."

269 *Abhor'd Slave.* Dryden and Davenant give this speech to Prospero rather than to Miranda in accordance with, Theobald argued, Shakespeare's original intention. The reasons for the Dryden-Davenant transfer were probably similar to those later set down by Theobald: that such a speech was too philosophical for a woman, that it would be an act of disobedience for Miranda to interrupt her father, and that it would be more likely for Prospero to have taught Caliban to speak. In transferring the speech to Prospero, Dryden and Davenant (and Theobald) seem to have given priority to questions of propriety and decorum rather than to the requirements of the stage, which would have dictated that Miranda not remain onstage without speaking. Modern editors of Shakespeare have almost unanimously disagreed with Theobald's assignment of the speech. See Lewis Theobald, ed., *The Works of Shakespeare* (1733), I, 18; Furness, p. 73; Kermode, p. 32.

273 *know thy own meaning.* The theory behind this statement is that without words and language there can be no understanding. For a discussion of this problem in relation to another wild, inarticulate creature, the famous "Peter the Wild Boy," see Daniel Defoe, *Mere Nature Delineated* (1726).

275 *wild race.* Substituted for Shakespeare's "vile race." Dryden and Davenant may have associated Caliban with the wild man, the free dweller of the forest who remained a myth in Europe throughout the Middle Ages and who is still a figure in folklore. He was often connected with the satyrs or the elemental beings who dwell on the earth and was a familiar stage figure in plays like the popular *Mucedorus.* See Richard Bernheimer, *Wild Men in the Middle Ages* (1952), pp. 9–11, 34.

279 *red botch.* Changed from Shakespeare's "red plague." *Botch* may be used in the sense of plague, ulcer, or boil. Perhaps the change was a deliberate attempt to avoid any reminder of the plague that had devastated London just a few years before.

279 *rid.* Destroy.

285 *old Cramps.* Either the cramps that old people experience or, more likely, cramps whose severity Caliban has experienced before.

290 *Setebos.* The god of the Patagonian giants whom Magellan en-

countered in his voyage around the world. Shakespeare probably derived the name from Richard Eden's *History of Travayle* (1577). See Furness, pp. 76–77.

292 + *s.d. Enter Dorinda.* Dorinda enters at the point where Ferdinand enters in Shakespeare's play.

II, i

3 *comfort.* At this point Dryden and Davenant cut ninety-two lines in which, in Shakespeare's play, Antonio and Sebastian mock Gonzalo's verbosity. Sebastian and supernumeraries like Adrian and Francisco are eliminated.

5 *against my stomack.* Contrary to a state of mind, or, using the food metaphor, contrary to what a man can digest at a given moment.

16 *we should have helpt it.* Dryden and Davenant provide Alonzo with an immediate sense of guilt and give Antonio a remorse that is entirely missing in Shakespeare's character. In preparing the audience for the penitence of these characters, the revisers probably felt they were adding psychological verisimilitude, which was hardly necessary in a play depending on magic and transformation for its main effects.

28 *Portugal.* The Moors entered Spain at the beginning of the eighth century and were driven from Portugal in the thirteenth century and from Spain on 6 January 1492. Thus Dryden and Davenant's revision is in almost as much of a chronological limbo as is Shakespeare's play.

42 *Blood pursu'd my hand.* The main source of the bleeding tree could have been Virgil, *Aeneid*, III, 24–48, but the theme was imitated by many poets; the groans of ghosts and voices are closer to Tasso, *Jerusalem Delivered*, Bk. XIII, trans. Edward Fairfax [1962], pp. 336–337, than to Virgil. See also Ovid, *Metamorphoses*, VIII, 758–776; Ariosto, *Orlando Furioso*, VI, 26; and Spenser, *Faerie Queene*, I, ii, 33.

97 *trills down.* Designating a flow more constant and continuous than a trickle.

106 *peid.* Pecked.

II, ii

s.d. Enter . . . Ariel, invisible. According to Henslowe's *Diary*, among the wardrobe of the Admiral's Men was "a robe for to goo invisibell." Wordsworth (*Prelude*, VII, 285–287) describes such a garment in use at Sadler's Wells:

> Delusion bold! and how can it be wrought?
> The garb he wears is black as death, the word
> "Invisible" flames forth upon his chest.

Such a garment must have been common even in the Victorian theater, since Dickens, like Wordsworth, was struck by its imaginative suggestiveness and mentions it frequently in his novels.

3 *kiss'd.* The comma after *kiss'd,* added by Dryden and Davenant in an attempt to clarify what modern editors consider a difficulty, makes the following line an absolute construction. The kiss described here, the

holding of hands, and the curtsy are part of a dance, though, as Kermode suggests, the kiss usually came when the dance was finished. See Furness, p. 78; Kermode, p. 34.

4 *whist.* Are silent.

6 *s.d. Burthen dispersedly.* The "burthen" was a continuous chorus or undersong playing behind the main melody. Dryden and Davenant follow the lineation of this song as it appears in the folios. Although various attempts have been made to give Shakespeare's lines, other than the barking chorus, to spirits besides Ariel, the problem has never been satisfactorily solved. The present editors' timidity on this particular problem (the lineation is left as it appears in the original) is matched only by their treatment of the lineation in general. See Furness, pp. 79–80; Kermode, p. 34.

13 *against.* Dryden and Davenant interpret Shakespeare's "againe" as against, or in full view of. This interpretation has not been accepted by most of Shakespeare's editors.

19 *Fathoms.* Shakespeare has "fadom," which his revisers felt was grammatically incorrect.

II, iii

1 *Runlet.* Cask or vessel.

6 *soop.* A draught or small amount of drink.

33 *marry agen.* After seven years' absence a person was declared legally dead. This practice became a law in 1666. See *The Statutes of the Realm* (1963), V, 614 (18 & 19 Car. II, c. 11).

35 *Bladders.* "The prepared bladder of an animal, which may be inflated and used from its bouyancy as a float" (*OED*).

38 *sorrow is dry.* A proverb usually applied to widows or widowers to excuse their drinking heavily to console themselves (see Tilley, S656).

42 *Poor heart.* A term of compassion, used especially among sailors. *dry.* A pun on *dry* meaning "barren" or "sterile."

43 *all is barren* etc. The landscape is taken from Fletcher's *Sea Voyage.* Cf. Sebastian's speech (I, i):

> It is so ominous.
> Serpents, and ugly things, the shames of nature,
> Roots of malignant tasts, foul standing waters;
> Sometimes we finde a fulsome Sea-root,
> And that's a delicate: a Rat sometimes,
> And that we hunt like Princes in their pleasure;
> And when we take a Toad, we make a Banquet.

43 *lye at Hull.* "To Hull, or Lie a-Hull, or Hulling; is said of a Ship, when either in a dead Calm, (to prevent her beating the Sails against the Masts, by Rolling;) or in a Storm, when she cannot carry them, she takes all her Sails in, so that nothing but her Masts, Yards and Rigging are abroad; the Helm is lash'd fast to the Lee-side of the Ship: In this Condition, if she is a good Sailer, she will lie easily under the Sea, and make her Way one Point before the Beam" (*Gentleman's Dictionary*, sig. Ddd3). See also Mainwaring, *Seaman's Dictionary,* II, 167–168.

44 *a Sail, a Sail.* The cry when a ship is sighted (see *Gentleman's Dictionary,* sig. Gff5v).

45 *Apron.* Within this context the reference is probably both to a sail that looks like an apron on a woman and to an apron on a woman which looks like a sail.

49 *Salvages.* Savages. Ventoso conceives of their returning to a state of nature in which they "may" (i.e., are permitted to) eat one another. Thus both the state of necessity, which was considered outside the bounds of law, and the stage of society before the establishment of law are suggested. Fletcher treated the first in his *Sea Voyage* (III, i) where the sailors claim the right to devour the heroine, Aminta, when they are starving—a right that the influential writer on natural law, Hugo Grotius, appeared to defend. In his commentary on Grotius, Caspar Ziegler brought up a specific case of seven English sailors who, after drawing lots, were forced to devour a member of the crew. The sailors were acquitted by the court. See Samuel Pufendorf, *Of the Law of Nature and Nations,* trans. Basil Kennett and William Percivale (Oxford, 1703), p. 158 (II, vi, 3). For a treatment of the primitive state of society, see Erwin Panofsky, *Studies in Iconology* (1962), pp. 33–67. See also Grotius, *De Jure Belli ac Pacis Libri Tres,* trans. Francis Kelsey (1925), pp. 193–194 (II, ii, 6–8), 172–173 (II, i, iii).

60 *a free Subject.* Cf. Strachey's account of the speech of Stephen Hopkins, one of the rebels in Bermuda, who held "that it was no breach of honesty, conscience, nor Religion, to decline from the obedience of the Governour, or refuse to goe any further, led by his authority (except it so pleased themselves) since the authority ceased when the wreck was committed, and with it, they were all freed from the government of any man" (*Purchas his Pilgrimes* [Glasgow ed.], XIX, 30–31). For the concept of the sailors as "Lords" of their island, see Smith, *Historie of the Bermudas,* in *Works,* p. 640; and *The Historye of the Bermudaes,* ed. J. Henry Lefroy (1882), p. 17.

78 *s.d. Both draw.* For a parallel conflict between Chard and Waters on Bermuda, see Smith, *Historie of the Bermudas,* p. 641.

89–96 *The Master* etc. Dryden and Davenant cut out Shakespeare's last line in this song: "Then to sea, boys, and let her go hang!"

102 *Old Simon the King.* The title of a song that recommends drink as the sovereign cure for all ills and exalts the man who drinks bravely as the king of his private world. The following stanza is typical (see (*Merry Songs and Ballads,* ed. John Farmer [1897], III, 1–4):

> But when a man is drunke to-day,
>   & laid in his grave to-morrow;
> will any man dare to say
>   that hee dyed ffor Care or sorrowe?
> but hang up all sorrow and care!
>   itts able to kill a catt;
> & he that will drinke till he stare
>   is never a-feard of that; . . .

sais old Simon the King, sais old Simon the King.
with his ale-dropt hose, and his malmesy nose,
with a hey ding, ding a ding, ding.

126 *swimmingly.* Smoothly, successfully.

132 *Common-wealth.* This scene is clearly a satire on the squabbling that took place during the interregnum, although there is surely some general satire on the way all governments are established. Stephano achieves his "election" by insisting on his power. Mustacho's claim that there is already a settled government and that Trincalo is an anarchist in saying "I'll have no Laws" (l. 140) must appear absurd under the circumstances. If the scene is a reflection of Davenant's attitude toward government, it shows his leaning toward the conventionalism that was so common in French libertine circles. And whatever Dryden's relationship to Hobbes might have been, Davenant, who wrote this section, was a professed admirer of that philosopher.

150 *Flats.* Low-lying marshy lands; swamps. *inch-meal.* Inch by inch.

152 *Urchin shows.* Tricks and antics of elves.

173 *Moon-calf.* "An abortion, a monstrosity. Moon-calf, *partus lunaris,* was an old name for a false conception—*mola carnea,* or foetus imperfectly formed, being supposed to be occasioned by the influence of the moon" (Summers, II, 490).

183 *out of the Moon.* Travelers sometimes told natives they came from the moon in order to impose on them (see Robert Cawley, "Shakespeare's Use of the Voyagers," *PMLA,* XLI [1926], 717).

193 *Crabs.* Crab apples.

194 *Pig-nuts.* A root with various names: earth chestnut, kippernut, hawknut. The scientific name is *Bunium flexuosum.*

196 *Marmazet.* Marmoset, a small monkey that was considered edible.

222 *by Alliance.* Trincalo takes the position that the original inhabitants own the island and that he may claim it by his marriage. Stephano, who thought the island uninhabited, bases his claim on the right of discovery. Dryden and Davenant follow Shakespeare in having Caliban claim the island on two grounds: right of inheritance from Sycorax, his mother, and right of prior possession. Prospero claims the island by the right of his superior nature. In this latter respect it is interesting that Purchas maintained that God had kept the pagan nations ignorant and weak so as to make the European's conquest of them the easier (*Purchas his Pilgrimes* [Glasgow ed.], I, 52–53).

II, iv

14 *kept me in a Rock.* The theme of a man kept isolated in a cave until maturity had a peculiar fascination for an age dominated by Cartesian philosophy and was widely used by writers. It found its fullest expression in Spain in the dramas of Calderón and in Baltasar Gracián's lengthy allegory, *El Criticón.* Through his struggle to understand the meaning of existence while locked in his cave, Andrenio, the hero of Gracián's work, became the archetypal hero of this motif.

19 *A black Star.* Perhaps a star connected with Saturn, the darkest planet and the one with the worst influence on human life. Agrippa (pp. 281–282) wrote:

> Know this that all the fixt stars are of the signification and nature of the seven Planets. . . . Now the natures of fixt stars are discovered by their colours, as they agree with certain Planets, and are ascribed to them: of Saturn, blew, and leaden. . . . For Celestial bodies, in as much as they are affected fortunately, or unfortunately, so much do they affect us, our works, and those things which we use. . . . And although many effects proceed from the fixt Stars, yet they are attributed to the Planets, as because being more neer to us, and more distinct and known, so because they execute whatsoever the superior Stars communicate to them.

19 *death unseen.* Both Saturn and Mars frequently indicate a "violent Death" (see Partridge, pp. 168–170).

25 *Man was Lord of.* That is, Prospero taught Hippolito the lesson of Genesis, 1, 26–28, that man was given dominion over the beasts of the field.

97 *rugged.* Rough with hair; hirsute.

106 *wild about the Woods.* The wild man was notorious for his sexual license and was often regarded as being free from the restraints imposed upon civilized man. He could be tamed by love. Prospero's image of the wild man of chambers and closets tends to associate the seventeenth-century libertine, who held a philosophic doctrine of sexual freedom, with the legendary wild man of the woods. In this respect the comparison to the bear is, perhaps, significant, since wild men were sometimes supposed to be suckled by bears. See Bern Connor, *The History of Poland* (1698), I, 342–349, for reports of some supposedly accurate accounts of these beings. For the way the legend of the wild man blended motifs of love and death, see Bernheimer, *Wild Men,* pp. 125–154.

II, v

3 *suck the poyson of the Earth.* In Shakespeare's *Richard II* (III, ii, 12–16) the King, after his return from Ireland, asks the earth of England to reject Bolingbroke:

> Feed not thy sovereign's foe, my gentle earth,
> Nor with thy sweets comfort his ravenous sense;
> But let thy spiders that suck up thy venom,
> And heavy-gaited toads, lie in their way,
> Doing annoyance . . .

The idea that venomous creatures served this purpose was a common teleological argument as late as the eighteenth century, when Archbishop William King wrote, "The very Serpents, tho' a Race hateful to us, have their uses; among the rest, they gather the Poison out of the Earth" (*An Essay on the Origin of Evil,* trans. Edmund Law [1731], p. 34).

60 *Serpents harmless to each other.* For contemporary illustrations of

Dryden's natural history of venomous serpents, see Edward Topsell, *The History of Four-footed Beasts and Serpents* (1658), p. 604; and M. Charas, *New Experiments upon Vipers* (1670), pp. 125–126. The harmlessness of venomous creatures to one another was one of the ideas that Richard Mead attempted to refute in *A Mechanical Account of Poisons* (1702), pp. 53–54.

III, i

86 *to tye him to a hair.* Bernheimer (*Wild Men,* p. 53) discusses a ritual in which the wild man was led into the village by a little girl who had tied a red ribbon on him. It is possible that, as the wild man became more of a symbol of sexual freedom, the significance of this ritual changed. In *The Faerie Queene* (VI, 4) Spenser has a scene in which the wild man is tamed by the sight of a beautiful woman in distress.

120 *lazy Ague.* Thomas Sydenham (*The Whole Works* [1697], pp. 37–59) distinguishes between the long agues that occur in the fall and the spring agues. The worst of the long agues is the "quatran" ague, which may last for six months with a fit every third day. Each fit, accompanied by shivering, may last up to five hours. Sydenham notes that the patient is often weakened psychologically by the recurrence of these fits over a long period of time.

121 *striving.* Struggling against.

127 *He hath no Claws.* In muted form this is the usual description of the limitations of man in his competition with *other* beasts of prey. In Gracián's *El Criticón,* Andrenio asks how man can do so much mischief: "He hath no claws like the Lyon, or Tyger, no Trunk like the Elephant, no Horns like the Bull, no Tusks like the Boar. . . . how then is that unarmed Malice able to wage such continual War?" Critilo then tells Andrenio a story of how a man rescued a criminal thrown into a cave with beasts. The beasts, including a tiger, showed their gratitude while the criminal murdered his rescuer for his wealth. Montaigne points out how greatly the beasts surpass man, but he denies that man is without weapons to defend himself. See Gracián, *The Critick,* trans. Paul Rycaut (1681), pp. 47–49; Montaigne, *Essays,* trans. John Florio, Tudor Translations (1893), II, 149–150.

144–146 *Now my designs* etc. A rewriting of Shakespeare, V, i, 1–39. Shakespeare's elaborate language and imagery are toned down, beginning with the elimination of "Time goes upright with his carriage."

188 *mop and moe.* Comic and grotesque gestures and grimaces.

III, ii

1–13 *I am weary* etc. From Shakespeare, III, iii, 1–17.

3 *forth-rights and Meanders.* A reference to the construction of mazes with paths sometimes straight and sometimes winding.

23 *Dry those eyes* etc. This song is adapted from Shakespeare's masque (IV, i) in which Juno and Ceres bless the marriage of Miranda and Ferdinand:

Earths increase, foyzon plentie,

Barnes, and Garners, never empty.
Vines, with clustring bunches growing,
Plants, with goodly burthen bowing:
Spring come to you at the farthest,
In the very end of Harvest.
Scarcity and want shall shun you,
Ceres blessing so is on you.

35+ *s.d. eight fat Spirits.* This expression was parodied in Buckingham's *Rehearsal* (II, v), when Bayes remarks to the soldiers, "Udzookers, you dance worse than the Angels in *Harry* the Eight, or the fat Spirits in *The Tempest,* I gad."

38 *Burgo-Masters.* Gonzalo puns on the resemblance of the fat burgomasters of Holland to the fat dancing devils, or burgomasquers. A burgomasque was an antimasque, such as appears in Milton's *Comus* and Davenant's *The Temple of Love.* It represented a baroque concept of playing the grotesque against the beautiful, and the cast usually included satyrs or devils.

39 *Collop.* Here meaning both a large fold of flesh on a heavy person and a slice of meat for eating.

41 *going to the door.* "That is, one of the permanent proscenium doors" (Summers, II, 491).

45 *to poyson us.* The danger of accepting food from the devil has its prime classical exemplum in the myth of Persephone, but it was also common in folk ballads like *Thomas Rymer.*

III, iii

12 *Blobber-lips.* Lips that are thick, swollen, and protruding.

13 *Fuss.* In defining this word as an abbreviated form of *fussock,* "a fat, unwieldy woman," the *OED* quotes this passage as an example. Summers (II, 491) suggests a misprint here for *fubs,* a term of endearment generally applied to a small, chubby person. In favor of Summers' suggestion, it might be pointed out that *fubs,* unlike *fuss,* would fit very well with "Chuck" and "Babby," the other loving words Trincalo used in addressing Sycorax.

19 *Babby.* Child or foolish child.

57 *flipant.* Sportive, playful. The word has sexual overtones, and there is unquestionably a good deal of stage action in Sycorax' attempt to make advances to Trincalo. Summers (II, 491) maintains the very doubtful position that Fainall's statement about Sir Wilful—"When he's drunk, he's as loving as the Monster in *The Tempest*"—in Congreve's *The Way of the World* refers not to Caliban but to his sister Sycorax.

57+ *s.d. Enter Ariel.* This comic action replaces Shakespeare's more elaborate and dramatically more effective scene in which the harpies snatch the food from the King and his followers just as they are about to eat.

78 *Simon the King.* See note to II, iii, 102.

109 *your Embassy.* This parody of diplomatic protocol may be related to the famous controversy over ambassadors which pervaded Europe at

this time. On 10 October 1661 the Spanish ambassador in London, Baron de Batteville, attempted to take precedence over the Count d'Estrade, the French ambassador. In an ensuing battle between the domestics attached to the embassies several servants and horses of the French ambassador were killed. On 14 November the King of Spain expressed his regrets over the incident, but the entire affair was not closed until 24 March 1662, when Spain formally apologized in the presence of foreign ministers, all the princes of the blood, and the ministers of state. Baron de Batteville assured Louis XIV that never again would the Spanish ambassador attempt to take precedence. Pepys's excellent account of the incident in his entry of 30 September 1661 echoed the anti-French and pro-Spanish sympathies of the mob. Charles II tried to calm Louis XIV by blaming the entire battle on the English mob, but Louis was furious over this attack on the dignity of France. See Benjamin Priolo, *The History of France under the Ministry of Cardinal Mazarine*, trans. Christopher Wase (1671), pp. 429–432; *The History of France . . . to the Year 1702* (1702), II, 959–961; Gabriel Daniel, *The History of France* (1726), V, 96–97.

120 *Blouze.* A woman with a ruddy complexion and a fat face.

121 *hectoring.* Bullying.

125 *natural.* Idiot.

142 *freshes.* Streams of fresh water.

148 *Spies than Embassadors.* Louis XIV refused to accept the new ambassador from Spain after he had expelled the Conde de Fuensaldagna, the Spanish ambassador to France during the "battle of embassadors" (see Bright's note to the entry of 4 October 1661 in *The Diary of Samuel Pepys,* ed. Henry Wheatley [1946], I, 326).

III, iv

27–44 *Go thy way* etc. After seeing *The Tempest* for the first time, Pepys commented: "The house mighty full; the King and Court there: and the most innocent play that ever I saw; and a curious piece of musique in an echo of half sentences, the echo repeating the former half while the man goes on to the latter; which is mighty pretty." This kind of echo refrain was, of course, a minor genre in the seventeenth century (see, for example, Lord Herbert of Cherbury, "Echo to a Rock" and "Echo in a Church," in *Poems,* ed. G. C. Moore Smith [1923], pp. 46–48).

III, v

1 *Advance the fringed Curtains of thine Eyes* etc. That this passage, which was attacked by Pope in his *Peri Bathous,* was retained by Dryden and Davenant with only a change in the syntax of the sentence suggests that the précieuse quality of Shakespeare's play was not at all uncongenial to the Restoration.

33 *third man that e're I saw.* Here Dryden and Davenant follow Shakespeare, though Hippolito rather than Caliban is to be understood as the second man seen by Miranda.

40–41 *light . . . light.* A play on *light,* which means "easy" in the first line and "little valued" in the second. Dryden and Davenant show little consistency in cutting quibbles of this kind. For example, they drop the pun on Miranda's name in Ferdinand's exclamation on first encountering her ("O you wonder!"), probably on the grounds that he could not have known her name and that such a pun was a kind of false wit.

46 *nothing ill.* For an interesting discussion of this Neoplatonic convention, see Kermode, p. 39.

53 *Acorn cradl'd.* The first edition has *Acorn crawl'd*, a misprint.

57 *gentle and not fearful.* Modern editors disagree on the meaning of this phrase, retained from Shakespeare. Kermode (p. 40) contends that it means "Of high birth and not a coward," whereas Furness (pp. 89–90) tends to agree with Joseph Ritson that Miranda means "mild and harmless, and not in the least terrible or dangerous." Dryden generally uses *gentle* in the sense of mild and *fearful* in the sense of frightened rather than frightening, but there are exceptions (e.g., "Upon Young Mr. Rogers of Glocestershire," l. 1, and *Annus Mirabilis*, l. 281). Certainly the context supports Furness and Ritson, for Miranda knows of her father's powers and is conscious of her feelings of tenderness for Ferdinand, but is of course unaware of the harm that swords might accomplish.

60–61 *Come from Thy Ward.* Drop your posture of defense, your position for parrying attacks.

62 *This Wand.* Shakespeare has "this stick" (I, ii, 475). Dryden and Davenant prefer to lose the contrast between the powerful sword and the seemingly weak stick, which is actually a magic wand. It is a typical example of the way the collaborators oversimplified Shakespeare's paradoxes in the name of clarity.

76 *Nerves.* Sinews or tendons. This usage was common in Dryden's day.

84 *liberty.* "Those who are free may have all the rest of the world; my prison, with Miranda near, is all the space I need" (Kermode, p. 41).

86–88 *It works* etc. Following the practice of most editors of Shakespeare's *Tempest*, we have introduced stage directions into this speech to indicate that Prospero is trying to carry on a dialogue with Ferdinand and Ariel at the same time. It is possible, however, that the collaborators read the entire speech as directed to Ariel.

154–155 *on what strange grounds* etc. This speech questioning the limitations placed on human freedom by fate begins by echoing the omitted speech of Prospero after the masque in Shakespeare's play (IV, i, 156–158):

> We are such stuff
> As dreams are made on; and our little life
> Is rounded with a sleep.

This skeptical philosophical disquisition, more typical of Dryden than of Davenant, is entirely relevant to the theme of freedom they found in Shakespeare's play. Unlike Shakespeare, however, the collaborators turned to the larger metaphysical problem of man's freedom of action. As a magician, Prospero should and does believe in the operation of fate, but he pauses for a moment to question his assumptions. If man is completely free, how can he be bounded in any way by the decrees of a deity? The problem is eventually resolved in favor of an overriding fate in the action of the play, but at this point Prospero is allowed to assume an ambiguous position. Although the last line must be read as a statement of resignation, it is difficult to tell whether Prospero resigns himself to faith in the absolute goodness of God and the wickedness of man —it is not easy to see how a benevolent deity would drive man to "ill" —or to a somewhat ironic statement of the unsatisfactory way men usually resolve the problem. For an analogous speech and situation, see the speech of King Basilio in Pedro Calderón de la Barca's *La Vida Es Sueño* (1635) (I, ii).

III, vi

60 *against my Nature.* The idea that marriage was an unnatural state and that in the state of nature man was allowed to have many women was one of the libertine arguments against marriage. The writers on natural law, such as Grotius, tended to regard monogamous marriage as a "custom" of Western nations, and even within these nations they attempted to establish certain laws giving concubines some kind of official status. The objections of the rakes to marriage (the usual metaphor was eating the same piece of meat every night) were based on a sense that the natural condition of man was sexually free. In Thomas Killigrew's *Thomaso; or, The Wanderer* (in *Comedies, and Tragedies* [1664], p. 346) the hero expresses the standard objection to marriage from the standpoint of the libertine ethic:

> I have a Woman without that boundless Folly, of better or worse; there's a kind of Non-sence in that Vow Fools onely swallow; I can now bid my Friends well-come without Jealousies; Our vows are built upon kindness only, they stand & fall together; We neither load, nor enslave the mind with Matrimony; no laws, nor tyes, but what good Nature makes, binds us; we are sure to meet without false well-comes, or dissembling smiles, to hide the Sallary of a sin, or blinde the Fornication of a Platonique Friendship; Our knots hold no longer then we love; No sooner with a liberty but we take it.

This libertine attitude gained support from the ever-expanding knowledge of other cultures which travelers were bringing back to Europe. Not only was there polygamy throughout the Turkish empire, but there was some knowledge of polyandry in India and Ceylon and rumors of complete sexual license in the Far East. The influence of such ideas on Restoration drama is obvious. In Aphra Behn's *The Young King* (1679), a play based partly on Calderón's *La Vida Es Sueño*, the hero, who like Hippolito has been reared in isolation, instead of seizing on the first available, beautiful woman, as in the original, grasps his own mother and offers to teach her "A new Philosophy inspir'd by Nature" (*The Works of Aphra Behn*, ed. Montague Summers [1915], II, 145).

73 *And will have yours.* Hippolito is depicted as very like the archetypal man of the Neo-Epicureans who is not able to live in society

without quarreling "about Food, Women, and other Commodities, which
the stronger alwaies took from the weaker" (*Epicurus's Morals,* trans.
Walter Charleton [1656], p. 150).

100 *for himself design'd.* That the natural man's contact with women
should lead to a rivalry with Hippolito's foster father, Prospero, is not
so much a brilliant foreshadowing of Freud's theory of sexual rivalry in
Totem and Taboo as a contemporary theory of man's instincts in the
state of nature before social restrictions were enforced by laws. Calderón's Segismund, in *La Vida Es Sueño,* feels no instinctive love for his
father, whom he perceives at once as a hated rival. Sir Sampson Legend's
rivalry with his son for the hand of Angelica in Congreve's *Love for Love*
and Aureng-Zebe's with the Emperor in *Aureng-Zebe* are typical expressions of this motif in Restoration drama.

IV, i

26 *envy freedom.* Dryden, revising the dialogue in this encounter between Ferdinand and Miranda from Shakespeare's tender meeting between the two lovers (III, i), stresses the theme of love as a loss of freedom. Ferdinand is relieved of the burden of carrying logs, probably on
the ground of neoclassical decorum.

75–76 *wants your conversation.* Lacks your social poise, manners, and
experience with the world. "Conversation" was a rich and complex word
in the seventeenth and eighteenth centuries.

192 *Is she your Sister.* The voyagers and writers on natural law had
discovered that Western taboos against incest were less the law of
nature than the rule of custom. Several decades later Pufendorf (*Law of
Nature and Nations,* p. 98 [IV, i, 28]) was to question why a taboo existed
against incest in the West and seemed not to exist elsewhere:

> But indeed this Repugnancy of Affections is not equally
> to be discover'd amongst all People, nor always, even
> amongst those who pretend to the Arts of Culture and
> Refinement: and when Authors urge it for a Reason, it
> would not be altogether absurd to answer them, that
> the Abhorrence may perhaps arise not so much from
> any in-bred Principle, as from long Use and Custom,
> which often counterfeit Nature. Nor in our Searches
> after Natural Law, is it very safe to rely upon the bare
> Judgment of our Senses and Affections; since at this rate
> we might conclude, that those things are by the same
> Law commanded, towards which our Senses and Affec-
> tions are carried on with a vigorous Inclination; where-
> as, on the contrary, it is manifest that those Acts to
> which we are so violently prone, Reason and Nature do
> really disallow."

209 *One is enough.* Discussions of polygamy and its lawfulness were
far more common than discussions of polyandry. Henry Neville's polygamous utopia, *The Isle of Pines* (1668), was published shortly after
Dryden and Davenant's revision of *The Tempest;* and at the end of

Killigrew's *Thomaso; or, The Wanderer* (p. 453), Edwardo and Ferdinando, the companions of Thomaso, contemplate going off to "the Indies; where we are promis'd six black wives apiece, smooth and comely beauties, naked truths, Eves, in the state of innocence. . . ." For a discussion of polygamy according to natural law, see Grotius, *De Jure Belli*, p. 234 (II, v, 9).

240 *lost*. A pun. Behind both Hippolito's and Dorinda's use of the word lies the meaning "sexually violated."

288 *what is right*. The misunderstanding about "rights" is in accord with Hippolito's stage of development as a natural man. Ferdinand uses the word "right" to imply a legal power over Miranda, a right to her as to a piece of property or to an island that one has first discovered and explored. Hippolito, who has no notion of property, thinks of his right to act freely, unlimited by anything but the passions that govern him. See *Epicurus's Morals*, trans. Charleton, p. 150.

322 *fit*. To suit or accustom oneself to.

IV, ii

8 *Linguist*. In the context of "a Monster of parts" at the beginning of Trincalo's speech (l. 5), this may be a sexual pun.

18 *Peace, and the Butt*. Peace and its benefits, symbolic and real (cf. *Works*, III, 434–435). The quarrel over the butt and sovereignty is reminiscent of the quarrel of Carter, Waters, and Chard over possession of the ambergris they found on Bermuda. But Dryden and Davenant may also be thinking about another peace. In 1663 Samuel Fortrey, attacking the trade with France according to the contemporary theory of the "balance of trade," had pointed out that while the French were raising their tariff on English woolens, England had not responded with an equally high tariff on wines. In January 1666 Charles II ordered all imports from France to halt until the end of the war. Thus a real peace including resumption of the flow of wine may have been in the minds of the audience as they watched the antics of the sailors. See *Historye of the Bermudaes*, ed. Lefroy, pp. 18–23; Henry Wilkinson, *Adventurers of Bermuda* (1958), pp. 53–73; Ephraim Lipson, *Economic History of England* (1948), III, 98–116.

23 *skink*. Pour out drinks.

24 *Rowse*. Sometimes *rouse;* a full draught of liquor.

25 *Haunse in Kelder*. Jack-in-the-cellar or the unborn child in the womb (see Tilley, J18).

34 *hearty*. Probably a sexual pun.

63 *Brindis*. From Italian *brindisi* or *brendisi:* a cup in which a person's health is drunk; a bumper.

74 *Up se Dutch*. From *Op Zyn,* in the fashion or manner of the Dutch.

97 *great Families in Lapland*. Unlike England, where witches were usually poor old women, Lapland held witchcraft in respect and recognized second sight as a talent. The most frequent reference to the craft of witches concerned their selling winds to sailors. The famous Duncan

Campbell, who gained wide notice in the eighteenth century for his claims to second sight, was supposed to have been the son of a Lapland woman. See Daniel Defoe, *The Life and Adventures of Mr. Duncan Campbell,* in *The Novels and Miscellaneous Works* (Oxford, 1841), XIX, 19–20; Peter Heylyn, *Cosmographie* (1657), p. 504; Margaret Cavendish, Duchess of Newcastle, *Poems and Fancies* (1653), p. 157.

98 *Mounsor De-Viles in France.* "Mounseer" was a common vulgarism according to the *OED,* but "Mounsor" is not listed. Dryden may have intended a pun on the word, however.

108–109 *Tory, Rory, and Ranthum, Scantum.* Words to indicate copulation, similar to those commonly used in a nursery rhyme in which nonsense words are substituted for improper words (see *OED;* Richard Head and Francis Kirkman, *The English Rogue* [1928], p. 637).

110 *O Jew* etc. Probably a reference to Lot's daughters (Genesis, XIX, 30–36), whose copulating with their father was sometimes defended on the ground that the species must be preserved by any means when threatened with extinction (see John Diodati, *Prose Annotations upon the Holy Bible* [1648], p. 15).

127 *Haws.* The fruit of the hawthorn.

127 *Wildings.* Wild apples or crab apples.

138 *Hackney-Devil.* That is, they will use one of the devils commanded by Sycorax' mother as a hackney coach to carry them through the air.

140 *Pigs-nye.* A term of endearment: sweet or darling.

156 *Hector.* A swaggering coward.

IV, iii

46 *as thou art thy self.* Prospero addresses Ariel as if he were a spirit of evil rather than as an astral spirit; the latter was regarded as amoral rather than evil and as controllable by the forces of either good or evil. Prospero is probably guilty of only a momentary lapse, but Scot (pp. 218, 222) makes less distinction between the astral and the evil spirits than does Paracelsus or Agrippa.

51 *malicious as the Earthy.* The earthy elemental spirits were usually under the control of the infernal spirits. According to Paracelsus (p. 240), their proximity to hell made the earthy spirits afraid of the power of their neighbors, and they might be possessed by devils in the same way as a human being.

52 *more approaching good.* Agrippa (p. 450) argued that spirits like Ariel were "not so noxious, but most neer to men"; "Anti-Scot" (p. 50), that "their Nature is wholly harmless"; and Villars (*Gabalis,* pp. 39–47), that they were more virtuous than men though of an inferior spiritual nature.

53 *we meet in swarms.* Scot (p. 225) similarly describes the wars of Luridan against the fiery spirits: "In this contest they do often totally extirpate and destroy one another, killing and crushing when they meet in mighty and violent Troops in the Air upon the Sea." And "Anti-Scot" (p. 41) is even more vivid:

They meet in mighty Troops, and wage warr one with

another: They do also procreate one another; and have
power sometimes to make great commotions in the Air,
and in the Clowds, and also to cloath themselves with
visible bodies, out of the four Elements appearing in
Companies upon Hills and Mountains, and do often
deceive and delude the Observers of Apparitions, who
take such for portents of great alterations, which are
nothing but the sports and pastime of these frolick Spirits: as Armies in the Air, Troops marching on the Land,
noises and slaughter, Tempest and Lightning etc.

For a partial discussion of Dryden's use of these two writers, see Maximillian E. Novak, "The Demonology of Dryden's *Tyrannick Love* and 'Anti-
Scot,' " *ELN,* IV (1966), 95–98.

59 *ill Genius of Hippolito.* Agrippa (p. 405) quotes Origen's *Periarchon*
on the question of a good and an evil genius for each man. "Now man,"
he concludes, "betwixt these contenders is in the midle, and left in the
hand of his own Counsell, to whom he will give the victory." "Anti-Scot"
(pp. 42–43) sees the good and the bad spirits fighting for control of
every man.

63 *My native fields.* For a similar image see Dryden's translation of
Virgil's *Aeneid,* I, 196. Pope probably drew on this passage for *The Rape
of the Lock,* I, 66.

65 *Mount Hecla.* Scot prints an illustration of this mountain, stating
(pp. 224–225) that the spirit, Luridan, whose "nature is to be at enmity
with fire . . . wageth continual warrs with the fiery Spirits that inhabit
the Mountain Hecla in Ise-land, where they endeavour to extinguish these
fiery flames, and the inhabiting Spirits defend the flames from his Master
and his Legions." In his discussion of the volcanoes in Iceland, Peter
Heylyn also comments on Hecla's reputation as an abode of evil spirits
and a gate to hell (*Cosmographie,* p. 496).

160 *I'm curs'd.* Prospero feels some guilt at using magic, even though
he does so as a theurgist rather than as a necromancer. Agrippa (p. 450)
argued that a pious man might even use evil spirits for good purposes,
but this position was very much in doubt; and he may have been
genuinely repentant when he renounced theurgy as "damnable" (see also
Scot, pp. 281–282). For a skeptical view of Agrippa's recantation, see
Walker, *Spiritual and Demonic Magic,* pp. 90–91.

219 *long of you.* Because of you.

271 *passions learn'd from man.* The idea that natives of the newly
discovered lands were corrupted by the invasion of the European was
common (see R. W. Frantz, *The English Traveler and the Movement of
Ideas, 1660–1732* [1934], pp. 79, 105, 111–114).

275 *In chains.* For an example of the kind of bond signed between a
spirit of the air and a conjuror, see Scot, pp. 225–226.

V, i

16 *Then you must be condemn'd.* This argument against capital punishment had strong roots in contemporary discussions based on natural

law and rights. If a man had a right to his life, should he surrender that right of self-defense even after he had entered society? Hobbes (*English Works,* III, 208–209) gave the magistrate the right to take away the life of a prisoner, but he also maintained that the prisoner had the right to defend his life to the utmost of his ability. Arguments similar to Miranda's were eventually to be advanced with great force by Cesare Beccaria in 1764, but Samuel Pufendorf's discussion of the problem shows that these arguments were bruited about long before (*Law of Nature and Nations,* pp. 160–162 [VIII, iii, 4–5]).

26 *his Executioner.* Miranda persists in regarding the action of Prospero as that of a private man, while Prospero acts on the idea that he is the ruler of the island. The distinction is obviously important. Were Prospero acting merely as a private man, he would be committing a sin, a worse sin, in fact, than Ferdinand's; but if he can justify himself as the agent of the law—as a monarch attempting to prevent the state from slipping into anarchy—he is not committing a sin. Through these means Ferdinand is to be punished for his crime rather than for his sin. Prospero is convinced by Miranda that the forms must be followed to the extent, at least, of separating judge and executioner. See Grotius, *De Jure Belli,* pp. 483–502 (II, xx, 12 ff.); Pufendorf, *Law of Nature and Nations,* pp. 157–158, 167–168 (VIII, iii, 2–4, 11).

52 *Moly.* The herb used by Odysseus to counteract the charms of Circe (see Homer, *The Odyssey,* X, 302–306; John Gerarde, *The Herball* [1636], pp. 182–189).

53–54 *trickling Balm.* Dryden was probably thinking of *Herba Judaica Lobelii,* Smith's Balm or Jew's Allheal. Gerarde (*Herball,* p. 692) says "Smiths Bawme or Carpenters Bawme is most singular to heale up greene wounds that are cut with yron; it cureth the rupture in short time; it staieth the whites. Dioscorides and Pliny have attributed like vertues unto this kinde of Bawme, which they call Iron-wort. The leaves (say they) being applied, close up wounds without any perill of inflammation. Pliny saith that it is of so great vertue, that though it be but tied to his sword that hath given the wound, it stancheth the bloud." Summers (II, 363, 493) suggests a Virgilian echo, paralleling Dryden's translation of the second *Georgic* (ll. 165–166), but there is no suggestion of healing here; and Dryden also refers to "trickling balm" in *Tyrannick Love* (IV, i, 134) as a cure for wounds.

55 *purple Panacea.* Perhaps *Panax Coloni,* "Clownes Wound-wort or All-heal." Gerarde (*Herball,* pp. 1004–1005) listed many cures of wounds attributable to the use of this herb. Although Summers (II, 493) may be right in arguing that by "purple" Dryden means "purpureus, brilliant, beautiful," the color of this flower was, in fact, purple. As Ariel's description of his travels would suggest, this plant was common in England. It was considered to be ironwort, of the genus *Sideritis* (see Parkinson, *Theatrum Botanicum,* pp. 584–589).

60 *Simples.* Single ingredients for use in a compound.

61 *Planet which o're-rul'd those Herbs.* For an excellent illustration of the way diseases were related to a given planet and cures derived from

a knowledge of astrology, see John Gadbury, *Thesaurus Astrologiae* (1674), pp. 257–272. Before listing the herbs that have curative powers he notes (p. 257) that "Diseases proceeding from the Planets must be withstood by Planets of contrary Effects and Inclinations, and contrary Natures, and by Remedies contrary to the Quality of the Sickness." Plants and herbs were always classified according to their qualities (i.e., hot, cold, liquid, dry), which in turn were associated with the qualities of the planets.

73 *vulnerary*. Healing. Used specifically in connection with herbs employed to cure external wounds.

79 *Weapon-Salve*. Weapon salves were closely associated with powders of sympathy. The most famous proponent of the powders was Sir Kenelm Digby, who cured James Howell of a wound sustained when he attempted to separate two duelists (see Sir Kenelm Digby, *A Late Discourse . . . Touching the Cure of Wounds by the Powder of Sympathy* [1658], pp. 6–11; R. T. Petersson, *Sir Kenelm Digby* [1956], pp. 262–274; Robert Fludd, *Mosaicall Philosophy* [1659], pp. 262–264, who bases his explanation on magnetism). Among many others who commented on the practice was Francis Bacon (*Sylva Sylvarum* [1635], pp. 258–259):

> It is constantly Received, and Avouched, that the Anointing of the Weapon, that maketh the Wound, will heale the Wound it selfe. In this Experiment, upon the Relation of Men of Credit, (though my selfe, as yet, am not fully inclined to beleeve it,) you shall note the Points following. First, the Ointment, wherewith this is done, is made of Divers Ingredients; whereof the Strangest and Hardest to come by, are the Mosse upon the Skull of a dead man, Unburied; and the Fats of a Boare, and a Beare, killed in the Act of Generation. . . . The other Ingredients are, the Bloud-Stone in Powder, and some other Things which seeme to have a Vertue to Stanch Bloud; As also the Mosse hath. . . . Secondly, the same Kinde of Ointment, applied to the Hurt it selfe, worketh not the Effect; but onely applied to the Weapon. Thirdly, (which I like well) they doe not observe the Confecting of the Ointment, under any certaine Constellation, which commonly is the Excuse of Magicall Medicines, when they faile, that they were not made under a fit Figure of Heaven. Fourthly, it may be applied to the Weapon, though the Party Hurt be a great Distance. Fiftly, it seemeth the Imagination of the Partie, to be Cured, is not needfull to Concurre; For it may be done, without the Knowledge, of the Partie Wounded; And thus much hath been tried, that the Ointment (for Experiments sake,) hath beene wiped off the Weapon, without the Knowledge of the Partie Hurt, and presently the Partie Hurt, hath beene in great Rage of Paine, till the Weapon was Reannointed. Sixtly, it is affirmed, that

if you cannot get the Weapon, yet if you put an Instrument of Iron, or Wood, resembling the Weapon, into the Wound, whereby it bleedeth, the Annointing of that Instrument will serve, and worke the Effect. . . . Seventhly, the Wound must be at first Washed cleane, with White Wine, or the Parties owne Water; And then bound up close in Fine Linnen, and no more Dressing renewed, till it be whole. Eighthly, the Sword it selfe must be Wrapped up close, as farre as the Ointment goeth, that it taketh no Wind. Ninthly, the Ointment, if you wipe it off from the Sword, and keepe it, will Serve againe; and rather Increase in Vertue, than Diminish. Tenthly, it will Cure in farre Shorter Time, than Ointment of Wounds commonly doe. Lastly, it will Cure a Beast, as well as a Man; which I like best of all the rest, because it subjecteth the Matter, to an Easie Triall.

V, ii

49 *naughty blood.* The belief that loss of blood would reduce the sexual drive was common enough. On this level, at least, Fujimura's argument that love in Dryden's plays is mainly physiological has some truth in it. See Robert Burton, *The Anatomy of Melancholy*, III, ii, 5, 1; Aphra Behn, *The Fair Jilt*, in *The Works of Aphra Behn*, V, 122; Thomas H. Fujimura, "The Appeal of Dryden's Heroic Plays," *PMLA*, LXXV (1960), 37–45.

51+ *s.d. Hippolito's Sword.* Summers (II, 493) suggests that it should be Ferdinand's sword, since Ariel gave instructions to wrap the weapon that pierced Hippolito. Although Summers seems logically correct, Bacon maintains that a man might be cured by any weapon of a similar shape, and Sir Kenelm Digby worked his famous cure through the garter that James Howell used to bind his hand after it had been cut by the sword (see Digby, *A Late Discourse*, pp. 8–10).

225 *controul the Moon.* According to Agrippa (p. 157), "the power of inchantments, and verses is so great, that it is believed they are able to subvert almost all nature, as saith Apuleius, that with a Magicall whispering, swift Rivers are turned back, the slow Sea is bound, the Winds are breathed out with one accord, the Sun is stopt, the Moon is clarified, the Stars are pulled out, the day is kept back, the night is prolonged . . ." (see also Scot, p. 6).

226 *deal in her command.* Wield the power of the moon.

226–227 *without Her power.* Kermode (p. 130) summarizes the interpretations of this passage: "This probably means, though to do so was not in her own power. Without means 'outside,' cf. MND., iv.i.157. That is to say, that she was dependent upon her diabolical agents for this power; which is orthodox witch-lore. Otherwise, the passage means either (1) beyond the moon's power to control her; or (2) she could command the moon to do that which the moon, but not Sycorax herself, was capable of performing; or (3) without having the power of the moon, she could meddle in the moon's realm of sovereignty." It is impossible to say in which of these senses Dryden and Davenant understood this passage. See also Furness, pp. 262–263.

259+ *s.d. Milcha.* Probably an abbreviation of Damilkar, the guardian spirit of Nagar, the Indian, who appears in "A Discourse concerning the Nature and Substance of Devils and Spirits," a work that influenced Dryden's treatment of magic in this play and in *Tyrannick Love* (see "Anti-Scot," p. 42).

260 *s.d. Saraband.* A dance in triple time of Spanish origin, possibly with Oriental sources, which became very popular in England during the seventeenth century. Usually a dance with majestic and stately movement, it could also be speeded up, as suggested by the appearance of a saraband in Playford's volume of country dances. Certainly Ariel's desire to "foot it featly" (l. 258) with Milcha suggests something different from the dignity of the common saraband. See *Grove's Dictionary of Music and Musicians*, ed. Eric Blom (1954), VII, 407–408.

263 *Promises of blooming Spring.* References to the perpetual spring of the golden age were especially common in works on Bermuda (see Smith, *Historie of the Bermudas*, in *Works*, p. 627; Andrew Marvell, "Bermudas," in *The Poems and Letters*, ed. H. M. Margoliouth [1952], I, 17–18). Marvell's image of Bermuda as a land for the persecuted is not very different from Dryden's vision of a "place of Refuge" (l. 262).

EPILOGUE

3 *Knaves abroad.* Probably a reference to Louis XIV's invasion of the Spanish Netherlands and conquest of Charleroy on 2 June 1667.

5 *The Rhyming Mounsieur and the Spanish Plot.* Summers (II, 494–495) interprets this line as a general criticism of Spanish intrigue plots and of the rhymed heroic play modeled on the French, and he points to Dryden's own writings as demonstrating the continuing vogue of the heroic play. That Dryden did not abandon the form until after *Aureng-Zebe* (1676) does not strike Summers as an argument against his interpretation, but it is unlikely that Dryden would criticize the rhymed play at a time when he considered himself the master of the form. One might more logically conclude that Dryden is referring to specific plays. The most likely candidate for the "Rhyming Mounsieur" is the Earl of Orrery's *The Black Prince*, which introduces King John of France into a somewhat preposterous love and honor plot. The play would have been fresh in the minds of the audience, since it was performed on 19 October 1667. Pepys, commenting on the long letter read in the fifth act, noted how the audience jeered: "I must confess it is one of the most remarkable instances that ever I did or expect to meet with in my life of a wise man's not being wise at all times, and in all things, for nothing could be more ridiculous than this, though the letter of itself at another time would be thought an excellent letter, and indeed an excellent Romance, but at the end of the play, when every body was weary of

sitting, and were already possessed with the effect of the whole letter, to
trouble them with a letter a quarter of an hour long, was a most absurd
thing. . . . I home by coach, and could not forebear laughing almost all
the way home, and all the evening to my going to bed, at the ridiculousness of the letter." Dryden may also have been distinguishing between
this play and James Howard's prose comedy, *The English Mounsieur,*
revived on 29 October 1667, ten days after *The Black Prince* had been
performed.

Dryden, still master of the rhymed heroic play, was also about to
dabble in a "Spanish Plot" with *An Evening's Love, or The Mock
Astrologer,* a play whose source was Calderón's *El Astrólogo Fingido,*
though he had previously attacked Spanish plots in the prologue to *The
Wild Gallant* (1663). In that instance he was probably casting aspersions
on Sir Samuel Tuke's *The Adventures of Five Hours* (see *Works,* VIII,
243), and he may once again be referring to a specific play. The most
likely candidate to exemplify the "rot" creeping into the English stage
since Tuke's success in 1663 was Thomas St. Serfe's *Tarugo's Wiles,*
produced on 5 October 1667. It was based partly on Agustín Moreto's
No Puede Ser, and St. Serfe confesses in the prologue that he had
decided to "cruise the Coast of Spain" for his plot. Pepys liked *Tarugo's
Wiles* the first time he saw it, but after a second viewing on 15 October
he said it was "the most ridiculous, insipid play" he ever saw.

On another level Dryden may be referring to the political situation of
the time, the machinations of Louis XIV and the peace completed between England and Spain (see Pepys, *Diary,* 27 September 1667).

6 *Defie or Court.* Perhaps a reference to *Tarugo's Wiles* and *The Black
Prince.* St. Serfe satirized the coffeehouses, the Royal Society, and rhymed
tags in contemporary comedies. Orrery's play was highly flattering to
King Charles, so much so that Mrs. Pepys criticized her husband for
daring to laugh at it.

6 *go to Pot.* To be cut in pieces like meat for the pot. The earlier
meaning of this proverb was more positively violent than it is today:
the playwrights have been cut to pieces by the audience (see Tilley,
P504).

9 *Visions bloodier than King Richard's.* Probably a reference to John
Caryll's *The English Princess; or, The Death of Richard the Third*
(1667) rather than to Shakespeare's *Richard III.* Summers (II, 495) suggests that there may have been a recent production of Shakespeare's play,
but the only evidence he offers is a prologue printed in *Covent Garden
Drollery* (1672, p. 13) where no date is given. Nor is there any internal
evidence for assigning a date. *The English Princess* was performed on 7
March 1667, and the visions in it are even bloodier than those in
Shakespeare, as the following passage from Caryll reveals (IV, ix):

> *The curtain is opened. The King appeares in a dis-
> tracted posture, newly risen from his Bed, walking in
> his Dream with a dagger in his hand, and surrounded
> by the Ghosts of those whom he had formerly killed.*
>
> *King.* Forrest! Rogue, Traitour! can thy Coward hands

Tremble, and faulter, when thy King commands?
They are not dead; they walk, they threaten me:
Dispatch; Kill them again, or I'le kill thee.
Varlet, make haste; Go poyson, strangle, drown
My Brother, Nephews, Wife, to save my Crown.
Small Victims may less Deities become;
To Soveraign Power belongs a Hecatome.
My Breast shall raise a Storm, my Hand a Flood,
And make this Isle float in a Sea of Blood.

Pepys did not find Caryll's play exceptional, but Downes (p. 27) remarks that "Richard the Third, or the English Princess, Wrote by Mr. Carrol, was Excellently well Acted in every Part; chiefly, King Richard, by Mr. Betterton; Duke of Richmond, by Mr. Harris; Sir William Stanly, by Mr. Smith, Gained them an Additional Estimation, and the Applause from the Town, as well as profit to the whole Company." Dryden might have taken offense at Caryll's prologue, which criticized borrowings from "Spanish Novel, or from French Romance," the source of most of Dryden's plays, and which mocked the "Indian Rarityes" that were a feature of his *Indian Queen* and *Indian Emperour*.

Tyrannick Love

Charles II wrote to his sister on the twenty-fourth day of June 1669, "I am just now going to a new play that I heare very much commended." [1] The play was almost certainly Dryden's *Tyrannick Love; or, The Royal Martyr*, which was performed at the end of June after a delay of more than a month.[2] Samuel Pepys had put aside his diary on the last day of May in that year and thereby deprived posterity of his comments on Nell Gwyn's delivery of what must be the most amusing epilogue ever written. But the records of a lawsuit brought by Thomas Killigrew, Charles Hart, and Michael Mohun of the Theatre Royal against the painter, Isaac Fuller, provide more than usual information about the composition, staging, and success of Dryden's play.[3] As might be expected of a lawsuit, however, there is conflicting testimony.

According to the players' version of the events, Fuller had been approached on 14 April 1669 to paint a "Scaene of an Elysium." They wanted to have the play ready for the Easter and Trinity terms, "sumer terme times being usually the greatest times of profitt to your Orators throughout the whole yeare." Although the players had requested that the scene be ready in a fortnight, it was not finished until the end of June 1669 and was ill painted. As a result, the play failed to make as much money for the King's Company as had been expected, and the actors "received very great blame from his said Majesty & by reason of his distast thereat he did much forbeare his coming to the said Theater or house." They estimated that the loss of court patronage cost them £500.

Fuller, replying to the actors' charges ten days later in a document dated 16 June 1670, stated that he had not been approached until the end of April or early May 1669, when Dryden came to Fuller's house accompanied by a scene maker to open negotiations that lasted some four or five days. The painter testified that no limitation had been placed on the time he might take to complete the work and that it was well executed and ready by 23 June. According to Fuller, the play had been a great success; it had been acted "about 14 dayes together" and had earned more than twice as much as an ordinary play. The scene he had painted, which was used in the spectacular fourth act, "gave greate content to the Spectators," and the King, far from being offended, was highly pleased by the play.

---

[1] Cyril H. Hartmann, *Charles II and Madame* (1934), p. 259.

[2] Van Lennep, pp. 162–163.

[3] P.R.O. C7 486/74. See Appendix for full text of the lawsuit. Leslie Hotson first uncovered the suit and printed most of the text in *The Commonwealth and Restoration Stage* (1928), pp. 250–253, 348–355. Fuller (1606?–1672), though an alcoholic, was apparently a painter of some talent. See *DNB*; Margaret Whinney and Oliver Millar, *English Art, 1625–1714* (1957), pp. 187, 291–292; Evelyn, *Diary*, III, 385–386.

In order to force Killigrew and his company to pay him for his work Fuller had previously brought and won an Exchequer suit for £335 10s. against the actors, who had apparently begun the countersuit in Chancery in order to avoid making the payment. There can be little doubt that Fuller was entitled to his money, and the Chancery suit was dropped. But the actors probably felt they had a grievance. The epilogue makes clear that Dryden intended the play for Easter term, which began on 28 April and ended on 24 May. Had Fuller succeeded in finishing the scene in a fortnight, the play would have been ready at the beginning of the term. As it turned out, the first performance came six days before the end of Trinity term.[4] Fuller's judgment on the success of the play was probably accurate enough, but after counting their losses and gains the players may have regretted their prodigality.

However much Fuller may have exaggerated on other matters, there is no reason to question his account of the initial success of the play. Part of the success must be laid to the extraordinary cast. Michael Mohun played the part of Maximin, a role similar to that of Cethegus in Ben Jonson's *Catiline*, which Mohun had acted in the ornate revival of that play in 1668.[5] Charles Hart, as usual, took the part of the heroic lover, Porphyrius.[6] But the person who attracted most attention must have been Nell Gwyn as Valeria. She had become so popular by that time that her presence alone might have assured the play's success.[7] The epilogue was written especially for her, its effectiveness clearly depending upon Valeria's being at once both a woman of perfect virtue and the very unvirtuous Nell Gwyn. Certainly no one else could have delivered these lines:

> *I come, kind Gentlemen, strange news to tell ye,*
> *I am the Ghost of poor departed* Nelly.
> *Sweet Ladies, be not frighted, I'le be civil,*
> *I'm what I was, a little harmless Devil.*

According to *The History of the English Stage* (1741), Nell, in the role of Valeria, "so captivated the King, who was present the first Night of the Play, by the humorous Turns she gave it, that his Majesty, when she had done, went behind the Scenes and carried her off to an Entertainment that Night." [8] Although this story may be apocryphal, what is certain is that Nell Gwyn did indeed become the mistress of Charles II shortly after acting in *Tyrannick Love,* and that she then left the stage. Returning to play Almahide in *The Conquest of Granada,* she retired permanently after 1671.[9]

It would be ironic if *Tyrannick Love* was indeed responsible for Nell

---

[4] See *Poor Robin* (1669), sig. A2.

[5] Van Lennep, pp. 149–150.

[6] For accounts of Mohun and Hart, see Thomas Betterton (?), *The History of the English Stage* (1741), pp. 90–91; "Memoirs of the Actors and Actresses Mentioned by Cibber," in *An Apology for the Life of Mr. Colley Cibber,* ed. Robert W. Lowe (1889), II, 322–329.

[7] Van Lennep, p. cii.   [8] Pp. 56–57.   [9] See Wilson, p. 148.

Gwyn's elevation to the role of royal mistress, for Dryden's play was certainly written to honor Charles's queen, Catherine of Braganza. The idea that the *"Persons of Honour"* who urged Dryden to write *"a Poem of this Nature"* could have been connected with the court has been dismissed on the grounds that Charles and his companions "were hardly noted for a deep enough interest in religion to urge the poet to write a play of 'good example.'" [10] But the court was indeed involved. If the suit against Fuller raises the question of whether the King was pleased or not, both sides nevertheless seem to agree that he was actively interested. And there can be little doubt what Dryden meant in his preface when he defended his play by stating, *"I am already justified by the sentence of the best and most discerning Prince in the World."*

The Queen had been painted as Saint Catherine by Jacob Huysmans in 1664, and both the artist and his portraits of the Queen attracted considerable attention. Huysmans came to England from Antwerp and brought to English painting a style described by one critic as "more nearly allied to what one may call the Continental Catholic Baroque than Lely's Protestant idiom." [11] Horace Walpole also suggests a rivalry between Huysmans and Lely, adding that Huysmans used the Queen as model for both his Madonnas and his Venuses, and that the portrait of the Queen as Saint Catherine was his favorite painting.[12] The painting could be seen by anyone who cared to visit Huysmans' studio, and Dryden may have had it in mind in Placidius' description of a vision of a virgin surrounded by cupids. After visiting the studio on 26 August 1664, Pepys remarked on two portraits of Catherine of Braganza: "The Queene is drawn in one like a shepherdess, in the other like St. Katherin most like and most admirably. I was mightily pleased with the sight indeed." Pepys was pleased enough by the great "picture drawer" to consider having Huysmans paint his wife.[13]

Dryden's play was written at a time when speculation over the Queen's pregnancy was widespread. Charles's letters to his sister are evidence of his concern. On 6 May 1669 he informed her that Catherine might be ready to present him with an heir to the throne, and on the twenty-sixth Pepys reported that such rumors had been confirmed.[14] That nothing came of these reports does not change the fact that a compliment to the Queen at this time was very much in order. Of course Dryden could not have foreseen that his graceful compliment would add to the Queen's bitterness by providing Charles with another mistress. On the other hand, given his experience in the court and the theater, Dryden would hardly have been surprised at Nell's triumphant rise to royal mistress. The

[10] Ward, *Life*, p. 74.

[11] Ellis Waterhouse, *Painting in Britain, 1530 to 1790* (1953), p. 65.

[12] *Anecdotes of Painting in England* (Strawberry Hill, 1762–1771), III, 38–39.

[13] 31 May 1665. Pepys changed his mind, but on 15 February 1666 he decided to have John Hayls paint Mrs. Pepys as Saint Catherine in imitation of a similar painting of Lady Peters.

[14] Hartmann, *Charles II and Madame*, pp. 209, 247–248.

audience must have experienced a kind of perverse pleasure in seeing the roles of women of exemplary virtue played by actresses who were anything but that in everyday life. Mrs. Hughes, who played Saint Catherine, was, in Pepys's words "a mighty pretty woman, and seems, but is not, modest." She became the mistress of Prince Rupert shortly after the initial run of *Tyrannick Love*.[15] Rebecca Marshall, who played Berenice, was, in the words of Nell Gwyn, "a whore to three or four, though a Presbyter's praying daughter," and was simply notorious.[16] The fascination of this contrast between role and reality is apparent in Pepys's report of the action backstage after Nell Gwyn had played an angel in Dekker and Massinger's *The Virgin Martyr* a few years previously.[17]

If we can believe Dryden when he says that he wrote *Tyrannick Love* in seven weeks, he may well have started the play in March when rumors about the Queen's condition were beginning to circulate. Certainly, when he visited Fuller in late April or early May, Dryden already knew exactly what the fourth act would be like. *Tyrannick Love* is not the only play of this time to compliment the Queen. On 6 November 1668 the King and Queen attended a revival of Fletcher's *The Island Princess; or, The Generous Portugal*, a play that glorifies Catherine's nation.[18] And there is some likelihood that Shadwell was paying a subtle compliment to the Queen in his pastoral, *The Royal Shepherdess*, which was acted by the Duke's Company in the presence of the King and Queen on 25 February 1669. In addition to his portrait of the Queen as Saint Catherine, Huysmans had also painted her as a shepherdess, and this play, which ends with the revelation that the shepherdess, whose marriage has been discovered by her pregnant condition, is actually a princess, could not but have provided the Queen with some moments of empathy.[19] So keen was the rivalry between the theaters that the King's Company responded with a revival of Fletcher's *The Faithful Shepherdess* on the following day.[20]

In writing *Tyrannick Love* Dryden attempted to draw upon many aspects of the drama which had proved popular during the preceding two years. It has long since been remarked that it is difficult to fit *Tyrannick Love* into any monolithic concept of the heroic play.[21]

---

[15] Mrs. Hughes was replaced as Saint Catherine by Elizabeth Boutell, whose name appears in all the casts listed after the quarto of 1670 (Wilson, pp. 120, 150).

[16] Pepys, *Diary*, 26 October 1667.

[17] *Ibid.*, 6 May 1668. See also John Harold Wilson, "Nell Gwyn as an Angel," *N&Q*, CXCIII (1948), 71–72.

[18] Oddly enough, this performance may have omitted Fletcher's most extravagant praise of Portugal (John Fletcher, *The Island Princess; or, The Generous Portugal* [1669], p. 8 [Act I]).

[19] Waterhouse, *Painting in Britain*, p. 65; Walpole, *Anecdotes*, III, 39.

[20] Van Lennep, p. 157.

[21] Margaret Sherwood, *Dryden's Dramatic Theory and Practice*, Yale Studies in English, no. 4 (Boston, 1898), pp. 72–80. For a general discussion of the heroic play, see commentary on *The Indian Queen* in *Works*, VIII, 284–293.

Although Dryden's contemporary, Martin Clifford, complained after examining Dryden's heroes, Montezuma, Maximin, and Almanzor, "I can't for my heart distinguish one from the other," Maximin is very different from Dryden's other creations.[22] And *Tyrannick Love* is not merely about love and honor, but also about religion and tyranny. The play is set at the time of the Roman Empire,[23] and there is a minimum of the cultural primitivism that had appeared in *The Indian Emperour* and *The Indian Queen* and was to appear in *The Conquest of Granada* and *Aureng-Zebe*.

In turning to a Roman theme, Dryden was following a trend apparent during the seasons of 1668 and 1669. The King's Company, to which Dryden was attached, put on Ben Jonson's *Catiline* on 18 December 1668 and continued to perform it into the following year. Their next recorded production, on 16 January 1669, was Katherine Philips' translation of Corneille's *Horace*. *Horace* had already been performed at court the year before, and there may be some significance in the participation of Dryden's patroness, the Duchess of Monmouth, in an important role and also as the speaker of the prologue.[24] The success of *Horace* probably suggested to the Duke's Company the idea of reviving another play with a Roman theme. *The Roman Virgin: or, The Unjust Judge*, an adaptation of John Webster's *Appius and Virginia*, was performed on 12 May 1669 and, according to John Downes, had a successful run of eight days.[25] Had Fuller delivered his scene for *Tyrannick Love* when the actors expected it, the King's Company might have been able to counter the success of the rival company. The trend toward plays about Rome continued into the following year with William Joyner's *The Roman Empress*, produced by the King's Company in the summer of 1670.

These plays have much more in common than a physical setting. *Catiline* gave Mohun and Hart an opportunity as Cethegus and Catiline to make speeches couched in terms of absolute villainy threatening society with rape, sodomy, murder, and treason. *Horace* demonstrated how that eccentric virtue, *gloire*, which belonged to the heroic man or woman might, under extreme circumstances, transcend the traditional morality of society. Why the Duke's Company revived Webster's play is not difficult to explain, for it contained, in Appius and Marcus Claudius, villains to rival Catiline and Cethegus, a Virginius to rival Horace in *gloire*,[26] and an innocent Virginia to rival Corneille's Camilla. To such ingredients, Joyner added even more murders and suicides. The focus in these plays seems to have centered upon extreme types of virtue and villainy

---

[22] *Notes upon Mr. Dryden's Poems in Four Letters* (1687), p. 7.

[23] Maximin died in A.D. 238 (Edward Gibbon, *The Decline and Fall of the Roman Empire*, ed. J. B. Bury [1909–1914], I, 460).

[24] Van Lennep, p. 128.   [25] Downes, p. 30.

[26] For discussion of the concept of *gloire* and its importance to the age, see Paul Bénichou, *Morales du Grand Siècle* (1967), pp. 19–79; Arthur C. Kirsch, "Dryden, Corneille and the Heroic Play," *MP*, LIX (1962), 248–264; Arthur C. Kirsch, *Dryden's Heroic Drama* (1965), 99–100.

rather than upon the contrast between societies which was common to the heroic play.

Although Maximin bears a certain similarity to the villains of these Roman plays, the presence of Saint Catherine dominates a large part of *Tyrannick Love;* and insofar as *Tyrannick Love* may be called a religious play, it belongs to a species of drama that was certainly not very common to the Restoration stage.[27] One play that did combine a Roman theme with martyrdom was *St. Cecily: or, The Converted Twins,* published in 1666 with a brief preface in praise of "Christian Tragedy" by Thomas Medbourne. It may never have been performed,[28] and if Dryden ever knew of it, he would have learned only what to avoid in attempting to write a religious play. More important was the successful revival of Thomas Dekker and Philip Massinger's *The Virgin Martyr,* acted on 27 February 1668 by the King's Company, with Nell Gwyn playing the part of an angel. Pepys, seeing a later performance of the play, found himself half shocked and half intrigued by the actresses: "Thence called Knapp from the King's house, where going in for her, the play being done, I did see Beck Marshall come dressed, off of the stage, and looks mighty fine, and pretty, and noble: and also Nell, in her boy's clothes, mighty pretty. But, Lord! their confidence! and how many men do hover about them as soon as they come off the stage, and how confident they are in their talk! Here I did kiss the pretty woman newly come, called Pegg, that was Sir Charles Sidly's mistress, a mighty pretty woman, and seems, but is not, modest." [29] The potentialities inherent in such a cast might have inspired Dryden to try his hand at a play similar to *The Virgin Martyr* but better suited to the Restoration audience. When Pepys first saw *The Virgin Martyr* he thought it "good but too sober a play for the company." Although he came to admire the scene with the angel, "which is so sweet that it ravished me, and indeed, in a word, did wrap up my soul so that it made me really sick, just as I have formerly been when in love with my wife," he reached the conclusion that on the whole the play was not "worth much." [30]

Dryden probably took some hints from *The Virgin Martyr,*[31] but he

---

[27] In addition to the play about Saint Cecilia discussed below, one might think of Milton's *Samson Agonistes* and Edward Ecclestone's *Noah's Flood; or The Destruction of the World,* first published in 1679, as well as Dryden's own *The State of Innocence.* It is possible that none of these plays was ever performed. Admittedly, all the tragedies written in England during the Restoration have Christian overtones, but they are not so generically religious as are these.

[28] Van Lennep (p. 91), noting that the edition published in 1666 "has no prologue, no epilogue, no actors' names," may have been convinced that there had been no performance. But both the 1666 edition and a reissue in 1667 do at least have an epilogue, an epilogue of such a nature as to suggest the author's expectation that the play would be performed. See Matthew Medbourne, *St. Cecily: or, The Converted Twins* (1666), p. 62.

[29] *Diary,* 7 May 1668.   [30] *Ibid.,* 16 February 1661; 27 February 1668.

[31] See Charles E. Ward, "Massinger and Dryden," *ELH,* II (1935), 263–266.

obviously thought religious drama could succeed in England in the year 1669 only by drawing upon those effects and methods that made for successful secular drama. If *Tyrannick Love* had a startling initial success, it was because Maximin outdid Catiline and Cethegus in his defiance of religion and morality, because Berenice was even more strictly concerned with her *gloire* and virtue than earlier heroines had been, because Saint Catherine represented chastity endangered by a brutal lust, because Nell Gwyn spoke an amazing epilogue, because the scenic and operatic effects of the fourth act surpassed anything seen up to that time on the English stage, and because the play was written in rhyme by England's poet laureate and foremost exponent of the rhymed heroic play. Yet it is not surprising that the play declined in popularity. Nell Gwyn left the stage shortly after its initial run, and a prompt copy indicates that after a fire on 25 January 1672 had destroyed the theater on Bridges Street, and along with it the scenery for which the King's Company had paid so dearly just a few years before, the entire scene with Damilcar and Nakar was cut. Some spectacular effects were preserved, but there was left nothing that could compete with productions like the "operatic" *Tempest* or *Psyche*.[32]

Admittedly records of performances are fragmentary, and John Downes may not have been too far from wrong in believing that *Tyrannick Love* was a stock play. But the only performance recorded after the initial fourteen-day run took place on 18 May 1676. Republication in 1677, 1686, 1695, and 1702 probably indicates revivals, as does the resetting of two songs by Purcell in 1695. The suggestion has been made that the play disappeared from the repertory with the death of Betterton in 1710, but if Betterton did play the part of Maximin, it was certainly not one of his more famous roles.[33] At any rate, there is no need to apologize for the popularity record of *Tyrannick Love*. Its decline paralleled that of the genre of the rhymed heroic play, which was no longer a viable dramatic medium after 1680.[34] *Tyrannick Love* may not have been so popular as *The Indian Emperour* or *Aureng-Zebe,* but it did as well as *The Conquest of Granada,* that paradigm of the genre, until the end of the century.

On 14 July 1669, shortly after the first performance, Dryden's publisher, Herringman, entered *Tyrannick Love* in the *Stationers' Register,* and publication probably came at some time around 22 November 1670 with the play's announcement in the *Term Catalogues*.[35] The second edition, "review'd by the Author," was published two years later with the addition of a paragraph in the preface to answer critics of the play and of thirty-nine lines in the fourth act, lines that had been omitted from all but a few copies of the first edition. The reply to the critics came at a time when

---

[32] Henry Hitch Adams, "A Prompt Copy of Dryden's *Tyrannic Love,*" *SB,* IV (1951–52), 170–174.

[33] Summers (II, 328) may be basing this opinion on Charles Gildon's remark that Betterton took over Mohun's parts after the latter's retirement (see *History of the English Stage,* p. 91; also the index to Van Lennep, pp. cxcii–cxciii).

[34] Eric Rothstein, *Restoration Tragedy* (1967), pp. 24–47.   [35] I, 56.

Dryden still felt confident about the worth of his play, in spite of *The Rehearsal*'s brilliant and severe parodies of several passages.[36] We cannot be entirely sure, of course, that Dryden ever turned against *Tyrannick Love*. In 1681 he wrote, "I remember some Verses of my own *Maximin* and *Almanzor* which cry, Vengeance upon me for their Extravagance, and which I wish heartily in the same fire with *Statius* and *Chapman:* All I can say for those passages, which are I hope, not many, is that I knew they were bad enough to please, even when I writ them: But I repent of them amongst my Sins." [37] Dryden was referring specifically to the kind of speech that, although theatrically effective, is an artistic failure; there is no indication that he ever regretted creating the character of Maximin or that he condemned the play as a whole.

Dryden devoted the period between the composition of *Tyrannick Love* and the dedication of the published play a year and a half later to writing *The Conquest of Granada* and to pondering new ideas on the relationship between the heroic play and the epic, ideas that evidence themselves throughout the dedication. Having mastered a form that he could claim as superior to anything done by the great dramatists of the age of Elizabeth and James I, Dryden dedicated his heroic play to the Duke of Monmouth, offering *Tyrannick Love* as a prelude to "a more noble Sacrifice," the "Heroick Poem" Monmouth might justly have expected. The dedication implies that Monmouth might see in the story of Porphyrius and Berenice a model for an epic on the House of Stuart with the Duke as its hero, and in the verse and in the rendering of "history" the suggestion of a poem glorifying himself and his wife. What has been called Dryden's "obsessive concern with the heroic" is certainly present in the dedication and preface, if not in the play itself, and Dryden defends his use of astral spirits on critical principles customarily employed to defend the use of the marvelous in the epic, rather than on dramatic grounds.[38]

Since *Tyrannick Love* was intended as a successful play in the theater, what Dryden has to say about it as drama suggests a great deal about his approach to the play. He is mainly concerned with defending the morality of *Tyrannick Love,* and he does so by suggesting that he aimed at an effect similar to what might be achieved by a religious opera. *"By the Harmony of words,"* wrote Dryden in the preface, *"we elevate the mind to a sense of Devotion, as our solemn Musick, which is inarticulate Poesie, does in Churches; and by the lively images of piety, adorned by action, through the senses allure the Soul."* By this identification with the spiritual, he implies, the audience will come to practice *"that which it admires."* The effect Dryden here describes is similar to the effect of the

---

[36] For parodies of the ghostly speech of Berenice at the end of Act III and of the duet of the spirits, Nakar and Damilcar, at the beginning of Act IV, see *The Rehearsal*, IV, i, 163–169; V, i, 45–75.

[37] Dedication of *The Spanish Fryar* (1681, sig. A2v; Watson, I, 276).

[38] H. T. Swedenberg, Jr., "Dryden's Obsessive Concern with the Heroic," *SP*, extra ser., no. 4 (1967), pp. 12–26. See also Ward, *Life*, pp. 93–115.

descending angel in *The Virgin Martyr* on Pepys, though the diarist could only compare the experience with his early love for his wife. The extraordinary scenic and musical qualities of the fourth act were definitely calculated to create an awesome religious feeling in the audience, but even some of the speeches of Maximin, Porphyrius, and Berenice must have been designed for similar emotional effect.

Dryden's defense of the character of Maximin is also based on moral grounds. Denying any adherence to Maximin's Hobbesian statements on power and will, Dryden maintains that the *"part of Maximin, against which these holy Criticks so much declaim, was designed by me to set off the Character of S. Catherine."* Dryden, finding his massive hero-villain in the pages of Herodian, created him as a symbol of physical strength, worldly power, and moral evil to contrast with the feminine weakness, religious dedication, and perfect virtue of Saint Catherine. Although Maximin falls in love with Catherine, his love—like that of Milton's Comus—grows out of the fascination of innocence for one who is entirely evil. Paradoxically, Maximin cannot harm Saint Catherine, though he may kill her, and Saint Catherine is incapable of changing the nature of Maximin. There can be no genuine understanding between the most striking figures in the play, and most of the action is carried by characters like Porphyrius, Berenice, Felicia, and Valeria, characters who hesitate before rushing into martyrdom and who do not attempt to exceed the bounds of human action.

In his "Examen" of *Théodore, Vierge et Martyre*, Corneille had suggested some of the problems inherent in a character similar to Saint Catherine, remarking that "une vierge et martyre sur un théâtre n'est autre chose qu'un Terme qui n'a ni jambes ni bras, et par conséquent point d'action." Corneille's play was a failure, and Dryden had to face the problem of writing a successful play with a heroine who, like Théodore, had to be "entièrement froid." [39] Dryden solved the problem in two ways: first, he allowed the audience to see Saint Catherine, in part, through the eyes of Maximin, who is incapable of regarding her as anything but proud and arrogant; second, he subjected her to temptations which made her argue the superiority of Christian martyrdom to ordinary Christian virtue. Unlike Corneille's heroine, Saint Catherine argues subtly for her particular role; shaping character through debate and argumentation was, as Dryden knew, one of his great gifts.

Swayed by his passions, inordinately proud, and sometimes extremely witty, Maximin is more human and vivid than Saint Catherine for much the same reason that Milton's Satan is more interesting than his Christ.

---

[39] *Œuvres de Pierre Corneille*, ed. Ch. Marty-Laveaux (Paris, 1862–1922), V, 12. For the suggestion that Dryden may have taken hints from *Théodore*, see Dorothy Burrows, "The Relation of Dryden's Serious Plays and Dramatic Criticism to Contemporary French Literature" (Ph.D. dissertation, University of Illinois, 1933), p. 205. The influence of Corneille's *Polyeucte* on Dryden's play has been argued in stronger but less convincing terms (P. Holzhausen, "Dryden's heroisches Drama," *Englische Studien*, XIII [1889], 431; XV [1891], 17).

But Maximin is more than an embodiment of evil. Although at times he seems the most outrageous of tyrants, he is, at other times, not very different from the comic old cuckold of Restoration comedy. Some of the grotesque quality given to the character may be owing to the line that Dryden borrowed from a French version of Saint Catherine's life, indicating that Maximin was the *"Son of a* Thracian *Herds-man, and an* Alane *Woman."* [40] Maximin is indeed the emperor of Rome, but he is also a usurper who has murdered the rightful emperor, Berenice's brother. He has strength, but he is also something of a boor. It is for this reason that Dryden described Maximin as a *"deformed piece,"* and that he could justify his dramatic craft by stating that there is *"as much of Art, and as near an imitation of Nature, in a* Lazare *as in a* Venus." [41] The comparison suggests the justification generally used for comic realism, and, given Dryden's patrician attitude, there is no reason to believe that he did not consider Maximin an ambiguous figure, heroic in stature and power, plebeian at heart.

Two other points in the preface merit attention: Dryden's statements concerning the regularity of his play and his remarks on his sources. Dryden seems to regard as only a minor accomplishment his adherence to the three unities and to the dramatic device that Aubignac almost elevates to a fourth unity, *liaison des scènes,* [42] alluding to the matter only because his admission to having written the work in so short a period of time might lead some critics to conclude that he had been careless. In fact, Dryden was obviously proud of having mastered a facet of dramatic writing which many neoclassical critics regarded as a necessary ingredient of true art. If he assumed the position that these techniques were not entirely necessary to tragedy and boasted that he did not follow them in *The Conquest of Granada,* he did so with the knowledge that not only the great English playwrights of the past, but also Corneille, to a certain extent, could serve as justification. [43] But for *Tyrannick Love* Dryden offered his adherence to the rules as a sign of his understanding of his craft.

Dryden may have been willing to admit that he had mastered the rules of tragedy as set down by contemporary French critics, but he would not admit that he had "stolen" his play from a French source. Yet, while denying any knowledge of Georges de Scudéry's *L'Amour Tyrannique,* he does confess to having read *"a* French *Play, called the* Martyrdom of S. Catharine." The reason for Dryden's seeking a French or continental source for a play on Saint Catherine should be perfectly obvious. Although Charles II and his queen might have been pleased by such a subject, a play based on the life of Saint Catherine would not

---

[40] Cf. Dryden's preface and *Le Martyre de Sainte Catherine* (Caen, 1650), p. 117 (V, v).

[41] For a detailed discussion of the significance of this theme in Dryden's critical writings, see *Works,* I, 274–276.

[42] *The Whole Art of the Stage* (1684), Pt. II, p. 88.

[43] *Œuvres de Corneille,* I, 111–112.

necessarily have been pleasing to a Protestant audience. John Foxe had remarked that some of the tales concerning her life and martyrdom "seem incredible, some also impudent," and among the strongest protests against the practices of the Catholic church before the Reformation and during the reign of Queen Mary were objections to the processions and celebrations connected with Saint Catherine's day, 25 November.[44] Just as Huysmans' painting of the Queen as Saint Catherine rendered its subject in a baroque, continental style, so Dryden looked to baroque, religious drama as it flourished on the continent during the seventeenth century for his model.

Several plays with the title *Le Martyre de Sainte Catherine* were written in France during the seventeenth century.[45] One by Puget de la Serre, published in 1643 with vivid illustrations, presents a traditional version of the story. The action is set at Alexandria where the Emperor has ordered a celebration after Porphire has brought him news of victory. Catherine feels that she must not avoid "l'occasion de combattre pour sa gloire," and that she must help the Christians by sacrificing her life.[46] She is arrested for her defiance, but the Emperor falls in love with her. She rejects his love, converts the Empress to Christianity, defeats the Emperor's chief philosopher, Lucius, and, after the torture and death of the Empress, Lucius, and Porphire, she too is tortured. After the destruction of the torture wheel and the failure of other methods of torture, Saint Catherine's head is chopped off. The Emperor, told that milk instead of blood came from her veins, is finally moved enough by this miracle to declare a general toleration.

Puget de la Serre's play is useful for showing how the legend of Saint Catherine could be presented on the stage with little variation from the traditional version, but that Dryden ever read it is doubtful. The play that he used was an anonymous work with the same title first published in 1649. Although Dryden denied borrowing more than one line from "*so dull an Author,*" he actually took much more. This play, variously ascribed to Aubignac, Desfontaines, and Saint-Germain,[47] provided Dryden with an emperor who compared himself to the gods ("Comme ils regnent au Ciel je regne sur la Terre") and with a subplot centered on the love of one of the Emperor's lieutenants, Maxime, for the Empress.[48] Like *Tyrannick Love,* the 1649 play emphasizes love and psychological analysis rather than action, and, unlike most versions of

[44] *The Actes and Monuments of John Foxe,* ed. Josiah Pratt (4th ed.; 1877), I, 273–274; VI, 82, 256, 413. By a Vatican decree in 1969, Saint Catherine was removed from the official lists of saints.

[45] See Lancaster, Pt. II, Vol. I, pp. 16n, 257n, 363; Pt. I, Vol. I, pp. 107–108. For an Italian play on this subject, see Federigo Venuti, *La Vincitrice Caterina* (Florence, 1615).

[46] Jean Puget de la Serre, *Le Martyre de Sainte Caterine* (Paris, 1643), p. 20 (II, ii).

[47] Lancaster, Pt. II, Vol. I, pp. 257n, 338n; Pt. II, Vol. II, pp. 657, 668–670.

[48] *Le Martyre de Sainte Catherine,* p. 10 (I, i).

the life of Saint Catherine, it has a political and historical background.[49] Maxime attempts to kill Maximin in a manner similar to the plot of Dryden's Porphyrius and Albinus, and the audience is informed that Rome has chosen two new emperors to take the place of Maximin.

The number of editions indicates that Dryden's model was a popular play.[50] Far more dramatic than Puget de la Serre's work, it follows both the unities and the practice of *liaison des scènes*. Dryden could not resist including Saint Catherine's battle with the philosopher, which is already over at the beginning of the French play, but he even borrows hints for the character of Berenice and her rejection of Porphyrius from this work. Because Dryden took so many suggestions from the 1649 play without acknowledging more than the debt of a line, his denial of any knowledge of *L'Amour Tyrannique*, Scudéry's play with the equivalent French title, has to be regarded skeptically. Scudéry's play, published in 1639, was hardly an obscure work by an obscure author. It was written to rival Corneille's *Le Cid*, and Sillac d'Arbois prefaced it with a "Discours de la Tragedie" proclaiming the greatness of the play and the genius of the author. And it has more in common with Dryden's play than the title.

Like *Tyrannick Love*, Scudéry's play is set before the walls of a besieged city. The main character, Tiridate, holds the same view on power as Maximin: that kings, unlike other men, are divinely inspired in every action. Tiridate is possessed by a brutal lust for the wife of his enemy, Tigrane, but he is cured through understanding the depth of his own wife's love for him. The final speech advises that happiness can come only when *"L'AMOUR TIRANIQUE"* is replaced by *"l'Amour raisonable."* [51] Although many of the striking parallels between the two plays exist also in other contemporary plays, a general Scudéry influence is possible.

Perhaps it was some such influence that Gerard Langbaine had in mind when, after listing a number of historians as Dryden's sources, he warned that "several Hints are borrow'd from other Authors, but much improv'd." [52] Although Langbaine was probably wrong in naming as Dryden's immediate historical source anyone other than Herodian, he was accurate enough in suggesting that Dryden had borrowed ideas from other dramatists. In creating the character of Maximin, for example, it is likely that Dryden looked to the heroic play as it had been shaped by Corneille, whose *Horace*, with its emphasis on what Dryden would have called "an excentrique vertue," had experienced a substantial success.[53] And in drawing the character of Maximin, Dryden may have

---

[49] See, for example, the speech of Vallerie in *ibid.*, p. 58 (III, iii).

[50] Lancaster, Pt. II, Vol. II, p. 668.

[51] Georges de Scudéry, *L'Amour Tyrannique* (Paris, 1639), p. 110 (V, viii).

[52] "As to the Plot of this Tragedy 'tis founded on History: see Zosimus, L. 4. *Socrates*, L. 5.C.14. *Herodiani Hist.* L. 7. and 8. *Jul. Capitolinus, in Vit. Max. Jun.*" (Langbaine, p. 174). Dryden refers to Herodian in the preface to justify his characterization of Maximin.

[53] See dedication of *The Conquest of Granada* (1672, sig. A4v; S-S, IV, 16).

recalled Corneille's praise of his own artistry in creating the totally evil Queen in his play, *Rodogune:*

> Cléopatre, dans *Rodogune,* est trés-méchante; il n'y a point de parricide qui lui fasse horreur, pourvu qu'il la puisse conserver sur un trône qu'elle préfère à toutes choses, tant son attachement à la domination est violent; mais tous ses crimes sont accompagnés d'une grandeur d'âme qui a quelque chose de si haut, qu'en même temps qu'on déteste ses actions, on admire la source dont elles partent.[54]

Although Maximin is sometimes described as a "Marlovian" hero, it seems quite correct to suggest, as has been done, that he shares with Cléopatre only half the qualities of the "Herculean hero," a type that easily embraces characters like Montezuma and Almanzor.[55] Like Cléopatre, Maximin is intended to arouse admiration by his defiant assertion of his will to power.

From *The Virgin Martyr* of Thomas Dekker and Philip Massinger Dryden took perhaps little more than the inspiration. Dryden's restraint in borrowing from this play may have stemmed from his feeling that the overtones of a medieval morality play were too dominant in it.[56] Good and evil are embodied in Angelo and Harpax, an angel and a devil who have assumed human form. Here was the problem that Dryden faced: even though magic was a successful ingredient in the drama of his day, the kind of religious drama that would have been acceptable to the audience of Dekker and Massinger would not have been welcomed by the Restoration audience. Dryden later regretted having brought Saint Catherine onto the stage, because he came to believe that showing the misfortunes of a "wholly perfect" character might, though it ought not, produce "impious thoughts" in the minds of the audience,[57] but he undoubtedly felt that some kind of religious drama was possible at the time he wrote *Tyrannick Love* and *The State of Innocence.* What he took from *The Virgin Martyr* was little more than an effective use of music, certain stage effects (like the descending angel), and one turn of plot: like *Tyrannick Love, The Virgin Martyr* has the daughter of the Emperor choose for her husband a man who is already in love and willing to give up an empire for his love.[58]

Although opinions about the worth of *Tyrannick Love* have varied, a majority of the critics have agreed on two points: first, the play is different in nature from Dryden's other heroic plays; second, it is es-

---

[54] *Œuvres de Corneille,* I, 32.

[55] John H. Winterbottom, "Stoicism in Dryden's Tragedies," *JEGP,* LXI (1962), 873; Eugene Waith, *The Herculean Hero* (1962), pp. 147–149.

[56] Robert Reed, Jr. (*The Occult on the Tudor Stage* [1965], pp. 226–227), refers to *The Virgin Martyr* as a "contemporized morality play" and compares it with Marlowe's *Doctor Faustus.*

[57] *A Parallel betwixt Painting and Poetry* (1695, p. xvii; Watson, II, 184).

[58] Ward, "Massinger and Dryden," pp. 264–265.

sentially a play of contrasts.[59] For the second point, Dryden's own remarks may be quoted as evidence. In his preface Dryden defends the character of Maximin as representing a contrast to the virtue of Saint Catherine; he repeats the idea in *A Parallel betwixt Painting and Poetry*, where he states his conception of the contrast in visual terms.[60] Although the two characters are united by the plot, it is only as the executioner and the victim are united. The love that Maximin feels for Saint Catherine is the love of a tyrant—a desire to possess and conquer—and this is one of the meanings of Dryden's title. But Catherine does not react to Maximin's love; she plays out her life on the same stage but in a different spiritual dimension from Maximin. Thus it is not Maximin who engages her in a dispute, but the philosopher Apollonius, and Maximin is not present at the attempt to seduce her through the use of magic and spirits. Such a scene is part of the supernatural element of the play to which Saint Catherine belongs and from which Maximin is excluded.

In spite of creating a mechanical unity in the play through the use of *liaison des scènes*, Dryden names in his prologue and epilogue the four contrasting elements that are never entirely unified: love, religion, magic, and tyranny. In the prologue he points out that for the poetry of magic he allowed *"his Fancy the full scope and swing,"* but for the poetry to express the thoughts of a tyrant he let *"his Muse run mad."* The epilogue, for all its humor, underscores the fact that Nell Gwyn was forced to die for love and to do it in a *"godly out-of-fashion Play."* The actress may have felt out of place in a tragic role,[61] but she would have been aware that her part as Valeria was conventional enough among the lovers in heroic plays, where the women have complete power over the men who love them. Berenice is, in a sense, a counterpart of Saint Catherine, for her gesture of saving Maximin's life to fulfill her duty as a wife in spite of the certainty that she and her admirer, Porphyrius, will be executed is equivalent in the code of love and honor to Saint Catherine's insistence on her martyrdom. Dryden does not merely deprive the Church of two martyrs in saving the lives of Berenice and Porphyrius; he transfers them to the ideal world of platonic love as the age absorbed that concept from French romances.[62]

---

[59] Holzhausen ("Dryden's heroisches Drama," p. 17) argues that *Tyrannick Love* is the most unified of the heroic plays and the only one with a central theme, which he identifies as the war between atheism and Christianity. Margaret Sherwood (*Dryden's Dramatic Theory and Practice*, p. 78) maintains that the religious theme and Saint Catherine were never successfully incorporated into the play and that the real center of the tragedy is suggested by the title, which describes the tyranny of love over the lives of all the characters. Bruce King (*Dryden's Major Plays* [1966], pp. 37–58) points to two central elements: the wit and humor inherent in the speeches of Maximin and the serious arguments for Christianity which Dryden puts into the mouth of Saint Catherine.

[60] *A Parallel betwixt Painting and Poetry* (1695, p. xlvii; Watson, II, 203).

[61] For evidence, see note to epilogue, l. 16.

[62] For a general discussion of this matter, see Kathleen Lynch, *The Social*

These perfect lovers are contrasted with Valeria and Placidius, whose love is mingled with passion. That Dryden regarded such love as lower in nature than the refined love of Berenice and Porphyrius is true enough, but the contention that he makes a severe moral judgment on his passionate lovers is untenable.[63] Since Dryden thought that the end of the heroic play was to arouse admiration, he would naturally want to create different effects for achieving that end.[64] The suicide of Valeria and the violent emotions of Placidius are as conducive to arousing admiration as the scenes of ideal love.[65] The nature of these lovers seems to be dictated more by the demands of dramatic form than by any particular moral statement.

Because she is beloved by Maximin, Saint Catherine becomes part of the love motif, but she belongs mainly to a specific religious theme, the superiority of Christianity over other beliefs. Perhaps Charles Wolseley exaggerated somewhat when he remarked that "Democritus is better believed [by the thinkers of the Restoration] than Moses, and Epicurus in better credit with them than St. Paul," but it was a time when a revival of Epicureanism and Stoicism was challenging Christianity.[66] In William Joyner's *The Roman Empress* (1671), acted a year after *Tyrannick Love* by Dryden's company, one of the main figures is an Epicurean philosopher, whose ideas are presented as true wisdom even though they include denial of an afterlife.[67] A comparison between Dryden's play and any of the religious plays of the time, whether *The Virgin Martyr*, the anonymous *Le Martyre de Sainte Catherine*, or any of Corneille's religious plays, reveals the extent to which Dryden was involved in staging a debate between Christianity and the challenge of atheism, Neo-Epicureanism, and Neo-Stoicism.

Dryden, taking advantage of Saint Catherine's reputed learning, allows her to turn the arguments of her enemies against themselves. Apollonius, a thoroughgoing Stoic, takes over the debate after Saint Catherine demolishes Maximin's arguments about the inability of reason to choose a faith. Saint Catherine's arguments have been identified as specifically Anglican in orientation, but there is little in them that could not be

---

Mode of Restoration Comedy (1926), pp. 43–79. See also Jean Gagen, "Love and Honor in Dryden's Heroic Plays," *PMLA*, LXXVII (1962), 208–220.

[63] Selma Zebouni, *Dryden: A Study in Heroic Characterization*, Louisiana State University Studies, Humanities Series, no. 16 (1965), pp. 20–34.

[64] See *A Defence of an Essay of Dramatique Poesie*, in *Works*, IX, 6.

[65] Although he overstates the case for a naturalistic basis of love in the heroic plays, Thomas H. Fujimura argues convincingly for the audience appeal of passionate love ("The Appeal of Dryden's Heroic Plays," *PMLA*, LXXV [1960], 37–45).

[66] *The Unreasonableness of Atheism* (1669), p. 37.

[67] See particularly p. 42 (IV). Although Honorius is described as an Epicurean, some of his statements would fit a Stoic equally well. His speech on death (p. 51 [IV]) is a rough translation of the same chorus from Seneca's *Troades* which Rochester imitated (see John Wilmot, *Poems*, ed. Vivian de Sola Pinto [1953], p. 49).

found in those writings of the Church Fathers accepted by most Christian sects.[68] It is certainly true that there was an increase in the number of Anglican works dedicated to proving the existence of God on rational grounds—an effort to defeat atheism on its own terms. This position, however, was not so opposed to the central Catholic position as had formerly been supposed.[69] Catherine defeats Apollonius because Christianity provided a reward for virtue; because, in regarding evil thoughts as sin, it held to an even more rigid doctrine than Stoicism; and because it preached the supreme virtue of forgiving one's enemies. As Dryden's friend, Dr. Charleton, wrote in his treatise, *The Immortality of the Human Soul* (1657), the Stoic could not actually live without some reward. If he pretended to be unconcerned about reward for his virtue, he was merely finding a private reward in what Saint Catherine calls "secret pride":

> That virtue is not a sufficient recompence to itself, may
> be naturally collected from hence; that all virtuous per-
> sons have an eye of Affection constantly levelled at
> somewhat beyond it. For, though the Stoicks affected
> this high-strain'd expression of the exceeding amiable-
> ness of virtue; yet could they never perswade them
> selves, or others, but that Glory and Honour, at least,
> were lookt upon, as the Consequents of Virtue: nor can
> it be affirmed, that Glory doth always seek out and
> court virtue, of its owne accord; forasmuch as really
> those persons were ever the most covetous of Glory, who
> have pretended the most to decline and avoid it.[70]

Placidius' identification of Saint Catherine's attitudes with those of the "Stoicks" suggests, as indeed Apollonius declares and as the saint herself admits, that Christianity shared many ideas with Stoicism.[71] Saint Catherine is equally adept at using the arguments of Epicurus and Lucretius against Placidius. Like Saint Paul speaking to the Stoic and Epicurean philosophers of Athens, she can offer a more meaningful solution to human hopes and fears than they can.[72]

In their first confrontation, Saint Catherine has little difficulty overcoming Maximin. His threats hold no fear for her, for she knows that her soul is immortal; and she is indifferent to his professions of love. Maximin himself is puzzled by his reactions. He claims she is so pure that in loving him her purity would change the nature of their love, and "Heav'n would unmake it sin." Saint Catherine takes the privilege of a

---

[68] Charles Ward finds "more than a tinge of the Anglican" in Saint Catherine's ideas, and Bruce King argues that Saint Catherine is actually mouthing the sentiments of Archbishop Tillotson (Ward, *Life*, p. 74; King, *Dryden's Major Plays*, pp. 50–58).

[69] Philip Harth, *Contexts of Dryden's Thought* (1968), pp. 106–108, 248–260.

[70] Pp. 148–149.

[71] See E. Vernon Arnold, *Roman Stoicism* (1911), pp. 408–436.

[72] Acts, XVII, 18–34.

woman loved and treats Maximin with contempt. She interprets her
power over him as the force of religion:
> Such pow'r in bonds true piety can have,
> That I command, and thou art but a Slave.

But Maximin is not certain. Is he in the grip of fate and impelled to
make Saint Catherine his victim? Or is he the victim of that ambivalent
emotion, "tyrannick love"? As a lover, he must indeed be a slave, but as
a tyrant, he has absolute power. As a lover, he wonders if he has the
"pow'r" to kill her; as a tyrant, he wants to have her tortured and
executed at once. His role, then, is similar to that of the antiplatonic
lover of the romances and of many of the English comedies of this
period.[73] Maximin is, after all, of plebeian stock, and the absurdity of
his love for the descendant of the royal family of Egypt acts as a cor-
rective force on the platonic lovers, Porphyrius and Berenice, and on
the passionate lovers, Placidius and Valeria. But in a comedy, the witty,
antiplatonic lover has none of the power over the lives of the other
characters which Maximin possesses.[74]

The relationship between Saint Catherine and Maximin is further
clarified in the scene where the saint pleads for Berenice. Here the confrontation is between the forces of moral control and those of complete
freedom. As emperor, Maximin can do what he wishes within the limitations of the human condition, but he aspires to a power beyond human
bounds. He threatens revenge against the gods, and even as he dies,
shouts defiance at them. He is a forceful figure, and it is not surprising
that Sir Walter Scott should have regarded him as a romantic hero [75] or
that contemporaries should have thought of the play by the title "Maximin." [76] In his love for Saint Catherine, Maximin views his passion as
a force beyond earthly control and, since he often sees himself in the
role of the god he will become after death, as beyond even the control
of the heavenly powers. To this expression of uncontained passion Saint
Catherine counters the ideals of self-control and the love of God. Maximin's failure to appreciate Saint Catherine's Christian message is probably best displayed in his contemptuous and sarcastic attitude toward
Berenice's conversion to Christianity and in his willingness to arrange
her speedy execution, which will at once rid him of a wife and satisfy
her longing for martyrdom.

---

[73] Lynch, *Restoration Comedy*, pp. 88–106, 137–181.

[74] Some critics have stressed a strong comic element in the actions and
speeches of Maximin, and support for this position may be found in Colley
Cibber's description of "a Laugh of Approbation" which might be used in
tragedy. But Cibber's discussion suggests that such attempts to arouse laughter
were infrequent. Eric Rothstein's argument that laughter was "one of Dryden's
most important devices for controlling the decorum of his heroic plays"
seems more accurate than Bruce King's attempt to find laughter where Dryden
was attempting a kind of wit intended to arouse admiration. See *Apology for
the Life of Mr. Colley Cibber*, I, 123–125; Rothstein, *Restoration Tragedy*, p.
134; King, *Dryden's Major Plays*, pp. 38–43.

[75] S-S, III, 371.   [76] Gerard Langbaine, *Momus Triumphans* (1688), p. 7.

The real temptations, so far as Catherine is concerned, are those that draw her to do good deeds on earth, deeds that would stand in the way of her martyrdom—the temptations to save the lives of Berenice and of her mother, Felicia. To the pleadings of Berenice and Porphyrius, Saint Catherine replies that Heaven has given her a part to play and that she is no more capable of abandoning her public role as a martyr than Maximin would be capable of abdicating his position as emperor:

> But I am plac'd, as on a Theater,
> Where all my Acts to all Mankind appear,
> To imitate my constancy or fear.

Refusing to question the judgment of heaven by fallible human reason, she explains her lack of action by rehearsing many of the ideas that Dryden was to use in *Religio Laici,* and she is actually horrified by her mother's suggestion that she deceive Maximin to save a parent's life. After a short speech on the transitory nature of life on earth, she rids herself of similar temptations to save the lives of others at the expense of her own martyr's crown by bringing on a speedy execution.

Catherine ensures her martyrdom by stating her physical revulsion for the Emperor. Her aversion toward him, rather than her contempt for the pagan gods and Rome, arouses Maximin's anger. The one passion or emotion that Saint Catherine shows at this point is her sense of disgust at the prospect of being exposed "bare and naked" during her torture and execution. Modesty, of course, was not considered a passion but a virtue, and, with the destruction of the torture wheel by the descending angel, the audience is spared all but the verbal suggestion of saintliness exposed to torture. Saint Catherine goes with pleasure to an "immortal birth" without the "blood" that makes birth on earth foul. She holds unfailingly to the heavenly glory she desires, and Dryden succeeds in showing her a saint by dramatic means without sacrificing some of her very human qualities.

The only other temptation to which Saint Catherine is subjected comes from the forces of magic, and these are combated entirely by angelic means. By using astral spirits rather than devils, Dryden avoided the division, found in *The Virgin Martyr,* between good angels and bad. These astral or middle spirits were regarded as amoral rather than immoral, and in the form in which Dryden presents them they provide a supernatural parallel to the world of love and heroism—the world of the heroic play—rather than to the theological conflicts in *Tyrannick Love.* Damilcar and Nakar are clearly of the same species of spirits that were to appear in the Abbé de Villars' *Comte de Gabalis,* a work almost contemporary with Dryden's play. Perhaps the use of middle spirits merely indicates the contemporary interest in them,[77] but by limiting the forces against Saint Catherine to those controlled by human power Dryden emphasizes the combat between religion and human folly rather than a combat between good and evil.

The presence of these spirits also introduces into *Tyrannick Love* a

---

[77] See notes to IV, i, 15–180.

different type of poetry. The beginning of the fourth act serves as a masque. Nigrinus begins with the poetry of incantation, and Nakar and Damilcar descend to sing a lyric based on the fairy way of writing. Then follows more incantation, two Restoration love lyrics, and, finally, the superb dialogue between Amariel and Damilcar with its sublime images of the angel's voyage from the "bright Empire of Eternal day." In itself this scene suggests something of the poetic variety of the play. In creating so many opposing elements, Dryden also created a contrast in techniques. All the main characters are identified not only as representatives of clearly defined types within the work, but also by individual verse styles. These vary from Maximin's often witty rants to Felicia's pathetic and tender description of Saint Catherine's childhood. In the speech of Berenice to Porphyrius on the subject of their love after death, Dryden captured a certain blend of extravagance and tenderness. Such speeches provided Buckingham with sufficient material for parody, but describing a moment between life and eternity was something Dryden did extremely well. Dryden had already attempted to portray the transition from life to death in *The Indian Emperour*,[78] and he achieved his goal in the speech of Saint Catherine to her mother which Sir Walter Scott so admired:

> Could we live always, life were worth our cost;
> But now we keep with care what must be lost.
> Here we stand shiv'ring on the Bank, and cry,
> When we should plunge into Eternity.
> One moment ends our pain;
> And yet the shock of death we dare not stand.

It should be apparent from this speech and from other passages mentioned above that Dryden's versification in *Tyrannick Love* is hardly a monotonous chime of couplets, but rather a variety of poetic styles with a free use of unrhymed half lines, alexandrines, triplets, and internal rhymes.[79]

Tyrannick Love was largely experimental in nature. Dryden was never again to create contrasting figures like Maximin and Saint Catherine, or to experiment with so wide a variety of poetic effects in a tragedy. Although the treatment of Porphyrius and Berenice was typical of what he had done in *The Indian Emperour* and of what he was to do in *The Conquest of Granada*, he was never again to deal with religion on the stage in the same way as he did in *Tyrannick Love*. *The State of Innocence*, written some four years later as a religious "opera" but never performed, shares few of the literary concepts of *Tyrannick Love*, although some of the intended stage effects seem to be parallel. Perhaps it is in his love of magical effects on the stage that *Tyrannick Love* seems most typical of Dryden. All the plays in this volume touch on magic and astrology in one form or another, and Dryden's continuing interest in

---

[78] *Works*, IX, 99 (V, ii).

[79] Otto Speerschneider, *Metrische Untersuchungen über den heroischen Vers in John Dryden's Dramen* (Halle, 1897), pp. 42, 48, 50, 74.

scenes that would enable him to write the "Enthusiastick parts of Poetry" —the poetry of spirits, ghosts, and incantation—is obvious enough, extending from the prologue to *The Wild Gallant* (a dialogue between two astrologers) to the conjuring of Merlin and Osmond in *King Arthur*.[80] Such scenes may be trivial, but they are marked by some of Dryden's most effective poetry. It must be remembered that when Dryden abandoned the rhymed play after *Aureng-Zebe*, he also abandoned the attempt to write a poetic drama in the sense of a play built on poetic rather than on dramatic principles. There is no question that *Tyrannick Love* contains effective poetry, and there is also little question that it has some effective characters. Unfortunately, for all Dryden's effort to create unity by the mechanical means of plot and *liaison des scènes,* the play does not hold together. The story of Berenice, Porphyrius, Valeria, and Placidius, although pathetic in itself, is somehow irrelevant to the struggle between Maximin and Saint Catherine. Theirs is the only relationship that is governed by impulses of desire and hatred, and the only one that moves to a conclusion large enough in scope to be considered tragic. The actions of the others are dependent on turns of plot and external circumstances, and our concern with them depends, in part, on our ability to interest ourselves in concepts of love which often seem, to a modern reader, inexplicably idealistic or extravagantly passionate. Anticipating his audience's favorable response to certain conventional presentations of passion which find their best exemplum in contemporary French romances, Dryden never bothered to render love in dramatic terms. In this regard, however, *Tyrannick Love* shares a flaw with all Dryden's rhymed heroic plays. Even though the quality of its poetry and its characterization of saint and emperor are insufficient to overcome its faults, *Tyrannick Love* yet remains Dryden's most explorative work in this genre.

Epigraph (title page). *Aeneid,* V, 194–196 (Loeb trans.: "No more do I, Mnestheus, seek the first place, no more strive to win; yet oh!—but let those conquer to whom thou, Neptune, hast granted it—it were a shame to return last!"). The context of the quotation is Virgil's description of the boat race and the heroic games held by Aeneas and his followers after their departure from Carthage. Cf. Dryden's *Aeneis,* V, 253–257.

DEDICATION

P. 107 *James, Duke of Monmouth.* James Scott, or Crofts (1649–1685), was the illegitimate son of Charles II and Lucy Walters. He was put under the charge of Lord Crofts and was formally presented to the King

---

[80] For Dryden's fullest discussion of the poetry associated with these themes, see *Of Heroique Playes,* prefixed to *The Conquest of Granada* (1672, sig. a4; Watson, I, 160–162).

in 1662. On 14 February 1663 he was created Baron Tyndale, Earl of
Doncaster, and Duke of Monmouth. When he married Anne Scott,
Countess of Buccleuch, on 20 April 1663, he was made Duke of Buccleuch
and assumed the surname of Scott. He later became the hero of the
Whig cause and is chiefly remembered as the unfortunate Absalom of
Dryden's *Absalom and Achitophel*. He was executed on 15 July 1685 after
leading a rebellion against James II. For an account of his life see
Elizabeth D'Oyley, *James, Duke of Monmouth* (1938).

107:2 *one of my former Plays.* A reference to *The Indian Emperour*,
dedicated to the Duchess of Monmouth. According to Pepys, the Duchess
acted in the *Emperour* at court along with her husband, "wherein they
told me things most remarkable: that not any woman but the Duchesse
of Monmouth and Mrs. Cornwallis did any thing but like fools and
stocks. . . ." See Pepys, 14 January 1667/8, and *Works*, IX, 23.

107:17–18 *Heroick Play . . . Heroick Poem.* Dryden expanded more
fully on the relationship between the heroic play and the heroic poem
and on the ideal heroes for such works, Achilles and Rinaldo, in his
essay *Of Heroique Playes,* which he published in 1672 prefixed to *The
Conquest of Granada*. Charles Ward (*Life,* p. 73) believes the compli-
ments to Monmouth were aimed at his father, Charles II, and his
uncle, James, Duke of York, but Dryden implies that Monmouth might
be the hero of such an epic, at least as great a warrior as Achilles and
Rinaldo, and perhaps the culmination of the entire line of Stuarts.
Certainly it is impossible that the compliment could have been directed
at James, whose jealousy of the Duke of Monmouth was well known,
and who had already expressed displeasure at similar compliments to
Monmouth in 1664. Pepys reports frequently on rumors that Monmouth
might become heir to the throne, and Dryden is writing before Monmouth's luster was somewhat dimmed by his assault on Sir John Coventry
and by another street brawl. Dryden does not specify what "uncommon
purpose" (107:27–108:1) Heaven had in mind when it gave Monmouth
such gifts, but surely Monmouth was to suppose that Dryden was referring
to the possibility that he might one day become England's ruler. See
D'Oyley, *James, Duke of Monmouth,* p. 57; Ogg, II, 644.

108:11 *Poetry.* Used in the now obsolete sense of fable or fiction.

PREFACE

109:2 *Commands of some Persons of Honour.* Leslie Hotson has shown
that members of the court were eager to see the play. Of the two suggestions put forward to explain this interest, Montague Summers' contention
that the "subject of S. Catharine was, no doubt, chosen in compliment to
Queen Catharine of Braganza" (II, 518) seems far more sound than that
of Bruce King, who argues that the court would have been eager to
witness a play that pitted the arguments of John Tillotson, the future
Archbishop of Canterbury, against those of the heathen philosophers. If
Charles was concerned about his queen, it was a somewhat belated
thought. Their marriage, which took place on 13 May 1662, was troubled

from the start when Charles took Lady Castlemaine as one of the Queen's waiting women. Gilbert Burnet described Catherine as "a woman of a mean shape, and of no agreeable temper," cause enough for Charles to begin visiting his mistresses. At about the time that Dryden wrote his play, Catherine was taking part in the frolics and masquerades of the court. Her political power and influence were insignificant, but Charles was still hoping she would give him an heir to the throne. See Leslie J. Hotson, *The Commonwealth and Restoration Stage* (1928), pp. 250–251; Bruce King, "Dryden, Tillotson, and *Tyrannic Love,*" *RES*, n.s., XVI (1965), 373; Burnet, *History of My Own Times*, ed. Osmund Airy (1897–1900), I, 306–308, 473–474; Ogg, I, 184–188; Cyril H. Hartmann, *Charles II and Madame* (1934), pp. 209, 247.

109:10–11 *Religion was first taught in Verse.* Richard Flecknoe, writing the same year as Dryden, also spoke of the ideal time "when Verse was wholly imployed in Devotion, that Poetry was called the language of the Gods, your Poets Prophets, and such as Moses and David were Poets" (*Epigrams of All Sorts* [1671], sig. A3v). A similar idea appears in Sir Philip Sidney's *The Defence of Poesie* (in *The Complete Works*, ed. Albert Feuillerat [1923], III, 6–9).

109:14 *conducing to Holiness.* William Prynne, the best-known opponent of the stage before Jeremy Collier, refused to accept the argument that there could be a religious or even a moral play (*Histrio-Mastix: The Player Scourge* [1633], pp. 101, 743–747). For a useful summary of attacks on the stage by Puritan and Anglican divines, see Lawrence A. Sasek, *The Literary Temper of the English Puritans* (1961), pp. 92–108.

109:17 *Enemies of the Stage.* Allardyce Nicoll comments on the antitheatrical tendencies in the city at this time, and the reissue in 1670 of Richard Baker's *Theatrum Redivivum, or the Theatre Vindicated* (1662) as *Theatrum Triumphans; or a Discourse of Plays* may indicate that a reply to William Prynne's *Histrio-Mastix* was needed to answer renewed attacks upon the theater. For one such criticism of the stage for arousing the passions and dulling the emotions, see *An Address to the Hopeful Young Gentry of England* (1669), pp. 16–18.

109:21–22 *Musick, which is inarticulate Poesie.* Dryden's comparison is reminiscent of Richard Baker's remarks on plays as sermons and the actors as musicians presenting "a Lesson in Musick, played unto us by the Master" (*Theatrum Triumphans*, pp. 133–136). Dryden's general attitude is similar to that expressed by Milton in his poem, "At a Solemn Musick." For interesting and relevant discussions of the power of music, see Jules de la Mesnardière, *La Poetique* (Paris, 1630), pp. 423–424; and Robert South, *Musica Incantans* (1700). See also *Works*, III, 459–462.

110:7 *Maximin.* Caius Julius Verus Maximinus Thrax, emperor of Rome from A.D. 235 to 238, was enrolled in the Roman bodyguard by Septimus Severus who admired the tremendous strength of the Thracian peasant. Herodian pointed out that after murdering Alexander Severus, Maximinus ruled through fear and in complete tyranny, well aware that he was the first man among the emperors to come of obscure parentage. Gibbon characterized him as cruel from "the fear of contempt" for his low birth. Herodian reports that he ravished the temples of the gods and melted down their statues to mint coins, though some citizens preferred "to die before the altars than to stand by and see their country ravaged." Dryden has made his Maximin a composite figure by combining in him the character of Maximinus with that of Galerius Valerius Maximinus, also a tyrant who ruled by fear and was possessed of fearful superstitions, a persecutor of Christians and a ravisher of Christian women. Dryden's violation of historical fact may be a lesson he learned from the famous *La Querelle du Cid,* but the confusion of the two emperors also appears in his sources. Eusebius identifies the year in which Maximinus "raised a persecution" against the Christians, but he does not indicate which emperor he refers to; and John Foxe seems to be equally uncertain. See Herodian, Bks. 7, 8; Eusebius Pamphili, *The Ecclesiastical History* (Loeb trans., II, 81); *The Actes and Monuments of John Foxe,* ed. Josiah Pratt (4th ed.; 1877), I, 273–274.

110:8–9 *S. Catharine.* Although Eusebius does not mention Saint Catherine, he tells (II, 309) how a "certain Christian lady, for example, most famous and distinguished among those at Alexandria, alone of those whom the tyrant ravished conquered the lustful and licentious soul of Maximin by her brave spirit. Renowned though she was for wealth, birth, and education, she had put everything second to modest behaviour. Many a time he importuned her, yet he was unable to put her to death though willing to die, for his lust overmastered his anger; but punishing her with exile he possessed himself of all her property." The story of how Saint Catherine overcame the Emperor's fifty philosophers and converted them, the Empress, the captain, Porphyry, and two hundred soldiers, withstood all the tortures inflicted upon her, and, after a beheading in which her veins poured milk instead of blood, was borne off to Mt. Sinai by angels was among the most popular of the saints' legends. Her festival day is 25 November. Pedro de Rivadeneira says she is usually painted "with a sword in her hand, and the head of an Emperor under her feet: to signify, that by the sword she obtained the crown of Martyrdom, and victory over the tyrant who Martyred her" (*The Lives of the Saints,* trans. W. P. [Saint-Omer, 1669], pp. 895–900). For the source of most accounts of her life, see Symeon Metaphrastes, "Martyrium Sanctae et Magnae Martyrus Aecaterinae," in *Patrologiae,* ed. J. P. Migne, CXVI (1891), cols. 275–302.

110:11 *vastus corpore, animo ferus.* Vast of body and savage of soul. Summers (II, 519–520) suggests that Dryden took this Latin paraphrase of a Greek author from the *breviarium* to the seventh chapter of Herodian's *History of the Roman Empire* as translated by Politian, where Maximin is described as *vasto corpore & crudeli animo.* Herodian speaks several times of Maximin's huge body and enormous strength, but nowhere does he use Dryden's exact words.

110:12–13 *sixth Persecution.* Beginning A.D. 237.

110:14 *life and manners.* Both Maximins were fierce and inhuman, slaughtering thousands without pity, but only the Thracian could be described as brave. The emperor who martyred Saint Catherine was a timid man, fearful of oracles.

110:17–18 *Lazare as in a Venus.* Although Dryden's statement here bears some resemblance to his remarks in the "Account" prefixed to *Annus Mirabilis* (*Works,* I, 56), he is not attempting to separate comedy or burlesque from the serious in art so much as he is defending his presentation of *a deformed piece* on the grounds of verisimilitude and *imitation of Nature.* On the one hand Dryden states that his character is drawn from history, but on the other he admits that he violated historical truth in order to present a proper moral. The contradiction, if it may be called that, was common in contemporary criticism. In the preface to his translation of Mateo Alemán's *Spanish Rogue,* Jean Chapelain praised the work for its use of details to gain a vivid sense of reality; he was also the chief critic of Corneille's *Le Cid* on the ground that it violated decorum, even though it followed history. But Chapelain's arguments are sensible enough when seen in relation to the separation of genres. Not everything was fit for presentation on the stage. What is unusual, then, is that Dryden should use an argument usually applied only to comedy and burlesque to defend a character in a heroic play. Whoever the *holy Criticks* of whom Dryden complains might be, he had already been attacked by "R. F." for his statements on nature, truth, and imitation in poetry and painting. For Dryden's changing attitude toward the Dutch art of the grotesque and the ideal art of Italy, see *Works,* I, 274–276. See also Jean Chapelain, *Opuscules Critiques,* with introduction by Alfred C. Hunter (1936), pp. 51–52; Chapelain, *Les Sentiments de l'Académie Françoise sur la Tragi-Comédie du Cid,* in *La Querelle du Cid,* ed. Armand Gasté (Paris, 1899), pp. 365–366; *A Letter from a Gentleman to the Honourable Ed. Howard Esq* (1668), pp. 4–5, 8–9.

110:22–23 *ought not to be presented.* William Prynne argued (*Histrio-Mastix,* pp. 96, 104) that the audience imitated the vices presented on the stage, no matter how dreadful the punishment for such vices might be, and that in some instances the mere hope of becoming the subject of a play provoked the spectators to commit crimes.

110:27 *Sea-marks.* A conspicuous object distinguishable at sea which serves to guide or warn sailors in navigation (*OED*).

110:33–34 *Walls of Aquileia.* Maximin, the Thracian, was murdered by his own soldiers during the unsuccessful siege of Aquileia, a Roman fortress at the head of the Adriatic, in A.D. 238. Maximin, emperor of the East, died in A.D. 313 after a dreadful illness.

111:20 *many accidents.* The opening performance was delayed because of difficulty with the production of paintings for the Elysium scene. The painter, Isaac Fuller, later sued the King's Company and recovered £335 10s. for his work. See Appendix to this volume, and Hotson, *Commonwealth and Restoration Stage,* pp. 250–253.

111:22 *Scenes are . . . unbroken.* A reference to the concept of *liaison des scènes* developed by contemporary French critics. The ideal was to prevent the stage from being empty at any time during the play. For an excellent summary of this concept of "Union of Presence," see François Hédelin, Abbé d'Aubignac, *The Whole Art of the Stage* (1684), Pt. II, p. 88.

111:23–24 *requisite in a Tragedy.* The action of *Tyrannick Love* occurs in an indeterminate number of hours within one day. Corneille, who had been criticized by Chapelain for fitting the action of *Le Cid* into twenty-four hours and thus violating the rules of nature for the sake of the rules of art, finally argued that a tragedy might extend to thirty hours or more, but rigid critics like Aubignac insisted that six hours would be "more reasonable." Aubignac contended that the action on the stage must always represent the actual passage of time for the audience, and that whereas some time might be supposed to have passed during the intermissions between acts, within twenty-four hours the characters in the play would have been forced to eat and sleep. See Cecil V. Deane, *Dramatic Theory and the Rhymed Heroic Play* (1931), pp. 90–95; and Aubignac, *Whole Art of the Stage*, Pt. I, pp. 113–120.

111:28 *slave to Syllables.* Although Dryden defended rhymed plays against Sir Robert Howard's attacks on rhymed dialogue as unnatural and improbable, he never upheld the warping of sense for the sake of rhyme. His statement here suggests Thomas Sprat's objections to rhyme in French plays (*Observations on Mons. de Sorbier's Voyage into England* [1665], p. 251).

111:34 *French Play.* Dryden is referring to the anonymous play, *Le Martyre de Sainte Catherine*, first published at Lyons in 1649. It has been attributed, on no very good grounds, to Aubignac, Desfontaines, and Saint-Germain; it appeared in three editions in 1649 and 1650. The line that caused Dryden to confuse the two emperors appears in the fifth act where Maximin is referred to as "Le fils d'un soldat Gots et d'une femme Alaine" (see Lancaster, Pt. II, Vol. II, pp. 668–670). For Dryden's confusion of the two Maximins, see 110:7n.

112:7 *Eusebius and Metaphrastes.* Eusebius Pamphili (A.D. 264?–339?) provides a thorough account of the reign of Maximin, though with only a suggestion of what was to become the legend of Saint Catherine. Symeon Metaphrastes, who lived in the tenth century A.D., was the principal compiler of the legends of the Byzantine church. His life of Saint Catherine became the principal source for the literature surrounding her.

112:15 *L'Amour Tyrannique.* Georges de Scudéry's *L'Amour Tyrannique*, first performed in 1639, was a deliberate effort on the part of the author to rival and surpass Corneille's *Cid.* Tremendously successful on the stage, it was published with a "Discours de la Tragédie" by Sillac d'Arbois which proclaimed the play as good as Sophocles' *Oedipus.* That Dryden was being perfectly honest about his ignorance of Scudéry's "Comedy" may be questioned. For one thing, he speaks as if the play were obscure, which is far from being true. And besides being set before the walls of a besieged city, *L'Amour Tyrannique* shares a number of parallel characters, scenes, and sentiments with *Tyrannick Love.* Tyridate, the king of Pontus, is almost a double for Maximin, and if Dryden was trying to conceal his borrowings by attacking the author of his source, it would not be the first time. For a discussion of *L'Amour Tyrannique,* see Lancaster, Pt. II, Vol. I, pp. 229–233. For further discussion of the parallels between the two plays, see p. 391, above.

112:21 *Astral or Aerial Spirits.* For discussions of the spirit world and the variety of angels therein, see Agrippa, pp. 390–451; Thomas Culpeper, "Of Spirits and Phantasmes," in *Essayes or Moral Discourses on Several Subjects* (1671), pp. 149–161. For attacks on the existence of such beings, see John Spencer, *A Discourse concerning Prodigies* (1665), pp. 210–223; Thomas Hobbes, *Leviathan,* in *English Works,* III, 637–650. In his essay *Of Heroique Playes,* prefixed to *The Conquest of Granada* (1672, a4r–v; Watson, I, 161), Dryden defended these "visionary objects" at greater length, with specific mention of Hobbes as his opponent.

112:28 *the little Critiques.* Both lines from *Tyrannick Love* mentioned by Dryden were parodied in Buckingham's *The Rehearsal* when it was performed on 7 December 1671. Dryden's "With empty arms embrace you while you sleep" (III, i) became "With empty arms I'll bear you on my back" (IV, i); the line from the prologue, "*And he who servilely creeps after sence,*" appears in Johnson's remark on Bayes, "Oh, for that, he desires to be excused; he is too proud a man to creep servilely after sense, I assure you" (IV, ii). The latter parody was not printed in the first edition of *The Rehearsal* in 1672, but appeared for the first time in the third edition of 1675, three years after Dryden added this passage to his preface. There is little question, however, that the line was included in the stage version.

112:32 *Horace. Ars Poetica,* II, 453. Horace warns against falling into one fault by trying to avoid another. (Loeb trans.: "One promising grandeur, is bombastic; another, overcautious and fearful of the gale, creeps along the ground.")

113:7–8 *vacuis amplectitur ulnis.* Dryden is probably thinking of the legend of Orpheus in Ovid's *Metamorphoses,* though the quotation is not exact. He may be confusing the passage in which Orpheus joins Eurydice in the Elysian fields after his death (XI, 63),

invenit Eurydicen cupidisque amplictitur ulnis

(Loeb trans.: "He found Eurydice and caught her in his eager arms"), with the passage describing the moment at which he looked back to see if she was following him out of Hades (X, 58–59),

bracchiaque intendens prendique et prendere certans
nil nisi cedentes infelix arripit auras

(Loeb trans.: "He stretched out his arms eager to catch her or to feel her clasp; but, unhappy one, he clasped nothing but the yielding air").

113:10 *And follow fate which does too fast pursue.* A line from *The Indian Emperour* (IV, iii, 5). Dryden was attacked for the line in *A Letter from a Gentleman to the Honourable Ed. Howard Esq,* pp. 5–6. The passage from Virgil (*Aeneid,* XI, 694–695) concerns Camilla's victory over Orsilochum before Camilla herself was slain by Arruns. (Loeb trans.: "Orsilochus she flees, and, chased in a wide circle, foils him, wheels into an inner ring and pursues the pursuer.") Dr. Johnson gives Dryden's defense as a supreme example of the foible of refusing to admit an error. Johnson thought that Dryden's "blunder" lay in "the double meaning of the word FATE, to which in the former part of the verse he had annexed the idea of FORTUNE, and in the latter that of DEATH." Even had he believed that Dryden had Virgil's passage in mind (which he did not), Johnson would hardly have thought that a justification for what he usually called a "quibble" (see *Rambler,* no. 31).

PROLOGUE

9 *censures.* Opinions (*OED*).

10 *equal.* Impartial (*OED*).

11 *They judge but half who only faults will see.* The editors of the Twickenham edition of Pope's *Essay on Criticism* suggest that this line is the origin of Pope's more famous couplet:

> Survey the Whole, nor seek slight Faults to find,
> Where Nature moves, and Rapture warms the Mind.

In his preface to *Sylvæ* (*Works,* III, 14) and his dedication of *Examen Poeticum* (1693, sigs. A3–A7; Watson, II, 156–160), Dryden attacked those critics who believed, to paraphrase Swift, that a critic was a collector of a writer's faults. Spingarn associates the tendency to regard harsh criticism as vicious with a school of "taste" in France and especially with the Chevalier de Méré, who wrote: "When we judge sincerely, . . . there is scarce any thing to be found that is perfect: but the more exquisite discernment one hath, the more it is for ones honour to be indulgent. . . ." The classical progenitors of this attitude are Horace, who warned that "shunning a fault may lead to error, if there be lack of art," and Longinus, who urged the poet to attempt great things even if he might thereby fall into bad poetry at times. These attitudes achieved their widest popularity after Boileau's translation of Longinus in 1674, but they had already found an important defender in Trajano Boccalini and his influential *I Ragguagli di Parnasso.* In one episode a critic appears before Apollo and angers the god by informing him that as a critic he ignores the beauties of a poem and concentrates solely on its faults. Apollo sets him the task of separating the darnel from the chaff in a bushel of corn, and after he has finished tells him to sell the chaff at a market. When the critic says that he would be ashamed to sell such a thing, Apollo draws the moral:

> ". . . in the reading of other mens labours, the wary Vertuosi imitated the Bee, which knew how to gather honey even from bitter flowres. And that there being no sublunary thing which was not kneaded with some imperfections; some bran would be found in the Works of Homer, Virgil, Livy, Tacitus, and Hyppocrates, who were the wonders of writing, if a man would be curious in sifting them; but that he was satisfied if the flowre of his Vertuoso's Composure were currant merchandize. That the defects of good Authors were conceal'd by the

juditious and freindly readers, and publisht only by
such as are malitious. And that to make profession of
taking out the worst things only out of other mens
writings, was the office of base beetles which spent their
lives with much gusto amidst the filth of excrements:
a thing very far from the practice of those honoured
Litterati who feed advantagiously upon good things."
See Spingarn, I, xcviii–ci; Antoine Gombard, Chevalier de Méré, *Conversations Written in French by Monsieur Clerombault* (1672), p. 113;
Horace, *Ars Poetica* (Loeb trans.), II, 453 (l. 31); Longinus, *On the Sublime*
(Loeb trans.), pp. 217–221; and Trajano Boccalini, *I Ragguagli di
Parnasso,* trans. Henry, Earl of Monmouth (1656), pp. 197–198.

12 *Poets, like Lovers.* Dryden was probably attempting a loose imitation of Horace's *Ars Poetica,* ll. 24–31, as he suggests in the preface. Dryden's
sentiments are exactly the same as those he later expressed in "The
Authors Apology for Heroique Poetry; and Poetique Licence" prefixed
to *The State of Innocence* (1677, b1v–b2; Watson, I, 196–198), which
was written under the direct influence of Longinus, whom he there
names "undoubtedly, after Aristotle, the greatest Critique amongst the
Greeks." Longinus had commented on this problem:

> In spite, then, of these faults I still think that great
> excellence, even if it is not sustained throughout at the
> same level, should always be voted the first place, if for
> nothing else, for its inherent nobility. Apollonius, for
> instance, in his *Argonautica* is an impeccable poet and
> Theocritus—except in a few extraneous matters—is
> supremely successful in his pastorals. Yet would you not
> rather be Homer than Apollonius? And what of Eratosthenes in his *Erigone?* Wholly blameless as the little
> poem is, do you therefore think him a greater poet than
> Archilochus with all the manifold irrelevance he carries
> on his flood; greater than those outbursts of divine
> inspiration, which are so troublesome to bring under
> any rule?

A Latin text of Longinus was available in 1650 and an English translation in 1652, but Dryden may merely have been echoing Boccalini or
contemporary French critics. See Longinus, *On the Sublime* (Loeb
trans.), pp. 219–221, and the remarks in the preceding note.

16 *Poet in his conjuring.* Throughout his life, Dryden alternated
between the view of Plato that poets "utter all those fine poems not
from art, but as inspired and possessed," and the argument of Aristotle
as interpreted by French critics like Rapin, which emphasized the craft
of the poet. Dryden used the image of the poet as a magician in the
prologue to *The Tempest* (ll. 19–23, above), and in the dedication of
Eleonora (*Works,* III, 231) he imagined himself as a priest of Apollo,
seized by a fit of poetic fury. He often quoted the famous statement of
Eumolpus in Petronius' *Satyricon,* that the "free spirit of genius must
plunge headlong into allusions and divine interpositions . . . so that

what results seems rather the prophecies of an inspired seer than the exactitude of a statement made on oath before witnesses." And he probably knew Agrippa's discussion of the "phrensie from the Muses," as well as Sidney's description of the poet as conjurer and sorcerer. Buckingham's remark in *The Rehearsal* (V, i) may be directed both to Dryden's statements about the poetic imagination and to his treatment of spirits in poetry: "Why, did you ever hear any people in Clouds speak plain? They must be all for flight of fancie, at its full range, without the least check, or controul upon it. When once you tye up spirits, and people in clouds to speak plain, you spoil all." See Plato, *Ion* (Loeb trans.), p. 421; Aristotle, *Poetics* (Loeb trans.), p. 65; Petronius, *Satyricon* (Loeb trans.), p. 253; Agrippa, pp. 500–501; Sir Philip Sidney, *Defence of Poesie*, in *Works*, ed. Feuillerat, III, 4–7; and René Rapin, *The Whole Critical Works of Monsieur Rapin*, trans. Basil Kennett (1731), II, 164. For an example of Dryden's attacks on those "who would justify the madness of Poetry," see his preface to *Troilus and Cressida* (1679, b1v–b2; Watson, I, 255).

PERSONS REPRESENTED

Metaphrastes gives names only to Catherine, Maxentius (for Maximin), and Porphyrio. The Empress is simply called Augusta, though Foxe, following later tradition, calls her Faustina. The author of *Le Martyre de Sainte Catherine* gives the Empress the name of Vallerie, similar to that of a woman who rejected the advances of the later Maximin, and also has a follower of Maximin called Valere. Other characters are Dryden's inventions, though they sometimes suggest obscure historical associations. For example, there was a tribune of horse named Nigrinus who seized Aquileia for Constantius sometime around A.D. 360. See Edward Gibbon, *The Decline and Fall of the Roman Empire*, ed. J. B. Bury (1909–1914), I, 461–465; Laurence Eachard, *The Roman History* (1724), III, 62.

I, i

3 *The German Lakes.* This speech refers to Maximin's victory over the Germans in A.D. 235. Having justified the murder of Severus Alexander on the ground that he had been a coward, Maximin was forced to demonstrate his own courage (Herodian, p. 176):

When the Germans rushed into a vast swamp in an effort to escape . . . Maximinus plunged into the marsh, though the water was deeper than his horse's belly; there he cut down the barbarians who opposed him. Then the rest of the army, ashamed to betray their emperor who was doing their fighting for them, took courage and leaped into the marsh behind him. A large number of men fell on both sides, but, while many Romans were killed, virtually the entire barbarian force was annihilated, and the emperor was the foremost man on the field. The swamp pool was choked with bodies,

and the marsh ran red with blood; this land battle had
all the appearance of a naval encounter.

17 *Two, tame, gown'd Princes.* After the death of Gordian, an assembly selected two of the eldest senators to lead the revolt against
Maximin: M. Clodius Pupienus Maximus, who was to direct the army,
and Decimus Caelius Balbinus, who was to head the civil government
in Rome. Herodian tells how the mob was displeased by the choice,
particularly of Maximus, and insisted that a young grandson of Gordian's
be chosen. In a compromise arrangement, the two senators became
regents during the minority of Gordian Caesar. But the army, which had
become accustomed to selecting the emperors, resented the Senate's
imposing a choice upon them. Eventually the Praetorian Guard broke
into open revolt against Maximus and Balbinus. The two emperors were
captured, led naked to the camp of the soldiers, and brutally murdered.
See Herodian, pp. 191–192, 212–213.

37 *Two equal pow'rs, two different ways will draw.* Maximin's predic-
tion was fulfilled when Maximus and Balbinus began to quarrel, but
Dryden was following Hobbes more than Herodian. Hobbes (*English
Works*, II, 141; III, 167–180, 317–318), arguing that there could be but
one source of power within the state, cited England as an illustration of
the failure of a mixed government (II, 141):

> But it is a manifest sign that the most absolute monar-
> chy is the best state of government, that not only kings,
> but even those cities which are subject to the people or
> to nobles, give the whole command of war to one only;
> and that so absolute, as nothing can be more. Wherein,
> by the way, this must be noted also; that no king can
> give a general greater authority over his army, than he
> himself by right may exercise over all his subjects. Mon-
> archy therefore is the best of all governments in the
> camps. But what else are many commonwealths, than
> so many camps strengthened with arms and men against
> each other; whose state, because not unrestrained by
> any common power, howsoever an uncertain peace, like
> a short truce, may pass between them, is to be accounted
> for the state of nature; which is the state of war.

40 *an Empire to increase.* According to Herodian (p. 177), Maximin
planned to extend the Roman Empire by subduing all of Germany.

42 *success should make him absolute.* Cf. Maximin's speech to his
army: "If anyone has informed you of the senate's action, do not be
surprised . . . and do not wonder that they call manly and moderate
acts fear-inspiring, and believe that unrestrained frenzy is civilized because it provides pleasure. They are, as a result, unfavorably disposed
toward my rule because it is disciplined and well ordered . . ." (Herodian,
p. 187).

48 *The thrifty State.* Surely Dryden meant this allusion to have contemporary significance. For Charles's problems in obtaining funds from
the Commons for financing his wars, see Ogg, I, 317–321, 334, 341.

53 *Crispinus and Menephilus.* Herodian (pp. 200–202) praises both

these men for wisdom in preparing for the siege and Crispinus, in particular, for inspiring the Aquileians with courage.

62 *That white one.* A white day was regarded as a fortunate day (see *OED*).

70 *Panonian Band.* Maximin sent the Pannonian troops into Italy ahead of his main force because "he had special confidence in these troops who had been first to proclaim him emperor and who wished and promised to risk their lives on his behalf" (Herodian, p. 188).

71 *Isters Banks.* "Hister" was the Roman name for the lower part of the Danube.

72 *bind the head-long flood.* The ability of magicians and witches to halt the flow of rivers, typical of their power to change nature, was called "nekyomantia." Lucan (*Pharsalia*, VI, 472–474) mentions this power in his discussion of the Thessalian witches. (Loeb trans.: "The waterfall is arrested on the steep face of the cliff; and the running river forsakes its downward channel.") See also Kirby F. Smith, "Magic (Greek and Roman)," in *Encyclopaedia of Religion and Ethics*, ed. James Hastings, VIII (1926), 286–287.

78 *Ghosts of slaughter'd Souldiers call.* Nigrinus is a necromancer. His art is well described by Agrippa (pp. 489–490):

> Hence Necromancy hath its name, because it worketh
> on the bodies of the dead, and giveth answers by the
> ghosts and apparitions of the dead, by certain hellish
> charms, and infernall invocations, and by deadly sacri-
> fices and wicked oblations. . . . there are two kinds
> of Necromancy, the one called Necyomancy, raising
> the carkasses, which is not done without blood. The
> other Sciomancy, in which the calling up of the shadow
> only sufficeth: to conclude, it worketh all its experiments
> by the carkases of the slain, and their bones and mem-
> bers, and what is from them, because there is in these
> things a spiritual power friendly to them. Therefore they
> easily allure the flowing down of wicked spirits, being
> by reason of the similitude and propriety very familiar.

80 *And loth to enter.* Dryden is unquestionably thinking of Lucan's description of Erictho's necromancy in the *Pharsalia*, particularly the passage (VI, 721–722)

> Exanimes artus invisaque claustra timentem
> Carceris antiqui. Pavet ire in pectus apertum

(Loeb trans.: "It feared the lifeless frame and the hateful confinement of its former prison; it shrank from entering the gaping bosom").

86 *in a Square he did a Circle draw.* Scot (pp. 251, 256) gives two excellent diagrams of this figure. The words in the corners are: *agla, el, panthon,* and *ya.* See also Cornelius Agrippa, pseud., *Fourth Book of Occult Philosophy*, trans. Robert Turner (1783), pp. 109–122.

90 *The Sky grew black.* For a similar description see Calpurnia's speech in Shakespeare's *Julius Caesar* (II, ii):

> A lioness hath whelped in the streets;

And graves have yawned and yielded up their dead;
Fierce fiery warriors fought upon the clouds,
In ranks and squadrons and right form of war,
Which drizzled blood upon the Capitol;
The noise of battle hurtled in the air,
Horses did neigh and dying men did groan,
And ghosts did shriek and squeal about the streets.

Dryden may also have been thinking of Lucan's *Pharsalia*, VI, 515–530.

92 *offer'd*. Attacked (*OED*).

93 *shrill and tender cry*. Summers suggests that "tender" here is being used in the obsolete sense of "thin," but Dryden may mean merely that their voices were weak (see *OED*).

97 *fenc'd within*. Pietro d'Abano speaks of the circles as "fortresses," for while the magician is within the circle he is entirely safe; he ought never to leave the circle without releasing the spirits beforehand (see *Heptameron, or Magical Elements*, in Agrippa, pseud., *Fourth Book*, p. 127).

102 *heaps of visionary Souldiers*. According to Herodian (p. 202), the Aquileians also had recourse to soothsayers and oracles, who informed them they would win through the favor of their god: "They call this god Belis, and worship him with special devotion, identifying him with Apollo, whose image, some of Maximinus' soldiers said, often appeared in the sky over the city, fighting for the Aquileians."

162 *An execrable superstition*. Dryden takes this phrase from Tacitus' brief description of the Christian religion (*exitiabilis superstitio*) from its origins to the time when Nero decided to blame the burning of Rome on the Christians (see *Annals*, XV, xliv).

167 *Mucius*. Gaius Mucius was given the name Scaevola (left-handed) for his bravery in thrusting his right hand into a fire in order to demonstrate to Porsena, leader of the Etruscan forces attacking Rome in 508 B.C., the indifference of the Romans to bodily suffering. Porsena freed Scaevola and, when told that three hundred others were willing to kill him even if they should die for it, made peace with Rome. See Livy (Loeb trans.), II, 255–261 (xii–xiii).

180 *murd'rers presence*. As Sir Francis Bacon says in his *Sylva*, "It is an usual observation, that if the body of one murthered be brought before the murtherer, the wounds will bleed afresh. . . . It may be that this participateth of a miracle, by God's just judgment, who usually bringeth murthers to the light: but if it be natural, it must be referred to imagination" (*Works*, ed. James Spedding, Robert Ellis, and Douglas Heath [1858–1870], II, 660 [N. 958]).

225 + *s.d. Charinus born in dead*. Maximin's son, Gaius Julius Verus Maximus, was killed at the same time as his father by army conspirators. Unlike his father, he was well educated, and though he was considered "insolent" many regarded him as a promising leader. See Julius Capitolinus, "The Two Maximini," in *Scriptores Historiae Augustae* (Loeb trans.), II, 368–371 (xxviii); Herodian, p. 207.

243 *fiery showrs of Sulphur*. "The Aquileians hurled down stones on

the besiegers; combining pitch and olive oil with asphalt and brimstone, they ignited this mixture and poured it over their attackers from hollow vessels fitted with long handles" (Herodian, p. 204).

246 *Capaneus*. One of the seven heroes who led the war against Thebes. In the midst of battle, while scaling a ladder, Capaneus addressed the gods with defiance and mockingly called upon Zeus to destroy him with fire as he had destroyed Semele. As soon as Capaneus spoke, he was struck by a thunderbolt from Heaven and consumed. Dryden was thinking of Statius' description of this scene and suggesting a resemblance between Charinus and heroic figures like Capaneus and Ajax, men of massive strength who thought themselves more powerful than the gods (see Statius, *Thebaidos*, x, 837–890).

273 *Antonin's was nam'd the Good*. Antoninus Pius (A.D. 86–161) ruled the empire from A.D. 138 and brought peace and harmony to Rome. He had been adopted by Hadrian, and he, in turn, adopted Marcus Aurelius Antoninus. Although the title "Antoninus" was a compliment to later rulers, the emperors actually deserving it were Antoninus Pius, Marcus Aurelius, and Lucius Verus. Dryden makes Berenice the sister of Aurelius Alexander Severus, who refused the title after Elagabalus had dishonored it.

278 *Images*. *Imagines* or funeral masks. These masks were set in a shrine and became, from their original significance as magical symbols of the departed ancestor, badges of ancient descent and focal points of snobbery about ancestry. Dryden probably believed in the *jus imaginum,* a law of doubtful existence which was supposed to limit the display of ancestral masks to the nobility. Summers (II, 525) confuses the *imagines* with the *lares,* or deities of the farm. Since Maximin was concerned about his social status, a reference to the *lares* would be meaningless. For a work tracing the evolution of the *imagines* in art and society, see Annie Zadoks-Josephus Jitta, *Ancestral Portraiture in Rome* (1932). See also Polybius, *The Histories,* vi. 53.

329 *my Cæsar him create*. The title of "Caesar" was given to the heir to the throne or to that person whose power put him next to the emperor. The family title had been extinguished with the death of Nero.

II, i

26 *I am to bear*. The attitude of Berenice is exactly the same as that of Vallerie in the anonymous French play, *Le Martyre de Sainte Catherine.* When Maxime, whose role is similar to that of Dryden's Porphyrius, urges her to revolt, she replies:

Il ne commettra rien dont i'oze murmurer,
Il peut tout entreprendre, Et moy tout endurer.

But unlike Berenice, Vallerie banishes her admirer as an enemy of her "gloire." See *Le Martyre de Sainte Catherine* (Caen, 1650), p. 68 (III, iii).

30 *who forfeits first*. Porphyrius argues on the basis of natural law that the person who first violates the contract of marriage, or any other contract, breaks the agreement for both parties. Grotius (*Of the Law of Warre and Peace* [1654], pp. 238–239), though agreeing with Porphy-

rius' legal position, praises the virtue of the man who, in the words of the psalmist, "Having sworn to his own hurt . . . changeth not." 38 *the wreck.* Porphyrius advances an argument based on a common error. Actually a wreck was not a lawful prize for anyone; it belonged to the owner when he could be found or to the crown when no owner could be discovered. Until 1771 a distinction was made between a wreck in which everyone perished (in which event the property went to the crown) and one in which even a single person survived. See *Select Pleas in the Court of Admiralty,* ed. Reginald G. Marsden (1897), II, xxiv–xli; A. Pearce Higgins and C. John Colombos, *The International Law of the Sea* (1952), pp. 241–242.

55 *on Cæsar's side.* Brutus and Cassius were defeated at Philippi in 42 B.C. by Octavius and Antony.

56 *'Tis vertue not to be oblig'd at all.* The problem of obligation is a central theme in this play, as it is in many of the tragedies of Corneille and Racine. In suggesting that all contracts are inviolable, whether of marriage or of obedience to the state, Berenice follows Hobbes, who argues that even such an obligation as is incurred by a sense of gratitude for gifts or favors must be binding: "For no man giveth, but with intention of Good to himselfe; because Gift is Voluntary; and of all Voluntary Acts, the Object is to every man his own Good; of which if men see they shall be frustrated, there will be no beginning of benevolence, or trust; nor consequently of mutual help; . . . and therefore they are to remain still in the condition of War" (*Leviathan,* in Hobbes, *English Works,* III, 138).

115 *Heav'n.* Here referring to the fixed vault of the sky.

126 *impetuous Tide.* For a discussion of contemporary theories of tides in relation to Dryden's imagery, see *Works,* I, 299–300.

142 *from Religion, all Rebellions grow.* Dryden may have taken this idea from Hobbes's argument that the Church is the only force within a state which, pretending to a "Soveraign Power over the People," is in competition with the political ruler of the state. The error of the Church, Hobbes suggests, lies in its leaders' belief "that the present Church now Militant on Earth, is the Kingdom of God" (*Leviathan,* in Hobbes, *English Works,* III, 689–700).

169 *Reason with our Faith.* For an excellent statement of this theme see *The Recognitions of Clement,* trans. Thomas Smith, in *The Ante-Nicene Fathers,* ed. Alexander Roberts and James Donaldson (1885–1896), VIII, 116. See also John Tillotson, *The Precepts of Christianity Not Grievous,* in *Works* (1696), pp. 70–79.

172 *many Gods are many Infinites.* See Thomas Aquinas, *Summa Theologica,* I, xi, iii.

173 *first Philosophers.* Speaking of Thales, whom he regarded as the first Greek philosopher, Thomas Stanley wrote (I, pt. i, p. 11): "He acknowledged God the first of beings, and Author of the world, asserting (according to Laertius) that the most antient of all things is God, for he is not begotten." See also Thomas Stanley, *The History of the Chaldaick Philosophy* (1662), p. 18.

178 *Cato blush'd to see.* Marcus Porcius Cato of Utica (95?–46 B.C.),

a man famous for his upright life. The event referred to is described in
Valerius Maximus, *Romae Antiquae Descriptio* (1678), p. 99 (II, x, 8):
"Beholding the Floral Plays which Messius the Aedil set forth, the
people were ashamed to require that the Mimicks should appear naked;
which when he understood from Favonius, his great friend, that sate
close by him, he departed out of the Theatre, lest his presence should
interrupt the custome of the Show, Whose departure the people loudly
applauding, renewed the ancient custome of Jesting in the Scenes." In
his attack on the stage, William Prynne retells this story to illustrate the
guilt and shame of audiences at spectacles rather than to demonstrate the
way a single moral man felt at such ceremonies (see *Histrio-Mastix*, fol.
529 [sig. Aaa*]).

183 *in pleasing Fables lye.* For an answer to this interpretation of the
fables of the gods, see Arnobius, *The Seven Books of Arnobius against
the Heathen*, trans. Hamilton Bryce and Hugh Campbell, in *The Ante-
Nicene Fathers*, VI, 502–506.

193 *Vertue, as its own reward.* A principle usually associated with the
thought of the Stoics. Similar statements appear throughout the *Medita-
tions* of Marcus Aurelius; and Seneca, in his essay "On the Happy Life,"
stated, "Do you ask what it is that I seek in virtue? Only herself. For she
offers nothing better—she herself is her own reward" (*Moral Essays*, VII,
ix, 4).

200 *Vertue grows cold without a recompence.* The Day of Judgment,
according to Sir Thomas Browne, "is the day whose memory hath onely
power to make us honest in the dark, and to bee vertuous without a
witnesse. *Ipsa sui pretium virtus sibi,* that vertue is her owne reward is
but a cold principle, and not able to maintaine our variable resolutions
in a constant and setled way of goodnesse." And Dryden's friend, Dr.
Charleton, has a lengthy dialogue on the subject in which Athanasius, his
own spokesman, explains that the Stoics were guilty of pride in pretending to shun a glory they coveted. Bruce King has argued that the source
of most of Saint Catherine's arguments is John Tillotson's writings, and
that Dryden was deliberately presenting them to a court audience that
wanted to hear them in the theater. Certainly the kind of debate that
Dryden staged was not to be found in his sources, but it was typical of
Dryden's method of handling argument on the stage. That he was
influenced by Tillotson's ideas, particularly those in *The Rule of Faith*,
is likely, but unless one accepts King's position that the play is *about*
Tillotson's arguments, it would seem naïve to believe that Dryden limited
his ideas on Christianity to the writings of one divine. See Thomas
Browne, *Religio Medici*, in *Works*, ed. Geoffrey Keynes (1964), I, 57;
Walter Charleton, *The Immortality of the Human Soul* (1657), pp. 148–
151; Tillotson, *Works*, pp. 64–65. See also Bruce King, "Dryden, Tillotson, and *Tyrannic Love*," pp. 364–377; Bruce King, *Dryden's Major Plays*
(1966), pp. 51–58.

208 *secret pride.* For an example of the kind of pride Saint Catherine
attacks, see Neo-Stoical works like Antoine le Grand, *Man without Passion*, trans. G. R. (1675), pp. 22–23, 115; and Guillaume du Vair, *The*

Morall Philosophy of the Stoicks, trans. Charles Cotton (1664), p. 13. For examples of attacks on Stoic pride, see *Essays of Montaigne,* trans. John Florio, Tudor Translations (1892–1893), I, 279; II, 507; and John Wilmot, Earl of Rochester, "Satyr against Mankind," in *Poems,* ed. Vivian de Sola Pinto (1953), pp. 118–124.

209 *our Moral virtues you obey.* The four moral virtues of the Stoics— prudence, temperance, fortitude, and justice—were praised and frequently adapted by the early Christian Fathers, especially Lactantius, who was an admirer of Seneca. The seventeenth-century philosopher Pierre Charron discusses these four virtues with a strong Stoical bias. See Stanley, II, pt. viii, pp. 1–140; Pierre Charron, *Of Wisdom,* trans. Samson Lennard (1658), pp. 330–521. See also Roger L'Estrange, trans., *Seneca's Morals by Way of Abstract* (1696), sigs. a8–b4.

214 *forbid ev'n to desire.* A reference to Christ's statement that sin is committed in the conception of a sin, whether acted upon or not. In distinguishing sharply between inclination and will, Hobbes was arguing against this idea. Cf. Matthew, v, 28; Hobbes, *Leviathan,* in *English Works,* III, 48–49. For an illuminating exposition of the Stoic concept of "intention," with its obvious relation to Christian attitudes toward sin, see E. Vernon Arnold, *Roman Stoicism* (1911), pp. 286–289.

215 *Revenge of injuries.* Perhaps a reference to the Stoic doctrine of following the law in matters of revenge. Thomas Stanley lists as one of the maxims of the Stoics: *"A wise man is not mercifull,* nor pardons any, remitting nothing of the punishments inflicted by Law, as knowing them to be proportioned to, not exceeding the offence, and that whosoever sinneth, sinneth out of his own wickednesse." Insofar as revenge might be regarded as a passion, however, both the Stoics and their seventeenth-century disciples attacked it. Dryden may be having Catherine answer a position held by Aristotle and the Peripatetic school, that virtue consists in action and that revenge need not be evil. See Epictetus, *Discourses* (Loeb trans.), II, 333–339 (IV, v, 9–21). See also Stanley, II, pt. viii, pp. 69–73, 94; II, pt. vi, pp. 83–88; Charron, *Of Wisdom,* pp. 504–506.

216 *forgiveness of our wrongs.* The Stoics admired the ability to forgive injuries, but Tillotson was probably correct in calling forgiveness "that peculiar Law of Christianity" (cf. Guillaume du Vair, *Morall Philosophy of the Stoicks,* trans. Cotton, p. 52; Tillotson, *Works,* p. 73).

222 *Where Truth prevails.* In almost all versions of the story of Saint Catherine the philosophers are quickly defeated and are won over to Christianity by a sudden awareness of the truth. Catherine, of course, has been visited by an angel who informs her that she will have supernatural powers of reasoning added to her natural genius and fine training in philosophy. See *The Life of Saint Katherine,* ed. Eugen Einenkel, E.E.T.S. no. 80 (1884), pp. 45–65; John Capgrave, *The Life of St. Katharine of Alexandria,* ed. Carl Horstman, E.E.T.S. no. 100 (1893), pp. 303 ff.; Jean Puget de la Serre, *Le Martyre de Sainte Caterine* (Paris, 1643), pp. 64–71 (IV, iv); and Metaphrastes, "Martyrium Sanctae," in *Patrologiae,* CXVI, cols. 283–290.

238 *baptiz'd in fire.* In some versions of the legend the philosophers worried about whether their conversion would be acceptable to Christ, and Catherine assured them that their blood would serve as their baptism (see, for example, *Life of Saint Katherine*, E.E.T.S. no. 80, p. 64; Metaphrastes, in *Patrologiae*, CXVI, col. 290).

256 *Consider she's a Queen.* Dryden thinks of Catherine as of the royal line of Egypt, but in most legends she is made the daughter of King Cost or Costus of Cypress; her mother was called Meliades (see Capgrave, *Life of St. Katharine of Alexandria*, E.E.T.S. no. 100, p. 31).

282 *new birds, and unknown beasts.* This reference to Jupiter's metamorphosis into a swan and a bull, respectively, in his amours with Leda and Europa was parodied in Buckingham's *The Rehearsal*, IV, ii, 58–60.

III, i

7 *loosen'd.* The context suggests that Dryden was using this word ambiguously by playing on a secondary meaning of loosening an animal for the purpose of procreating. Cf. Dryden's translation of Virgil's description of spring, *Georgics*, II, 438–450.

16 *stiff with age.* Maximin, who was sixty-five at this time, was sometimes upbraided for acting like a young man in his wrestling and military activities. See Julius Capitolinus, "The Two Maximini," in *Scriptores Historiae Augustae* (Loeb trans.), II, 325 (vi).

42 *a happiness so mean.* The Stoics were related to the Cynics both in despising any kind of material comfort or position as a means of happiness and in believing that the only true evil lay in the failure of virtue. Placidius is not wrong in referring to the Stoics, but Saint Catherine voices an attitude shared by Stoicism and Christianity. In a similar passage advising that "the shortest way to be rich is not by enlarging our estates, but by contracting our desires," Dryden's contemporary, Tillotson, immediately refers to the Stoic Seneca as his authority. See Stanley, II, pt. viii, p. 67; Tillotson, *Works*, p. 54; Seneca, *Epistolae Morales* (Loeb trans.), II, 409.

52 *the tenth wave.* Ovid (*Tristia*, I, ii, 49–50) writes of "a wave that o'er tops them all—the wave after the ninth and before the eleventh." In his notes to Sir Thomas Browne's confutation of this superstition, Simon Wilkin shows that it persisted as a belief among sailors at least as late as 1835 (see Browne, *Works*, ed. Simon Wilkin [1835], III, 355–357).

53 *silent joy.* Catherine echoes the beginning passage of the second book of Lucretius, *De Rerum Natura*, which Dryden later translated (see *Works*, III, 46):

> Tis pleasant, safely to behold from shore
> The rowling Ship; and hear the Tempest roar:
> Not that anothers pain is our delight;
> But pains unfelt produce the pleasing sight.

Sensing the Epicurean drift of Placidius' arguments, Catherine turns his own weapons against him. Interestingly enough, this passage from Lucretius was a key passage in contemporary theories of tragedy (see Baxter Hathaway, "The Lucretian Return upon Ourselves in Eighteenth-Century Theories of Tragedy," *PMLA*, LXII [1947], 672–689).

64 *If happiness . . . be rest.* Placidius advances some Epicurean doc-
trines in an erroneous belief that they were similar to Christian doctrine.
According to Aquinas (*Summa Contra Gentiles,* III, xxv, xxxvii; *Summa
Theologica,* I, xxv, i), true happiness consists in an intellectual contemplation of God, but Aquinas means an active contemplation in imitation
of God, whom he conceives of as a continually active principle. In his
picture of the happiness to be experienced in heaven, Tillotson (*Works,*
p. 93) rejects the idea of rest: "Not that I imagine the happiness of
Heaven to consist in a perpetual gazing upon God, and in an idle
contemplation of the glories of that place. For as by that blessed sight
we shall be infinitely transported, so the Scripture tells us we shall be
also transform'd into the image of the divine perfections; we *shall see
God, and we shall be like him,* and what greater happiness can there
be than to be like the happiest and most perfect Being in the world?
Besides, who can tell what employment God may have for us in the
next life?"

Just as Catherine combated the Stoic position of Apollonius, Dryden
now has her refute the Epicurean idea. Epicurus argued (*Epicurus's
Morals,* trans. Walter Charleton [1656], pp. 116–117): "Gods, in truth,
there are; for the knowledge of them is evident, as we have elsewhere
declared: but, they are not such as men commonly conceive and describe
them to be. For, when they have described them to be Immortal and
Blissful, they contradict themselves, by affixing other Repugnant Attributes
upon them; as that they are alwaies taken up with business themselves,
. . . at the good or bad Actions of men; that they are delighted with
human adoration and sacrifices, *etc.* all which presuppose great Disquiet,
Imbecility, Fear, and the want of external assistance." And Lucretius
held (*De Rerum Natura* [Loeb trans.], II, 646–651) that "the very nature
of divinity must necessarily enjoy immortal life in the deepest peace, far
removed and separated from our troubles; for without any pain, without
danger, itself mighty by its own resources, needing us not at all, it is
neither propitiated with services nor touched by wrath." Probably the
most complete statement of this image of a god above the strife of
human life appears in Cicero (*De Natura Deorum,* trans. in Stanley, III,
v, 148), who insists that "God doth nothing, he is not intangled in any
employments, he undertakes no works, but joyeth in his own wisdome
and vertue. He knowes for certain, that he shall ever be in pleasures,
both greatest and eternall. This God we justly style Blessed, who our
selves place a blessed life in security of mind, and in disengagement from
all businesse; but not, such as others describe him, laborious, involved in
great and troublesome employments."

69 *A casual world.* Thomas Stanley summarizes the Epicurean position on the creation of the world (III, pt. v, pp. 145, 171). The universe
is infinite, and the world was not created out of nothing; since God
would have no reason for creating a world such as ours, it must have
been made by either nature or chance:

> By nature; for such is the nature of the Atoms, running
> through the immensity of the Universe, that in great
> abundance running against one another . . . and, vari-

ously commixing themselves, first roll up a great kind
of Chaos, in manner of a great Vortex, (clue or bottom)
and then after many convolutions, . . . trying all kinds
of motions and conjunctions, they came at last into that
forme which this world beares.

By chance; for the Atoms concurrre, cohere, and are
co-apted, not by any designes, but as chance led them.
Wherefore, as I said, Chance is not such a Cause, as
directly, and of it selfe, tends to mingle the Atoms and
dispose them to such an effect; but the very Atoms
themselves are called chance, in as much as meeting one
another, without any premeditation, they fasten on one
another, and make up such a compound, as chanceth
thence to result.

Lucretius contended that the world was far too faulty to be considered as
the product of a deity and argued (II, 1058) for an analogy with the
operation of chance in nature: "This world was made by nature, even
as the seeds themselves of their own accord knocking together and
collected in all sorts of ways, heedless, without aim, without intention,
have allowed some to filter through which suddenly thrown together
could become in each case the beginnings of mighty things, of earth and
sea and sky and the generation of living creatures."

70 *order in each chance we see.* In accepting the idea of "chance,"
Dryden has Saint Catherine advance a doctrine best stated by Aquinas,
who argued that certain effects under the law of secondary causes might
be regarded as effects of chance even though they are ultimately connected with the final will of God. Aquinas is less deterministic than
Augustine in his emphasis upon what Dryden calls God's "workmanship"
rather than His control. In associating such passages with the influence
of Hobbes, Mildred E. Hartsock fails to realize that the chain of causes
was part of traditional Christian doctrine as well as a tenet of Hobbesian
determinism. See Aquinas, *Summa Theologica,* I, ciii, i; I, cxvi, iv;
Hartsock, "Dryden's Plays: A Study in Ideas," *Seventeenth Century
Studies,* 2d ser. (1937), pp. 107–109.

87 *my anger did from Love proceed.* Maximin suggests that his anger
and love are the same passion, an idea much in keeping with Descartes's
attack on the theory of a division between concupiscible and irascible
appetites. Thus Descartes finds that desire is a passion without a contrary: "Me thinkes, it is still the same motion which enclines to the
seeking after good, and withall, to the avoyding evil, which is contrary
to it, I onely observe this difference, that the desire he hath, when he
tends towards some good, is accompanied with Love and afterwards with
Hope, and Joy: whereas the same Desire, when he tends to the avoyding
an evil contrary to this good, is attended with Hatred, Fear, and Sorrow:
which is the reason why it is conceived contrary to it self. But if it be
considered when it relates equally at the same time to a good sought
after, and an opposite evill to shunne it, it may be clearly perceived but
one Passion onely which causeth both the one and the other" (*The*

Passions of the Soule [1650], p. 69; see also pp. 46, 53). For other interpretations of the interchangeability of love and hatred in Dryden's plays, see Thomas H. Fujimura, "The Appeal of Dryden's Heroic Plays," *PMLA*, LXXV (1960), 42–43; and Hartsock, "Dryden's Plays," p. 125.

177 *threw their Rings.* Dryden was thinking of the story told by Livy about the daughter of Spurius Tarpeius, who betrayed the Roman citadel to the Sabines (not the Gauls) in return for what they wore on their left arms (gold bracelets). Instead of or along with the bracelets, the Sabines threw their shields, also worn on their left arms, and crushed her to death (see Livy, I, xi).

224 *constancy it self rewards my Love.* This is almost the précieuse-platonic love equivalent of Apollonius' "Vertue, as its own reward." The platonic lover was supposed to be above jealousy, and Alvaro, a character in Davenant's *Love and Honour*, states his satisfaction at the discovery that two men are in love with Melora, the woman he loves (*Dramatic Works*, ed. James Maidment and W. H. Logan [Edinburgh, 1872–1874], III, 169):

> And why should ladies, then, that imitate
> The upper beauty most to mortal view,
> Be barr'd a numerous address? or we
> Envy each other's lawful though ambitious aim?

See also Kathleen Lynch, *The Social Mode of Restoration Comedy* (1926), pp. 44–78.

306 *like Jews upon their Sabbath, fall.* Josephus claims that Pompey saved much labor by attacking Jerusalem on the sabbath when "the Jews, from religious scruples, refrain from all manual work, and then proceeded to raise the earthworks, while forbidding his troops to engage in hostilities; for on the sabbaths the Jews fight only in self-defence" (Josephus, *The Jewish War* [Loeb trans.], II, 66–69 [I, 146–147]).

312 *My earthy part* etc. One of the longest sections of *Tyrannick Love* parodied in *The Rehearsal* (IV, i):

> Since Death my earthly Part will thus remove,
> I'll come a Humble-Bee to your chaste Love:
> With silent Wings I'll follow you, dear Couz;
> Or else, before you, in the Sun-beams, buz.
> And when to melancholy Groves you come,
> An airy Ghost, you'll know me by my Hum;
> For Sound, being Air, a Ghost does well become.
> *Smith. (After a Pause.)* Admirable.
> *Bayes.* At night, into your Bosom I will creep,
> And buz but softly, if you chance to sleep:
> Yet in your Dreams I will pass sweeping by,
> And then both hum and buz before your Eye.
> *Johns.* By my troth that's a very great Promise.
> *Smith.* Yes, and a most extraordinary Comfort to boot.
> *Bayes.* Your bed of Love from Dangers I will free;
> But most from Love of any future Bee.
> And when with Pity your Heart-Strings shall crack,

With empty Arms I'll bear you on my Back.
Smith. A pick-a-pack, a pick-a-pack.
Bayes. Ay, I'gad, but is not that *tuant* now, ha? Is it not *tuant?*
Here's the end.
Then at your Birth of Immortality,
Like any winged Archer hence I'll fly,
And teach you your first flutt'ring in the Sky.

After Johnson gives his ironic praise of the speech, Bayes replies: "Yes, I think, for a dead Person, it is a good way enough of making love: for being divested of her terrestrial Part, and all that, she is only capable of these little, pretty, amorous Designs that are innocent, and yet passionate."

Although there is no question that Buckingham and his friends were attacking Dryden, they may have intended also to satirize very similar speeches in the plays of Dryden's contemporaries. Cowley has his heroine, Lucia (*Cutter of Coleman-Street,* IV, ii), imagine herself as a ghost protecting her lover:

. . . when I'm dead,
My busie Soul shall flutter still about him,
'Twill not be else in Heaven; it shall watch
Over his sleeps, and drive away all dreams
That come not with a soft and downy wing;
If any dangers threaten, it shall becken
And call his spirit away, till they be past,
And be more diligent than his Guardian Angel;
And when just Heaven, as I'm assur'd it will,
Shall clear my Honor and my Innocence,
He'l sight, I know, and pity my misfortunes,
And weep upon my Grave
For my wrong'd Virtue, and mistaken Truth,
And unjust Death; I ask no more.

In 1663 Katherine Philips added to her translation of Corneille's *Pompée* a genuine ghost singing a song very much in the manner of Cowley. And the Duke of Newcastle (*The Humorous Lovers,* IV, i) has a man threaten to return as a ghost:

At Courfew time, and at the dead of night
I will appear, thy conscious soul to fright,
Make signs, and beckon thee my Ghost to follow
To sadder Groves, and Church-yards, where we'l hollow.

All these writers were drawing upon legends about amorous ghosts which were common in occult literature (cf. Agrippa, p. 483) and ballads (see, for example, "The Unquiet Grave" and "Sweet William's Ghost" in *A Collection of Ballads,* ed. Frances Child [1886], II, ii, 226–238). In giving his ghost very human traits of love and jealousy, Dryden could have called upon no less an authority than Joseph Glanvill, who in 1668 argued that apparitions, such as that of Samuel raised by the witch of Endor, might very likely be the souls of departed men rather than angels, since those "happy departed souls . . . are nearer allyed to our Natures" (*A Blow at Modern Sadducism* [1668], p. 77). In 1681 Glanvill was even more emphatic, arguing that the souls of the dead were "like unto Angels, and they are as proper at least for the service of Men. They have the same nature and affections. They feel our infirmities, and consider us more than abstract Spirits do. . . . Souls departed have Life and Sense and Motion, capacity of being employed, and no doubt inclination to it; and whether more properly may they be sent, than to those of their own nature, whom they affect, are allied to, and so lately come from?" (*Sadducismus Triumphatus* [1681], Pt. II, pp. 73–74).

IV, i

S.d. Indian Cave. "No doubt the scene which had already been used for Ismeron in *The Indian Queen*, III, and for the incantation scene in *The Indian Emperor*, II, i, 'the Magician's Cave' " (Summers, II, 527). Directions in a prompt copy at the Folger Library suggest that the cave was represented by a black curtain, but this usage prevailed after fire had destroyed the Theatre Royal in Bridges Street on 25 January 1671/2 and with it all the original sets to *Tyrannick Love* (see Henry Hitch Adams, "A Prompt Copy of Dryden's *Tyrannic Love*," SB, IV [1951–52], 170–174).

9 *and they on Will.* Dryden has the pagan Nigrinus regard "will" as caprice. Hobbes (*English Works*, III, 48–49) objected to the idea that will was a servant of reason: "In deliberation, the last appetite, or aversion, immediately adhering to the action, or to the omission thereof, is that wee call the WILL; the act, not the faculty, of willing. . . . The definition of the will, given commonly by the Schools, that it is a rational appetite, is not good. For if it were, then could there be no voluntary act against reason. For a voluntary act is that, which proceedeth from the will, and no other. . . . Will therefore is the last appetite in deliberating." For a traditional interpretation of will see Peter de la Primaudaye, *The French Academie* (1605), Pt. II, pp. 203–208.

15 *Astral forms.* Dryden is relying here mainly on the account given in the anonymous "A Discourse concerning the Nature and Substance of Devils and Spirits" appended to the third edition of Reginald Scot's *The Discovery of Witchcraft* (1665). The author, sometimes called "Anti-Scot" for his opposition to the skepticism of the original, distinguishes these elemental beings, which are part of the "outward World" and are subject to beginning and dissolution and also to the commands of conjurors, from both the infernal spirits and the angels (p. 41): "But to speak more nearly unto their natures, they are of the source of the Stars, and have their degrees of continuance, where of some live hundreds, some thousands of years: Their food is the Gas of the Water, and the Blas of the Air: And in their Aspects, or countenances, they differ as to vigour and cheerfulness: They occupy various places of this world; as Woods, Mountains, Waters, Air, fiery Flames, Clouds, Starrs, Mines, and hid Treasures. . . . They are capable of hunger, grief, passion, and vexation: they have not any thing in them that should bring them unto God: being meerly composed of the most spiritual part of the Elements: And

when they are worn out, they return into their proper essence or primary quality again." On Dryden's indebtedness to "Anti-Scot" see Maximillian E. Novak, "The Demonology of Dryden's *Tyrannick Love* and 'Anti-Scot,'" *ELN*, IV (1966), 95–98.

16 *purest Atoms of the Air*. The Abbé N. de Montfaçon de Villars, whose fanciful work, *Comte de Gabalis*, was published shortly after the performance of Dryden's play, uses this phrase to describe the sylphs only, the other elemental beings—salamanders, nymphs, and gnomes— being composed of the purest elements of fire, water, and earth, respectively (*Gabalis*, p. 47). For the possibility that Villars' work may have existed in some form by 1668, see René-Louis Doyon, ed., *Le Comte de Gabalis* (1921), p. ix.

18 *subservient to bad Spirits will*. Villars states that the sylphs are devout and desire to mate with men and women to gain immortality, but that the gnomes are easily terrified by the devils who use them to attack man (see *Gabalis*, pp. 39, 179; see also Paracelsus, pp. 228–239).

20 *eighty Legions*. Speaking of the elemental spirits, Agrippa (p. 393) quotes "the opinion of the Platonists" that "there are so many Legions, as there are Stars in the Heaven, and so many spirits in every Legion, as in heaven it self Stars, but there are (as Athanasius delivereth) who think that the true number of the good spirits, is according to the number of men, ninety nine parts, according to the parable of the hundred sheep; others think only nine parts, according to the parable of the ten groats; others suppose the number of the Angels equal with men. . . ." Scot (pp. 233–238) lists the various devils and their legions and states that each legion is composed of 6,666 devils.

22 *Nakar . . . Damilcar*. These names are adapted from "Anti-Scot's" account of the relation between "Nagar the Indian" and his good demon or genius, Damilkar. Since resort to Indian manuscripts was a common device in hermetic and occult writings, there is not necessarily a genuine source for the account of how Damilkar appears to warn Nagar of a dangerous troop of devils who might attack him on a trip through the air, then entertains him in the form of a beautiful virgin, and finally carries him to a mystical contemplation of God (see "Anti-Scot," p. 42; Novak, "Demonology of Dryden's *Tyrannick Love*," pp. 95–98).

23 *In Aery Chariots*. Villars (*Gabalis*, pp. 189, 191) speaks of the "aerial ships" of the elemental spirits, and Dryden must have been aware of the debate going on concerning visions of armies in the air. Jacques Gaffarel (*Unheard-of Curiosities*, trans. Edmund Chilmead [1650], pp. 343–348), considering the reality of the figures seen in the air during battle in 2 Maccabees, x, concluded that they were part of the "wonderful workes of God." His conclusions were attacked by John Spencer in *A Discourse concerning Prodigies* (1665, p. 213): "The running to and fro of Horsemen and armed Companies may be represented to an active Fancy by the Clouds of differing colors carried by the uncertain force of the Winds to very unequal figures. The stands of Pikes and Spears may possibly be but the ragged and deformed protuberances of the disturbed Clouds. Onely I am apt to believe the representations of these things

are in themselves so rude, that men are forc'd much to quicken the deadness of the Types by the fictions of Imagination. . . ."

25 *in Love have pow'r.* Villars (*Gabalis,* p. 39) depicts the spirits as far superior to human mates. The Comte de Gabalis tells him that theirs is a purer kind of love with none of the "revulsion" that follows love on earth.

28 *'Tis Venus hour.* Seven is the number associated with Venus (see Agrippa, p. 243).

29 *With Chalk I first describe a Circle.* Reginald Scot (pp. 215–216) notes that a circle made for the purpose of calling upon elemental beings differs from a circle for calling evil spirits. Both circles are to be drawn during a storm or during "the brightest Moon-light," but for evil spirits the circle should be drawn in black and should have holy names and triangles or crosses between an inner and an outer circle. For elemental spirits the circle is to be drawn in chalk, and the magical talisman of the element to which the spirit belongs should be substituted for the crosses and triangles. In both instances the circle acts as a protection against the spirits, and Nigrinus is right in urging Placidius to enter the circle before they arrive.

33 *to Venus, just.* "For Venus," writes Agrippa (p. 88), "take Musk, Ambergryse, Lignum-aloes, red Roses, and red Corall, and make them up with the brain of Sparrows, and the blood of Pigeons."

42+ *s.d. Nakar and Damilcar descend . . . and sing.* This lyric section of *Tyrannick Love* was parodied mercilessly in *The Rehearsal* (V, i), where elemental spirits are replaced by the two kings of Brentford, who sing mainly about food. The main inspiration for what Buckingham and his collaborators called "the tune and style of our modern spirits" was probably the following fanciful passage from "Anti-Scot" (p. 50): "Innumerable are the Spirits that inhabit the Aiery Region, germinating amongst themselves as Magicians affirm, and begetting one another after a Mystical manner. It is their property to be instant in storms and boistrous weather, which is said to be joy and delight unto them; And in such a season they may with most facility be calld upon, and make their appearance, which they do accordingly to their age, and youthfulness, seeming young or old at their appearance answerable to their years. Besides they march in mighty Troops through the Aiery Region, waging warr amongst themselves, and destroying one anothers beings or Existences, after which they are reduced to the primary source or nature of the Starrs."

55 *Gelly of Love.* In a list of some of the wild notions of astrologers made by Henry More in 1656 was the idea that "the Starres eat and are nourished, and therefore must ease themselves, and that those falling Starres, as some call them, which are found on the earth in the form of a trembling gelly are their excrement." The material thought to be the remains of a star was, according to the *OED,* "the alga *Nostoc,* which appears as a jelly-like mass on dry soil after rain." See Henry More, *Enthusiasmus Triumphatus* (1656), p. 45.

57 *The Spirits of Fire.* Paracelsus (pp. 235–240) pictures these "sala-

manders" or "vulcans" as "long, narrow and lean" spirits who never enter into marriage with human beings but who frequently serve them as agents of the devil. "Anti-Scot" (pp. 54–55) describes their playful "tumbling, and fooling one with another when the flames are most impetuous, and violent in the Mountains," but he warns against those who believe the spirits do good by punishing evil men, arguing that they are wholly under the control of infernal spirits for "such is their innate Affinity, and Unity with the dark World, or infernal Kingdome that they do often become the Devils Agents to propagate his works upon the face of the Earth." Villars, on the other hand, insists that the salamanders are beautiful and pure, capable of mating with human beings and of achieving immortality (*Gabalis*, pp. 31–33, 109–111).

62 *The wind is for us.* Dryden's description of the spirits struggling against the wind bears some resemblance to Robert Fludd's account of the innumerable good and bad spirits who struggle to control the winds: "By reason of these spirits of a contrary fortitude in the aire, sometimes good and propitious events befall the creatures of this lower world, namely when the good spirits raigne, and wholsome winds do blow, which happen, when the benign starrs and Planets have dominion in heaven, and consequently their influences below; and again, sometimes bad and dysastrous accidents, armed with privative and destructive effects, befall the creatures of this Elementary region, by reason of severe emissions of beams from the winds, which animate those evill spirits, that in infinite multitudes do hover, though invisible, in the aire; who are rejoyced and revived at the blasts which issue from the stations of their cruell Princes, and are as it were summons and all-arms to stir and excite them unto wrath, and to blow the coles of their sleeping malice" (*Mosaicall Philosophy* [1659], p. 189).

64 *leaves in the Autumn.* Perhaps an echo of Virgil's *Aeneid*, VI, 309–310, rather than of Milton's *Paradise Lost*, I, 302. For similar images from Homer, Dante, and Tasso, see Henry Todd, ed., *Milton's Poetical Works* (2d ed.; 1809), II, 319–320.

81 *North quarter.* In Scot's directions (pp. 249–250) for binding a spirit in a crystal stone, the spirits are supposed to come from the north. They kneel before five small circles in the north section of a large square which encloses the larger circle in which the magician stands.

82 *Sev'n foot around.* "Anti-Scot," in discussing the costume and instruments of conjurers (p. 72), notes that "the Circles by which they defend themselves are commonly nine foot in breadth, but the Eastern Magicians give but seven."

84 *thy thousand years.* Jean Bodin (*De la Démonomanie des Sorciers* [Paris, 1581], p. 3) allows the elemental spirits this span of life. Villars (*Gabalis*, p. 31) speculates that they live for two hundred years; "Anti-Scot" (p. 41), that "some live hundreds, some thousands of years."

89 *Astral source.* "But to speak more nearly unto their natures, they are of the source of the Stars . . ." ("Anti-Scot," p. 41).

90 *Gemory.* Scot (p. 236) includes Gemory in his list of devils and

spirits: "Gemory, a strong and mighty Duke, he appeareth like a fair woman, with a Dutchess crownet about her middle, riding on a Camel; he answereth well and truly of things present, past and to come, and of treasure hid, and where it lyeth; he procureth the love of women, especially of maids, hath Twenty six Legions."

122+ *s.d. A Scene of a Paradise.* The scene painted by Isaac Fuller for the King's Company (see Appendix, p. 539, below).

143 *Spring-tides.* For a contemporary discussion of spring tides, see *Philosophical Transactions of the Royal Society,* no. 16 (1666), pp. 276–277, 282–283.

163 *the task assign'd you.* The idea that the fairies controlled the weather was part of English folklore, and Dryden may be recalling Shakespeare's Oberon and Titania, whose quarrels caused such strange and violent weather. Thomas Heywood, arguing more seriously for the same idea (*The Hierarchie of the Blessed Angels* [1635], p. 505), saw these creatures as servants of God who were capable of being subverted by magicians:

> Spirits of th'Aire are bold, proud, and ambitious,
> Envious tow'rd Mankinde, Spleenful, and malicious:
> And these (by Gods permission) not alone
> Have the cleare subtill aire to worke vpon,
> By causing thunders and tempestuous show'rs,
> With harmefull windes: 'tis also in their pow'rs
> T'affright the earth with strange prodigious things,
> And what's our hurt, to them great pleasure brings.

178 *Changlings and Fooles of Heav'n.* "Besides, it is credibly affirmed and believed by many," writes "Anti-Scot" in his discussion of the terrestrial spirits (p. 51), "That such as are real Changlings, or Lunaticks, have been brought by such Spirits and Hobgoblins, the true Child being taken away by them in the place whereof such are left, being commonly half out of their wits, and given to many Antick practices, and extravagant fancies. . . . Such jocund and facetious Spirits are sayd to sport themselves in the night by tumbling and fooling with Servants and Shepherds in Country houses, pinching them black and blew. . . ."

180 *Gross-heavy-fed.* Paracelsus (p. 228) insists that since these spirits have bodies, they must eat, and "Anti-Scot" (pp. 50–53) lists their preferences. By threatening to feed Damilcar, an aerial spirit delighting in "the choisest Daynties" with the *damps of Earth* (l. 186), Amariel suggests a diet destructive to his elemental nature.

180 *next man in ignorance.* Paracelsus (pp. 226–229) ranks the elemental beings below man because they lack an immortal soul; but he holds, as does Villars, that they are both more beautiful and more intelligent than human beings.

211 *Possess her Love.* Maximin is repeating the words of Damilcar as whispered to him by Placidius.

270 *their Parents int'rest.* Maximin seems to strike a pose toward his children with which few writers but Hobbes would have agreed. Hobbes

(*English Works,* III, 186–188) bases his theory of sovereignty of parent over child not on generation but on an implicit consent. The child owes absolute obedience to his parent for having preserved his life.

288 *obnoxious.* Used in the rare sense (*OED* 3) of "subject to" or "answerable to."

298 *Free will's a cheat.* Mildred Hartsock ("Dryden's Plays," p. 113) suggests that this notion is "characteristically Hobbist in tone," but it was standard psychology for a tyrant. For a similar speech from the mouth of a tyrant, see Scudéry's *L'Amour Tyrannique* (III, i), where Tiridate holds forth in the same manner as Maximin:

> Il n'est pas d'autre Loy, que le vouloir des Rois:
> C'est de nous qu'elle vient, tous puissant que nous sommes;
> C'est nous qui sommes Dieux, qui la donnons aux hommes;
> Mais bien que les mortels la doivent respecter,
> Celuy qui fait un joug, ne le dois pas porter.

303 *Spirit of the World.* Stanley (II, v, 73) associated this concept with Platonic doctrine, though it is part of Stoic philosophy as well: ". . . it is manifest, that the World was endued by God, both with a Soul and mind. For, intending it to be the best, he must have made it animate and intelligent, since an animate thing is more excellent then an inanimate, and an intelligent then an unintelligent; perhaps the mind also could not subsist without a Soul. This Soul being diffused from the Center of the world to the extreams comprehendeth the whole body of the World, so as it is extended throughout the Universe, and in that manner joyneth and conserveth the whole." Robert Fludd (*Mosaicall Philosophy,* pp. 145–146) relates such a spirit to Virgil's famous passage on the spirit that is infused through all matter.

313–351 This exchange between Maximin and Porphyrius, added in a cancel to some copies of the first edition, was retained thereafter. Perhaps it was a passage that had been cut for performance but reinserted in the published version.

326 *Lapwing-like.* A proverb: "The Lapwing cries most when farthest from her nest" (Tilley, L68).

372 *Prætorian Bands.* The Praetorians were much more than the emperor's private guard; they were often the determining force in choosing the emperor. In rebelling against Maximin, the citizens of Rome attacked the Praetorians encamped outside the city, and they, in turn, burned a large part of Rome. Refusing to accept Balbinus and Maximus, the choices of the Senate, as successors to Maximin, the Praetorians asserted their *Arbitrary pow'r* (l. 373) by murdering the two emperors (see Herodian, pp. 194, 212–213).

377 *no man can resist.* Mildred Hartsock ("Dryden's Plays," pp. 99–110) argues that this concept of the passions owes much to Hobbes's theory of shifting passions and his tendency to see man as being at the mercy of his appetites (Hobbes, *English Works,* III, 49, 277), but such a doctrine was a basic tenet of the libertines (see Théophile de Viau, "Satyre Première," in *Les Libertins au XVIIᵉ Siècle,* ed. Antoine Adam [1964], p. 60).

381 *An Eagle mounting.* See Dio Cassius' description of the releasing of an eagle at the funeral of Augustus; the bird was supposed to carry the soul to heaven (*Roman History*, LVI, 42, iii). For a Christian attack on the pride that lay behind such a ceremony, cf. George Hakewill, *An Apologie or Declaration of the Power and Providence of God* (1635), Pt. I, pp. 473–480.

384 *never are at rest.* Catherine presents the impossibility of finding happiness in worldly activity and change. Hobbes (*English Works*, IV, 33) argued that "for an utmost end, in which the ancient philosophers have placed felicity, and disputed much concerning the way therto, there is no such thing in this world, nor way to it, more than to Utopia: for while we live, we have desires, and desire presupposeth a further end. . . . Seeing all delight is appetite, and presupposeth a further end, there can be no contentment but in proceeding: and therefore we are not to marvel, when we see, that as men attain to more riches, honour, or other power; so their appetite continually groweth more and more. . . . Felicity, therefore, by which we mean continual delight, consisteth not in having prospered, but in prospering." And in excusing himself on the basis of "faults which Nature made," Maximin is obviously arguing (as might be expected) a libertine and Epicurean position (cf. Saint-Evremond, "Sur la Morale d'Epicure," in *Les Libertins au XVIIe Siècle*, pp. 229–235). Catherine's contention that true content is to be found only in Christianity may be influenced by Tillotson's sermon, "The Precepts of Christianity Not Grievous" (see King, "Dryden, Tillotson, and *Tyrannic Love*," pp. 369–371), but the arguments are as old as Christianity itself.

395 *humour his disease.* Robert Burton suggests that the cause of love may frequently be found in an excess of power, wealth, and idleness, and that the best cure lies in giving way to it (*Anatomy of Melancholy*, III, ii, 2, 1; III, ii, 5, 3; III, ii, 5, 5).

406 *Erre.* Wander or ramble (*OED*).

440 *envy.* Odium (*OED*).

472 *Now death draws near.* Summers (II, 530) suggests a comparison between this speech and that of Vallerie in the anonymous *Le Martyre de Sainte Catherine,* but the momentary fear of Berenice was traditional and there is certainly no verbal borrowing. For a similar situation, see Puget de la Serre, *Le Martyre de Sainte Caterine,* p. 55 (III, v).

516 *private interest.* This statement would probably have had political overtones for Dryden and his audience (see Grotius, *De Jure Belli ac Pacis Libri Tres,* trans. Francis Kelsey [1925], p. 138 [I, iv, 1, 3]; Hobbes, *English Works*, III, 310–311).

522 *its Being would prolong.* For a discussion of contemporary attitudes toward the rival claims of self-preservation and honor or ideals, see Maximillian E. Novak, "The Problem of Necessity in Defoe's Fiction," *PQ*, XL (1961), 513–524. See also Grotius, *De Jure Belli,* trans. Kelsey, p. 172 (II, i, 3); Hobbes, *English Works*, II, 8.

544 *Heav'ns deep.* Perhaps an echo of Job, xi, 8.

548 *Faith's necessary Rules.* Catherine's position is the same as that of

Tillotson in *The Rule of Faith,* an attack on the writings of John Sergeant
and other Catholics who argued for the superiority of the oral tradition
over Scripture. "If the Rule be plain and certain," wrote Tillotson, "the
most acute Adversary may be convinced by it, if he will; that is, if he be
not obstinate; but if he be obstinate, that is, such a one as will not be
convinced, but will persist in his Errour in despite of all evidence that
can be offered to him, then I must profess that I do not know any kind
of evidence that is apt to convince that man. . . ." Tillotson also objects
to the skepticism of his opponents in their insistence that "Reason cannot
be otherwise than a most blind and fallible guide." Like Tillotson,
Dryden repeats the word "plain," but in this regard both Dryden and
Tillotson may have been indebted to Richard Hooker: "Some things
are so familiar and plain, that truth from falsehood, and good from
evil, is most easily discerned in them, even by men of no deep capacity.
And of that nature, for the most part, are things absolutely unto all men's
salvation necessary. . . ." See Tillotson, *The Rule of Faith* (1666), pp.
57, 155; Hooker, *Of the Laws of Ecclesiastical Polity,* ed. John Keble
(1888), I, 143.

551 *Religion all Contemplative.* Perhaps an answer to Hobbes, who
regarded the proposition—"faith and sanctity are not to be attained by
study and reason, but by supernatural inspiration, or infusion"—as pernicious to the stability of the state (*English Works,* III, 311–312; see also
II, 156–157; III, 588–597).

564 *'Tis not a Crime.* "Since therefore no man is tied to impossibilities,
they who are threatened either with death (which is the greatest evil to
nature), or wounds, or some other bodily hurts, and are not stout enough
to bear them, are not obliged to endure them" (Hobbes, *English Works,*
II, 25; see also Grotius, *De Jure Belli,* trans. Kelsey, pp. 172–175 [II, i, 3–
5], 148–156 [I, iv, 7]).

568 *horrour of this deed.* Dryden may have been influenced by a similar
speech by Vallerie in *Le Martyre de Sainte Catherine* (p. 58; III, iii):

> Non, je ne prendray point cette fausee allegeance
> Qu'il ne craigne de moy, ny depit, ny vengeance;
> Bien que son changement m'afflige au dernier point,
> Il s'offence luy-mesme & ne m'offence point:
> Il n'a point fait de voeux àquoy ie ne consente,
> Qu'il vive seul coupable, Et moy seule innocente,
> Il ne commettra rien dont i'oze murmurer,
> Il peut tout entreprendre, Et moy tout endurer.

573 *Ungrateful man.* Although Porphyrius may seem to be caught
between the traditional forces of love and honor, it is important to realize
that by revolting against Maximin he would be guilty of ingratitude, a
crime that was particularly fascinating to the age. Descartes decided that
ingratitude was not a passion but a vice, and Hobbes, though listing
gratitude as the fourth law of nature, made ingratitude a violation of
the first law which impels man to seek peace. See Descartes, *Philosophical
Works,* trans. Elizabeth Haldane and G. R. T. Ross (1965), I, 418;
Hobbes, *English Works,* III, 138.

602 *none believe, because they will, but must.* "If the things which we believe be considered in themselves," wrote Richard Hooker, "it may truly be said that faith is more certain than any science. That which we know either by sense, or by infallible demonstration, is not so certain as the principles, articles, and conclusions of Christian faith. Concerning which we must note, that there is a Certainty of Evidence, and a Certainty of Adherence. Certainty of Evidence we call that, when the mind doth assent unto this or that, not because it is true in itself, but because the truth is clear, because it is manifest unto us" (*A Learned and Comfortable Sermon of the Certainty and Perpetuity of Faith in the Elect,* in *Laws of Ecclesiastical Polity,* ed. Keble, III, 470).

606 *Conscience is without the pow'r of Kings.* William Ames (*Conscience* [1639], pp. 6, 155, 158) argues that "though men are bound in Conscience by God to observe in due and just circumstances the lawes of men, yet the same lawes of men so far as they are mans lawes, doe not bind the Conscience," and that if the magistrate passes a law that violates the conscience to obey, the citizen must assume that the magistrate never meant the law to be obeyed. Richard Hooker believed such an attitude wrong and identified it with the Puritans (*Laws of Ecclesiastical Polity,* ed. Keble, I, 168; III, 457–460). Dryden does not slip into anachronism, for Porphyrius' theory of conscience is inherent in the Christian tradition, but it is apparent that he meant this debate over private conscience and regicide to have contemporary significance.

610 *the worst Weapon.* Maximin counters with an argument drawn from Hobbes's theory that only one sovereign may exist within the state. Hobbes attacked the concept that to act against one's conscience in a civil society was a sin: "For a man's conscience, and his judgment is the same thing, and as the judgment, so also the conscience may be erroneous. Therefore, though he that is subject to no civil law, sinneth in all he does against his conscience, because he has no other rule to follow but his own reason; yet it is not so with him that lives in a commonwealth; because the law is the public conscience, by which he hath already undertaken to be guided" (*English Works,* III, 310–311). He also argued that a king could not be a heretic, since "heresy is nothing else but a private opinion obstinately maintained, contrary to the opinion which the . . . representant of the commonwealth, hath commanded to be taught" (*ibid.,* p. 579).

616 *safely may release.* Porphyrius argues a position that may have been close to that of Charles II, and the conflict between king and counselor may recall that between Charles and his chief adviser, Clarendon. Charles's efforts to allow "liberty to tender consciences" were defeated by Clarendon, who felt that religous dissent and sedition were inseparable. Porphyrius argues for liberty of conscience at the expense of loss of "Civil pow'r" (l. 613). See Ogg, I, 27, 201–209; II, 516–517.

667 *adoption.* Adopted son.

669 *Old as I am.* Maximin, who was sixty-five when he was killed at Aquileia, was famous for his refusal to grow old or to act like an old man. He was supposed to have wrestled from five to seven soldiers, one after

another, in his old age, and he boasted that death was afraid to encounter him for fear of having his javelin thrown back at him (see Edward and Henry Leigh, *Analecta Caesarum Romanorum* [1664], pp. 267–270).

V, i

70 *Mine.* An image taken from the art of warfare. In a process called "sapping," mines were dug under fortifications to destroy them by removing the supports (see *A Military Dictionary* [1702], sigs. E4*v*, F7).

76 *wink.* By closing his eyes, Placidius would follow the Cartesian concept of annihilating his world by a wink, an idea inherent in the scholastic precept. Dryden may have been thinking of Tillotson's warning against beliefs that would eventually lead to Berkeley's rejection of matter and of an objective world: "For our belief or dis-belief of a thing does not alter the nature of the thing; we cannot fancy things into being, or make them vanish into nothing by the stubborn confidence of our imaginations; things are as sullen as we are, and will be what they are, what-ever we think of them; and if there be a God, a man cannot by an obstinate disbelief of him make him cease to be, any more then a man can put out the Sun by winking" (*The Wisdom of being Religious* [1664], p. 40).

141 The four lines that followed this line in the first edtion were deleted from the second edition by Dryden for obvious reasons of decorum.

157+ *s.d. Enter at one door.* "One of the permanent proscenium doors" (Summers, II, 530).

168 *Seas.* High swells and winds.

182 *witness.* Testimony for Christ or martyrdom (*OED*).

187 *a Monarch, and her Mother dye.* Dryden's introduction of Felicia and the conflict between duty to parents and duty to God appear in none of the accounts of Saint Catherine, but Dryden may have taken the hint from Georges de Scudéry's *L'Amour Tyrannique* (1639, p. 19; I, v), where the hero must face a decision that will lead to the death of his father, whose life, like Felicia's, is threatened by a tyrant.

193 *it is not you I hear.* Summers (II, 381) suggests a parallel here with Tourneur's *The Revenger's Tragedy.* Neither the passage quoted nor the play as a whole bears any resemblance to *Tyrannick Love.*

250 *Her Paps.* In Metaphrastes (*Patrologiae*, CXVI, cols. 297–298) and in medieval versions of the legend it was the Queen who was tortured in this manner. If Dryden seems to combine religion with a certain prurience and sadism, he is following a long tradition. A medieval writer described how the Emperor "commanded, in hot heart to seize her rudely; and immediately without judgment, to pierce through her nipples with iron nails, and rend them up cruelly with the breast-roots. . . . And they did so; and drew her without the gates of the city; and pulled off the paps from her breasts, by the bare bone, with iron awls" (*Life of Saint Katherine,* E.E.T.S. no. 80, pp. 105, 108).

250 *bearded Tenters.* Barbed hooks (*OED*).

251 *Gobbet.* A piece of raw flesh (*OED*).

314 *Bilbilis.* A town in Spain famous for the manufacture of iron and

steel for use in war (see Pliny, *Natural History* [Loeb trans.], IX, 233 [XXXIV, xli, 144]).

374 *Gods 'cause they have pow'r and will.* Mildred Hartsock ("Dryden's Plays," p. 137) maintains that this speech is based on Hobbes's *Leviathan*, where it is argued that the "right of nature whereby God reigneth over men, and punisheth those that break the laws, is to be derived, not from his creating them, as if he required obedience as of gratitude for his benefits; but from irresistible power. . . . To those therefore whose power is irresistible, the dominion of all men adhereth naturally by their excellence of power; and consequently it is from that power, that the kingdom over men, and the right of afflicting men at his pleasure, belongeth naturally to God Almighty; not as Creator, and gracious; but as omnipotent. And though punishment be due for sin only, because by that word is understood affliction for sin; yet the right of afflicting, is not always derived from men's sin, but from God's power." In this sense the state or "Leviathan" is a "mortal God" (see Hobbes, *English Works*, III, 345–346, 158; IV, 295). Although Dryden may owe a good deal to Hobbes, Maximin's speech is also typical of the mentality of tyrants as they appeared in English and French drama. Very similar is the thought of Tiridate in Scudéry's *L'Amour Tyrannique* (1639, p. 55; III, i), a play published more than a decade before *Leviathan* (see note to IV, i, 298, above). Scudéry's theorizing is close to that of Hobbes, and he has some of the same kind of witty logic as Dryden.

390 *Ætherial musick.* In Puget de la Serre's *Le Martyre de Sainte Caterine* (p. 75) the scene depicting the angels receiving the spirit of Saint Catherine is one of the illustrations included before each act. Saint Catherine's body was brought to Mount Sinai by the angels.

412+ *s.d.* For a discussion of the impressionistic stage technique employed at this point, see Staging, p. 488.

497+, 499+ *s.d.* Two stage directions calling for Porphyrius and Berenice to kiss their hands and blow kisses to each other were cut in the second edition. Such précieuse gestures could obviously be open to ridicule.

603+ *s.d.* The stage direction "Stabbing upward with his Dagger" in the first edition was cut in the second, probably because such a gesture, however much in keeping with Maximin's character, might appear absurd and excessive on the stage.

675 *Cypress with my Myrtle Wreath.* Symbols of death and love. Venus was called Myrtea, or goddess of myrtles.

EPILOGUE

12 *dance about your Beds at nights.* An echo of Berenice's speech near the end of the third act.

13 *taking.* Passion or excitement.

16 *Out of my Calling in a Tragedy.* In the epilogue to Sir Robert Howard's *The Duke of Lerma* (1668), Mrs. Ellen, or Nell Gwyn, is made to speak out on her preference for comedy:

We have been all ill us'd, by this days Poet.
'Tis our joynt Cause; I know you in your hearts
Hate serious Plays, as I do serious Parts,
To trouble us with Thoughts and State-designs,
A melancholly Plot ty'd with strong Lines,
I had not the least Part to day you see,
Troth, he has neither writ for you, nor me,

and Pepys put into his diary on 22 August 1667 how "infinitely displeased" he was with her in *The Indian Emperour* where she was "put to act the Emperours daughter, which is a great and serious part, which she doth most basely." On 26 December Pepys made the same objection again, but in fact, during her seven-year career, Nell Gwyn played numerous serious parts, including the role of an angel in *The Virgin Martyr*. See Wilson, pp. 146–148; *Works*, IX, p. 293 and n.

20 *Easter-Term*. If the play was acted on 24 June, Easter term had ended a month before on 24 May. In fact, Trinity term was to end in six days on 30 June.

An Evening's Love

Samuel Pepys was traveling through Somersetshire on Friday, 12 June 1668, viewing the tombs in the church at Philips-Norton, when John Dryden's new play, *An Evening's Love, or The Mock-Astrologer,* was performed before the King and Queen at the Theatre Royal on Bridges Street. This play was the first one Dryden wrote as a shareholder in the King's Company, and he had the satisfaction of seeing it performed for at least nine consecutive days.[1] Mrs. Pepys went to see it on 19 June and told her husband that "though the world commends" *An Evening's Love,* she could not. Accompanied by his wife, Pepys went to a performance on the following day and recorded in his diary his agreement with his spouse:

> Up, and talked with my wife all in good humour, and so to the office, where all the morning, and then home to dinner, and so she and I alone to the King's house, and there I saw this new play my wife saw yesterday, and do not like it, it being very smutty, and nothing so good as "The Maiden Queen," or "The Indian Emperour," of his making, that I was troubled at it; and my wife tells me wholly (which he confesses a little in the epilogue) taken out of the "Illustre Bassa."

Pepys's reaction may have been influenced to some extent by his effort to conciliate his wife, with whom he had been quarreling. Certainly his comparison of Dryden's comedy with a heroic play and a tragicomedy seems odd, and his confession of being "troubled" by his experience, as well as his objections to the play's morality, tells us more about his state of mind than about Dryden's play.

Pepys returned to the theater two days later after his wife had verified her suspicions of the play's origins by showing him Madeleine de Scudéry's *Ibrahim, ou l'Illustre Bassa.* Although remaining for only "an act or two," he thereafter found reason to trust his own taste in the confession of Dryden's publisher that the author himself did not think highly of his play. "Calling this day at Herringman's," wrote Pepys, "he tells me Dryden do himself call it but a fifth-rate play." Pepys never changed his mind. On 8 March 1669 he went to the theater again, only to confirm his judgment that *An Evening's Love* was "but an ordinary play." John Evelyn, who attended on 19 June 1668, the same day that Mrs. Pepys first saw the play, made Dryden's comedy the subject of one of his customary attacks upon the age. "To a new play, with severall of my Relations, the *Evening Lover,*" wrote Evelyn with a significant misquotation of the title, "a foolish plot, & very prophane, so as it afflicted

---

[1] Van Lennep, p. 138.

me to see how the stage was degenerated & poluted by the licentious times." [2]

In spite of these severe judgments, *An Evening's Love* retained some popularity through the Restoration and into the first quarter of the eighteenth century. It was performed in April 1705 with the notice, "Not Acted these six Years," and after revivals in 1713, 1714, and 1716 its last recorded performance came on 18 October 1717.[3] Herringman first entered *An Evening's Love* in the *Term Catalogues* for 13 February 1671, and it was published in that year with a lengthy preface.[4] The second edition appeared in 1675 and the third in 1691, dates that probably indicate revivals.[5] John Downes lists *An Evening's Love* among "both Old and Modern Plays being the Principal in their [the King's Company's] Stock." [6] Given the fragmentary nature of the records, it is difficult to determine the popularity of *An Evening's Love*, but the play was certainly successful enough to please Dryden and his company.

The initial popularity of Dryden's comedy may have had some connection with its topicality, but part of the reason for the play's success was surely the cast. The great actors, Hart and Mohun, were doubtless brilliant in their roles as English rakes on the prowl in Madrid, but the actresses must have attracted everyone's attention. Surely Nell Gwyn was perfectly cast as the witty heroine, Jacinta, and Theodosia was played first by the beautiful Mrs. Hughes and, after a year or so, by Mrs. Boutell.[7] The affected coquette Aurelia was acted by Mrs. Quin, formerly Anne Marshall,[8] and the clever servant Beatrix by the excellent singer and dancer, Mary Knep. They were among the most beautiful women of their time, and *An Evening's Love* gave them a perfect opportunity to display their talents. Pepys must have been in a bad mood indeed if he could not appreciate hearing Mrs. Knep's performance of the song beginning "Calm was the Even, and Cleer was the Skie" (IV, i, 47–70).

The sources of *An Evening's Love* have received considerable attention. Gerard Langbaine complained that though Dryden had recorded his literary debt to Thomas Corneille's *Le Feint Astrologue*, he had neglected to mention his plagiarisms from

Molliere's *Depit amoreux*, and his *Les Precieuses Ridi-*

---

[2] *Evelyn, Diary*, III, 510–511.

[3] Van Lennep, pp. 158,. 347, 353; *The London Stage, 1660–1800*, Pt. II: 1700–1729, ed. Emmett L. Avery (1960), Vol. I, pp. 92, 95, 103, 114, 309, 310, 314, 404; Vol. II, p. 465.

[4] *Term Catalogues*, I, 66. Herringman had previously entered the play in the *Stationers' Register* on 20 November 1668.

[5] See Textual Notes, pp. 514–515. See also Van Lennep, pp. 187, 220, 316, 386, who erroneously lists an edition of 1672.

[6] Downes, pp. 7, 15. Downes made the mistake of listing *An Evening's Love* among the older plays.

[7] *Ibid.*, p. 8. Downes lists Mrs. Hughes in the role though the cast printed with the edition of 1671 lists Mrs. Boutell. This change is similar to the substitution of Mrs. Boutell for Mrs. Hughes in *Tyrannick Love*.

[8] See Wilson, pp. 168–170.

cules; and Quinault's *L'Amant Indiscreet:* not to mention little Hints borrow'd from Shakespear, Petronius Arbiter &c. The main Plot of this Play is built on that of Corneille's, or rather Calderon's Play call'd *El Astrologo fingido,* which Story is likewise copied by M. Scudery in his Romance call'd *Ibrahim,* or the Illustrious *Bassa* in the Story of the French Marquess. Aurelia's affectation in her Speech p. 31. is borrow'd from Molliere's *Les Precieuses Ridicules.* The Scene between Alonzo and Lopez p. 39. is translated from Molliere's *Depit amoreux,* Act 2. Sc. 6. Camilla's begging a new Gown of Don Melchor p. 61. from the same. Act 1. Sc. 2. The Love Quarrel between Wild-blood, Jacinta; Mascal and Beatrix; Act 4. Sc. the last: is copied from the same Play, Act 4. Sc. 3, and 4. The Scene of Wild-blood, Jacinta, &c. being discover'd by Aurelia's falling into Alonzo's Arms, p. 73. Etc. is borrow'd from Quinault's *L'Amant Indiscreet,* Act 5. Sc. 4.[9]

As if these sources were not sufficient, later critics have been eager to discover new ones, among them three other plays by Molière—*L'Étourdi, Le Tartuffe,* and *Dom Juan*—as well as Ben Jonson's *Epicoene.*[10] Indeed, one scholar, who regarded Langbaine's remark about the borrowings from Shakespeare and Petronius as "plagiary-hunting run stark wood," himself added to Langbaine's list by the tentative suggestion that Dryden took some hints from Antoine Le Métel's (d'Ouville's) *Jodelet Astrologue,* and from Plautus' *The Pot of Gold.*[11] It has further been claimed that "Dryden's pillage of the French theatre" extended to Molière's *Le Misanthrope.*[12]

One other possible source might be added to the list. The flirtation scene that takes place in the temple in Madeleine de Scudéry's *Le Grand Cyrus* is similar to the scene in Dryden's play where Wildblood makes advances to Jacinta in the church.[13] But these scenes, like others in many of the supposed sources, are merely analogues, and there is no evidence that Dryden actually had them in mind when he wrote. They tell us what we already know—that, as a writer, Dryden was a man of his time.

One major assessment of the claims about Dryden's sources dismisses

---

[9] *An Account of the English Dramatick Poets* (Oxford, 1691), pp. 163–164.

[10] See J. E. Gillet, "Molière en Angleterre," *Mémoires,* Académie Royale de Belgique, Classe des Lettres, 2d ser., IX (1913), 88–89. André de Mandach, who accepts Gillet's statements, calls *An Evening's Love* a "véritable mosaïque de plagiats" (*Molière et la Comédie de Mœurs en Angleterre (1600–68)* [1946], p. 86).

[11] Summers, II, 233–235.

[12] M. J. O'Regan, "Two Notes on French Reminiscences in Restoration Comedy," *Hermathena,* XCIII (1959), 63–66.

[13] *Artamenes; or Cyrus the Great,* trans. F. G. (1653–1655), Pt. IX, Bk. III, pp. 137–138. For Dryden's borrowings from this section of Scudéry's romance for his play *Secret Love* see Allen, pp. 82–86. See also *Works,* IX, 338–340.

the contention that Dryden borrowed from Shakespeare's Beatrice and Benedick in *Much Ado About Nothing*, says nothing about any plays by Molière except *Le Dépit Amoureux, Les Précieuses Ridicules,* and *L'École des Maris,* and argues that "it is evident that the likeness between Mlle de Scudéry's story [in *Ibrahim*] and Dryden's play results from the fact that she used Calderón, while Dryden used Corneille's play, which was also imitated from Calderón." [14] An even more skeptical appraisal dismisses any influence of *L'École des Maris* on *An Evening's Love* and attempts to limit Dryden's major debt to Thomas Corneille's *Le Feint Astrologue* to two plays by Molière and to one by Quinault.[15] Nevertheless, in view of the way in which Dryden and Newcastle apparently drew upon both Quinault and Molière for *Sir Martin Mar-all,*[16] it may be possible to assume, as a working principle, that Dryden used whatever materials he could find. There is no reason to believe that he was unaware of either Calderón's or Le Métel's account of the story, and it is certain that he knew and used the novella that Mlle de Scudéry inserted in her *Ibrahim*.

Because Mrs. Pepys's assertion concerning Dryden's debt to Scudéry has been questioned, and because Dryden's borrowing reveals his familiarity with a variety of sources, it is important to demonstrate his use of *Ibrahim*. The most obvious evidence is in the names, which vary considerably from version to version: Calderón calls the lady who is being deceived by the lover Violante, and her maid Beatriz; in Le Métel she is Jacinte and her maid is Jule; in Corneille she is Leonora and her maid is Jacinth. Only in Scudéry are the two women called Aurelia and Camilla, the names they have in *An Evening's Love*. This could be a coincidence, of course, but there is also some direct verbal borrowing. For example, Dryden transfers to his play a phrase from the note written by Scudéry's Aurelia in order to conjure up the spirit of her absent lover. In the English translation of Scudéry's *Ibrahim*, Hortensio, entering the garden to see Aurelia, echoes her note which had contained the statement, "Although you goe in the night like an Angel of darkness, yet pass you with me for an Angel of light." At this point Scudéry tells us that although Hortensio "was come thither onely to appease her, he said unto her that at last this Angell of darkness was come by conjurations to see an Angell of light." Dryden changes Aurelia's note to a direct statement of passion, but his Don Melchor enters the garden announcing, "This Spirit of darkness is come to see an Angel of light by her command; and to assure her of his constancy, that he will be hers eternally." [17] This

---

[14] Allen, pp. 154–162. Thomas Corneille himself used a variety of sources, including Scudéry's *Ibrahim* (Arpad Steiner, "Calderón's *Astrólogo Fingido* in France," *MP*, XXIV [1926], 27–30).

[15] See John Wilcox, *The Relation of Molière to Restoration Comedy* (1938), pp. 109–112.

[16] *Ibid.*; see also *Works*, IX, 364–367.

[17] See *Ibrahim, or the Illustrious Bassa*, trans. Henry Cogan (1652), Pt. II, Bk. II, pp. 32, 35. Cf. *Ibrahim, ou l'Illustre Bassa* (Paris, 1723), II, 107, 116 (I, vii).

direct transfer of a key phrase reveals not only that Dryden was using Scudéry's romance, but that he was using the English translation, for there is nothing comparable in the French.

Before looking at Dryden's use of other French sources, we should consider the possibility that he borrowed from Plautus and Petronius. The suggestion that Dryden took his hint for the dialogue between Don Alonzo and Don Melchor (in which the one is speaking of a stolen jewel and the other about a metaphoric jewel, Don Alonzo's daughter, Theodosia) from Plautus' *Pot of Gold* is recommended by the fact that this particular dialogue is found only in Dryden's version of the feigned-astrologer story.[18] Dryden may well have recalled here Plautus' dialogue between Euclio and Lyconides, and he may even have recalled it in the exchange-of-gold scene between Jacinta and Wildblood, but there is no verbal borrowing; insofar as Alonzo feels a certain embarrassment at having to ask Don Melchor for the stolen jewel, the situation is common to every account of the story. In suggesting that Dryden took a hint from Petronius, surely Langbaine was thinking of the parallel between the burlesque peace treaty drawn up among the mock-heroic protagonists of the *Satyricon* and the treaty made by Maskall and Beatrix. Admittedly Dryden had already made use of the scene from Petronius in *The Rival Ladies,* but there is no reason to conclude that he was thinking more of the *Satyricon* than he was of the proviso scenes of French romance.[19]

When we turn from Langbaine's "little Hints" to Dryden's borrowings from Corneille, Molière, and Quinault, the problems concern direct translation and paraphrase rather than what Dryden knew or had in mind. The following passages from *An Evening's Love* show how Dryden merely changed French to suit the manner of English conversation:

Corneille	*Dryden* (III, i, 118–121)
D. FERNAND.	
D'où vient que vostre cœur soû-pire?	*Bell.* But why that sigh, Madam?
LEONOR.	
Vous pourriez m'épargner la honte de le dire,	*Aur.* You might spare me the shame of telling you; since I am
Puisque ce haut sçavoir dont chacun est jalous,	sure you can divine my thoughts: I will therefore tell you nothing.
Vous fait connoistre assez ce que je veux de vous.[20]	

Farther on in the same dialogue, after the false astrologer has discovered the identity of the woman to whom he is speaking, Dryden once more translates:

---

[18] Summers, II, 233–235.

[19] See Petronius, *Satyricon* (Loeb trans.), p. 225 (sec. 109). For Dryden's debt to Petronius in *The Rival Ladies,* see *Works,* VIII, 268–269. See also Kathleen Lynch, *The Social Mode of Restoration Comedy* (1926), pp. 83–84, 146.

[20] Thomas Corneille, *Poëmes Dramatiques* (Paris, 1661), I, 166 (III, ii). Corneille's play, first performed in 1650, was published by Thornycroft in a more

Corneille	Dryden (III, i, 210–213)
D. FERNAND.	
Puisque la mer enfin ne m'embarrasse plus, Madame, il ne me reste aucun lieu de refus. Regardez-moy l'oeil fixe.	*Bell.* Well, Madam, since the Sea hinders not, you shall have your desire. Look upon me with a fix'd eye———so———or a little more amorously if you please.———
LEONOR.	Good. Now favour me with your
O fille fortunée!	hand.
D. FERNAND.	
Montrez-moy vostre main. Quel jour estes-vous née? [21]	

It has been suggested that Dryden may have borrowed several other passages from Corneille, including the one in which Camilla fears that the astrologer will be able to read her thoughts, but this incident may be found in Scudéry's *Ibrahim* as well. The same objection can be made to the claim that Dryden took from Corneille the scene in which Don Alonzo demands the return of Theodosia's jewel from Don Melchor.[22] Since Corneille and Scudéry both copied Calderón rather closely at this point, it would be impossible to decide where Dryden's debt lay. There is little question, however, that he took numerous hints from Corneille.

Dryden's borrowing from Molière and Quinault, on the other hand, is very specific. From *Les Précieuses Ridicules* (III, i) he took the suggestion of satirizing Aurelia's pretensions by having her ask her bewildered maid for "le conseiller des Graces" instead of her mirror. He also adapted the dialogue of four scenes from *Dépit Amoureux:* that between the talkative Métaphraste and Albert (II, vi); that between the pairs of lovers, master and servant, lady and maid, who quarrel and make up along parallel emotional lines distinguished by class behavior (IV, iii); a brief bit of dialogue in which the servant, Marinette, succeeds in wheedling some money from Eraste (I, ii); and the final interchange between Mascarille and Gros-René.[23] From Quinault's *L'Amant Indiscret*

---

literal translation in 1668 as *The Feign'd Astrologer.* In the English version the scene is shifted to London, and some contemporary references are added. A few minor characters are introduced, and the old man, who wishes to return to his country in the farcical subplot, is given a farcical French accent, but the play is substantially as Corneille wrote it.

[21] Corneille, *Poëmes Dramatiques*, I, 171 (III, ii).

[22] Philipp Ott, *Über das Verhältnis des Lustspiel-Dichters Dryden zur gleichzeitigen französischen Komödie insbesondere zu Molière* (Landshut, 1885), pp. 27–29.

[23] Carl Hartmann correctly suggested that Bellamy's threat to cuckold Maskall ("Why, thou would'st not be so impudent, to marry *Beatrix* for thy self only?") came from Mascarille's "Tu crois te marier pour toi tout seul, compère?" But Beatrix's reply ("For all his ranting and tearing now, I'll pass my word he shall degenerate into as tame and peaceable a Husband as a civil Woman would wish to have") was proverbial and not so close to

(IV, iv) Dryden took his scene in which the couples pretend to be spirits, attempt to leave after candles have been extinguished, and are finally captured when Aurelia's attempt at pretending that Alonzo has actually taken hold of Maskall is revealed by her voice.

Probably no speech more thoroughly reveals the degree of Dryden's indebtedness to French comedy than Dryden's adaptation in Act III of Métaphraste's diatribe in *Dépit Amoureux:*

Molière MÉTAPHRASTE.	*Dryden* (III, i, 359–380)
D'où vient fort à propos cette sentence expresse D'un philosophe: "Parle, afin qu'on te connaisse." Doncques si de parler le pouvoir m'est ôté, Pour moi, j'aime autant perdre aussi l'humanité, Et changer mon essence en celle d'une bête. Me voilà pour huit jours avec un mal de tête. Oh! que les grands parleurs sont par moi détestés! Mais quoi? si les savants ne sont point écoutés, Si l'on veut que toujours ils aient la bouche close, Il faut donc renverser l'ordre de chaque chose: Que les poules dans peu dévorent les renards, Qu'a les jeunes enfants remontrent aux viellards, Qu'à poursuivre les loups les agnelets s'ébattent, Qu'un fou fasse les lois, que les femmes combattent,	*Alon. at the same time [as Lopez].* 'Tis the sentence of a Philosopher, *Loquere ut te videam;* Speak that I may know thee; now if you take away the power of speaking from me . . . Oh, how I hate, abominate, detest and abhor, these perpetual Talkers, Disputants, Controverters, and Duellers of the Tongue! But, on the other side, if it be not permitted to prudent men to speak their minds, appositely, and to the purpose and in few words———If, I say, the prudent must be Tongue-ty'd; then let Great Nature be destroy'd; let the order of all things be turn'd topsy-turvy; let the Goose devour the Fox; let the Infants preach to their Great-Grandsires; let the tender Lamb pursue the Woolfe, and the Sick prescribe to the Physician. Let Fishes live upon dry-land, and the Beasts of the Earth inhabit in the Water.———Let the fearful Hare———

Molière as Allen (p. 162n) would have it. Hartmann's suggestion of parallels between two speeches of Maskall and those in Molière's *Le Dépit Amoureux* is also very likely, particularly Maskall's "Now could I break my neck for despair; if I could find a precipice absolutely to my liking" (IV, i), and Mascarille's (III, ii):

> Je me vais d'un rocher précipiter moi-même,
> Si, dans le désespoir dont mon coeur est outré,
> Je puis en rencontrer d'assez bout à mon gré.

See Hartmann, *Einfluss Moliere's auf Dryden's komisch-dramatische Dichtungen* (Leipzig, 1885), pp. 26–27.

Que par les criminels les juges
soient jugés
Et par les écoliers les maîtres
fustigés,
Que le malade au sain présente le
remède,
Que le lièvre craintif . . .
Miséricorde! à l'aide!

Enter Lopez *with a*
Bell, and rings it
in his ears.

Alon. Help, help, murder, murder, murder!

(Albert lui vient sonner aux oreil-
les une cloche qui le fait fuir.) [24]

Although this rendering might be considered translation, Dryden does
not servilely follow Molière. He retranslates Molière's proverbial tag into
Latin; he cuts in some places and amplifies in others. He has the first
part of Alonzo's speech shouted out at the same time as the frustrated
Lopez attempts to put into absurd legal jargon his suggestion that Don
Melchor be allowed to marry Theodosia. The latter innovation is typical
of Dryden's effort to heighten the comic effect in a scene that is already
very funny and to adapt his material so that it makes sense within the
structure of *An Evening's Love.* Thus the famous scene (Act V)
in which the lovers and their servants quarrel and come together again
is changed to suit the different situation, characters, and setting. The
men are kept very English and the imagery of the peace treaty between
England and Spain has no parallel in Molière.

Dryden's debt to Quinault needs little comment:

Quinault	*Dryden* (V, i, 380–392)
LIDAME, *attrapant Cléandre.*	
Il est pris, le galant!	*They all come out upon*
CLÉANDRE.	*the Stage, groaping their*
Que le sort m'est contraire!	*way. Wildblood falls into*
PHILIPIN.	Alonzo's *hands.*
Vous tenez Philipin; ne vous abusez	
pas:	*Alon.* I have caught some body;
Peste! que rudement vous me ser-	are these your Spirits? Another
rez le bras!	light quickly, *Pedro.*
LIDAME.	*Mask. slipping between Alonzo*
Quoi! c'est toi, Philipin: ce succès	*and Wildblood.* 'Tis *Maskall* you
m'embarrasse?	have caught, Sir; do you mean to
Je croyois avoir pris notre fourbe	strangle me that you press me so
en ta place.	hard between your Arms?
PHILIPIN.	*Alon. letting Wildblood go.* Is it
Plût à Dieu qu'il fût vrai que le	thee *Maskall?* I durst have sworn
Ciel, par bonheur,	it had been another.

[24] Molière, *Le Dépit Amoureux,* in *Œuvres,* ed. Eugène Despois, I (Paris, 1873),
451–452 (II, vi).

Eût en vos mains livré ce lâche
suborneur!

LIDAME, *prenant la main
de Cléandre une
seconde fois.*

Ha! c'est donc à ce coup; je le
tiens, que je pense.
CLÉANDRE.
Vous tenez Philipin.
PHILIPIN
Dieu! quelle impertinence!
LIDAME.
L'artiface est grossier; je connois
bien sa voix.[25]

Bell. Make haste now before the
Candle comes.

Aurelia *falls into*
Alonzo's *armes.*

Alon. Now I have another.
Aur. 'Tis *Maskall* you have
caught Sir.
Alon. No I thank you Niece, this
artifice is too gross! I know your
voice a little better. What ho, bring
lights there.
Bell. Her impertinence has ruin'd
all.

In *An Evening's Love* it is not the lover who is caught but Alonzo's niece, Aurelia. The scene is a garden, not a lady's chamber. Dryden's captor is not the fierce mother but a rather more dangerous Don Alonzo with a band of servants. And the end of the play is not a reconciliation as in Quinault, but rather a rejection of parental control—that perennial theme of Restoration comedy. Don Alonzo barely escapes with his life from the enraged English cavaliers and his rebellious daughters.

The important question to ask about all this borrowing is whether Dryden succeeded in blending such disparate material into a unified comedy. That he failed to do so has been argued more than once. Corneille's drama of intrigue, it is claimed, could not possibly mix with "the atmosphere of *commedia dell'arte* which is so much a part of early Molière." Dryden's prologue, moreover, has been cited as evidence that the playwright tried to provide as much variety as possible merely to please his audience. And while it is admitted that Dryden's lovers, Wildblood and Jacinta, may well have more charm and wit than his gay couple of *Secret Love,* Celadon and Florimell, even their charm, it is said, can scarcely overcome the impossible mixture of styles.[26]

It seems, however, that an exactly opposite opinion of the play is at least equally tenable. Surely no one but a critic who has approached *An Evening's Love* through its various sources can sense a disparity of styles. In spite of all the contempt for comedy Dryden expressed as a man and as a critic, he had an excellent sense of the comic, and he approached his material like the craftsman he thought the ideal comic poet ought to be. The story of the false astrologer had proved to be an

---

[25] Philippe Quinault, *Théâtre* (Paris, 1778), I, 343–344 (V, iv).
[26] See Gillet, "Molière en Angleterre," pp. 88–91; Allen, pp. 162–164. André de Mandach (*Molière et la Comédie des Mœurs en Angleterre,* p. 86) agrees with their estimate and argues that Sir Walter Scott's high praise of *An Evening's Love* (S-S, III, 236) was attributable to his poor judgment and to certain romantic qualities he thought he perceived in Dryden's comedy.

entertaining play and story, and by the time Dryden came to adapt it for the English stage it had gone through a variety of transformations. In the hands of Madeleine de Scudéry it had become a charming novella with a précieuse framework which occasionally entered the tale itself. In Le Métel's version the farcical element—the subplot of how the clever servant tricks a man into believing that he can be transported to his native land by means of magic and so avoid thieves—became the tonal center. In Corneille's version there was still an emphasis on the cleverness of the valet, but the plot had been tightened. Attempting to make the plot even tighter, Dryden reduced the time scheme of his play to a single evening as compared with Corneille's full day or with Calderón's loose, extended three-day structure, typical of Spanish drama. And Dryden also made the time dramatically significant: it is the last evening of the carnival, when marriage has to be consummated or be delayed until the end of Lent. In typical English fashion he doubled the main plot by introducing Wildblood and Jacinta, a witty couple—already established as a hallmark of his comedies—while at the same time dropping the farcical subplot that marked all the previous transformations of Calderón's play.

But most of Dryden's innovations were changes in character and dialogue. The astrologer Bellamy, who in Dryden's sources acts from revenge after being rejected by the heroine, is given an active and sympathetic role; Theodosia is transformed from an object of revenge into a very real woman, worthy of being won away from her deceitful suitor, Don Melchor. Aurelia, who in all the other versions is never more than a somewhat silly woman, gullible about astrology and love, is made into a character whose affectation of précieuse language throws doubt on her professions of deep love ("this furious tender") for Don Melchor and makes her transfer of affection to Don Lopez both credible and amusing. In a similar manner Don Melchor is changed from a stereotyped, sentimental lover into a genuinely comic figure. Whereas in the other versions he is awarded the hand of the heroine, in *An Evening's Love* he is punished for his attempt at making love to two women at the same time by being knocked down, carried off violently several times, and rejected by both ladies. In Scudéry's *Ibrahim*, the gentleman in love with several women at once is an object of light amusement, but Dryden makes Don Melchor a comic villain who becomes the victim of the English wits; in addition to his other humiliations, he has to suffer the indignities of being mistaken first for a ghost and then for a thief. At the end Theodosia tells him, "You are justly punish'd for loving two," and he exits resolving to despise the women he has failed to deceive.

Dryden's method, it has been suggested, was to conceive the kind of character he wanted and then to search for material that would heighten the comic effect.[27] This procedure is nowhere so obvious as in the development of Don Alonzo. With a vague sketch in mind and working within the decorum of comic types, Dryden made Don Alonzo an old

---

[27] See Wilcox, *Relation of Molière to Restoration Comedy*, p. 111.

man, a pedant on the subject of astrology, an incessant talker, and a stern but ineffectual guardian of his husband-hunting daughters. Some previous opinions to the contrary, there is nothing inconsistent in having Don Alonzo speak so much that he will not allow Don Lopez to get in a word. Certainly the credit for the comedy in this scene should go to Molière from whom Dryden borrowed it, but Dryden's addition is completely compatible with the character of Don Alonzo as he appears in the later scene, so fearful that his demand for the return of the jewel will embarrass Don Melchor that he will not allow the supposed thief to explain the situation—a scene found in all versions of the story. Dryden is unquestionably open to the charge of plagiarism, but at least it may be said that his borrowings show a true awareness of how he might make his characters more complex and his play more amusing.

For all these borrowings, it is Dryden's own distinct contribution—the addition of Wildblood and Jacinta—which transforms the nature of the comedy. Although Wildblood and Jacinta are similar to Celadon and Florimell in *Secret Love,* they are even less restrained and more witty. Dryden changes Scudéry's Cerinthe, a woman of malicious wit who was capable of neither love nor jealousy, into the ideal Restoration comic heroine, possessed of Cerinthe's wit but lacking her cold heart. When Jacinta announces that she intends "to bury this man e're *Lent* be done, and get me another before *Easter,*" she is communicating to Wildblood her understanding of the libertine code by which her future husband has lived, and she is throwing out to him a sexual challenge which he is not likely to misunderstand. Although models for characters like Jacinta may be found in English comedy, she is essentially new, whereas Wildblood is merely a direct development of Fletcher's rakes—Mirabel in *The Wild Goose Chase* or Young Loveless in *The Scornful Lady.* Dryden criticized Fletcher's treatment of women but obviously admired his mad, witty rakes.

If there is any mixture of styles in *An Evening's Love,* it is a mixture commensurate with the subject. Dryden places his English rakes in an alien culture and merges Restoration comedy with Spanish comedy in a literary parallel to England's attempt to establish a political and commercial treaty with Spain. A somewhat similar socioliterary confrontation between the two nations had already been tried less successfully by Thomas Killigrew in *Thomaso; or, The Wanderer.*[28] It has been asserted that *An Evening's Love* may have had roots in a broader dramatic subgenre referred to as "the Spanish romance."[29]

---

[28] See *Comedies, and Tragedies* (1664), pp. 313–464. This play has some of the same details about Madrid as Dryden's, but Killigrew's cynical world-weary Thomaso is far different from Dryden's English wits.
[29] According to Van Lennep (p. cxxiii), "This kind of play, based upon a Spanish source, placed its emphasis upon a rigid code of conduct, had a plot filled with intrigue, and emphasized one or more high-spirited women in the *dramatis personae.*" On this basis Van Lennep classifies Dryden's comedy in the same category with Sir Samuel Tuke's *The Adventures of Five Hours*

But *An Evening's Love* is actually very much in the vein of Beaumont and Fletcher, who, as Dryden remarks in his preface, borrowed many of their plots from Spanish novels. As original as the character of Jacinta is, she has some of the same qualities as Margarita, the libertine heroine of Fletcher's *Rule a Wife and Have a Wife*. Like Jacinta, Margarita lifts up her veil to flirt with her rakish lover and confesses her desire to marry:

> I find it as all bodies are that are young and lusty
> Lazy, and high-fed; I desire my pleasure,
> And pleasure I must have.[30]

The point is not that Dryden was more influenced by English than by foreign sources, but that he drew upon Corneille, Quinault, Scudéry, and Molière with the same end in view as when Beaumont and Fletcher drew upon Spanish novels. That end was to write a thoroughly English style of comedy which would please an English audience.

Dryden's most important statement on comedy appears in the preface to *An Evening's Love*, written almost three years after the first performance of the play. Like so many of his critical statements, it must be read, at least in part, as a reply to his detractors, and in 1671 Dryden was

---

(first performed in 1663), Lord Digby's *Elvira,* Thomas Porter's *The Carnival,* and Dryden's *The Rival Ladies* (all in 1664), and Thomas St. Serfe's *Tarugo's Wiles* (1668). He might also have added William Davenant's *The Man's the Master* to his list, a comedy performed on 26 April 1668, the prologue to which suggests that a new kind of play was indeed being written (*Dramatic Works,* ed. James Maidment and W. H. Logan [Edinburgh, 1872–1874], V, 7):

> Well our old poet hopes this comedie
> Will somewhat in the fine new fashion be.

Except for a certain amount of disguise and intrigue, however, it is difficult to see that these plays have very much more in common than their Spanish setting. The plays of Tuke and Digby have a high moral tone and little true comedy; Davenant's has similar debates on love and honor but is far more amusing; St. Serfe's play is actually, in part, a parody of Tuke's *The Adventures of Five Hours.* Porter's *The Carnival* might seem to have much in common with *An Evening's Love,* including a man in love with two women at once, another who complains about flirtations being carried on in churches, a carnival setting, and a witty couple. But most of the comedy is dull and farcical, and the plays are entirely different in tone. As Dryden does in the preface to his comedy, St. Serfe uses his prologue to attack farce. He also contrasts England and Spain and has a character assuming numerous disguises in the manner of Jacinta. But the only true resemblance between *Tarugo's Wiles* and *An Evening's Love* is that both plays adapt foreign sources to the taste of an English audience. A grouping that makes little distinction among tragicomedy, comedy, and farce is hardly useful. Despite the interest in Spanish plays created by *The Adventures of Five Hours,* it would be better to recognize Spanish influence, particularly of the *comedias de capa y espada,* than to call *An Evening's Love* a "Spanish romance," a classification that creates more problems than it answers. For a brief discussion of this type of play, see Gerald Brenan, *The Literature of the Spanish People* (1951), pp. 278 ff. See also Max Oppenheimer, Jr., "The *Burla* in Calderón's *El Astrólogo Fingido,*" PQ, XXVII (1948), 241–263.

[30] Francis Beaumont and John Fletcher, *Works,* ed. R. Warwick Bond (1908), III, 388 (II, i).

under attack for what some of his critics regarded as his slighting remarks upon the comedy of Ben Jonson. In the epilogue to *Cambyses* (1671), a play performed close to the time when Dryden was writing his preface, Elkanah Settle, who was soon to number himself among Dryden's enemies, had described the quarrels of the "monstrous factions" among critics:

> Nay, Poets too themselves, of late, they say,
> The greatest Hectors are that e're huff'd Play.
> Like the Issue of the Dragons teeth, one brother
> In a poetick fury falls on t'other.
> 'Tis thought you'll grow to that excess of Rage,
> That Ben had need come guarded on the Stage.

Dryden's epilogue to the second part of *The Conquest of Granada* (1671) and his preface to *An Evening's Love* were anything but conciliatory and provoked new controversy. Apparently Dryden was irritated enough by this time to be willing to fight to an end the battle over the superiority of modern comedy to the comedy of Jonson.

Who were Dryden's opponents in this critical skirmish? The most obvious were Sir Robert Howard, Edward Howard, Richard Flecknoe, a writer signing himself R. F., Elkanah Settle, and Thomas Shadwell, all defenders of the drama of the past age. Some of them had already attacked Dryden in print, but none so outspokenly as that confessed disciple of Ben Jonson and the comedy of humours, Thomas Shadwell. If R. F. had stung Dryden into a deliberate effort to refute charges of plagiarism,[31] Shadwell forced him to reconsider and restate some of his remarks on comedy in his reply to Sir Robert Howard.[32] In *Defence of an Essay of Dramatique Poesie,* written in 1668, Dryden had deliberately pretended to misunderstand Sir Robert Howard's contention that "in the difference of Tragedy and Comedy, and of Fars it self, there can be no determination but by the Taste." [33] Dryden had insisted on a hierarchy of genres in which comedy was to be considered inferior to what he called "serious" plays. And he set out to establish a hierarchy of sub-genres within comedy in which his own comedy of wit would take precedence over Jonson's comedy of humour, and in which every form of comedy would take precedence over farce.

Although in the preface to *An Evening's Love* Dryden sometimes seems close to Molière's position on comedy in *La Critique de l'École des Femmes,* [34] he frequently betrays some of the same snobbery that may be

---

[31] *A Letter from a Gentleman to the Honourable Ed. Howard Esq; Occasioned By a Civiliz'd Epistle of Mr. Dryden's* (1668), p. 3. For a summary of some of the arguments against ascribing this work to Richard Flecknoe, see Maximillian E. Novak, "Dryden's 'Ape of the French Eloquence' and Richard Flecknoe," *Bulletin of the New York Public Library*, LXXII (1968), 503–504.

[32] See R. Jack Smith, "Shadwell's Impact upon John Dryden," *RES*, XX (1944), 30–37.

[33] See the preface to *The Great Favourite, or, The Duke of Lerma,* in Spingarn, II, 106.

[34] Particularly Dorante's remarks in scene vi on the difficulty of writing in a genre in which the characters and events are more capable of being tested by the experience of ordinary life than in tragedy (Molière, *Œuvres*, III, 351–352).

found in Aubignac, who complained that modern comedy had fallen into a type of farce that was beneath contempt.[35] Dryden too complained that most contemporary comedies were *"ally'd too much to Farce,"* blaming this situation on the translation and performance of French plays. And if we recall that Dryden was among those English playwrights who regarded the comedies of Molière, or at least their English adaptations, as farce, it will not be difficult to identify some of those whom Dryden was attacking in his preface to *An Evening's Love.* Shadwell adapted Molière's *Les Fâcheux* for *The Sullen Lovers,* and perhaps used *Le Tartuffe* for *The Hypocrite;* Flecknoe used *Sganarelle, L'École des Femmes,* and *Les Précieuses Ridicules* for his *Damoiselles à la Mode,* adding new farcical sections to Molière's scenes and praising himself in the preface for his ability to translate the "Language of the Pretieuse." Among other adapters of Molière were Davenant, Sedley, Caryll, Medbourne, Lacy, and Betterton. Dryden himself, of course, had helped Newcastle with his adaptation of *L'Étourdi (Sir Martin Mar-all),* and he had taken some scenes from Molière for the very play he was prefacing, *An Evening's Love.* Yet when Ravenscroft was successful with *The Citizen Turn'd Gentleman* in 1672, Dryden attacked this adaptation of *Monsieur de Pourceaugnac* and *Le Bourgeois Gentilhomme* as the worst kind of farce. The quarrel over comedy and farce continued among the critics long after Dryden's preface was written, and whatever his practice, Dryden's stance as a critic remained fairly consistent.

Perhaps no one caught Dryden's hauteur so well as Joseph Arrowsmith in his play, *The Reformation* (1673), where a parody of Dryden's own condescending remarks is spoken by a character named Tutor: "Then as for Comedy, which I was saying my Genius does not lead me to, but that the world may know I can at idle houres, when I please out-write them, I do venture at." [36] Dryden's attitude to comedy had already been apparent in the epilogue to *The Wild Gallant* revived (1667), where he expressed his dislike for comedy in general and for farce in particular, exhorting the audience to abandon such "fripperies of France":

> *Would you but change for serious Plot and Verse*
> *This mottley garniture of Fool and Farce,*
> *Nor scorn a Mode, because 'tis taught at home,*
> *Which does, like Vests, our Gravity become.*[37]

In this epilogue and in *Of Dramatick Poesie,* Dryden stressed the idea that comedy was an imitation of the natural and that it gave pleasure for that very reason, a pleasure separable from the laughter produced by the element of malice inherent in a comic imitation. Farce was different from comedy in being unnatural. For all Dryden's attacks on farce, however, Molière became increasingly popular on the Restoration stage, and farce

---

[35] *The Whole Art of the Stage* (1684), Pt. II, p. 141. See also Frank Harper Moore, *The Nobler Pleasure* (1963), pp. 63–68.

[36] P. 48 (IV, i).

[37] See *Works,* VIII, 89–91, 262–263. See also Moore, *The Nobler Pleasure,* p. 65.

found its first true advocate in Richard Flecknoe, who, a few months after publication of Dryden's preface to *An Evening's Love,* wrote a poem defending farce as an appeal to man's most distinct trait, his capacity for laughter.[38] By 1693 Nahum Tate was confidently treating farce as an accepted literary mode with its own distinct rules and values.[39]

Dryden admits in his preface that *An Evening's Love* might justly be accused of containing elements of low comedy and that he has borrowed some of its materials from French sources, but this customary modesty should not be mistaken for self-denigration. From his confession of shame at having pleased the audience, we learn that the play was a success. And from his willingness to defend the play against its detractors, we can feel certain that he thought his play a satisfactory comedy based more on a *"lively representation"* of the *"imperfections of humane nature"* than on the *"forc'd humours, and unnatural events"* of farce, which appeal to the fancy alone rather than to a combination of fancy and judgment.

The opponent toward whom Dryden appears to be directing most of his remarks is Thomas Shadwell, who in the prefaces to both *The Sullen Lovers* and *The Royal Shepherdess* had implicitly attacked Dryden's comedies for their lack of manners and morals. In his preface Dryden is conciliatory enough toward Shadwell's self-proclaimed discipleship to Ben Jonson to argue for a blend of Fletcher's wit and Jonson's humour as the ideal of comedy. But he is far more concerned with defending his own concept of the character of wit than with humour.

Dryden does use Jonson pointedly in defending himself against the charge of immorality in *An Evening's Love,* for Jonson too did not punish his rakish heroes. The problem with his critics, Dryden insinuates, is that they do not understand the true nature of comedy, the chief end of which is *"divertisement and delight";* instruction *"can be but its secondary end."* Therefore the best comedy is not that of Jonsonian humours but a comedy of wit which moves the audience *"to a pleasure that is more noble"* because it appeals to the judgment. What Dryden offers in the way of a theory of comedy is cathartic. Comedy moves laughter, and laughter brings with it a sense of shame which causes us to recognize and reform the defects in our *"manners."* The priority that Dryden gives to delight in comedy, then, is determined by the sequence of psychological response: we laugh first and learn through laughter. His attitude toward what Thomas Rymer was to call "poetic justice" is based on the very nature of a comic action, for comedy, as Dryden conceives it, cannot encompass crimes of any magnitude. Dryden fails to take into account the theory that every action presented on the stage may

---

[38] *Epigrams of All Sorts* (1671), p. 52. Dryden eventually replied to Flecknoe's argument in *A Parallel betwixt Painting and Poetry* (1695, p. xxvi; Watson, II, 190): "Laughter is indeed the propriety of a Man, but just enough to distinguish him from his elder Brother, with four Legs." The *"Farce-Scriblers"* appeal to one of the lowest of human instincts.

[39] See the preface to *A Duke and No Duke* (1693). Tate had already defended farce in the first preface to this play published in 1685.

move the audience to a similar action. When Collier published his attack on the stage in 1698, he maintained that Dryden's theory and practice in comedy had been immoral on these very points: delight, poetic justice, and moral example. Dryden thought the marriage of his rake a sufficiently moral conclusion for comedy.[40]

Dryden turns next to the question of plagiarism. The author of *A Letter from a Gentleman to the Honourable Ed. Howard Esq*, written shortly after Dryden's play was acted, argued that Dryden deserved the title of "Ingrossing Plagiary" rather than "Esquire" for his thefts in both *The Indian Emperour* and *An Evening's Love*.[41] And in the preface to *The Sullen Lovers*, so largely devoted to attacking Dryden's ideas on wit, Shadwell also suggested that there were some writers who "by continual Thieving, reckon their stolne goods their own." [42] In his reply Dryden explained his ends and means in using the writings of others. His main interest was to make his play amusing for the English audience, and this objective required him to *"heighten"* the comic material. He speaks of rejecting some *"adventures"* because they were not *"divertising,"* an obvious reference to the farcical sequences in his sources concerning the gulling of a servant, sequences he eliminated more for artistic reasons than for their lack of comic possibility. But his claim to originality in creating the characters of Wildblood and Jacinta is completely justifiable.

Dryden ends his essay with a comparison between the common craftsman and the master craftsman. The writer of Jonsonian comedy is merely a common craftsman, an exact observer, a realist, a man of judgment. The true artist is the master craftsman who possesses fancy as well as judgment; the value of his work lies not in the base materials (i.e., the works Dryden has been accused of plagiarizing) but in the *"workmanship."* Shadwell had acknowledged the lack of design in *The Sullen Lovers*, arguing that the real art of comedy lay in creating new humours. His main objection to the style of comedy developed by Dryden and Etherege was that it sacrificed the creation of "perfect Character" for a reliance on witty dialogue between a stereotyped "Swearing, Drinking, Whoring, Ruffian for a Lover, and an impudent ill-bred tomrig for a Mistress." [43] In his reply, then, Dryden is willing to allow some of Shadwell's distinctions, but he argues that Shadwell's craft is inferior to that of the true artist. Bringing in the serious play once more as the test of the true artist, Dryden remarks that *"he who works dully on a Story, without moving laughter in a Comedy, or raising concernments in a serious Play, is no more to be accounted a good Poet, than a Gunsmith of the Minories is to be compar'd with the best workman of the Town,"* a reminder to Shadwell that Dryden's plays have been more successful than his as well as more artful. The quarrel between Shadwell and Dryden is

[40] See Jeremy Collier, *A Short View of the Immorality and Profaneness of the English Stage* (1698), pp. 148–165.

[41] *Letter from a Gentleman*, p. 3.   [42] Shadwell, *Works*, I, 10.

[43] *Ibid.*, I, 11.

a familiar one in literature. It is not very different from that between Richardson and Fielding or Arnold Bennett and Virginia Woolf. The realistic artist often confuses the materials of art with art itself and is usually scornful of imposing a design on his slice of life. The artist interested in form usually says that design is what art is all about.

If Dryden was more than a match for his enemies in defending his artistic practice, he probably satisfied few moralists by his definition of the comic ethos. Although some have professed to be puzzled that Pepys thought *An Evening's Love* "smutty" and that Evelyn found it "very prophane," [44] Jeremy Collier singled out the play and the characters of Jacinta and Wildblood as particular examples of licentiousness and immorality. "If Delight without Restraint, or Distinction, without Conscience or Shame, is the Supream Law of Comedy, 'twere well if we had less on't," wrote Collier in replying to Dryden's preface.[45] Clearly *An Evening's Love* is one of those plays that made wit and obscenity closely allied terms throughout the Restoration, and it must be confessed that Dryden, though occasionally falling behind Etherege in wit, was second to no one in his honest and amusing treatment of sex on the stage. Perhaps it is time to praise Dryden for his urbanity and sophistication instead of apologizing for his obscenity.

Both the prologue and the epilogue rely on sexual images to describe the playwright's relation to his audience: the prologue uses the relation of a complacent husband to his wayward wife; the epilogue, that of a mistress to her lover. In the prologue, which contains one of his most brilliant extended metaphors, Dryden asks his audience to allow him the rights of a seaman who returns to his spouse only three times a year (a reference to his new contract with the King's Company):

> *That only time from your Gallants he'll borrow;*
> *Be kind to day, and Cuckold him to morrow.*

The reactions of the wife-audience are conveyed by suggestions of movement, weight, orgasm, and detumescence, sometimes in traditional double entendres, sometimes in direct description of sexual intercourse. The total effect is witty and broadly comic, and behind the jest lies the implication that the audience is wedded to Dryden, that the playgoers, for all their occasional lovers, understand that Dryden is their only true spouse.

This kind of imagery has been part of realistic comedy and satire from Aristophanes to the present. Wildblood can hardly open his mouth without making some kind of sexual pun. Like Fletcher's Mirabell in *The Wild Goose Chase*, he offers himself to any woman who comes by, whether Spanish, Moor, or mulatto, Catholic, Moslem, or pagan. In Bellamy's disguise as an astrologer, Wildblood merely sees a chance for more sexual encounters. Adding to the general preoccupation with sex are the songs *"After the pangs of a desperate Lover"* [46] and *"Calm was*

---

[44] See, e.g., Summers, II, 236; Evelyn, *Diary*, III, 510.

[45] *Short View*, pp. 163–164.

[46] Dryden was apparently proud of the popularity of this song. He has Doralice in *Marriage A-la-Mode* report that a year after the song had gone

the Even, and cleer was the Skie," which provide vivid and spirited descriptions of sex play and intercourse. Two other songs in the play, though somewhat less suggestive of physical love, are explorative of the psychology of lovers. *"You charm'd me not with that fair face"* concerns the combination of aggression and fear underlying courtship and love, while *"Celimena, of my heart"* concerns the way anger and quarreling feed the flames of passion. Dryden may not have been so skillful as Etherege, Congreve, and Vanbrugh in tracing the subtle and tender passions of his lovers, but he was certainly as insightful and amusing concerning their physical response.

Many of the double entendres of *An Evening's Love* are related to the three image patterns running through the play as analogies of love: images of war and peace, of hawking and hunting, of astrology and magic. Such consistent patterns of images may be unusual in a prose comedy, but they provide a unifying element in the play, drawing together the disparate strains of the plot: the problem of matching two English wits with two Spanish ladies and the story of the false astrologer. The play is set in 1665, when negotiations for a peace between England and Spain were being conducted by Fanshawe, and there is much in the play to make it thoroughly contemporary. The commercial treaty between England and Spain was not signed until 13 May 1667 and did not arrive in England until 27 September of that year. Speaking of some of the strange customs of Spain, Pepys said that what "pleases me most indeed is, that the peace which he [Sandwich] hath made with Spain is now printed here, and is acknowledged by all the merchants to be the best peace that ever England had with them: and it appears that the King thinks it so." The *London Gazette* carried news of the final ratification of the treaty on 12 February 1668, only four months before Dryden's play was performed.

The general atmosphere of the play, then, is colored by foreign relations, especially a treaty between England and Spain to protect both nations from Louis XIV's "Universal Monarchy." [47] There are sly references to the "Battle of the Ambassadors" which resulted in France's diplomatic victory over Spain and to the violation of the law of nations in France's sudden invasion of Flanders. When Dryden stated in the epilogue that he had *"us'd the* French *like Enemies"* in stealing their plots, his remark was intended to have political overtones. Pepys had cheered the Spanish during their brawl with the French in the streets of London, and England was eagerly seeking allies to counter French power.

The meeting of Jacinta and Wildblood is deliberately constructed in terms of wars, treaties, and leagues. Dryden uses realistic details to suggest his picture of Spain. We learn that the Spanish wore their shoes too

---

stale in London a person visiting the country "heard nothing else, but the Daughters of the house and the Maids, humming it over in every corner, and the Father whistling it" (1673, p. 34 [III, i]; S-S, IV, 301).

[47] For a good contemporary discussion of these problems, see François Paul de Lisola, *The Buckler of State and Justice against the Design Manifestly Discovered of the Universal Monarchy* (1667).

tight and that they suffered from a shortage of meat, and we even discover something about the way they moved. Although there is a certain amount of satire, Dryden's main purpose seems to be to suggest the parallel between courtship and marriage and the arranging of a treaty between two nations. Wildblood and Jacinta agree to discuss "Leagues offensive and defensive," while Beatrice and Maskall, who think that marriage would be too rigid for them, are willing to sign a "Treaty of commerce." These images appear at the end of the fourth act, but suggestions of war and peace are scattered throughout. Even *"You charm'd me not with that fair face,"* on the surface simply a decorative lyric, draws upon references to unjust invasions by *"young Monarchs"* and the *"dull defensive warr"* required to protect conquered territory.

More obvious, perhaps, in *An Evening's Love* are the imagery and language of astrology. Even before Maskall conceives of claiming that his master is a great astrologer in order to save Beatrix her position and her reputation for secrecy, there are discussions about lovers in alchemical and astrological terms. This language, clearly connected with the central plot of the play, needs little explanation. The contrary is true about Dryden's use of images from hunting and hawking. Such comparisons may be suitable enough for a play in which two rakes are in search of women, but the unusually large number of them must appear eccentric. Perhaps Dryden gave these images to his English gallants to suggest the sports of their country in the same way that references to the *Juego de cannas* adds realism to the Spanish atmosphere; perhaps such imagery came naturally to Dryden from the sports of his youth. When the imagery is not from astrology and the related ideas of magic and conjuring, when Dryden is not having his characters speak in terms of war and peace or of hawking, he is using some other comparison. The particular quality of wit in this play is not to be found in that subtle conversation that Etherege had already perfected, but in an exchange of apt metaphor and simile which even the servants have at their fingertips. None of this verbal structure is present in Dryden's sources. Small wonder that he claimed in the epilogue that he *"did not steal their Plots, but made 'em prize."*

An Evening's Love is probably not so good a play as *Secret Love* or *Marriage A-la-Mode,* though, like *Sir Martin Mar-all,* it may be more amusing. It is realistically set in a neighboring country rather than in the romantic never-never land of Sicily, where both *Secret Love* and *Marriage A-la-Mode* are set, but whatever it gains by an avoidance of romance it loses in being deprived of those occasionally splendid passages of poetry which appear in the serious plots of the tragicomedies. Wildblood and Jacinta are of the same blood as Celadon and Florimell, or Rhodophil and Doralice. Like Florimell and Doralice, Jacinta falls in love at once and, having decided on an ideal mate, tortures him for the rest of the play until he is willing to do anything, even marry, to attain her. If Jacinta seems also to bear some resemblance to Etherege's Gatty in *She Would If She Could,* it should be borne in mind that Florimell of Dryden's play, *Secret Love,* preceded Etherege's heroine on the stage by almost a year. But if critics are reluctant to place Dryden squarely in the comedy-of-manners tradition along with Etherege, it is perhaps because Dryden's heroes and heroines concentrate rather more directly on sex itself than do the heroes and heroines of his contemporaries. Even Horner in Wycherley's *The Country Wife* seems to be pursuing sex for rather complicated reasons, compared with Dryden's heroes, who seem to have no difficulty in comprehending where the main business of love lies. One might simply call plays such as *An Evening's Love* witty, sexual comedies.

Epigraph (title page). Martial, *Epigrams,* IX, lxxxi:
>   Lector et auditor nostros probat, Aule, libellos,
>   sed quidam exactos esse poeta negat.
>   non nimium curo: nam cenae fecula nostrae
>   malim convivis quam placuisse cocis.

(Loeb trans.: "Reader and hearer approve of my works, Aulus, but a certain poet says they are not polished. I don't care much, for I should prefer the courses of my dinner to please guests rather than cooks.")
  The reference is too general to assume that Dryden was answering any one of his critics. Hugh Macdonald (p. 106) assumes that the preface is a direct response to Thomas Shadwell's attack upon immoral comedies, specifically in the preface to *The Sullen Lovers.* That Dryden was responding to Shadwell seems likely enough, but Robert Howard and Edward Howard also attacked Dryden in print, and the number of "coffeehouse critics" is incalculable.

DEDICATION

  P. 197 *William, Duke of Newcastle.* William Cavendish, Duke of Newcastle (1592–1676), is chiefly known today through the biography by his wife, Margaret, who praised him as "the best lyrical and dramatic poet of this age" and as "a pattern for all gentlemen." He was the author of four plays and probably wrote most of the adaptation of Molière's *L'Étourdi* before giving it to Dryden for revision. He was a generous patron to many of the writers of the time including both Ben Jonson and his disciple, Thomas Shadwell, who, like Dryden, dedicated plays to the Duke and Duchess. Cavendish was awarded the Order of the Garter shortly after the Restoration and was created Duke of Newcastle on 16 March 1665. His later years were spent away from politics, improving his estate and engaging in his favorite pastime of training horses.
  197:8 *Pattern and Standard of Honor.* Dryden may be echoing the praise given the Duke in the biography written by his adoring wife (*The Life of William Cavendish,* ed. C. H. Firth [1906], p. 111).
  197:9–10 *Heroick vertue.* Taking the hint from the Duchess of Newcastle's comparison of her husband with Caesar, Dryden attempts to establish a comparison between Plutarch's noble Greeks and Romans and the Duke (*Life of Cavendish,* ed. Firth, p. 142).
  197:12–13 *noble Birth and Education.* For an account of the Duke's

noble ancestors, see *Life of Cavendish,* ed. Firth, pp. 1–3. Cavendish was educated at St. John's College, Cambridge.

197:20 *her favour to Cymon and Lucullus.* Plutarch is not so direct as Dryden would pretend in regard to the activity of fortune in the lives of Cimon and Lucullus. He says that Cimon's death occurred "through ill fortune pure and simple" (Loeb trans., II, 617), and that at a certain point in his life Lucullus was abandoned by fortune. Perhaps Dryden was using the North translation, which omits any reference to fortune at this point (*Plutarch's Lives of the Noble Grecians and Romans,* trans. Sir Thomas North, Tudor Translations [1895], III, 356, 410). North's rendering of the final comparison of the two, however, does stress the favors of fortune: "So that all thinges weyed and considered, it were hard to judge which of them two proved the worthiest man: for that it seemeth, that the goddes did favor both the one and the other, telling the one what he should doe, and the other what he should not doe. And thus it appeareth by testimonie of the goddes, they were both good men, and that they both obtained everlasting glorie" (*ibid.,* p. 430). In taking up the subject of fortune, Dryden picks one that the Duke had commented upon in his writings; but Dryden is more interested in drawing a comparison between the Duke and Plutarch's two heroes, both of whom retired to private life after a career of glorious deeds in military and political life (*Life of Cavendish,* ed. Firth, pp. 133–134).

197:22 *than Hannibal could boast.* Hannibal was defeated by Scipio at Zama in 202 B.C.

197:24–25 *the last smiles of victory were on your armes.* This compliment is tactful, if not wholly accurate. The Duchess describes her husband's victories over the forces of Parliament and presents his actions at Marston Moor on 2 July 1644 in such a way that he appears to have won his part of the field. After the defeat at Marston Moor Cavendish decided to go to Holland because, the Duchess explained, he was out of funds and ammunition, but Clarendon deemed his action inexplicable and inexcusable. It is reported that Cavendish told the King, "I will not endure the laughter of the Court," though up to this point he had been successful in a number of engagements and had almost all of Yorkshire except Hull under his control. See Samuel Gardiner, *History of the Great Civil War* (1886), I, 439–448; *Life of Cavendish,* ed. Firth, pp. 13–42.

199:5 *Caius Marius.* See Plutarch, trans. North, Tudor Translations, III, 205: "Marius too ambitiously striving like a passioned young man against the weakenes and debility of his age, never missed day but he would be in the field of Mars to exercise him selfe among the young men, shewing his body disposed and ready to handle all kinde of weapons, and to ryde horses: albeit that in his latter time, he had no great health of body, bicause he was very heavy and sad." The first part of Dryden's paragraph continues to echo Plutarch's "Life of Lucullus," and Lucullus continues to function as Dryden's main comparison between Newcastle and the ancients. Caius Marius is criticized by Plutarch for his excessive ambition, his brutality, and his greed, but the bulk of Dryden's compliment refers to Newcastle's vigor at the age of seventy-eight.

199:9 *Silius Italicus.* A Roman poet and statesman (A.D. 26–101) who wrote an epic, *Punica,* and, according to Pliny (Letters, III, vii), after retiring from political life "spent his time in philosophical discussion, when not engaged in writing verses" (Loeb trans.). He imitated Virgil in his style and revered Virgil's tomb as if the poet had been a deity.

199:15 *your excellent Lady.* Margaret Cavendish, Duchess of Newcastle (1623–1673), was the author of philosophical treatises, poems, essays, and romances. In addition to affecting an eccentric manner of dress, Margaret attracted attention by her claims to literary greatness. After her death her husband published a volume of letters and poems by eminent men, scholars of both Oxford and Cambridge and philosophers like Joseph Glanvill, Henry More, and Walter Charleton, testifying to her genius. One named her "Margaret the First: Princess of Philosophers: who hath dispelled Errors: Appeased the differences of Opinions: And restored Peace, To Learnings Commonwealth." Edward Howard called her "the unequal'd Daughter of the Muses," and in his *Elegy* Thomas Shadwell wrote,

> Her Books are the best Patterns for the Pen,
> Her Person was the best of Subjects too;
> In Wit and Sense She did excel all Men;
> And all her Sex in Virtue did outgoe,

but behind the public display of admiration there existed considerable scorn. Margaret became the pattern of the female virtuoso, a common literary stereotype in the eighteenth century. See *A Collection of Letters and Poems . . . Upon Divers Important Subjects to the Late Duke and Dutchess of Newcastle* (1678), pp. 123, 152, 165–166. For a recent biography, see Douglas Grant, *Margaret the First* (1957).

199:15–16 *Partner of your studies.* The Duke of Newcastle contributed something to almost every book Margaret wrote, whether letters or scenes of plays. In her volume of plays she acknowledged his contribution: "My Lord was pleased to illustrate my Playes with some Scenes of his own Wit, to which I have set his name, that my Readers may know which are his, as not to couzen them, in thinking they are mine; also Songs, to which my Lords name is set; for I being no Lyrick Poet, my Lord supplied that defect of my Brain with the superfluity of his own Brain; thus our Wits join as in Matrimony, my Lords the Masculine, mine the Feminine Wit, which is no small glory to me, that we are Married, Souls, Bodies, and Brains, which is a treble marriage, united in one Love, which I hope is not in the power of Death to dissolve; for Souls may love, and Wit may live, though Bodies dye" (*Playes* [1662], sig. A6).

199:16–17 *Sappho of the Greeks, or the Sulpitia of the Romans.* The comparison between the Duchess and Sappho (fl. seventh century B.C.) and Sulpicia (fl. first century A.D.), both writers of love lyrics, is particularly meaningful in the context of Margaret's pose as a platonic lover. In her autobiography Margaret speaks with great simplicity and tenderness of her love for the Duke (see "A True Relation of My Birth, Breeding and Life," in *Life of Cavendish,* ed. Firth, pp. 172, 176).

199:19 *the History of your life.* Margaret Cavendish's *The Life of the Thrice Noble, High and Puissant Prince William Cavendishe, Duke, Marquess, and Earl of Newcastle* . . . was published in 1667.

199:29 *Præsenti tibi* etc. Horace, *Epistles,* II, i, 15:

praesenti tibi maturos largimur honores,
iurandasque tuum per numen ponimus aras,
nil oriturum alias, nil ortum tale fatentes

from the famous "Epistle to Augustus" (Loeb trans.: "Upon you, however, while still among us, we bestow honours betimes, set up altars to swear by in your name, and confess that nought like you will hereafter arise or has arisen ere now").

200:13 *manes.* Shades or spirits.

200:13 *Johnson and D'avenant.* For an account of Newcastle as the "English Maecenas" and patron of Ben Jonson and Sir William Davenant, see *Life of Cavendish,* ed. Firth, pp. xvi–xvii; Arthur Nethercot, *Sir William D'Avenant* (1938), pp. 203–204. Dryden seems to be apologizing for the failure of the two poets to show sufficient thanks in their works for the favors granted them by Newcastle. Jonson wrote two masques for Newcastle, but Nethercot denies that Davenant was greatly indebted to the Duke for favors. Davenant did begin a poem commemorating the marriage of Newcastle's eldest daughter to Charles Cheney (Davenant, *Works* [1673], [Pt. I], p. 293); and Margaret considered *Gondibert* the best epic ever written: "I had rather read Sir W.Ds. Work ten times, than Homer twice, as he is Translated" (*Sociable Letters* [1664], pp. 258–259).

200:31–32 *the wit of my Predecessors* etc. In acknowledging Jonson's wit Dryden may be apologizing somewhat for remarks considered irreverent to Jonson's genius. In his preface to *The Sullen Lovers,* Shadwell (*Works,* I, ii) leaped to Jonson's defense:

> Though I have known some of late so Insolent to say, that Ben Jonson wrote his best Playes without Wit; imagining, that all the Wit in Playes consisted in bringing two persons upon the Stage to break Jests, and to bob one another, which they call Repartie, not considering that there is more wit and invention requir'd in the finding out good Humor, and Matter proper for it, then in all their smart reparties. For, in the Writing of a Humor, a Man is confin'd not to swerve from the Character, and oblig'd to say nothing but what is proper to it: but in the Playes which have been wrote of late, there is no such thing as perfect Character, but the two chief persons are most commonly a Swearing, Drinking, Whoring, Ruffian for a Lover, and an impudent ill-bred tomrig for a Mistress, and these are the fine People of the Play.

Shadwell was probably referring to Dryden's comment in his essay *Of Dramatick Poesie* that if Jonson did not lack wit he was nevertheless "frugal of it" (1668, p. 49; Watson, I, 69). Shadwell might also have taken some of the lines in the prologue to *The Tempest* as a slur on his favorite author. Dryden may appear somewhat humble in the prologue, but he clarified his position on Jonson's wit in the epilogue to 2 *Conquest of Granada* (1672, p. [159]; Watson, I, 167), as well as in the *Defence of the Epilogue*, where he argued that when Jonson "aim'd at Wit, in the stricter sence, that is, Sharpness of Conceit, [he] was forc'd either to borrow from the Ancients, as, to my knowledge he did very much from *Plautus:* or, when he trusted himself alone, often fell into meanness of expression" (*Conquest of Granada* [1672], p. 170; Watson, I, 178).

PREFACE

202:9 *Conquest of Granada*. Dryden is referring to his essay *Of Heroique Playes*, prefixed to *The Conquest of Granada* when it was published in 1672.

202:12–13 *refining the Courtship, Raillery, and Conversation of Playes*. Dryden undertook this task in his *Defence of the Epilogue* which he appended to *The Conquest of Granada*. Perhaps he was anticipating the inevitable reply to the epilogue, in which he attacked the manners and "conversation" of Jonson's era:

Thus *Johnson* did mechanic humour show,
When men were dull, and conversation low. . . .
Wit's now arriv'd to a more high degree;
Our native language more refin'd and free.
Our Ladies and our men now speak more wit
In conversation, than those poets writ.

Dryden was eventually attacked for this concept of the primitive manners of the "last age" in *The Friendly Vindication of Mr. Dryden from the Censure of the Rota* (1673), p. 11.

"Raillery" was a relatively new word in English. In 1653 Robert Loveday explained that the "word Raillery you return'd me for interpretation, signifies a kind of jesting, scoffing, dissimulation, and is now grown here so common with the better sort, as there are few of the meaner that are not able to construe it" (*Letters* [1663], p. 245). Dryden was obviously thinking of the new comedy of wit which had been assailed by Shadwell in the preface to *The Sullen Lovers*.

202:14 *Opiniatre*. "Stiff or stubborn in opinion" (*OED*). Dryden may be referring to specific antagonists, and the best candidate may be Sir Robert Howard whom all believed to be the model for Shadwell's opinionated fool, Sir Positive At-all in *The Sullen Lovers* (cf. *Works*, IX, 322–323). There are, however, at least three other possibilities: Edward Howard, Thomas Shadwell, and Richard Flecknoe. For *The Womens Conquest*, performed in November 1670, Edward Howard wrote three prologues praising Jonson and attacking the immorality of modern comedies, and he sided with his brother in the quarrel between Sir Robert Howard and Dryden on rhymed plays. It was to Edward Howard that the person giving his initials as "R. F." addressed the first personal attack upon Dryden in 1668. Howard attacked Dryden more specifically in the prefaces to *The Womens Conquest* and *The Six Days Adventure*, both published in 1671. For Shadwell's attacks, see R. Jack Smith, "Shadwell's Impact upon John Dryden," *RES*, XX (1944), 29–44. For the quarrel between Flecknoe (the only *old* opponent) and Dryden, see Maximillian E. Novak, "Dryden's 'Ape of the French Eloquence' and Richard Flecknoe," *Bulletin of the New York Public Library*, LXXII (1968), 499–506.

202:17–20 *Comedy . . . inferiour to all sorts of Dramatick writing.* Dryden repeats an idea he advanced in the epilogue to *The Wild Gallant* revived, that comedy is to be ranked below tragedy in a scale of genres. This position has support from Aristotle who put the genres on an ethical scale (see S. H. Butcher, *Aristotle's Theory of Poetry and Fine Art* [1951], pp. 230–237; Frank Harper Moore, *The Nobler Pleasure* [1963], p. 66; and *Works*, VIII, 262). Comedy was not in high esteem among the French critics who had so much influence upon Dryden at this time. In 1657 François Hédelin, Abbé d'Aubignac, remarked: "Comedy among us has remain'd long, not only in meanness and obscurity, but look'd upon as infamous, being chang'd into that sort of Farce, which we still retain at the end of some of our Tragedys; though they are certainly things without Art, or Grace, and only recommendable to the Rascally sort of Mankind, who delight in obscene, infamous words and actions" (*The Whole Art of the Stage* [1684], p. 143).

203:4 *Zany of a Mountebank.* The mountebank used a Jack-pudding or Merry-Andrew to attract the crowd by his pranks. Jonson has a famous scene with a mountebank in *Volpone*, and so has Thomas Killigrew in *Thomaso; or, The Wanderer* (IV, ii). See also Samuel Butler, "The Character of a Mountebank" (in *Characters*, ed. A. R. Waller [1908], pp. 130–131); Dryden, prologue to *The Pilgrim*, ll. 38–40.

203:7 *habit and . . . Grimaces.* Summers (II, 498–499; III, 514–515) suggests that Dryden is referring specifically to James Nokes and Edward Angel of the rival Duke's Company. The reference is a general one to the techniques of the *commedia dell'arte* and to popular farces, but in England Angel and Nokes were the best examples to choose, and Dryden must have realized that his readers would have thought of them in connection with such a definition. In his first prologue to *The Womens Conquest* (1671), performed a few months before publication of Dryden's preface, Edward Howard has the great comedians of the Duke's Company —Angel, Underhill, and Nokes—carry on a dialogue on farce (sigs. c2v–c3). In reply to Underhill's objections that it is destroying comedy, Angel defends farce mainly on the basis of its popularity and the lack of good comedies. At this point Nokes enters to suggest a new kind of prologue. "What think you then," says Nokes, "if I speak to all the Judges in the pit by looks and grimisks." Angel approves, and Nokes argues that it will please everyone, including "the moderate Wits"; but Underhill brings in a changeling, a figure directly out of *commedia dell'arte*, who is to dance for the prologue. With this final plunge into theatrical chaos, the ghost of Ben Jonson appears to frighten off these masters of grimace.

203:9 *Farce.* This term came into currency shortly after the Restoration and may be associated with the visit of a troupe of French actors to

England in 1661 (see Sir William Davenant, *The Playhouse to be Let,*
in *Dramatic Works,* ed. James Maidment and W. H. Logan [Edinburgh,
1872–1874], IV, 18–19, for a dialogue between the director of a playhouse
and the head of a troupe of French actors). The words "farce" and
"troupe" are both treated as neologisms. See also Richard Flecknoe, "Of
Farces," in *Epigrams of All Sorts* (1671), p. 52, for a defense of farce,
perhaps in deliberate opposition to Dryden; and Leo Hughes, "The Early
Career of Farce in the Theatrical Vocabulary," *Texas Studies in Literature,* no. 4026 (1940), pp. 82–95.

203:10–11 *the sullenness of my humor.* Dryden and Howard disagreed
on the question of the comparative value of the genres. In his *Defence
of an Essay* Dryden quoted Howard's argument as it had appeared in the
preface to *The Duke of Lerma* (see *Works,* IX, 11): ". . . *in the difference of* Tragedy *and* Comedy, *and of* Farce *it self, there can be no
determination but by the taste."* Dryden called the statement obscure and
then proceeded to misinterpret it. In the same essay he also confessed to
a "saturnine" humor and a psychological set against comedy. In this
passage he corrects what must have been a deliberate misunderstanding of
Howard's general position to focus on farce as an *"unnatural"* and
therefore inferior genre. Although Flecknoe defended farce as "merrier
than Comedy by half" and as productive of more laughter (*Epigrams,* p.
52), the first formal critical defense was made by Nahum Tate in his
preface to *A Duke and No Duke* (1693). See Leo Hughes, "Attitudes of
Some Restoration Dramatists toward Farce," *PQ,* XIX (1940), 268–287;
Watson, I, 116, 119–120.

203:23 *judgment and fancy.* Although common enough, this division
was popularized by Thomas Hobbes and his disciple Walter Charleton
(see Clarence Thorpe, *The Aesthetic Theory of Thomas Hobbes* [1940],
pp. 107–108, 178; *Works,* I, 271–272).

203:25 *more of scorn.* Dryden's distinction between the laughter occasioned by comedy and that aroused by farce suggests Hobbes's theory of
laughter. "Sudden glory," wrote Hobbes in *Leviathan* (*English Works,*
III, 46), "is the passion which maketh those grimaces called Laughter;
and is caused either by some sudden act of their own, that pleaseth them;
or by the apprehension of some deformed thing in another, by comparison whereof they suddenly applaud themselves." In regarding excessive laughter as the sign of a foolish and inferior person seeking an
object of "scorn" in order to feel superior to it, Hobbes may have been
following Ben Jonson's translation of Heinsius' misreading of Aristotle
(see Jonson, *Timber,* in Spingarn, I, 58, 231–232; and Thorpe, *Aesthetic
Theory of Hobbes,* pp. 145–147).

Dryden's distinction between that which merely arouses laughter and
that which brings a sense of pleasure became part of the accepted critical
principles of the eighteenth century. In his essay *Of Dramatick Poesie*
(1668, p. 52; Watson, I, 73) Dryden distinguished between the *"ridiculum"*
aroused by the old comedy, still followed by the French in their farces,
and the humour comedy of the English, where the laughter occasioned
was "accidental" and the chief experience a "malicious pleasure." The

comedy of humour is described as "natural" in opposition to the "unnatural" comedy of the ridiculous. In his example here and in his defense of a kind of laughter without malice, Dryden may have been influenced by Walter Charleton's *Of the Different Wits of Men*, written in 1664 but not published until 1669. Charleton defends witty jests (pp. 112–137), and though he follows Hobbes in warning against laughing at one's own jests, he applauds that wit "whereby a Man modestly and gently touches upon the Errours, Indecencies, or Infirmities of another, without any suspicion of hate or contempt of his Person, pleasantly representing them as only ridiculous, not odious." Aristotle actually broke with Plato's theory of laughter as malicious and suggested the possibility of a laughter "more of satisfaction," as Dryden puts it. Richard Flecknoe (*Epigrams*, p. 52) may have been replying to Dryden in praising the laughter raised by farce:

> Nature of man they do not know then, who
> For causing laughter discommend them so,
> Since next to Rational, there's nothing can
> Than laughing be more natural to man.

203:32–33 *Loam, or with the Rinds of Trees.* See Samuel Butler, "A Duke of Bucks" (in *Characters,* p. 32): "His Appetite to his Pleasures is diseased and crazy, like the Pica in a Woman, that longs to eat that, which was never made for Food, or a Girl in the Green-sickness, that eats Chalk and Mortar." See also Théophile Bonet, *A Guide to the Practical Physician* (1684), p. 93, where it is argued that the longing after "Lime, Chalk, Ashes, Oatmeal" is merely a temporary state in women suffering from greensickness and that the patient should be prevented from having such food. The literary parallel is implicit in Dryden's attitude.

204:1 *Empirique.* A quack.

204:12 *translation of French Plays.* Dryden confessed himself guilty of such translations; indeed, not only had his patron, Newcastle, collaborated with him on the translation of *Sir Martin Mar-all* from Molière's *L'Étourdi,* but Dryden took a large part of *An Evening's Love* from the French playwrights Thomas Corneille and Molière. The English tended to regard Molière mainly as a writer of farce, but such stated opponents of farce as Dryden and Shadwell continued to translate and adapt Molière to the English stage. For borrowings from Molière and other French writers, particularly Pierre and Thomas Corneille and Philippe Quinault, see Allardyce Nicoll, *A History of Restoration Drama, 1660–1700* (4th ed., rev.; 1952), pp. 186–191. See also Leo Hughes, *A Century of English Farce* (1956), pp. 142–148.

204:17–18 *I have given too much to the people.* This confession is a change from Dryden's assertion in *Defence of an Essay* (see *Works,* IX, 7): "I confess my chief endeavours are to delight the Age in which I live. If the humor of this, be for low Comedy, small Accidents, and Raillery, I will force my Genius to obey it. . . ."

204:28 *humour.* Jonson defined his theory of humour in the induction to *Every Man Out of His Humour* (1599), where Asper links comic theory to the bodily humours:

> So in every humane body
> The choller, melancholy, flegme, and bloud,
> By reason that they flow continually
> In some one part, and are not continent,
> Receive the name of Humours. Now thus farre
> It may, by Metaphore, apply it selfe
> Unto the general disposition:
> As when some one peculiar quality
> Doth so possesse a man, that it doth draw
> All his affects, his spirits, and his powers,
> In their confluctions, all to runne one way,
> This may be truly said to be a Humour.

In denying that he was writing the comedy of humour, Dryden was taking a stand in opposition to Thomas Shadwell, who in his preface to *The Sullen Lovers* had attacked the new witty heroes and heroines. In arguing that his opponents (probably Edward Howard as well as Shadwell) were unsuccessful in writing the comedy of humours, Dryden may have been indicating the change in dramatic representation since Jonson's day: Shadwell's introduction of farcical elements, his borrowings from Molière, and his use of a character like Crazy in *The Humourists* (performed on 10 December 1670), a person suffering from venereal disease and hence a figure suffering from a natural infirmity rather than a humourous character.

204:32 *Crambe bis cocta.* Literally, twice-cooked cabbage. Dryden probably paraphrases Juvenal's satire upon repeated themes in poetry (VII, 154; Loeb trans.: "Served up again and again, the cabbage is the death of the unhappy master"). Summers (II, 499) points out that Erasmus listed a similar statement in his collection of proverbs.

204:34–35 *the follies of particular persons.* Shadwell was accused of having represented Sir Robert Howard as Sir Positive At-all in *The Sullen Lovers,* and Summers (Shadwell, *Works,* I, 270–271) suggests Edward Howard as the poet, Ninny, and the actress Susanna Uphill as Lady Vaine, among other characters being satirized by Shadwell. Pepys wrote on 8 May 1668: "But, Lord! to see how this play of Sir Positive At-all, in abuse of Sir Robert Howard, do take, all the Duke's and every body's talk being of that, and telling more stories of him, of the like nature, that it is now the town and country talk, and, they say, is most exactly true." In the preface to *The Humourists,* Shadwell (*Works,* I, 186) seems to be answering Dryden: "But I have had the fortune to have had a general humour (in a Play of mine) applied to three, or four men (whose persons I never saw, or humours ever heard of) till the Play was acted. . . . Mr. Jonson, I believe, was very unjustly taxed for personating particular men, but it will ever be the fate of them that write the humours of the Town, especially in a foolish, and vicious Age." In 1673 an anonymous author accused Dryden himself not only of libeling men on the stage but also of getting Shadwell to attack Howard in *The Sullen Lovers* (see *The Friendly Vindication of Mr. Dryden,* p. 8). For an account of Jonson's habit of pillorying his enemies on the stage, see Jonson, *Works*, I, 24–31.

204:35–205:1 *Parcere personis dicere de vitiis*. Martial, *Epigrams*, X, xxxiii (Loeb trans.): "To spare the person, to denounce the vice."

205:4–6 *In vitium libertas* etc. Horace, *Ars Poetica*, ll. 282–284 (Loeb trans.): "But its freedom sank into excess and a violence deserving to be checked by law. The law was obeyed, and the chorus to its shame became mute, its right to injure being withdrawn."

205:9, 11 *Neve immunda crepent* etc. Horace, *Ars Poetica*, ll. 246–247. Horace does not refer to the old comedy, but defends the dignity of the comedy that employs satyrs and their blunt humor. (Loeb trans.: "When the Fauns are brought from the forest, they should, methinks, beware of behaving as though born at the crossways and almost as dwelling in the Forum, playing at times the young bloods with their mawkish verses, or cracking their bawdy and shameless jokes. For some take offence—knights, free-born, and men of substance—nor do they greet with kindly feelings or reward with a crown everything which the buyers of roasted beans and chestnuts approve.") Dryden misquotes Horace's first word, which is *aut* rather than *neve*.

205:22 *they can practice it*. Shadwell's claim to following Jonson in his comic technique was couched modestly in the epilogue to *The Humourists*:

> Expect not then, since that most flourishing Age,
> Of BEN, to see true Humor on the Stage.
> All that have since been writ, if they be scan'd,
> Are but faint Copies from that Master's Hand.
> Our Poet now, amongst those petty things,
> Alas, his too weak trifling humors brings.
> As much beneath the worst in Johnson's Plays,
> As his great Merit is above our praise.

206:3–5 *Stulta reprehendere* etc. Quintilian, *Institutio Oratoria* (Loeb trans.): "It is easy to make fun of folly, for folly is laughable in itself: and laughter is never far removed from derision, but we may improve such jests by adding something of our own." Summers (II, 499) suggests that "Dryden, as is his wont, does not quote Quintilian's words, but using his own phrase and Latinity summarizes none too closely the great critic." Dryden is actually drawing upon two passages in Quintilian (VI, iii, 8 and 71).

206:7–8 *Non displicuisse illi jocos* etc. Quintilian, *Institutio*, VI, iii, 2 (Loeb trans.): "That he lacked the power, not merely that he disliked to use it."

206:10 *so little of humour as Fletcher*. This comparison of Fletcher and Jonson was common in contemporary criticism. Dryden had indulged in a similar exercise in *Of Dramatick Poesie* (1668, p. 48; Watson, I, 68–69).

206:16 *Urbana, venusta, salsa, faceta*. These are Quintilian's terms for different aspects of wit (*Institutio*, VI, iii, 17–20). They may be rendered as an urbane wit, a charming wit, a sharp wit, and a gentle wit.

206:22–23 *sunt, enim, longè venustiora* etc. Quintilian, *Institutio,* VI,
iii, 13 (Loeb trans.): "For wit always appears to greater advantage in
reply than in attack."

206:27 *Character of Wit.* See Cowley's ode "Of Wit," ll. 33–40:

> Yet 'tis not to adorn, and gild each part;
> That shows more Cost, then Art.
> Jewels at Nose and Lips but ill appear;
> Rather then all things Wit, let none be there.
> Several Lights will not be seen,
> If there be nothing else between.
> Men doubt, because they stand so thick i'th' skie,
> If those be Stars which paint the Galaxie.

206:31–32 *In omni ejus* etc. Quintilian, *Institutio,* VI, iii, 5 (Loeb
trans.): "In any case, as in regard to all the manifestations of his genius
[his detractors will] find it easier to detect superfluities than deficiencies."
Dryden quotes the last two words incorrectly; they should be *possit, in-
venient* instead of *potest, invenies.* Quintilian was speaking of Cicero,
not of Ovid.

207:1 *Repartie.* The *OED* assigns to this preface the first usage of this
word in this way, but Dryden was probably referring to Shadwell's attack
on "Repartie" in the preface to *The Sullen Lovers.* See 202:12–13n,
above.

207:7 *different characters in wit.* Dryden chooses for his examples
characters from Pierre Corneille's *The Lyar,* which Dryden mentioned in
Of Dramatick Poesie; from Fletcher's *The Chances,* a play recently revised
by George Villiers, Duke of Buckingham; and from Beaumont and
Fletcher's *Wit without Money.* The wits in these plays differ from one
another. Don John in *The Chances* is concerned only with women who
may be had without marriage; Valentine in *Wit without Money* dislikes
women and is interested only in railing wittily against them. Happy to
be rid of his estate, he announces, "my wit's my plough." Dorant in *The
Lyar* uses his wit to weave "lofty fictions" or to lie at every opportunity.
The Lyar, less popular than the other two plays, was performed only
twice during the Restoration and was not printed until 1685. Dryden
may have been using it to provide support from the French for his "character of wit," though, in fact, he was actually defending Fletcher, Shakespeare, and the new Restoration comedy of wit against the attacks of the
disciples of Jonson.

207:17 *translated verbatim.* See Jonson, *Works,* X, 7–8, 14–18; V, 167–
168, 179–183.

208:1 *'Tis charg'd upon me.* Dryden may be thinking of Shadwell's
remarks in the preface to *The Royal Shepherdess,* which was advertised
in the *Term Catalogues* for 22 November 1669. Shadwell compared his
play with the immoral plays of his contemporaries:

> I shall say little more of the Play, but that the Rules of
> Morality and good Manners are strictly observed in it:
> (Vertue being exalted, Vice depressed) and perhaps it

might have been better received had neither been done
in it: for I find, it pleases most to see Vice incouraged,
by bringing the Characters of debauch'd people upon
the Stage, and making them pass for fine Gentlemen,
who openly profess Swearing, Drinking, Whoring,
breaking Windows, beating Constables, etc. and that is
esteem'd among us a Gentile gayety of Humour, which
is contrary to the Customs and Laws of all civilized
Nations.

Shadwell also attacked the new plays in the prologue, pointing out that
his play was unlike the new witty comedies in providing a moral distribu-
tion of rewards:

It is a Vertuous Play, you will confess,
Where Vicious men meet their deserv'd success.
Not like our Modern ones, where still we find,
Poets are onely to the Ruffians kind.

Although Dryden seems on occasion to echo Shadwell's language, it is
always possible that the attacks to which he is referring were merely made
by the wits in the coffeehouses and were never printed. For a comment
on coffeehouse criticism, see Edward Howard, *The Six Days Adventure*
(1671), sig. A3.

208:4 *Law of Comedy.* For a discussion of the growth of the concept
of poetic justice, see Joseph Wood Krutch, *Comedy and Conscience in
the Restoration* (1962), pp. 77–82.

209:10 *Oedipus.* Dryden is probably drawing from Pierre Corneille's
Discours de la Tragédie (in *Œuvres de Pierre Corneille,* ed. Ch. Marty-
Laveaux [Paris, 1862–1922], I, 56–57), where he speaks of the problem of
an ideal tragic hero:

Il reste donc à trouver un milieu entre ces deux ex-
trémités, par le choix d'un homme qui ne soit ni tout
à fait bon, ni tout à fait méchant, et qui, par une faute,
ou foiblesse humaine, tombe dans un malheur qu'il ne
mérite pas. Aristote en donne pour exemples Œdipe et
Thyeste, en quoi véritablement je ne comprends point
sa pensée. Le premier me semble ne faire aucune faute,
bien qu'il tue son père, parce qu'il ne le connoit pas, et
qu'il ne fait que disputer le chemin en homme de coeur
contre un inconnu qui l'attaque avec avantage."

See also Corneille's "Examen" before his *Œdipe* (*Œuvres,* VI, 130).

209:16–17 *it is disputed . . . by Heinsius.* Dryden is in error here.
Contrary to Dryden's contention, Daniel Heinsius (1580–1655), in his
edition of Horace published in 1610, argued that the purpose of comedy
was both to teach and to delight. Whatever the source, Dryden's theory
became a *locus classicus* for the concept of delight as the end of comedy,
especially after Jeremy Collier's vigorous attack on it. For a brief discussion of pleasure as the end of comedy, see Edward Niles Hooker, ed.,
The Critical Works of John Dennis (1939), I, 514–515. For an applica-

tion of this principle to all forms of drama, see Bernard Weinberg, "Castelvetro's Theory of Poetics," in *Critics and Criticism*, ed. R. S. Crane (1952), 349–371.

209:21–22 *a pleasure that is more noble.* Dryden associates the new comedy of wit with a superior form of art. Since Hobbes and Charleton agreed that laughter was somewhat beneath the dignity of those people who did not need to laugh at the infirmities of others, Dryden is able to rely on their theories for the argument that a comedy of wit is necessarily superior to a Jonsonian comedy of humours. His theory that the audience feels a sense of shame at laughing and that this shame is what causes the audience to reform its own ridiculous habits is probably based on Jonson's and Heinsius' misreading of Aristotle, though in its implications Dryden's theory is not very different from the cathartic theories of comedy offered by Renaissance critics. See Bernard Weinberg, *A History of Literary Criticism in the Italian Renaissance* (1961), I, 538, 582, 587, 625–626; Spingarn, I, 58–59, 231–232.

210:19 *stealing all my Playes.* Dryden may be thinking specifically of the remark in *A Letter from a Gentleman to the Honourable Ed. Howard Esq* (1668), p. 2, where the writer points out that Howard acknowledged all his borrowings, "But the Squire perhaps is justly angry to see any one use the least thing of another Writer, and enter into his Jurisdiction, claiming the right of Theft perhaps by continual Custome; witness his *Maiden Queen* stoln out of the Queen of Corinth: a great part of his *Indian Emperour*, and most of his *Mock Astrologer*, [by] which he means (for he is a Critick) the *Feign'd Astrologer*, out of French Playes and Romances." Dryden may also have taken Shadwell's remarks in the preface to *The Sullen Lovers* as a reference to him. "But I freely confess my Theft," wrote Shadwell (*Works*, I, 10), "and am asham'd on't, though I have the example of some that never yet wrote Play without stealing most of it. . . . I cannot but believe that he that makes a common practice of stealing other mens Witt, would, if he could with the same safety, steal any thing else." Dryden himself attacked the plagiarizing of plays in his prologue to *Albumazar*.

210:23 *Et spes & ratio* etc. Juvenal, *Satires*, VII, 1 (Loeb trans.): "On Caesar alone hang all the hopes and prospects of the learned." Watson (I, 153) suggests that this passage is "No doubt a second compliment to the Duke of Newcastle, himself the author of several comedies, to whom *An Evening's Love* is dedicated." Dryden may, however, be referring to the King, who would certainly be in a better position to command his poet laureate than Newcastle.

211:3–4 *Hulk of Sir Francis Drake.* Drake's ship, the *Golden Hind*, in which he sailed around the world and which was visited by Queen Elizabeth on 4 April 1581, was kept as a national monument at Deptford. After a century it was so badly decayed that it had to be broken up. See Cowley, "Upon the Chair Made Out of Sir Francis Drakes Ship" (in *Poems*, ed. A. R. Waller [1905], p. 453). Gerard Langbaine thought Dryden was alluding to Plutarch's "Life of Theseus" (*Lives*, trans. John Dryden *et al.* [1683], I, 32).

211:6–7 *El Astrologo fingido*. By Pedro Calderón. *Le Feint Astrologue* was an adaptation by Thomas Corneille, produced in 1648 and published in 1651. *The Feign'd Astrologer*, an anonymous translation of Corneille, was published in 1668. See the discussion of the sources of Dryden's play (pp. 434–443, above).

211:14 *Walk*. Course of action assigned to one person in a drama (*OED*).

211:27 *help't . . . by . . . Lælius*. Cicero mentions this accusation (see *Letters to Atticus*, VII, 3). In his prologues to *The Self-Tormentor*, *Phormio*, and *The Brothers*, Terence himself refers to it as being leveled at him by a "malignant old Playwright," Luscius Lanuvinus.

212:1 *Hecatommithi*. Giraldi Cinthio's *Hecatommithi* (1566) was the source for *Othello* and a partial source for *Two Gentlemen of Verona*, *Twelfth Night*, and *Measure for Measure;* but if Dryden saw an Italian source for *Romeo and Juliet*, it was probably in Matteo Bandello's *Novelle*. Shakespeare may have taken the story from a more readily available English source.

212:4 *Spanish Novels*. Cervantes' *Exemplary Novels* (1613) supplied the plot for *The Chances* and the underplot of *Rule a Wife and Have a Wife*. *The Little French Lawyer* is derived from Mateo Alemán's *Guzman de Alfarache* (1599; trans. 1622); and *The Spanish Curate* was drawn from Leonard Digges's English translation (1622) of the Spanish novel, *Gerardo the Unfortunate Spaniard*, written by Gonzalo de Cespedes in 1615. Some of the other plays Dryden may have had in mind are *The Coxcomb*, *The Custom of the Country*, *The Double Falsehood*, and *Love's Pilgrimage*, all of which have Spanish sources.

212:18 *variety of the English Stage*. In his *General History of the Stage* (1754) Luigi Riccoboni observed (p. 172) that "the English Comedies are crowded with Incidents, insomuch that having adapted to their Stage some French Plays, the Authors have doubled the Intrigue, or they have joined them with another Plot to keep the Spectator in Breath, and not allow him time to wander with his Thoughts. The Miser of Molière among others, which in the Original is perhaps too full of Intrigue, has much more in the English Translations." Dryden had already criticized French comedy for its lack of "variety" in his essay *Of Dramatick Poesie* (1668, p. 38; Watson, I, 57).

212:26 ποιητὴς. This word means a maker, an author of a poem, a lawgiver, or a workman. Dryden's concept of the poet's function follows that of Aristotle (see Butcher, *Aristotle's Theory of Poetry and Fine Art*, pp. 190–225; Gerald F. Else, *Aristotle's Poetics: The Argument* [1957], pp. 9, 304–307).

212:26 *imployes*. In an obsolete sense, means "implies" or "signifies" (*OED*).

212:27 *fancy that gives the life touches*. Dryden repeats a theme he expressed in slightly different terms in the "Account" prefixed to *Annus Mirabilis* (*Works*, I, 53, 271–272). Here he puts more weight upon fancy than upon judgment, probably in order to stress his own feeling of confidence in the writing of successful heroic plays with their fanciful scenes of ghosts and spirits, and also in order to clarify his running argument with the disciples of Jonson.

213:3 *Gunsmith of the Minories.* John Stow (*A Survey of London,* ed. Charles Kingsford [1908], I, 126) reported "diverse faire and large storehouses, for armour, and habiliments of warre, with diverse worke-houses serving to the same purpose" in the Minories, a street running alongside the Tower of London where a nunnery was once located. In 1720 the editor of Stow remarked that in addition to the warehouses, the Minories was "of chief note for the Gunsmiths there inhabiting, and driving a considerable Trade." In Dryden's time the area may already have had an unsavory reputation for its open ditch and its dung heaps. See *A Survey of the Cities of London and Westminster,* corrected by John Strype (1720), Bk. II, pp. 15, 28.

PROLOGUE

As late as 1924 Joseph Wood Krutch called this prologue "unprintable" (*Comedy and Conscience in the Restoration,* p. 85). Although it indeed ranks among the most obscene of Dryden's works, this quality should not hinder the recognition of Dryden's brilliance in sustaining the single simile of the audience as a wayward wife and the playwright as an understanding cuckold. Had Dryden merely been trying to titillate the audience, the prologue might well have deserved the judgment that Krutch thought his readers would make, but Dryden succeeded in making the comparison a profound one. The double entendres should be as obvious to a modern reader as they were to the Restoration audience.

16 *gets.* Used in the sense of begets.

19 *janty.* Jaunty, meaning genteel or well-bred.

33 *but thrice a year.* A reference to Dryden's contract with the King's Company to provide three plays a year in return for a share and a quarter of the profits. As Ward points out (Ward, *Life,* p. 57), the contract gave Dryden the same financial terms as the best actors of the company enjoyed.

PERSONS REPRESENTED

the last Evening of the Carnival. That is, Shrove Tuesday. According to the English calendar, it would be the evening of 21 March 1665; the date on the Continent would have been ten days later.

I, i

19 *I'll perform it.* In the opening lines of the play Dryden retains the theme of honor and friendship which is present in all his sources— Calderón, Scudéry, and Quinault. If Dryden's use of verse in this passage is any indication, he may have initially conceived of his play along the more traditional lines of Spanish comedy. Only in Scudéry's version, however, does the character represented by Dryden's Don Melchor have his friend deliver a letter explaining his supposed departure.

22 *Guests of the English Embassador's Retinue.* Since Dryden is very

specific concerning the time of the action, it is possible to set the milieu of the play and to suggest some knowledge on the part of the audience of events that were still fresh in their minds. The English ambassador at this time was Sir Richard Fanshawe, who arrived in Spain on 18 June 1664 to negotiate a treaty between the two nations. Although his reception at the court was ceremonious, Fanshawe was kept waiting pending the expected death of Philip IV. When this event occurred on 7 September 1665, Fanshawe was surprised to find himself presented with a treaty. He signed it with the provision that it would have to be approved by Charles II, who decided against it. Lord Sandwich was sent to Spain to replace Fanshawe, and on 13/23 May 1667 he succeeded in negotiating a new treaty plus an additional commercial treaty. Fanshawe died on 18/28 May 1666, shortly after being relieved of his duties. See Anne Fanshawe, *Memoirs*, ed. Herbert Fanshawe (1907), pp. 234–251; Keith Feiling, *British Foreign Policy, 1660–1672* (1930), pp. 168–183, 232–233.

36 *till we came to taste it.* Reports on the scarcity and the poor quality of the food in Spain were common. According to the anonymous author of *The Character of Spain: or an Epitome of Their Virtues and Vices* (1660), "Happy are they that were never so unhappy as to see the sterility of Spain, but to believe it onely. 'Tis an excellent Countrey to travel in, for you shall scarce meet with Meat for money, but Sawce good store, nor an Inne to entertain you; for the Master and the Mule usually lodge together, and the latter perhaps meets with better fare than the former" (p. 2). This image of Spain appears in several other Restoration plays (see Thomas Killigrew, *Thomaso; or, The Wanderer*, in *Comedies, and Tragedies* [1664], p. 320; John Wilson, *The Projectors* [1664], in *Works*, ed. James Maidment and W. H. Logan [Edinburgh, 1874], p. 259).

56 *reconquest of Flanders.* By the treaties of Munster (1648), Pyrenees (1659), and Aix-la-Chapelle (1668), Spain lost portions of Flanders to Holland and France.

56–57 *fly 'em to a Mark.* This image, the first of many from hunting and falconry in the play, refers to the action of a goshawk when she takes a stand to indicate a covey of partridges.

58 *Courtezans.* Antoine de Brunel's *A Journey into Spain*, which Dryden may have read in French when it appeared in 1665, contains a description of the "bizarre" courtesans with their gaudy apparel and painted faces: "They which are well acquainted with Madrid," he wrote, "assure, that most Families are ruined by Women: every man keeps a Mistress, or is besotted on a Curtisan. . . ." (1670, pp. 34–35; see also pp. 100–101).

59 *rash.* A rustling noise.

70 *projection.* In alchemy, the casting of a powder on a metal to effect its transmutation into gold or silver.

81 *light of Nature.* The "conventionalists" contended that marriage was an unnatural custom, and argued that social laws were merely set up to make man tractable for society. The attitude was a commonplace among Neo-Epicureans and libertines.

82 *Prado.* The wide boulevard in Madrid. Wildblood's objection may

be based on the number and the brazenness of the courtesans there (see Brunel, pp. 36–37).

90 *feathers.* Beaux, gallants.

97 *let us pull up our Vails.* According to Brunel (pp. 35–36), respectable women in Spain "scarce ever go abroad, neither by Coach, nor otherwayes, to take the Air. Most of them hear Mass in their own Houses, and excepting some few Visits, never appear in Publick and then in Sedans." The courtesans, on the other hand, wore black veils which left one eye uncovered. Dryden is transplanting the conditions of English comedy to Spain, but Bellamy's complaint about his shoes (ll. 114–115) adds some accurate local color. Brunel (p. 57) reports that "shooes are shaped exactly to their feet, with narrow soles; and a little Foot and large calf of the leg, are in such request that Gallants bind their feet about with Riband, to their no small torment. . . ."

126 *Alguazile.* An officer of the law.

131–132 *I am your Spaniel . . . I'll wait on you.* A proverb (see Tilley, S704, S705, W644). In his copy of the play (now owned by the Folger Library), Gerard Langbaine compared this passage with *A Midsummer Night's Dream,* II, i, 203.

138 *Juego de cannas.* Sometimes refers to bullfighting in general, sometimes to placing the small barbs in the neck of the bull from horseback. Brunel (p. 80) writes that "the serious part, and that in which the activity consists, is the darting certain Arrows or little Javelines, which the skilful fix between the Bulls horns, with admirable dexterity, without which they would be torn in pieces." Dryden mentions the *juego de cannas* at the beginning of *The Conquest of Granada.*

152–153 *Atalanta in the fable.* Atalanta, warned against marriage by an oracle, challenged her suitors to a foot race and killed them after she had overtaken them. Hippomenes defeated her by dropping three golden apples which Aphrodite had given him. Atalanta stopped to pick up the apples and, having lost the race, was forced to marry Hippomenes. But Hippomenes failed to thank Aphrodite for her gift, and through her wrath both he and Atalanta were changed into lions. See Ovid, *Metamorphoses,* X, 560–707.

188 *Calle major.* The Calle Major, the most important commercial street in Madrid at this time, ran from the Puerta de Guadalajara to the Puerta del Sol (see Luis Martínez Kleiser, *Guia de Madrid Para El Año 1656* [1926], p. 41).

I, ii

18–21 *in other Countries* etc. Cf. the speech of Lucetta in Killigrew's *Thomaso; or, The Wanderer,* p. 323 (I, iii): "Lament in my behalf the sad condition of a Woman of quality in this Nation, whose jealous customes will admit no occasions for Men to make their addresses to us, which exposes us thus to their censure, forced against the modesty and custome of our Sex to speak first. . . ."

26–27 *no other Prayer, but only that they may not mistake us.* Summers (II, 503) suggests that Evelyn had the chapel scene in mind when he called *Evening's Love* "very profane," but Dryden may merely have been staging what was thought to be a common practice in Spain. Pepys reports a conversation with a friend about Spain on 27 September 1667, which repeats this gossip: "He tells me of their wooing by serenades at the window, and that their friends do always make the match; but yet that they have opportunities to meet at masse at church, and there they make love."

85 *Their wit and beauty.* Brunel (p. 36) says it "must needs be granted that this Sex hath here a great deal of Wit, exercising it self in Reparties; and this with much liberty. . . ."

103 *Monsieurland.* See Wycherley's characterization of Monsieur de Paris in *The Gentleman Dancing Master* (1672) for a good example of satire on the aping of French manners.

107 *Gennits.* Jennets, small Spanish horses.

144 *old law of pawns.* Deuteronomy, XXIV, 10–13: "When thou dost lend thy brother any thing, thou shalt not go into his house to fetch his pledge. Thou shalt stand abroad, and the man to whom thou dost lend shall bring out the pledge abroad unto thee. And if the man be poor, thou shalt not sleep with his pledge: In any case thou shalt deliver him the pledge again when the sun goeth down, that he may sleep in his own raiment, and bless thee: and it shall be righteousness unto thee before the Lord thy God."

146–147 *a man's a pool if love stir him not.* Dryden is arguing that passions are valuable, that man is dull and lifeless without them, and that though they may lead him to evil they are also the source of the greatest good. Dryden's friend, Dr. Walter Charleton, who defended the "Use" of the passions in general (*Natural History of the Passions* [1674], pp. 106–109), described the physical effects of love upon the body and its general improvement of the spirit: "For, they who are affected there-with . . . feel a certain agreeable heat diffused in their breast; they find their brain invigorated by abundance of Spirits, and thereby grow more ingenuous; and in fine they digest their meat quickly, and perform all actions of life readily and with alacrity" (p. 108; see also pp. 168–171).

149–150 *a strong imagination is requir'd . . . . in a Witch.* Dryden echoes the position of Reginald Scot and his followers (see Scot, pp. 29–34; John Gaule, *The Mag-Astro-Mancer, or the Magicall-Astrologicall-Diviner Posed, and Puzzled* [1652], pp. 50, 105).

II, i

17 *retrieve.* This term and the entire image are taken from the language of hawking. A retrieve is the second discovery and flight of a bird (especially a partridge) that is already sprung; the bells with the attachments that tie them to the legs of the hawk are called bewits (see Cox, Pt. II, frontispiece and pp. 162, 167).

26–27 *opiniatre.* Stubborn.

50 *swinge.* Full liberty to follow her inclinations.

71–74 *'Tis so wild . . . 'Tis a meer Bajazet* etc. See Marlowe's *Tambur-*

laine the Great, Part I, V, ii. Dryden's passage seems to echo Marlowe's stage direction, "He brains himself against the cage." Bajazet became chief of the Ottoman Turks in 1389 and was defeated on 28 July 1402 by Tamerlane, dying nine months later (see Summers, II, 503, for a learned note on the subject). The imagery itself is explained by contemporary directions concerning methods for preventing tame birds from "beating their tender bodies against the top and Wyres of the Cage" (see Cox, Pt. III, pp. 56–57; Richard Blome, *The Gentleman's Recreation* [1686], Pt. II, p. 166).

87 *Æsop's Frog.* See *Fables of Æsop,* ed. Sir Roger L'Estrange (1699), I, 129. The moral drawn by L'Estrange is, " 'Tis Good Advice to Look before we Leap."

93 *racy.* The first use of this word in the sense of "Having a distinctive quality of vigour or character or intellect, lively, spirited, full of 'go' " (*OED*).

111 *a whole Ægyptian year.* Two days of the month which were considered ill-omened were called "Egyptian days," and Jacinta may be totaling up the twenty-four Egyptian days in the year to suggest that a month of marriage would be the distillation of all the bad days in the year. Jacinta's "dismally" refers to these *dies mali.*

117 *your Spanish Planet, and my English one.* The planet governing Spain was Jupiter; Mars was the governing planet of England (see Partridge, pp. 73, 75).

118 *some by-room or other in the 12 houses.* "The Zodiack is divided into 12 equal parts, called Houses, which Houses the Signs of the Zodiack do always possess" (Partridge, p. 38; see also William Lilly, *Christian Astrology* [2d ed.; 1659], pp. 47–48). For a somewhat similar play on words involving planetary houses and human houses, see Samuel Butler, *Hudibras,* ed. John Wilders (1967), p. 18 (I, i, 583–586).

120 *take up.* Stop.

128 *Passa-calles.* Passacaglia. The *OED* lists the occurrence here as one of the earliest usages of this word. *Grove's Dictionary of Music and Musicians,* ed. Eric Blom (1954), VI, 575, defines *passacaglia* as an "early Italian or Spanish dance, similar in character to a chaconne." Apparently no contemporary setting for this song has survived.

162 *tear you a pieces.* The conjurer, always in danger from the spirits, had to be cautious about leaving the magic circle, which served him as a fortress; the spirits might be irritated either by too much employment or by too little (see Scot, pp. 215–239; Pietro d'Abano, *Heptameron, or Magical Elements,* in Cornelius Agrippa, pseud., *Fourth Book of Occult Philosophy,* trans. Robert Turner [1783], p. 127).

169–170 *Ladies . . . Banquiers of their Servants. Banquier* was a common term for banker in the seventeenth century. Jacinta's statement is confirmed by a contemporary account: "They which are well acquainted with Madrid, assure, that most Families are ruined by Women: every man keeps a Mistress, or is besotted on a Curtisan; who . . . as soon as they ensnare any, plume them to the quick. . . ." (Brunel, pp. 34–35).

175 *Cordial.* For a discussion of the use of gold as a cordial see John

Schroder, *The Compleat Chymical Dispensatory*, trans. William Rowland (1669), pp. 178–186.

188 *French Fashion*. Although Boulenger reports one invasion (of Valtellina on 25 November 1624) before 1665 in which France did not declare war, the reference must be regarded, on the whole, as anachronistic and contemporary. In May 1667 and February 1668 France suddenly invaded Flanders and Franche-Comté. The treaty of Aix-la-Chapelle forced France to give up some of her gains, but required Spain "to quit Charleroy, Binch, Ath, Douay, Tournay, Oudenard, L'Isle Armetier, Courtray, Bergh and Furnes, with all their Dependencies, Appurtenances and Jurisdictions" (see *The Bounds Set to France by the Pyrenean Treaty* [1694], pp. 35–36; Jacques Boulenger, *The Seventeenth Century in France* [1963], pp. 41, 221–223). For a detailed account of the progress of the war see the *London Gazette*, 13–16 May 1667; 13–17 February 1668.

190–191 *to be in the middle of the Country*. France conquered Flanders in less than three months and Franche-Comté in less than three weeks.

254–255 *Captaining to Flanders*. The contemporary response to such a remark must have turned to the war then going on against the French in Flanders. England had signed an alliance with Holland and Sweden (the Triple Alliance) against France in order to restore to Spain her possessions in Flanders. But Calderón's Don Juan also goes to Flanders (see Pedro Calderón de la Barca, *El Astrólogo Fingido*, in *Obras Completas*, ed. Angel Valbuena Briones, II [2d ed.; 1960], 130 [Jornada I]).

288 *Oph. Oaf*.

291 *Astrologer*. Boulenger reports that sorcery and magic were "tremendously in fashion" at this time in France. The ideal of the court, he remarks, quoting Molière, was simply to transform "everything into gold, carry on life for ever, cure by spoken words, make themselves loved by any one they chose, know all the secretes of the future, command evil spirits" (*Seventeenth Century in France*, p. 191). In 1668 two quacks who had assisted Mme de Montespan in giving love philters to the King were arrested. How much of this interest in sorcery and magic carried over to England is difficult to say, but the *Oxford Gazette* (no. 3, 20 November 1665) reported news of a famous astrologer in Vienna as an exciting event, and both revivals and contemporary plays revealed an interest in magic and astrology.

318 *Chrystal*. For a formula to conjure up a spirit and visions in a crystal, see Scot, pp. 257–258.

323 *Lilly*. William Lilly (1602–1681), the famous astrologer and writer of almanacs, was considered something of a hoax by the time Dryden was writing. Pepys reports a conversation with a friend who accused Lilly of having changed the rules of the art of astrology in order to please his friends (24 October 1660), and he tells of one occasion (14 June 1667) when they laughed at Lilly's predictions. Nevertheless, Lilly says the parliamentary forces used him at the siege of Colchester to predict victory, and when London was destroyed by fire, he was questioned concerning a picture of a city in flames which had appeared in 1651 (see Lilly, *History of His Life and Times* [1715], pp. 67, 95–97).

343 *Gorget.* An article of female dress covering the neck and bosom.

364–365 *Nostradamusses.* Nostradamus, or Michel de Nostredame (1503–1566), achieved fame through the publication of his *Centuries* in 1555. He was appointed physician in ordinary to the French court through the help of Catherine de' Medici. The pretenders to astrology in Dryden's sources claimed to have studied under him (see Madeleine de Scudéry, *Ibrahim, or the Illustrious Bassa,* trans. Henry Cogan [1652], Pt. II, Bk. II, p. 25; Thomas Corneille, *Le Feint Astrologue,* in *Poëmes Dramatiques* [Paris, 1661], I, 149 [II, ii]).

389 *gravels.* Perplexes.

391 *Præmunire.* Predicament, scrape.

395 *trine Aspect of the two Infortunes in Angular houses.* The trine aspect is that of two heavenly bodies 120 degrees distant from each other. The two infortunes are Saturn and Mars. The angular houses are the first, fourth, seventh, and tenth signs of the zodiac, or Aries, Cancer, Libra, and Capricorn. Although the infortunes would threaten some disaster, the trine aspect is so beneficial as to change their potentially evil influence to good. See, for example, Partridge, pp. 24, 38–39, 339; John Bishop, *The Marrow of Astrology* (1688), Pt. I, pp. 4, 34–38, 44–48.

398 *quærent.* A technical term in astrology signifying the person who questions the astrologer.

409 *taking Hyleg.* Signifying a way of casting a nativity on the basis of a ruling planet or of a place in the heavens (see Lilly, *Christian Astrology,* p. 531 [CIV]).

409–410 *rectification for a Nativity.* Finding out the precise time of birth in order to cast a nativity (see Bishop, *Marrow of Astrology,* Pt. II, p. 1).

410–411 *Centiloquium of Trismegistus.* The hundred aphorisms on astrology ascribed to Hermes Trismegistus. They are printed in Partridge, pp. 290–304.

411 *Mars in the tenth.* Mars, as one of the infortunes, is always harmful, though least so in the sixth house. The harm from Mars, however, does not usually afflict the person himself, but, as the result of his malignant power, is more likely to be inflicted by him upon another (see Partridge, pp. 153, 278–279, 290).

412 *Jupiter.* One of Hermes' aphorisms is that "Jupiter in a good Aspect of the Infortunes changeth their Malevolency into good," but that only with difficulty can the power of Jupiter in a bad aspect prevail over the infortunes. Jupiter has the particular power of dissolving the malevolence of Saturn. See Partridge, pp. 278, 284, 289, 290, 294.

445 *Squire Widdrington.* The character in the ballad "Chevy Chase" who fights on his "stumps" after his legs have been cut off (*The English and Scottish Ballads,* ed. Francis Child [1890], III, 313).

448–449 *Haly, and the spirit Fircu in the Fortune-book.* "Haly, Alis-Ibn-Isa, chief astronomer at the court of Haroun Alraschid's famous son, Abul Abbas Abdallah Momoun, seventh Abasside caliph, 786–835. . . . Fircu is a fantastic name given to a supposed familiar of whom mention may be found in the old almanacs" (Summers, II, 507). Both Haly and

Fircu are depicted in *The Book of Fortune* (1698), with quatrains of predictions below their pictures. Fircu's picture is merely that of one of the three icons for astrologers used in the work, but Haly is individualized with a sharp nose and a strong jaw (see illustration facing p. 243). Scot (p. 235) lists Furcas as one of the demons of hell.

465 *all the trade of Lapland.* The witches in Lapland were known to sell winds to sailors, and as late as 1727 Defoe reported the efficacy of their magic: "Whether these good spirits are not those, who at the request of some certain people on all the coasts of Norway, are said to procure fair winds for ships going to sea, I will not undertake to say; but this I have upon strict inquiry learnt: First, that it really is so in fact; that upon going to certain people there, and upon paying them a small consideration (not above two dollars), they have been assured of a fair wind, exactly at such a time, from such a certain point of the compass, and to last so many hours, as been agreed for." Defoe reports that "they have never failed" and never raised a harmful wind. The price seems to have gone up from the time that Fletcher said they sold winds for "dead drink and old doublets." See Defoe, *A System of Magick,* in *The Novels and Miscellaneous Works* (1840), XII, 318; *The Chances,* in Francis Beaumont and John Fletcher, *Works,* ed. E. K. Chambers (1912), IV, 521 (V, iii).

475–476 *Lilly . . . if our sins hinder not.* Lilly frequently modified his predictions with phrases like "if we over-do not" or "if God give a blessing" (see Lilly, *Englands Propheticall Merline* [1644], p. 108).

483 *Tinker in the Play.* A reference to Christopher Sly in the induction to Shakespeare's *The Taming of the Shrew.*

485–486 *throwing out a handkerchief.* Whatever its general import in Europe, this gesture was the indication given by the grand seignior in selecting a woman from his seraglio (see Paul Rycaut, *The Present State of the Ottoman Empire* [1668], p. 39; Samuel Purchas, *Purchas his Pilgrimes* [Glasgow ed.; 1905–1907], VIII, 158).

491 *Musick.* A company of musicians.

514+ *s.d. above.* In the balcony located over the proscenium door.

563–564 *back-sides.* Italians were noted for sodomy. See Defoe's delineation of various national sins in *The True Born Englishman* (in *A True Collection of the Writings of the Author of the True Born Englishman* [1703], I, 2):

> Lust chose the Torrid Zone of Italy,
> Where Blood ferments in Rapes and Sodomy.

Summers (II, 508) quotes James Howell's *Paroimiologia* (1659): "Tres Italianos, dos bugerones, el otro Atheista."

III, i

16 *Argol.* Almanac. The word is derived from Andrea Argoli (1570–1650), whose treatises on astrology were frequently used as the basis for almanacs.

17 *Cant.* Bellamy has learned the basic terms of astrology. Conjunction is the position of two planets when they are in the same or nearly the

same direction from earth. Trine denotes a distance of 120 degrees between two planets; opposition is a distance of 180 degrees between planets. Partridge (pp. 23–24) states that whereas trine is an aspect of perfect love and amity, opposition is an aspect of perfect hatred. Square or quartile comprehends the distance of 90 degrees and is an aspect of "imperfect hate." Sextile, which is "an aspect of Friendship, though imperfect," is the aspect of two heavenly bodies that are 60 degrees, or one-sixth part of the zodiac, distant from each other.

24 *New Prophet*. Summers (II, 509) is probably correct in taking this phrase as a reference to the Fifth Monarchy Men and perhaps as a specific reference to Thomas Venner's preaching that "the sword of the Lord was whetted and going forth against the enemies of His people." Venner, along with fifty of his followers, staged an abortive revolution on 6 January 1660/1. They were overpowered after all but twenty had been killed. All but four were hanged; Venner and Roger Hodgkin were drawn and quartered. See *A Relation of the Arraignment and Trial of those who made the late Rebellious Insurrections in London,* in *Somers Tracts* (1748), IV, 520–523; P. G. Rogers, *The Fifth Monarchy Men* (1966), pp. 110–122.

42 *Boracho's*. Drunkards.

50 *Begging-box*. For a description of those imprisoned for debt and their begging, see *Spectator,* no. 82.

90 *Counsellor of the Graces*. A direct borrowing from Molière's *Les Précieuses Ridicules,* scene vii, where Magdelon scolds her maid in much the same manner as Aurelia does. Molière was satirizing the précieuse diction and language of the salons of the time; the salon of Madame de Rambouillet, the most famous of them, reached its height of renown between 1630 and 1645. The précieuse mode was a major influence on the literature of the court of Charles I, and the popularity of French romances maintained its influence through the rest of the century. Richard Flecknoe used the phrase "Councellor of the Graces" in his translation of Molière's *The Damoiselles à la Mode* (1667), p. 36 (II, iii).

171 *Genius, or Idea*. See Agrippa, pp. 410–412, for a discussion of the good genius who rules each man.

182–183 *bottle of hay*. See Christopher Marlowe, *Doctor Faustus* (scene xi). The horse courser finds that his mount has turned into a "bottle of hay" when he rides it into a pond after being warned by Faustus against riding into water.

201 *smickering*. Casting lewd glances.

249 *Lancashire Devils*. For an account of this "proverbial" phrase, see Montague Summers, *The Geography of Witchcraft* (1927), pp. 133–138.

250 *Tybert and Grimalkin*. "Tibert is the name of the cat in the apologue of Reynard the Fox, and hence is generically used for any cat. Grimalkin (probably from *grey* and *Malkin, Matilda*) is an old she-cat. Cats are proverbially connected with witches, and in the Lancashire of 1612 Elizabeth Sothernes, alias Old Dembdike, confessed to the Justice of Peace Roger Nowell that she entertained a spirit 'called Tibb, in the shape of a black cat'" (Summers, II, 511).

250 *wet their feet.* Dryden is running together the superstition of the devil's fear of water with the proverb, "The Cat would eat fish but she will not wet her feet" (Tilley, C144).

287 *five Hylegiacalls.* To erect a nativity according to the five hylegiacals named by Dryden was considered an alternative to judging the lord of the nativity according to the moon (see Partridge, pp. 83–84; Lilly, *Christian Astrology,* pp. 525–531, 656–657). What Dryden calls *Sors* is probably a reference to the *pars fortunae,* or "Part of Fortune."

306–307 *Aldeboran, and there Cor Scorpii.* According to Ptolemy, both Aldebaran, in the constellation Taurus, and Cor Scorpio or Antares, in the constellation Scorpio, had the same action as Mars, though Antares had some degree of Jupiter in its influence. Both stars signified either difficulties or, when in conjunction with Mars, a violent death for the person born under their influence. See Ptolemy, *Tetrabiblos* (Loeb trans.), pp. 46–51 [I, ix]; E. Sibly, *A New and Complete Illustration of the Celestial Science of Astrology* [1817], pp. 234–239).

353–354 *impetus dicendi.* Literally an onslaught of speaking (see Quintilian, *Institutio,* III, viii, 60; IX, iv, 35).

360 *Loquere ut te videam.* "Say somthing, that I may see what you are like." Apuleius, in his *Florida,* ascribes this phrase to Socrates, who insisted that men must be seen through the "mind's eye" (see Apuleius, *The Apologia and Florida,* trans. H. E. Butler [1909], p. 160). Dryden took this phrase as well as Alonzo's entire speech from Molière's *Le Dépit Amoureux* (in *Œuvres,* ed. Eugène Despois, I [Paris, 1873], 451 [II, vi]):

> D'où vient fort à propos cette sentence expresse
> D'un philosophe: "Parle, afin qu'on te connoisse."

436–437 *break no squares.* Cause no harm.

447 *Your Prophet's a Cavalier.* The Koran promises a paradise of black-eyed houris and sensual delights to satisfy any libertine. For a typical reaction to these passages in the Koran see Sir Thomas Herbert, *Some Yeares Travels into Africa & Asia the Great* (1665), pp. 346–347. After describing the women in paradise ("their hairs being threads of Gold, their eyes Diamonds as big as the Moon: their lips resemble Cherries, their teeth Pearl, their tongues Rubies, their cheeks Corral, their noses Jasper, their fore heads Saphire: round-faced, courteous and mercifull"), Herbert sneers at the "fanatic Dogmataes of the Alcoran" and wonders that so many people can believe such stories.

458 *Hamets . . . Zegrys . . . Bencerrages.* Moorish factions in Granada before the fall of the city in 1492. Dryden was already clearly familiar with the material he was eventually to work into the two parts of *The Conquest of Granada.* For a fictionalized presentation of the conflict within Granada, see Georges and Madeleine de Scudéry, *Almahide,* trans. John Phillips (1677), pp. 1–10.

463 *high-running Dice.* Dice loaded or filed in such a way as to turn on a high number (see Charles Cotton, *The Compleat Gamester* [1674], pp. 12–13).

471 *Raffle.* "A game with three Dice, wherein he that throws the

greatest Pair-Royal, wins" (Thomas Blount, *Glossographia* [1661]).

472 *Duplets.* Sometimes doublets, the same number turning up on two of the three dice at a throw.

473 *In and In.* What Dryden describes appears to be a combination of the English game in-and-in and the French game raffle. In-and-in was played with four dice. The term was used to describe any combination of pairs, but in raffle it signified a throw of three dice with the same number (see Cotton, *Compleat Gamester,* pp. 164–165).

477 *two quaters and a sice.* Two fours and a six.

548–549 *commend to you.* Give me you by choice (*OED*).

570 *Maravedis.* "A kind of Spanish coin of very small value, 34 of them amounting but to a Royal, which is about 6 pence of our money" (Edward Phillips, *The New World of English Words* [1658], sig. Bb2).

603 *sinews of warr.* Money. A mercantilist commonplace. See Tilley, M1067.

631 *throw out.* To make a losing cast; in raffle, failure to make a doublet.

632 *Bulli-Ruffin.* Cotton tells of the "Bully-Huffs" and "Bully-Rocks" who rob the winners after the game is over, and also notes, "some I have known so abominably impudent, that they would snatch up the Stakes, and thereupon instantly draw, saying, if you will have your money you must fight for it; for he is a Gentleman and will not want" (*Compleat Gamester,* pp. 8–9). *A New Canting Dictionary* (1725), sig. C2v, defines "Bully-Ruffins" as "Highway-men or Padders, of the most cruel and desperate kind: Who attack with Oaths and Curses, plunder without Mercy, and frequently murder without Necessity."

IV, i

24 *Mathematicks.* A common term for astrology.

34 *bleeding.* Losing. The *OED* records this as the first use of the word in this figurative sense.

75 *Laws of Nations.* Surely a reference to the famous "battle of the ambassadors" which created such a stir in Europe. In 1661 the Spanish ambassador, Baron de Watteville, representing Philip IV, tried to take precedence over the Comte d'Estrades, the French ambassador, and caused a battle in the streets of London. According to the law of nations, an ambassador was to be considered as an extension of the king of the country he represented, and it was not surprising that Louis XIV was affronted. The Treaty of Lisbon was almost left unratified because the Earl of Sandwich allowed the Spanish ambassador, the Marquess of Carpio, to put his signature above Sandwich's. See F. R. Harris, *The Life of Edward Montagu* (1912), II, 147; Pepys, *Diary,* 30 September 1661.

91 *Universal-Monarchy.* A term applied to the aspirations of various monarchs to gain control of Europe, but by 1667 it was beginning to be applied almost exclusively to the schemes of Louis XIV, whose conquest of Flanders and Franche-Comté suggested that he had the power to overcome all Europe (see François Paul de Lisola, *The Buckler of State and Justice against the Design Manifestly Discovered of the Universal Monarchy* [1667], sig. A6).

99 *the sight of black.* For a somewhat similar stereotyped image of sensuous Negro women, see Killigrew, *Comedies, and Tragedies,* p. 453.

115 *Et la lune & les estoiles.* According to Saintsbury, "The quotation is hardly sufficient to identify the song. Moons and stars were not infrequent in that description of literature" (S-S, III, 320). Unfortunately nothing more has been discovered about Wildblood's song.

119 *stoop . . . Sowse.* Both terms are from hawking. Stooping describes the flight of the hawk as it descends from aloft upon its prey; to sowse is to swoop down with speed and force (see Cox, Pt. II, p. 167).

146 *Piquing.* To pique is to strive or to view with thorough envy or jealousy. The *OED* lists this occurrence as the single example of this usage.

149 *Heron and Jerfalcon.* For the "high-flying" of these birds, see Cox, Pt. II, pp. 203–205, 210.

192 *nick.* To win at dice. See *A New Canting Dictionary,* sig. H2.

194 *butters.* "To double or treble the Bet or Wager, in order to recover all Losses" (*A New Canting Dictionary,* sig. C3).

197 + *s.d. The Scene opens* etc. Although we have not indicated a new scene here, this section, concluding with the overthrown table and lights (l. 239 +), may, from the standpoint of staging, at least, be regarded as a separate scene. For a discussion of this impressionistic technique, see Staging, p. 488, below.

217–218 *Specter . . . Fantome . . . Idea.* Aurelia is uncertain whether she is going to meet Don Melchor's genius or guardian spirit, which has assumed his form, or some kind of shadowy representation of him such as the spiritualists believed in. The ambiguity exists in Dryden's sources (see Calderón, *El Astrólogo Fingido,* pp. 145, 149–150 [Jornada II]).

299 *Ambages.* Circuitous means of speech.

302–303 *Table Diamond.* A diamond cut with a flat upper surface which is large in proportion to the faceted sides.

313–314 *Degree ascending.* One of the major claims made by astrology was its ability to locate goods stolen or lost. Lilly does not require the information that Alonzo seems to consider crucial for recovering the object (see *Christian Astrology,* pp. 319–366).

340 *erect a Scheme.* "Before you come to set a Scheme or Figure of Heaven, it will be convenient to let you know what a Scheme is; and therefore be pleased to take notice, that a Figure or Scheme is nothing else but a Delineation of the Heavens in Plane, according to the division of the Sphear—Thus,—The Zodiack is divided into equal parts, called Houses, which Houses the Signs of the Zodiack do always possess, the principle Angles of these 12 are the Ascendant and Mid-heaven, with their Opposites; these 12 Houses are divided by the Horizon into two Hemisphears, the one *Supra terram,* the other *Infra terram;* that Hemisphear above the Earth is divided by the Meridian into Oriental and Occidental, East and West" (Partridge, p. 38).

351 *nimble Master Mercury.* "This nimble messenger Mercury . . . is the Author of subtile tricks, as thefts, perjuries, cliping, and coyning, also all manner of deceit whatsoever" (Bishop, *Marrow of Astrology,* Pt. I, p. 59).

367 *reliefe.* To do acts of charity.

411 *the Dragons tail.* "The Dragons-head and Tail are no Stars, but Nodes, or imaginary points in the Heavens, and is not more but the Intersection of the Ecliptick and Orbite of the . . . [moon], to which points when she comes, she changes the denomination of her Latitude; . . . the Dragons-tail is esteemed an Infortune, and doth increase the Evil of the Infortunes, and abateth the good of the fortunate Stars" (Partridge, p. 18).

466 *Albricias.* A Spanish word signifying a reward given to the bearer of good news.

632 *Is the wind in that door.* A proverbial expression analogous to knowing which way the wind blows. Observing that Wildblood has decided the best defense is an attack, Maskall groans at his master's strategy (see Tilley, W419).

708 *take back your Picture.* This scene of quarrel and reconciliation on the level of masters and servants is taken from Molière's *Le Dépit Amoureux* (in *Œuvres*, ed. Despois, I, 486–494 [IV, iii]).

720 *Mutton haft.* A knife handle of sheep bone.

720–721 *knives are of little use.* Another remark on the poverty of Spain (see note to I, i, 36, above).

722 *Cizars.* Scissors.

726 *ferret Ribbaning.* Ferret is a stout tape most commonly made of cotton, but also of silk.

765 *Venice-glass.* Renowned for its beauty, Venetian glass was also known for its brittleness.

780 *The prime Articles between Spain and England.* The concept of the lovers as representatives of their nations in their quarrels and agreements is entirely original with Dryden. The final treaty with Spain was not signed until April 1667 after the original commercial treaty which Sir Richard Fanshawe had provisionally accepted on 7 December 1665 was rejected. Beatrice's objections to "Leagues offensive and defensive" is wise, for such a treaty would have brought Spain into war with France, though Maskall's suggestion that both may "fall to privateering" is ominous for future English-Spanish relations, since the treaty itself suspended privateering. What Wildblood means by "the Article of Navigation" (ll. 783–784) is difficult to determine, though the phrase may refer to the provision giving English merchants a part of the carrying trade so long dominated by the Dutch. Dryden conveys his concept through a series of witty sexual puns in which sex throws light on foreign policy, and the art of diplomacy enlightens the war of the sexes. See Harris, *Life of Edward Montagu*, II, 39–102; Feiling, *British Foreign Policy, 1660–1672*, pp. 168–235; and Pepys, *Diary*, 27 September 1667.

V, i

20 *Law of Arms.* See Hugo Grotius, *De Jure Belli ac Pacis Libri Tres*, trans. Francis Kelsey (1925), pp. 842–843 (III, xxi, 25–28).

34 *furious tender.* Aurelia imitates the concept of tendresse as it appeared in French romances. Cathos in Molière's *Les Précieuses Ridicules* (scene iv) complains that her own suitors and those of her cousin

Magdelon "n'ont jamais vu la carte de Tendre," the allegorical map of the land of love in Madeleine de Scudéry's *Clelia*.

80–81 *my humours circulate like my blood.* In his *Natural History of Nutrition, of Life, and Voluntary Motion* (1659), Dr. Charleton argued that "all the blood in the body is transmitted through the heart, once in a quarter, or half, or a whole hour, or in two hours at most" (p. 73); and he later wrote: "In the state of Tranquility, it seems probable that the whole Corporeal Soul being coextens to the whole body inshrining it (as the body is to the skin envesting it) doth at the same time both inliven all parts with the vital flame of the blood, to that end carried in a perpetual round (as the vulgar conceive the Sun to be uncessantly moved round about the Earth, to illuminate and warm all parts of it) and irradiate and invigorate them with a continual supply of Animal spirits, for the offices of Sense and Motion" (*Natural History of the Passions*, p. 69). Charleton believed that one of the chief functions of the blood was to circulate the humours.

157–158 *spoyl'd our English Playes.* Wildblood's remark may be applied both to the form of Spanish plays and to the content of plays about Spain. Van Lennep (p. cxxiii) discusses the "Spanish romance" as a distinct genre, the first distinct genre, in fact, to emerge after the Restoration. He distinguishes it as a play based on a Spanish source with an "emphasis upon a rigid code of conduct," a plot full of intrigue and "one or more high-spirited women in the dramatis personae." Hugo Rennert describes the *Comedias de Capa y Espada* as being "based entirely upon external circumstances," as plays of intrigue and turns of plot without any depth of character motivation (*The Spanish Stage* [1909], p. 276). Taken in this sense, Wildblood's remark provides an amusing commentary on the structure of *An Evening's Love.*

In another sense Wildblood may be commenting on the most famous of all "Spanish" plays, Corneille's *Le Cid*, in which discussions of love and honor are central to the motivations of all the characters. Thus Dryden's *Conquest of Granada* in which Almanzor "faces about" several times may be an example of the "Spanish" influence that Wildblood deplores. There is some talk of honor in the most famous of all the Spanish adaptations, Samuel Tuke's *The Adventures of Five Hours* (1663), but the French made it part of the précieuse code.

161–162 *yarely . . . yarly.* Briskly, nimbly.

212 *go snip with you.* To go shares.

230 *Wilderness.* A technical term in gardening indicating a piece of ground divided into geometrical forms in which the trees are planted without order (see Philip Miller, *The Gardeners Dictionary* [1737], I, sig. 9y).

232 *Corigidore.* Magistrate.

246 *a Legion of spirits.* The devils were often listed according to their rank and their power over a certain number of lesser spirits organized into military divisions called legions, each legion composed of 6,666 spirits (see Scot, pp. 229–238).

253 *Rear-mice.* Bats.

258 *Agrippa*. Heinrich Cornelius Agrippa of Nettesheim was born 14 September 1486 and died at Grenoble or Lyons in 1534 or 1535. His *Three Books of Occult Philosophy*, written about 1510 and published some twenty years later, is an exploration of magic, astrology, alchemy, and spiritualism as a way of learning more about the world created by God. Only a small section is devoted to conjuring, but a spurious fourth book on this subject was thought to be his.

259 *Pari die* etc. Appear by God and the waxing moon. Spirits should always be called when the moon is new. See Agrippa, pseud., *Fourth Book of Occult Philosophy*, p. 110; Scot, p. 256.

294 *Baptista Porta*. Like Agrippa, Giambattista della Porta (1538–1615) dabbled in magic, but Dryden is here thinking of him as the author of *De humana physiognomonia* (1586), a study of the characters of men as revealed by their facial characteristics. Calderón's astrologer claims to have studied with Porta (see *El Astrólogo Fingido*, pp. 139–140 [Jornada II]).

315 *Monstrum hominis*. As used by Terence in *The Eunuch*, this phrase means "beast of a man" and is addressed to the eunuch when he is being scolded by his master, but Alonzo means it as a compliment in the sense of "O prodigy of a man." Dryden may have expected the audience to catch the allusion. See Terence, *Works* (Loeb trans.), I, 304–305 (l. 696).

404 *baggage*. A pun on this word which might mean portable equipment or a young woman (sometimes used pejoratively).

411 *weeson*. Weasand, the throat.

466 *bate you an Ace*. Abate you the slightest amount.

472–473 *what do you lack*. A street cry of shopkeepers and pedlars to attract customers.

477 *Critical minute*. This concept of a psychological moment at which love and marriage become possible was a commonplace in Restoration drama and in the literature of the age (see, for example, Thomas D'Urfey, *Sir Barnaby Whigg* [1681], p. 39 [IV, i]).

516 *Anger sets it on the lees*. This image is drawn from the method of reclaiming wines that are turning bad. "The general and principal Remedy for the preternatural or sickly Commotions incident to Wines after their first Clarification, and tending to their Impoverishment or Decay, is Racking, i.e. drawing them from their Lees into fresh Vessels" (Miller, *Gardeners Dictionary*, I, sig. 10D).

523 *Put me in a Feavor*. The cure of ague fits by violent sweats induced by Jesuits' powder was common at the time; and Dryden's juxtaposition of the fermentation of wine and a fever has some support from contemporary medical treatises (see John Archer, *Every Man His Own Doctor* [1682], p. 111; Daniel Sennertus, *Practical Physick*, trans. Nicholas Culpeper and H. Care [1679], p. 137).

559 *Plate-fleet*. The fleet bringing riches from the mines in America to Spain.

EPILOGUE

4 *Like Jews.* For the dispersion of the Jews through the world at this time, see Jacques Basnage, *The History of the Jews,* trans. Thomas Taylor (1708), pp. 714–748.

7 *Club of jests.* Summers (II, 517) connects this with "selling bargains," the practice of making a fool of one's neighbor in the theater by an obscene remark, but Dryden seems to be speaking about the critics in the audience such as those described by Ned Ward in his picture of the "Scatter-Wit Club." See *Satyrical Reflections on Clubs* (1710), pp. 238–256, or Dryden himself in the epilogue to *Sir Martin Mar-all* (*Works,* IX, 209).

14 *French stoop.* French gestures and movements were frequent subjects for satire in Restoration literature; see especially the character of Monsieur de Paris in Wycherley's *The Gentleman Dancing Master* (1672). James Howard has one of his characters in *The English Mounsieur* (1666, p. 5 [I, i]) remark on a mock Frenchman, "Look how he throws his legs as if he would fain be rid of them—what distance there is between 'em." And a later writer described their gestures in detail (*A Satyr against the French* [1691], p. 5):

> Their Tongues not only wag, but Hands and Feet.
> Each part about them seems to move and walk;
> Their Eyes, their Noses; nay, their Fingers talk.

15 *cocks.* This word could have two different meanings, both supported by the context. It may describe the Monsieur's absurd posture as he speaks; we have already seen his *French stoop* and his *pull-back o'th' arm.* But it may also be simply a swear word he speaks, an English equivalent of *Morbleu.* A. Smythe Palmer (*Folk Etymology* [1882], pp. 69–70) lists *cocks* as a word commonly used in combinations: "Cock's-Bones, cock's passion, etc. by cock, a corruption of the name of the Deity, slightly disguised, as is common in most languages, to avoid the open profanity of swearing. So odds bodikins, . . . Fr. corbleu, ventrebleu, mortbleu, parbleu."

16 *the feint Astrologue.* A play by Thomas Corneille and one of Dryden's sources.

28 *us'd the French like Enemies.* A reference to the Triple Alliance against France consisting of England, Holland, and Sweden which had been formed in January 1668.

STAGING

STAGING

In her beautifully illustrated study, *The Baroque Theatre,* Margarete
Baur-Heinhold has attempted to generalize about the European stage
during the seventeenth and eighteenth centuries in cultural as well as in
artistic terms: "On every stage in Europe *periaktoi* were turning, wings
sliding in and out, divine apparitions ascending and descending on flying
machines; the earth was opening, spewing forth devils and demons and
swallowing the damned; the sea raged and the heavens stormed. Space
had broken its bounds and become indeterminate." [1] To explain why
seventeenth-century audiences demanded more and more magic and illusion, both in the dramatic text and in the staging, Baur-Heinhold refers
to the illusions of transcendent political power propagated by the mon-
archies of the period, an explanation that seems oversimplified for so
complex a phenomenon.[2] But in approaching three plays that are concerned in a variety of ways with astrology, magic, miracle, illusion, and
their presentation on the stage, we should have at least some idea of
the effects that were available to the two theatrical companies, especially
because John Dryden was interested enough in stage scenery to explain
precisely what he wanted to the scene painter, Isaac Fuller. Since John
Harrington Smith's careful analysis of contemporary staging and particularly of the staging of Dryden's plays [3] provides full details, this section is
limited to brief comments on the three plays under consideration.

From the standpoint of staging, the most difficult of the plays to deal
with is *The Tempest.* We know that Pepys praised the play for its
"variety," its dancing and its music, of which there was a great deal. But,
because of the inadequacy of the scene directions, we do not know very
much about the scenery. It seems likely, however, that even before
spectacular stage effects were added in 1674 to the Dryden-Davenant play,
the Duke's Company would have employed as many effects as the small
theater in Lincoln's Inn Fields would allow.[4] Lines from a poem called
The Country Club (1679) have often been quoted to suggest what performances of *The Tempest* were like:

> Such noise, such stink there was you'd swear
> The *Tempest* surely had been acted there.
> The cryes of Star-board, Lar-board, cheerly boys,
> Is but as demy rattles to this noise.[5]

But this comment, like almost all the comments we have, refers to the
operatic version of *The Tempest.* Perhaps a glance at the text of that

---

[1] Trans. Helga Schmidt-Glassner (1967), pp. 122–123.   [2] *Ibid.,* pp. 7–24.
[3] *Works,* VIII, 307–316.
[4] According to E. K. Chambers, Shakespeare's *Tempest* was "in some ways,
under the mask influence, the most spectacular performance attempted by the
King's men at Globe or Blackfriars" (*The Elizabethan Stage* [1951], III, 108).
There can be little doubt that Davenant would have used whatever theatrical
effects were available for staging the play (see G. C. D. Odell, *Shakespeare
from Betterton to Irving* [1920], I, 189).
[5] P. 2.

version, with its fuller and more elaborate descriptions, will help us to visualize the scenery used for the Dryden-Davenant play.

In addition to the sections involving flying spirits and an elaborate use of traps in the opening scene, the expanded masque in the second act, and the closing masque of Neptune (all possible through the facilities of the Dorset Garden Theatre which were lacking at Lincoln's Inn Fields), there were at least three painted "scenes": the scene at the opening, depicting "a thick cloudy Sky, a very Rocky Coast, and a Tempestuous Sea in perpetual Agitation"; the scene representing the vicinity of Prospero's habitation, "compos'd of three Walks of Cypress-trees, each Side-walk leads to a Cave, in one of which Prospero keeps his Daughters, in the other Hippolito: The Middle-Walk is of great depth, and leads to an open part of the Island"; and the scene of "the wilder part of the Island, . . . compos'd of divers sorts of Trees, and barren places, with a prospect of the Sea at a great Distance." [6] Since these scenes correspond roughly to those that may have been used for the Dryden-Davenant version, there is a strong possibility that some of the scenery provided for the Lincoln's Inn Fields production was used again in 1674. Although the opening directions describe a "new Frontispiece," the scene of the ship in a storm is not so designated. It seems likely enough that the frantic actions of the sailors in the first scene were played before some kind of painted representation of a sea in storm, and that they were accompanied by the traditional effects for producing the illusion of thunder and lightning.[7]

The second scene in the Dryden-Davenant version begins after the last cry of the sailors and with the entry of Prospero and Miranda. Miranda's mention of a walk in her answer to Prospero's query about her sister Dorinda—"I left her looking from the pointed Rock, at the walks end, on the huge beat of Waters"—is reminiscent of the scene described in the operatic *Tempest,* which, incidentally, retains this speech. At the end of this scene Dorinda enters and again refers to the rock from which she observed the storm. It would seem not improbable, then, that the "pointed Rock" was a feature of the "open part of the Island" revealed at the end of the "Middle-Walk," and that this scene was similar to, if not the same as, the one used in the operatic version. Such a continuity in scenery between the two versions is what one might expect, and thus we can assume that the representation of "the wilder part of the Island," used for the scenes involving shipwrecked courtiers and sailors, was also not very different in the Dryden-Davenant version from that used in 1674.[8]

One distinction, however, is possible. It has been argued that the scenes of the operatic *Tempest* which are described as taking place in

[6] See Christopher Spencer, ed., *Five Restoration Adaptations of Shakespeare* (1965), p. 409.

[7] For a description of the means used in producing such effects, see Lily B. Campbell, *Scenes and Machines on the English Stage during the Renaissance* (1923), p. 39.

[8] For a discussion of the way old scenes were adapted for use in new plays,

"a Cave" (III, vii; V, ii) are actually played in front of one of the caves designated in the scene representing the area around Prospero's habitation. This conclusion is possible in spite of the direction, "Enter Miranda and Dorinda peeping" (III, vii). But in the Dryden-Davenant version there seems to be a specific reference to the interior of a cave. The fifth scene of Act II is a "discovery" scene, revealed by drawing apart the flats: *"The Scene changes, and discovers* Hippolito *in a Cave walking, his face from the Audience."* The direction for the sixth scene of Act III is simply *"a Cave."* These scene directions are the most specific in the Dryden-Davenant version, and, whatever may have been used in the operatic version, there seems little question that the interior of a cave was used in 1667. Since Dorinda moves Hippolito toward the audience in the cave scene where he is *"discovered on a Couch"* (V, ii), this scene must have been located at the very rear of the stage.

Lacking the equipment that made the operatic version at Dorset Garden so delightful a spectacle throughout the Restoration and the eighteenth century, Dryden and Davenant could still provide "variety" by the highly dramatic effect of suddenly drawing a flat to reveal a vividly painted scene. Similar effects were used at the Bridges Street Theatre of the King's Company, where *An Evening's Love* was performed, but this play presents fewer problems than *The Tempest.* All the action takes place in Madrid, and the wings, stationary throughout the play, could have shown a generalized cityscape. Much of the action occurs in a street of Madrid. For the second scene of Act I the street scene is drawn to reveal *"A Chappel."* The second act is played entirely on the street, while the third is set in a room in the house of Don Lopez, with a few tables and chairs for props. Like the first act, the fourth begins with the street scene, which is later drawn to reveal *"a Garden with an Arbour,"* containing a table with some lights placed upon it. Soon the flats are closed on the garden scene, and at the end of the act we are once more in the street scene. The final act again utilizes the garden scene with the addition of a tableau within a garden house. The tableau was presumably at the very rear of the stage, since the characters are described as *"standing all without motion in a rank,"* perhaps indicating that they had just enough room to fit behind the rear flat. The rear flat is closed quickly, and the remainder of the play is acted in the garden.

Tyrannick Love was unquestionably the most spectacular of the three plays. The effects come suddenly in the last two acts, the first three acts having been played before a single scene—*"A Camp or Pavilion Royal."* The fourth act opens with what is somewhat inappropriately described as an "Indian *Cave,"* not because the action has been transferred to the Indies but as an indication that the scene had been used in *The Indian Queen* (III, ii) and *The Indian Emperour* (II, i).[9] The cave scenes from

---

see Roger Boyle, Earl of Orrery, *Dramatic Works,* ed. W. S. Clark (1937), II, 792, 800–802. This suggestion may be strengthened by William Milton's argument that the "operatic *Tempest*" was produced as a "quickie" when the opera, *Psyche,* was delayed.

[9] See Summers, II, 527.

these plays resemble the scene in *Tyrannick Love* insofar as all make ample use of the equipment available in the Bridges Street Theatre: traps for ghosts and demons to rise from under the stage and machines above the stage to raise and lower spirits and deities. Nakar and Damilcar descend in clouds,[10] and Saint Catherine rises in her bed from below; the flats of the cave draw to reveal Isaac Fuller's painting of paradise; Saint Catherine's guardian angel, Amariel, *"descends to soft Musick,"* dismisses the middle spirits, delivers a warning to them, and ascends as the scene shuts. Although no scene direction is given, the fifth act probably begins once more with the royal pavilion, but this scene soon opens to reveal the wheel of torture by which the intended victims, Saint Catherine and Felicia, are to be torn apart. The torture instrument was not a painted scene but rather a prop made to come apart at the touch of Amariel's sword, as he descends from above. After this vision the scene is shut, probably to allow for the removal of the shattered wheel and the placing of the scaffold upon which, when the scene reopens, Berenice is seen standing. The scaffold scene is retained until the end, when Nell Gwyn, acting the part of Valeria, refuses to be carried off as a suicide victim and leaps up to speak the epilogue.[11]

It has been suggested that the opening of the garden door in Act IV of *An Evening's Love* is a good example of impressionistic "cinema technique" in Restoration staging.[12] As Wildblood is soliloquizing on his plans to win money at the gaming house, the scene behind him draws to reveal Aurelia and Camilla in the garden. By exclaiming "The Garden dore opens!" he establishes a liaison with this scene and then goes off to gamble. The scene shuts when Aurelia and Camilla flee from what they believe to be the spirit of Don Melchor, and the very real Don Melchor, now before a scene representing the street in front of Don Alonzo's house, soliloquizes on the strange behavior of the two ladies. The versatility of Restoration staging also appears in Act V when Maskall, asked to open the door to the garden house, moves to the side of the scene, which draws to discover the supposed spirits, and even more spectacularly in Act V of *Tyrannick Love,* when the scene suddenly opens behind Maximin to reveal Berenice on the scaffold. Such sudden changes did not merely provide the pleasure of surprise. Dryden's stage benefited from a sense of space, movement, and scenery which was both representational and symbolic, satisfying the desire for spectacle without being confined to a literal realism.

---

[10] For illustrations of cloud machines, see Baur-Heinhold, *Baroque Theatre,* pp. 134–135.

[11] The illustration of this scene (facing p. 192) reveals what seems to be a royal pavilion rather than a camp or a royal camp; the indication in a prompt copy, now in the Folger Library, of "stairs" in the scenery of Act I where the scene is described as *"A Camp or Pavilion Royal"* suggests that, at least after the fire of 1672, the opening scene was played before a pavilion (see Henry Hitch Adams, "A Prompt Copy of Dryden's *Tyrannic Love,*" SB, IV [1951–52], 170–174).

[12] Richard Southern, *Changeable Scenery* (1952), pp. 135, 137.

TEXTUAL NOTES

Introduction

CHOICE OF THE COPY TEXT

The copy text is normally the first printing, on the theory that its accidentals are likely to be closest to the author's practice; but a manuscript or a subsequent printing may be chosen where there is reasonable evidence either that it represents more accurately the original manuscript as finally revised by the author or that the author revised the accidentals.

REPRODUCTION OF THE COPY TEXT

The copy text is normally reprinted *literatim,* but there are certain classes of exceptions. In the first place, apparently authoritative variants found in other texts are introduced as they occur, except that their purely accidental features are made to conform to the style of the copy text. These substitutions, but not their minor adjustments in accidentals, are recorded in footnotes as they occur. In the second place, the editors have introduced nonauthoritative emendations, whether found in earlier texts or not, where the sense seems to demand them. These emendations are also listed in the footnotes. In the third place, accidentals, speech headings, stage directions, scene headings, and so forth, are altered or introduced where it seems helpful to the reader. All such changes also are recorded in footnotes as they occur. In the fourth place, turned b, q, d, p, n, and u are accepted as q, b, p, d, u, and n, respectively, and if they result in spelling errors are corrected in the text and listed in the footnotes. The textual footnotes show the agreements among the texts only with respect to the precise variation of the present edition from the copy text; for example, in *An Evening's Love* at V, i, 97, the footnote "a-bed] Q3, F, D; a bed Q1-2" has reference to the addition of a hyphen; F and D actually read "a-Bed."

Certain purely mechanical details have been normalized without special mention. Long "s" has been changed to round "s," "VV" to "W"; swash italics have been represented by plain italics; head titles and any accompanying rules, act and scene headings, and display initials and any accompanying capitalization, have been made uniform with the style of the present edition; except in *The Tempest* (see p. 494, below), speeches beginning in the middle of verse lines have been appropriately indented; the position of speech headings and stage directions and their line division have been freely altered (braces in the speech tags have been omitted; those in the stage directions have been replaced by brackets; erratic uses of capitals in stage directions have been normalized); wrong font (e.g., the indiscriminate use of "*I*" for "I" in *Evening's Love*), and turned letters other than q, b, p, d, u, and n have been adjusted; medial apostrophes that failed to print have been restored; italicized plurals in -'s have been distinguished (by italic final "s") from possessives (roman final "s"); spacing between words and before and after punctuation has been normalized when no change in meaning results; the common contractions have been counted as single words, but otherwise words abbreviated by elision have been separated from those before and after if the apostrophe is present (for example, "bind 'em both"); if the elided syllable is written out as well as marked by an apostrophe, the words have been run together (*"speak'it"*).

TEXTUAL NOTES

The textual notes list the relevant printings and manuscripts, assign them sigla, and give references to the bibliographies where they are more fully described. Normally only the seventeenth-century printings and manuscripts, the folio edition of the plays (1701), and Congreve's edition (1717) are cited, since there is little likelihood that authoritative readings will be found in any later manuscripts or editions. The textual notes also outline the descent of the text through its various manuscripts and printings, indicate which are the authorized texts, and explain how the copy text was selected in each instance. A list of copies collated follows. If the differences between variant copies of an edition are sufficient to warrant a tabular view of them, it will follow the list of copies collated.

The sigla indicate the format of printed books (F = folio, Q = quarto, O = octavo, etc.) and of parts of printed books (f = folio, q = quarto, o = octavo, etc.) and the order of printing, if this is determinable, within the format group (F may have been printed after Q1 and before Q2; f may have been printed after q1 and before q2). If order of printing is in doubt, the numbers are arbitrary, and they are normally arbitrary for the manuscripts (represented by M).

Finally the variants in the texts collated are given. The list is not exhaustive, but it records what seemed material, viz.:

All variants of the present edition from the copy text except in the mechanical details listed above.

All other substantive variants and variants in accidentals markedly affecting the sense. The insertion or removal of a period before a dash has sometimes been accepted as affecting the sense; other punctuational variants before dashes have been ignored. Failure of letters to print, in texts other than the copy text, has been noted only when the remaining letters form a different word or words, or when a word has disappeared entirely.

All errors of any kind repeated from one edition to another, except the use of -'s instead of -s for a plural.

Spelling variants where the new reading makes a new word (e.g., *then* and *than* being in Dryden's day alternate spellings of the conjunction, a change from *than* to *then* would be recorded, since the spelling *then* is now confined to the adverb, but a change from *then* to *than* would be ignored as a simple modernization).

In passages of verse, variants in elision of syllables normally pronounced (except that purely mechanical details, as *had'st, hadst,* are ignored). Thus *heaven, heav'n* is recorded, but not *denied, deny'd.*

Relining, except when passages printed as prose are reprinted as prose.

When texts generally agree in a fairly lengthy variation, but one or two differ from the rest in a detail that would be cumbrous to represent in the usual way, the subvariations are indicated in parentheses in the list of sigla. For example:

land Devils] Q1, D (Land D); Land-Devils Q2-3, F.

This means that D agrees with Q1 in lacking a hyphen, but that D has a capital ("Land") where Q1 has a lowercase letter ("land"); Q2, Q3, and F have a hyphen, and capitals for both parts of the compound word ("Land-Devils").

When variants in punctuation alone are recorded, the wavy dash is used in place of the identifying word before (and sometimes after) the variant punctuation. A caret indicates absence of punctuation.

As in the previous volumes, no reference is made to modern editions where the editor is satisfied that reasonable care on his part would have resulted in the same emendations, even if he collated these editions before beginning to emend.

The Tempest

The first edition of the Dryden-Davenant version of *The Tempest* was published in 1670 (Q; Macd 73a; W&M 328, 329). Three states of inner *A* and two of inner B have been discovered in Q. The second edition of this version (set from a copy of Q with corrected inner *A* [second state] and uncorrected inner B) was published in Dryden's *Comedies, Tragedies, and Operas* (1701), I, 226–274 (F; Macd 107ai–ii [two issues, the differences not affecting this play]). The "echo" song of Ariel and Ferdinand (III, iv, 27–44) was reprinted in *Windsor-Drollery* (1672), pages 12–13 (d).

An "operatic" revision of the Dryden-Davenant *Tempest* was published in 1674 (Macd 73b; W&M 330). The second edition of this revision appeared in 1676 (Macd 73c; W&M 331); the third, in 1676 (W&M 333); the fourth, in 1690 (Macd 73d; W&M 334); the fifth, probably *c.* 1692 ([title page date is 1676] Macd 73e; W&M 332); the sixth, in 1695 (Macd 73f; W&M 335); the seventh, in 1701 (Macd 73g). It was also reprinted in Congreve's edition of Dryden's *Dramatick Works* (1717), II, 163–254 (Macd 109ai–ii). The songs of the operatic version were reprinted time and again in the last quarter of the seventeenth century and the first half of the eighteenth century. That Dryden had a hand in the operatic revision or in the subsequent publication of any of the editions of it is quite unlikely (see Commentary, pp. 323–325); consequently, a Clark copy of Q (*PR3418.J1.1670) has been chosen as the copy text, and only those variants uncovered in the collation of Q, F, and d are given in the textual notes.

The Dryden-Davenant play is a mosaic of passages of Shakespeare, revised Shakespeare (both condensed and expanded), Davenant, Dryden, and revised Dryden (*"my writing received daily his [Davenant's] amend-*

ments" [Preface, 4:14, above]). To George Saintsbury the result was a
"strange disjointed blank verse, half prose" (S-S, III, 103). The lineation
of the copy text reflects the mixed nature of this cooperative effort. After
a great deal of unsatisfactory experimentation, the present editors have
decided to follow the lineation of the copy text [1] (except for passages
printed as prose in the copy text and reprinted as prose in the present
edition), partly because much of the play—as Saintsbury wrote of some
particularly frustrating passages in V, i—"may be versified in several
ways, but all bad" (III, 207n), and partly because most of the lineation of
the copy text very likely reflects the condition of the copy sent to the
printer rather than compositors' errors or sophistications.

The following additional copies of the two editions of the Dryden-
Davenant version and *Windsor-Drollery* have been examined: Q: Clark
(*PR3418.J1), Folger (S2944 [2 cop.]), Harvard (*EC65.D8474.670t2a),
Huntington (122923); F: Clark (*fPR3412.1701 [2 cop.], *fPR3412.1701a);
d: Huntington (148513).

Press Variants by Form

Q
Sheet *A* (inner form)
Uncorrected (first state): Harvard
Corrected (second state): Clark (1 copy), Folger (1 copy), Huntington
Sig. *A2*
  3:4 *which] who*
Sig. *A3v*
  3:17 Davenant] D'avenant
Corrected (third state, the above corrections and the following): Clark
  (1 copy), Folger (1 copy)
Sig. *A3v*
  5:12 DRIDEN] DRYDEN
Sheet B (inner form)
Uncorrected: Clark (1 copy), Folger (1 copy)
Corrected: Clark (1 copy), Folger (1 copy), Harvard, Huntington
Sig. B1*v*
  I, i, 21 is] ∼ :
    40+ *s.d. aud] and*
    44 Vall's] Viall's
Sig. B2
  I, i, 64 sttar-board] star-board
Sig. B4
  Pagination 5] 7

*Preface: 3:1–5:10 writing . . . [to] . . . Decemb.] italics and romans
reversed in F but normalized in the textual footnotes and the following*

---

[1] Summers (II, 157–228) solved the problem much the same way. He followed
the lineation of F, which is, with a few exceptions, that of Q.

textual notes.   3:3   French] *French* Q, F.   3:4   *who*] Q *(corrected [second state])*, F; *which* Q *(uncorrected [first state]).*   3:17, 4:2   D'ave-nant] Davenant Q, F.   4:24   Latine] *Latine* Q, F.   5:9   D'avenant] Q *(corrected [second state])*, F; Davenant Q *(uncorrected [first state]).* 5:12   DRYDEN] Q *(corrected [third state])*; DRIDEN Q *(uncorrected [first and second states])*, F *(Driden* F).

Prologue: 2   shoot;] F; ~∧ Q.   4   *Play:*] ~ . Q, F.   38   abed] Q; *in Bed* F.

Dramatis Personæ: Nobleman] F; Noble man Q.   Spirits,] ~∧ Q, F. Caliban and] F *(Caliban / and)*; *Caliban* Q.

I, i

THE] Q; THE / TEMPEST, / OR, THE F.   ACT I. SCENE I.] ACT I. Q, F.   1   What,] ~∧ Q, F.   2–2+   *s.d.* weather. / *Enter*] F; ~ . [~ Q *(s.d. at right margin).*   9–9+   *s.d.* Boy! / *Enter*] F; ~ ! [~ Q *(s.d. at right margin).*   14–15   Master? / Play] Q; ~ ? ~ F.   21 is:] Q *(corrected state)*; ~∧ Q *(uncorrected state)*, F.   32   *s.d. Exeunt Alonzo, Antonio, and Gonzalo] Exit* Q, F.   35+   *s.d. [Exeunt two Mariners.]* omitted *from* Q, F.   36   jeere-Capstorm] seere-Capstorm Q; Seere-Capstorm F.   40+   *s.d. and]* Q *(corrected state)*, F; aud Q *(uncorrected state).*   41   Capstorm!] ~ ? Q, F.   43+   *s.d. two Mariners]* Mustacho *and* Ventoso Q, F.   44   Viall's] Q *(corrected state)*; Vall's Q *(uncorrected state)*, F.   48   Bullys] F *(Bullies)*; *Bullys* Q.   53   Cat . . . cat] Cut . . . cut Q, F.   63   *Steph.] Steph. within.* Q, F.   64 star-board] Q *(corrected state)*, F; sttar-board Q *(uncorrected state).*   70 there. [*Exit* Mustacho.] there. Q, F.   74–74+   *s.d.* weather. / *Enter*] ~ . [~ Q, F *(s.d. at right margin).*   91–92   Heaven! / [*A cry within.* / . . . farewell!] Q (Heaven! [*A*); Heaven! / . . . farewell! [*A cry within.* F.   95+   *s.d. and]* F; and Q.   96   What,] ~∧ Q, F.   102   wide-chopt] wide chopt Q, F.   104   be] F; he Q.

I, ii

SCENE II.] *omitted from* Q, F.   28   attentive.] ~ , Q, F.   41 Millain] Millan Q, F.   52–53   Uncle———Do'st . . . Child?] Uncle (do'st . . . Child?) Q, F.   68, 75, 79   Millain] Millan Q, F.   79 for] F; For Q.   93   Nobleman] F; Noble man Q.   106   approach,] ~∧ Q, F.   107–107+   *s.d.* Come. / *Enter*] F; ~ . [~ Q *(s.d. at right margin).*   108   hail, . . . hail;] ~∧ . . . ~ , Q, F.   122–123   soul / But] Q; Soul but F.   127   *in romans in* Q, F.   130   by,] F; ~∧ Q.   140–145   Ship; . . . hid; . . . stow'd; . . . asleep:] ~ , . . . ~ , . . . ~ , . . . ~ , Q, F.   190   I,] F; ~∧ Q.   192–198   Saylors: . . . servant; . . . commands, . . . Pine;] ~ , . . . ~ , . . . ~ , . . . ~ , Q, F *(Servant* F; *Commands* F).   210–211   in; . . . Bears:] ~ , . . . ~ , Q, F.   217   thee] F; the Q.   234   us. What] ~ : what Q, F *(What* F).   238–238+   *s.d.* when? / *Enter*] ~ ? [~ Q, F *(s.d. at right margin).*   243–243+   *s.d.* forth. / *Enter*] ~ . [~ Q, F *(s.d. at right margin).*   262   from me] Q; me from F.   267   would't had] would t'had Q, F.   283   (malice)?] (~)∧ Q, F *(Malice* F).   289   [*Aside.*]

I] I Q, F.   310 side-long] side long Q, F.   321 us,] F; ~∧ Q.
334 Sister,] sister∧ Q, F (Sister F).   342 Man. [*Exeunt.*] F; Man. Q.

II, i

ACT II. SCENE I.] ACT II. Q, F.   5 stomack. How] ~, how Q, F
(Stomach F).   10–12 him; . . . shore:] ~, . . . ~, Q, F.   32
guilt.] ~, Q, F.   33 price] Q; prize F.   42 hand.] ~ ; Q, F.   47
1.] F; ~∧ Q.   47 D.] D. Q, F.   47 *Where does proud*] Where does
proud Q, F.   47–55 *dwell? . . . Crowns,*] *words of song in romans in*
Q, F.   55 Chor.] *Chor.* Q, F.   55 &c.] *&c.* Q, F.   61 *Who are*
the Pillars of] Who are the Pillars of Q, F.   61–62 *Court? . . . and*
. . . it support.] *in romans in Q, F.*   63–71 *What . . . Crowns,*]
words of song in romans in Q, F.   63 *Her . . . tread,*] *not set over*
to right in F.   71 Cho.] *Cho.* Q, F.   71 &c.] *&c.* Q, F.   72+
s.d. in the] Q; *in* F.   73 open'd] Q; open F.   74–76 *1. . . . 2.*
. . . 1.] 1. . . . 2. . . . 1. Q, F.   76 side.] ~ : Q, F.   77–77+ *s.d.*
Pride. / Enter Pride] Pride. [*Enter Pride* Q, F (*s.d. at right margin*).   79
Ambition] Ambition Q, F.   79–79+ *s.d.* betray. / *Enter Fraud*] ~ .
[*Enter Fraud* Q, F (*s.d. at right margin*).   80 *Fraud does*] Fraud does
Q, F.   83–83+ *s.d.* steer. / *Enter Rapine*] ~ . [*Enter Rapine* Q, F
(*s.d. at right margin*).   84 *Fraud*] Fraud Q, F.   84 *Force*] Force
Q, F.   85 *Rapine*] Rapine Q, F.   85–85+ *s.d.* drive. / *Enter*
Murther] ~ . [*Enter Murther* Q, F (*s.d. at right margin*).   89+ *s.d.*
&c.] F; *&c.* Q.   95 unmann'd] unman'd Q, F.   99 *indented in F.*

II, ii

SCENE II.] *omitted from Q, F.*   7–8 Bow-waugh . . . Bow-waugh]
Bow-waugh . . . Bow-waugh Q, F.   9 Chanticleer] *Chanticleer* Q, F.
10 Cock a doodle do] *Cock a doodle do* Q, F.   21 *eyes;*] ~, Q, F
(*Eyes* F).   22 *fade,*] Q; ~ : F.   25 *his knell*] his Q, F.   26 Ding
dong Bell] *Ding dong Bell* Q, F.

II, iii

SCENE III.] *omitted from Q, F.*   31 putting me] F; putting Q.
44 *a Sail, a Sail*] a Sail, a Sail Q, F.   62 hear?] ~, Q, F.   68
there] Q; they F.   72 well agreed] Q; all agreed F.   85–86 *I . . .*
[italics] . . . ashore] F; *in romans in Q.*   89–94 *The . . . [to] . . .*
Saylor,] F; *romans and italics reversed in Q.*   94 go hang:] Q;
go hang: F.   95–96 *as in F; in romans in Q.*   128 Island?] ~ . Q,
F.   141 *s.d.* Vent. Must. draw] *Vent. Must.* draw Q, F.   151 curse;]
~, Q, F (Curse F).   161–162 Isle; . . . painted,] ~, . . . ~ ; Q, F.
169 thee] Q; the F.   178 Monster. Monster,] ~ ; ~∧ Q, F.   184
———[*Aside.*] By] By Q, F.   192 drink. [*Aside.*] drink. Q, F.   198
race. [*Aside.*] race; Q, F (Race F).   211 *Sings*] Q; Sings F.   211–215
No . . . [to] . . . man] F (*Man*); *italics and romans reversed in Q.*
213 *Dish;*] F; Dish, Q.   216 *indented as part of Caliban's song in*
Q, F; in italics in F.   220–221 Mistress Monster,] ~, ~∧ Q, F (Mistriss
F).   222 Alliance.] ~ : Q, F.

II, iv

SCENE IV.] *omitted from Q, F.*   9 nigh.————] nigh: Q, F.   9–
9+ *s.d. Hippolito! / Enter*] ~ ! [~ Q, F *(s.d. at right margin).*   25
of;] ~ , Q, F.   35 'em] Q; them F.   42 should] Q; shall F.   46–
47 Eyes; . . . Nightingales;] F; ~ , . . . ~ , Q.   48 enchantment;]
F (Enchantment); ~ , Q.   55 'em] Q; them F.   56 revenge;] F;
~ , Q.   85 hath] Q; has F.   87 behind;] ~ , Q, F.   88–88+
s.d. disperst. / *Enter*] ~ . [~ Q, F *(s.d. at right margin).*   90 enough.
————] ~ :∧ Q, F.   96 ill is] F; is ill Q.   115 way?] ~ , Q, F.
134 Sister;] ~ , Q, F.   141 lose] Q; loose F.

II, v

SCENE V.] *omitted from Q, F.*   7 and] Q; and he F.   13
Heaven] Q; Heav'n F.   13 is!] ~ ? Q, F.   28 you?] F; ~ ! Q.
35 his] Q; its F.   49 lose] Q; loose F.   51 warn'd;] Q; ~ : F.
52 are.] ~ ? Q, F.   82–83 *indented in F.*

III, i

ACT III. SCENE I.] ACT III. Q, F.   14 him.] ~ ? Q, F.   34
full blown-flower] Q; full blown Flower F.   43 spreads;] ~ , Q, F.
44+ *s.d. Enter*] [~ Q, F *(s.d. at right margin).*   48 clear.] Q; ~ , F.
54, 55 to] Q; too F.   57 man.] ~ ? Q, F (Man F).   72 Nay, . . .
so;] ~∧ . . . ~ , Q, F.   102 Go to] Go too Q, F.   105 trembled;]
~ , Q, F.   106 ground;] ~ , Q, F.   146+ *s.d. Enter*] F; [~ Q
(s.d. at right margin).   151 On . . . sixth you] Q; On . . . sixth /
You F.   165 *the good*] the good Q, F.   167 Reeds;] ~ , Q, F.   185
come . . . go] come . . . go Q, F.   186 *so, so,*] so; so, Q; so; so. F.
188 moe;] ~ , Q, F.   189 I,] Q; ~∧ F.

III, ii

SCENE II.] *omitted from Q, F.*   1 further] Q; farther F.   1–3
Sir; . . . ake: . . . Meanders:] ~ , . . . ~ , . . . ~ , Q, F.

III, iii

SCENE III.] *omitted from Q, F.*   5+ *s.d. Enter*] [~ Q, F *(s.d. at
right margin).*   7 well,] F (Well); ~∧ Q.   9 beauty. [*Aside.*]
beauty. Q, F (Beauty F).   19 Babby,] ~∧ Q, F.   24 God-a-mighty]
F (God-A-Mighty); God a mighty Q.   33 Pimp. [*Aside.*] Pimp. Q, F.
37 Sycorax. Wilt] ~ , wilt Q, F.   45–46 Fens, / Where] Q; Fens,
where F.   57+ *s.d. Enter*] [~ Q, F *(s.d. at right margin).*   65
then!] ~ ? Q, F.   77 gulp] Q; gulph F.   78 Predecessor,] ~∧ Q,
F.   99–99+ *s.d.* Monster; / *Enter Stephano, Mustacho, and Ventoso.*]
~ ; [*Ent. Steph. Must. Vent.* Q, F (*Enter* F; *s.d. at right margin*).   101
know, Rebels,] ~∧~∧ Q, F.   101 I'm] Q; I am F.   110 us.] ~ :
Q, F.   125 *Lord*] Lord Q, F.   138 cannot,] F; ~∧ Q.   152 you]
F; your Q.   156 I!] ~ ? Q, F.

III, iv

SCENE IV.] *omitted from* Q, F.   5 frowns:] ∼ , Q, F (Frowns F).
11 men,] ∼∧ Q, F (Men F).   21, 22 further] Q; farther F.   27–44
*italics and romans reversed in d but normalized in the following textual
notes.*   27–28 way. / Ariel. Go] Q, F; *way, go* d.   28–29 *way. /
Ferd.*] Q, F; *way;* d.   29–30 *stay? / Ariel. Why*] Q, F; *stay, why* d.
31 Ferd. *Where*] Q, F; *Where* d.   32 yond] Q, F; *yon* d.   34–35
gone. / Ariel. For] Q, F; *gon, for* d.   36 Ferd. *What*] Q, F; *What* d.
40 Ariel.] Q, F; Cho. d.

III, v

SCENE V.] *omitted from* Q, F.   13–14 it.————[*Aside to* Ariel.]
. . . fine Spirit,] it: . . . fine Spirit. Q, F.   25 weep;] ∼ , Q, F.   30
this. [*Aside.*]————Young] this————young, Q, F (young∧ F).   34 for;]
∼ , Q, F.   39 [*Aside.*] They] They Q, F.   41 light.————One] ∼∧
————one Q, F.   46 Temple;] ∼ , Q, F.   49 Traytor.] ∼ , Q, F.
53 cradl'd] crawl'd Q, F.   58 up,] ∼∧ Q, F.   63 you,] ∼∧ Q, F.
86 Prosp. aside. . . . works.————[*To* Ferd.] Come on.] *Prosp.* . . .
works: come on: Q, F.   87 *Ariel.*————[*To* Ferd.] Follow] *Ariel:*
follow Q, F.   103 Prince.] ∼∧ Q, F.   105 *s.d. Exit*] F; ∼ . Q.
110–110+ *s.d. Hippolito. / Enter*] ∼ . [∼ Q, F (*s.d. at right margin*).
127 wish.————Yet] ∼∧————yet Q, F.   132 two] F; too Q.   137
can never] Q; can / Never F.   147–151 virtue: . . . birth; . . . Affliction:] ∼ , . . . ∼ , . . . ∼ , Q, F (Virtue F; Birth F).   153 lives;] ∼ ,
Q, F.   155 fears;] ∼ , Q, F.

III, vi

SCENE VI.] *omitted from* Q, F.   *s.d. Scene, a Cave. / Enter* . . .
Ferdinand.] F (SCENE, *A*); *Enter* . . . Ferdinand. / *Scene, a Cave.* Q.
10 are.] ∼ ? Q, F.   14 so.] ∼ : Q, F.   15 time [*Aside.*] time Q,
F.   19 world;] ∼ , Q, F (World F).   49, 77 Why,] ∼∧ Q, F.   80
Well,] ∼∧ Q, F.   86 Further] Q; Farther F.   88 are] Q; were F.
99–100 *indented in F.*

IV, i

ACT IV. SCENE I.] ACT IV. Q, F.   52 than] F; then Q.   69
Yes,] ∼∧ Q, F.   100–101 hopes! / . . . this [*Aside.*] hopes! [*Aside.* /
. . . this Q, F.   105 Ferd. aside.] Ferd. Q, F.   118 me!] ∼ ? Q, F.
118 *s.d. Ferdinand.*] F; ∼∧ Q.   123–123+ *s.d. Love. / Enter*] F; ∼ .
[∼ Q (*s.d. at right margin*).   154 him!————Well] him? well Q, F
(Well F).   166 *s.d. Dorinda. / Enter* . . . Dorinda. / I'le . . . let]
Dorinda. I'le . . . let [*Ent.* . . . Dorinda. Q, F (I'll F; *Enter* F).   228
Yes,] ∼∧ Q, F.   237 Before] F; before Q.   246–246+ *s.d. so. /
Enter*] F; ∼ . [∼ Q (*s.d. at right margin*).   262 Besure] Q; Be sure
F.   269 self,] ∼ ; Q, F.   272 Sir.] F; ∼ , Q.   273 Women,]
∼ . Q, F.   282 Arms.] Q; ∼ ? F.   286 force. [*Aside.*]————Pray]
force: pray Q, F.   320 *s.d. [Gives . . . sword.]* for . . . Cave] for . . .

Cave [*Gives . . . sword.* Q, F.   333–334 Agreed, / And] Q; Agreed: And F.

IV, ii

SCENE II.] *omitted from Q, F.*   22 joy.] ~ : Q, F.   25 Haddock in] Q; *Haddock in* F.   46–49 *We . . .* [*italics*] *. . . us*] F; *in romans in* Q.   47 *Up, Dam,*] Up Dam Q; *Up Dam* F.   51 for't!] ~ ? Q, F.   51 come,] F (Come); ~∧ Q.   52–53 the / Humour] Q; the Humour F.   58 agen. [*Exit* Caliban.] agen. Q, F.   61 Subject,] ~∧ Q, F.   61+ *s.d. Enter*] [~ Q, F (*s.d. at right margin*).   66 thee.] ~ , Q, F.   70–71 lost, / For] Q; lost, For F.   74 *Up se Dutch*] Up se Dutch Q, F.   76 agen;] ~ , Q, F.   76 hands?] ~ ; Q, F.   77–78 thee. [*Drinks.*]——Now] thee, now Q, F.   84 lose] Q; loose F.   89 sounds. [*Exit* Caliban.] sounds: Q, F.   92 matter,] ~∧ Q, F.   94 Princess.] F; ~ ? Q.   95 as on] Q; as F.   96 Noble?] Q; ~ ! F.   98 Mounsor *De-Viles*] Q; Monsieur *de Viles* F.   106+ *s.d. Enter*] [~ Q, F (*s.d. at right margin*).   108 an] Q; and F.   110 Tribe?] Q; ~ ! F.   113 agen. Give] agen, give Q, F.   123–124 hem!——[*To* Calib.] Skink . . . agen.——] hem! skink . . . agen. Q, F (Skink F).   127 Black-berries;] F (Black-Berries); ~ , Q.   143 so?——Hah] ~∧——hah Q, F (Hah F).   151–152 Bosom.——[*Whispers . . . hastily.*] *Mustacho,*] Bosom. / [*Whispers . . . hastily.* / *Mustacho*∧ Q, F.   154 *Ventoso,*] F; ~∧ Q.

IV, iii

SCENE III.] *omitted from Q, F.*   29–29+ *s.d. help!* / *Enter*] F; ~ ! [~ Q (*s.d. at right margin*).   34 Heaven!] ~ ? Q, F.   42–42+ *s.d. thou?* / *Enter*] F; ~ ? [~ Q (*s.d. at right margin*).   50–52 glad; . . . good:] ~ , . . . ~ . Q, F.   65–67 *Hecla; . . .* smoak;] *Heila,* . . . ~ , Q, F (Smoak F).   86 hope;] ~ , Q, F.   87–87+ *s.d. enter.* / *Enter*] F; ~ . [~ Q (*s.d. at right margin*).   97 Why,] ~∧ Q, F.   102 me;] ~ , Q, F.   103+ *s.d. Antonio, and*] Antonio. Q, F.   123 ne're] F (ne'er); n'ere Q.   135 ended;] ~ , Q, F.   139 Corps;] ~ , Q, F.   159 then, . . . Guards!——[*Aside.*] I] then∧ . . . Guards∧ ——I Q, F.   160 I'm] Q; I am F.   191 help, *Ariel,*] ~∧~∧ Q, F.   216+ *s.d. again,*] ~ . Q, F.   231 Sister,] ~∧ Q, F.   233 satisfi'd.] ~ ? Q, F.   251 I'le] F (I'll); I'e Q.   276–277 *indented in* F.

V, i

ACT V. SCENE I.] ACT V. Q, F.   9 punishing;] ~ , Q, F.   32–33 Father, . . . Son; . . . here;] ~∧ . . . ~ , . . . ~ , Q, F.   34–34+ *s.d.* him. / *Enter*] F; ~ . [~ Q (*s.d. at right margin*).   54 *British*] F; British Q.   71 air;] ~ , Q, F.   81 done. Be] done, be Q, F.

V, ii

SCENE II.] *omitted from Q, F.*   *s.d.* Hippolito] F (*s.d. at right margin*); [~ Q (*s.d. at right margin*).   3 Sun? . . . walk.] ~ , . . .

~ ? Q, F.   4+ *s.d. nearer*] Q; *nearer to* F.   29 made] Q; make F.
35 Father] F; ~ , Q.   39 off,] F; ~ ; Q.   40 do;] ~ , Q, F.
45–46 it: . . . blood;] ~ , . . . ~ , Q, F (Blood F).   49 live;] ~ ,
Q, F (Live F).   51 lest] Q; least F.   60 and so] Q; so F.   65
unconstant] Q; inconstant F.   78 Of] Q; of F.   79 her?] ~ ! Q,
F.   98 Sir;] ~ , Q, F.   105 away,] Q; ~ . F.   156 back?] ~ ,
Q, F.   167 can] Q; shall F.   175 Prophecy;] ~ . Q, F.   190 you
yet] Q; you F.   196+ *s.d. Enter*] F; [~ Q (*s.d. at right margin*).   199
look, the] ~ʌ ~ Q, F.   201 ne're] F (ne'er); n'ere Q.   205 What,]
~ʌ Q, F.   233 world!] ~ ? Q, F (World F).   238 draws] Q; dawns
F.   259–259+ *s.d. thee. / Enter*] F; ~ . [~ Q (*s.d. at right margin*).
265–266 *indented in F*.

   Epilogue: 5 Mounsieur] *Mounsieur* Q, F (*Monsieur* F).   5 Spanish]
Spanish Q, F.   *FINIS.*] Q; *omitted from* F.

Tyrannick Love

The first edition of *Tyrannick Love* was published in 1670 (Q1; Macd
74a); the second, in 1672 (Q2; Macd 74b); the third, in 1677 (Q3; Macd
74c); the fourth, in 1686 (Q4; Macd 74d); and the fifth, in 1695 [1] (Q5;

---

[1] The "1694 edition" (Montague Summers, *A Bibliography of the Restoration Drama* [1934], p. 57; Macdonald, p. 105n; James M. Osborn, "Macdonald's
Bibliography of Dryden: An Annotated Check List of Selected American
Libraries," *MP*, XXXIX [1941], 86) is a ghost. The compositor was setting Q5
from a copy of Q4; following the title page of Q4 closely, he first set the title
page of Q5 as follows: "Tyrannick Love; | OR, THE | Royal Martyr. | A
| TRAGEDY. | As it is Acted by His Majestie's Servants at the | THEATRE
ROYAL. | [rule] | By *JOHN DRYDEN,* Servant to His Majesty. | [rule] | *Non
jam prima peto——neq; vincere certo;* | *Extremum rediisse pudet.*——Virg.
| [rule] | *LONDON,* | Printed for *H. Herringman,* and are to be sold by *Joseph
| Knight,* and *Francis Saunders,* at the Sign of the *Blue An-* | *chor* in the
Lower Walk of the *New Exchange,* 1694." Both the Folger Library and the
Harvard Library have copies of this edition (D2397; *EC65.D8474.670te), including a title page with these readings, the Folger copy containing a "1695" title
page as well. But the partnership between Joseph Knight and Francis Saunders
had been dissolved about 1688 (Henry R. Plomer, *A Dictionary of the Printers
and Booksellers Who Were at Work in England, Scotland and Ireland from
1668 to 1725* [1922], pp. 181, 262), and the press was stopped so that the title
page could be corrected to reflect more accurately the current business relationships of Francis Saunders. The publication date was also changed from
1694 to 1695, the new title page reading: "Tyrannick Love; | OR, THE |
Royal Martyr. | A | TRAGEDY. | As it is Acted by His Majesty's Servants at
the | *THEATRE ROYAL.* | [rule] | By *JOHN DRYDEN,* Servant to His
Majesty. | [rule] | *Non jam prima peto——neq; vincere certo;* | *Extremum
rediisse pudet.*——Virg. | [rule] | *LONDON,* | Printed for *Henry Herring-
man,* and are to be sold by | *R. Bently, J. Tonson, F. Saunders,* and *T. Bennet.*
1695." According to Gertrude L. Woodward and James G. McManaway (W&M,
p. 54), "The title page of this issue [1695] is set from the same type as that
of the 1694 issue through 'London' in the imprint." Comparison of the two

Macd 74e). The play was published later in Dryden's *Comedies, Tragedies, and Operas* (1701), I, 337–378 (F; Macd 107ai–ii [two issues, the differences not affecting this play]), and in Congreve's edition of Dryden's *Dramatick Works* (1717), II, 369–444 (D; Macd 109ai–ii [two issues, the differences not affecting this play]).

Dryden altered Q1 after it had started through the press. James M. Osborn ("Annotated Check List," p. 85) first noticed this major revision: "The Yale copy contains an important difference in collation; sheet F has a fifth leaf, with the pagination 39–40 repeated, but no duplication in the text. Examination of the watermark and chain lines shows that F3 was canceled and two leaves, apparently conjugate, were inserted. The new text contains the scene between Maximin and Porphyrius which was previously thought to have been added in the second edition. The text of this additional passage is almost identical with that printed two years later. This copy is thus of considerable importance, for it indicates that this scene was added two years earlier than has hitherto been known. Mr. A. T. Hazen suggests that this copy may have been a remainder." Describing a Folger prompt copy (2d ed.; 1672) of the play, Henry Hitch Adams later accepted Hazen's suggestion as fact: "Dryden had revised this second edition by adding thirty-nine lines and reviewing the whole. . . . Note that these additions had actually been made in at least one remainder copy of the 1670 edition: see J. M. Osborn, 'Macdonald's Bibliography of Dryden: An Annotated Check List . . .' " ("A Prompt Copy of Dryden's *Tyrannic Love*," *SB*, IV [1951–52], 170 and n.).

In response to these conjectures one might, first of all, point out that additional canceled copies of the first edition have turned up at the Clark Library, the Huntington Library, and the University of Texas Library. Second, inspection of the canceled and uncanceled Clark copies reveals that the watermark on the cancel is identical with the watermark on the cancelandum. In addition, the width of the type page in the cancel corresponds to the width of the type page in the cancelandum, and the type font of the cancel is apparently the same as that of the cancelandum. All the evidence indicates, then, that F3 was canceled, at the very latest, shortly after the printing of the last sheet of the play.

Q2 (title page: "review'd by the Authour") was evidently printed from a copy of Q1 containing the cancel (IV, i, 266–377). Dryden added a paragraph to the preface (112:28–113:15) and two lines (76–77) to Act III, scene i; from Act V, scene i, he omitted four lines (following 141), two stage directions (497+ and 499+), and part of a third stage direction (603+). He also regularized a short line (674) in Act V, scene i. Q3 was printed from a copy of Q2, Q4 from a copy of Q3, Q5 from a copy

---

title pages on a Hinman Collator reveals that, except for "THEATRE ROYAL" and "Majestie's" of the first version and *"THEATRE ROYAL"* and "Majesty's" of the second, Woodward and McManaway are correct. That the "1694" title pages in the Folger and Harvard copies were not intended for use is evidenced by tears or cuts which begin at the bottom and extend to the middle of the page.

of Q4, F from a copy of Q5, and D from a copy of Q2. Since Dryden seems not to have revised the accidentals for any later edition, the Clark copy of Q1, with canceled F3 (*PR3418.L1.1670), has been chosen as the copy text.

The following seventeenth-century collections of songs have been examined: *Windsor-Drollery* (1672), page 41 (d), for Damilcar's song ("Ah how sweet it is to love" [IV, i, 125–148]); *Deliciæ Musicæ* (1695), I, 16–[23] and 6–7 (f1; D&M 131), for the song sung by Nakar and Damilcar ("Hark, my Damilcar, we are call'd below" [IV, i, 43–78]) and the first two stanzas of Damilcar's later song ("Ah how sweet it is to love" [ll. 125–136]), both set to music by Henry Purcell; and *Orpheus Britannicus* (1698), pages 148–154 and 3 (f2; Macd 32b), for "Hark, my Damilcar, we are call'd below" and the first stanza of "Ah how sweet it is to love" (ll. 125–130). Probably Q1 or Q2 was the source of d. The source of f1 is unknown; the source of f2 was f1.

The first two stanzas of "Ah how sweet it is to love" were printed in a broadside ("*A Song sung by Mrs* Aliff *in the Play call'd* Tyrannick-Love *or the Royall Martyre set by Mr* Henry Purcell") about 1696 (b1). A second edition ("*set by Mr* Henry Purceell") (b2) probably appeared within a year or so. About 1710 a third edition ("A *SONG in the* Play *call'd* Tyrannick Love *Set by* Mᵣ Henry Purcell") (b3) was published. The source of b1 is unknown; the source of b2 was b1, and the source of b3 was b2.

"Hark, my Damilcar, we are call'd below" occurs in two late seventeenth-century or early eighteenth-century manuscripts: British Museum MS Add. 19,759, folios 29*v*–30*r* (M1), and Folger MS V.b.197, pages 136–140 (M2). M2 appears in a musical commonplace book containing settings mainly by Henry Purcell; it was once owned by William Penn. The source of M1 is uncertain, but M2 was copied from f2. "Ah how sweet it is to love" appears in a late seventeenth-century or early eighteenth-century manuscript in the Edinburgh University Library (Laing III.798, pp. 38–39; M3); although its source is not entirely certain, it may have been copied from F or D. The first two stanzas of this song are contained in two other late seventeenth-century or early eighteenth-century manuscripts: Bodleian MS Mus. Ch. Ch. 580, folios 7*v*–8*r* (M4), and the Guildhall Library's Gresham Coll. MS, folios 60*v*–61*r* (M5). The source of M4 was a copy of f1. M5 was copied from b1, b2, or b3. The first stanza of "Ah how sweet it is to love" is found in an early eighteenth-century (*c.* 1704) British Museum manuscript (MS Add. 22,099, fol. 59; M6). It was copied from either b1 or b2.

The following additional copies of the various editions have also been examined: Q1: Clark (*PR3418.L1 [2 cop.]), Harvard (*EC65.D8474. 670t), Yale (Ij.D848.670U); Q2: Clark (*PR3418.L1.1672), Folger (Prompt T 40; Wing D2394 bd. w. D2291; Wing D2394), Harvard (*EC65.D8474. 670tb); Q3: Clark (*PR3418.L1.1677), Folger (Wing D2395), Harvard (*EC65.D8474.670tc); Q4: Clark (*PR3418.L1.1686; *PR3410.C93), Huntington (123021); Q5: Clark (*PR3418.L1.1695; *PR3410.C91; *PR3412.

1679), Harvard (*EC65.D8474.670te); F: Clark (*fPR3412.1701 [2 cop.]; *fPR3412.1701a); D: Clark (*PR3412.1717 [2 cop.]; *PR3412.1717a); d: Huntington (148513); f1: Folger (P2429); f2: Clark (*fM1549.P98); b1: British Museum (K.7.i.2); b2: Clark (*fPR3418.L2P9), British Museum (G.306.[17]; G.304.[15]); b3: Huntington (81013.IV.2).

Dedication: Caption: Illustrious] Q2-5, F, D (Illustrious Q4-5, F, D); *Illustrious and High-born* Q1. James,] Q3-5, F (JAMES); ~ʌ Q1-2, D (JAMES D). *Privy-Council*] Q1-2, F, D; *Privy Council* Q3-5. 107:22 Person.] Q1-4, F, D; ~ , Q5. 107:22 and the] Q1-4, D; and Q5, F. 108:6 derived to] Q1-4, D; derived Q5, F. 108:6 best-belov'd] D; best belov'd Q1-5, F (beloved Q5, F). 108:12 ever] Q1, Q3-4, F, D; ~ . Q2, Q5.
Preface: PREFACE] Q1-5, F; THE / PREFACE D. 109:5 *were . . . inclinations*] Q2-5, F, D (Inclinations F, D); *was . . . inclination* Q1. 109:6 *considered*] Q1-5, D; *consider* F. 109:11 *Verse*] Q1, F; ~ : Q2-5, D. 109:12 *Prose.) And*] Q2-5, F, D; ~ :) and Q1. 109:16 *maintain,*] Q2-5, F, D; ~ʌ Q1. 109:18 *extremes*] Q1-5, D (Extremes Q3; *Extreams* D); *extream* F. 109:22 *Churches; and*] Q1; ~ . And Q2-5, F, D. 109:26 *wound*] Q2-5, F, D; *woond* Q1. 110:9 *who have*] Q1-4, D; *who* Q5, F. 110:9 *the* Roman *History*] Q3-5, F, D (The Roman History D); *the Roman History* Q1-2. 110:24 *persons*] Q5, F; ~ , Q1-4, D (Persons D). 110:32 *Play,*] Q4-5, F; ~ʌ Q1-3, D. 110:34 *slain;*] F; ~ , Q1; ~ : Q2-5, D. 111:2 *honest,*] Q5, D (Honest D); ~ʌ Q1-4, F. 111:12 *Reader. For*] Q1-4, D; ~ , for Q5, F. 111:12 *my own*] Q1-5, D; *my* F. 111:13 *Poets.*] Q1-4, D; ~ : Q5, F. 111:16 *in*] Q2-5, F, D; *in the* Q1. 111:21 *best*] Q1-2, D; *just* Q3-5, F. 111:22 *every where*] Q1-2, Q4-5, F, D; *every-where* Q3. 111:25 Conquest of] F; *Conquest of* Q1-5, D. 111:26 *every where*] Q1-2, Q4-5, F, D; *everywhere* Q3. 111:34 French] Q3-4, D; *French* Q1-2, Q5, F. 111:34 Martyrdom of S.] *Martyrdom of S.* Q1-5, F, D (St. Q3-5, F, D). 112:4 French] Q3-5, F, D; *French* Q1-2. 112:4 Thracian] Q3-5, F, D; *Thracian* Q1-2. 112:6 Herodian. *Till*] Q1-4, D; ~ ; *till* Q5, F. 112:7 *French-man*] Q3-5, F, D (Frenchman); *French-man* Q1-2. 112:10 the Great] Q3-5, F; *the Great* Q1-2, D. 112:19 French] Q3-5, F, D; *French* Q1-2. 112:28-113:15 omitted from Q1. 112:30 safe, &c.] Q3-5, F, D; ~ʌ &c. Q2. 112:32 Horace.] Q2, D; ~ , Q3-5, F. 112:32 tutus,] Q3-5, F, D; ~ʌ Q2. 113:5 useing] Q5, F (using); ~ , Q2-4, D (using Q3-4, D). 113:8 ulnis] ~ , Q2-5, F, D. 113:9 the] Q2-5, F; The D. 113:10-11 pursue; which] Q4-5, F; ~ . Which Q2, D; ~ : which Q3. 113:11 XIth] xith Q2; 11th Q3-5, F; sixth D. 113:11 Æneids] D; *Æneids* Q2-5, F. 113:13 writ] Q3-5, F; write Q2, D.
Prologue: 6 *Mad-men*] Q1-3, F, D (mad-men F); *Mad men* Q4-5 (mad men Q5). 6 *judge . . . write*] Q1-3, Q5, F, D; *judge . . . write* Q4. 8 *you*] Q3-5, F; ~ , Q1-2, D. 8 *writes*] Q1-2, Q5, F; ~ , Q3-4, D. 12 *Poets, . . . Lovers,*] Q3-5, F, D (Poetsʌ D; lovers

Q5, F); ~∧ . . . ~∧ Q1-2.　16 *'tis,*] Q4-5, F (*tis* Q4-5); ~∧ Q1-3,
D.　16 *Poet*] Q1-2, Q4-5, F; ~ , Q3, D.
　　Persons Represented: Persons Represented] Q1-5, F; Dramatis Personæ
D.　*D heads the two sections* "MEN." *and* "WOMEN."　By] Q1-5,
F; *omitted from* D.　*Harris*] Q1-5, D (Harris D); *Horris* F.　Amariel,
Guardian-Angel] Q1-4, D; Ameriel, *Guardian Angel* Q5, F.　Apol-
lonius, *a Heathen Philosopher.*] Q2-5, F, D (*Philosopher,* Q4-5, F, D);
omitted from Q1.　Mr. *Cartwright.*] Q2-5, F, D (*Mr.* Cartwright. D);
omitted from Q1.　By] Q1-5, F; *omitted from* D.　*Hughes*] Q1;
Bowtell Q2-5, F, D (Bowtel D).　Mrs. *Uphill*] Q1-5, F (*corrected
state*), D (*Mrs.* Uphill D); Mos. *Uphill* F (*uncorrected state*).　SCENE,]
Q3-5, F; ~∧ Q1-2, D.　*The Camp of*] Q1-5, F; the Camp of D.　Max-
imin] Q4-5, F; *Maximin* Q1-3, D.　*under the Walls of* Aquileia] F;
under the Walls of *Aquileia* Q1-5, D.

I, i

S.d. A] Q1-5, F; SCNE *a* D.　*s.d. Pavilion Royal*] Q1-3, D;
Pavilion-Royal Q4-5, F (*Pavillion-Royal* F).　*s.d. Enter*] D; *omitted
from Q1-5, F.*　*s.d. Guards*] Q1-5, F; *and Guards* D.　1 *Max.* Thus]
Q1-5, F (THUS); MAXIMIN. / THUS D.　3 *German*] F, D; German Q1-
5.　6 expos'd,] F; ~ . Q1-4, D; ~∧ Q5.　9 *Roman*] F, D; Roman
Q1-5.　15 would too much their sloth] Q3-5, F (Sloth Q4-5, F); would
their sloth too much Q1-2, D (Sloth D).　17 Two, tame,] Q1-5, F;
~∧~∧ D.　17 ease,] Q1-3; ~∧ Q4-5, F, D.　17 debate] Q1-5, F
(Debate F); ~ , D.　18 Chairs,] Q1-3, D; ~∧ Q4-5, F.　21 *Char.*]
Q1-2, F, D; *Clar.* Q3-5.　22 breathe] Q1-4, D; breath Q5, F.　22
Walls.] Q1-4, D; ~ , Q5; ~ : F.　23 Souls] Q1-5, D; Soul F.
25 Summons] Q1-5, D; ~ , F.　30 despair:] Q1-4, D (Despair D);
~ . Q5, F (Despair F).　31 guilty,] Q1-4, F, D (Guilty D); ~∧ Q5.
36 pow'r] Q1-4, D (Pow'r D); power Q5, F (Power F).　37 pow'rs]
Q1-4, D (Pow'rs Q3-4, D); powers Q5, F (Powers F).　47 half-Kings]
Q1-5; Half Kings F, D (half D).　61 day,] Q4-5, F; ~ ; Q1-3, D (Day
D).　66 lose] Q1-5, F; loose D.　67 Heav'ns] Q1-5, D (Heav'n's
D); Heaven's F.　68 as] Q1-5, D; at F.　70 Tribune] Q1-5, D;
Tribute F.　70 *Panonian*] F, D (*Pannonian* D); Panonian Q1-5.
79 wounded] Q1, F; wounden Q2-5, D.　81 dread] Q1-4, D; dread-
ful Q5, F.　82 Battels] Q1-4, D; Battle Q5, F (Battel F).　83
Placidius,] Q1-2, Q4-5, F, D; ~∧ Q3.　87 Angles] Q1-4, F, D;
Angels Q5.　88 sence.] Q1-4, D (sense Q3-4; Sense D); sense, Q5;
Sense; F.　90 low;] F; ~ , Q1-5, D.　91 fields] Q1-2, D (Fields D);
field Q3-5, F (Field F).　100 drawn] Q1-5, D; ~ , F.　100 view]
F; ~ , Q1-5, D.　101 besieg'd;] Q1-4, D; besieg'd∧ Q5; Besieg'd, F.
101 neighb'ring] Q1-4, D (neighbring Q2); Neighbouring Q5, F (neighbouring F).　101 Plain] Q1-3, F, D; ~ . Q4-5.　106 strove] Q1-3,
Q5, F, D; stove Q4.　107 voice] Q1-5; Voice, F, D.　107 *to morrow . . . to morrow*] F; to morrow . . . to morrow Q1-5; To Morrow
. . . to Morrow D.　119 *indented in* Q4-5.　123 resign,] Q1-4,
F, D; ~∧ Q5.　123 Command;] F; ~ , Q1-5 (command Q5); ~∧ D.

127 obey'd] Q1-3, D; ~ . Q4; ~ , Q5, F.   131 *s.d. omitted from* Q5,
F.   132 pow'r] Q1-4, D (Pow'r D); power Q5, F (Power F).   138
Wood.] Q3-5; ~ , Q1-2, D; ~ : F.   145 twin Stars] Q1-2, D; Twin-
Stars Q3-5, F.   148 Lovers,] Q2-5, F, D; ~∧ Q1.   150 *Por.*] Q1-2,
D; *Per.* Q3-5, F.   164 Require] Q1-2, Q4-5, F, D; Requires Q3.   173
pow'rs] Q1-3, D (Pow'rs Q3, D); Powers Q4-5, F.   175 shall;] Q1-4,
D; ~∧ Q5; ~ , F.   175 Laws] F; ~ , Q1-5, D.   177 here.] Q3-5,
F, D; ~ , Q1-2.   178 those] Q1-2, D; these Q3-5, F.   178 appear!]
Q1-4, D; ~ ? Q5, F.   178+ *s.d. Aside, looking] Looking* Q1-5, F, D.
179 view!] Q1-4, D; ~ ? Q5, F.   180 anew!] Q1-4, D; ~ ? Q5; ~ ; F.
183 did *Porphyrius*] Q1-5, D; ~ , ~ , F.   191 *s.d. Lower*] F, D; *lower*
Q1-5.   194 nor] Q1-4, F, D; not Q5.   194 rise!] Q1-5, D; ~ . F.
195 tongue!] Q1-5, D (Tongue Q3, D); Tongue. F.   197 long,]
Q1-4, F; ~∧ Q5; ~ ! D.   199 *s.d. Rising]* Q3-5, F, D; *rising* Q1-2.
201 *Vale.*] *Val.* Q1-5, F, D.   201 be] Q3-5, F, D; ~ , Q1-2.   203
cause] F, D (Cause); ~ , Q1-5.   218 more.] Q1-2, D; ~ ? Q3-5, F.
221 Sir————] Q1-4, D; ~ .————— Q5, F.   226 wo;] F (Wo); ~ ,
Q1-5, D (Wo D).   228 You've] Q3-5, F, D; Youv'e Q1-2.   236
Gods] Q1-5, D; ~ ! F.   237 pray'r] Q1-5, D (Pray'r Q5, D); Prayer F.
237 you,] Q3-5, F; ~∧ Q1-2, D.   239 brought,] Q4-5, F; ~ . Q1-3,
D.   240 all humane force] Q2-5, F, D (human D; Force F, D);
humanity Q1.   245-246 strove, . . . *Jove;*] ~ ; . . . ~ . Q1-5, F, D.
248 Town,] Q4-5, F; ~ . Q1-3, D.   250 mistook;] ~ . Q1-5, F, D.
251 Till,] F; ~∧ Q1-5, D.   251 late,] Q1-5, D; ~ . F.   253 *Vale.*]
Q1-2; *Valer.* Q3-5, F; *Val.* D.   253 Heav'n] Q1-3, D; Heaven Q4-5,
F.   258 in] Q1-5, D; to F.   262 dye.] F (die); ~ : Q1-5, D (die
Q3-5, D).   267 trust,] F (Trust); ~ ; Q1-5, D (Trust D).   267
infamy,] Q3, F (Infamy F); ~∧ Q1-2, D (Infamy D); ~ . Q4-5.   270
obey'd.] Q1-3, F, D; ~ , Q4; ~ ; Q5.   272 know.] Q1-4, F, D; ~ ,
Q5.   279 more,] Q3-5, F, D; ~∧ Q1-2.   280 *Thracian*] D; Thra-
cian Q1-5, F.   287 day,] F, D (Day D); ~ ; Q1-5.   293 me,] F;
~ ; Q1-5, D.   297 *Por. aside.* . . . mind!] *Por. aside.*] . . . mind!
Q1-5, F (aside∧ Q3); *Por.* . . . Mind! [*Aside.* D.   298 kind!] Q1-
5, D (Kind D); ~ , F.   299 stand:] Q1-5, D; ~ ! F.   300 Heav'n]
Q1-2, D; Heaven Q3-5, F.   302 *s.d. Going]* Q3-5, F, D; *going* Q1-2.
304 *s.d. leading]* Q1-4, F, D; *leading to* Q5.   307, 313 *Vale.*] *Val.*
Q1-5, F, D.   313 [*rule*] *Placidius*] [*rule omitted*] ~ Q1-5, F, D.
325 you,] F; ~∧ Q1-5, D.   325 remain] Q1-2, F, D; ~ , Q3-5.
326 bed,] Q3-5, F, D (Bed); ~∧ Q1-2.   330 him you] Q1-2, D; you
him Q3-5, F.   331 *Vale.*] *Val.* Q1-5, F, D.

II, i

SCENE I. / *The*] Q1-4, Q5 (*corrected state*); SCENE / *The* Q5 (*un-
corrected state*); SCENE I. *The* F; SCENE I. / SCENE *The* D.   *s.d.*
Enter] D; *omitted from Q1-5,* F.   *s.d. Berenice, Porphyrius*] Q4-5;
Berenice, Porphyrius Q1-3, F; *Berenice and Porphyrius* D.   12 giv'n]
Q1-4, D; given Q5, F.   13 bear,] Q1-5, D; ~ . F.   17 sin,] Q1,
Q4-5, F, D (Sin F, D); ~ . Q2-3.   18 Wife] Q1-2, Q4-5, F, D; Wise

Q3.　　19　will?] Q1-4, F, D (Will Q3-4, F, D); Will∧ Q5.　　26　bear,] Q1-4, F, D; ∼∧ Q5.　　27　pow'r] Q1-5, D (Pow'r D); Power F.　　32 avails the . . . take?] Q1-5, D; avails? The . . . take. F.　　34　Pirate] Q1-4, F, D (Pyrate Q4, F); Pyrates Q5.　　34　ill-gotten] Q1-4, F, D; ill gotten Q5.　　36　fall;] Q3-5, F; ∼ : Q1-2, D.　　39　lawfully] Q1-4, F, D; unlawfully Q5.　　46　instrument,] Q4-5, F (Instrument); ∼∧ Q1-3, D.　　53　But was] Q1-2, D; But 'twas Q3-5, F.　　70　use.] Q1-3, D; ∼ , Q4-5; ∼ ; F.　　71　lose.] Q1-3, D; ∼ , Q4-5; ∼ : F.　　85+　*s.d.* hand.] Q3-5, F, D (*Hand* D); ∼ .] Q1-2.　　90　alone] F; ∼ , Q1-5, D. 92　grow!] Q1-5, D; ∼ . F.　　94+　*s.d.* Erotio] Q3-5, F; *Erotio* Q1-2; *Erotion* D.　　95　cast] Q1-4, F, D; ∼ . Q5.　　96+　*s.d.* Placidius,] Q1-5, F; ∼ , *and* D.　　102　face,] Q1-5, D (Face Q4, D); Face. F.　　109 thoughts] Q1-4, D (Thoughts D); thought Q5, F (Thought F).　　109 ambition lift?] Q1-4, F, D (Ambition F, D); ambitious life; Q5.　　109 *s.d.* [*Kneeling*] Q1-5, F (*some copies*), D; Kneeling F (*some copies*). 115+　*s.d. Raising*] F, D; raising Q1-5.　　115+　*s.d.* him.] Q3-5, F, D; ∼ .] Q1-2.　　119+　*s.d.* again.] Q3-5, F, D; ∼ .] Q1-2.　　135　Ev'n] Q1-4, D; Even Q5, F.　　136　assistants] Q1-4, F, D (Assistants F, D); assistance Q5.　　138-139　punishment. [*Exit* Valerius. / . . . provide,] F; punishment. / . . . provide, [*Exit* Valerius. Q1-5, D (Punishment D; Val. D).　　143　Teachers] D; ∼ , Q1-5, F (teachers Q5).　　150　then proceed . . . a new] Q1-4, D (New D); then . . . anew Q5; then presume . . . a new F.　　153　Male-contents] Q1-4, F, D; Male contents Q5. 158+　*s.d.* Apollonius,] Q1-5, F; Apollonius, *and* D.　　160　Queen.] Q1-5, D; ∼ ! F.　　166　mind,] F, D (Mind); ∼ ; Q1-5.　　168　Heav'n] Q1-4, D; Heaven Q5, F.　　169　*S. Cath.*] Q1-5, D; *Cath.* F.　　174 one;] ∼ . Q1-5, F, D.　　176　ev'ry] Q1-4, D; every Q5, F.　　179 Province;] Q1-5, D; ∼ , F.　　180　Heav'n] Q1-4, D; Heaven Q5, F. 193　Vertue, as] Q1-3, D (Virtue∧ Q3; Virtue D); Vertue∧ is Q4-5, F (Virtue Q5; Virtue, F).　　194　without,] Q1-4, D; ∼∧ Q5, F.　　198 nor] Q1-4, D (Nor D); not Q5, F.　　205　*S.*] Q3-5, F, D; S. Q1-2. 205　ev'n] Q1-2, D; even Q3-5, F.　　206　yours] Q3-5, F, D; your's Q1-2.　　211　*S.*] Q3-5, F, D; S. Q1-2.　　211　virtues] Q1-2, D (Virtues D); riches Q3-5 (Riches Q4-5); Precepts F.　　214　ev'n] Q2, D; e'vn Q1; even Q3-5, F.　　221　heard] Q1-2, Q4-5, F, D; herd Q3. 222　weak.] Q1-2, Q5, F, D; ∼ , Q3-4.　　224　Truth,] Q3-5, F; ∼∧ Q1-2, D.　　237　*S.*] Q3-5, F, D; S. Q1-2.　　237　Heav'n] Q1-4, D; Heaven Q5, F.　　247　this] Q1-4, D (ths Q4); the Q5, F.　　247　come:] Q1-4, D; ∼∧ Q5, F.　　251　just:] Q1-5, D; Just∧ F.　　251　shall] Q1-5, D; should F.　　254　fear] Q1-2, Q4-5, F, D; ∼ , Q3.　　254 sed] Q1-2, D (said D); fed Q3-5, F.　　258　her!] Q1-2, D; ∼ ? Q3-5, F. 261　too] Q2-5, F, D; to Q1.　　266　find———] ∼———∧ Q1-5, F, D. 267　confest: [*Aside.*] confest: Q1-5, F, D (confess'd Q3-5; confess'd; F). 270+　*s.d.* [*Exit*] Q1-3, F, D; *Exit.* Q4-5.　　270+　*s.d.* guarded.] Q3-5, F, D (guard- Q5); Guarded.] Q1-2.　　273　which] Q1-4, D; that Q5, F.　　275　me;] D; ∼ . Q1-2; ∼ , Q3-5, F.　　275+　*s.d. Kneeling.*] Q3-5, F, D; ∼ .] Q1-2.　　288　———Devotion] Q1-3, D; ∧Devotion Q4-5, F.　　293　Natures,] Q3-5; Natures∧ Q1-2, F; Nature's∧ D.

299 sooth] Q1–5, D; smooth F.   299 passion,] F (Passion); ~∧ Q1–5, D (Passion D).   300 care;] D (Care); ~ . Q1–5; Care, F.

III, i

S.d. The] Q1–5, F; SCENE *The* D.   s.d. *Enter*] *omitted from Q1–5, F, D.*   2 age.] Q1–2, F, D (Age F, D); ~ , Q3–5.   19 assaults,] F (Assaults); ~ ; Q1–4, D (Assaults Q4, D); ~∧ Q5.   24 Iron heart] Q2–5, F, D (Heart F, D); Ironheart Q1.   25+ *s.d. Exit*] Q1–2, Q4–5, D; ~ . Q3, F.   31 Heav'n] Q1–4, D; Heaven Q5, F.   34 Heav'n] Q1–3, Q5, F, D; Heaven Q4.   34 th'] Q1–4, D; the Q5, F.   34 *Ægyptian*] D; Ægyptian Q1–5, F.   55 yours,] ~ . Q1–5, F, D.   57 asks] Q1–4, F, D; askt Q5.   68 well befitted] Q1–2, F, D; well-befitted Q3–5.   76–77 *omitted from Q1.*   78 Th'] Q1–4, D; The Q5, F.   78 *Ægyptian*] F, D; Ægyptian Q1–5 (Egyptian Q4).   82 *Roman*] Q3–4, F, D; Roman Q1–2, Q5.   82 be] Q1–2, Q4–5, F, D; *be* Q3.   85 Princess] Q1–3, F, D; Princes Q4–5.   93 sin.] ~∧ Q1–5, F, D (Sin D).   97 *s.d. Exit*] Q5; ~ . Q1–4, F; *Ex.* D.   99 ill nature] Q1–5, F (Nature Q4–5, F); Ill-Nature D.   105 *Ægyptian*] F, D; Ægyptian Q1–5.   107 on] Q1–4, D; of Q5; off F.   109 *s.d. omitted from Q5, F.*   131 me,] Q1–4, F, D; ~ . Q5.   134 weak,] Q1–4, F, D; ~∧ Q5.   137 free:] Q1–2, D; ~ , Q3–5, F.   150 Funeral-torch] Q1–2, D; Funeral Torch Q3–5, F.   151 too,] Q1, F, D; ~ . Q2–5.   152 'Gainst] Q2–5, F, D; Gainst Q1 (*but* " 'Gainst" *in catchword*).   157 Rock, I . . . Port] Q4–5, F, D; ~∧ ~, . . . ~, Q1–3.   158 *Vale.*] Val. Q1–5, F, D.   172 *Vale.*] Val. Q1–5, F, D (*Val*∧ Q3).   180 *Vale.*] Val. Q1–5, F, D.   181 float] Q1, Q3–5, F, D; flout Q2.   184 *Vale.*] Val. Q1–5, F, D.   184 Quick-sands] Q1–3, Q5, F, D (Quick-Sands F); Quick sands Q4.   187 way,] Q1–3, F, D; ~ . Q4–5.   190 *Vale.*] Val. Q1–5, F, D.   191 guess.———] Q1–2, D; ~∧——— Q3–5, F.   193 gagg'd] Q3–5, F, D; gag'd Q1–2.   194 *Vale.*] Val. Q1–5, F, D.   198 it!] Q1–5, D; ~∧ F.   202 *Vale.*] Val. Q1–5, F, D.   207 obey.] Q1–4, D; ~ : Q5, F.   208, 216 *Vale.*] Val. Q1–5, F, D.   221 who e're] Q1–4, D (e'r Q3–4; e'er D); whoe'er Q5, F (whoe're F).   223 ingrateful] Q1–5, D; ungrateful F.   232+ *s.d.* Berenice,] Q1–5, F; ~ , *and* D.   233 *Porphyrius*,] Q1–4, D; ~∧ Q5, F.   239 'tis] Q1–4, D; it is Q5; it's F.   240 it is] Q1–4, F, D; tis Q5.   246 indiff'rence] Q2–5, F, D (Indiff'rence F, D); indifference Q1.   256 Prison-door] Q1–5, D (prison-door Q5); Prison Door F.   263–264 score? . . . more.] F; ~ , . . . ~ ? Q1–5, D (Score D).   271 dye.] Q1; ~ , Q2–5, F, D (die Q3–5, D; Die F).   278 try?] Q1–4, F, D; ~ ; Q5.   284, 288 *Ægyptian*] F, D; Ægyptian Q1–5.   288 Princess] Q1–4, F, D; Princes Q5.   288 heard] Q3–5, F, D; hard Q1–2.   290 *s.d. omitted from Q5, F.*   294 his] Q1–5, D; this F.   306 *Jews*] F, D; Jews Q1–5.   306 Sabbath,] Q3–4; ~∧ Q1–2, Q5, F, D.   307 not] Q1–4, F, D; nor Q5.   311 me?] Q1–3, F, D; ~ . Q4–5.   317 Groves,] Q1–4, D; ~ . Q5, F.   336 o'repow'rd] Q1–2; o'r-pow'rd Q3–4; o'r-power'd Q5, F, D (o'er-power'd D).   336 overcome] Q1–2, F, D; over-come Q3–5.   337 Forc'd back] Q2–5, F, D; Forc'dback Q1.

IV, i

S.d. Indian] D (SCENE *an* Indian); *Indian* Q1–5, F.   *s.d. Enter*]
D; *omitted from Q1–5, F.*   *s.d.* Placidius, Nigrinus] Q1–5, F; Placidius,
and Nigrinus D.   *s.d. upward*] Q1–2, D; *upwards* Q3–5, F.   11
pow'r] Q1–4, D (Pow'r D); power Q5, F (Power F).   12 you] Q1–4,
F, D; yon Q5.   15 pray'r] Q2–5, F, D (Pray'r F, D); prayer Q1.   19
these] Q1–2, D; those Q3–5, F.   33 *Venus,*] Q1–5, D; ∼∧ F.   40
death-like] Q1–4, F, D; death like Q5.   43–74 *italics and romans
reversed in f1–2 but normalized in the following textual notes.*   43
Hark,] Q1–5, F, D, f1–2, M2 (*Heark* Q3–4, F; *Heark*∧ Q5; *HArk*∧ f1–2;
Hark∧ M2); *Hark hark* M1.   43 Damilcar,] Q1–5, F, D, M1 (Damilkar
F; ∼∧ M1); Daridcar! f1–2, M2.   43 *we are*] Q1–5, F, D; *we're* f1–2,
M2; *wee're* M1.   43 *below!*] Q1–5, F, D; ∼ ; f1–2, M2; ∼∧ M1.   44
go!] Q1–5, F, D; *goe*∧ f1–2, M1–2 (*go* M2).   45 Go] Q1–5, F, D;
omitted from f1–2, M1–2.   45–46 *care / Of*] Q1–5, D (*Care* D); *Care
of* F, f1–2, M1–2 (*care,* f1; *care* M1–2).   46 *despair!*] Q1–5, F, D
(*Despair* Q5, F, D); ∼ ; f1–2 (*dispair* f1); *disspair*∧ M1; ∼ , M2.   48
a] Q1–5, F, D; *the* f1–2, M1–2.   49 *Moon-shine*] Q1–4, F, D, f1;
Moon shine Q5; *Moonshine* f2, M1–2.   49 *while*] Q1–5, F, D; *whilst
the* f1–2, M2; *when the* M1.   50 *we . . . we*] Q1–5, F, D, f1–2, M2;
wee'l . . . wee'l M1.   51 *racking*] Q1–5, F, D, f1–2, M2; *rocking* M1
(?).   51 *downy*] Q1–5, F, D, M1 (*Downy* Q5); *dawny* f1–2, M2.   52
lest] Q1–5, F, D, f2, M2; *least* f1, M1.   52 *too*] Q1–5, F, D, f1–2, M2;
to M1.   53 *We*] Q1–5, F, D; *we'll* f1–2, M1–2 (*wee'l* M1).   53
new-falling] Q1–2, D; *new falling* Q3–5, F, f1–2, M1–2.   53 *Star.*] Q1–
5, F, D; ∼ , f1–2, M2 (*Starr* f2; *star* M2); ∼∧ M1.   55 *Love!*] Q1–5,
F, D; ∼ . f1–2, M2; *love*∧ M1.   56 *Sun's*] Q1–5, F, D, f1–2, M2; *suns*
M1.   56 *Element's*] Q1–4, F, D, f1–2, M2; *Elements* Q5, M1 (*Ellements*
M1).   57 *head!*] Q1–5, F, D; *Head;* f1–2; ∼∧ M1; ∼ , M2.   59
Alas] Q1–5, F, D, f1–2, M2 (*alas* f1–2; *Alass* M2); *and alass* M1.   59
Fair] Q1–5, F, D, f1–2, M2 (*fair* M2); *dear* M1.   60 *light Horse-men*]
Q1–5, D, f1; *Light-horse-men* F; *light Horsemen* f2, M1–2 (*horsmen* M1;
horsemen M2).   61 *'em*] Q1–5, F, D, f1–2, M2; *them* M1.   63 *we*]
Q1–5, F, D, f1–2, M2; *wee* M1.   63 *fight!*] Q1–4, D; ∼ : Q5; ∼ .
F; ∼ ; f1–2; ∼∧ M1; ∼ , M2.   66 *drown!*] Q1–5, F, D; *down:* f1–2;
drownd∧ M1; *drown.* M2.   67 *But their*] Q1–5, F, D, f1–2, M2;
your M1.   68 *a Trumpeter-Hornet*] Q1–5, F, D; *a Trumpetter,
Hornet* f1–2 (*Trumpeter* f2); *the trumpetts and Hornetts* M1; *Trumpeter
Hornet* M2.   69 *Now*] Q1–5, F, D, M1 (*now* M1); *no* f1–2, M2.   70
we] Q1–5, F, D, f1–2, M2; *wee* M1.   71 *will*] Q1–5, F, D, f1–2, M2;
shall M1.   72 *pass!*] Q1–5, F, D; ∼ , f1–2, M2; ∼∧ M1.   73 *will*]
Q1–5, F, D; *wou'd* f1–2, M1–2 (*would* M1; *woud* M2).   74 *Then
call*] Q1–5, F, D, f1–2, M2; *Re call* M1.   75 *ready and quick is a
Spirit*] Q1–5, F, D, f1–2, M2; *quick*[?] *and so kind*[?] *are the spirits* M1.
77 *the*] Q1–2, D, f1–2, M1–2; *that* Q3–5, F.   78 *and*] Q1–5, F, D,
f1–2, M2; *but* M1.   79+ *s.d.* Damilcar.] Q3–5, F, D (Damil. Q3–5, F);
∼ .] Q1–2.   80 Wand,] Q3, Q5, F (wand Q5); ∼∧ Q1–2, D; ∼ .

Q4.   82 Sev'n] Q1–5, D; Seven F.   88 pain] Q1; ∼ . Q2; ∼ ,
Q3–5, F, D (Pain D).   91 whate're] Q1–2; what e'r Q3–4; whate'er
Q5, F, D.   97 She,] F; ∼∧ Q1–5, D.   97 Suppliant-like] Q1–4, F,
D; Suppliant like Q5.   99 thy] Q1–5, D; the F.   100 *Ægyptian*]
D; Ægyptian Q1–5, F.   102 dream:] Q1–2, D (Dream D); ∼ ; Q3–4;
∼ ? Q5; Dream, F.   106 'em] Q4, D; e'm Q1–3; them Q5, F.   120
ly,] Q1–2, Q4–5, F, D (*lye* F, D); *lie.* Q3.   122 'em] Q3–5, F, D; *e'm*
Q1–2.   122 *ever-laughing*] Q4–5, F, D; *ever laughing* Q1–3.   125–
148 *in romans in d, 125–136 in romans in f1, and 125–130 in romans in*
f2; but normalized in the textual footnote and the following textual notes.
125 Dam.] Q1–5, F, D; *omitted from d, f1–2, b1–3, M3–6.*   125 *love,*]
Q1–5, F, D, f1 (*Love* D, f1); ∼ ! d, M3; *Love;* f2, b1–3; *Love*∧ M4–6 (*love*
M6).   126 *desire!*] Q1–5, F, D, d, M3 (*Desire* F, D); ∼ : f1–2; ∼ .
b1–2; ∼ , b3; ∼∧ M4–6.   127 *pains*] Q1–5, F, D, d, b1–3, M3, M5
(*Pains* D; *paines* M5); *pain* f1–2, M4, M6.   128 *we first approach*
Loves fire!] Q1–5, F, D, d, M3 (*Love's* D, M3; *Fire!* M3; *fire?* M3 [*?*]); *first*
we feel a Lovers fire; f1–2, b1–3, M4–6 (*wee* M5; *feell* M6; *fire:* f2; *fire.*
b1–2; *fire*∧ b3, M6; *fire,* M4; *Fire*∧ M5).   129 *Pains*] Q1–5, F, D, d,
f1–2, b1–3, M3–4, M6 (*paines* f1; *pains* f2, M4); *Pangs* M5.   129 *be*]
Q1–5, F, D, d, M3, M5; *are* f1–2, b1–3, M4, M6.   130 *Than*] Q1–5, F,
D, d, b1–3, M3, M6 (*than* b1–3, M6); *then* f1–2, M4–5.   131 *which*]
Q1–5, F, D, d, M3, M5 (?); *that* f1, b1–3, M4.   132 *Do but gently*]
Q1–5, F, D, d, M3; *Gently move and* f1, b1–3, M4–5 (*Gentle* b1–3; *gently*
M4–5; *Move* M4; *&* M5).   132 *Heart:*] Q1–5, F, D, M3 (*heart* Q3);
heart, d, b1–2, M4; ∼ ; f1; ∼∧ b3; *heart*∧ M5.   133 *Ev'n*] Q1–5, F, D,
d, b1–3, M3; *Even* f1, M4; *And* M5 (?).   134 *Cure, like trickling Balm,*
their] Q1–5, F, D, d, M3 (*Balm*∧ Q1–5; *balm* d); *Like trickling balm cure*
the f1, b1–3, M4–5 (*Balsome* f1, M4; *Balm* M5; *Cure* M4).   135 *lose*]
Q1–5, F, D, d; *loose* f1, b1–3, M3–5.   136 *in*] Q1–5, F, D, M3, M5; *an*
d, f1, b1–3, M4.   137 *reverence*] Q1–5, F, D (*Reverence* Q5, F);
Rev'rence d, M3.   144 *Swells*] Q1–5, F, D, d; *Swell's* M3.   144
every] Q1–5, F, D, d; *ev'ry* M3.   146 *they . . . shrink*] Q1–5, F, D, d;
they're . . . shrunk M3.   147 *flow in*] Q1–5, F, D, M3 (*Flow* F, M3);
flowing d.   148+ *s.d. Guardian-Angel*] Q1–5, D; *Guardian Angel* F.
151 flies.——— [*To* S. Cath.] A] flies: (a Q1–5, F, D, (A D).   158–159
behind. / ———Vain] behind.) / Vain Q1–5, F, D (behind∧) F).   163
Hence,] Q1–2, D; ∼∧ Q3–5, F.   168 'em] Q1–4, D; them Q5, F.   171
feel] Q1–3, F, D; ∼ : Q4–5.   173 Thou,] Q1–4, D; ∼∧ Q5, F.   175
th'] Q1–4, D; the Q5, F.   182 sight,] Q1–4, F, D (Sight); ∼ . Q5.
183 and stagger] Q1–4, D; I stagger Q5, F.   193 steams] Q1–2, F, D
(Steams F, D); streams Q3–5.   194–195 Go . . . dreams. . . ./ But . . .
more [*To* S. Cath.] D (Dreams); *to* S. Cath. Go . . . dreams. . . . / But
. . . more (*Cath.*) Q4–5; dreams∧ Q3–5); Go . . . Dreams. . . . /
To S. Cath.] But . . . more F.   200 *s.d. omitted from* Q5, F.   202
and twi-light] Q1–4, F, D (Twi-light F); twi-light Q5.   208 it be]
Q1–4, F, D; be it Q5.   211 *in romans in Q1–5, F, D.*   212 fair:]
Q1–5, D; ∼ , F.   214 wakes.] ∼∧ Q1–5, F, D.   226 *s.d. Valeria*]
Q3–5, F, D (Val. D); *Valeria* Q1–2.   230 Vale.] *Val.* Q1–5, F, D (Val.

F).   230   *Venus*] Q1-4, F, D; *Venns* Q5.   231   him] Q1-4, F, D; no Q5.   234, 238   *Vale.*] *Val.* Q1-5, F, D.   240   amaz'd.] Q1-3, F, D; ∼∧ Q4-5.   242   *Vale.*] *Val.* Q1-5, F, D.   242   how e're] Q1-3 (how e'r Q3); howe'er Q4-5, F, D (howe're F).   246   You] Q1-3, Q5, F, D; Yon Q4.   247, 254   *Vale.*] *Val.* Q1-5, F, D.   258   Lab'rinth] Q2-5, F, D; Labyrinth Q1.   260   I must] Q1-5, F; must I D.   264   *Vale.*] *Val.* Q1-5, F, D.   266   see,] Q1-5, F; ∼∧ D.   267   effect] Q1-2, D; effects Q3-5, F.   275   lov'd,] Q4-5, F; ∼. Q1-3, D.   276   confest] Q1 (*cancel*), Q2-5, F, D; confest, Q1 (*cancelandum*).   278   knew,] Q1, Q4-5, F, D; ∼. Q2; ∼∧ Q3.   280   Tempest] Q1; Tempests Q2-5, F, D.   281   my] Q1-4, D; her Q5, F.   282   *Vale.*] *Val.* Q1-5, F, D.   292   [*rule*] I'le] [*rule omitted*] ∼ Q1-5, F, D (I'll Q3-5, F, D).   293   may] Q1 (*cancel*), Q2-5, F, D; my Q1 (*cancelandum*).   294   Pris'ner] F; Prisoner Q1-5, D.   296   *Vale.*] *Val.* Q1-5, F, D.   298   Free will's] Q1-5, F (Will's Q3-5, F); Free-will's D.   299   slavery,] ∼. Q1-5, F, D (Slavery Q4-5, F, D).   300   desire,] Q4-5, F; ∼: Q1-3, D (Desire D).   307   and when] Q1, F, D; when Q2-5.   309   *Vale.*] *Val.* Q1-5, F, D.   312   *s.d. Exit* Valeria] Q1 (*cancel*), Q2-5, F, D (Val. D); *Exeunt* Porphyrius *and* Valeria *severally* Q1 (*cancelandum*).   313–351   *omitted from Q1 cancelandum*.   326   Lapwing-like] Q1 (*cancel*), Q2-5, D; Lap-wing like F.   328   affronts] Q1 (*cancel*), Q2-5, F (Affronts F); affront D.   332   *Ægyptian*] F, D (Egyptian D); Egyptian Q1 (*cancel*), Q2-5 (Ægyptian Q4-5).   332   Princess] Q1 (*cancel*), Q2-4, F, D; Princes Q5.   343   Mistress,] Q1 (*cancel*), Q2-5, D (Mistris Q4); ∼∧ F.   346   Your] Q1 (*cancel*), Q3-5, F, D; You Q2.   351+   *s.d. Enter*] Q1 (*cancel*), Q2-5, F, D; *To* Maximin *enter* Q1 (*cancelandum*).   353   Heav'ns] Q1-2, Q5, F, D (Heav'n's D); Heaven's Q3-4.   354   fulfill] Q1 (*cancelandum*), Q3-4; fulfil Q1 (*cancel*), Q2, Q5, F, D.   361   close.] Q1-4, D; ∼, Q5, F.   363   Seeks] Q1-2, Q4-5, F, D; Seek Q3.   380   *Roman*] Q3-4, F, D; Roman Q1-2, Q5.   384–386   rest, . . . possest; . . . before,] ∼ ; . . . ∼ . . . . ∼ : Q1-5, F, D (Rest F, D).   394   change, the . . . ease;] ∼ (∼ . . . ∼) Q1-5, F, D (Ease F).   411   a while] Q1-2, Q4-5, F, D; awhile Q3.   415   swift] Q1-2, D; sweet Q3-5, F.   416   And] Q1-4, D; In Q5, F.   417   would] Q1-5, D; could F.   425–426   strife, . . . life;] ∼ ; . . . ∼ . Q1-5, F, D (Life F, D).   428   too] Q2-5, F, D; to Q1.   433   pow'rful] Q1-2, D; powerful Q3-5, F.   433   blandishments] Q1-4, D (Blandishments D); banishments Q5, F (Banishments F).   436   blest,] Q1-5, D; Blest! F.   446   Tribune . . . strait, *To* Val.] D ([*To*); *To Val.* Tribune . . . strait, Q1-5, F ([*To* Val.] F; *line indented*).   450   Tribune,] Q1-4, D; ∼∧ Q5, F.   465   Faith's] Q1-3, F, D; Faiths Q4-5.   466   so e're] Q1-2, D (e'er D); soe're Q3-5, F (soe'er Q5, F).   482   do's] Q1-5, D; does F.   489   with] Q1-4, D; will with Q5, F.   495   farther] Q1-5, D; further F.   500   Tyrants] Q1, F, D (Tyrant's F, D); Tyrant Q2-5.   506   you] Q1-4, F, D; yon Q5.   509   try] Q1-4, D; ∼. Q5, F.   518   weigh.] Q1-5, D; ∼∧ F.   522   is,] Q1-5, D; ∼∧ F.   522   its] Q3-5, F, D; it's Q1-2.   531   you] Q3-5, F; ∼, Q1-2, D.   544   sound,] Q1-4, D; ∼∧ Q5, F.   546   launce] Q1-3; launch Q4-5, F, D (Launch F).   547

Discov'rers] Q1–4, D; discoverers Q5, F (Discoverers F). 549 We,] Q1–2, D; ~∧ Q3–5, F. 549 needless] Q1–5, F; ~, D. 554 All-great] Q1, Q3–5, F, D; All great Q2. 555 will . . . crime,] F, D (Crime); ~ , . . . ~∧ Q1–5 (Crime Q3–5). 555 prepare.] Q1, Q3–5, F; ~∧ Q2, D. 556 decreed,] F; ~∧ Q1–5, D. 557 life,] Q4–5, F (Life); ~∧ Q1–3, D (Life D). 557 shall] Q1–5, D; should F. 562 brought;] Q1; ~ . Q2; ~ , Q3–5, F, D. 576 Guards,] ~∧ Q1–5, F, D. 577 Heav'n] Q1–3, Q5, F, D; Heaven Q4. 583 Guardian-Angel] Q1–2, Q4–5, F, D; Guardian Angel Q3. 588+ *s.d. and Guards*] Q1–5, D; *with Guards* F. 589 *Max.*] Q2–5, F, D; ~∧ Q1. 596 Yes,] D; ~∧ Q1–5, F. 596 fame.] Q1–3, F, D (Fame Q3, F, D); Fame, Q4–5. 609 leaves] Q1–5, F; leave D. 610 a] Q1–4, D; the Q5, F. 611 Its] Q3–5, F, D; It's Q1–2. 611 therefore,] Q4–5, F, D; ~∧ Q1–3. 612 its] Q3–5, F, D; it's Q1–2. 615 secure] Q1–4, D; rescue Q5, F. 616 may] Q1–4, F, D; my Q5. 627 down,] Q1, F, D; ~ . Q2–5. 637 thou wert] Q1–4, F, D; that thou were Q5. 641 your] Q1–4, F, D; thy Q5. 646 the] Q1–4, D; a Q5, F. 659 when e're] Q1–3, D (e'er D); whene'r Q4–5, F (whene'er F). 659 please,] Q1–3, D; ~ . Q4–5, F. 661 fed,] Q1, Q3–5, F; ~ . Q2, D. 666 Nay,] Q5, F; ~∧ Q1–4, D. 666+ *s.d. omitted from Q5, F*. 667 ———I] Q1–5, F; ∧~ D. 669 am,] Q1–4, D; ~∧ Q5, F.

V, i

S.d. Enter] D; *omitted from Q1–5,* F. *s.d.* Valeria, Placidius] Q4–5, D (Valeria *and* Placidius D); *Valeria, Placidius* Q1–3, F. 1, 7, 12 *Vale.*] *Val.* Q1–5, F, D. 19+ *s.d. Exit.*] Q3–5, F, D; ~ .] Q1–2. 20 *Vale.*] *Val.* Q1–5, F, D. 24 loves] Q1–5, D; love F. 29, 37 *Vale.*] *Val.* Q1–5, F, D. 37 elsewhere] Q1–2, F, D; else-where Q3–5. 45, 51 *Vale.*] *Val.* Q1–5, F, D. 57 Besides, what can I] Q2–5, F, D (Besides∧ Q2; What F); Besides——— / What is it I can Q1. 59 *Vale.*] *Val.* Q1–5, F, D. 63 pray'rs] F (Pray'rs); prayers Q1–5, D (Prayers Q4–5, D). 65 *Vale.*] *Val.* Q1–5, F, D. 72 away.] ~ . ——— Q1–2, D; ~∧——— Q3–5, F. 73 set: *Aside.*] set: Q1–5, F, D. 82 *Vale.*] *Val.* Q1–5, F, D. 82 here] Q2–5, F (heere Q2); hear Q1, D. 83 *Placidius,*] F; ~∧ Q1–5, D. 86 *Vale.*] *Val.* Q1–5, F, D. 92 in] Q1–5, F; is D. 95 *Vale.*] *Val.* Q1–5, F, D. 99+ *s.d.* Porphy.] Q3–5, F, D (Porph. Q3–5, F; Porphyrius. D); ~ .] Q1–2 (Porph. Q2). 100 *Vale.*] *Val.* Q1–5, F, D. 101+ *s.d. face.*] Q3–5, F, D (*Face* Q4–5, F, D); ~ .] Q1–2. 104 o're-rated] Q1–3, F, D (o'r-rated Q3; O'er-rated F; o'er-rated D); o'r rated Q4–5 (o'er rated Q5). 104 price] Q1–5, D (Price D); Prize F. 109 Lest] Q1–5, F; Least D. 110 back-way] Q1–4, D; back way Q5, F. 113 *Vale.*] *Val.* Q1–5, F, D. 113+ *s.d. away.*] Q3–5, F, D; ~ .] Q1–2. 115+ *s.d. him.*] Q3–5, F, D; ~ .] Q1–2. 119 one] Q1–4, F, D; once Q5. 123 where ever] Q1–5, F; where-ever D. 124 wear:] F; ~ . Q1–5, D. 128 you;] ~ . Q1–5, F, D. 131+ *s.d. [Going . . . it.]* Q4–5, F, D (*s.d. at line 122*); *[Going . . . it∧]* Q1–2 (*s.d. at line 122*); *[Going . . . it.]* Q3 (*s.d. at line 122*). 134 *Vale.*] *Val.* Q1–5, F, D. 137 Misleading]

Q1–5, F; Mis-leading D.   140 driv'n] Q1–2, D; driven Q3–5, F.   141
sake.] Q2–5, F, D; sake. / He, like a secret Worm, has eat his way; /
And, lodg'd within, does on the kernel prey: / I creep without; and hopeless to remove / Him thence, wait only for the husk of Love. Q1.
141+ *s.d.* Valerius, *and Guards.*] Valerius. Q1–5, F, D.   146 *Ægyptian*] F, D; Ægyptian Q1–5.   147 *Valerius,*] Q1–2, F, D; ~∧ Q3–5.
148 *Ægyptian*] F, D; Ægyptian Q1–5.   149 defer;] Q3–5, F; ~ .
Q1–2, D.   151 Love.———] Q1–2, D; ~∧——— Q3–5, F.   153
swiftly] Q1–2, D; quickly Q3–5, F.   160 than] Q1–4, F, D; then Q5.
163 disdain,] Q4–5, F (Disdain F); ~ . Q1–3; ~ : D.   168 Tempests]
Q3–5, F, D; Tempest Q1–2.   168 hear] Q1, F, D; shear Q2–5.   171
combine: *To* Max.] combine: Q1–5, F, D.   179 Whatever] Q1; What
ever Q2–5, F, D.   179 dye.] Q1–4, D (die Q3–4, D); die, Q5, F (Die
F).   181 it] Q1–4, D; he Q5, F.   183 Truths] Q1–5, D; Truth's F.
190 *s.d.* Cath.] Q2–5, F, D; *Cath.* Q1.   206 Too] Q1–5, D; To F.
208 deaths] Q1–4, D (Deaths Q4, D); Death's Q5, F.   212 If you but]
Q2–5, F, D; (Ah) if you Q1.   214 than] Q1–4, F, D; then Q5.   215
Oh!———] Q1; ~ !∧ Q2–5, F, D.   216+ *s.d. set below line 219 in* D.
216+ *s.d.* Privately] Q3–5, F, D; *privately* Q1–2.   216+ *s.d.* Cath.]
Q3–5, F, D; ~ .] Q1–2.   218 ask] Q1–5, D; ask that F.   218 some
false] Q1–4, D; some Q5, F.   244 torments] Q1–4, D (Torments D);
torment Q5, F (Torment F).   246 the] Q1–4, D; that Q5, F.   251
take;] ~ . Q1–5, F, D.   252 piece-meal] Q1, Q4–5, F, D; piece meal
Q2; peace-meal Q3.   254 Daughter,] D; ~∧ Q1–5, F.   261 bed;]
Q4–5, F, D (Bed); ~ . Q1–2; ~ , Q3.   269 breath,] Q3–5, F (Breath
F); ~∧ Q1–2, D (Breath D).   274 short.] ~ ; Q1–5, F, D.   275
sport. *To his Guards.*] sport. Q1–5, F, D.   276+ *s.d.* Daughter.] Q3–5,
F, D (*s.d. set below line 277 in* D); ~ .] Q1–2.   278 What,] Q3–5, F,
D; ~∧ Q1–2.   280 pay.] ~ : Q1–5, F, D.   280+ *s.d.* Mother.] Q3–
5, F, D; ~ .] Q1–2.   292+ *s.d.* breast.] Q3–5, F, D (Breast Q4–5, D;
Breast∧ F); ~ .] Q1–2.   294 loth.] ~ , Q1–5; ~ ; F, D (loath D).
295 both. *To his Guards.*] both. Q1–5, F, D.   306 Heav'n,] Q4–5, F,
D; ~∧ Q1–3.   308+ *s.d.* pieces;] Q3–5, F; ~ , Q1–2, D.   309 skill?
To Valerius.] skill? Q1–5, F, D (Skill F, D).   310 will?] Q1–3, D (Will
D); Will; Q4–5, F.   312 sinewy] Q1–4, D; sinew Q5, F (Sinew F).
315 ne're] Q1–2, Q4–5, F, D (ne'er Q4–5, F, D); near Q3.   319
Whirlwind-like] Q1–5, D; Whirl-wind like F.   322 me?] Q1–2, D;
~ ! Q3–5, F.   323 Iron-free] Q3–5, F; Iron free Q1–2, D.   326
death] Q1–3, D (Death D); Deaths Q4–5, F.   333 its] Q1–3, D; it
Q4–5, F.   342 see him] Q1, F, D; ~ , ~ Q2–5.   342 pursue,] F,
D; ~ . Q1–5.   345 Mother;] D; ~ , Q1–5, F.   351–351+ went. /
Aside.] went. Q1–5, F, D.   356 would'st] Q1–3, D; would Q4–5, F.
379 sin] Q2–5, F, D (Sin F, D); ill Q1.   380 for,] Q3–5, F; ~∧ Q1–2,
D.   382 dead!] Q1–5, D; ~ ? F.   401 tracks] Q1–2, D (Tracks
D); tracts Q3–5, F.   406+ *s.d.* speaks on.] Q3–4, D; *speaks on.*] Q1–2;
speaks. Q5, F (*speaks∧* Q5).   409 too,] Q5, F; ~ . Q1–4, D.   412+
s.d. Moors] *Moors* Q1–5, F, D.   421 Yet, *Berenice,*] Q3–5, F, D (Yet∧
D); ~∧ ~∧ Q1–2.   423 will] Q1–2, D; well Q3–5, F.   427 live]

Q3–5, F (Live F); ~, Q1–2, D. 430 mind. *To his Guards.*] mind.
Q1–5, F, D (Mind F, D). 434 part.] Q1, F, D (Part D); ~, Q2–5.
435 done.] ~ ∧ Q1–5, F, D. 440 Gods! . . . see?] Q4–5, F; ~ , . . .
~ ! Q1–3, D. 444 which,] Q3–5, F, D; ~ ∧ Q1–2. 445 *Roman*]
F, D; Roman Q1–5. 446 *s.d.* Ah . . . design, *To* Ber.] D (Design,
[*To*); *To* Ber. Ah . . . design, Q1–5, F (*line indented; Ber.*] Q4; Design
F). 450 *s.d.* Porphyrius.] Q3–5, F; Porphyriu ∧ Q1; ~ ∧ Q2; Por. D.
451 walks] Q1; walk Q2–5, F, D (Walk Q4–5, F). 454–460 endure:
. . . side: . . . fire: . . . glass:] ~ . . . . ~ . . . . ~ . . . . ~ . Q1–5, F,
D (Fire Q4–5, F, D; Glass Q4–5, F, D). 456 cherisht] Q1; cherish
Q2–5, F, D. 459 which] Q3–5, F; ~, Q1–2, D. 465 *Barbarian*]
D; Barbarian Q1–5, F. 466 head:] ~ . Q1–5, F, D (Head Q4–5, F,
D). 469 *Porphyrius,*] Q3–5, F, D; ~ ∧ Q1–2. 480 pray'r] Q1;
prayer Q2–5, F, D (Prayer Q4–5, F, D). 485 first,] Q3–5, F, D; ~ ∧
Q1–2. 490 fear,] Q4–5, F; ~ . Q1–3, D. 491 there;] ~, Q1–5,
F, D. 493 *Soul*] Soul Q1–5, F, D. 497 heart.] Q2–5, F, D (Heart
Q4–5, F, D); heart. / *Porphyrius kisses his hand, and blows it to* Berenice
saying, Q1. 499 breath.] Q2–5, F, D (Breath F, D); breath. / *Berenice
kissing hers in the same manner.* Q1. 501 giv'n] Q1–2, D; given Q3–
5, F. 501+ *s.d.* Cydon] Q2–5, F, D; Cydon *her Woman* Q1. 502
Vale.] Val. Q1–5, F, D. 503 *Vale.* [*rule*]] *Val.* [*rule omitted*] Q1–5,
F, D. 506 *Vale.*] Val. Q1–5, F, D. 509 ev'ry] D; every Q1–5, F.
512 Bed;] Q1–5, F; ~ ! D. 515 I] D;——I Q1–5, F. 518
Max.] Q2–5, F, D; ~ ∧ Q1. 518 *s.d.* Vale.] Val. Q1–5, F (Val ∧ F);
Valeria. D. 520, 530 *Vale.*] Val. Q1–5, F, D. 537 off your] Q1,
Q4–5, F, D; off you Q2–3. 537 Love.] Q1, F, D; ~ , Q2–5. 539
Med'cine] Q1–5, D; Medicine F. 548+ *s.d.* Porphyrius,] Q1–5, F;
Por. *and* D. 549 *Vale.*] Val. Q1–5, F, D. 549+ *s.d.* Porphy.]
Q4–5, F, D (Porph. Q4–5; Por. D); ~ .] Q1–3 (Porph. Q2–3). 554
gloomy] Q1, Q3–5, F, D; groomy Q2. 558 *Vale.*] Val. Q1–5, F, D.
558 away.] ~ : Q1–5, F, D. 562 this, *Porphyrius,*] F, D; ~ ∧ ~ ∧
Q1–5. 563 help] Q1–5, F (Help F); ~ , D. 565 *Vale.*] Val. Q1–5,
F, D. 568 th'] Q1–4, D; the Q5, F. 569 yet.] ~ : Q1–5, F, D.
572 *Vale.*] Val. Q1–5, F, D. 581 live.] ~ ∧ Q1–5, F, D. 588
down,] D; ~ . Q1–2; ~ : Q3–5, F. 592 *Maximin,*] D; ~ ∧ Q1–5, F.
594 declare:] Q3–5, F (Declare F); ~, Q1–2, D. 600+ *s.d.* him.]
Q4–5, F, D; ~ .] Q1–3. 602 giv'n] Q1–5, D; given F. 602+ *s.d.*
Placid.] Q4–5, F, D (Placidius. D); ~ .] Q1–3. 603 thus;] Q3–5, F;
~, Q1–2, D. 603+ *s.d.* Placidius] Q2–5, F, D; *Stabbing upward with
his Dagger.* Placidius Q1. 603+ *s.d.* him;] Q3–5, F; ~, Q1–2, D.
603+ *s.d.* come] Q2–5, F, D; come in Q1. 607 *Rome*] Q1–4, F, D;
Room Q5. 608 pity . . . went,] Q1–5, F (Pity F); Pity, . . . went ∧
D. 610 new-attempted] Q1–4, D; new attempted Q5, F. 615
be.] ~ ∧ Q1–5, F, D. 616 pow'r] Q2–5, F, D (Pow'r F); strength Q1.
627 Tyrants] Q1–5, D (Tyrant's Q4, D); Tyrant' F. 627+ *s.d.*
Souldiers.] Q3–5, F, D (Soldiers Q3, F, D); ~ .] Q1–2. 632 th'] Q1–
4, D; the Q5, F. 634+ *s.d. Entring,* Porphyrius . . . *Bodies*] Porphyrius . . . *Bodies entring,* Q1–5, F, D (Bodys Q5, F). 635 Fate!]

Q1-5, D; ~ . F.   636   our] Q1-5, D; your F.   645   dumb-show] Q1-
2, D; dumb show Q3-5, F (Show Q4; Dumb Q5).   648   Emp'rours]
Q1-4, D (Emp'rour's Q3-4; Emp'ror's D); Emperor's Q5, F.   650
sake, . . . live,] Q4-5, F, D; ~∧ . . . ~∧ Q1-3.   654   *Cen.*] Q1-3, D;
Cent. Q4-5, F.   654   th'] Q1-4, D; the Q5, F.   656   *Porphyrius*]
Q1-2, Q5, F, D; ~ , Q3-4.   658   you] Q1-4, F, D; yon Q5.   664+
s.d. hand.] Q1 (*some copies*), Q2-5, F, D; ~∧ Q1 (*period did not print in
copy text*).   669   troubles] Q1-4, D (Troubles D); trouble Q5, F
(Trouble F).   671+   *s.d.* Souldiers.] Q3-5, F, D (*Soldiers* Q3, Q5, F,
D); ~ .] Q1-2.   673   *Aquileia*] Q1-3, Q5, F, D; *Aqnileia* Q4.   674
Gates our peaceful Ensigns bear.] Q2-5, F, D (peacefull ensignes Q2);
Gates—— / Our peaceful Ensigns crown'd with Olives bear: Q1.
676+   *s.d. omnes.*] Q1-3, D; *omnes. / FINIS.* Q4-5, F.

Epilogue: Epilogue.] Q5, F, D (EPILOGUE); ~∧ Q1-4.   *s.d.* Bearers]
Q1-3, Q4 (*some copies*), Q5, F, D; Bierers Q4 (*some copies*).   1   *s.d.*
Bearer] Q1-3, Q4 (*some copies*), Q5, F, D; Bierer Q4 (*some copies*).
3   *s.d.* Audience.] Q1-3, D; ~∧] Q4-5, F.   7   *Sprights*] Q4-5, F, D;
~ , Q1-3.   7   *Natures*] Q2, D; ~ , Q1, Q3-5, F (natures Q5, F).   8
had,] Q4-5; ~∧ Q1-3, F, D.   11   Gallants,] Q1-4, D; Gallant's∧ Q5,
F.   17   *O Poet,*] Q1-5, D; *O Poet!* F.   18   sensless!] Q1-2, D; ~ ,
Q3-4; ~∧ Q5, F.   18   Love;] Q2-4, D; ~ , Q1; ~ : Q5, F.   20
Cheese-cake time] Q1-2, D (Cheese-Cake D); Cheesecake-time Q3-5, F.
22   godly] Q1-2, D; ~ , Q3-5, F.   22   out-of-fashion] D; out of
fashion Q1-5, F.   22   Play:] ~ . Q1-5, F, D.   24   devout.] Q1, Q3-
5, F; ~∧ Q2, D.   25   But farewel,] Q3-5, F; ~ , ~∧ Q1-2, D.   30+
FINIS.] Q1-3; omitted from Q4-5, F, D.

An Evening's Love

The first edition of *An Evening's Love* was published in 1671 (Q1; Macd
75a). The copies of Q1 collated for this edition disclosed press variants in
inner [A], *a*, and *b;* outer A; inner D; outer G, I, and K; and inner L
and *M.* L. A. Beaurline and Fredson Bowers (Dryden, *Four Comedies*
[1967], p. 276) record a Newberry Library copy with uncorrected inner
F, which has since been sold; and one University of Texas copy and the
Huntington Library copy with a different variant in the uncorrected
state of K3 ("*Melch.*" rather than "*Mel.*" [V, i, 160; their line 178]). We
have examined only one Texas copy as against their five, but they are
mistaken about the Huntington copy (which actually reads "*Mel.*"). The
second edition was probably published in 1675 (Q2; title page with press-
variant dates of 1671 [Macd 75b] and 1675 [Macd 75c]).[1] Copies of Q2

---

[1] Macdonald (p. 107) had not seen a copy of 75c and naturally assumed that
the differing dates on the title pages indicated different editions. Fredson
Bowers ("Variants in Early Editions of Dryden's Plays," *Harvard Library
Bulletin,* III [1949], 278–279) first noticed that copies of 75b and 75c had been

revealed press variants in outer *A* and *B*, inner *E* and *G*, outer *K*, and inner *M*. The third edition was published in 1691 (Q3; Macd 75d). The play was reprinted in Dryden's *Comedies, Tragedies, and Operas* (1701), I, 275–326 (F; Macd 107ai–ii [two issues, the differences not affecting this play]), and in Congreve's edition of Dryden's *Dramatick Works* (1717), II, 255–368 (D; Macd 109ai–ii [two issues, the differences not affecting this play]). Q2 was printed from a copy of Q1 with corrected inner *a* and outer A; Q3 from a copy of Q2 with uncorrected outer K; F from Q2 (probably a copy with uncorrected outer K); and finally, a part of D (the dedicatory epistle) from F, the rest being printed from a copy of Q1 with uncorrected inner *a*. Since Dryden seems not to have revised the text after the publication of Q1, the Clark copy of Q1 (*PR3417.K1) has been chosen as the copy text.

The following seventeenth-century collections of songs have been examined: *Merry Drollery, Complete* (1670, reissued in 1691 with a cancel title page [o1; Case 132(a) and 132(b)]), pages 171–172, for "After the pangs of a desperate Lover" (II, i, 499–514), and pages 220–221 (o1a) and 292 (o1b) for two versions of "Calm was the Even, and cleer was the Skie" (IV, i, 47–70); *The New Academy of Complements* (1671 [d1; Case 148]), pages 191–192, for "After the pangs of a desperate Lover," pages 192–193 for "Calm was the Even, and cleer was the Skie," and page 106 for "Celimena, of my heart" (V, i, 504–533); *Westminster-Drollery* (1671 [o2; title page: "Never before publish'd"]), pages 32–33, for "Celimena, of my heart"; *Westminster-Drollery* (1671 [o3; title page: *"With Additions"*]), pages 30–31, for "Celimena, of my heart"; *Westminster-Drollery* (1671 [o4; Case 150 (1) (b); title page: *"With Additions"*]), pages 30–31, for "Celimena, of my heart"; *Westminster-Drollery* (1671 [o5; title page: *"With Additions"*]), pages 30–31, for "Celimena, of my heart"; *Westminster-Drollery* (1672 [o6; Case 150(1)(d)]), pages 30–31, for "Celimena, of my heart"; *Windsor-Drollery* (1672 [d2; Case 154]), page 139, for "After the pangs of a desperate Lover," page 100 for "Calm was the Even, and cleer was the Skie," and pages 101–102 for "Celimena, of my heart"; *The Canting Academy* (1673 [d3; Case 155]), pages 184–185, for "Calm was the Even, and cleer was the Skie"; *Choice Songs and Ayres for One Voyce* (1673 [f1; D&M 35]), page 8, for "After the pangs of a desperate Lover," and page 9 for "Calm was the Even, and cleer was the Skie"; *The Canting Academy* (1674 [d4; title page: "The Second Edition"]), pages

---

made up from the same sheets and were therefore the same edition. Bowers, although thinking it "possible that a few early pulls of a second edition in 1671 were misdated 1675," felt that the "more normal hypothesis is certainly that in 1675 (not 1671), when Herringman ordered a second edition, the printer used the first edition as a copytext and carelessly set its 1671 date on his title, later making the correction to 1675 in press." This hypothesis is a convincing one, but, for some reason, Bowers seems recently to have changed his mind. In the introduction to his edition of *An Evening's Love* (*Four Comedies*, p. 181), he assigns Q2 to 1671: "Q2 1671 (Macd. 75b, W&M 410)." He adds that the "supposed edition of 1675 (Macd. 75c, W&M 411) was a reissue of Q2 with a new title page."

138–139, for "Calm was the Even, and cleer was the Skie"; *Choice Ayres, Songs, & Dialogues* (1675 [f2; D&M 40]), page 4, for "After the pangs of a desperate Lover," and page 8 for "Calm was the Even, and cleer was the Skie"; *Choice Ayres, Songs, & Dialogues* (1676 [f3; D&M 42]), page 4, for "After the pangs of a desperate Lover," and page 8 for "Calm was the Even, and cleer was the Skie"; *The New Academy of Complements* (1681 [d5]), pages 191–192, for "After the pangs of a desperate Lover," and pages 192–193 for "Calm was the Even, and cleer was the Skie"; *The Compleat Courtier* (1683 [d6; Case 168]), pages 14–15, for "Calm was the Even, and cleer was the Skie"; and *Wit and Mirth: or, Pills to Purge Melancholy* (1699 [d7; D&M 182]), pages 177–178, for "Calm was the Even, and cleer was the Skie." For "After the pangs of a desperate Lover" the sources of o1, d1, d2, and f1 are not clear. The source of d5 was, however, d1; f2 derived from f1 and f3 derived from f2. For "Calm was the Even, and cleer was the Skie" the sources of o1a, o1b, d1, d2, d7, and f1 are not apparent. It is probable that d3 derived from d1, d4 from d3, d5 from d1, d6 from d2, f2 from f1, and f3 from f2. For "Celimena, of my heart" the sources of o2 and d1 are unknown. The source of o3 was o2, and the source of o4 was o3; o5 was set from either o3 or o4; o6 was set from o5. That d2 is related to d1 is obvious, but the exact relationship is not apparent; d5 was set from d1.

A number of late seventeenth-century and early eighteenth-century manuscripts of parts of the play are in existence. There is a copy of the prologue in the Huntington Library (MS EL 8922 [M1]). Although the evidence is tenuous, M1 may be distantly related to F or D. The William Salt Library, Stafford, contains a manuscript (D 1721./3/246[M2]) of "After the pangs of a desperate Lover," and the British Museum contains another (MS Harley 3991, fols. 92r–92v[M3]). The source of M2 is not clear, but M3 was copied from o1. Manuscripts of "Calm was the Even, and cleer was the Skie" are located in the British Museum (MS Harley 3991, fols. 149r–149v [M4]), the Edinburgh University Library (Laing III.491, pp. 58–59 [M5]), and the Bodleian Library (MS Rawl. Poet. 65, fol. 33r [M6]). The sources of M4, M5, and M6 cannot be determined. Finally, the British Museum has a manuscript of "Celimena, of my heart" (MS Harley 3991, fols. 89r–90r [M7]); M7 was copied from either d1 or d5 (most likely d5).

The following copies of the various editions have also been examined: Q1: Folger (D2273), Harvard (*EC65.D8474.671e), Huntington (123016), Yale (Ij.D848.671. copy 1); Q2: Clark (*PR3417.K1.1671; *PR3417.K1. 1675), Harvard (*EC65.D8474.671ec), Huntington (123004); Clark (*PR3410.C91; *PR3412.1679; *PR3417.K1.1691); F: Clark (*fPR3412. 1701 [2 cop.]; *fPR3412.1701a); D: Clark (*PR3412.1717 [2 cop.]; *PR3412.1717a); o1: British Museum (C.39.b.29), Huntington (55771); d1: British Museum (1076.e.29); o2: Harvard (*EC65.A100.671w); o3: Bodleian (Douce D27); o4: Harvard (*EC65.A100.671wba); o5: Bodleian (Mal. 381); o6: Harvard (*EC65.A100.671wc); d2: Huntington (148513); d3: Huntington (X82254); f1: Clark (*fM1623.5.P72a); d4: Clark (*PR3506.H97C2); f2: Clark (*fM1623.5.C54); f3: Huntington (14173);

d5: Huntington (86952); d6: Bodleian (Mal. 350); d7: British Museum (C.117.a.19).

Press Variants by Form

Q1
Sheet [A] (inner form)
Uncorrected: Folger, Harvard, Huntington, Yale
Corrected: Clark
Sig. [A4]
202:5 *humonr*] *humour*
      19 *noture*] *nature*

Sheet *a* (inner form)
Uncorrected: Yale
Corrected: Clark, Folger, Harvard, Huntington
Sig. *a*2
207:16 *the long*] *the*

Sheet *b* (inner form)
Uncorrected: Clark, Harvard
Corrected: Folger, Huntington, Yale
Sig. *b*1*v*
Catchword *Peersons*] *Persons*

Sheet A (outer form)
Uncorrected: Clark, Huntington
Corrected: Folger, Harvard, Yale
Sig. A1
I, i, 2 business.] ~ ?

Sheet D (inner form)
Uncorrected: Harvard, Huntington, Yale
Corrected: Clark, Folger
Sig. D3*v*
III, i, 1 *Mel- / Melchor*] *Mel- / chor*
Sig. D4
III, i, 46 you] your

Sheet F (inner form)
Uncorrected: Newberry (as recorded by Beaurline and Bowers)
Corrected: Clark, Folger, Harvard, Huntington, Yale
Sig. F1*v*
III, i, 398–399 Gui- / tars] Guit- / tars
        404 Guittarrs] Guittars
Sig. F3*v*
III, i, 540 *Maskall*] ~ ,
Sig. F4
III, i, 557 Heaven,] ~ !
        569 *Perue*] *Peru,*

Sheet G (outer form)

Uncorrected: Clark, Huntington
Corrected: Folger, Harvard, Yale
Sig. G4*v*
 IV, i, 242 unfathfulness] unfaithfulness
Sheet I (outer form)
Uncorrected: Folger, Harvard, Huntington
Corrected: Clark, Yale
Sig. I3
 IV, i, 682 aud] and
Sig. I4*v*
 V, i, 8 coufidence] confidence
Sheet K (outer form)
Uncorrected: Clark, Huntington, Yale
Corrected: Folger, Harvard
Sig. K3
 V, i, 160 *Mel.* Must] Must
Sheet L (inner form)
Uncorrected: Harvard
Corrected: Clark, Folger, Huntington, Yale
Sig. L2
 V, i, 379 tronble] trouble
Sig. L4
 V, i, 506 *leaue] leave*
Sheet M (inner form)
Uncorrected: Clark
Corrected: Folger, Harvard, Huntington, Yale
Sig. M1*v*
 Catchword *omitted] He*

Q2
Sheet A (outer form)
Uncorrected (?): Clark [1671], Huntington
Corrected (?): Clark [1675], Harvard
Sig. [A1]
 Title page 1671] 1675
Sheet B (outer form)
Uncorrected (?): Huntington
Corrected (?): Clark [1671], Clark [1675], Harvard
Sig. B4*v*
 212:26 *imploys]* implies
Sheet E (inner form)
Uncorrected (first state): Clark [1675], Huntington
Corrected (second state): Clark [1671]
Sig. E1*v*
 II, i, 160 think] thing
  174 your mistrust] you mistrust
Sig. E2
 II, i, 198 inconveniece] inconvenience
  209 in them] in the

Corrected (*third state, the above corrections and the following*): Harvard
Sig. E4
  II, i, 345 Fathers] Father
      347–348 happi- / piness] happi- / ness
      348 acqnaintance] acquaintance
                    Sheet G (inner form)
Uncorrected: Clark [1671]
Corrected: Clark [1675], Harvard, Huntington
Sig. G4
  Catchword *Lo*] *Lop.*
                    Sheet K (outer form)
Uncorrected: Harvard
Corrected: Clark [1671], Clark [1675], Huntington
Sig. K3
  IV, i, 412 shall enjoy never] never shall enjoy
                    Sheet M (inner form)
Uncorrected (first state): Huntington
Corrected (second state): Harvard
Sig. M1*v*
  V, i, 76 whom c] whom I
Corrected (third state, the above correction and the following): Clark
    [1671], Clark [1675]
Sig. M3*v*
  V, i, 216 shorr] short

Dedication: caption: WILLIAM] D; WILLIAM Q1–3, F.   Privy
Council] Q1–2, F; Privy-Council Q3, D (*Privy-Council* D).   197:1–
201:2 *May . . . [to] . . . were,*] *romans and italics reversed in D but
normalized in the textual footnotes and the following textual notes.*
197:1 May it please your Grace,] F, D (Your D); *omitted from Q1–3.*
197:11 *former?*] Q1–2, F, D (*Former* D); ~. Q3.   197:13 *both*] D;
~, Q1–3, F.   197:17 *it;*] Q3; ~. Q1; ~, Q2, F, D.   197:17 *most,*]
Q2–3, F, D; ~∧ Q1.   197:22 *boast,*] Q2–3, F, D; ~; Q1.   197:27
flight] Q2–3, F, D (*Flight* D); *fiight* Q1.   198:6 *than*] Q2–3, F, D; *then*
Q1.   198:18 *you,*] Q2–3, F, D; ~∧ Q1.   198:19 *that*] Q1; *that*
Q2–3, F, D.   198:23 *spirits*] Q1–3, F (*Spirits* F); *Spirit* D.   198:35
prophesie] Q1–3; *Prophecy* F, D.   199:13 *lest*] Q1–3; *least* F, D.
199:16 *studies: a*] ~. *A* Q1–3, F, D (*Studies* F, D).   199:17 Romans:
who] ~. *Who* Q1–3, F, D.   199:18–19 *Genius; and*] ~: *And* Q1–3,
F, D.   199:23 *latter*] Q1–3, F; *later* D.   199:29 *&c.*] Q3, F, D; &c.
Q1–2.   199:30 *indented in F.*   200:6 *affect*] Q1–3, D; *effect* F.
200:10 *and*] Q1; *and* Q2–3, F, D.   200:12 *name*] Q1–3; *Names* F, D.
200:12 *Poets.*] Q1; ~, Q2–3; ~; F, D.   200:31–32 *Predecessors*] Q1;
Predecessor Q2–3, F, D.   200:32 *'em*] Q1–3; *them* F, D.   200:33
Scene] Q1; *Scene* Q2–3, F, D.   201:2 *were,*] Q3, F, D; ~∧ Q1–2.
201:4 Servant,] Q3, F, D (*Servant* D); ~∧ Q1–2.
Preface: PREFACE] Q1–3, F; THE / PREFACE D.   202:1–213:12
had . . . [to] . . . this.] *romans and italics reversed in Q3 and F but*

normalized in the textual footnotes and the following textual notes.
202:5 *humour*] Q1 (corrected state); *Humour* Q2–3, F, D; *humonr* Q1
(uncorrected state). 202:9 Conquest of] *Conquest of* Q1–3, F, D.
202:10 *improvement*] Q2–3, F, D (*Improvement* D); *improvemeni* Q1.
202:14 *Opiniatre*] Q1–3, D (*opiniatre* Q2–3); *opiniative* F. 202:19
nature] Q1 (corrected state), Q2–3, F, D (*Nature* D); *noture* Q1 (uncorrected state). 203:6 *Actor*] Q1, Q3, F, D; *Acter* Q2. 203:11
Farces] Q2–3, F, D; *Farees* Q1. 203:17 *events.*] D (*Events*); ~ : Q1–
3, F. 203:18 *nature:*] D (*Nature*); ~ . Q1–3, F. 203:19 *chimerical.
The*] D; ~ : *the* Q1–3, F. 203:20 *manners,*] D (*Manners*); ~ ; Q1–3,
F (*Manners* Q2–3, F). 204:12 Plays] Q1–3, F; *Plays* D. 204:16
defend] Q2–3, F, D; *de fend* Q1. 204:23 *than*] Q2–3, F, D; *then* Q1.
204:24 *Poets.*] Q1, D (*Poet's* D); ~ ; Q2–3, F. 204:25 *it as*] Q2–3,
F, D (~ , ~ D); *as it* Q1. 204:25 *other*] Q1; *others* Q2–3, F, D.
204:30 *who*] Q2–3, F, D; *wo* Q1. 205:8 *precept,*] D (*Precept*); ~ .
Q1–3, F (*Precept* Q3, F). 205:19 *Philosophy?*] Q1, D; ~ʌ Q2; ~ .
Q3; ~ , F. 206:3 *words.*] Q1, D (*Words* D); ~ , Q2–3, F. 206:7–8
contigisse.] D; ~ , Q1–3, F. 206:10–11 *both: neither . . . Johnson:
neither*] *both. Neither . . . Johnson. Neither* Q1–3, F, D. 206:27
Character of Wit] Q1, D; Character of Wit Q2–3, F. 206:28 *all*] Q1–
3, F; *all be* D. 206:28 *I think*] Q1–3, F; *think* D. 207:5 *it:
whereas*] D (*Whereas*); ~ . *Whereas* Q1–3, F. 207:9 *witty*] Q2–3, F,
D; *wity* Q1. 207:10 *Lyar*] ~ , Q1–3, F, D. 207:11 *Money.*] Q1,
D (*Mony* D); ~ , Q2–3, F. 207:16 *the*] Q1 (corrected state), Q2–3, F;
the long Q1 (uncorrected state), D. 207:17–18 *Amandi; to*] ~ . *To*
Q1–3, F, D. 207:28 *Preface, and*] ~ . *And* Q1–3, F, D. 208:2
Astrologer] *Astrologer* Q1–3, F, D. 208:7 *Chærea*] F, D; *Chœrea* Q1–3.
208:8 *Eunuch*] D; *Eunuch* Q1–3, F. 208:15 *in*] Q1–3, D; *it* F.
208:27 *singular:*] D; ~ :) Q1–3, F. 209:17 *art of Poetry*] Q1–3, F
(*Art* Q2–3, F); Art of Poetry D. 209:35 *obnoxious;*] D; ~ , Q1–3, F.
209:35 *such*] Q2–3, F, D; ~ , Q1. 210:1 *horror:*] ~ ; Q1–3, F, D
(*horrour* Q3; *Horror* D). 210:9 *lest*] Q1–2, F, D; *least* Q3. 210:9
vice. For] Q1, D (*Vice* D); *Vice; for* Q2–3, F. 210:22 *things,*] Q2–3, F,
D; ~ . Q1. 210:23 *tantum,*] ~ . Q1–3, F, D. 210:24 *and*] D; *And*
Q1–3, F. 210:25 *mine;*] Q2–3, F; ~ , Q1, D. 210:29 *where ever*]
Q1–3, F; *where-ever* D. 210:34 *it for*] D; ~ , ~ Q1–3; ~ ; ~ F.
211:3 Sir] Q1; *Sir* Q2–3, F, D. 211:18 *Romance*] Q3; ~ , Q1–2, F,
D. 211:27 *help't*] Q2–3, F, D (*helpt* D); *help'* Q1. 212:1 Heca-
tommithi] Hecatommuthi Q1–3, F, D. 212:2 *and*] Q1, D; *and* Q2–3,
F. 212:4 Novels] Q1, D; *Novels* Q2–3, F. 212:4 Chances] Q1,
Q3, D; Ceances Q2; Ceanthes F. 212:5 Wife, *the*] Q1, F, D; ~ ; ~
Q2–3. 212:26 ποιητὴς *did not print in F.* 212:26 *imployes*] Q1,
Q2 (uncorrected state?), D (*imploys* Q2, D); *implies* Q2 (corrected state?),
Q3, F. 212:27 *life touches*] Q1, F (*Life* F); *life-touches* Q2–3, D
(*Life-touches* Q3, D). 213:2 *accounted*] Q1–3, D; *counted* F. 213:
11 *after ages*] Q1–3, F (*Ages* Q3, F); *after-Ages* D.
Prologue: 1–2 *write, . . . Bridegroom on*] Q1–3, F, D; ~ʌ . . .
Bridegroome. On M1. 2 *Wedding-night*] Q1–3, F, D (*Wedding-Night*

D); *Wedding night* M1.   3 *about*] Q1–3, F, D; *a bout* M1.   5
Honey-moon] Q1–3, F, D (*Hony-moon* F); *Hony moone* M1.   7 *do*]
Q1–3, F, D; *doe* M1.   10 *smackings*] Q1–2; *smacking* Q3, F, D, M1.
10 *after-kiss*] Q2–3, F, D (*after-Kiss*); *after kiss* Q1, M1 (*After Kisse* M1).
12 *Monsieur*] Q2–3, F, D; *Monsieur* Q1, M1 (*Mounsieur* M1).   12 *a*]
Q1–3, F, D; *your* M1.   17 *by-stroke*] Q1–3, F, D; *by stroak* M1.   18
some] Q1–3, F, D; *a* M1.   18 *cranny,*] Q1 (*some copies*), Q2–3, F, M1
(*Cranny* M1); ~∧ Q1 (*comma did not print in copy text*), D (*Cranny* D).
19 *janty*] Q1 (*some copies*), Q2–3, F, D, M1; *jant* Q1 ("*y*" *did not print
in copy text*).   20 *good man*] Q1–3, F, D (*Man* Q2–3, F, D); *goodman*
M1.   21 *small-timber'd*] Q1 (*hyphen printed faintly in copy text*), D;
smalltimber'd Q2; *small timber'd* Q3, F, M1 (*smale tymberd* M1).   21
would] Q1–3, F, D; *will* M1.   22 *are Gallants but*] Q1–3, F, D; *are but
Poetts* M1.   23 *had*] Q1–3, F, D; *have* M1.   24 *Whom*] Q1–3, F,
D; *Who* M1.   26 *overstraining*] Q1, M1 (*overstraineing* M1); *overstraining* Q2–3, F, D.   30 *an*] Q1–3; *a* F, D, M1.   34 *time from
your Gallants he'll*] Q1–3, F, D; *time He'll from your gallants* M1.

Persons Represented: Persons Represented] Q1–2; Persons Represented
Q3; *Dramatis Personæ* F; Dramatis Personæ D.   By] *omitted from* D.
Wildblood . . . [to] . . . and Don Alonzo.] *romans and italics generally
reversed in* D *but normalized in the textual footnotes and the following
textual notes.*   English] D; English Q1–3, F.   Spanish] Q2–3, F, D;
Spanish Q1.   Spaniard] Q2–3, F, D; Spaniard Q1.   By] *omitted from*
D.   Jacinta] Jacintha Q1–3, F, D.   Cousin.] Q2–3, F, D (Consin D);
~∧ Q1.   Marshall;] Q1; Marshal. Q2, F; Marshal, Q3, D.   Sisters.]
Q2–3, F, D; ~∧ Q1.   Time,] Q2–3, F, D (*Time* Q3); ~∧ Q1.

I, i

ACT] Q2–3, F, D; ~ . Q1.   s.d. Don] *Don* Q1–3, F, D.   2 busi-
ness?] Q1 (*corrected state*), Q2–3, F, D (Business Q3, D); ~ . Q1 (*uncor-
rected state*).   3 Letter;] ~ . Q1–3, F, D.   6 *Melchor* 'tis] Q1–3,
F; ~ / 'Tis D.   14 whiles] Q1; whilst Q2–3, F, D.   15 Cousin;]
~ . Q1–3, F, D.   21+ s.d. Maskall] Q1–3, F (Maskal Q2–3, F); *and*
Maskall D.   22 2^d.] 2^d Q1; 2. Q2, F; 2 Q3, D.   22 *English*] Q2–3,
F, D; English Q1.   26 however,] Q2–3, F; ~∧ Q1, D.   31, 33 *Don*]
Q2–3, F; Don Q1, D.   43 to] Q1–3, D; into F.   45 *Indies*] Q2–3,
F, D; Indies Q1.   54 Why,] Q1–3, D; ~∧ F.   56 reconquest] Q1,
D (Reconquest D); re-conquest Q2–3, F (Re-conquest Q3).   58–59 Silk-
Gown] Q1–3, D (Silk-gown Q2); Silk Gown F.   65 in Embrio] Q1–2,
F, D (Embryo D); *in Embryo* Q3.   66 some ten] Q1–3, F; some D.
68 under kind] Q1, D; under-kind Q2–3, F.   71 *Frank*] Q2–3, F, D;
Franck Q1.   75 it.] ~∧ Q1–3, F, D.   78 what,] D; ~∧ Q1–3, F
(What Q3).   83–84 *Hide-Park.*] Q1–2, F, D; ~ ! Q3.   90 *English*]
Q2–3, F, D; English Q1.   96–97 aside. However] ~ : however Q1–3,
F, D (However D).   105 Madman;] Q1–2, F, D; ~ ! Q3.   107
throats; what,] D (Throats); ~ , ~∧ Q1–3, F (Throats Q2, F; Throats;
Q3).   116 Shoomaker] Q1–2, F, D (Shoemaker D); Shooe-maker Q3.
117 our man's] Q1–3, F (Man's Q2–3, F); our D.   117 s.d. Bell.]

Q1–3, F; Bell. *and* D. 118 *Alon. . . . off.*] D; Alon. . . . *off.*
———— Q1–2; Alon. . . . *off.* Q3; Alon. . . . *off*——— F. 123 be-
fore,] D; ~∧ Q1–3, F. 125 begone] Q1, D; be gone Q2–3, F. 125
or I'll] Q1–3, D; I'll F. 133 thee] Q1–3, D; you F. 145 himself.]
Q3; ~ : Q1–2, F, D. 146 *Englishman*] Q2–3, F, D; Englishman Q1
(English- / man). 148 Sir!] Q1–2, F, D; ~ , Q3. 152 *Atalanta*]
Q1–2, F, D; *Atlanta* Q3. 153+ *s.d.* Jacinta] Q1–3, F (Jacint. Q3);
and Jacintha D. 153+ *s.d.* Maskall] D; Maskal Q1–3, F. 162
Names,] Q3, D; ~∧ Q1–2, F. 164 Servant,] Q2–3, F, D; ~∧ Q1.
167 you,] Q3; ~∧ Q1–2, F, D. 168 Woman,] Q2–3, F; ~∧ Q1, D.
170 then,] Q2–3, F, D; ~∧ Q1. 171 Secrets,] Q2–3, F, D; ~∧ Q1.
187 out:] Q1–2, F, D; ~ ! Q3. 188 *major*] Q3; *maior* Q1–2, F, D.
192 too.] Q1, F, D; ~ ! Q2 (?), Q3. 199 Sir;] Q3; ~ , Q1–2, F, D.
203 going.———] Q1–2, F, D; ~∧——— Q3. 209 mouth.] ~∧ Q1–
3, F, D (Mouth Q3, F, D). 210 again.———] Q1, D; ~∧——— Q2–3,
F. 214 *major*] Q1–3, F; *maior* D. 217–218 present.———] Q1–2,
F, D; ~∧——— Q3.

I, ii

SCENE II. / *A*] Scene II. *A* Q1–3, F, D (SCENE Q3, F, D). *s.d.*
Ladies . . . Cavaliers] Q3, D; Ladies . . . Cavaliers Q1–2, F. *s.d. as*
at] Q1–3, F; *at* D. *s.d. Devotion*] Q1–3, F; *Devotions* D. 8 suddenly.] Q1–2, F, D (suddainly Q2); ~ ! Q3. 9 Faith,] Q3, D; ~∧
Q1–2, F. 14 Madam;] Q3; ~ , Q1–2, F, D. 19 not;] Q3; ~ ,
Q1–2, F, D. 20 Windows,] ~ ; Q1–3, F, D. 23+ *s.d.* Maskall]
Q1–3, F (Maskal Q2–3, F); *and* Maskall D. 27 us.] ~∧ Q1–3, F, D.
31 on's] Q1–3, F; of us D. 32 Madam;] Q3; ~ , Q1–2, F, D. 39
besworn] Q1; be sworn Q2–3, F, D. 44 fix;] ~ , Q1–3, F, D. 60
to] D; to Q1–3, F. 61 civil;] Q3; ~ , Q1–2, F, D. 72+ *s.d.*
Alonzo] Q2–3, F, D; Alonso Q1. 72+ *s.d.* devotion.] Q3, D (*Devo-*
tion); ~∧ Q1–2, F (*Devotion* Q2, F). 75 Father?] Q1, Q3, D; ~ : Q2,
F. 77 *Englishmen*] Q2–3, F, D; Englishmen Q1. 80+ *s.d. at end*
of preceding speech in D. 80+ *s.d.* English] Q3, D; *English* Q1–2, F.
81 to] D; to Q1–3, F. 82 *Spanish*] Q2–3, F, D; Spanish Q1. 84
Castilians.] Q1–2, F, D; ~ ? Q3. 86 *St.*] Q2–3; St. Q1, F, D (S. F).
87 Faith,] Q2–3, F; ~∧ Q1, D. 100 call'd] Q1–3, D; call F. 102
Beast] Q1, Q3, D; Beasts Q2, F. 106 'em to't] Q1–3, D; them to it
F. 111 Father,] Q3, D; ~∧ Q1–2, F. 112 Daughters!] Q1–3, D;
~ ; F. 114 devotions.———] ~ : ∧ Q1–2, F, D (Devotions Q2, F, D);
Devotions.∧ Q3. 116 *s.d.* Aside] Q2–3, D; *aside* Q1, F. 117 my]
Q1, Q3, F, D; me Q2. 118–119 *Tuesday . . . Tuesday*] Q3, D;
Tuesday . . . Tuesday Q1–2, F. 125 *s.d.* Aside] Q2–3, F, D; *aside*
Q1. 127 Sir.] Q1, D; ~ , Q2, F; ~∧ Q3. 129 than] Q3, F, D;
then Q1–2. 129+ *s.d.* Aside] Q2–3, F, D; *aside* Q1. 141 this]
Q1–2, F, D; these Q3. 143 Faith,] Q3; ~∧ Q1–2, F, D. 147 pool]
Q1–2, F, D (Pool Q2, F, D); Fool Q3. 147 it] Q1, D; him Q2–3, F.
158–159 *as in* Q3, F (*in italics in* Q*3*); *not indented in* Q*1*–2, D.

II, i

ACT II. SCENE I.] D; ACT. II. Q1-2; ACT II. Q3, F.   *s.d.   Enter*]
Q3, D; *omitted from Q1-2, F.*   *s.d.* Wildblood, Bellamy, Maskall] Q3,
F, D (Wildbloud Q3; Maskal Q3, F; *and* Maskall D); *Wildblood, Bellamy,
Maskall* Q1-2 (*Maskal* Q2).   6 purpose.————] D; ~.∧ Q1-3, F
(Purpose Q3).   9 knee-deep] Q1, Q3, D (Knee-deep D); knee deep
Q2, F.   28 out!] ~? Q1-3, F, D.   28 why,] Q3 (Why); ~∧ Q1-2,
F, D (Why D).   37 'St,] Q1-2, F, D; ~ ! Q3.   38 their] Q1-3, D;
this F.   43 sails,] Q3 (Sails); ~∧ Q1-2, F, D.   50 If I'll] Q1-3, F;
If I D.   53 beforehand] Q1, D; before hand Q2-3, F.   57 Pilot]
Q1, D; Pilate Q2-3, F.   62 profess] Q1, D; professes Q2-3, F.   64
him.] ~∧ Q1-3, F, D.   67 come.] Q1-3, D; ~? F.   69 *to*] D; to
Q1-3, F.   69 What,] D; ~∧ Q1-3, F.   72 were well] Q1, D; were
Q2-3, F.   85 parables] Q1-3, D (Parables Q2-3, D); Parable F.   90
Faith,] ~∧ Q1-3, F, D.   97 hear] Q1-2, F, D; here Q3.   99 'em]
Q1-3, D; them F.   102 Climate?] Q1-3, D; ~ ; F.   103 born
here,] Q2-3, F, D; ~ ~ ; Q1.   105 Faith,] Q3, D; ~∧ Q1-2, F.   108
twelvemonths] Q1-3, F (twelve- / months Q1; Twelvemonths Q3); twelve
Month's D.   111 year. If] D (Year); ~ , if Q1-2, F; Year: If Q3.
123-124 forward; . . . married?] Q1-2, F, D; ~? . . . ~. Q3.   128
Passa-calles] Q1-2, D (*hyphen printed very faintly in Q2*); *Passa calles*
Q3, F.   133 Gods] Q1, Q3, D; God's Q2, F.   141 *every*] Q1-2, F,
D; *ev'ry* Q3.   157 Madam? why,] D; ~ , ~∧ Q1-2, F; ~ ! ~∧ Q3.
160 thing] Q1, Q2 (*corrected* [*second state*]), Q3, F, D; think Q2 (*un-
corrected* [*first state*]).   167 such] Q1, D; such a Q2-3, F.   168 fie;]
Q1-2, F, D (fy Q2); fie! Q3.   168 mercinary!] Q1-2, F (mercenary
Q2, F); mercenary? Q3, D (Mercenary D).   174 you mistrust] Q1, Q2
(*corrected* [*second state*]), Q3, F, D; your ~ Q2 (*uncorrected* [*first state*]).
176 mine's Q2-3, F, D; mines Q1.   186 *s.d.* Wild., . . . *severally.*]
Q2-3, F, D; ~∧ , . . . ~ , Q1.   186+ *s.d.* Maskall] D; Maskal Q1-3,
F.   188 What,] Q3, D; ~∧ Q1-2, F.   198 inconvenience] Q1, Q2
(*corrected* [*second state*]), Q3, F, D (Inconvenience Q3, D); inconveniece
Q2 (*uncorrected* [*first state*]).   200 Valet] Q1, D; Varlet Q2-3, F.
205 suffice] Q1, D; ~ , Q2, F; ~ ; Q3.   207-208 world, . . . agoe] D
(World, . . . ago); ~∧ . . . ~ , Q1; World∧ . . . ago, Q2-3, F (world
Q2).   209 in the] Q1, Q2 (*corrected* [*second state*]), Q3, F, D; in them
Q2 (*uncorrected* [*first state*]).   225 invents] Q1, D; invents new Q2-3,
F.   227 company:] Q1, D (Company D); ~ ; Q2, F (Company F);
Company. Q3.   239-240 however,] D (However); ~∧ Q1-3, F.   244
Madam;] Q3; ~ , Q1-2, F, D.   246 Maskall] D; Maskal Q1-3, F.
246, 257 me.] Q1-2, F, D; ~ ! Q3.   259 knows] Q2-3, F, D; know's
Q1.   263 Bell.] Q1, D (Bel. D); Bea. Q2, F; Beat. Q3.   268 Theo.]
Q2-3, F, D (Theod. Q3); ~∧ Q1.   268 to] D; to Q1-3, F.   270
Well;] Q1-2, F, D; ~ ! Q3.   270+ *s.d. Going.*] Q3, D; *going*∧ Q1-2,
F.   271 stay;] Q1-2, F, D; ~? Q3.   272 should] Q1, D; shall
Q2-3, F.   273-274 ————[*Aside.*] If . . . me.————] (If . . . me:)

Q1–3, F, D (if F). 278–279 me, . . . uppon't;] Q1–2, F, D (up- / pon't Q1; upon't Q2, F, D); ~ ; . . . upon't, Q3. 281–282 grimaces. [*To Bellamy.*]———In] grimaces, in Q1–3, F, D (Grimaces; Q3; Grimaces D). 287 Devils. In] ~ : in Q1–3, F, D (In D). 291 *Christendome*] Q3 (*Christendom*); Christendome Q1–2, F, D (Christendom Q2, F, D). 295 is;] Q1–2, F, D; ~ ? Q3. 296 out.———] Q1–2; ~‿——— Q3, F, D. 303 what,] D (What); ~‿ Q1–3, F (What Q3). 305 in it,] Q1–2, F, D; it? Q3. 307 ground? So] ~ ; so Q1–3, F, D (Ground Q3, D). 308 love.] Q1, Q3, D (Love Q3, D); Love? Q2, F. 309 *Astrologie*] Q2–3, F (*Astrology*); Astrologie Q1, D (Astrology D). 316 me] Q1, D; me to Q2–3, F. 317 what,] Q3, D (What D); ~‿ Q1–2, F. 319–320 window?] Q2–3, F, D (Window); ~ ; Q1. 324 then;] Q1–2, F, D; ~ ? Q3. 326 *Astrologer*] Q2–3, F; Astrologer Q1, D. 331 You] Q2–3, F, D; you Q1. 338 so.———] Q1–2, F; ~‿——— Q3, D. 345 Father] Q1, Q2 (*corrected* [*third state*]), Q3, F, D; Fathers Q2 (*uncorrected* [*first and second states*]). 346 begone] Q1; be gone Q2–3, F, D. 347–348 happiness . . . acquaintance] Q1, Q2 (*corrected* [*third state*]), Q3, F, D (Happiness . . . Acquaintance Q3, D); happipiness . . . acqnaintance Q2 (*uncorrected* [*first and second states*]). 357 knowledge ———] Q3 (Knowledge); ~ .——— Q1–2, F, D (Knowledge D). 359–360 ———[*Aside.*] One . . . lost.] (one . . . lost.) Q1–3, F, D. 361 *to*] F, D; to Q1–3. 369 is in] Q1–2, F, D; is Q3. 380 *s.d. Aside*] Q2–3, F, D; *aside* Q1. 397 *s.d.* Maskall] D; Maskal Q1–3, F. 403 devil,] D (Devil); ~‿ Q1–3, F (Devil F). 408 him. What] ~ : what Q1–3, F, D (What Q3, D). 411 *Trismegistus?*] Q3; ~ : Q1–2, F, D. 418 School-boyes questions] Q1, Q3, D (School-boys Questions Q3, D); School-boys-questions Q2, F (School-Boys-Questions F). 419 ——— But . . . this.] (But . . . this.)——— Q1–3, F, D (this.)‿ Q2–3, F). 419+ *s.d.* Maskall] D; Maskal Q1–3, F. 420 Sir.] Q1, D; ~ ? Q2–3, F. 422–423 *Michaelmas . . . Hillary . . . Easter . . . Trinity . . . Long Vacation*] Q2–3, F, D; Michaelmas . . . Hillary . . . Easter . . . Trinity . . . Long Vacation Q1. 433+ *s.d. Servant*] F, D; Servant Q1–3. 434 Sir,] Q1–2, D; ~‿ Q3; ~ . F. 434 *s.d. Whispers*] Q2–3, F, D; *whispers* Q1. 442–443 immediately. Come] ~ ; come Q1–3, F, D. 443+ *s.d.* Alonzo, Theodosia, Beatrix] Q2–3, F, D (Alon. Theo. Beat. *and* D); *Alonzo, Theodosia, Beatrix* Q1. 450 *Wild.*] Q2–3, F, D; *Widl.* Q1. 450 wrath?] Q2–3, F, D; ~ , Q1. 453–454 errant . . . errant] Q1, D; errand . . . errand Q2–3, F (Errand . . . errand Q3). 454 I am] Q1, D; I'm Q2–3, F. 467 me?] F, D; ~ . Q1–3. 468 boy:] Q1, D (Boy D); ~ , Q2, F (Boy F); Boy; Q3. 477 *Christendom*] Christendom Q1–3, F, D. 486 'lif] Q1, D ('life D); 's lif Q2; 'slife Q3, F. 489 back. But] D (Back); back. / But Q1–3, F (*second line indented in Q1–2, F, but not in Q3*). 492 Mistresses] Q1–3, F; Mistress D. 493 discovery,] Q2–3, F, D (Discovery Q3, D); ~‿ Q1. 494 too.———] Q1–2, F; ~‿——— Q3, D. 498+ SONG.] Q1–3, F, D; *Loves Fancy.* o1; *Song* 181. d1, d5; *Song* 229. d2; *omitted from f1–3, M2; Evening Love* M3. 499–514 *italics and romans reversed in o1, d1–2, d5, f1–3, but normalized in the textual foot-*

notes and the following textual notes. 499 *pangs*] Q1-3, F, D, d1-2, d5, f1-3, M2 (*Pangs* D; *panges* M2); *pains* o1, M3. 500 *have*] Q1-3, F, D, d1-2, d5, f1-3, M2-3; *had* o1. 501 *Ah*] Q1-3, F, D, o1, d1-2, d5, f1-3, M3; *O* M2. 501 *pleasure*] Q1-3, F, D, o1, d1, d5, f1-3, M2-3 (*Pleasure* D); *Joy* d2. 502 *who causes*] Q1-3, F, D, o1, d1, d5, f1-3, M2-3; *that causeth* d2. 502 *pain!*] Q1-3, F, D (*Pain* D); *pain,* / *Chorus* Ah what, &c. o1, d1, d5 (*pain!* d1, d5; *Chorus.* d1, d5); *pain!* / *Cho.* Ah what a *Joy!* &c. d2; *pain.* f1-3 (*Pain* f2-3); *pain*∧ M2-3 (*paine* M2). 503-510 *stanzas 2 and 3 transposed in o1, d1-2, d5, M3.* 505-506 *Ah . . . Ah*] Q1-3, F, D, o1, d1-2, d5, f1-3, M3 (*ah . . . ah* M3); *O . . . Oh* M2 (?). 505 *is,*] Q1-3, F, D, d2; ~ ! o1, d1, d5, f1-3; ~∧ M2-3. 506 *again!*] Q1-3, F, D, f1-3; *again!* / *Chor.* Ah what, &c. o1, d1 (A what d1); *again!* / *Cho.* Ah what a joy, &c. d2; *again!* / *Chor.* Ah what, &c. d5; *againe*∧ M2; *again.* M3. 507 *the denyal comes*] Q1-3, F, D, o1, d1, d5, f1-3, M3 (*denial* Q2-3, F, o1; *Denial* D, d1, d5; *Denyall* M3); *her denial comes* d2; *her denyalles come* M2. 507 *fainter,*] Q2-3, F, D, o1, d1-2, d5, f1-3; ~ ,, Q1; ~∧ M2-3. 508 *give*] Q1-3, F, D, d1-2, d5, f1-3, M2-3; *gives* o1. 508 *does*] Q1-3, F, D, d1-2, d5, M3 (*dos* M3); *doth* o1, M2. 509-510 *Ah . . . Ah*] Q1-3, F, D, o1, d1-2, d5, f1-3, M3 (~ . . . *ah* M3); *Oh . . . Oh* M2(?). 509 *venture,*] Q1-3, F, D, o1, d1 (*venter* o1, d1); ~ ! d2, d5, f1-3 (*venter* d5); *venter*∧ M2-3 (*Venter* M3). 510 *does*] Q1-3, F, D, o1, d1-2, d5, f1-3, M3 (*dos* M3); *doth* M2. 510 *joy!*] Q1-3, F, D, f1-3 (*Joy* D, f1-3); *Joy!* / *Chor.* Ah what, &c. o1, d5; *Joy!* / Ah what, &c. d1; *Joy!* / *Cho.* Ah what a trembling, &c. d2; *joy*∧ M2-3 (*Joy* M3). 511 *accords me the*] Q1-3, F, D, o1, d1, d5, f1-3, M3; *affords me her* d2; *accordes with a* M2. 512 *'twixt*] Q1-3, F, D, o1, d1-2, d5, f1-3; *twixt* M2; *twix* M3. 513-514 *Ah . . . Ah*] Q1-3, F, D, o1, d1-2, d5, f1-3, M3 (*ah . . . ah* M3); *Oh . . . Oh* M2(?). 513 *joy 'tis*] Q1-3, F, D, f1-3, M2 (*Joy,* D; *Joy* f1-3; *tis* M2); *Joy!* oh o1, d1, d5, M3 (*Oh* d1, d5, M3); *joy* d2. 513 *expressing,*] Q1-3, F, D, d2; ~ ! o1, d1, d5, f1-3; ~∧ M2-3 (*Expressing* M3). 514 *Shall we again?*] *shall we again!* Q1-3, F, D, f1-3, M2 (*Shall* f2-3; *again?* f1-3; *a gaine* M2); *it again!* / *Chor.* Ah what, &c. o1; *it again!* / *Chor,* A what, &c. / *When with delight we have surfeit our senses,* / *And like a Deer that retires from the Chace,* / *Ah what a thousand of pretty pretences,* / *Doth she use to be brought to the second Embrace!* / *Chor.* A what, &c. d1, d5 (*again! Chor.* Ah d5; *a second* d5; *Chor.* Ah d5); *it again!* / *Cho.* Ah what a joy, &c. d2; *it again.* M3. 514+ *s.d. Enter*] *omitted from Q1-3, F, D.* 514+ *s.d.* Theodosia . . . Jacinta] Q2-3, F, D (*Jacintha* D); *Theodosia . . . Jacinta* Q1. 516 *silence.*] Q1-3, F; *Silence*∧ D. 519 *hear;*] Q1-3, F; ~ ? D. 523+ *s.d. Enter* Don] *Don* Q1-3, F, D ([*Don* Q3, D; *Don* Q2, F). 524 *Bellamy:*] Q1, D; ~ ? Q2-3, F. 526+ *s.d.* Maskall] D; *Maskal* Q1-3, F. 530 *small-guts*] Q1, D (*Small-guts* D); *small Guts* Q2-3, F. 534 *English*] Q2-3, F, D; *English* Q1. 536 *here?*] Q2-3, F, D; ~ : Q1. 541 *agoing*] Q1-2, D; *a going* Q3, F. 541 *discover'd*] Q2-3, F, D; *disover'd* Q1. 567 *friends.*] Q1-3, F (*Friends* Q3, F); *Friends*∧ D. 567 ——[*Aside.*] So] ——So Q1-3, F, D. 568 Springe.——]

Q1–3; ~ ·∧ F; Spring∧——— D.   575 in] Q1–2, F, D; in the Q3.
579 *s.d. Exit.*] *omitted from F.*

III, i

ACT III. SCENE I.] D; ACT. III. Q1; ACT III. Q2–3, F.   *s.d.*
Bellamy, Maskall] Q2–3, F, D (Maskal Q2–3, F; *and* Maskall D); *Bellamy,*
Maskall Q1.   1 *Melchor*] Q1 (*corrected state:* "Mel- / chor"), Q2–3,
F, D; *Mel- / Melchor* Q1 (*uncorrected state*).   8 women, . . . know,]
Q3 (Women); ~∧ . . . ~∧ Q1–2, F, D (Women Q2, F, D).   16 *En-*
glish-Almanack] Q1, D; *English Almanack* Q2–3, F.   17 half-hour]
Q1, D; half hour Q2–3, F.   25 Trumpet?] Q2–3, F, D; ~ . Q1.   31
knew] Q1; ~ , Q2–3, F, D.   41 me. *What*] ~ : What Q1–3, F, D.
41–44 *must . . . [italics] . . . person!*] must . . . [*romans*] . . . person∧
Q1–3, F, D (Person Q3, F, D).   46 your] Q1 (*corrected state*), Q2–3,
F, D; you Q1 (*uncorrected state*).   49–50 cleft-Cane] Q1, D (Cleft-
cane D); cleft Cane Q2–3, F.   54–55 Gaming house] Q1; Gaming-
house Q2–3, F, D (Gaming-House Q2–3).   56 here is] Q1–2, F, D;
here's Q3.   79 you!] Q3; ~ ? Q1–2, F, D.   86 nothing] Q1, Q3, F,
D; no thing Q2.   91 what,] D (What); ~∧ Q1–3, F (What F).
94–96 *Madam . . . Mam . . . yes Mam . . . no Mam . . . Madam*]
Madam . . . Mam . . . yes Mam . . . no Mam . . . Madam Q1–3, F,
D (Yes Q2–3, F; No Q2–3, F).   98 again ignorance:] Q1–3, F (Igno-
rance Q3); again, Ignorance! D.   98 *par-don Madam,*] par-don Madam,
Q1–3, F, D (Par-don F, D; Madam! D).   99 superfluity] Q1, F, D
(Superfluity D); super fluity Q2; super-fluity Q3.   100 *parn me Mam*
. . . your Ladyship, your] parn me Mam . . . your Ladyship, your Q1–3,
F, D (Parn F).   100 *Laship.*] Laship∧ Q1–3, F, D (~ . F).   105
Mam,] Q2–3, F; ~∧ Q1, D.   106 *to*] D; to Q1–3, F.   108 upon it]
Q1–3, D; upon't F.   108 speak,] D; ~∧ Q1–3, F.   117 *s.d. Sighs*]
Q2–3, F, D; *sighs* Q1.   119 since] Q2–3, F, D; sioce Q1.   139 than]
Q1, Q3, F, D; then Q2.   146 do? [*Aside.*]] do? Q1–3, F, D.   156
La] Q1–3, D; Lau F.   168 Hero] F, D (Heroe D); Heros Q1–3.
169 me most] S-S; most Q1–3, F, D.   175–176 [*Aside.*]——] [*aside*]
Q1; [*Aside.*] Q2, D; [*Aside.* Q3 (*at right margin*); (*aside.*) F.   180 I,] D
(Ay); ~∧ Q1–3, F.   200 redemption.] Q1–3, F; Redemption∧ D.
200 *Maskall*] Q1, D; *Maskal.* Q2–3, F.   201+ *s.d.* [*Aside.*] Q2–3, F,
D; [*aside.*] Q1.   202 [*Aside.*] ——] [*aside*] Q1; [*aside.*] Q2; [*Aside.*
Q3 (*at right margin*); (*Aside.*) F; [*Aside.*] D.   212 please.] Q1–3, F; ~∧
D.   219 *Idea's*] Q1–2; Idea's Q3, F; Idea's D.   222 *to*] D; to Q1–
3, F.   235 Madam;] ~ , Q1–3, F, D.   241 *s.d. schreeks*] Q1, D
(shrieks D); screeks Q2–3, F (skreeks F).   249 water!] ~ ? Q1–3, F, D
(Water Q2–3, F, D).   251 land Devils] Q1, D (Land D); Land-Devils
Q2–3, F.   251 foot Posts] Q1; Foot-Posts Q2–3, F, D.   257 see,]
Q1, D; ~∧ Q2–3, F.   276 sides.] Q2–3, F, D; ~ , Q1.   288 *Sors*]
F; Sors Q1–3; Stars D.   291 besworn] Q1; be sworn Q2–3, F, D.
291 not.] ~∧ Q1–3, F, D.   295–296 occasions. . . . without [*Tears*
it.] . . . *Sir.*——] ~ . . . . ~ [*tears it.*∧ . . . ~∧—— Q1–2 (*Tears*
Q2); ~ . [*Tears it.*] . . . ~ . . . ~∧—— Q3; ~ . . . . ~ [*tears it*∧] . . .

~_∧_————— F; ~ .... ~ ... ~_∧_————[*Tears it.*_∧_ D.   296 Sir.] ~_∧_
Q1-3, F, D.   297 us.] Q2-3, F; ~ : Q1, D.   299+ *s.d. Papers.*] Q2-3,
F, D; ~ , Q1.   299+ *s.d.* Don] Q2, F; *Don* Q1, Q3, D.   304 Love.
[*Aside.*] Love Q1-3, F, D.   308 Roof:] Q1, D; roof! Q2-3, F.   311
here.] Q1-3, F; ~_∧_ D.   311-312 ————[*To* Bellamy.] But, . . . Sir,]
D; [*to Bellamy*————But, . . . Sir, Q1-2 (*To* Bellamy. Q2); ————But_∧_
. . . Sir, [*To* Bellamy.] Q3; [*to* Bellamy.]————But, . . . Sir, F.
314+ *s.d.* [*Aside.*] Q3, F, D; ————*Aside.* Q1-2.   315 *s.d.* [*To*
Alonzo.] Q3, D; to *Alonzo.* Q1-2 (*in middle of line as dialogue*); (to
Alonzo.) F (*in middle of line*).   318 service. But] ~ : but Q1-3, F
(service; F); Service: But D.   322+ *s.d.* Maskall] D; Maskal Q1-2, F;
Mask. Q3.   325 it.] Q1-2, F, D; ~ ? Q3.   330 patience,] Q1-2, F,
D (Patience F, D); Patience? Q3.   336 more,] Q2-3, F, D; ~_∧_ Q1.
336 me:] Q1-3, F; ~ ! D.   338 Sir————] ~; Q1-2; ~ . Q3, F, D.
339 me to be] Q1-2, F, D; me, be Q3.   342 Why,] Q3; ~_∧_ Q1-2, F,
D.   351 Sir?] Q3; ~ ; Q1-2, D; ~ : F.   354 *dicendi;*] Q3, D; ~ ,
Q1-2, F.   363 Gibberish.] ~_∧_ Q1-3, F, D.   366 aforesaid.————
Not] ~_∧_————not Q1-3, F, D (Not Q3).   366 yet;] Q3; ~ , Q1-2, F,
D.   367 silent.] Q3; ~_∧_ Q1-2, F, D.   368 at] F; At Q1-3, D.
368-369 *Lopez . . . Lopez*] Lopez . . . Lopez Q1-3, F, D.   369 out.]
Q2-3, F, D; ~_∧_ Q1.   374 Tongue-ty'd;] Q1-2, F, D; ~ ? Q3.   376
Great-Grandsires] Q1, D; Great Grandsires Q2-3, F.   378 dry-land]
Q1 (dry- / land); dry Land Q2-3, F, D.   380 murder!] Q3, D; ~ .
Q1-2, F.   381 *Lop.*] omitted from Q2, F.   384 *s.d.* [*Exit Servant.*]
Q3 (*Ex.*); omitted from *Q1-2*, F, D.   387+ *s.d.* Maskall] D; Maskal
Q1-3, F.   388 Gaming-house] Q1-3, F (Gaming-House Q3); Gaming
house D.   388 i'faith;] ~ , Q1-3, F, D (y'faith Q2-3).   392 Visor
Masques] Q1, D (Masks D); Visor-Masques Q2-3, F.   398-399 Guit-
tars] Q1 (*corrected state:* "Guit- / tars"), Q2-3, F, D; Guitars Q1 (*uncorrected state recorded by Beaurline and Bowers:* "Gui- / tars").   401
s.d. Servant] Q3, F, D (*Serv.* D); Servant Q1-2.   402 to] Q3, D (*To*
Q3); to Q1-2, F.   404 Guittars] Q1 (*corrected state*), Q2-3, F, D;
Guittarrs Q1 (*uncorrected state recorded by Beaurline and Bowers*).
405+ *s.d. Cavaliers . . . Ladies*] D; Cavaliers . . . Ladies Q1-3, F.
405+ *s.d.* Jacinta.] Q3, F, D (Jacintha Q3, D); ~ ; Q1-2.   406-407
been . . . prove equal] Q1, Q2 (*some copies*), Q3, F, D; een . . . provb
qual Q2 (*press damage in some copies*).   408 a] Q1, D; an Q2-3, F.
431 *African-Cupid*] Q1, D; *African Cupid* Q2-3, F.   431 surer Archer]
Q1, Q3, F, D; sure Acher Q2.   434 it;] D; ~ , Q1-3, F.   449
Fresh-Maidenheads] Q1; Fresh Maidenheads Q2-3, F, D (fresh Q3, D).
461 true,] F, D; ~_∧_ Q1-3.   473 Duplets] Q1-3, F; Duplet D.   473
and] Q2-3, F; and Q1, D.   475 it.] ~ : Q1-3, F, D.   476 *s.d.*
Jacinta] Q2-3, F, D (Jacintha D); *Jacinta* Q1.   478 *s.d. Sweeps*]
Q2-3, F, D; *sweeps* Q1.   480 here,] Q3, D; ~_∧_ Q1-2; ~ ? F.   482
Sir.] Q1, D; ~ , Q2-3, F.   482 [*Aside.*] *Beatrix*] Beatrix Q1-3, F,
D.   487 *Christian*] Q2-3, F; Christian Q1, D.   488 Infidel] D; ~ .
Q1-3, F (Infidel Q1).   492 *Mask.*] Q2-3, F, D; Mask. Q1.   496 be
gone] Q1, F, D; begone Q2-3.   497 however,] ~_∧_ Q1-3, F, D.   518

————A] D; ∧~ Q1-3, F.   518   fortune!] Q1, D (Fortune D); Fortune?
Q2-3, F (fortune Q2).   518   *s.d. Aside*] Q2-3, F, D; *aside* Q1.   540
Maskall,] Q1 *(corrected state)*, Q2-3, F, D *(Maskal Q2-3, F)*; ~∧ Q1 *(un-*
corrected state recorded by Beaurline and Bowers).   542   stares;] Q1,
D; ~ ! Q2-3, F.   547   Why] Q1-3, F; ~ , D.   547   it.] Q1-2, F, D;
~ ? Q3.   548   it,] Q1, F, D; ~ . Q2-3.   548-549   commend to] Q1;
commend me Q2-3, F; commend me to D.   556   why,] D; ~∧ Q1-3, F.
557   Heaven!] Q1 *(corrected state)*, Q2-3, F, D (Heav'n D); ~ , Q1 *(un-*
corrected state recorded by Beaurline and Bowers).   559   *Jac.*] Q1 *(some*
copies), Q2-3, F, D; *Jac*∧ Q1 *(period did not print in copy text)*.   560
nothing, . . . warrant,] D; ~∧ . . . ~∧ Q1; ~∧ . . . ~ , Q2-3, F.
563+   *s.d. Aside.*] Q2-3, F, D; *Aside.*] Q1.   569   *Peru,*] Q1 *(corrected*
state), Q2-3, F, D; *Perue*∧ Q1 *(uncorrected state recorded by Beaurline*
and Bowers).   576   neighbour Princes] Q1-3, D (neighbor Q2; Neighbour Q3); Neighbour-Princes F.   578, 579   *Christendome*] Q2-3, F
(Christendom); Christendome Q1, D (Christendom D).   583   *Christian*]
Christian Q1-3, F, D.   588   of] Q1, D; of the Q2-3, F.   614   score,]
F, D (Score D); ~ . Q1-3.   625   to't.] Q1-3; ~∧ F, D.   625-626
Melchor.————] Q1; ~ . ∧ Q2-3, F; ~∧———— D.

IV, i

ACT IV. SCENE I.] D; ACT. IV. Q1; ACT IV. Q2-3, F.   *s.d. Enter*]
D; *omitted from Q1-3, F*.   *s.d.*   Bellamy, Wildblood: Maskall] Q3, F,
D (Wildblood, Q3, F; Maskal F); *Bellamy, Wildblood: Maskall* Q1-2
(Wildblood, Q2).   4+   *s.d. Don Melchor*] Q3, F; *Don Melchor* Q1;
Don Melchor Q2; *Don* Melchor D.   10+   *s.d.* Maskall] Maskal Q1-3,
F; Mask. D.   13   Town?] Q1, D; ~ ! Q2-3, F.   13-14   pretensions]
Q2-3, F, D (Pretensions D); pretentensions Q1 (preten- / tensions).
26+   *s.d.* Beatrix;] Q1-3, D; ~ , F.   26+   *s.d.* Mulatta] D; *Mulatta*
Q1-3, F.   32   inconstant;] Q1, D; ~ , Q2-3, F.   46+   SONG.]
Q1-3, F, D; *A Loves Song.* o1a; *Ha, Ha, Ha, Ha, Ha.* o1b; *Song* 182.
d1, d5; *Song* 171. d2; *The Rapture.* d3-4; *Song.* d6; *A SONG.* d7; *omitted*
from f1-3, M6; In Evening Love M4; *Song. by John Dryden* M5.   47-
70   *italics and romans reversed in o1a, o1b, d1-7, f1-3 (except 54-55,*
62-63, 70-71 of o1b, which are in italics) but normalized in the textual
footnotes and the following textual notes.   47   *Even*] Q1-3, F, D;
Evening o1a, o1b, d1-6, M4, M6; *Ev'ning* d7, f1-3, M5 *(ev'ning* M5).
48   *the new*] Q1-3, F, D, d2; *new* o1a, d1, d3-6; *the sweet* o1b, d7, f1-3,
M5-6 *(Sweet* M6); *Sweet* M4.   48   *flowers*] Q1, o1b, d2, d6, M4, M6;
Flowers Q2-3, F, D, o1a, d1, d3-5, d7, f1-3; *flowrs* M5.   49   Amyntas]
Q1-3, F, D, o1a, d1-6, M6 (Amintas d1, d3-5; *Amyntas* M6); Amintor
o1b, d7, f1-3, M4-5 *(Amyntor* d7; *Amintor* M4-5).   51   *me,*] o1a, o1b,
d1-7, f1-3; ~ ; Q1-3, F, D; ~∧ M4-5; ~ . M6.   52   *But*] Q1-3, F, D,
M6(?); *And* o1a, o1b, d1-7, f1-3, M4-5 *(and* f1-3, M4-5).   53   *For*
when] Q1-3, F, D; *But when* o1a, o1b, d1-7, f1-3, M4-5 *(but* M4-5); *then*
strait M6.   53   *fear he*] Q1-3, F, D, o1b, d7, f1-3, M4-6 *(fear,* Q2-3,
F; *Fear* D); *fear, / He* o1a, d1-6 *(fear*∧ d2, d6; *he* d4).   53   *draw*]
Q1-3, F, D, d2, d4, d6, M5-6; *come* o1a, o1b, d1, d3, d5, d7, f1-3, M4

(*Come* M4). 54 *He*] Q1-3, F, D, o1a, o1b, d1-7, f1-3, M4-5 (*he* f1-3, M4-5); *But* M6. 54 *dash'd*] Q1-3, F, D, d6-7, f1-3, M6 (*dashd* M6); *dasht* o1a, o1b, d1-5, M4-5 (*dash't* M5). 54 A ha ha ha ha!] *A ha ha ha ha!* Q1-3, F; *A ha, ha, ha, ha!* D; *a ah, ah, ah.* o1a, d1, d3, d5 (*an ah*∧ d3); *a ha ha ha ha ha ha ha,* &c. o1b, M4 (*ha*∧ *&c* M4); *a ha ha ha ha.* d2; *an ah ha, ha, ha.* d4; *a ha ha ha.* d6; *a Ha, ha, ha, ha, ha, ha, ha, ha, ha, ha, ha, ha, ha, ha, ha, ha, ha, ha.* d7; *a Ha ha ha ha ha ha ha ha ha ha ha ha ha ha ha ha ha ha.* f1-3, M5 (*a ha* M5); *an Ha ha ha ha hhah* M6. 55 *blush'd*] Q1-3, F, D, d6-7, f1-3; *blusht* o1a, o1b, d1-5, M4-5 (*blush't* M5 [?]); *blush* M6. 55 *lay*] Q1-3, F, D, o1a, d1-6, M6; *laid* o1b, d7, f1-3, M4-5. 55 *for a*] Q1-3, F, D, o1a, d1-7, f1-3, M5-6; *a* o1b, M4. 56 *And his*] Q1-3, F, D, o1a, d1, d3-5; *For his* d2, d6; *His* d7, f1-3, M5 (*his* M5); *'Twas* o1b, M4, M6 (*'twas* M4, M6). 56 *curb'd*] Q1-3, F, D, o1a, o1b, d1-7, f1-3, M4-5 (*Curb'd* M4); *coold* M6(?). 57 *But*] Q1-3, F, D, o1a, o1b, d1-7, f1-3, M4-5 (*but* M4); *then* M6(?). 57 *streight I*] Q1-3, F, D, o1b, d1-7, f1-3, M4-6 (*strait* d6-7, f1-3, M5-6); *streightly* o1a. 57 *fear*] Q1-3, F, D (*Fear* D); *fears* o1a, o1b, d1-7, f1-3, M4-6. 58 *Which*] Q1-3, F, D, d3-4, M6; *And* o1a, o1b, d1-2, d5-7, f1-3, M4-5 (*and* M4-5). 59 *O*] *O* Q1-3, F, D; *Ah* o1a, o1b, d1-7, f1-3, M4-6 (*ah* M5). 59 *Sylvia,*] Q1-3, F, D, o1a, o1b, d1, d5-6 (*Silvia* o1a, o1b, d1); ~ ! d3-4, d7, f1-3, M5 (*Silvia* f1-2; *Silvia* M5); ~∧ d2, M4 (*Silvia* M4); *Celia* M6(?). 59 *said*] Q1-3, F, D, o1a, o1b, d1-7, f1-3, M4-5; *quoth* M6. 59-60 you . . . [*to*] . . . awe;] *in italics in Q1-3, F, D, o1a, o1b, d1-7, f1-3, M4-6.* 59 you are] Q1-3, F, D, o1a, o1b, d1-7, f1-3, M4-5 (*you are*); thou art M6 (*thou art*). 60 your] Q1-3, F, D, o1a, o1b, d1-5, d7, f1-3, M4-5 (*your*); a d6 (*a*); thy M6 (*thy*). 61 *Then*] Q1-3, F, D, o1a, o1b, d1-7, f1-3, M4-5 (*then* M4); *And* M6. 61 *prest with*] Q1-3, F, D, o1b, d7, f1-3, M4-6; *prest / With* o1a, d1-6 (*prest,* d3-4). 61 *hand*] Q1-3, F, D, o1b, d6-7, f1-3, M4-6 (*Hand* D); *hands* o1a, d1-5. 61 *to*] Q1-3, F, D, o1a, o1b, d1-5, d7, f1-3, M4-6; *on* d6. 62 *dash'd*] Q1-3, F, D, d6-7, f1-3, M6 (*dashd* M6); *dasht* o1a, o1b, d1-5, M4-5 (*dash't* M5). 62 A ha ha ha ha!] *A ha ha ha ha.* Q1-3, F (*ha!* F); *A ha, ha, ha, ha.* D; *a ah, ah, ah.* o1a, d1, d3, d5 (*on ah* d3); *a ha ha ha ha ha ha,* &c. o1b, M4 (*ha*∧ *&c.* M4); *a ha ha ha ha.* d2; *an ah ha, ha, ha.* d4; *a ha ha ha.* d6; *a Ha, ha, ha, ha, ha, &c.* d7; *a ha, ha, ha, ha, ha,* &c. f1-3 (*a Ha* f2-3); *a ha ha &.* M5; *an ha ha ha ha ha ha*∧ M6. 63 *'twas*] Q1-3, F, D, o1a, o1b, d1-3, d5-7, f1-3, M4; *'t was* d4; *it was* M5; *twas* M6 (?). 63 *passion that*] Q1-3, F, D, o1b, d2, d6-7, f1-3, M4-6 (*Passion* Q3, D, d2, d7, f1-3, M4); *passions* o1a, d1; *passion* d3-4; *passions that* d5. 63 *all his*] Q1-3, F, D, o1a, d1-6, M6; *his* o1b, d7, f1-3, M4-5. 63 *fear*] Q1-3, F, D, o1a, o1b, d1-7, f1-3, M4-5 (*Fear* Q3, D, d2); *fears* M6. 65 *him softly*] Q1-3, F, D, o1a, o1b, d1-5, d7, f1-3, M4-6; *softly* d6. 65 *there's*] Q1-3, F, D, o1a, o1b, d1-7, f1-3, M4-5 (*There's* D, d5; *ther's* d4; *thers* M5); *there was* M6. 65 *near*] Q1-3, F, D, o1a, o1b, d1-7, f1-3, M4, M6 (*neer* M6); *hear* M5. 66 *And*] Q1-3, F, D, o1a, o1b, d1, d3-5, d7, f1-3, M4-6 (*and* M5); *And I* d2, d6. 66 *cheek*] Q1-3, F, D, o1a, o1b, d1-7, f1-3, M4-5 (*Cheek* Q2-3, F, D, o1b, d7, f1-3, M4); *cheeks* M6. 67 *But as*] Q1-3, F, D, o1a,

O_{1b}, d_{1-7}, f_{1-3}, M_{4-5} (*Bur* f_1 [?]; *but* M_5); *As* M_6 (?).   67 *he*] Q_{1-3}, F, D, O_{1a}, O_{1b}, d_{1-6}, M_4, M_6; *we* d_7, f_{1-3}, M_5 (*wee* M_5).   67 *bolder and bolder*] Q_{1-3}, F, D, O_{1a}, O_{1b}, d_{1-2}, d_{4-7}, f_{1-3}, M_{4-6} (*bolder, and* d_4; & M_6); *bolder* d_3.   69 *And just*] Q_{1-3}, F, D, O_{1a}, d_{1-7}; *And straight* O_{1b}, f_{1-3}, M_{4-5} (*strait* f_{2-3}, M_5); *just* M_6.   69 *bliss we began*] Q_{1-3}, F, D, d_7, f_{1-3}, M_5 (*bliss*, d_7, f_{1-3}; *blisse wee* M_5); *bliss / Began* O_{1a}, d_{1-6}; *bliss, began* O_{1b}, M_4, M_6 (*Bliss*∧ M_4; *bliss*∧ M_6).   69 *with a*] Q_{1-3}, F, D, O_{1a}, d_{1-7}, f_{1-3}, M_{4-6}; *with* O_{1b}.   70 *laugh'd*] Q_{2-3}, F, D; *laughd* Q_1, M_6; *burst* O_{1a}, d_{1-6}; *laughs* O_{1b}, M_4; *laught* d_7, f_{1-3}, M_5. 70 *with A ha ha ha ha!*] *with A ha ha ha ha.* Q_{1-3}, F (*ha!* F); *with A ha, ha, ha, ha.* D; *with a Ha, Ha, ha, Ha.* O_{1a}; *with a ha ha ha ha ha ha,* &c. O_{1b}, M_4 (*ha*∧ &c. M_4); *with a ha, ha, ha, ha. / I bade him be quiet for fear of the Swain, / And follow me down to the Grove, / Where we crope in a Cave, and we chatter'd again, / The dangers that prosecute Love. / He plaid with my pretty white shooe-strings. / My legs he did tickle and claw, / But do what I could, / Yet he forced my bloud, / And I squeek't with a ha, ha, ha, ha, / The small of my leg he did prettily praise, / And my calf that so roundly did rise, / I wink'd, and I frown'd, at his foolish delays, / Which made him skip up to my thighs, / He plaid with my soft panting Belly, / I bade to his fingers no law, / But when he did touch, / What he loved so much, / He burst out with a ha, ha, ha, ha.* d_1, d_{3-5} (*with ha, ha, ha, ha.* d_1; *with ha, ha, ha, ha,* d_3; *with an ah, ha, ha, ha.* d_4; *bad him* d_{3-4}; *and chatter'd* d_{3-4}; *Love,* d_{3-5}; *shooe-strings;* d_{3-4}; *shooe-strings,* d_5; *claw;* d_{3-4}; *claw:* d_5; *blood* d_{3-4}; *with an ha, ha, ha.* d_3; *with an ah, ha, ha, ha.* d_4; *with a ha, ha, ha, ha.* d_5; *rise;* d_{3-5}; *wink'd*∧ d_{3-5}; *frown'd*∧ d_{3-5}; *thighs:* d_{3-4}; *thighs.* d_5; *Belly;* d_{3-4}; *belly* d_5; *bad to* d_{3-4}; *law:* d_{3-4}; *law;* d_5; *touch*∧ d_{3-5}; *much.* d_4; *with an ha, ha, ha.* d_3; *with an ah, ha, ha, ha.* d_4; *with a ha, ha, ha.* d_5); *with a ha ha ha ha.* d_2; *with a ha ha ha.* d_6; *with a Ha, ha, ha, ha, ha,* &c. d_7; *with a Ha ha ha ha ha,* &c. f_{1-3}; *with a ha ha ha & . & . & .* M_5; *with A ha ha ha ha*∧ M_6.   73 *Song.*] ~∧ Q_{1-3}, F, D.   74 *hold;*] Q_{1-3}; ~ , F, D.   74 *Sir,*] Q_{1-3}, F; ~ ; D.   78 *mankind.*] Q_1; *Mankind*∧ Q_{2-3}, F, D.   82 *should*] Q_1, D; *shall* Q_{2-3}, F.   83 *do't.*] Q_3; ~ , Q_{1-2}, F, D.   90 *o're-run* Q_1, D (*o'er-run* D); *over-run* Q_{2-3}, F. 91 *Universal-Monarchy*] Q_1, D; *Universal Monarchy* Q_{2-3}, F.   99 *than*] Q_3, D; *then* Q_{1-2}, F.   103 *Compliment's*] Q_{1-2}, F, D; *Compli-ments,* Q_3.   125 *I'll*] Q_{1-3}, F (*I'll* Q_1); *I* D.   129 *six,*] Q_1, D (*six*∧ D); *six Horses* Q_{2-3}, F.   130, 136 *than*] Q_3, F, D; *then* Q_{1-2}. 146 *like the*] Q_{1-3}, F; *like* D.   160 *Changeling.*——— *[Aside.]*] ~∧——— Q_{1-3}, F, D (*Changling* Q_3, F).   170 *beholding*] Q_{1-3}, F; *beholden* D.   177 *Beatrix!*] Q_{1-2}, F; ~ . Q_3, D.   182 *Maskall*] D; *Maskal* Q_{1-3}, F.   185 *Mask.*] Q_{2-3}, F, D; *Mak.* Q_1.   187+ *s.d.* *Maskall*] Q_{2-3}, F, D (*Maskal* Q_{2-3}, F; *Mask* D); *Maskall* Q_1.   188 *Wild.*] Q_{2-3}, F, D; ~∧ Q_1.   194 *kindles,*] Q_1, Q_3, D; ~∧ Q_2, F. 197+ *s.d. on*] Q_{1-2}, F, D; *upon* Q_3.   198 *The . . . [romans] . . . opens!*] Q_1, D; *The . . . [italics] . . . opens.* Q_{2-3}, F (*set as part of preceding s.d.*).   198 *now,*] Q_1, D; ~ ! Q_{2-3}, F.   199 *door;*] Q_{1-3}, F; *Door!* D.   199 *lest*] Q_{1-3}, F; *least* D.   214 *s.d.* Don

Melchor] Q2–3, F, D (*Don*); *Don Melchor* Q1.   217 he;] Q1–2, F,
D; ∼ ! Q3.   218 *Idea*] Idea Q1–3, F, D.   219 himself] Q2–3, F,
D; nimself Q1.   221 self.] Q3, F, D; ∼∧ Q1–2.   221 *s.d. Runs*]
Q2–3, F, D; *runs* Q1.   222+ *s.d. Running*] Q2–3, F, D; *running*
Q1.   224–225 too. Avoid, avoid, Specter!] too; avoid, avoid∧ Spec-
ter. Q1–3, F, D.   235 *s.d. [Runs]* Q2–3, F, D; ∧*runs* Q1.   237
me.] ∼ : Q1–3, F, D.   242 unfaithfulness] Q1 (*corrected state*), Q2–3,
F, D (Unfaithfulness D); unfathfulness Q1 (*uncorrected state*).   245
Melchor!] Q1–3, D; ∼ ? F.   266+ *s.d.* Don] *Don* Q1–3, F, D.   273
Don] Don Q1–3, F, D.   273, 278 St.] Q2, F; St. Q1, Q3, D.   280
Law Sute] Q1, D; Law-Sute Q2–3, F (Law-Suit F).   280 St.] Q2, F; St.
Q1, Q3, D.   285 on] Q1–3, F; upon D.   294 servants.] D (Servants);
∼∧ Q1–3, F (Servants Q3, F).   300 Ring.] ∼∧ Q1–3, F, D.   301
him. [*Aside*.]] him Q1–3, F, D.   302–303 Table Diamond] Q1–3, D;
Table-Diamond F.   306 too] Q1–2, F, D; to Q3.   320 you.] D;
∼∧ Q1–3, F.   320 *s.d. Aside.*] Q2–3, D; ∼ .] Q1; ∼∧) F.   323 Dis-
eases] Q1–3, F; Disease D.   325 Earthquake.] ∼∧ Q1–3, F, D.   327,
330 *Don*] Don Q1–3, F, D.   335 How . . . Devil] Q1–2, F, D; ∼ ,
. . . ∼ , Q3.   335 come] Q1–3; came F, D.   335 me? [*Aside.*] me?
Q1–3, F, D.   341 me.] ∼∧ Q1–3, F, D.   343 out.] Q1–2, D; ∼∧ Q3,
F.   346 speculation.] D (Speculation); ∼∧ Q1–3, F (Speculation Q3).
348 *Astrologer*] Q2–3, F; Astrologer Q1, D.   349 all.] D; ∼∧ Q1–3, F.
349 *s.d. Aside*] Q2–3, F, D; *aside* Q1.   352–353 ingeniously] Q1–3, F;
ingenuously D.   356 like] Q1–2, F, D; by Q3.   360 Science;] Q3,
D; ∼ , Q1–2.   366 Gentlewoman.] ∼∧ Q1–3, F, D.   375 eare.] ∼∧
Q1–3, F, D (ear Q2; Ear Q3, F, D).   376 *Don*] Don Q1–3, F, D.
377 Garden door] Q1–2, F, D (Door D); Garden-Door Q3.   379
answer.] D (Answer); ∼∧ Q1–3, F.   380 Sir.] D; ∼ , Q1–3, F.   391
Who] Q3, D; ∼ , Q1–2, F.   394 better,] Q2–3, F, D; ∼∧ Q1.   395
theft:] ∼ ; Q1–3, F, D (Theft Q2–3, F, D).   398+ *s.d. Servant*] Q2–3,
F, D; Servant Q1.   399 you?] D; ∼ ; Q1–3, F.   407 Bell.] Q2–3, F,
D (*Bel.* D); ∼ , Q1.   409 means. [*Aside.*]———] D; ∼∧——— (aside∧)
Q1, F (*Aside* F); ∼∧———[*Aside.*] Q2; ∼∧——— [*Aside.*∧ Q3 (*at right
margin*).   412 never shall enjoy] Q1, Q2 (*corrected state*), D; shall
enjoy never Q2 (*uncorrected state*), Q3; shall never enjoy F.   415–416
double dealing] Q1–3, D (Dealing D); double-dealing F.   424 *Turk*]
Q2–3, F, D; Turk Q1.   427 than] Q2–3, F; then Q1, D.   429 you.]
Q1–3, D; ∼∧ F.   438 *Bellamy!*] Q1, D; ∼ ? Q2–3, F.   445 *Idea*]
F; Idea Q1–3, D.   446 whom] Q1–3, D; who F.   449 *Idea*] F;
Idea Q1–3, D.   466 *Albricias*,] Q3, F, D; ∼∧ Q1–2.   471 Good-
night] Q1, D (Good- / night Q1); Good night Q2–3, F (Night Q3).   477
this is] Q2–3, F, D; this Q1.   480 Lady.] Q3; ∼ ; Q1–2, F, D.   492
where,] Q2–3, F; ∼∧ Q1, D.   499 it.] Q3; ∼∧ Q1–2, F, D.   499+
s.d. [Gives . . . money.] Q2–3, F, D (*Money* Q2–3, F; *Mony* D); ∧∼ ₃ . . .
∼ .] Q1 (*at left margin*).   502 sake.] Q1–2; ∼∧ Q3, F, D.   502–503
immediately] Q2–3, F, D; immedeiately Q1.   504 possibly.] ∼∧ Q1–3,
F, D.   506–507+ me. [*Aside.*]———Sir, . . . you. / [*To* Alonzo.] D
(Alon.); me.——— / [*Aside.*] / *To Alonzo.* Sir, . . . you. Q1 ("*To*

Alonzo" indented); me.——— / [*Aside.* / *To* Alonzo. Sir, . . . you. Q2,
F (me∧——— F; *"To* Alonzo" *indented in* Q2, F); me∧——— [*Aside.* /
[*To* Alonzo.] Sir, . . . you. Q3.   509+   *s.d. Aside*] Q2-3, F, D; *aside*
Q1.   511 Son in law] Q1; Son-in-Law Q2-3, F, D.   511 law!
[*Aside.*] Q3, D; law! Q1-2, F.   523 point,] Q2-3, F, D (Point D); ~∧
Q1.   524 Sir.] Q1, D; ~ , Q2-3, F.   528 Sir.] Q1, D; ~∧ Q2-3, F.
529 Sir———] Q3, D; ~ .∧ Q1-2, F.   537 respect———] Q3, F, D
(Respect Q3); ~ .——— Q1-2.   548 *in tenebris*] Q2-3, F, D (in Q2,
F); in tenebris Q1.   549, 553 Sir] Q1, Q3, F, D; ~ . Q2.   576
Daughter. [*Aside.*]———] Daughter. Q1-3, F; Daughter.——— D.   581
why,] Q3, D (Why D); ~∧ Q1-2, F (Why F).   583, 584   Son in Law]
Q1; Son-in-Law Q2-3, F, D.   601 it.] ~∧ Q1-3, F, D.   601+   *s.d.*
Maskall, Jacinta, Beatrix] Q2-3, F, D (Maskal Q2-3, F; Jacintha, *and* D);
Maskal, Jacinta, Beatrix Q1.   602 Honour?] Q1-3, D; ~ . F.   606
in your] Q1-3, D; in F.   612 good natur'd] Q1-3, F; good-natur'd D.
627 you.———Sir———] ~∧———~ .∧ Q1-3, F, D.   634 with] Q1-
3, F; without D.   641 come———] D; ~ . Q1-3, F.   655-656
———[*Aside.*] Help . . . abominably.———] (Help . . . abominably∧)
Q1-3, F, D.   656 Maskall] D; *Maskal* Q1-3, F.   666 Heyday] Q1;
Hey day Q2, F, D; Hey-day Q3.   668-669 for't.———*Maskall,* . . .
gone. [*Aside.*] for't: (*Maskall,* . . . gone.) Q1-3, F, D (*Maskal* Q2-3, F).
671 poverty] Q1, D (Poverty D); ~ . Q2-3, F (Poverty Q3, F).   674-
674+ Money———I . . . Sir. / [*Aside.*] Money (I . . . Sir.) Q1-3, F,
D (Mony. D; *I* Q1).   675-676 *to* Mask. Forward, . . . throat.———
And] (Forward, . . . throat;) and Q1-3, F, D (Throat Q3, F, D).   680
it?] Q2-3, F; ~ . Q1, D.   682 and] Q1 (*corrected state*), Q2-3, F, D;
aud Q1 (*uncorrected state*).   683 *to*] D; to Q1-3, F.   686 *to Beat.*]
omitted from Q1-3, F, D.   716 wearing,] Q2-3, F, D; ~∧ Q1.   720
Mutton haft] Q1-2, D (Haft Q2, D); Mutton-Haft Q3, F.   722 brass
chain] Q1-2, F, D (Brass Chain Q2, F, D); Brass-Chain Q3.   725
dandriffe Comb] Q1-2, D (Dandriffe Q2; Dandriff D); Dandriff-Comb
Q3, F.   729 Letter,] D; ~∧ Q1-3, F.   743 are so] Q1-3, D; are F.
756 Why,] F; ~∧ Q1-3, D.   756 off?] Q1-3, D; ~ . F.   757 Why,]
F; ~∧ Q1-3, D.   759 quarrelling,] Q2-3, F (quarreling F); ~∧ Q1, D.
760 disguisements,] Q2-3, F; ~∧ Q1, D (Disguisements D).   765
Venice-glass] Q2-3, F, D (*Venice*-Glass Q2-3, D; *Venice* Glass F); Venice-
glass Q1.   773 *Beatrix?*] Q1, D; ~ : Q2-3; ~ ; F.   781 alliance,]
D; ~ ; Q1-3, F (Alliance Q2-3, F).   784 Navigation,] Q2-3, F, D;
~∧ Q1.   784 you.] Q1-3, F; ~——— D.   788 *as in Q3; not
indented in Q1-2, F, D.*   788+   *s.d. Exeunt*] Q2-3, F, D; Exeunt Q1.

V, i

ACT V. SCENE I.] D; ACT. V. Q1; ACT V. Q2-3, F.   *s.d. Enter*]
D; *omitted from Q1-3, F.*   *s.d.* Lopez, Aurelia, . . . Camilla] Q3, F,
D; *Lopez, Aurelia,* . . . *Camilla* Q1-2 (*Aurelia*∧ Q2).   8 confidence]
Q1 (*corrected state*), Q2-3, F, D (Confidence D); coufidence Q1 (*uncor-
rected state*).   9 upon you] Q2-3, F, D; upon Q1.   18 withall,]
Q3 (withal); ~∧ Q1-2, F, D (withal Q2, F, D).   18 me to] Q2-3, F,

D; me Q1.   26 the] Q1-2, F, D; thy Q3.   29 Mam,] Q2-3, F, D;
~∧ Q1.   38 fruit.] Q1-2, F, D (Fruit Q2, F, D); Fruit! Q3.   40
mignonne] Q1, D; *magnonne* Q2-3, F.   43 surpriz'd.] Q1-2, F, D;
~ ! Q3.   44 'em.] ~ : Q1-3, F, D.   45 come] Q1, D; came Q2-3,
F.   45 here!] Q1-2, F, D; ~ ? Q3.   53 her.] ~ ? Q1-3, F, D.   57
withall,] Q3 (withal); ~∧ Q1-2, F, D (withal Q2, F, D).   61 you not]
Q1, D; not you Q2-3, F.   61 tender] Q1, D (Tender); tender Love
Q2-3, F.   64 is,] Q2-3, F, D; ~∧ Q1.   65 his Q1-3, F; He D.
69 in] Q1, D; in Don Q2-3, F.   72 to] D; to Q1-3, F.   72 promise,] F, D (Promise D); ~ : Q1-3 (Promise Q3).   76 whom I] Q1, Q2
(*corrected [second state]*), Q3, F, D; whom c Q2 (*uncorrected [first state]*).
83 Autumn] Q1-2, F, D; *Autumn* Q3.   84 you] Q1-2, Q3 (*corrected
state*), F, D; you you Q3 (*uncorrected state*).   91 rest,] Q2-3, F; ~∧
Q1, D.   95 Cavaliers,] Q3, D; ~∧ Q1-2, F.   96+ *s.d.* Don
Melchor] *Don Melchor* Q1; *Don* Melchor Q2-3, F, D.   97 *Melchor,*]
Q2-3, F, D; ~∧ Q1.   97 a-bed] Q3, F, D (a-Bed F, D); a bed Q1-2.
108 self.] Q1-2, F, D; ~ ! Q3.   110 Cousin?] Q2-3, F, D; ~ . Q1.
112 How,] Q3, D; ~∧ Q1-2; ~ ! F.   112 ingratitude,] Q1-2, D
(Ingratitude Q2, D); Ingratitude; Q3; Ingratitude! F.   116 that,] Q3,
F, D; ~∧ Q1-2.   122 *as in Q3, F, D; indented in Q1-2.*   124
Garden door] Q1-3, D (Door D); Garden-door F.   128+ *s.d.* Wild-
blood, Maskall, Jacinta, Beatrix] Q2-3, F, D (Maskal Q2-3, F; Jacintha,
and D); *Wildblood, Maskall, Jacinta, Beatrix* Q1.   129 to] Q2, F, D;
to Q1, Q3.   131 you,] Q1-2, F, D; ~ ! Q3.   132 alarme?] Q2-3,
F, D (allarm Q2, F; Alarm Q3, D); ~ . Q1.   135 Garden-door] Q1-2,
F, D (Garden-Door D); Garden door Q3.   137 running] Q2-3, F, D;
runing Q1.   146 too. Dear] Q3; ~ ; dear Q1-2, F, D.   148 Dog,]
Q3, D; ~∧ Q1-2, F.   149 *s.d.* To Maskall] Q2-3, F, D (Maskal Q2-3,
F); *to Maskall* Q1.   151 *s.d.* To Melchor] Q2-3, F, D; *to Melchor* Q1.
160 Must] Q1 (*corrected state*), Q2-3, F, D; *Mel.* Must Q1 (*uncorrected
state*).   165 Madam;] ~ , Q1-3, F, D.   168 Cavaliers.] ~∧ Q1-3,
F, D.   172 what ever] Q1-3; whatever F, D.   178 me] Q1-3, F;
me to D.   180 credit,] Q2-3, F, D (Credit Q3, D); ~∧ Q1.   193
Sir?] F, D; ~ . Q1-3.   194-197 *Astrologie . . . Astrologie*] Astrologie
. . . Astrologie Q1-3, F, D (Astrology . . . Astrology Q2-3, F, D).
197 Sir?] Q1-2, F, D; ~ ; Q3.   198 Art Magick] Q1-3, D; Art-
Magick F.   199 *Astrologie*] Astrologie Q1-3, F, D (Astrology Q2-3,
F, D).   206 Garden door] Q1-2, D (Door D); Garden-Door Q3, F
(Garden-door F).   209 me,] F; ~∧ Q1-3, D.   209-210 advice]
Q1, Q3, D (Advice D); ~ . Q2, F.   211 in? [*Aside.*] in? Q1-3, F, D.
214+ *s.d. omitted from Q1-3, F, D.*   216 short] Q1, Q2 (*corrected
[third state]*), Q3, F, D; shorr Q2 (*uncorrected [first and second states]*).
216 Sir,] Q2-3, F, D; ~∧ Q1.   218 further] Q1-3, D; farther F.
220 *You*] You Q1-3, F, D.   222 Squire. [*To* Maskall *aside.*] Squire.
Q1-3, F, D.   231 Parterre. You] ~ : you Q1-3, F, D (You F, D).
237 Sir,] Q3, F, D; ~∧ Q1-2.   238 mad!] F; ~ . Q1-3, D.   244
private.] ~∧ Q1-3, F, D.   254 again. [*Aside.*] again. Q1-3, F, D.
262 arising. [*Aside.*] arising. Q1-3, F, D.   266 in,] F, D; ~∧ Q1-3.

266 a Gods] Q1–3, D (God's Q2–3, D); a-God's F.   267 all at] Q1–3,
F; all D.   268 this? [*Aside.*] this? Q1–3, F, D.   272 fellows] Q1,
D (Fellows D); fellow Q2–3, F (Fellow Q3, F).   274 mean? [*Aside.*]
mean? Q1–3, F, D.   276 *s.d.* [*Goes . . . door.*]] Q2–3, F, D (*door*∧)
F; *Door.*] D); ∧~ . . . ~ ·∧ Q1.   279 boldly.] Q1–2, F, D; ~∧ Q3.
279 *Maskall* open the door] Q3, D (*Maskal,* Q3; *Maskall,* D; Door D);
Maskal *open the door* Q1–2, F (*printed as s.d.*).   282 *s.d.* [*Going . . .
them.*] Q1–3, D (*them*∧ Q2); omitted from F.   286 Why,] Q3, D; ~∧
Q1–2, F.   287 blood.] ~∧ Q1–3, F, D (Blood Q3, F, D).   289
Devil:] Q1–3, D; ~ ? F.   290 clutches:] Q1–2, D (Clutches D);
Clutches∧ Q3, F.   292 *Jacinta*] Q1; ~ , Q2–3, F, D (*Jacintha* D).
303 I lay] Q1–3, F (*I* Q1); I'll lay D.   304 *s.d. claps*] Q2–3, F, D;
Claps Q1.   309 her,] D; ~∧ Q1–3, F.   311 you have] Q1, D; have
you Q2–3, F.   316 lost. [*Aside.*] lost. Q1–3, F, D.   320 *Mel.*] Q1
(*some copies*), Q2–3, F, D; ~∧ Q1 (*some copies*).   320 Sir, your] Q1–
2, F, D; ~ ! ~ Q3.   321 gone,] Q3, D; ~∧ Q1–2, F.   321 it. But]
~ : but Q1–3, F, D (But F, D).   324 you. [*Aside . . . Master.*]——]
you∧——*Aside . . . Master.* Q1–2; you∧——[*Aside . . . Master.* Q3;
you∧——[*Aside . . . Master.*] F, D (*Master*∧] F).   332 him,] Q2–3,
F, D (him); ~∧ Q1.   334 honor.] Q1–3, F (Honour Q3, F); Honour.
—— D.   337 case] Q1–2, F, D (Case D); Cause Q3.   345 *Alon.*]
F, D; Alon. Q1–3.   347 *Bell. Mask.*] F, D (*Bell.* and *Mask.* F; *Bel.*
D); Bell. Mask. Q1–3 (Bell. *and* Mask. Q3).   358 Devilship,] Q2–3,
F, D; ~∧ Q1.   359 *to*] D; to Q1–3, F.   364 than] Q1, Q3, D; then
Q2, F.   365 I'll] Q1–2, F, D; I will Q3.   366 No,] Q2–3, F, D;
~∧ Q1.   367 help!] D; ~ . Q1–3, F.   369+ *s.d. Enter* Maskall
again] Q1–2, F, D (Maskal Q2, F); *Re-Enter* Maskal, Q3.   371 me]
Q1, D; me all Q2–3, F.   374 *Bell.*] F, D (*Bel.* D); Bell∧ Q1; Bell. Q2–
3.   374 *them within.*] Q1–3, D; *them* F.   376 Garden-door] Q1,
F, D; Garden door Q2–3.   379 trouble] Q1 (*corrected state*), Q2–3,
F, D; tronble Q1 (*uncorrected state*).   379 further. Go] ~ : go Q1–3,
D (Go D); ~ ; go F (farther).   382 *Mask. . . . Alonzo . . . Wild-
blood*] D; Mask. . . . Alonzo . . . Wildblood Q1–3, F (*Mask.* Q2, F;
Alon. F; Wild. F).   385 *Alon. . . . Wildblood*] F, D (Wildblood F);
Alon. . . . Wildblood Q1–3 (Alon∧ Q2).   390 gross!] Q1, D; ~ ; Q2–
3, F.   391 ho,] Q3, F, D; ~∧ Q1–2.   394 Garden doors] Q1, D
(Doors D); Garden-doors Q2–3, F (Garden-Doors Q3).   403 match,]
~∧ Q1–3, F, D.   406 him.——[*To* Alonzo.] In] D (him:); him: [*to
Alonzo*] in Q1; him: [*To* Alonzo.] in Q2–3 (Alonzo∧] Q3); him: (*To
Alonzo*) In F.   406 time] Q1, D; ~ ! Q2–3, F.   422 what ever]
Q1–3, F; whatever D.   434 Carnival merriment] Q1–3, D (Merriment
Q3, D); Carnival-merriment F.   436 *Jac.*] Q1 (*some copies*), Q2–3, F,
D; *Jac*∧ Q1 (*some copies*).   438 Among] Q1–2, F, D; Amongst Q3.
440 Carnival device] Q1–3, D (Device D); Carnival-device F.   440–441
ending] Q1–3, D; ended F.   443 *Astrologer*] Q2–3, F; Astrologer Q1,
D.   450 *Astrologie*] Q2–3, F (*Astrology*); Astrologie Q1, D (Astrology D).
451 way,] Q2–3, F, D; ~∧ Q1.   453 *Cid*] Cid Q1–3, F, D.   454
Romanes] Q2–3, F, D (*Romans*); Romanes Q1.   459 *Theo.*] Q1 (*some*

copies), Q2–3, F, D; *Theo*∧ Q1 *(some copies)*.   459   *to*] Q2, D; to Q1,
Q3, F.   459   have had] Q1, D; have Q2–3, F.   461   gratitude] F, D
(Gratitude D); ~ , Q1–3.   463–467 *Lent . . . Lent . . . Lent*] Q2–3,
F; Lent . . . Lent . . . Lent Q1, D.   468   *Easter*] Q2–3, F, D; Easter
Q1.   470   *Jacinta*] Q1, D *(Jacintha* D); ~ , Q2–3, F.   470   *Wild-
blood,*] Q1, F, D; ~ . Q2–3.   470   me:] Q1–3, D; ~ ; F.   471   so,] Q2–
3, F, D; ~∧ Q1.   472   unawares;] F; ~ : Q1–3, D.   472   us in] Q1,
D; us Q2–3, F.   472–473 *what do you lack*] what do you lack Q1–3, F,
D.   476   upon] Q1–3, F; upon the D.   494   Fala, fala, fala] Q1–3,
D; Fa la, fa la, fa la F.   494   best,] Q2–3, F, D (Best D); ~∧ Q1.
496   I,] D (Ay); ~∧ Q1–3, F.   499   singer] Q1–3, D (Singer Q3, D);
Finger F.   502–503 *St. . . . St.*] Q2; St. . . . St. Q1, Q3, F, D.
503+ SONG.] Q1–3, F, D; *A Song.* 02–6; Song 33. d1, d5; *Song 172.* d2;
Dyalogue in Evening Love∧ M7.   504–533 *italics and romans reversed
in 02–6, d1–2, d5 but normalized in the textual footnote and the following
textual notes.*   504 Damon. Celimena Q1–3, F, D (Cᴇlimena Q3);
CᴇEllamina 02; Cᴇllamina 03–6; Cᴇlemana d1, d5, M7 *(Celemana* M7);
Damon. / Cᴇlamina d2.   506   *If, with*] Q1–3, F, D, d1–2, d5, M7 (If∧
Q2, F, d1–2, d5); If by 02–6.   506   leave] Q1 *(corrected state)*, Q2–3, F,
D, 02–6, d1–2, d5, M7 *(Leave* D, M7); leaue Q1 *(uncorrected state)*.
506 may] Q1–3, F, D, 03–6, d1–2, d5, M7; ~ , 02.   507   day,] Q1,
Q3, D, 02–3, d1, d5 *(Day* D); ~ . Q2, F; ~∧ 04–6, M7; ~ : d2.   508
will] Q1–3, F, D, 02–6, d1, d5, M7; *shall* d2.   509   Celimena. *Passion's*
Q1–3, F, D; *Passion's* 02–6; Celemana. / *Passion's* d1–2, d5, M7 (Celamina
d2; *Celemana*∧ M7).   512   burn] Q1–3, F, D, d1–2, d5, M7; *dam* 02–6.
514 Damon. *Love*] Q1–3, F, D; *Love* 02, 03(?), 04–6; Damon. / Love
d1–2, d5, M7 *(Damon*∧ M7).   514   dull] Q1–3, F, D; *pale* 02, 03(?),
04–6, d1–2, d5, M7 *(Pale* M7).   517   refines] Q1–3, F, D, 02–6, d1–2,
d5; *Refine's* M7(?).   518   it quicker] Q1–3, F, D, 02–6, d1, d5, M7; *the
quicker* d2.   519   Celimena. *Love*] Q1–3, F, D; *Love* 02–6; Celemana.
/ *Love* d1–2, d5, M7 (Celamina d2; *Celemana*∧ M7).   519   quarrels]
Q1–3, F, D (Quarrels D); *anger* 02–6; *quarrel* d1–2, d5, M7 (Quarrell
M7).   521   grave] Q1–3, F, D, 02–6, d1, d5, M7; *brave* d2.   521
Physician's] Q1–3, F, D, d1–2, d5, M7 (Physitian's Q2–3; Physicians d1–2;
Physitians d5, M7); Physician 02–6 (Phisician 02).   521   wit,] Q3, F,
D, 02–6, d1–2, d5 (Wit Q3, D); ~∧ Q1, M7 (witt M7); ~ . Q2.   522
Ague fit] Q1–3, D, 02–6, d2, d5, M7 (ague 05–6, d5); fitt M7); *Ague-fit* F,
d1.   523   *Put*] Q1–3, F, D; *Puts* 02–6, d1–2, d5, M7.   524   Damon.
Anger] Q1–3, F, D; *Anger* 02–6; Damon. / *Anger* d1–2, d5, M7 *(Damon*∧
M7).   524   rouzes] Q1–3, F, D, d2; *rowseth* 02–6; *rouses* d1, d5, M7
(Rouses M7).   525   his] Q1–3, F, D, d1, d5, M7; *its* 02–6, d2.   526
spurre] Q1–3, F, D, d1–2, d5, M7 *(spur* Q3, F, d1–2; *Spur* D, d5, M7);
guide 02–6.   526   dull] Q1–3, F, D, 02–6; *vain* d1–2, d5, M7 *(Vain*
M7).   528   at] Q1–3, F, D, 02–6, d1, d5, M7; *at the* d2.   528+ 6]
Q1–3, F, 05–6; 5 02–4; *omitted from* D, d1–2, d5, M7.   529   Celimena.
If] Q1–3, F, D; *If* 02–6; Celemana. / *If* d1–2, d5, M7 (Celamina d2;
Celemana∧ M7).   529   such] Q1–3, F, D, 02–6, d1, d5, M7; *you* d2.
529 can] Q1–3, F, D, d1–2, d5, M7 *(Can* M7); *do* 02–6.   530   wooing]

Q1-3, F, D, o3-6, d1-2, d5, M7 (*Wooing* D, M7); *woing* o2.   531   *can*]
Q1-3, F, D, d2, M7 (*Can* M7); *do* o2-6, d1, d5.   532   *the Devil*] Q1-3,
F, D, o2-6, d1, d5, M7 (*devil* d1, d5; *Devill* M7); *Devils* d2.   537
Christendome] Christendome Q1-3, F, D (Christendom Q2-3, F, D).
546   *Beat.*] Q1-3, F; *Theo.* D.   549   Why,] F, D; ∼ʌ Q1-3.   549-
550   *Beatrix*] Q2-3, F, D; ∼ : Q1.   550   only?] Q1, F, D; ∼ : Q2; ∼ .
Q3.   557   Why,] F, D; ∼ʌ Q1-3.   566   as soon] Q1, D; assoon
Q2-3, F.

   Epilogue: 8   *o'th'*] Q2-3, F, D; *oth'* Q1.   10   Astrologer] Q2-3, F, D;
Astrologer Q1.   13   Monsieur] Q2-3, F, D (Mounsieur Q2-3, F); *Monsieur* Q1.   14   *pull-back*] Q1, D (*Pull-back* D); *pull back* Q2-3, F.
14   *o'th'*] Q2-3, F, D; *oth'* Q1.   15   *Morbleu*] Morbleu Q1-3, F, D.
15-16   I . . . [*to*] . . . the] *in italics in Q1-3, F, D.*   16   *feint*] Q1;
fein'd Q2; *feign'd* Q3, F, D.   17   Pox] *Pox* Q1-3, F, D.   17-22
here's . . . [*to*] . . . next?] *in italics in Q1-3, F, D.*   22   Whither] Q1
(*Whither*); *Whether* Q2-3, F, D.   26   nor] Q1-3, F; *or* D.   41+
FINIS.] *omitted from F, D.*

APPENDIX

Chancery Suit Concerning Scenery
for Tyrannick Love

[In reproducing Document C 7 486/74/1-2, Crown-copyright, Public Record Office, London, we have expanded abbreviations, lowered superior letters, and silently added punctuation where necessary to the sense.]

Sexto Junii 1670

To the Right Honorable Sir Orlando Bridgman knight &
Barrister: Lord Keeper of the Great Seale of England.

Humbly Complaining shew unto your Lordship your daily orators Thomas Killigrew Esquire, one of the Groomes of the now kings Majesties Bedchamber, Charles Hart & Michaell Moone of the parish of Covent Garden in the County of Middlesex, gentlemen, That your orator Thomas Killigrew being Master of the Company of his said now Majesties Comedians or Actors at his said Majesties house called the Theater Royall, & your orator Thomas Killigrew being intended according to his Majesties appointment in that behalfe that the said Company of Comedians or Actors should Act a new play or Tragedy called the Royall Martir or St. Katherine about the latter end of Aprill one thousand six hundred six nine and there being a necessity of making a new Scaene of an Elysium to be presented in the said Tragedy or play of St. Katherine and one Isaack Fuller of the parish of St. Gyles in the Fields & County of Middlesex, gentleman, being a Painter & one who sometimes did apply himselfe for painting of Scaenes, & your orators Charles Hart & Michaell Moone being two of the said Company of Comedians or Actors, your said orators Charles Hart & Michaell Moone were appointed by your orator Thomas Killigrew to treat & agree with the said Isaack Fuller touching his painting of the said Scaene of Elysium & accordingly treating with him about the same. It was upon or about the Fourteenth day of the said moneth of Aprill one thousand six hundred sixty nine agreed by and between your said orators Charles Hart & Michaell Moone for and on your orators Thomas Killigrews behalfe and the said Isaack Fuller that the said Isaack Fuller shold paint the said Scaene of Elysium of such largenes as should fitt the stage of the said house or Theater Royall and that he should paint the same so well as other Scaenes belonging to the said Theater were usually painted by other painters and as was fitting for the same to be painted for the best advantage of the said Tragedy or play of St. Katherine, and that he shold soe paint & perfect the same within a fortnight then next following, and that your orators Charles Hart & Michaell Moone shold in consideration thereof for and on your orators Thomas Killigrews behalfe pay unto the said Isaack Fuller what he shold

reasonably deserve for painting of the said Scaene. And your orators shew
that at the making of the said agreement your Orators Charles Hart and
Michaell Moone did acquaint the said Isaack Fuller that your said orators
who were to have considerable shares in the benefitt and profitt to be
gotten by the said play or Tragedy and your Orator Thomas Killigrew
were exceedingly concerned to have the said Scaene finished by the time
agreed on, for that the said play was appointed by the said Kings Majesty
to be Acted presently after the said time wherein by the said agreement
the said scaene was to be finished, and alsoe for that notice was given to
your orators that a very great number of persons of Honor & of the
greatest quality attending on his said Majesties person & his Royall consort the Queenes Majestie in & about the Cort were very urgent to see
the Acting of the said Tragedy or play, and for that at the time of the
said agreement the parts in & about London were very full of nobility
& Gentry & persons of quality who daily called on your Orators & pressed
them to see the Acting of the same, and also for that Easter & Trinity
termes were then coming on which were times for great resort of Gentry
& persons of quality to the parts in & about the Cittys of London &
Westminster (& very many at that time more then ordinary for that it was
in Parliament time also) so that great numbers did resort to the said
house or Royall Theater to see Comedyes or playes Acted, these sumer
terme times being usually the greatest times of profitt to your Orators
throughout the whole yeare. And therefore your Orators Charles Hart &
Michaell Moone did give great caution & warning to the said Isaack Fuller
that he shold not fail to paint & finish the said Scaene by the said time
agreed on & to paint the same so as might be for the best advantage of the
said Tragedy or play. But your orators shew that the said Isaack Fuller
not regarding the said agreement or your Orators advantage in presenting
or Acting the said play as aforesaid, he the said Isaack Fuller did wilfully
neglect & delay the painting & perfecting of the said Scaene till the latter
end of June then next after & till both the said termes of Easter &
Trinity were past, though Your Orators did from time to time importune
& presse him to paint & finish the same with all expedition according to
his said promise & agreement, acquainting him with the great losse &
damages which your orators did & shold susteine by reasons of the not
painting & finishing thereof by the time agreed on & with the further
losse & damage which they shold receive in case the same were not
finished with all expedition. By meanes of the said Isaack Fullers breach
of which agreement in not finishing the said Scaenes untill the time
aforesaid your Orators received very great blame from his said Majesty
& by reason of his distast thereat he did much forbeare his coming to the
said Theater or house to see other playes or Comedyes presented or Acted
& did alsoe occasion the Nobility & Gentry & persons of quality attending
upon his Majestys & his Royall consorts persons & Cort to forbeare very
much their coming thereunto for the said purposes, & also your Orators
lost the advantage of presenting or Acting the said Tragedy or play
during the said two Termes, the parts in & about London during that
time being very full of other Nobility & Gentry & persons of quality who

wold have byn present at the presenting or Acting of the said play &
where by reason of the not Acting thereof came not too frequently to the
said Theater or house to see playes Acted as otherwise they wold have
done, the said play not being to be presented with such benefit to your
orators without the said Scaene by much as otherwise it wold have byn.
And the said Isaack Fuller having att or about the end of the said moneth
of June as aforesaid finished the said Scaene the same was painted very
meanly & inconsiderably & not at all answearable to what became such a
play or to the curiosity wherewith the said Isaack Fuller agreed to
paint the same, by reason whereof the said play when it was Acted was
disparaged & lost its reputation, & not halfe the company resorted to see
the acting thereof which wold have come in case the said Scaene had byn
painted according to the said Agreement, the painting & finishing of the
said Scaene not being worth Fifty pounds whereas if the same had byn
painted according to the said Agreement the painting & finishing thereof
wold have byn worth as much more. By meanes of which said breaches
of the said agreement by the said Isaack Fuller your orators were damnified five hundred pounds at least. And your Orators shew that they being
so damnified did resort to the said Isaack Fuller acquainting him there-
with & did propose to him to make them recompence & satisfaction for
their said damnifications hoping that he wold have borne so just a mind
as to have made them recompence for the same, which the said Isaack
Fuller did seeme willing to doe or at least in some considerable proportion to what your Orators were damnified insomuch that your Orators
were perswaded & had some reason not to doubt but that he would accordingly have satisfyed the same, and your Orators had the greater reason
to be confident therein for that your Orators or one of them the more to
indulge & incourage him to be just in the performance of the said Agreement did presently after the making thereof at severall times pay unto
him Forty pounds towards satisfaction for painting & finishing the said
Scaene. But your Orators shew that the said Isaack Fuller being since
designed to avoyd if by any meanes possibly he can his making your
Orators satisfaction for their said damnifications, he the said Isaack
Fuller hath since refused to make any recompence or satisfaction to your
orators for the same, giving out in speeches (& as the truth is) that the
said agreement was made in the presence of such wittnesses as he is
sure are gone so farr beyond Seas or into other remote parts unknowne to
your orators that it will be long enough before they will retorne whereby
your orators may bee able to bring them to give evidence upon any triall
to be had at law touching the witnesses & that he doubts not but that
by reason of your Orators want of proofe he shall totally avoid giving
your Orators any recompence for their said damnifications. And not
content therewith the said Isaack Fuller hath lately brought an action
att Law against your Orators Charles Hart & Michaell Moone for painting
& finishing the said Scaene & hath recovered three hundred thirty five
pounds ten shillings against them for the same. And the said Isaack Fuller
also gives out in speeches that he is sure that the cheife of your Orators
wittnesses who shold proove the said Agreement upon which your

Orators should recover their said damnifications shall be so kept under his power that your Orators shall never be able to produce them att any triall at Law touching the same. Which doeings of the said Isaack Fuller are contrary to all right equity and good Conscience and tend to your orators very great wrong. In tender consideration Whereof and for that your orators wittnesses who can proove the premisses are in parts remote or beyond Seas whereby your Orators are & hitherto have byn unable to produce them att any triall att law to be had touching the premisses so punctually as by the strict rules of the Comon Law is required whereby your Orators are & hither to have bynn remedilesse at law touching the premisses without the ayd of this honorable Cort. And that the said Isaack Fuller may set forth whether he did not make the agreement aforesaid or what agreement hee made touching his said painting & finishing the said Scaene either as to time or goodnes And to the end that your Orators may be releived in the premisses by the Ayd of this honorable Cort. Mayst please your Lordship the premisses considered to grant unto your orators his Majesties most gracious writt of subpoena issuing out of this honorable Cort to be directed to the said Isaack Fuller thereby comanding him at a certeine day & under a certeine paine therein to be limitted personally to be and appear before your Lordship in this honorable Cort then & there upon his tryall oath to Answeare all & synguler the premisses. And further to stand to & abide such other order and direct[ion?] therein as to your Lordship shall seeme meet. And your Orators will ever pray for your Lordshipps health & happiness.

* * *

Jurat 16 Junii 1670 w a Littleton

The Answere of Isaac Fuller to the Bill of Complaynt of
Thomas Killigrew Charles Hart and Michaell Moone Complaynants

This Defendant saving to him selfe now and att all times hereafter all benefitt and Advantage of Exceptions to the many Incertaintyes Insufficiencyes and Imperfections of the said Complaynants said Bill of Complaynt For Answere thereunto, or unto so much thereof as any way materially concerneth him, this Defendant, to make answere unto: Hee Saith hee knoweth nothing of any appointment of his Majestie for the Acting of the Play or Tragedy in the Bill mentioned, Save only that the plaintiff Thomas Killigrew a few dayes before this Defendant had made and Perfected the Scheane of an Elizyum in the Bill mentioned as an Argument or motive to perswade this defendant to hasten the finishing thereof Did tell this Defendant that his Majestie was desirous to See the Said Tragedy acted within a day or two after or to that effect. Whereupon this Defendant did Sitt upp all night to finish the Said Scheane. Butt this Defendant Saith true it is that about the latter end of Aprill or the beginning of May in the yeare of our Lord 1669 One Mr. Dryden (a Poett as this Defendant hath heard that Sometimes makes Playes [for] the Company of **Comedians or Actors in the Bill mentioned) and one Mr.**

Wright (a Joyner belonging to the Said Company) by the Order or direction as this Defendant believes of the said Company or Some of them did come unto this Defendant then lying Sicke att his owne house and did propose unto him the painting of the said Scheane of an Elizyum for the said Company in their house called the Theatre Royall in the Bill mentioned, and to encourage this Defendant to undertake the painting thereof the said Dryden and Wright or one of them told this Defendant hee should bee well Satisfyed for the S[ame?] or used Severall expressions to that effecte. And this Defendant saith that about foure or five dayes after, this Defendant haveing recovered his health went to the said Company att their said house and there mett with all or most of them togeather particularly with the Complaynants Hart and Moone and then and there treated with them about the painting the said Scheane, and then (and not about the 14th of Aprill 1669 as in the Bill is Suggested) it was att length agreed by and betweene this Defendant and the said Company or Some of them on the behalfe of the rest of them, to this or the like effect that this Defendant should paynte the said Scheane of an Elizyum so as should fitt the Stage of the said house or Theatre Royall and so as was fitting for the same to be paynted. Butt this Defendant doth not remember that it was expressely Agreed that hee should paynte the same as well as other Scheanes belonging to the said Theatre were usually paynted by other Paynters as the Bill suggests. Howbeit this Defendant saith hee believeth and hopeth if need bee to prove that the Same was paynted as well as any other Scheane belonging to the said Theatre was or had been paynted by any other Paynter whatsoever And this Defendant doth positively deny that it was then or att any other time agreed betweene this Defendant and the said Company or any of them that this Defendant should or would paynte or perfect the said Scheane within a Fortnight as the Bill very unreasonably suggests (the same beeing in truth impossible for this Defendant or any other as this Defendant believeth to doe within that time) And denyeth that any other certaine time was agreed for the finishing thereof. And this Defendant saith that by the said Agreement the said Company or some of them were to pay unto this Defendant what hee should deserve for painting the said Scheane, And to encourage this Defendant to undertake the painting thereof they or Some of them, particularly the said Hart and Moone, did not onlie promise that this Defendant should have satisfaction for doeinge the said worke but did also expressly Say that hee should not Stay a minute for his moneye after his worke was done. And this Defendant saith that there was noe other Agreement betweene this Defendant and the Said Company or any of them or any other on their behalfe but Such or to Such effecte as herein before is Sett forth, And denyeth that att the time of the said Agreement the Complaynants or any of them did acquainte this Defendant that they were exceedingly concerned to have the said Scheane finished by the time in the Bill pretended to bee Agreed on for any of the reasons in the Bill for that purpose alleadged or for any other reason whatsoever, And denyeth that att the time of the said Agreement the plaintiffs Hart and Moone or either of them or any other of the said Company did give any Caution or Warneing to this Defendant that hee Should not fayle to painte and finish the said Scheane by the said time pretended to bee agreed on. Butt this Defendant believeth that while the said worke was goeing on they or some of them might call upon him to dispatch the same with what expedition hee could, and might use Some Such Arguments as in the Bill are alleadged, to quicken him therein. And this Defendant Saith hee did make what haste therein hee could and believeth hee finished the Same in as little time as any other painter could have done the same and believeth that the said plaintiffs or some of them might mind him to painte the said Scheane well and for the best Advantage of the Said Play. And this Defendant believeth for the reasons herein after expressed that hee did and hath painted the Same very well and that the said Company of Actors have had very greate Advantage thereby. And this Defendant denyeth that hee did willfully neglect or Delay the painting and Perfecting of the said Scheane. For hee saith hee painted the Same within the Space of Six weekes or thereabouts, beginning to painte the Same about the 12th Day of May in the said yeare of our Lord 1669 and Perfecting the Same about the 23th of June then next following And hath reason to believe that noe painter in England could have finished the same and have done the worke Soe well as this Defendant did it in Soe Short a Space. For that att the tryall att Law hereafter mentioned had touching the premisses wherein the now plaintiffs Hart and Moone were Defendants, and this Defendant was plaintiff, One Mr. Streeter an eminent Paynter beeing produced by the now plaintiffs themselves as a wittnesse on their behalf, did acknowledge that this Defendant had a quicker hand att painting then any other, And if hee Performed the Said Worke in Six weekes time it was very fayre, And did also acknowledge that the Said worke was excellently well done. And this Defendant saith that hee was so farre from neglecting or delaying the said worke that for three weekes of the said Six weekes hee did not putt off his Cloathes but lay upon a pallatt-bed in the Roome and rose upp to worke as Soone as hee could See and for the rest of the Said Six weekes hee made what haste hee could and entred upon no other worke till the said worke was finished. And if in the meane time the two Termes of Easter and Trinity that yeare were past as is Suggested in the Bill, this Defendant conceiveth it not materiall to him for that hee beganne the Said worke within Three or foure dayes after the Said Agreement, which three or foure dayes was time little enough to provide materialls and Servants for the entring upon Such a worke, and finished the Same within Six weekes after as aforesaid. And if the plaintiffs would have had the said worke perfected against the said two Termes they should have Employed this Defendant about it Sooner, [a] good part of Easter Terme that yeare beeing in truth Spent before the Said Agreement for doing thereof. Nor is it materiall to this Defendant as hee humbly conceiveth [that] the Complaynants or any of them did importune and presse this Defendant to finish the Said Scheane with all expedition or acquainte him with the greate losse and damage that they had or should Sustaine by reason of the not finishing thereof

Sooner, this Defendant denying that by any Agreement with them hee was to finish the Same against any certaine time, And denying that hee did willfully neglect or delay the finishing thereof as aforesaid. For which reason also this Defendant humbly conceiveth it no way materiall to him if the Plaintiffs did receive any blame from his Majestie or that by reason of his Distaste thereof his Majestie did forbeare the comeing to the said Theatre to See other Playes presented and acted Or if the Nobillity and Gentry or any others did forbeare comeing thereunto or if for any other cause they received any losse or Damage by reason the said Scheane was not finished Sooner. Howbeit this Defendant saith hee doth not believe that they did receive any blame from his Majestie for that the said worke was not done Sooner as is pretended by their Bill and hee doth the rather So believe for that the Complaynant Thomas Killigrew Some few dayes after the finishing thereof gave this Defendant thankes for the Same And told him that hee this Defendant had very well pleased his Majestie and the whole house And then also told this Defendant that hee the said Thomas Killigrew would See him, this Defendant, payd for the doeing thereof, And this Defendant doth utterly deny that the said Scheane was painted very meanely or inconsiderably and not att all Answerable to what became Such a play, or to the curiosity wherewith this Defendant Agreed to paynt the Same as in the Bill is very falsely and unworthyly Suggested. Nor doth this Defendant believe that by reason thereof the said Play when Acted was disparaged or lost any reputation or that not halfe the Company resorted to see the Acting thereof which would have come in Case the said Scheane had been well painted. For this Defendant Saith it appeared att the said tryall as well by the testimony of Wittnesses produced by this Defendant as also by wittnesses produced by the plaintiffs themselves, Some of them beeing their owne Servants, that the said Scheane was very well paynted and gave greate content to the Spectators that came to see the said Play Acted And that the plaintiffs and their said Company acted the Same about 14 dayes together and received all that while about 100 li. per diem Whereas att other playes they are not wont usually to receive above 40 or 50 li. per diem, And that their said House all the said 14 dayes was very full, the Pitt Boxes and other Places thereof beeing thronged with Spectators. And for that also this Defendant hath been informed and hopeth if need bee to prove by diverse Persons of Quallity whoe in the said 14 dayes time did See the said Play Acted and the said Scheane therein presented, that the said Scheane did give a generall content to the Spectators thereof. For which reasons also this Defendant taketh the said Allegation touching the meane performance of the said worke and the Disparagement the said Play received thereby to bee not only false but also a very greate and unjust Scandall to this Defendant in his Profession, which he humbly hopeth will in due time bee considered by this Honorable Court. And as for the Suggestion in the Bill that the painting & finishing of the said Scheane was not worth 50 li., And that if the Same had been done according to the said Agreement the Same would have been worth as much more, this Defendant taketh the Same to bee a very vaine and idle

Suggestion after that by a verdict upon full Evidence att the said Tryall the said worke hath been found to bee worth 335 li: 10s. And in truth this Defendant was in disburse well nigh 100 li. in providing materialls and paying Servants for and about the Same. And this Defendant denyeth that the plaintiffs or any of them did resort unto this Defendant and acquaint him that they were dampnifyed 500 li. or any other sume by his, this Defendants, breach of the said Agreement and proposed to him to make them satisfaction for the Same. Howbeit it may bee true that when this Defendant did resort unto them or Some of them or to some of the said Company to bee payd for his said worke, to delay and putt off this Defendant they might pretend Some Such Damage as by their now Bill the Plaintiffs Suggest. But this Defendant doth absolutely deny that hee ever was willing or did expresse him selfe to bee willing to make them any recompence or Satisfaction in any proportion whatsoever for such their pretended damages. Nor doth this Defendant believe that they were att all dampnifyed, but on the contrary hee verily believeth that they received greate benefitt and Advantage by the Performance of the said worke in Such good and workeman-like manner as this Defendant performed the Same. And if they did receive any losse or Damage this Defendant doth utterly deny that they received the Same by any breach of Agreement on his Part, this Defendant haveing made no breach of Agreement att all as herein before is declared. And this Defendant confesseth that while the said worke was carrying on the said plaintiffs Some or one of them did pay or cause the sume of 40 li. to bee payd to this Defendant towards his Satisfaction for painting and finishing the said Scheane which this Defendant did acknowledge att the said Tryall, And the same was considered by the Jury whoe were Summoned to try the said Cause. And this Defendant also confesseth it to bee true that after hee had often in vaine resorted unto the Complaynants or Some of them or of the said Company to bee payd for his said worke They Still delaying and putting him off from time to time and offering him very inconsiderable Satisfaction for his great paynes taken therein, Hee this Defendant did bring or cause to bee brought an Action att Law in his Majesties Court of Exchequer against the said Plaintiffs Charles Hart and Michaell Moone upon a quantum meruit as this Defendant is informed by his Attourneye in the said Cause the said Action was call'd. And it is true that upon full Evidence given on both Sides att the Tryall of the said cause in Yield hall London about the end of Easter Terme last, this Defendant did obtaine a Verdict for 295 li: 10s., The said Jury who were to try the said Cause valueing the Said worke at 335 li: 10s. but diducting the said 40 li. this Defendant did acknowledge hee had received as aforesaid. And that Judgment is thereupon entred as this Defendant is likewise informed by his said Attourneye in the said Court of Exchequer for the said Sume of 295 li: 10s. and Costs of Suite, Upon which Judgment this Defendant is likewise informed as aforesaid that Execution is Since taken out and Executed upon the said Hart and Moone or one of them And that thereupon they or one of them have payd or caused the said moneyes recovered against them by the said Judgment to be payd into the hands of the Sheriffe to whome the said Execution was directed, and this Defendant expecteth that the said Sheriffe will very Suddenly pay the Same over unto him this Defendant, As this Defendant humbly conceiveth under the favour of this Honorable Court hee is and ought to doe. And this Defendant Saith that before hee brought his Said Action hee did desire the plaintiffs or Some of them or of the said Company to referre the matters in difference betweene them to any indifferent Persons, this Defendant beeing very unwilling to contend with them att Law, which would distract and hinder him in his worke & businesse by which hee Supports himselfe and family. And this Defendant further Saith that before hee could bring his said Action att Law the said Company of Actors did putt him, this Defendant, to great trouble charge and expence of time to gett liberty to bring his said Action against them, they insisting upon their priviledge as his Majesties Servants and refuseing to appeare gratis thereunto. Butt att length the Earle of Manchester beeing fully Satisfyed as this Defendant believeth of the greate Justice and honesty of his Cause did give this Defendant liberty to bring his said Action against them And did Order the said Hart and Moone to appeare thereunto on the behalf of the said Company. And this Defendant Saith that att the Said Tryall att Law the most materiall allegations in the plaintiffs now Bill, particularly the allegation touching the time by the Bill pretended to bee Agreed on for the doeing of the said Worke and touching the goodnesse thereof, were insisted on by the now plaintiffs Hart and Moone and were endeavoured to bee proved, but no such Agreement as to time Appeareing to the said Court and Jury and it appeareing that the said Worke was very well done, One of the now plaintiffs owne Wittnesses then affirmeing that the Same was excellently well done, this Defendant did obteyne Such Verdict as aforesaid. And this Defendant positively Saith that hee would not doe the like worke againe for the Same moneye as is given him by the said Verdict for the painting and finishing the said Scheane, And that in the Same time hee was about the Said worke hee could have gotten more else where if hee had not been Employed therein, And this Defendant doth utterly deny that hee ever agreed to make the plaintiffs or any of them any manner of recompence or Satisfaction for any their pretended Damnifications or for any other Damnifications whatsoever as by their Bill is very falsely Suggested. Without that that any other matter or thing whatsoever in the Complaynants Said Bill of Complaynt Contained materiall or effectuall [in] [t]he Lawe for this Defendant to make Answere unto and not herein or hereby sufficiently answered unto, confessed or avoided, traversed or denyed, is true to the knowledge of this Defendant. All which matters and things this Defendant is and willbee ready to Averre and prove as this Honourable Court shall Award, And prayeth to bee hence Dismissed with his reasonable Costs and Charges in this behalfe most wrongfully Sustained.

Will. Moses.

INDEX TO THE COMMENTARY

DATE DUE

GOSHEN COLLEGE - GOOD LIBRARY

3 9310 01089160 2